Director 7 and Lingo

AUTHORIZED

macromedia®
PRESS

Director 7 and Lingo Authorized
Macromedia, Inc.

  Published by Macromedia Press, in association with Peachpit Press, a division of Addison Wesley Longman.

Macromedia Press
1249 Eighth Street
Berkeley, CA 94710
510/524-2178 • 800-283-9444
510/524-2221 (fax)
Find us on the World Wide Web at:
http://www.peachpit.com
http://www.macromedia.com

ISBN 0-201-35416-0

Notice of Liability
The information in this book and on the CD-ROM is distributed on an "as is" basis, without warranty. While every precaution has been taken in the preparation of the book and the CD-ROM, neither Macromedia, Inc., its licensors, nor Macromedia Press shall have any liability to any person or entity with respect to liability, loss, or damage caused or alleged to be caused directly or indirectly by the instructions contained in this book or by the computer software and hardware products described herein.

Trademarks
Macromedia and Director are registered trademarks; Director Multimedia Studio, Lingo, Macromedia Studios, Shockwave, Xtras, and the Made With Macromedia logo are trademarks of Macromedia, Inc.

Apple, QuickTime, and Macintosh are registered trademarks of Apple Computer, Inc. Sound Forge is a trademark of Sonic Foundry, Inc. Other product names mentioned within this publication may be trademarks or registered trademarks of other companies.

Printed and bound in the United States of America

9 8 7 6 5 4 3 2 1

CREDITS

Producer
Karen Tucker, Macromedia

Authors
Phil Gross, Frank Elley, Karen Tucker

Programmers
Phil Gross
Frank Elley, Behind the Curtain
Mark Castle, Castle Productions

Production
Rick Gordon, Emerald Valley Graphics
Myrna Vladic, Bad Dog Graphics
Debbie Roberti, Espresso Graphics

Editors
Lisa Theobald, Judy Ziajka

Indexer
Karin Arrigoni

Cover Design
Carolyn Crampton
Lisa Brazieal

Thanks to the following people:
Jay Armstrong, Marjorie Baer, Jennifer Bennett, Peri Cumali, Darcy DiNucci,
Brian Ellertson, Mike Gross, Mimi Heft, Barbara James, Martha Kuhl,
Becky Morgan, Bill Mowrey, Andy Rose, Ilona Sturm

table of contents

introduction

Macromedia Director 7 is the best-selling multimedia authoring program and the leading tool for creating interactive media for the World Wide Web, CD-ROM, information kiosks, presentations, and interactive TV. Director's easy-to-use interface lets you combine graphics, sound, video, and other media in any sequence and then add interactive features with Lingo, the program's powerful scripting language. This Macromedia Authorized training course introduces you to the major features of Director 7 and guides you step by step through the development of several real-world Director projects. This 50-hour curriculum includes these lessons

Lesson 1: Director Basics
Lesson 2: Animated Bullet Lists
Lesson 3: Reversing Animations
Lesson 4: Transitions, Sounds, and Video
Lesson 5: Adding Interactivity
Lesson 6: More Animation Techniques
Lesson 7: Keyframes and Layers
Lesson 8: Film Loops and Buttons
Lesson 9: Built-in Behaviors
Lesson 10: Custom Cursors
Lesson 11: Alpha Channels
Lesson 12: Sprite Properties and Palettes
Lesson 13: Markers and Navigation
Lesson 14: Color Cycling and Blends
Lesson 15: Shockwave for Director
Lesson 16: Learning Lingo

Each lesson begins with an overview of the lesson's content and learning objectives and is divided into short tasks that break the skills into bite-size units. Lessons also include these special features:

Tips: Shortcuts for performing common tasks and ways to solve common problems by applying the skills you've learned.

Boldface terms: New vocabulary that will come in handy as you use Director and work with multimedia.

Menu commands and keyboard shortcuts: Alternative methods for carrying out commands in the Director Multimedia Studio. Menu commands are shown like this: Menu › Command › Subcommand. Keyboard shortcuts (when available) are shown in parentheses after the step; a plus sign between the names of keys means you press the keys simultaneously.

Lingo Equivalents: Almost everything that you can do in Director can also be done through Lingo, Director's scripting language that you will learn to use beginning in Lesson 16. When appropriate, the Lingo equivalent for an operation will be listed below the operation. Those with programming knowledge will find the Lingo equivalent interesting. However, you shouldn't worry if Lingo makes no sense to you now; understanding it is not required to complete the lessons.

Appendices A and B provide a quick reference to the Windows and Macintosh shortcuts you can use to give commands in Director.

2

As you complete these lessons, you'll be developing the skills you need to complete your own Director projects. By the end of the course, you should have mastered all the skills listed under "What You Will Learn" at the end of this introduction.

All the files you need for the lessons are included in the Lessons folder on the enclosed CD-ROM. Files for each lesson appear in their own folders, titled with the lesson number. You do not need to copy the Lessons folder to your hard drive. You can complete the lessons by running the files from the CD-ROM.

The folder for each lesson contains a Complete folder, a Media folder, and a Start folder. The Complete folder contains completed files for the lesson, so you can compare your work or see where you're headed. The Media folder contains any media elements you need to complete the lesson. Certain projects require you to use prebuilt files. The prebuilt files you will need are identified at the beginning of each lesson and can be found in the Start folder for that lesson.

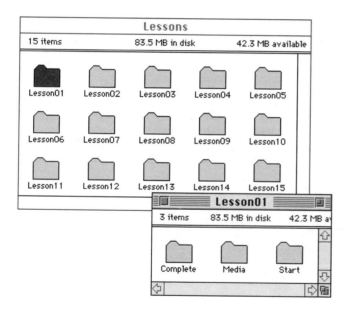

Files for each lesson appear in their own folders, titled with the lesson number. The Complete folder contains completed Director files for each lesson. The Media folder contains the media elements you need to complete each lesson. If a lesson requires a prebuilt file, the file, usually named Start.dir, is found inside the Start folder.

AUTHORIZED TRAINING FROM MACROMEDIA

The lesson plans in this book were developed by some of Macromedia's most successful trainers and refined through long experience to meet students' needs. Macromedia Authorized courses offer the best available training for Macromedia programs.

The instructions in this manual are designed for multimedia developers, graphic artists, instructional designers, illustrators, Webmasters, and anyone who wants to become a multimedia developer or Web designer. This course assumes that you're a beginner with Director but are familiar with the basic methods of giving commands on a Windows or Macintosh computer, such as choosing items from menus, opening and saving files, and so on. For more information on those basic tasks, see the documentation provided with your computer or operating system software.

The instructions in this book also assume that you already have Director 7 installed on a Windows or Macintosh computer and that your computer meets the system requirements listed at the end of this chapter. This minimum configuration will allow you to run Director 7 and open the files included on the enclosed CD-ROM.

We hope you enjoy the course.

WHAT YOU WILL LEARN

In this course you will:

- Create, import, and sequence media elements in Director multimedia presentations
- Incorporate graphics, sound, and text into your projects
- Create screen transitions
- Animate media elements to include movement in Director movies
- Create film loop animations
- Add interactive navigation to presentations
- Create buttons that provide user feedback
- Use Shockwave to produce movies for playback on the World Wide Web
- Create effects with Director's Alpha Channel support
- Create custom cursors for your program
- Learn to use Lingo, Director's scripting language
- Control the screen with the keyboard
- Make a database
- Link to the Internet
- Create hypertext

MINIMUM SYSTEM REQUIREMENTS

Windows

- Pentium processor or or compatible, 100 MHz or faster
- 32 MB available RAM
- CD-ROM drive
- 25 MB available disk space
- 640 × 480 screen resolution
- 8-bit color (256 colors) monitor depth
- Windows 95 or later or Windows NT 4.0 or later
- Windows-compatible sound card
- QuickTime 3 for Windows
- The Shockwave plug-in and a Web browser that supports Shockwave (such as Netscape Navigator version 4.0 or later or Microsoft Internet Explorer version 3.0 or later)
- 14.4 modem and Internet access

Macintosh

- PowerPC, 100MHz or faster
- 32 MB available RAM
- 25 MB available disk space
- 640 × 480 screen resolution
- 8-bit color (256 colors) monitor depth
- System 7.6.1 or later
- QuickTime 3
- The Shockwave plug-in and a Web browser that supports Shockwave (such as Netscape Navigator version 4.0 or later or Microsoft Internet Explorer version 3.0 or later)
- 14.4 modem and Internet access

director basics

LESSON 1

Director lets you easily create visual presentations or interactive multimedia software with audio and video. You can add visual interest to oral presentations by creating animated slides. You can create eye-catching effects simply by using interesting images and adding movement to objects that appear in the presentation. This lesson introduces you to Director's basic tools. Then you'll jump right in and create a simple presentation.

Before you begin working on a presentation of your own, you need to understand some basic Director concepts. Director is based on the metaphor of a theater

Director lets you create attention-grabbing presentations, as you'll see when you complete the simple movie in this lesson. This project uses just a background graphic and text that changes color on the screen to create a memorable introduction to a speaker's presentation.

The background graphic, titled Artist's Studio, *was created with Extreme 3D by graphic artist Joe DiCesare of JDC Illustration in Brooklyn, New York.*

production. All the action takes place on the stage, and the cast appears on the stage as **sprites**, according to a timeline called the **score**, which tells cast members where to be and when to be there. A Director file is called a movie.

Each movie, cast member, sprite, and point in time (**frame**) can also have its own **script** (which is where Lingo comes in).

You follow four basic steps to create any Director movie:

Step 1: Assemble the media elements. Media elements include graphics, digital video, movies, sound, text, and animation. You can either create new media elements or use ones that have already been developed. Director provides numerous tools for creating elements, including a paint tool and text creation tools. You can also import elements from a variety of other sources.

Step 2: Position the media elements on the stage and sequence them in the score. You use the Director stage to create the look and feel for your production; you use the stage and score together to arrange the media elements in space and time. The stage is the screen that the user will see, and the score is the timeline you use to organize what happens when and where.

Step 3: (optional) Add interactivity and scripting. Interactivity can include buttons or other navigation elements that branch the user to different parts of the Director movie or the Internet depending on the user's input. Scripting allows you to extend your movie beyond what is possible using the stage and the score.

Step 4: Package the movie into a projector and distribute it to end users, or use Shockwave to prepare a movie that end users can play back in a Web browser. Projectors are the actual, stand-alone, software programs that the user will run. By distributing your movies in Projector form, end users can run your multimedia movie without needing their own copy of Director. Of course, they can't change the movies; they can only play them back. Or, you can save your work as a Shockwave movie when you want end users to see and interact with the movie on a Web page using a Web browser.

The media you use, your decision regarding the use of interactivity, and how you package your movie will vary from project to project. However, by following these four basic steps, you can effectively organize any Director project. In this lesson, you will perform Steps 1 and 2. Later in this book, you will perform Steps 3 and 4. For now, it is most important that you become familiar with Director's features and learn how to create, assemble, and sequence media elements in a Director movie.

If you would like to view the final result of this lesson, open the Complete folder in the Lesson01 folder and play Artist.dir.

WHAT YOU WILL LEARN

In this lesson you will:

- Open Director and create a new movie
- Learn about Director's basic components
- Create a new Director file
- Import a graphical image
- Create and modify text
- Display images on the screen
- Change the opacity of displayed objects
- Create an animation
- Play an animation

APPROXIMATE TIME

This lesson should take about 1½ hours to complete.

LESSON FILES

Media Files:
Dir7\Lessons\Lesson01\Media\Artiststudio.tif

Starting File:
None

Completed Project:
Dir7\Lessons\Lesson01\Complete\ Artist.dir

CREATING A FOLDER ON YOUR HARD DRIVE

Before you begin working with Director, you should create a folder on your hard drive named *Projects* to hold all the projects you will create as you work through the lessons in this book.

OPENING DIRECTOR

Your first task is to open Director.

1] Double-click the Director icon to open Director 7.

You will see the menu bar and stage. Depending on your Director settings, you may also see other features, such as the toolbar, control panel, score, and cast. These features are described in this lesson.

The stage is where the action occurs. The stage window may cover the entire screen, or only a portion, or it may be hidden altogether. If it is hidden now, make it visible by choosing Window > Stage (Windows Ctrl+1, Macintosh Command+1). Unlike other windows, the stage has no scroll bars. The default size of the stage is 640 × 480 pixels.

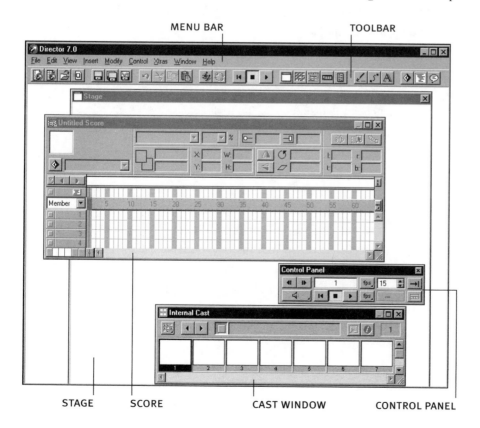

MENU BAR   TOOLBAR

STAGE SCORE   CAST WINDOW   CONTROL PANEL

2] Open the Director menus to see the available commands.

Most Director commands are available through the menus as well as through keyboard shortcuts. The keyboard shortcuts, which you can use to activate a command without using the menus, are listed next to the command name.

The menus you see reflect the **Macromedia user interface standard**, which ensures that menus and other interface elements are consistent across Macromedia applications. This standard makes it easy for you to learn to use the programs as a single powerful tool for creating multimedia applications rather than as a group of separate programs.

OPENING THE TOOLBAR

The buttons on the toolbar provide shortcuts for common commands and functions, such as Open, Save, Print, Rewind, Stop, and Play. The toolbar is one of many windows you can open in Director. As you open windows in the following tasks, leave them open unless you are instructed to close them. Arrange the windows that remain open on the screen so you can see them completely.

1] If the toolbar isn't visible, choose Window › Toolbar to open it (Windows Ctrl+Shift+Alt+B, Macintosh Command+Shift+Option+B).

The toolbar contains the most common control buttons used in Director. It is a good idea to keep the toolbar open while you work on Director movies so you can quickly select a Director command with a mouse click. For example, instead of choosing File > Save you can click the disk icon on the toolbar.

CLICKING THE DISK ICON IS THE SAME AS CHOOSING FILE › SAVE

2] Slowly move the cursor over the tools in the toolbar to see the names of the tools.

The pop-up labels you see are called **Tooltips**. Move the mouse over the tools to identify the commands and Director features they activate. If the Tooltips don't appear, you may need to turn them on by choosing File > Preferences > General and checking Show Tooltips in the dialog box.

USING THE CONTROL PANEL

You can use the control panel to play, stop, and rewind movies. In this task, you will play the movie in the Complete folder provided in the Lesson01 folder to see how the control panel works.

1] If the control panel is not visible, choose Window › Control Panel to open the control panel (Windows Ctrl+2, Macintosh Command+2).

The control panel provides buttons like those on a VCR for controlling a movie. The other buttons let you control the way the movie plays. You will learn to use these controls later in this book.

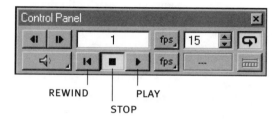

REWIND   PLAY

STOP

2] Choose File › Open and locate the Lesson01 folder. Then select Artist.dir to open it. (In the Open window this is Dir 7\Lessons\Lesson01\Complete\Artist.dir.)

You see the first frame of the movie on the stage.

3] Use the buttons on the control panel to rewind the movie, play it, and stop it.

This movie is the beginning of the speaker's presentation that you will start creating in this lesson and then complete in Lesson 2.

4] Choose Window › Control Panel to close the control panel (Windows Ctrl+2, Macintosh Command+2).

Because three of the most important control buttons—Rewind, Stop, and Play—are duplicated on the toolbar, you can use the toolbar to play the movie you create in this lesson. Closing the control panel gives you more work space on the screen. When you need to use the control panel again, the instructions in this book will direct you to open it.

VIEWING THE CAST

Like a theater production, a Director movie needs a **cast**. Actually, Director can have more than one cast available, and each cast can have its own unique set of **cast members**. In Director's case, the cast members are not people but media elements, such as graphics, sounds, digital video, text, or other Director movies. All of these are stored in the Cast window. The Cast window is like an off-stage area where the cast members wait until they're called to the stage. Unlike the theater, though, in Director the same cast members can appear on stage in multiple places at once. This feature allows you to conserve valuable disk space (or download time) by reusing the same image or text as necessary.

1] If the Cast window is not visible, choose Window › Cast to open the Cast Window (Windows Ctrl+3, Macintosh Command+3).

The Cast window shows you the cast members of the current movie. Each cast member can be identified by a number and, optionally, a name. For every cast member in the Cast window, a thumbnail image appears along with an icon that represents that cast member's type. For example, a paintbrush icon means the cast member is a graphic, and the letter A means the cast member is text.

THUMBNAIL IMAGE

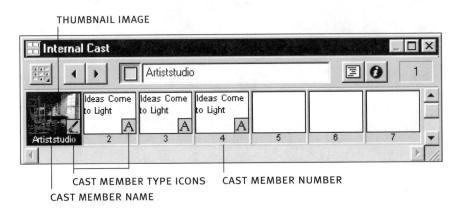

CAST MEMBER TYPE ICONS   CAST MEMBER NUMBER
CAST MEMBER NAME

A movie's cast can consist of up to 32,000 cast members. You control the row width and the number of visible rows by sizing the window or setting the Cast window's preferences. In the next steps you'll use preferences to change Director's default cast member label setting.

2] Choose File › Preferences › Cast.

A dialog box opens and shows you the default settings for the way Director displays the Cast window and its cast members.

SELECT THE NUMBER OF CAST MEMBERS THE CAST WINDOW DISPLAYS

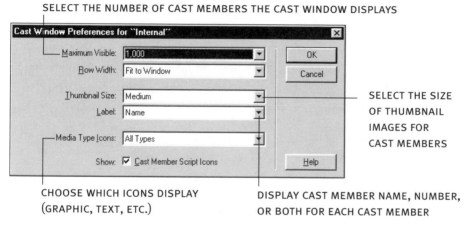

SELECT THE SIZE
OF THUMBNAIL
IMAGES FOR
CAST MEMBERS

CHOOSE WHICH ICONS DISPLAY
(GRAPHIC, TEXT, ETC.)

DISPLAY CAST MEMBER NAME, NUMBER,
OR BOTH FOR EACH CAST MEMBER

3] Open the Label pop-up menu and choose Number:Name for the label. Click OK to close the dialog box.

Displaying the number and the name of cast members in the Cast window helps you identify cast members you want to use in your movies more quickly.

OPENING THE SCORE

To tell cast members when to appear on the stage, what to do, and when to exit, the cast members need a script. In Director, the script is known as the **score**. You use the score to sequence and synchronize the actions of the cast.

The horizontal rows in the score are called **channels**. The channels are used for different jobs. You'll learn how to use these channels later in this book.

1] Choose Windows › Score to open the Score window (Windows Ctrl+4, Macintosh Command+4).

When you first open the Score Window, all of the channels may not be visible. If the upper channels, called the effects channels, are not visible, you can display them using the Hide/Show Effects Channels arrows on the right side of the window. Notice the icons that appear to the left of some of the channels. These are the effects channels and are reserved for specific types of information.

The **tempo channel** is used to adjust the speed of the movie as it plays. The **tempo** determines how many frames per second are displayed in the movie.

The **palette channel** sets the available colors for the movie.

The **transition channel** allows you to set screen transitions such as fades and wipes.

You can use the two **sound channels** to add music, sound effects, and voice-overs.

The **behavior channel** (sometimes called the **script channel**) provides a place to write frame scripts. Frame scripts provide one way to add interactivity to a movie.

The **frame channel**, or **timeline**, is the shaded channel that contains the numbers 5, 10, 15, 20, and so on. These numbers identify the frame number. **Frames** represent a single step in a movie, like the frames in traditional film. Each column in the score is a frame, and frames are numbered from left to right.

The object in the frame channel is the **playback head**; it moves through the score, indicating the frame that is currently displayed on the stage. The playback head moves to any frame you click in the score's timeline or when you click any cell in the score.

The numbered channels are **sprite channels**. You use these channels to assemble and synchronize all the visual media elements such as graphics, backgrounds, buttons, additional sounds, text, and digital video. A **sprite** is a representation of a cast member that has been placed on the stage or in the score, much as an actor on a stage is a representation of a character in a film script. There are 1000 available sprite channels.

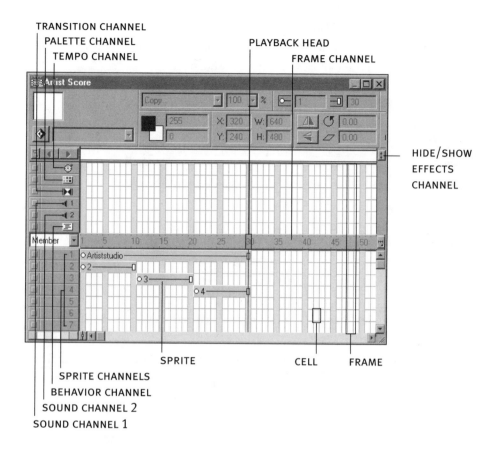

TRANSITION CHANNEL
PALETTE CHANNEL
TEMPO CHANNEL
PLAYBACK HEAD
FRAME CHANNEL

HIDE/SHOW
EFFECTS
CHANNEL

SPRITE
CELL
FRAME

SPRITE CHANNELS
BEHAVIOR CHANNEL
SOUND CHANNEL 2
SOUND CHANNEL 1

The smallest unit in the score—a single rectangle—is a **cell**. As Director plays a movie, the playback head moves from left to right across the frame channel in the score. As the playback head enters a frame, Director draws the sprites that it finds in the sprite channels for that frame. When the playback head moves to another frame, Director redraws the stage with the sprites in the frames it enters. This is how animation effects are created.

When drawing each frame on the stage, Director draws the contents of each sprite channel starting with sprite channel 1, and the remaining channels overdraw the lower numbered channels wherever they might overlap. As a result, the highest numbered sprite will always be visible and the lower numbered sprites will be visible only if no higher numbered sprite appears at that same location. For this reason, the background image, if any, is usually kept in sprite channel 1 (the lowest numbered sprite).

You should know one other score feature. The shaded panel at the top of the score is the **sprite toolbar**, which you can use to change the properties of sprites. You will learn how to use the sprite toolbar in the next lesson.

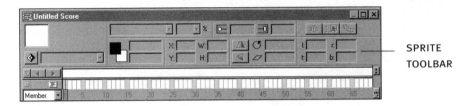

SPRITE
TOOLBAR

OPENING THE TEXT AND PAINT WINDOWS

Director includes tools for creating and editing cast members: the Text and Paint windows. You'll look at these windows next.

1] Choose Window › Text to open the Text window (Windows Ctrl+6, Macintosh Command+6).

The Text window is used for creating and editing text. In addition to changing fonts, font styles, and point sizes, you can also adjust the space between lines of text (leading) and between characters (kerning). You can enter text from the keyboard or import the text from other sources.

FONT   TYPE STYLE   TYPE   LINE SPACING SETTING
MENU   BUTTONS   SIZE MENU   TEXT ALIGNMENT BUTTONS

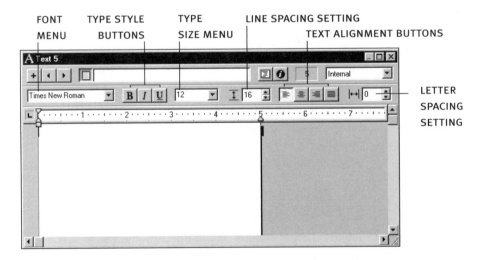

LETTER
SPACING
SETTING

2] Close the Text window by clicking the close box.

3] Choose Window › Paint to open the Paint window (Windows Ctrl+5, Macintosh Command+5).

The Paint window includes a number of tools for creating and editing graphics. All images you create using the Paint window become members of the cast. In addition to creating filled and unfilled shapes, you can use the tools to create many interesting effects with color. You'll use some of these tools later in this book to create as well as edit images for use in Director movies.

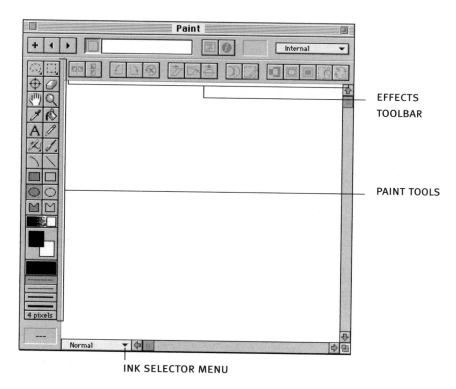

4] Close the Paint window.

USING THE HELP SYSTEM

Although Director is capable of performing many complex tasks, it remains simple to use. Director's help system can be especially useful because it includes complete documentation of all of Director's commands and features and is always available from the desktop. Here's how you use Director's help system:

1] Choose Help from the menu bar.

The Help menu appears. You can navigate to a particular area of the help system by clicking the corresponding menu item.

From here you can view contents, the index, or specific help topics.

2] Close the help window.

You've now seen how to open the most common windows in Director. As you work with Director, opening and closing these windows will become second nature to you. Here are two more steps that will make Director easier for you to use.

3] Choose View > Sprite Overlay. If either Show Info or Show Paths is checked, click on it to uncheck it. This will affect what shows up on the stage and will make the stage less crowded.

4] Choose View > Sprite Toolbar to make sure the command is checked and the Sprite Toolbar will be visible.

CREATING A NEW MOVIE

Now you'll learn how to use the cast, stage, control panel, and score to create a Director movie. You are going to create the beginning of the speaker presentation. Remember how the text changed color over the background graphic? You are going to add the same effect to a presentation you create. Open a new Director file.

1] Choose File > New > Movie to start a new movie (Windows Ctrl+N, Macintosh Command+N). If Director asks you whether you want to save changes, click No.

You see an empty stage on screen. This simple command is similar to the command used to create a new file in any application.

IMPORTING AN IMAGE

Director can import many types of image files for you to use in your movies. In both the Windows and Macintosh versions of Director, you can import BMP, GIF, JPEG, Photoshop 3.0 and later, and other graphics formats.

Now you will import the graphic that appears as the background for the speaker's presentation. The graphic will be cast member number 1 of the new movie you are creating. In the Cast window, you see that cast member 1 is highlighted.

1] Choose File › Import (Windows Ctrl+R, Macintosh Command+R). In the Import dialog box, open the Media folder for Lesson01. Then select Artiststudio.tif and click Add.

The Media folder contains only one file, Artiststudio.tif. This is the graphic you will import into your presentation. When you click Add, Artiststudio.tif appears in the file list panel of the dialog box.

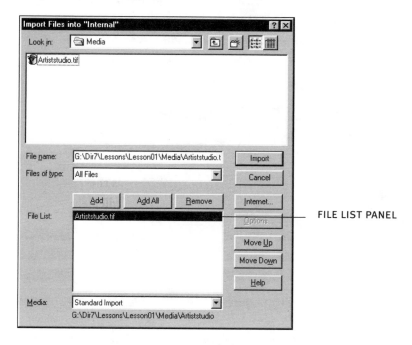

FILE LIST PANEL

2] Click Import.

Director displays the Image Options dialog box, indicating that the graphic you are importing has a different color depth than the system into which you're importing it. The number of colors a graphic or a computer system can display is called the **color depth**. Your computer monitor and the images you import into a movie can have different color depths.

An image with a 1-bit color depth appears only in black and white, and a monitor with a 1-bit color depth setting displays only black-and-white images. The higher the color depth value, the greater the number of colors that can be displayed. The most common color depths display colors like this: 2-bit displays 4 colors, 4-bit displays 16 colors, 8-bit displays 256 colors, 16-bit displays 32,768 colors, and both 24-bit and 32-bit display 16.7 million colors. (With 32-bit color, 8 bits are reserved for transparency, or "alpha," information.)

By default, the original 32-bit color depth of the graphic is selected in the dialog box. For the entire range of colors in the graphic to appear in the movie, a large amount of memory will be required. In most cases, you should transform graphics with higher color depth settings to the lower setting listed next to the Stage radio button. This value reflects the color depth set for your system, so an 8-bit stage setting reflects an 8-bit monitor setting.

If your computer monitor is set to a higher color depth than 8 bits, the stage setting in this dialog box will be a higher number, such as 16 bits. If your monitor is set to 32 bits, the same color depth as the graphic, this dialog box will not appear. Unless otherwise stated, all instructions in this course assume that your monitor is set to 8-bit color.

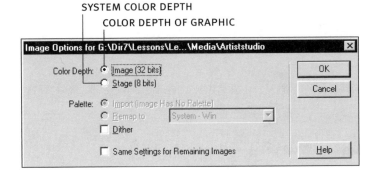

tip *Since many low-end systems support only 8-bit graphics, you should change graphical media elements to 8-bit graphics when you import them, especially if you intend to distribute a movie to a wide audience. Also, changing graphics to a lower color depth requires less storage space and memory, which is important if your movie will be used on the Internet. On the other hand, if you know you will be distributing or playing back on systems that support greater bit depths, you should stay with the higher bit depth because you can then take advantage of features like Director's Alpha Channel support and anti-aliasing for terrific special effects and appearances.*

If you don't change a graphic to the stage color depth when you import it, you may see ugly color flashes when the graphic appears on the stage. The flashes occur because the stage color depth setting (the system color depth used when the movie was created) takes precedence over the cast member color depth. As the movie plays, the cast members that contain more color information than the stage can display cause conflicts in the colors that appear on the stage. To avoid this, choose an appropriate color depth when you begin creating a movie and use graphics with the same color depth.

3] Select the Stage (8 bits) color depth and then click OK.

You have imported the graphic and reduced its color to 8 bits. In the Cast window, you can see that the graphic is now cast member 1. A thumbnail version of the graphic appears along with the name of the graphic.

4] Choose File › Save to save your work (Windows Ctrl+S, Macintosh Command+S). Name your file *Artist.dir* and save it in the Projects folder.

ADDING SPRITES TO THE STAGE

You can create a sprite by dragging it onto the stage. Remember that a sprite is only a representation of a cast member. If you look in the Cast window after you drag a cast member to the stage, you will see that the cast member remains in the Cast window. The image that appears on the stage is the sprite that represents the cast member.

As you will see, you can reposition sprites on the stage and make other changes to them without affecting the original cast members. In this task, you will place a sprite that represents the imported graphic on the stage.

1] Click frame 1 in the frame channel to move the playback head to frame 1.

Now when you add a media element to the stage, it will be placed in frame 1.

CLICK FRAME 1 TO PLACE THE PLAYBACK HEAD THERE

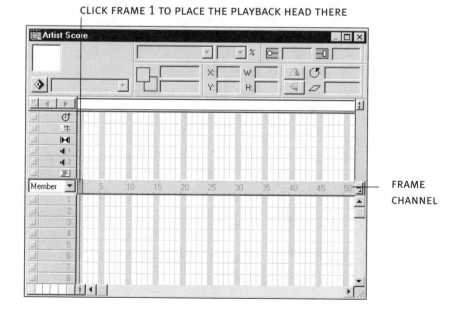

FRAME CHANNEL

2] Drag cast member 1 from the Cast window to the center of the stage.

Only the outline of the graphic appears as you drag the cast member. Use the outline to determine when the image is centered between the stage borders (you can adjust it again later). You can see the sprite on the stage when you release the mouse button. It appears wherever the cursor was when you released the mouse button.

DRAG AND CENTER THE CAST MEMBER ON THE STAGE

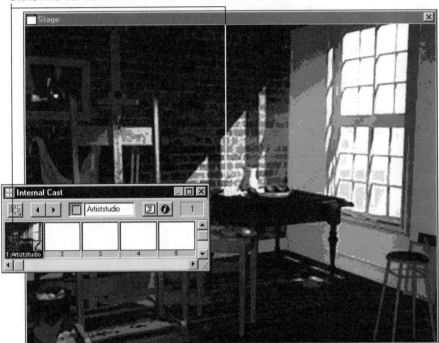

In channel 1 of the score, the sprite is represented by a shaded bar labeled Artiststudio. The sprite appears from frame 1 to frame 28 in channel 1, which means that the background graphic will appear for 28 frames of the presentation. The choice of 28 frames is the default number used by Director 7. You can change this value at any time.

note   *If the Score window does not show the Sprite toolbar (the sprite information area at the top of the score, shown in the illustration above), you can display it by choosing View > Sprite Toolbar.*

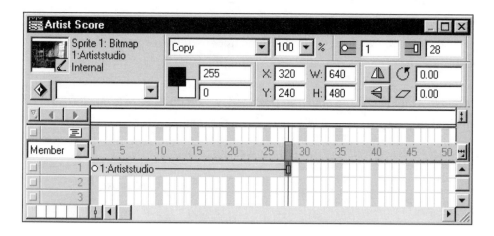

Notice the small dot in frame 1 in the score. This dot indicates the **start frame**, or the first frame of the sprite. The small bar in the last frame of the sprite is the **end frame** indicator, or the last frame of the sprite. You can drag these indicators to make a sprite appear in fewer frames or more frames in the score.

START FRAME INDICATOR   END FRAME INDICATOR

3] Click and drag the end frame indicator to frame 30.

The sprite will now appear on the stage from frame 1 to frame 30. By dragging the end frame, you have just made the presentation longer, since Director will play as long as there are sprites to display.

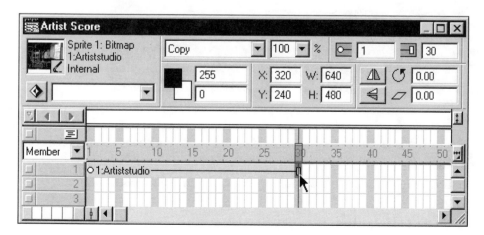

CREATING TEXT CAST MEMBERS

In the next task you will add another cast member to the presentation. Instead of importing a cast member, you will create it yourself using the Text window.

1] Choose Window › Text to open the Text window (Windows Ctrl+6, Macintosh Command+6), or click the Text window icon on the toolbar.

TEXT WINDOW

In the Text window you will create text for the presentation. You can select a font, style, size, line spacing, and letter spacing for the text.

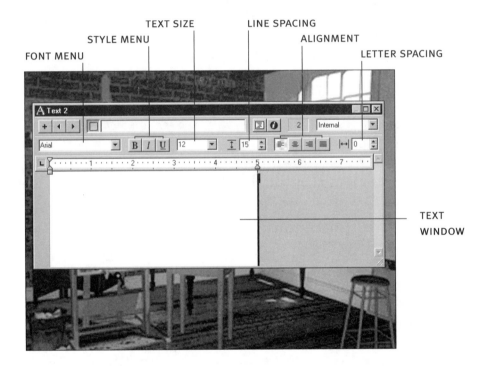

2] Select Times as the font, click the Bold style button, and choose 36 points as the text size.

The Text window's controls are similar to those of many word processors.

3] Enter the following text:

Ideas Come to Light

24

CAST MEMBER NUMBER

The text you enter in the Text window automatically becomes a cast member. Look in the Cast window to see that cast member 2 now contains text. Cast members you create within Director itself are generally placed in the first blank position in the Cast window. You could choose a different cast location by selecting an empty position before creating the new cast member. The new cast member would then be placed in the selected position.

You won't add this text to the stage yet. First you will create two more cast members that are identical to the text you just entered and assign each a different color. Then you will create an animation that uses the different-colored text to add interest to the presentation.

tip   *The Text window uses any font installed in the system. If you play the final version of a Director presentation and the text doesn't appear as you expect it to, the font may not be installed on the system on which you're running the presentation. To correct this, install the missing font(s) on the system or select replacement fonts for the text in the movie. (Alternatively, you can use Shockwave fonts in your movie.) When you create a projector or a Shockwave movie, Director can turn the font outlines of text into images called* **bitmaps** *of the font shapes, so the text looks correct even if the fonts are not installed. With bitmapped text, the systems that play the movie don't need to have installed the same fonts that were used to create the movie. Director can also embed font outlines in a projector if you don't want the text displayed as bitmaps.*

4] Highlight the text in the Text window and then choose Edit › Copy Text (Windows Ctrl+C, Macintosh Command+C).

You are going to paste this text into a new Text window.

5] Click the New Cast Member icon on the Text window toolbar to add a new cast member.

CLICK HERE TO CREATE A NEW CAST MEMBER

An empty Text window labeled Text 3 appears. The text you enter in this window will become cast member number 3.

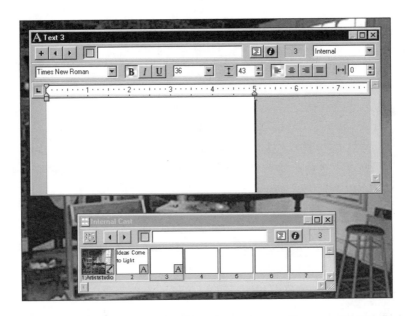

6] Choose Edit › Paste Text (Windows Ctrl+V, Macintosh Command+V).

Director pastes the text you copied into the new Text window. Check the Cast window to see the text you pasted into cast member 3.

7] Click New Cast Member to add another cast member. Then choose Edit › Paste Text.

Now when you look in the Cast window, you should see three identical text cast members.

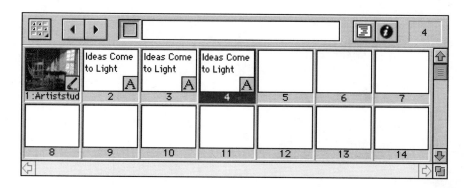

Notice that the Cast window displays information about each cast member. The graphic you imported is identified by its original file name. The cast members you just created don't have names, though you could add names to them if you wanted. You will learn how to name cast members in the next lesson.

8] Save your work.

You have finished creating the cast members you will use in this presentation. As you look at the cast, you're probably wondering why you have created three identical text cast members. In the next task, you will change them so that each is a different color.

CHANGING THE COLOR OF CAST MEMBERS

Remember how the text in the Artist.dir movie changed colors? That is the effect you will create for the text in the presentation. Right now the text color of each of the cast members is black and will not show up well on the graphic you have placed in the background. In the following steps, you will change each cast member to a color that will stand out against the background graphic.

1] Select the text in the Text window for cast member 4.

Make sure you highlight all the text.

2] Choose Window › Tool Palette (Windows Ctrl+7, Macintosh Command+7).

This displays the tool palette. You can use the tool palette to create shapes and other objects. As you can see, the tools are similar to those found in drawing programs. You use the foreground color chip to assign a color to the filled shapes you draw. In the next step, you will use the foreground color chip to assign a color to the text you have selected.

FILLED SHAPE TOOLS

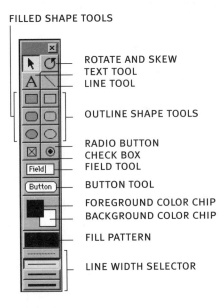

ROTATE AND SKEW
TEXT TOOL
LINE TOOL

OUTLINE SHAPE TOOLS

RADIO BUTTON
CHECK BOX
FIELD TOOL

BUTTON TOOL

FOREGROUND COLOR CHIP
BACKGROUND COLOR CHIP

FILL PATTERN

LINE WIDTH SELECTOR

3] Click the foreground color chip to open the color palette. Then select a light color for the text.

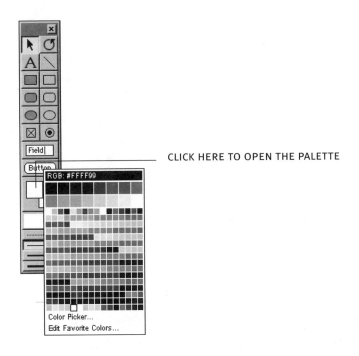

CLICK HERE TO OPEN THE PALETTE

RGB: #FFFF99

Color Picker...
Edit Favorite Colors...

When you deselect the text, you will see that the color is changed.

4] In the Text window, click the Previous Cast Member arrow.

CLICK HERE TO DISPLAY THE PREVIOUS CAST MEMBER

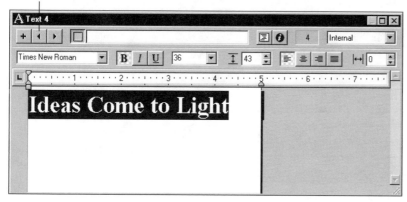

The Text window should already be open on the screen, displaying cast member 4. When you click Previous Cast Member, cast member 3 is displayed. Now you will change the color of this text.

5] Select the text in the Text window. Then click the foreground color chip in the tool palette again and choose a different color for this text.

As you select colors, try to choose colors that you think will show up well against the background graphic and that are different from one another.

6] Click Previous Cast Member to display cast member 2.

7] Select the text and then choose another color from the tool palette.

Now you have changed the text colors for each cast member. Look at the cast members in the Cast window and notice that the text is still black. Director displays the thumbnail text in black so you can read it against the white background in the Cast window. When these cast members appear on the stage, the colors you selected will appear.

8] Close the Text window.

ADDING SPRITES TO THE SCORE

All your media is now assembled, and you can begin to sequence it by placing the media elements in the presentation where they will appear.

1] Drag cast member 2 to frame 1, channel 2, in the score (not the stage). Dragging cast members is another way to create sprites.

Notice that once again, by default, Director puts the sprite in 28 frames of the movie; you will change this placement later. The sprite is also labeled with the cast member number it represents, cast member 2.

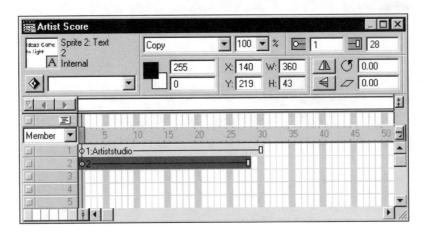

Look at the stage to see how Director has automatically centered the sprite. When you drag a sprite to the score (instead of the stage), it is automatically centered on the stage.

2] Drag cast member 3 to frame 1, channel 3. Then drag cast member 4 to frame 1, channel 4.

Now cast members 2, 3, and 4 have sprites in the score. These sprites occupy channels 2, 3, and 4.

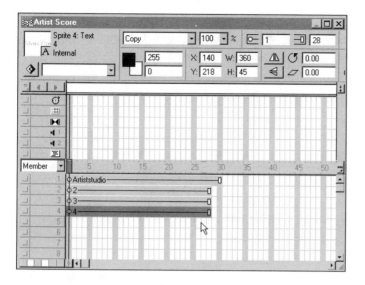

You can see only one of the sprites on the stage, although you added three sprites to the movie. In the middle of the stage you see the text in the color you selected for cast member 4. This is the sprite for that cast member. The handles around the sprite show that it is selected.

The sprites in channels 2 and 3 are stacked behind the sprite you see on the stage. These sprites are stacked in the order in which you placed the cast members in the score. Director always displays the sprites in higher-numbered channels in front of those in lower-numbered channels when they overlap each other on the stage. The sprites appear centered on the stage because Director automatically centers the sprites when you drag cast members to the score.

The white box that appears around the text is the default background. Though you can't see the other two sprites right now, they also have white backgrounds. In the next task, you will select all the text sprites and remove their white backgrounds. You will also place them in the movie to create the color-change effects for the movie.

3] Save your work.

MAKING CHANGES TO MULTIPLE SPRITES

In this task, you will move all the sprites for the text to the upper-left corner of the stage and then remove the white background that surrounds the text. In the Score window, only the sprite in channel 4 appears highlighted. To move all three text sprites at once, all three sprites must be selected.

1] Hold down the Shift key and click between the start and end frames of the sprite in channel 3.

Pressing Shift as you click lets you add to the current selection. When you click between the start and end frames of a sprite, the whole sprite is selected. (If you click either of the end frames, only that particular end frame is selected.) The sprites in channels 3 and 4 should now be selected.

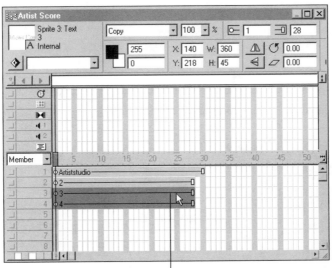

CLICK HERE TO SELECT THE SPRITE IN CHANNEL 3

2] Hold down the Shift key and select the sprite in channel 2.

All three text sprites are selected in the score. Now you can move them all together to their new location on the stage.

3] Drag the text sprite shown on the stage to the upper-left corner of the stage.

If one of the windows blocks the view of the sprites on the stage, you can click the title bar of the stage to bring the stage to the foreground. When you want to view the other windows, you can bring them to the foreground by using the Windows menu.

Although you can see only one sprite selected on the stage, the two other sprites behind it are also selected because you selected them in the score. When you drag the sprite, all three sprites move to the new location.

Check the score to see that the sprites in channels 2 through 4 are still selected.

In the next step, you will remove the white background around the text by using an **ink effect**. Ink effects modify the appearance of a sprite on the stage, affecting the way the sprite is displayed against the objects or background behind it. Applying an ink effect to sprites does not affect the cast members themselves, only the appearance of the sprite. You will often need to apply ink effects to sprites to make them appear exactly the way you want them.

4] In the sprite toolbar at the top of the score, open the Ink menu and select Background Transparent.

The Ink menu is currently set to Copy.

INK MENU

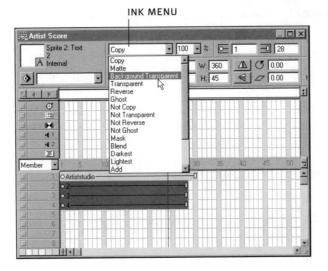

Changing the ink effect to Background Transparent removes the white background of the sprite. In this case, you removed the white boxes around three sprites all at once. Inks are used most often to remove the backgrounds from media elements, but they can also create interesting and useful effects.

For example, the Background Transparent ink makes the pixels in the background color of the sprite appear transparent and permits the background to be seen, and the Reverse ink effect reverses overlapping colors. You will use other ink effects later in this book.

Until now you have been busy gathering and creating the movie's media elements and placing them on the stage. Now it's time to order the sprites in the score so you can show a change in color.

SEQUENCING SPRITES

In this task, you will sequence the text sprites in the score so they appear one after the other when the presentation plays, thereby creating the effect of the text changing color. To do this, you must work with one sprite at a time. You will begin by working with the sprite in channel 2.

1] Select the sprite in channel 2.

The sprites in channels 3 and 4 become unselected, while the sprite in channel 2 remains selected.

2] Drag the end frame indicator in channel 2, frame 28, to frame 10.

Now the sprite is on the stage from frame 1 through frame 10.

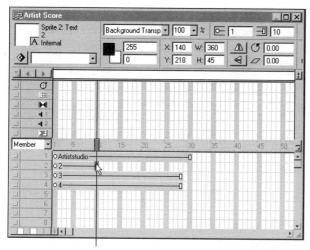

DRAG THE END FRAME TO FRAME 10

3] Select the sprite in channel 3 and then drag the end frame to frame 10.

You want channels 2, 3, and 4 each to contain sprites that are 10 frames in duration. You can then easily sequence the sprites in these three channels to fill 30 frames. Since the background graphic sprite in channel 1 occurs in 30 frames, making the text change colors within 30 frames creates a complete movie.

4] With the sprite in channel 3 still selected, click between the start and end frames and drag to the right to place the start frame in frame 11.

Be sure not to drag the sprite's start or end frame indicator; otherwise, you will change the number of frames in which the sprite appears.

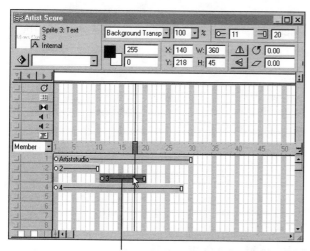

CLICK BETWEEN THE START AND END FRAMES
OF SELECTED SPRITES TO DRAG THEM

For the sprite in channel 3 to appear directly after the sprite in channel 2, the start frame must be in frame 11. Once you have repositioned the sprite that appears in channel 3, you should begin to see how Director will display the text in channel 2 for 10 frames and then display the text in channel 3 for the next 10 frames. You can probably guess what must be done to the sprite in channel 4 to make it appear directly after the sprite in channel 3.

5] Click channel 4 and drag the sprite's end frame to frame 10. Then drag the entire sprite so its start frame is in frame 21.

The sprites for each color of text in the movie now appear in their own sets of frames.

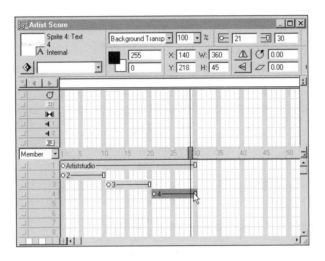

6] Click frame 1 in the frame channel to move the playback head to frame 1.

Notice that the text you see on the stage is a different color than the text you last saw on the stage. With the playback head in frame 1, you now see the sprite for the background graphic and the sprite for cast member 2.

7] Save your work.

You have assembled the media elements for the presentation, placed them on the stage where they belong, and sequenced them in the score so they will appear when you want them. The only thing left to do is play the presentation to see how it looks.

PLAYING A MOVIE

In this task you will use the control panel to play the movie you have created.

1] Click on the title bar of the stage to bring it to the foreground so the Score and Cast windows do not block your view of the stage.

2] Choose Window › Control Panel to open the control panel.

3] Click Loop Playback to turn on this feature.

You turn on Loop Playback so Director will play the presentation continuously. If Loop Playback isn't active, the presentation will stop playing after the playback head reaches the last frame of the movie.

LOOP PLAYBACK BUTTON

STOP   PLAY

4] Click Play.

Watch the text change from one color to the next. Congratulations! You created that effect, and it's a great animation for the beginning of a speaker's presentation.

Now watch the Score window to see how the playback head determines what you see on the stage. If the Score window is not visible, you can display it from the Director menu by choosing Windows > Score. The movement of the playback head through the frames makes the sprites display the simple color animation you sequenced in the score. Because Loop Playback is on, after the playback head moves to the last frame of the movie, it returns to frame 1, and the movie plays again.

5] Click Stop and close the control panel.

You've created your first animation in a short period of time. Of course, if you were developing a complete interactive presentation, you would add many more media elements and the presentation would be much longer and more complex. In the remaining lessons in this book, you will add more complex features to Director projects. In the next lesson, you will finish this presentation by adding an animated bullet list.

WHAT YOU HAVE LEARNED

In this lesson you have:

• Created a new movie [page 18]

• Imported a graphic background image [page 18]

• Created cast members using the Text window [page 24]

• Applied the Background Transparent ink effect to text sprites to make their backgrounds transparent [page 33]

• Created a simple animation that shows text changing color [page 34]

animated bullet lists

LESSON 2

Animation is the core of Director's power. Director lets you create animations in many ways, but one of the simplest is by using **keyframes**. To use a keyframe, you select a frame within a sprite where you want the sprite to appear different in size or position or in some other way. Then you use the Insert › Keyframe command and make the change to the sprite as it appears on the stage in that keyframe.

A simple way to show movement is to set up a start position and an end position for a sprite and let Director take care of the movement in between. You accomplish this by inserting a keyframe in the sprite and moving the sprite to the new location. The new location you select should be a place on the stage where you want the sprite to appear

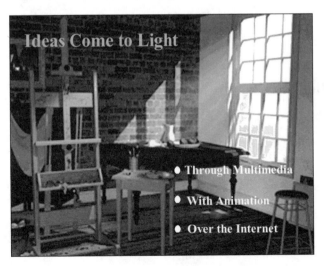

The speaker's presentation you began in the last lesson can be enriched with another popular effect: a bullet list in which the bullet points animate onto the stage as the speaker makes each point.

in the frame you identify as a keyframe. For instance, to show a fish swimming across the stage, you might position the fish at the left side of the stage in the start frame of the sprite, and then insert a keyframe in the end frame of the sprite and move the fish sprite to the far right side of the stage. Director will automatically supply the positions for the sprite in all the frames in between the start and end positions. In this lesson, you'll use this method to create a simple bullet list that slides onto the stage, one bullet at a time, to support a speaker's presentation. You will also learn about a few new tools for creating and positioning sprites.

If you would like to view the final result of this lesson, open the Complete folder in the Lesson02 folder and play ArtList.dir.

WHAT YOU WILL LEARN

In this lesson you will:

- Practice using the Text window to create sprites
- Practice applying ink effects to sprites
- Practice sequencing sprites in the score
- Use the Paint window to create a graphic cast member
- Apply a gradient color effect to a graphic cast member
- Use the score's Zoom menu
- Align sprites using the Align panel
- Name sprites to help identify them in the score
- Set sprite end frames using the sprite toolbar
- Insert keyframes to create animations

APPROXIMATE TIME

It should take about 1 hour to complete this lesson.

LESSON FILES

Media Files:
None

Starting Files:
Dir7\Lessons\Lesson02\Start\Start.dir

Completed Project:
Dir7\Lessons\Lesson02\Complete\ArtList.dir

OPENING THE FILE

Start by opening the prebuilt file, Start.dir, for Lesson 2.

1] Choose File › Open to open Start.dir in the Lesson02 folder (Windows Ctrl+O, Macintosh Command+O).

Notice that the score is already filled with the sprites used in Lesson 1 to create the Artist.dir movie. In addition, the sprite for the background graphic has been extended to make the movie longer, and the sequence of the sprites that change color repeats to the end of the movie. This work has been done for you so you can concentrate on creating new cast members for this movie and placing them in the score.

2] Choose File › Save As and save the file as *ArtList.dir* in your Projects folder.

This step places a copy of the prebuilt file on your computer, since you can't save files on the CD.

ADDING TEXT CAST MEMBERS

You need to create the text that will be animated. You used the Text window in Lesson 1 to create cast members, and you will use it again here to create the lines of text in the bullet list.

1] Choose Window › Text to open the Text window (Windows Ctrl+6, Macintosh Command+6).

You will create three lines of text as separate cast members.

2] Select Times as the font, the Bold style, and a size of 24 points for the text.

The font for these new cast members should be identical to the font you selected for the title, but the font size should be reduced.

3] Enter this line of text:

Through Multimedia

The color of the text will be the color that was last used for creating text. Check the Cast window to see the text. It should appear as cast member 5.

LINGO EQUIVALENT

```
newTextMem = new(#Text)
newTextMem.text = "Through multimedia"
newTextMem.font = "Times"
newTextMem.fontStyle = [#Bold]
newTextMem.fontSize = 24
```

4] Select all the text in the Text window. Then open the tool palette and click the foreground color chip to select a light color for the text.

You can also reverse the actions in steps 3 and 4, choosing a color first and then typing the text. We are changing the color so we can select a color that will show up well against the background graphic.

5] Click New Cast Member to create a new cast member. Then enter this text:
With Animation

This text appears in the color you selected in the tool palette.

6] Create one more text cast member and then enter this text:
Over the Internet

7] Close the Text window.
The cast should now have seven members.

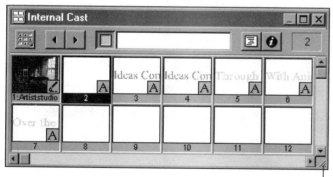

DRAG TO RESIZE

If you can't see cast member 7, either use the scroll bar or drag the lower-right corner of the Cast window to resize the window. You can also choose File > Preferences > Cast to choose the number of thumbnails you want to see per row.

8] Close the tool palette. Then choose File › Save to save your work (Windows Ctrl+S, Macintosh Command+S).
You have finished creating the cast members that will be the lines of text in the bullet list. In the next task, you'll create another cast member that you will use as the bullet that begins each line; you will create this new cast member in the Paint window.

USING THE PAINT WINDOW

The Paint window provides common paint tools such as the Air Brush and Paint Bucket and the shape tools for creating and editing graphic cast members. In the next task, you will use one of the shape tools, the Filled Ellipse tool, to create a bullet for the presentation's bullet points. You will also use another Paint window tool, Gradient Colors, to add more visual interest to the bullet.

1] Choose Window > Paint to open the Paint window (Windows Ctrl+5, Macintosh Command+5), or click the Paint window button on the toolbar.

PAINT WINDOW

An empty Paint window appears. In the next steps, you will select gradient colors for the Gradient Colors tool and then create a bullet object and apply a gradient setting to it.

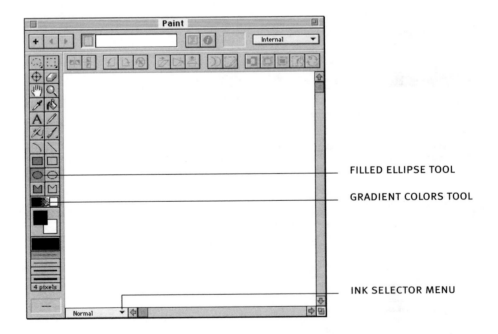

FILLED ELLIPSE TOOL

GRADIENT COLORS TOOL

INK SELECTOR MENU

2] Click the foreground color chip on the Paint window's Gradient Colors tool and select the same color you assigned to the bullet point text.

This is the beginning color of the color blend you will create with this tool. You will also select a destination color that the Gradient Colors tool will use as the end color of the blend it will create in an object.

42

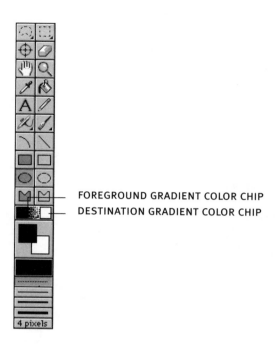

FOREGROUND GRADIENT COLOR CHIP
DESTINATION GRADIENT COLOR CHIP

3] Click the destination gradient color chip and choose a bright color as the destination color.

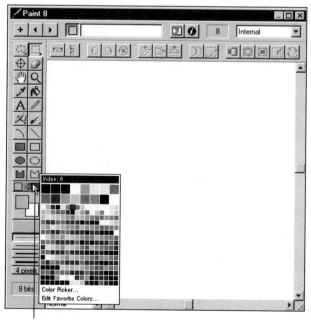

CLICK THE DESTINATION GRADIENT COLOR CHIP

The Gradient Colors tool now displays the foreground and destination gradient colors you chose. A blend of these colors will fill objects you create in the Paint window when you apply Gradient ink to them.

4] Click the Filled Ellipse tool.

Select the Filled Ellipse tool to draw an ellipse or a circle that is filled with the currently selected ink.

5] Click the Ink Selector and choose Gradient.

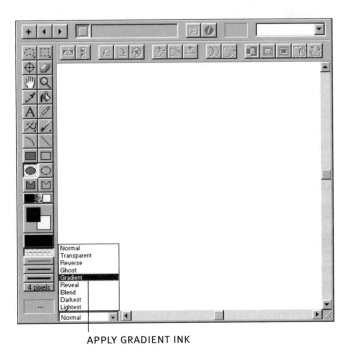

APPLY GRADIENT INK

You have just assigned Gradient ink to the Filled Ellipse tool you selected. The objects you draw using the Filled Ellipse tool will be filled with a gradient blend of the colors you chose for the Gradient Colors tool. In the next step, you will select a gradient pattern that Director will use to blend the colors.

6] Click the Gradient Colors menu and select Sun Burst. The Gradient Colors menu selector is the small area between the gradient foreground and destination color chips.

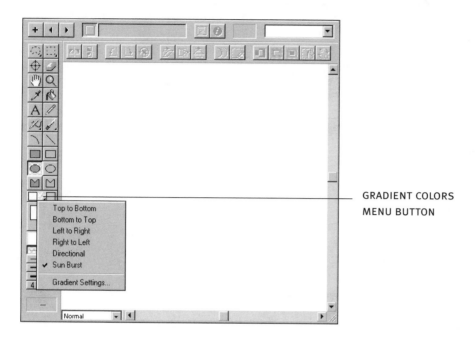

GRADIENT COLORS
MENU BUTTON

The Sun Burst pattern blends the gradient colors from the center of an object outward. The color at the center of the object will be the destination color, and the foreground gradient color will appear at the outer edge.

7] With the Filled Ellipse tool still selected, hold down the Shift key and drag to create a small circle shape in the Paint window.

Holding down the Shift key as you drag creates a perfect circle. To create a bullet that is the appropriate size, keep this shape very small, just a little larger than the Filled Ellipse tool in the Paint window's tool palette.

MARQUEE TOOL

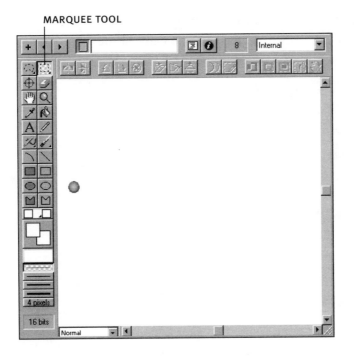

tip *To remove an object from the Paint window, use the Marquee tool in the Paint window's tool palette. Click the Marquee tool and drag a marquee around the object; then press Delete. You can also double-click the Eraser tool. If you don't like the bullet you created, you can remove it and try again.*

8] Close the Paint window.

In the cast, the thumbnail view of the bullet shows the blend of the gradient colors you selected.

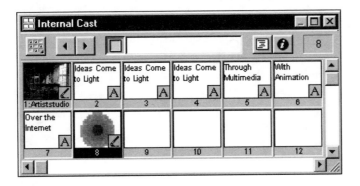

You have finished creating the text and the bullet for the presentation's bullet list. The next step is to place these items in the score and animate them.

PLACING SPRITES IN THE SCORE

To prepare the new cast members for animation, you'll first drag them to the score to create sprites for the bullets and the text. Before you begin work, change the view of the score so you can see more frames.

1] In the score, click the Zoom menu and choose 50%.

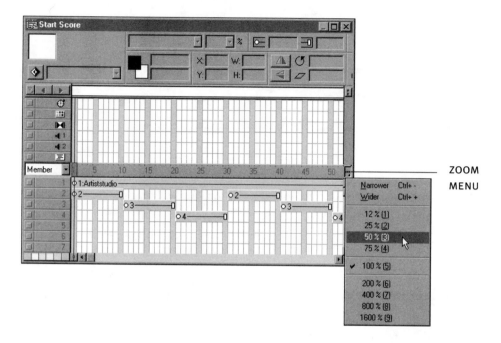

ZOOM
MENU

The Score window changes to display up to 100 frames of the score. The selections in the Zoom menu let you control how you view the score. Choose zoom out selections (12%, 25%, 50%, and 75%) to see more frames. Choose zoom in selections (200%, 400%, 800%, and 1600%) to view fewer frames. The Narrower and Wider options let you change the width of the cells in the zoomed view you select.

Now you are ready to create bullet sprites and arrange them in the score. The presentation needs three bullets, one for each of the three lines of text. Before the bullet makes its first appearance on the stage, you will let the text at the top of the stage cycle once through its three colors. The first color cycle ends at frame 30. That makes frame 31 a logical choice for the bullet's first appearance.

2] Drag the bullet cast member to channel 5, frame 31 in the score.

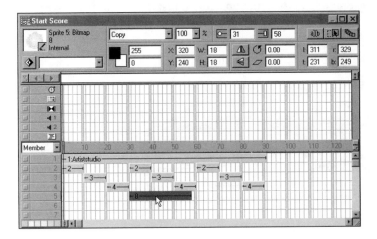

Since you need a bullet for three lines of text, you must drag the bullet cast member to two more locations in the score. In the next step, you will drag the bullet cast member to the score twice, leaving an empty channel between each set of the bullet sprites. This will make it easier later in this lesson to work with the bullet-and-text sprite pairs in the presentation.

3] Drag the bullet cast member to channel 7, frame 31. Then drag the cast member to channel 9, frame 31.

All the sprites are on the stage now and appear in 28 frames of channels 5, 7, and 9. The sprite for the third bullet in channel 9 remains highlighted since it was the last to be added to the score.

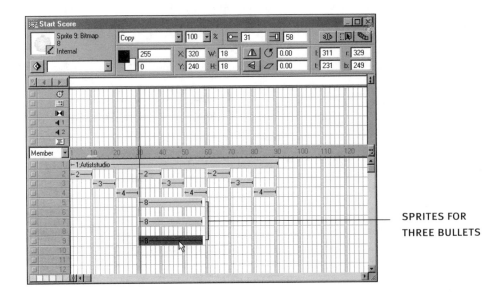

SPRITES FOR
THREE BULLETS

At this point, the sprite you see on the stage with handles around it represents all 28 frames of the sprite in channel 9. As long as the entire sprite is selected in the score, a single change on the stage affects the entire sprite. This is true regardless of the position of the playback head. This means that dragging the sprite currently selected to a new location on the stage will make the bullet appear in its new location for all of frames 31 through 58.

You have probably guessed that the empty channels that follow the bullet sprites will contain sprites for the lines of text. In the next step, you will create sprites in channels 6, 8, and 10.

4] Drag cast members 5, 6, and 7 to channels 6, 8, and 10 in frame 31 in the score.
All the sprites for the bullet list now appear in the score. Arranging the sprites on the stage will be your next task.

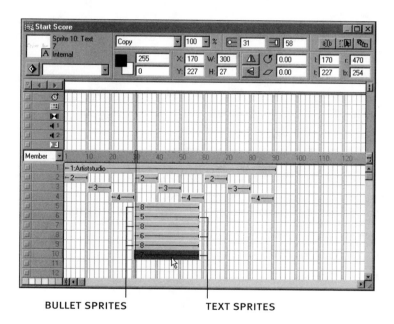

BULLET SPRITES   TEXT SPRITES

POSITIONING SPRITES ON THE STAGE

In this presentation, the bullets and lines of text fit neatly into the lower-right quadrant of the stage. The following instructions tell you how to place the sprites for the bullet list in this area, but when you create your own bullet list presentations, you'll determine the best positions for the sprites you create. A bullet list with longer lines of text, for example, would need to be positioned further to the left or in the center of the stage so all the text can be seen.

Now you will drag the bullets and text on the stage to their proper positions. You know by now that all the sprites in channels 5 through 10 are stacked in the center of the stage. You also know that the sprite you see on the stage is the sprite highlighted in channel 10, the third line of text for the bullet list and the last item you placed in the score. Before you move this sprite, you will hide the effects channels to make the score even easier to work with.

1] Click the Hide/Show Effects Channel button in the score to collapse the channels above the frame channel.

This increases the number of sprite channels you can see. You'll be filling the sprite channels with more sprites in the next few steps; so hiding the effects channels lets you see more sprite channels without scrolling or resizing the Score window.

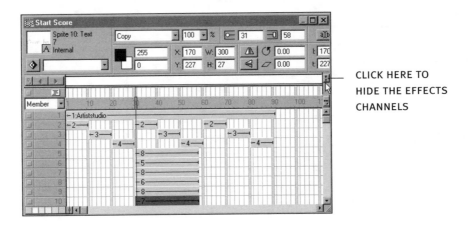

CLICK HERE TO HIDE THE EFFECTS CHANNELS

2] Drag the selected sprite to the lower area of the stage where you want the third line of text to appear.

Choose the darker area of the image where there is good contrast for the text against the image.

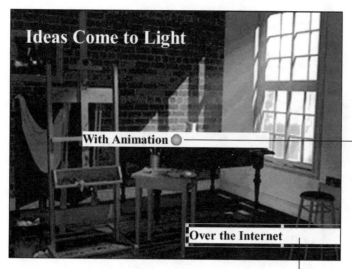

Ideas Come to Light

With Animation ⬤

Over the Internet

SPRITES IN CHANNELS 5 THROUGH 9 REMAIN CENTERED ON THE STAGE

DRAG THE SELECTED SPRITE INTO POSITION FOR THE THIRD LINE OF TEXT

LINGO EQUIVALENT

(sprite 10).loc = point(253,367)   --Takes effect on the next redraw

The other sprites that complete the bullet list are still stacked in the center of the stage. Though you can see the next line of text, the bullet is actually above it because the bullet is in channel 9 and the text is in channel 8. You will move the remaining sprites for the bullet list in the next step.

3] Click the bullet sprite in the middle of the stage to select it and then drag it next to the text sprite you moved. Because the sprite is so small, you must pay careful attention where you place the mouse to drag the sprite. As you see in the figure below, the corner areas and center-side areas are for resizing the sprite and not for dragging. If you accidentally use the wrong area you can undo your mistake using Edit › Undo Score from the Director menu (Windows Ctrl+Z, Macintosh Command+Z).

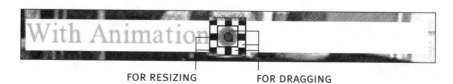

FOR RESIZING   FOR DRAGGING

4] Drag each of the remaining sprites and position them to create a completed bullet list.

Don't worry too much about exact location; we will adjust that soon.

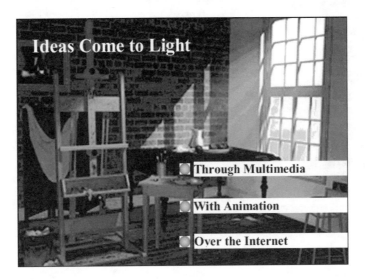

If you look at the sprites on the stage, you'll see a problem you recognize: the white backgrounds of the sprites look wrong against the presentation's background. As you know, you can solve this by applying the Background Transparent ink effect to the sprites.

To apply the ink effect to all the bullets at once, you will now select all the sprites for the bullet list in the score.

tip   *If you do not see the sprite toolbar at the top of the score, choose View > Sprite Toolbar.*

5] In the score, select the sprite in channel 5, if it's not already selected. Then hold down the Shift key and select the sprite in channel 10.

6] In the sprite toolbar, choose Background Transparent from the Ink Effects menu.
Because all of the bullet sprites are selected, this operation removes the white backgrounds for all of them at once.

LINGO EQUIVALENT

```
repeat with x = 5 to 10
    (sprite x).ink = 36                    --36 is background transparent
end repeat
```
You can find the ink numbers in Help under "ink of sprite" properties.

ALIGNING SPRITES WITH THE ALIGN PANEL

You have positioned the sprites on the stage by dragging them into place—an easy way to get them into position, but not very effective if you want them to be precisely aligned. Director offers a useful tool for aligning sprites on the stage, which you will use in this task. In these steps, you'll align just the bullets. Later you'll align the text sprites.

1] Click the stage or an empty cell in the score to deselect the sprites.

You're going to work with the three bullet sprites only. To deselect the currently selected sprites you can click an empty cell in the score.

2] On the stage, click one of the bullet sprites. Then hold down the Shift key and click each of the other bullet sprites.

This is a way to select sprites without using the score. If you look at the score, you'll see that the sprites in channels 5, 7, and 9 are selected.

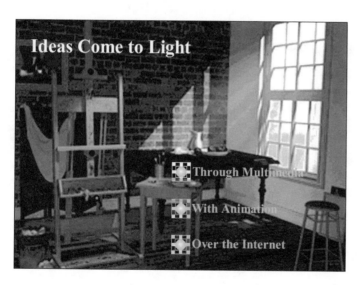

3] Choose Modify › Align (Windows Ctrl+K, Macintosh Command+K).

The Align panel appears.

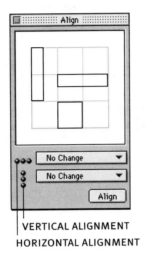

VERTICAL ALIGNMENT
HORIZONTAL ALIGNMENT

4] Click the Vertical Alignment pop-up menu and choose Align Lefts from the menu.

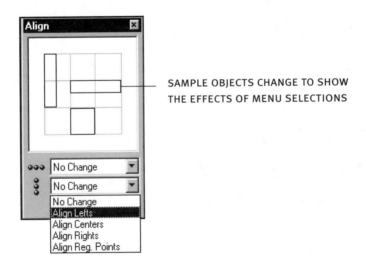

SAMPLE OBJECTS CHANGE TO SHOW
THE EFFECTS OF MENU SELECTIONS

The objects in the Align panel appear with their left sides aligned. This gives you a preview of how the sprites on the stage will be aligned.

5] Click the Align button.

All the bullet sprites appear vertically aligned on the stage.

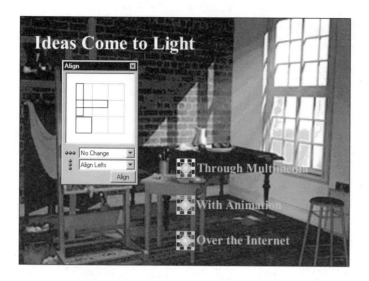

6] Close the Align panel.

In the animated bullet list, the bullets and lines of text will appear one at a time and not all at once as they appear now. The next step, then, is to sequence the sprites in the score so they appear in the same locations you have carefully established for them, but at different times.

Before you sequence the sprites, you will perform a task to make the score easier to read.

NAMING CAST MEMBERS

Naming cast members makes them easier to identify in the score. The Artiststudio cast member in channel 1 got its name from the graphic you imported. You created the other sprites in the score using the Text and Paint windows, and you can give their cast members' names in those windows; but the easiest way to name a sprite and the cast member it represents is in the Cast window.

1] In the Cast window, click cast member 8 to select it.

2] In the Name field at the top of the Cast window, type *Bullet* and then press Enter (Windows) or Return (Macintosh).

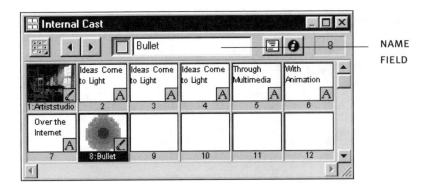

Cast member 8 and the sprites in channels 5, 7, and 9 now have names.

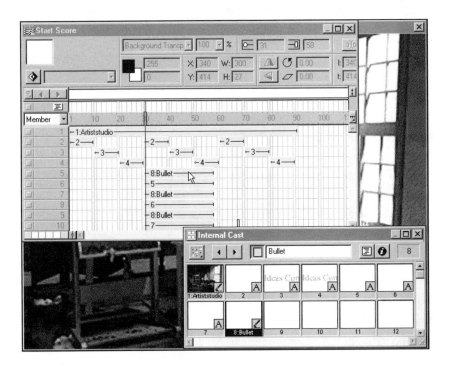

As you look through the score, it's much easier to see what's in each frame when names are attached to sprites. How would you name the sprites for the text in this presentation? That's right; click the text cast members and type a name in the Cast window's Name field.

In Director, the information shown in the sprite is a **sprite label**. As you've seen, the labels appear within the sprites in the score and include the name and number of the sprite's cast member. They can include other information about a sprite, such as its ink effect or the X and Y coordinates of the sprite's location on the stage.

You can choose the kind of information contained in sprite labels using the View > Display command or by selecting an option from the Display pop-up menu in the score. The Member option is selected by default and includes the information you see in the sprites now. You will find other options more helpful as you increase your Director skills.

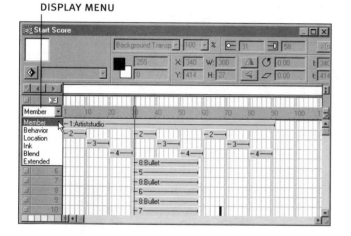

DISPLAY MENU

ANIMATING TEXT USING KEYFRAMES

At this point, you have assembled all the media elements for the presentation and placed them in the score. What you see on the stage is the way the movie will look in the last frame when all the lines of text have moved onto the stage. You now need to sequence the sprites in the score to create an animated bullet list.

In an animated bullet list, the first bullet and line of text are usually the first things you see. Then the second bullet and line of text come into view, followed by the third bullet point. To set up these appearances, each bullet-and-text sprite pair needs to be sequenced in the score so they appear in the right order. Once they are in the proper frames, you can animate the text sprites so they move onto the screen from right to left.

In the next step, you'll work with just the first bullet and line of text to appear in the presentation. As the score stands now, these sprites disappear from the stage after the playback head moves into frame 59. They should first appear in frame 31 and remain on the stage to the end of the movie at frame 90.

To make these sprites appear for more frames in the movie, you'll use the sprite toolbar in a new way. You've already used the Ink Effects menu on the toolbar. Now you will use the End Frame field to change the end frames of sprites.

1] Select the sprites in channels 5 and 6. Then type 90 in the End Frame field on the sprite toolbar and press Enter (Windows) or Return (Macintosh).

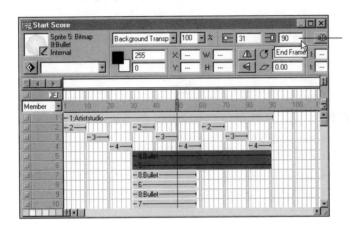

END FRAME FIELD

In Lesson 1 you changed a sprite's end frame by dragging it. In this lesson, you just used the End Frame field on the sprite toolbar to accomplish the same thing for two sprites at once. You can use either method, but you'll find the End Frame field approach most helpful when you've zoomed your view of the score to 50% or less, making the cells smaller and more difficult to select by dragging.

With the new end frame setting, these sprites appear on the stage from frame 31 to frame 90. Now you want the line of text to move onto the stage from right to left. In the next step, you will create the animation for this line of text.

The simplest way to make a sprite move from one position to another is through **tweening**. Tweening is a traditional animation term that describes the process in which an animator draws the frames where major changes take place and then the animator or assistants draw all the frames in between.

To tween the animation for the line of text, you need to set the frames in the score that correspond to the positions you want the sprite to move from and to. These frames are the **keyframes** in the animation. A keyframe is a frame in which a sprite appears in a new location, or as a different size, or changed in some other way within the entire sprite you see in the score.

In typical animations, you set a keyframe in the sprite and then move the sprite on the stage to the location where you want it to appear. As you place keyframes in the sprite, Director automatically tweens the sprites between the keyframes. You can set many keyframes in a sprite, but for the line of text in the bullet list, you will create only two keyframes. This means Director will tween all the frames between your keyframes to make the text appear to move.

2] In channel 6, click the start frame of the sprite. Because the cells are so small, you must be careful to select only the first cell. If you select a different cell, the entire length of the sprite will be selected.

By default, a sprite's start frame is a key frame. Selecting the start frame of the sprite lets Director know you want to make a change to the sprite in this frame. You want this line of text to move onto the stage from the right, so you are going to move the sprite that appears on the stage to its start position.

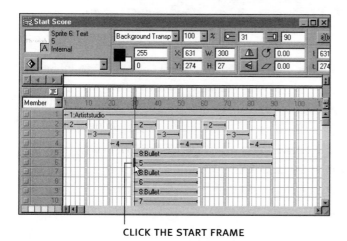

CLICK THE START FRAME

3] On the stage, hold down the Shift key and drag the sprite in a straight path to the right edge of the stage.

Holding down the Shift key as you move a sprite either horizontally or vertically moves the sprite in a straight line right to left or up and down, whichever direction you choose. Since you want the line of text to end up next to the bullet as it appears now, you should drag it straight to its start location using the Shift key.

DRAG THE
SPRITE TO
THE EDGE
OF THE PAGE

With this step, you've set the start position of the text in a keyframe of the animation (the start frame). Now you need to set up a keyframe and position the text where it should appear next to the bullet at the end of the animation.

4] Click frame 40 in channel 6. Then choose Insert › Keyframe (Windows, Ctrl+Alt+K, Macintosh Command+Option+K).

Choosing frame 40 for a keyframe makes the animation occur in frames 31 through 40. This 10-frame animation will get the text in place quickly. After frame 40, the line of text will remain in place.

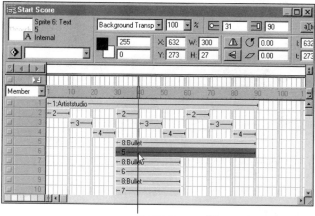

CLICK FRAME 40 IN THE CHANNEL

After you insert a keyframe, Director places a **keyframe indicator** in the sprite. After every keyframe, Director inserts a sprite label in the sprite so you can identify what appears after the keyframe. In a more complex animation, you could choose another sprite to appear after a keyframe, and this label would identify the sprite you selected. In this animation, your keyframe simply signifies a change in location for the same sprite, so the two sprite labels you see in channel 6 are identical.

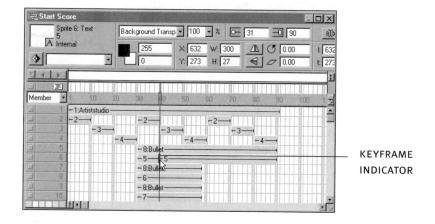

KEYFRAME
INDICATOR

5] On the stage, hold down the Shift key and drag the text sprite to its end position next to the bullet.

DRAG THE SPRITE TO ITS END POSITION NEXT TO THE BULLET

You've now assigned two different positions to the sprite: one position in frame 31 and another in frame 40. Director has already tweened the frames in between, so you can now see the text move across the screen when you play the movie.

6] Rewind the movie by clicking Rewind on the toolbar. Then click Play to see what you have created so far.

STOP

REWIND   PLAY

Clicking Rewind moves the playback head to frame 1. You can click Rewind on the toolbar or the control panel. It's always a good idea to rewind before playing a Director movie to make sure you're viewing it from frame 1.

When you play the movie, notice that the line of text moves onto the stage and then stays in the position you set for it in frame 40.

To quickly view a section of a movie, you can drag the playback head in the frame channel back and forth. This is called **scrubbing**. *Scrubbing helps you quickly see the effects of changes you make to a movie.*

7] Click Stop.

REPEATING THE ANIMATION PROCESS

Now you'll sequence the remaining sprites to complete the animation.

1] In the score, select the sprites in channels 7 and 8. Then drag them so their start frames are in frame 45.

Having these sprites appear on the stage in frame 45 gives the first bullet point some time on the stage without the second bullet point appearing. In a moment, you will move the sprites for the last bullet point so they appear in a frame after the second animation ends.

2] In the sprite toolbar, set 90 as the end frame for both sets of sprites.

Just as you set the end frames of the sprites in channels 5 and 6 to frame 90, you must set the end frames of these sprites so they stay on the stage until the end of the movie.

3] Click the start frame (frame 45) for the sprite in channel 8.

This sprite makes up the second line of text. Next you will move the sprite to its beginning position on the stage. You want this line of text to slide onto the stage just as the text above it does.

4] On the stage, hold down the Shift key and drag the sprite in a straight path to the right edge of the stage.

5] In the score, click the sprite in frame 55, channel 8. Then choose Insert › Keyframe.

6] On the stage, hold down the Shift key and drag the sprite to its end position next to the second bullet.

Looking at the score now, you can see that the second line of text will be moving onto the stage between frames 45 and 55. Director has already tweened the frames between frames 45 and 55. From frame 55 to the end of the movie, the text will remain in its end location on the stage.

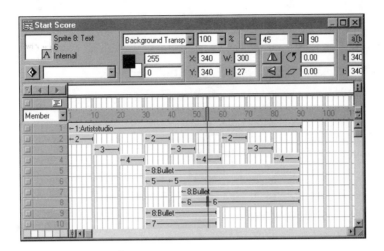

Now you need to animate the last line.

7] Select the sprites in channels 9 and 10 and then drag them so the start frame for each set of sprites appears in frame 60.

8] Click either of the end frames of these sprites and drag to frame 90.
As you see, you can also drag the end frames to frame 90. You cannot, however, drag both end frames together. That's why using the End Frame field on the toolbar is a better method. Now adjust the final sprite so it, too, ends at frame 90.

9] Click the start frame of the sprite in channel 10.
The sprite in this channel is the third line of text.

10] On the stage, hold down the Shift key and drag the sprite in a straight path to the right edge of the stage.

11] In the score, insert a keyframe in frame 70, channel 10.

12] On the stage, hold down the Shift key and drag the sprite to its end position next to the last bullet.

The animation for this sprite will occur during frames 60 to 70. Then the sprite will remain on the stage in the location you set in frame 70.

You've probably been wondering how you can align the text sprites. To get them to appear aligned vertically once they've all moved onto the stage, you'll use another tool: the **Sprite inspector**.

ALIGNING SPRITES USING THE SPRITE INSPECTOR

All the text sprites should appear aligned vertically when they arrive in their end positions next to the bullets. For these three sprites, you will set the same coordinate for their left edges so they will appear vertically aligned. In the following steps, you'll use the Sprite inspector to set these coordinates.

1] Click frame 40, channel 6, to select this frame in the sprite. Then choose Window › Inspectors › Sprite.

The Sprite inspector is a floating window that contains the same information found in the sprite toolbar at the top of the score. All the properties that define the currently selected sprite are displayed in both areas. When you select multiple sprites, the Sprite inspector displays any settings that all the selected sprites have in common, just as the sprite toolbar does. If you enter new settings, the change affects all selected sprites. If you'd rather use the Sprite inspector than the sprite toolbar, use the View > Sprite Toolbar command to remove the toolbar from the top of the score. This makes the score smaller and more convenient, and you can bring up the Sprite Inspector any time you need it.

In the Sprite inspector, you can see all the values in one window. To see all the values in the sprite toolbar, you must resize the Score window to see the values at the far right of the toolbar.

You are familiar with some of the information in the Sprite inspector, such as the thumbnail image, the ink effect, and the start and end frames of the selected sprite. In this task, you'll learn about the sprite's left, right, top, and bottom coordinates, shown at the bottom of the Sprite inspector. These numbers represent the distances of the sprite's edges in **pixels** from the upper-left corner of the stage. Pixels are the basic unit of measure for computer displays.

The numbers for the left and right coordinates, shown in the *l* and *r* fields of the Sprite inspector, represent the distances of the left and right edges of the sprite from the left edge of the stage. Likewise, the top and bottom coordinates in the *t* and *b* fields of the Sprite inspector are the distances of the top and bottom edges of the sprite from the top of the stage.

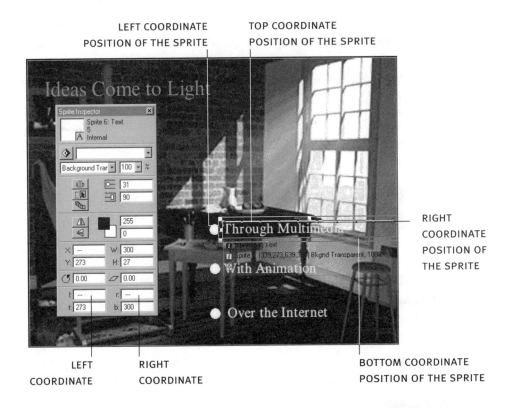

LEFT COORDINATE
POSITION OF THE SPRITE

TOP COORDINATE
POSITION OF THE SPRITE

RIGHT
COORDINATE
POSITION OF
THE SPRITE

LEFT
COORDINATE

RIGHT
COORDINATE

BOTTOM COORDINATE
POSITION OF THE SPRITE

In the Sprite inspector, notice the left coordinate value for the sprite in this keyframe. This is the value you want the other sprites to have as the left coordinate of their corresponding keyframes. You'll need to enter this value at the end of this task, so you may want to write it down before you continue. In the next steps, you will select all the keyframes of the text sprites and set a left coordinate for them.

2] Hold down Ctrl (Windows) or Command (Macintosh), and then click frame 55, channel 8.

You've now selected the corresponding keyframe for the second line of text. Holding down the Ctrl (Windows) or Command (Macintosh) key and clicking a frame in a sprite allows you to select the individual frames you want to work with in the score. You have one more keyframe to select.

3] Hold down Ctrl (Windows) or Command (Macintosh), and then click frame 70, channel 10.

Now you've selected the keyframes in each sprite where the text has moved onto the stage and remains in position to the end of the movie. These positions are the ones in which you want the text to appear aligned.

KEYFRAME SELECTIONS IN THE TEXT SPRITES

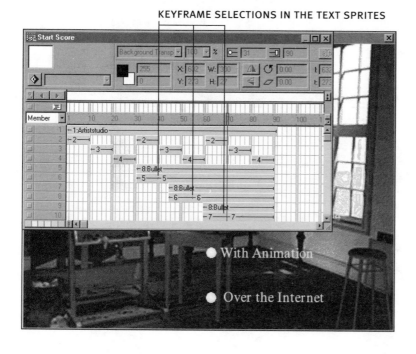

4] In the left coordinate (*l*) field of the Sprite inspector, type the coordinate value you recorded in step 1 and then press Enter (Windows) or Return (Macintosh).

The sprites shift into alignment on the stage. As the movie plays now, each line of text will move onto the stage and end with its left edge at the pixel position you specified. Since the positions are all the same, the lines of text will appear vertically aligned.

With this step, you've completed the animated bullet list. Look over the score to determine what will appear on the stage as the movie plays. As the movie begins, the background graphic and the text changing color plays for 30 frames. Then the first bullet appears and the first line of text begins moving across the stage. By frame 40, the bullet point has arrived at its destination.

The second bullet and line of text appear in frame 45, and by frame 55, the second bullet point is in place. In frame 60, the third bullet and line of text make their entrance. From frame 70 on, all the media elements are in place on the stage. Throughout the movie, the text at the top of the stage changes color every 10 frames.

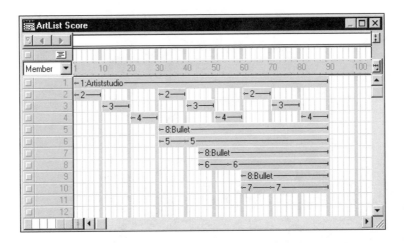

5] Save your work.

6] Click Rewind and then click Play to watch the movie.

It works! Now you're ready to create visually dynamic presentations for yourself and others.

WHAT YOU HAVE LEARNED

In this lesson you have:

• Created a cast member using the Paint window [page 42]

• Applied a gradient effect to a Paint cast member [page 43]

• Changed the view of the Score window using the Zoom menu [page 47]

• Aligned sprites using the Align panel and the Sprite inspector [page 53, 65]

• Named a cast member [page 55]

• Used keyframes to create simple animations that move lines of text across the screen [page 57]

animations
reversing

LESSON 3

Throughout the next three lessons you will create a small multimedia travelog, bringing together sound, graphics, text, animations, video, and interactivity. You will work on different parts of the presentation in each lesson.

In this lesson, you will set up basic movie properties and create a small portion of this project. You will start by importing some media elements, setting the movie tempo and the color of the stage, and putting a few of the elements into the score.

First there was a dream veiled in mist, like something in your subconscious...

Your next Director projects will take you on a fantastic journey. You will bring to life the sights and sounds of the Taj Mahal as you build a small multimedia travelog of your own.

The images, sounds, and digital video you'll use to create this project were produced for the CD-ROM Taj Mahal—Sights and Sounds *by Icon Softec, a multimedia development company based in New Delhi, India.*

You learned to create bulleted text animations in the last lesson. Here you will create an animation that moves an image onto the stage; then you will reverse the animation to show the image moving back off the stage.

If you would like to view the final result of this lesson, open the Complete folder in the Lesson03 folder and play TajMah1.dir.

To give you a jump-start, part of the travelog piece has been prebuilt for you. Many of the media elements have been assembled in the cast, and one of them—the TajMist image—has been sequenced in the score. The prebuilt movie, Start.dir, is located in the Start folder in the Lesson03 folder.

WHAT YOU WILL LEARN

In this lesson you will:

• Set a background color for a movie

• Set a movie tempo

• Practice importing graphics and text files

• Practice using ink effects

• Practice creating animations

• Reverse animations

APPROXIMATE TIME

It should take about 1 hour to complete this lesson.

LESSON FILES

Media Files:
Dir7\Lessons\Lesson03\Media

Starting Files:
Dir7\Lessons\Lesson03\Start\Start.dir

Completed Project:
Dir7\Lessons\Lesson03\Complete\TajMah1.dir

SETTING THE STAGE COLOR AND MOVIE TEMPO

In this task, you perform two steps that are common preliminaries to most projects: applying a color to the stage to create a background for the movie and setting the movie **tempo** in frames per second. The tempo is the speed at which the playback head moves from frame to frame—and the speed at which Director plays the animations in your movies. Start by opening the prebuilt Start.dir file.

1] Choose File › Open to open Start.dir in the Start folder in the Lesson03 folder (Windows Ctrl+O, Macintosh Command+O).

Notice that some cells in the score have already been filled in to give you a jump-start on this project, and most of the cast members you need have already been imported.

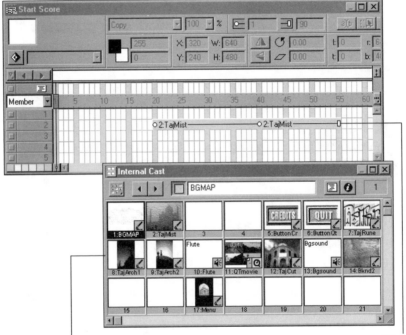

CAST MEMBERS ALREADY IMPORTED   PREBUILT ANIMATION

2] Choose File › Save As. Save the file as *TajMah1.dir* in your Projects folder.

This step preserves the original prebuilt file in case you want to repeat this lesson.

3] Choose Modify › Movie › Properties to open the Movie Properties dialog box (Windows Ctrl+Shift+D, Macintosh Command+Shift+D).

The Movie Properties dialog box lets you specify options such as the stage size and color for the movie that is currently open. You want to change the stage color so your movie stands out against the background.

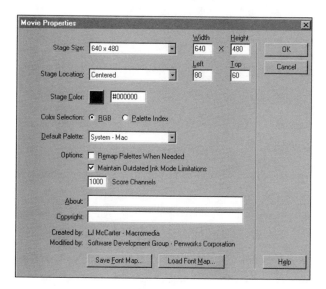

tip *It is a good idea to have the stage centered in your Director movies. All users who view your movies will then see the action centered on their screens, no matter what size their screens are. Setting a stage location that moves the stage into a corner of your screen could crop part of your movie from view on smaller screens. If the Stage Location is not already set to Centered, use the drop-down menu to change it.*

4] Click the Stage Color chip and choose black from the palette.

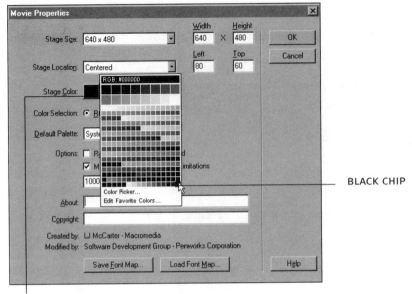

STAGE COLOR CHIP

BLACK CHIP

The stage color changes so the movie is set against a black background. With the stage color set to black, the gray map image that is cast member 1 will stand out against it.

LINGO EQUIVALENT

the stageColor = 255

The colors in the palette range from 0 (white) to 255 (black).

5] Click OK to close the dialog box.

Now you will set a tempo for the movie. The movie tempo is measured in **frames per second**, or **fps**. As you increase the tempo, Director plays animations faster. For instance, a fast tempo of 60 fps makes sprites speed across the stage, and a slower tempo such as 10 fps or less creates slow-motion effects. A movie's tempo is set in the tempo channel of the score. Although one tempo can be used for an entire movie, you can also vary the tempo as you please within a movie.

In the next step, you'll increase the movie's tempo to 60 fps to see how quickly the prebuilt animation plays at that tempo.

6] In the score, click Hide/Show Effects Channels to display the effects channels. Then, double-click frame 1 of the tempo channel to display the Tempo dialog box.

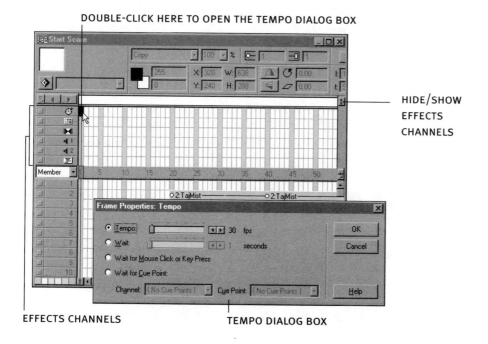

DOUBLE-CLICK HERE TO OPEN THE TEMPO DIALOG BOX

HIDE/SHOW EFFECTS CHANNELS

EFFECTS CHANNELS   TEMPO DIALOG BOX

You're now going to set a tempo that is faster than the 30 fps default tempo currently set in this movie. Since the movie is currently less than 60 frames, setting a 60 fps tempo setting will make the image in the prebuilt animation zoom onto the stage in less than 1 second.

7] In the Tempo dialog box, select Tempo and set the frames per second (fps) to 60 by dragging the slider and using the arrow keys.

SET FRAMES PER SECOND WITH THE SLIDER AND THE ARROW KEYS
FRAMES PER SECOND SETTING

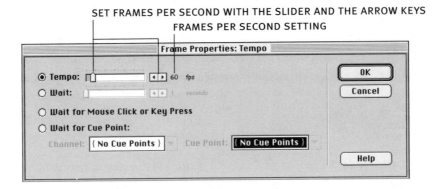

8] Click OK to close the dialog box.

The first frame of the tempo channel is highlighted to indicate that you've set a tempo for the movie. The movie will run at 60 fps until Director encounters a new tempo setting in the channel.

THIS TEMPO SETTING IS IN EFFECT UNTIL ANOTHER TEMPO
IS SET IN ANOTHER FRAME OF THE TEMPO CHANNEL

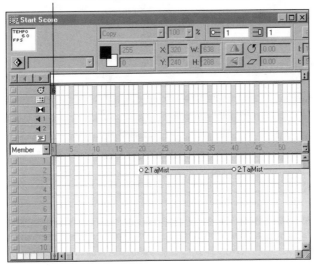

LINGO EQUIVALENT

puppetTempo 60

9] On the toolbar, click Rewind and then click Play to view the effect of the tempo setting on the prebuilt animation.

The TajMist image zooms onto the stage from the top of the screen. This doesn't give your audience much time to see the image. In a travelog presentation, you want your audience to have time to experience the images you include.

There may be times at which you prefer to have animations move quickly across the screen. In these instances, a tempo of 30 fps or higher would be appropriate, but only if your computer's processing speed is fast enough to keep up with the pace. If your computer can't keep up, Director will slow down the tempo automatically and stretch out the time it takes to play the movie. This is very different from movies created in QuickTime. Given a 60-frame movie with a 30 fps tempo, QuickTime drops frames from the movie to play the movie in exactly 2 seconds rather than stretch out the movie to display all the media. Remember, too, that the user's machine on which your movie plays may not be as fast as your machine. When you set the tempo in your projects, you need to keep in mind the end user's requirements.

You're now going to set a slower tempo. Slowing down the tempo will slow the animation and help to create the atmosphere a project like this needs. By setting a slower movie tempo for a Director movie, you can help ensure that everyone who views your movie will see the action at a nice pace—even those who have fast computers.

tip   *Increasing or decreasing tempo settings changes the speed at which Director plays animations, but the playback rate for sounds and digital videos in the movie are not affected. However, a slower animation rate means that Director can free up more time for other activities, like playing video. In fact, reducing the Director tempo may actually improve the performance of digital video playback. You'll work with sounds and digital video in the next lesson.*

10] Click Stop to stop the movie. Then double-click frame 1 of the tempo channel to display the Tempo dialog box again.

tip   *To set the tempo in frame 1 of the movie, you can also click frame 1 in the frame channel and then choose Modify > Frame > Tempo.*

11] Select Tempo and set the frames per second (fps) to 10 by dragging the slider and using the arrow keys. Then click OK to close the dialog box.

Now the movie will run at 10 fps until Director encounters a new tempo setting in the channel.

IMPORTING MEDIA ELEMENTS INTO THE CAST

To save you the trouble of building this Taj Mahal travelog from scratch, the cast and score in the prebuilt file are partially filled in. As you can see in the Cast window, many media elements have already been imported for you, but nothing has yet been imported into cast members 3 and 4. In this task, you'll import additional media elements into these cast members. As you work, you'll learn more about how Director manages cast members.

1] Choose File › Import (Windows Ctrl+R, Macintosh Command+R) to display the Import dialog box.

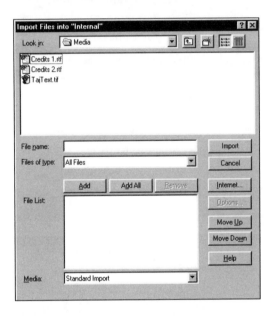

You'll be importing a graphics file and two text files. Director imports many types of files. You can see the types when you open the menu under List Files of Type (Windows) or Show (Macintosh). The file types PICT and Bitmap Image in these lists represent images you can import for your movies. File types that allow you to import multiple images at once are listed as FLC and FLI for Windows, and as PICS and Scrapbook for Macintosh. The graphic you will import is a TIFF file. The text files you'll import are in Rich Text Format (RTF), which is supported by the Text file type listed in these menus.

WINDOWS FILE TYPES

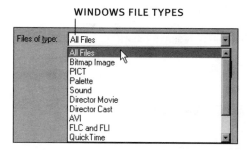

MACINTOSH FILE TYPES

tip *Becoming familiar with the types of files Director can import is important so that you and your colleagues know what file formats to assign to files you want to import into Director. Images can be saved in a variety of formats such as BMP, PICT, and TIFF, and all of these can be imported into Director, but each has a different effect on a movie's file size.*

2] Open the Media folder for Lesson 3. Then select the TajText.tif file and click Add.

This file contains a graphic that consists of a block of text.

3] Select Credits 1.rtf and click Add. Select Credits 2.rtf and click Add.

This adds the two RTF files to the import list. An RTF file contains text as well as font information, paragraph information, and other formatting information that makes text look nice on the screen or on a printed page. In Lessons 1 and 2 you created RTF files using Director's Text window. The files you just imported were created in an application outside of Director, but they were saved as RTF documents.

4] Click Import. In the Image Options dialog box that appears, make sure that the Remap radio button is selected under the palette. Then click OK.

The Cast window now includes new cast members for the media you imported.

importfileinto(member 1, "d:\dir7\lessons\lesson03\media\credits.rtf")

TAJTEXT IS CAST MEMBER 3

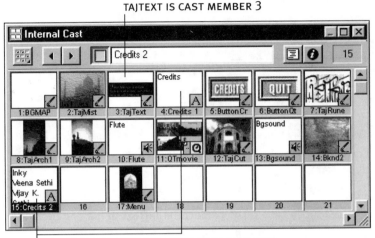

CREDITS.RTF IS SPLIT INTO TWO CAST MEMBERS

The TajText.tif file was placed in cast member 3 in the movie. This cast member position was the first empty cast member, so Director imported the graphic into this position by default. If you first select an empty cast member and then import media, Director places the media in the cast member you selected.

As you work with casts in Director you may delete unwanted cast members, leaving blank positions throughout the cast as shown in this example. As you have seen in this task, importing two RTF files adds cast members to non-consecutive cast member positions. This is an example of how you can expect to find related cast members scattered throughout the cast when you delete cast members and then import new ones.

You can shuffle cast members in the Cast window to place them where you want them. Dragging one or more cast members in the Cast window is a simple way to organize your cast members. In the following steps, you'll put the two Credits.rtf cast members in positions next to each other. Then you'll close the gap between positions 3 and 5.

5] Select cast member 15 and drag it to position 16. Then drag cast member 4 to position 15.

The two Credits.rtf files now appear next to each other in the cast. By dragging cast members to new locations, you can organize the cast so that related cast members appear next to each other. Next you will close the gap left behind.

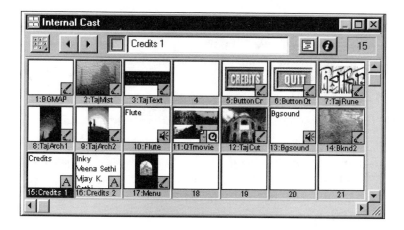

6] **Select cast member 5 and then hold down the Shift key and select cast member 17, so cast members 5 through 17 are selected. Then drag the selected cast members into the blank cast member 4.**

All the cast members you selected move to new cast positions.

> **tip** *If you select a range of cast members, you can put them in order by choosing Modify > Sort. You can use this feature to organize cast members by type, name, usage, or size, or to simply get rid of empty cast members in between.*

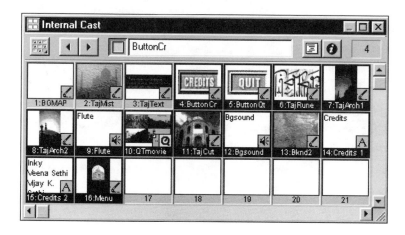

7] **Choose File › Save to save your work (Windows Ctrl+S, Macintosh Command+S).**

USING INK EFFECTS ON THE BACKGROUND IMAGE

In this task you place a background sprite on the stage. The sprite is a gray outline of a world map and will remain on the stage throughout the presentation.

1] Select and drag cast member 1 (Bgmap) to channel 1, frame 2, in the score.

Because you dragged the background graphic to the score, the image appears in the center of the stage. In addition, the sprite labeled 1:Bgmap now extends for 28 frames in the Score window, beginning at frame 2 and ending in frame 29 of channel 1. Frame 1 of channel 1 will present only the black background. Then frame 2 will be the first frame in the movie that displays a sprite.

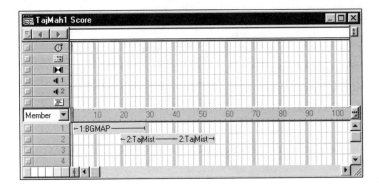

2] With the Bgmap sprite selected in the score, choose Matte from the Ink menu in the sprite toolbar.

Matte ink removes all the white pixels around the edges of an image. In the sprite here, the white pixels that remain inside the image could not be removed because they do not appear outside the image's outline. Some of the interior pixels of the image were removed because there are breaks in the image's outline. This ink doesn't seem to work so well, so you'll try another one.

**3] With the Bgmap sprite still selected in the score, choose Background
Transparent from the Ink menu.**

This ink effect makes all the white space in the image transparent, so the black stage
shows through. You should use Background Transparent when an image has a hole or
windows through which you want the background to show.

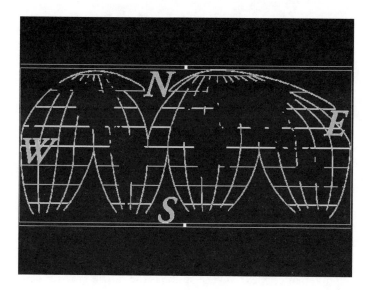

tip *If Background Transparent or Matte ink effects don't work well, the background of the image may not be true white. To change the background to white, double-click the cast member. This will open a Paint window that contains an editable version of the image. To replace the area that appears to be white in the image with true white, click the Paint window's toolbar foreground color chip. Change the color of the foreground color chip to white and click the Paint Bucket tool. The Paint Bucket will fill an entire area with the Paint window's foreground color; so with the Paint Bucket tool selected, click the area in the image you want to be true white. This changes the background of the image to true white. Close the Paint window and check the sprite on the stage to see that the ink effect now applies.*

If a rim of white appears around your image, this is usually due to anti-aliasing by your original paint program. These white and near-white pixels might have to be removed one by one in the paint window.

You may have noticed that the default ink for sprites is Copy. The Copy ink copies the image directly onto the stage, surrounding white and all. Using the Copy ink is the fastest drawing technique. Some of the other drawing techniques you see in the ink menu require more calculation time while the movie is playing. The amount of overhead varies by ink effect. The ink effects that are the least calculation intensive are Copy, Matte, and Background Transparent. The ink effects toward the bottom of the menu are the most calculation intensive.

tip *When you are preparing Director movies for use in a Web page, using ink effects is a great way to alter the appearance of a sprite without having to create new artwork. This also improves the movie's download speed because only a single graphic needs to be downloaded rather than many versions of a graphic. However, you should keep in mind that applying the more calculation-intensive inks to sprites may slow the playback speed of the movie. To preview ink effects, choose the Show Me movie "Ink Effects" under the Help menu.*

In this movie the map background needs to be visible from frame 2 through frame 100 so it remains on the stage long enough for the movie to display the animations you will be adding. Although you may not always know exactly how many frames long your movie is going to be, it is good practice to extend the sprites that will appear throughout the movie to a frame number further to the right in the Score window. This saves you from having to repeatedly extend the sprite as the movie grows.

You already know two ways to set the end frame of a sprite: by dragging the sprite's end frame in the score and by using the End Frame field in the Sprite Inspector or toolbar.

4] In the Sprite Inspector, double-click the End Frame field. If the Sprite Inspector is not visible, display it by choosing Window › Inspectors › Sprite. Then type *100* and press Enter (Windows) or Return (Macintosh).

The sprite's end frame now extends to frame 100 in sprite channel 1 of the score.

5] Rewind and play the movie.

You should see the stage color and the background graphic you just incorporated. You also see an image animate onto the stage—the effect that was already in the prebuilt file.

As the movie plays, notice the playback head move in the score. You may recall from the previous lesson that as Director plays a movie, what appears on the stage are the sprite images in the frame that contains the playback head. As the playback head moves from frame to frame, Director erases the sprite images in the frame it is leaving and redraws the stage with the sprites in the frame it enters. This is how the animation effects are created.

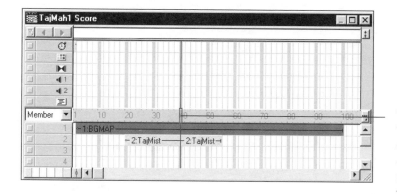

THE SPRITES IN THIS FRAME IN CHANNEL 1 AND CHANNEL 2 ARE DISPLAYED ON THE STAGE

tip *You can also play the movie and temporarily close all open windows by using the keyboard shortcut Alt+Ctrl+Shift+P (Windows) or Option+Command+Shift+P (Macintosh). Try this—it's a useful way to see your movie without having to move or close the windows you are working with. Using the numeric keypad, you can rewind, stop, and play a movie. Press 0 to rewind, the decimal point (.) to stop, and Enter to play. If you press Shift+Enter, all the open windows will close temporarily and you will see only the stage while the movie plays.*

6] Save your work.

ANIMATING A GRAPHIC IMAGE

Your next task will be to animate the TajText image you imported at the beginning of this lesson. The movie already contains an animation of the TajMist graphical image moving onto the stage from top to bottom; to accompany this, you will create an animation of the TajText image that moves onto the stage from left to right.

1] Drag cast member 3 to frame 20, channel 3, in the score.
You will start the TajText image at the same time in the movie that the TajMist image enters the stage.

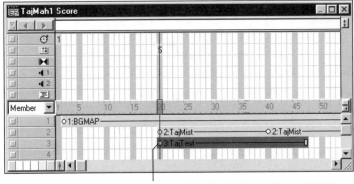

PLACE THE TAJTEXT SPRITE DIRECTLY
BENEATH THE TAJMIST SPRITE

Notice that the ink for the sprite is Copy, but no white bounding box surrounds the sprite on the stage. This is because the TajText image was created with a black background so it blends right in with the black background you assigned to the stage at the beginning of this lesson.

2] With the sprite still selected in the score, click the sprite's start frame. Then drag the sprite on the stage to the left edge where the animation will begin.

DRAG THE TAJTEXT SPRITE TO THE STARTING POSITION OF THE ANIMATION

**3] Click frame 40, channel 3, to select this frame of the sprite. Then choose Insert ›
Keyframe (Windows Ctrl+Alt+K, Macintosh Command+Option+K).**

Looking at the score, you can see that the sprite in channel 2 has a keyframe in
frame 40, too. In this frame, the TajMist image arrives at the end of its animation
path from the top of the stage. Now you will move the TajText image to the end of
its animation path in the same keyframe.

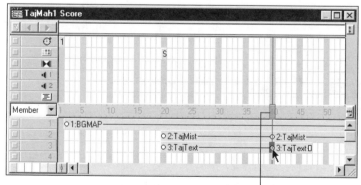

INSERT A KEYFRAME IN FRAME 40

4] Hold down the Shift key and drag the TajText sprite on the stage to its end position.

Place the TajText image in a position that will be pleasing to the eye as both images
arrive at the end of their animations on the stage.

5] Drag the TajText sprite's end frame to frame 55.

As you drag the end frame, the Score window scrolls to show you more frames. This allows you to drag the end frame to frame 55 even though you couldn't see frame 55 when you began.

By dragging the end frame, you also advanced the keyframe you just inserted. Whenever you extend a sprite, the keyframes you inserted in the sprite retain their positions relative to the entire sprite. For instance, if you insert a keyframe at the halfway point of a sprite, the keyframe will continue to appear at the halfway point no matter how many frames you extend or shorten the sprite. You don't want the keyframe to move, so in the next step you'll move it back to the same frame in which the TajMist sprite has a keyframe.

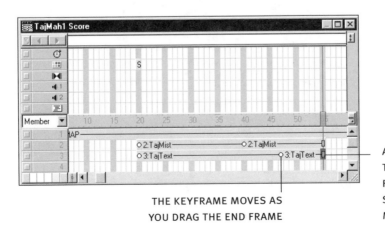

THE KEYFRAME MOVES AS
YOU DRAG THE END FRAME

AS YOU DRAG
THE SPRITE'S END
FRAME, THE SCORE
SCROLLS TO SHOW
MORE FRAMES

6] Drag the keyframe in TajText back to frame 40, channel 3.

With this operation, the keyframes for the TajMist and TajText images are synchronized again. Note that moving a keyframe within a sprite doesn't affect the positions of the sprite's start and end frames.

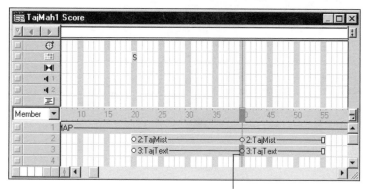

DRAG THE KEYFRAME BACK TO FRAME 40

7] Rewind and play the movie.

As you watch the movie, you see the TajMist and TajText images move onto the screen and remain in their end positions until frame 55; then they disappear. The animations for these two sprites are identical in the number of frames in which they occur. The only difference is that TajMist moves onto the stage from the top of the screen, and the TajText sprite you animated moves onto the stage from the left. Having these animations occur at the same time creates a connection between the two of them that you want your audience to notice. To add some more interest to this segment of the movie, you'll now reverse the animations.

REVERSING ANIMATIONS

Director's Reverse Sequence command reverses the cells in the selected sprites so they are placed in the exact opposite order. In effect, reversing an animation creates a duplicate, reversed, set of score entries—though it requires only a few keystrokes. In the reverse animations you'll create next, the TajMist and TajText images will move off the stage along the same paths they took to move onto the stage.

1] Choose 50% from the score's Zoom menu to see more of the score. Then select the sprites in channels 2 and 3.

2] Choose Edit › Copy Sprites (Windows Ctrl+C, Macintosh Command+C). Then click frame 56, channel 2, and choose Edit › Paste Sprites (Windows Ctrl+V, Macintosh Command+V).

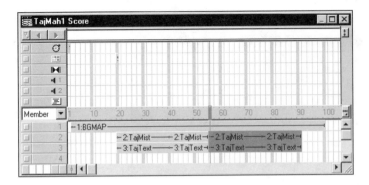

Director pastes the sprites you copied into the score right after the original sprites, using frame 56, channel 2, as the beginning cell of the pasted sprites. Playing the movie now would show you the same animations twice. Now reverse the animations.

3] With the sprites still selected, choose Modify › Reverse Sequence.

In the score, you can see that the sprites are reversed since the keyframes in the sprites you just pasted into the score moved to frame 71 from frame 76. The sprites in channel 2 are mirror images of themselves, as are the sprites in channel 3.

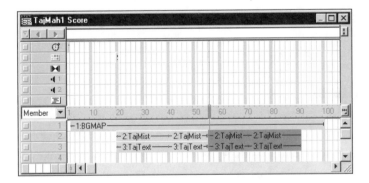

4] Drag the end frame of the sprite in channel 1 to frame 91.

Now the gray map image ends at frame 91 with the end of the reverse animations.

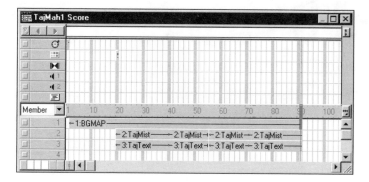

5] Save your work.

6] Rewind and play the movie.

The TajText and TajMist images now move onto the stage, remain in place for a few frames, and then move off the stage. As you can see, reversing animations is not only easy but adds balance to the movie.

WHAT YOU HAVE LEARNED

In this lesson you have:

• Used movie properties to set a background stage color for a movie [page 73]

• Used the tempo channel to set a movie tempo [page 75]

• Imported an additional graphic and an RTF text file into the cast [page 78]

• Organized cast members in the Cast window [page 80]

• Used the Matte and Background Transparent ink effects [page 82]

• Created an animation and reversed it using Reverse Sequence [page 86]

and video

transitions, sounds,

In this lesson you will continue building the Taj Mahal travelog by adding sound, selecting transitions such as dissolves and wipes from a list of transition types built in to Director to help you present new scenes, and adding a digital video to end the movie.

If you would like to view the final result of this lesson, open the Complete folder in the Lesson04 folder and play TajMah2.dir.

With special effects such as transitions, sound, and digital video you can capture your audience's attention and keep it. These effects let you create a montage of images, as shown here.

LESSON 4

WHAT YOU WILL LEARN

In this lesson you will:

• Exchange cast members in the score

• Use screen transitions

• Add sounds to a movie, including a sound that plays repeatedly

• Add a digital video to a movie

APPROXIMATE TIME

It should take about 1½ hours to complete this lesson.

LESSON FILES

Media Files:

None

Starting Files:

Dir7\Lessons\Lesson04\Start\Start.dir

Completed Project:

Dir7\Lessons\Lesson04\Complete\TajMah2.dir

SETTING REGISTRATION POINTS

Registration points are the main way of locating images on the stage in Director. A registration point provides a fixed reference point within an image. By default, Director assigns a registration point in the center of all images, but in many instances you may want to move the registration point. In the next task you'll set the registration point of an image.

1] Open Start.dir in the Start folder in the Lesson04 folder and save it as TajMah2.dir.

Alternatively, you can use the file you worked on in the previous lesson and save it as TajMah2.dir.

2] Drag cast member 7 (TajArch1) from the Cast window to channel 1, frame 92, in the score. Then drag the end frame of the sprite to frame 100.

The sprite now occupies frames 92 through 100 in channel 1.

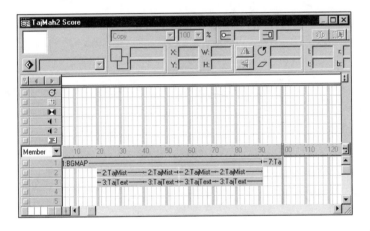

On the stage, notice that the sprite appears in the center as usual. Sprites that appear in the center of the stage have a registration point at the center of the image. This is Director's default registration point for images.

3] Double-click the sprite on the stage.

This opens the Paint window and displays an editable version of the image. You get the same result when you double-click the cast member for this sprite.

4] Click the Registration Point tool in the Paint window.

Once you click the Registration Point tool, you'll see the intersecting lines at the center of the image that make up the registration point. You can move these crosshairs to a new location on the image to change the way Director displays the image in a movie. The registration point can be set for an image in the application used to create it, or you can set the registration point in Director's Paint window.

REGISTRATION POINT TOOL

REGISTRATION POINT
OF THE IMAGE

95

5] Click and drag the crosshairs to the right edge of the image to reset the registration point. Then close the Paint window.

Now the registration point is at the right edge and near the center of the image.

```
newRegpoint = (member 7).regpoint
newRegpoint.locH = (member 7).width
(member 7).regpoint = newRegpoint
```

NEW REGISTRATION POINT

The sprite also appears in a new location on the stage. The image appears at the left side of the stage because of the new location of the image's registration point. Director automatically centers the registration point on the stage; thus, the registration point of this image is at the center of the stage, which positions the image at the left of the stage's center.

Next you'll copy and paste the TajArch1 sprite into channel 1 directly after its current position. Then you'll use the Exchange Cast Members command to exchange the pasted TajArch1 sprite with TajArch2 on the stage.

EXCHANGING CAST MEMBERS

1] In the score, select the TajArch1 sprite in channel 1 and then choose Edit › Copy Sprites (Windows Ctrl+C, Macintosh Command+C).

2] Click frame 101, channel 1, and then choose Edit › Paste Sprites (Windows Ctrl+V, Macintosh Command+V).

3] Click frame 110, channel 1, and choose Edit › Paste Sprites again.
The sprite labeled 7:TajArch1 now appears three times in channel 1 in frames 92 through 118.

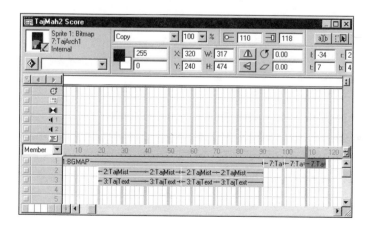

In the next step, you'll exchange one of the TajArch1 sprites you pasted into channel 1 with a TajArch2 sprite.

4] In the score, select the sprite you pasted into channel 1, frames 101 through 109.

5] In the cast, select cast member 8 (TajArch2)

Be sure the Cast window is active (in the foreground) and cast member 8 is selected, or the following step won't work.

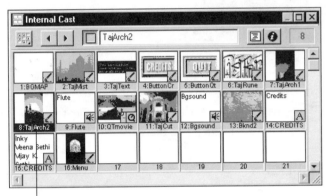

SELECT CAST MEMBER 8

6] In the toolbar at the top of the screen, click the Exchange Cast Members tool (Windows Ctrl+E, Macintosh Command+E).

EXCHANGE CAST MEMBERS

The sprite label changes to 8:TajArch2. Now when the playback head arrives in frame 101, the TajArch2 image will appear on the stage. Next, you'll exchange the cast member in the last sprite you pasted into channel 1, frames 110 through 118, with the TajRune cast member.

7] In the score, select the sprite in channel 1, frames 110 through 118; in the Cast window, select cast member 6; and in the toolbar at the top of the screen, click the Exchange Cast Members tool.

The last sprite in channel 1 is now labeled 6:TajRune.

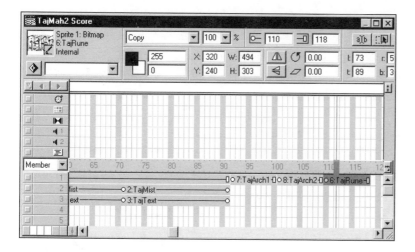

8] Rewind and play the movie.

Note that the images you exchanged, TajArch2 and TajRune, appear in different positions on the stage than the TajArch1 image. You didn't have to position them. The registration point on each of the three images in this sequence is in a different location on the art itself.

You set the registration point on the TajArch1 image at the right edge, near the center. For the TajArch2 image, the registration point is at the left edge, near the center, and the TajRune image has a registration point at its center. When you exchange cast members, Director aligns the registration point of the exchanged image with the original image. Having different locations for the registration points on the images themselves makes one image appear to the left, another to the right, and the last image at the center of the stage.

You may want to look at the registration points of each of the images you exchanged to determine where the registration points are in each of them. Then you can determine how Director aligned the registration points in the TajArch2 and TajRune images with the one in the TajArch1 image.

tip *You have seen that you can open the Paint window by double-clicking a cast member or a sprite on the stage. Another way to do this is to double-click the sprite in the score.*

You just used Director's Exchange Cast Members feature to produce a simple montage of graphical images that appear in different areas on the stage. You could have accomplished the same effect by dragging the TajArch2 and TajRune images to the score and then resizing the sprites; but using Exchange Cast Members requires fewer keystrokes to get the same job done.

9] Save your work.

USING A SCREEN TRANSITION

In this task you will select a screen **transition** to introduce your viewers to the images as they appear in the travelog presentation. You've probably heard of dissolves, wipes, and fades in traditional filmmaking. In Director, screen transitions are visual effects used to reveal or remove objects on the stage. For example, a Wipe Left transition displays the next frame of the movie by wiping it onto the screen starting from the right side of the stage and moving toward the left side, as if the viewer is pushing aside a curtain. You can apply the transition to the entire stage or only to the areas that are changing on the stage, and you can adjust the duration and smoothness of most transitions.

1] In the transition channel, double-click frame 2 to display the Transition dialog box.

TRANSITION CHANNEL

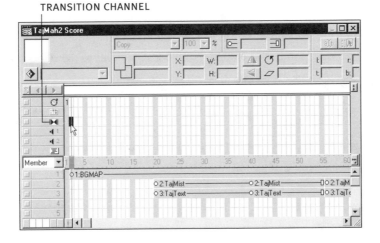

Frame 1 contains the black stage, and frame 2 contains the background sprite that you added earlier (in Lesson 3). Always place a transition in the frame where the new sprites appear on the stage so the transition effect can reveal the sprites. In this case, the new sprite that appears in frame 2 is the Bgmap sprite. With the transition applied to frame 2, the Bgmap sprite will be revealed as the playback head moves from frame 1 (the black stage) to frame 2 (where the Bgmap sprite first appears). The transition actually begins to take effect when Director begins to draw frame 2.

2] In the Categories list, select All, and in the Transitions list, select Dissolve, Bits Fast. Then click OK.

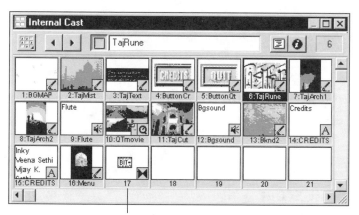

SELECT ALL CATEGORIES

SELECT DISSOLVE, BITS FAST FROM THE TRANSITIONS LIST

The transition now becomes cast member 17 in the Cast window.

THE TRANSITION BECOMES CAST MEMBER 17

You'll use the same transition in one other part of the piece; you can copy and paste a transition just like any other cast member.

3] Select frame 2 in the transition channel and copy it.

4] Select frame 92 in the transition channel and paste the transition.

At frame 92 the TajArch1 sprite appears on the stage. Placing transitions where new sprites appear on the stage is a good way to introduce new scenes in a presentation. Since the image will change to the TajArch2 image and then to the TajRune image, you'll also place a transition in the frames where those images appear on the stage.

5] Paste the transition in frames 101 and 110 in the transition channel.

Now you have placed Dissolve, Bits Fast transitions throughout the score where new images appear on the stage.

LINGO EQUIVALENT

    puppetTransition member 17

or

    puppetTransition 50

tip *You can either specify a transition member or give a transition number. Transition numbers are listed in Help under "PuppetTransition."*

6] Rewind and play the movie.

Now you can see how the transition looks in all four places.

7] Save your work.

tip *Many transition effects are available as Xtras—extensions that add new capabilities to Macromedia products. Xtras use the Macromedia Open Architecture (MOA) standard to ensure that the same Xtra can work with more than one product. For example, Transition Xtras now available from third parties work in Authorware 5 Attain as well as in Director. Go to Macromedia's Web site for information on Transition Xtras currently available. Once you have purchased or created an Xtra, you need to make it available to Director by copying it to Director's Xtras folder.*

ADDING SOUNDS TO THE SCORE

The next part of this project calls for you to add sound in two places in the score. In one case, the sound will **loop**, or play continuously throughout the movie. In the other case, the sound will play for only a few frames.

1] Drag cast member 12 (Bgsound) from the Cast window to sound channel 1, frame 1, in the score.

You should see the sound appear in the sound channel just as a sprite does in the sprite channels. This sound will play in the background throughout the production, so you should start it in frame 1.

SOUND CHANNEL

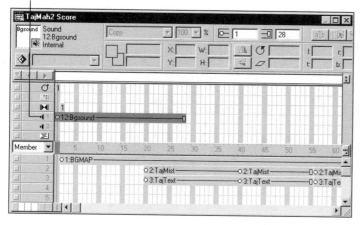

2] Select cast member 12 in the Cast window and click Cast Member Properties in the Cast window.

CAST MEMBER PROPERTIES

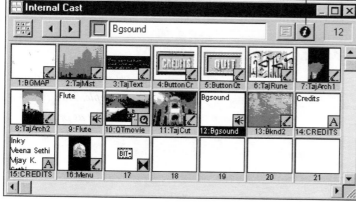

3] In the dialog box, check the Loop box. Then click OK.

Often you'll want a particular sound to play repeatedly throughout a movie. Setting the Loop option starts the sound again at the beginning of the sound file once it finishes playing. This is a good way to establish background music for a movie. If you don't check Loop, the sound will stop playing at the end of the sound file.

(member "bgsound").loop = TRUE

CLICK TO HEAR THE SOUND

CHECK THE LOOP OPTION

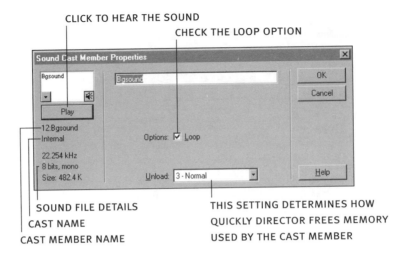

SOUND FILE DETAILS

CAST NAME

CAST MEMBER NAME

THIS SETTING DETERMINES HOW
QUICKLY DIRECTOR FREES MEMORY
USED BY THE CAST MEMBER

4] Drag the end frame of the Bgsound sprite in sound channel 1 to frame 118.

Even when you have set a sound file to loop, the sprite for the sound must extend through every frame in which you want the sound to play. Extending the sprite ensures that the sound plays through to the end of the presentation in frame 118. Your score should now look like this:

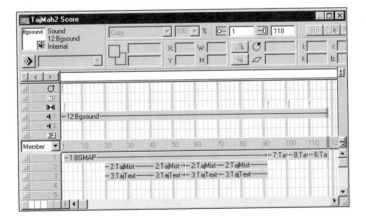

5] Rewind and play the movie.

The sound plays throughout the movie and adds life to this presentation.

Now you will make the movie more dramatic by adding another sound to sound channel 2. Adding a second sound in the sound channels is one way you can add more audio interest to a movie. The sound you'll add to the Taj Mahal travelog will play only when the TajArch and TajRune graphics are displayed, but it will play at the same time the background sound is playing.

tip *Many small sounds add life to movies and can be reused throughout a movie without dramatically affecting the movie's file size. Since file size is always a consideration when downloading movies over the Web, you'll want to limit the size of the sound files you use in a movie. Also, sound effects can be sampled at a lower rate than a voice-over file. Sampling reduces the dynamic range of a sound file—removing the sound file's highest and deepest sounds—so the sound can still be heard but only at its middle ranges. When digitized speech is sampled, it typically never runs at less than 8-bit 22 kHz, and at this rate quality it is drastically reduced, whereas sampled sound effects can run at half that size, at 8-bit 11 kHz, and still sound fine. Also, using mono instead of stereo can cut the size of the sound media in half.*

6] Drag cast member 9 (Flute) to sound channel 2, frame 92, in the score. Change the sound's end frame to 99.

The Flute sound will play now when the TajArch1 image appears on the stage. To make the sound play for each of the images that follow, you'll copy the sound sprite and paste it in the frames where the remaining images appear.

7] Select the Flute sound sprite, then copy and paste it into frames 101 and 110 in sound channel 2.

This will make the Flute sound play three times in the presentation, announcing each of the images as they appear on the stage. Notice that a blank cell is necessary between each of the Flute sound sprites.

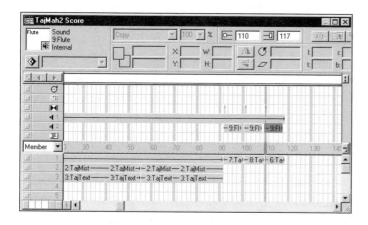

TRANSITIONS, SOUNDS, AND VIDEO

8] Rewind and play the movie.

Great sound effects! Notice that as the Flute sound plays the sound in channel 1 continues playing. The transitions you placed in frames 92, 101, and 110 also help to announce images in the movie. Now you can see how sound and Director's transitions can bring a presentation to life even more.

9] Click the on/off toggle in sound channel 1 to turn off the looping music.

During long projects you'll get tired of hearing the sounds playing over and over. To temporarily turn off the sounds, click inside the box at the far left of the channel. This will highlight the box and indicate that the sounds in that channel have been toggled off. To hear the sounds again at any time during this project, click inside the box to toggle the sound on. Notice that every channel has an on/off toggle.

LINGO EQUIVALENT

the soundLevel = 0

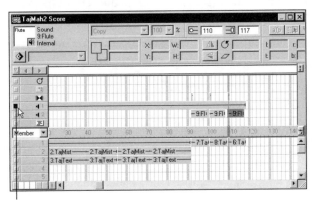

WHEN YOU CLICK HERE, THE INDICATOR HIGHLIGHTS
AND THE SOUND IS TURNED OFF IN THE CHANNEL

tip *When you open any movie, all the toggles are turned on by default. Toggle off states are not saved when you save a movie.*

10] Save your work.

ADDING DIGITAL VIDEO

Now it's time to assemble the ending of the presentation by adding a digital video file. Digital videos are digital movies you can incorporate into a Director movie as you would any other graphical cast member: by placing it in the score or on the stage.

1] Drag cast member 11(TajCut) from the Cast window to channel 1, frame 119, of the score. Then set the sprite's end frame to 130.

This is a new background graphic that the digital video will play on top of.

2] Drag cast member 10(QTmovie) to channel 2, frame 119, of the score. Change the end frame of the QTmovie sprite to 130.

This file is a QuickTime movie that was created for the *Taj Mahal—Sights and Sounds* CD-ROM. To make sure the video will play to completion, you'll need to add a tempo setting that will make the playback head wait until the movie is finished playing before it continues.

3] Select the background music sprite in sound channel 1 and set its end frame to 130.

Remember that a sound's sprite must appear in the sound channel of every frame where you want the sound to play. This action ensures that the sound continues to play during the new part of the movie you are adding.

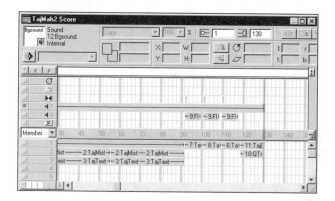

4] Double-click frame 120 in the tempo channel to open a Tempo dialog box. In the dialog box, click Wait for Cue Point. In the Channel field, select 2:QTmovie and in the Cue Point field, select {End}. Click OK to close the dialog box.

In frame 119, Director begins to display the TajCut and QTmovie sprites. By setting a tempo that affects the digital video sprite one frame later, Director will not have to process the tempo instructions at the same time it starts to display a new image and play the digital video. This makes the presentation smoother since there are not so many instructions to process all at once.

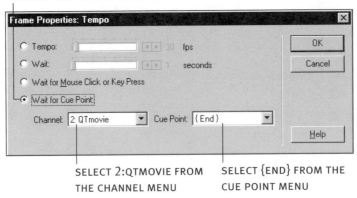

These tempo selections will allow the digital video to play before the playback head moves ahead in the movie.

5] On the stage, center the sprite for the digital video (10:QTmovie) over the cutout in the image (11:TajCut).

The cutout area is a different size than the digital video sprite; but you can scale a digital video so that its dimensions match those of any rectangular area. In the following steps, you resize the QTmovie sprite to fit inside the cutout in the background image.

CENTER THE DIGITAL VIDEO OVER THE WHITE
CUTOUT AREA IN THE TAJCUT IMAGE

6] If the resizing handles are visible on the QTmovie sprite, go ahead and resize the sprite and then skip to step 9.

7] Select the QTmovie cast member in the Cast window and then click Cast Member Properties.

CAST MEMBER PROPERTIES

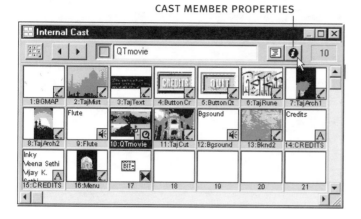

8] In the Cast Members Properties window, click the Options button to bring up the QuickTime Xtras Properties window. Check the Scale option, and then click OK. Click OK again in the Cast Members Properties window.

With the Scale option selected, Director allows you to drag the handles on the digital video sprite to resize the sprite so it will fit inside the cutout area on the image. When the Scale option is not selected, the sprite can't be resized and must appear in your movie at the same size it was when you imported it.

CHECK THE SCALE OPTION TO RESIZE THE DIGITAL VIDEO SPRITE

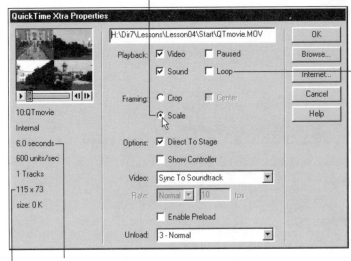

PLAYBACK
OPTIONS ALLOW
YOU TO PAUSE
OR LOOP THE
DIGITAL VIDEO,
OR INCLUDE THE
SOUND IN THE
DIGITAL VIDEO

TIME LENGTH OF THE DIGITAL VIDEO

PIXEL SIZE OF THE DIGITAL VIDEO

note *Performance of digital video is best when scaled up or down by multiples of 2—for instance, double height and width or half height and width. Otherwise a lot of time-consuming calculations are involved to convert the image, resulting in possible dropped frames and/or poor performance.*

9] In the score, select the entire QTmovie sprite. On the stage, drag the handles that surround the digital video sprite to make it fit inside the cutout in the background image.

110

10] Rewind and play the movie.

After the TajArch and TajRune images appear, the digital video plays inside the cutout area in the TajCut image. You see the entire digital video because you used the tempo channel to instruct Director to play the whole digital video before advancing the playback head.

In the next step, you use the tempo channel again to instruct Director to wait in the last frame of the presentation for 2 seconds. Setting wait times at the end of movies is a good idea so the stage doesn't simply go blank at the end of the action. This is a nice finishing touch to add to any movie.

11] In the tempo channel, double-click frame 130. Then click Wait, set the slider to 2 seconds, and click OK to close the dialog box.

After the movie finishes playing, the last frame of the movie will stay on the stage for 2 more seconds because the playback head will stay on this frame for 2 seconds.

12] Save your work.

Now you're ready to set up a menu and buttons for the Taj Mahal travelog. In the next lesson, you'll use the remaining cast members to build a menu and incorporate interactive branching into the travelog.

WHAT YOU HAVE LEARNED

In this lesson you have:

• Set the registration point of a cast member [page 94]

• Used the Exchange Cast Members tool to swap cast members in the score [page 97]

• Used the transition channel to add screen transitions to the movie [page 100]

• Added sounds and used the Loop option to make a sound continuous [page 102]

• Placed a digital video in a movie and scaled it to fit inside a rectangular area [page 107]

adding interactivity

LESSON 5

In this lesson you complete the Taj Mahal travelog project you've been working on for the past two lessons. You'll create a menu and buttons for the presentation and then use **Lingo**, Director's scripting language, to add interactivity. Interactive movies involve users by allowing them to click images to explore other parts of the movie or to exit when they are ready. Typically, this kind of user interaction is provided in Director movies through a written instruction called a **script**. Scripts are written in a Script window using commands and words that are part of Lingo. In Lesson 9 you'll learn to use prewritten scripts from the behavior library. You'll write two simple Lingo scripts in this lesson for the Credits and Quit buttons of the Taj Mahal travelog. The scripts you

By adding just a few concluding interactive elements, you can bring your Director movies to a smooth close. To complete the Taj Mahal travelog, you'll create a simple menu with interactive buttons that let users decide what parts of the movie to view. By adding Lingo scripts to the button cast members, you provide the interactivity that displays another segment of the movie or lets users exit the movie.

write will allow users to click the Credits button to see another screen you'll build for the presentation, and to click the Quit button to quit the presentation. You'll also add other Lingo scripts to the score in the behavior channel that help you display the screen containing the buttons when you want it to appear in the movie.

Buttons are important features in interactive presentations because they are the keys to navigating through the presentation. With button scripts Director moves the playback head to another frame in the movie or executes other commands included in the script. Whenever a script instructs Director to move the playback head to another frame, the playback head actually moves, or **branches**, to another frame and then can return to the original frame through the instructions of another script. You'll see how easy it is to implement branching in your movies by working through the tasks in this lesson. Once you've finished the travelog presentation, you'll create a stand-alone projector so users can view and interact with the movie without having to install Director.

If you would like to view the final result of this lesson, open the Complete folder in the Lesson05 folder and play TajMah3.dir.

WHAT YOU WILL LEARN

In this lesson you will:

• Align sprites on the stage using a grid

• Add navigation markers to the score

• Use Lingo commands for navigation

• Create a play-only version of a movie to distribute to end-users

APPROXIMATE TIME

It should take about 1 hour to complete this lesson.

LESSON FILES

Media Files:
None

Starting File:
Dir7\Lessons\Lesson05\Start\Start.dir

Completed Project:
Dir7\Lessons\Lesson05\Complete\TajMah3.dir

BUILDING A MENU SCREEN

In this task you create a menu with two buttons that allow a user to navigate to a Credits screen or to exit the movie.

1] Open Start.dir in the Lesson05 folder and save it as *TajMah3.dir*.

Start.dir is the prebuilt file. If you completed the previous lesson, you can use the movie you worked on there and save it as *TajMah3.dir* in your Projects folder.

2] Drag cast member 16 (Menu) from the Cast window to channel 1, frame 131, in the score.

This is the background for the menu screen.

When you read the score now, you see that the Menu image will appear on the stage after the digital video finishes playing and the movie pauses for 2 seconds, according to the tempo setting in frame 130. You added the digital video and set the 2-second pause in the tempo channel in the last lesson.

TEMPO SETTING WITH 2-SECOND WAIT SETTING

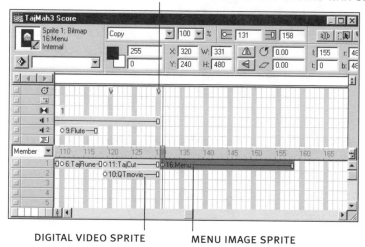

DIGITAL VIDEO SPRITE   MENU IMAGE SPRITE

3] Drag cast member 4 (ButtonCr) from the Cast window to channel 2, frame 131, in the score.

This is the Credits button users will click to get to the Credits screen. You'll build the Credits screen in the next task.

4] Drag cast member 5 (ButtonQt) from the Cast window to channel 3, frame 131.

This is the button users will click to leave the movie.

5] On the stage, drag the Credits and Quit buttons so they appear side by side at the lower edge of the stage.

Though you have used the Modify > Align feature to align sprites in Lesson 2, precise alignment isn't necessary for these sprites. Simply align these buttons manually on the stage.

6] In the score, select the sprites for the menu image and the two buttons you placed in channels 1, 2, and 3, frame 131, and set their end frames to frame 132.

This changes the duration of the sprites to two frames. This is a good length for sprites used to create a menu in Director since most menus do not include animation, sound, or digital video that require a larger number of frames. However, now you can't read the sprite labels in the score, which makes it difficult to read what sprites are in those frames.

When you can't read the sprite labels in the score, move the cursor over the sprite and read the **data tip**. Data tips are the small pop-up panels that display the cast member name and number when the cursor is over a sprite; they're like the Tooltips that appear when you rest the cursor on a tool. Data tips come in handy when a sprite's length is too short for the sprite label to appear in the score and you want to know what sprites will appear on the stage without playing the movie.

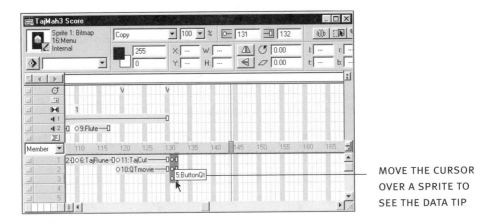

MOVE THE CURSOR OVER A SPRITE TO SEE THE DATA TIP

Now that the menu screen has been built, you need to write the Lingo script that will keep it on display when the movie plays. The screen should remain on display so users can click the buttons. Without a script to hold the playback head in place on the screen, the playback head continues to move to other frames you add to the movie.

WRITING A LINGO SCRIPT

To write a Lingo script that holds the playback head in place on a frame, you add a script to the **behavior channel**, also called the **script channel**. As the playback head moves into a frame that contains a script, Director reads the instructions included in the script and performs them. These instructions are organized into groups of Lingo statements called **handlers.** Handlers "handle" events such as mouse clicks and keyboard commands as well as environment changes such as the start of a movie or the entrance or exit of a frame. A handler consists of a set of instructions, grouped like sentences in a paragraph. Every handler begins with *on* and ends with *end*.

Here you'll create a handler that causes the menu screen to remain on the stage while Director waits for a button to be clicked.

1] In the behavior channel, double-click frame 132 to open a Script window.

Frame 132 is the last frame that displays the menu and its buttons. This is the logical place to write instructions for Director to wait for the user to click one of the buttons.

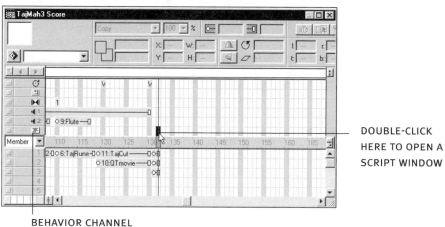

DOUBLE-CLICK HERE TO OPEN A SCRIPT WINDOW

BEHAVIOR CHANNEL

You'll use the Script window to write the instruction that Director will follow when the playback head reaches this frame. Note that a cast member number has been assigned to this script; it is cast member 18.

CAST MEMBER NUMBER

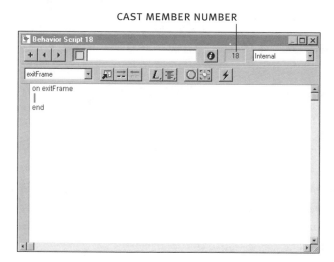

The two default statements *on exitFrame* and *end* are already in the Script window, and the insertion point is indented under the first line. Whenever you double-click the behavior channel, the Script window opens and contains these two statements. You could script a handler for a different event, or even multiple handlers for multiple events, but the exitFrame handler shows up by default. The on exitFrame statement applies to the action of the playback head moving through the score. The end statement simply tells Director that the end of the instructions has been reached. In the next step, you'll add the statement to the script that represents the action you want Director to take when the playback head exits the frame. More detailed information about scripts is covered in later chapters.

2] Type *go to the frame* in the Script window below *on exitFrame* as shown here in bold:

```
on exitFrame
   go to the frame
end
```

Recall that handlers handle events. In this case, this handler will handle the exitFrame event, which occurs when the playback head exits a frame. The phrase *the frame* is a built-in Lingo function that identifies the number of the frame where the playback head is currently located. If the playback head is on frame 50, 50 is returned by the function. If it's on frame 10, 10 is returned. The value returned is completely dependent on the current location of the playback head.

Go to is a command that sends the playback head to the frame location that follows the go to command. Typing *go to the frame* will make the playback head go to the frame in which it's already located. In other words, the playback head stays in the same frame, and all sprites in that frame remain displayed on the stage.

The *on exitFrame* statement tells Director to follow the instructions in the handler as soon as the playback head leaves the frame. In this case, upon leaving the frame the playback head is sent right back to that same frame. The result is that the playback head never leaves the frame.

tip   *Never add a* go to the frame *script to a frame that also contains a transition because the transition will play over and over, and keep the mouse pointer from being displayed long enough to click a menu button. The transition will begin again before the pointer can be displayed and used to click a selection.*

3] Close the Script window. Then rewind and play the movie.
The movie plays and then pauses at the menu screen. Look at the playback head and notice that it's paused on this frame. It pauses here because of the script you added in the previous step.

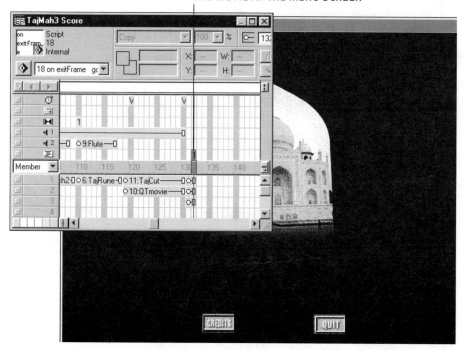

THE SCRIPT AT FRAME 132 PAUSES
THE MOVIE AT THE MENU SCREEN

CREATING A DESTINATION SCREEN

Now you'll create the Credits screen that will appear when the Credits button is clicked. In other words, the playback head will branch to the Credits screen when a user clicks the Credits button in the movie. The Credits screen will consist of a background and text. You imported this text into the cast in Lesson 3 so it's already available for you in the movie's cast.

1] Drag cast member 14 (Credits 1) to channel 2, frame 135, in the score.
Make sure you drag the cast member to channel 2. Channel 1 will contain a sprite for a background upon which the Credits 1 and Credits 2 sprites will appear. You don't always have to begin placing sprites in channel 1, but you must always be aware of the channel number order of sprites and how it affects the appearance of sprites. For instance, if you placed the Credits 1 sprite in channel 1 and then placed a background sprite in channel 2, you wouldn't be able to see the Credits 1 sprite on the stage because the background is large enough to hide the sprite in channel 1. Since sprites are drawn from the lowest number channel first to the highest channel last, the first channel is often used for the background image.

This cast member is a text cast member you imported in Lesson 3. Notice that you didn't drag the cast member to the next available frame in the channel, frame 133.

119

Skipping a few frames makes a visual break in the score that helps you read the score. For instance, this break helps you differentiate between the flow of the movie and a screen that users will branch to.

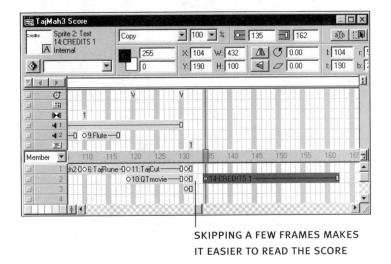

SKIPPING A FEW FRAMES MAKES
IT EASIER TO READ THE SCORE

2] Drag cast member 15 (Credits 2) to channel 3, frame 135.

Now you need to use an ink effect to remove the white backgrounds of these sprites.

3] Select the Credits 1 and Credits 2 sprites in the score. Then from the Ink menu, choose Background Transparent.

4] Drag cast member 13 (Bknd2) to channel 1, frame 135.

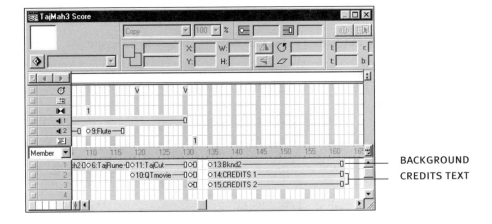

BACKGROUND
CREDITS TEXT

All of the elements of the Credits screen are now on the stage. It's time to position them so everything looks symmetrical and centered.

5] Choose View › Grids › Show (Windows Alt+Ctrl+Shift+G, Macintosh Option+ Command+Shift+G).

A grid overlays the stage; you can use the lines to align sprites.

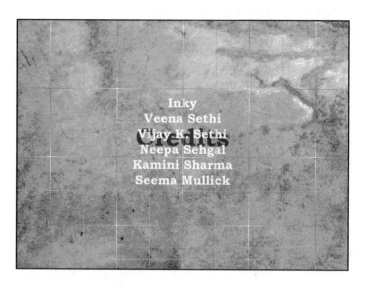

6] On the stage, click the Credits 2 sprite and move it toward the bottom of the stage. Then align the sprites on the stage so the screen looks like the illustration below.

Clicking a sprite on the stage selects the whole sprite in the score. This is another way of selecting sprites. You can easily select the Credits 2 sprite containing a list of names because it is in front of the Credits 1 sprite. Remember that Director layers sprites in channel order, placing sprites in higher-numbered channels in front of those in lower-numbered channels. Once you have the Credits 2 sprite in place, drag the text of the Credits 1 sprite toward the top of the stage.

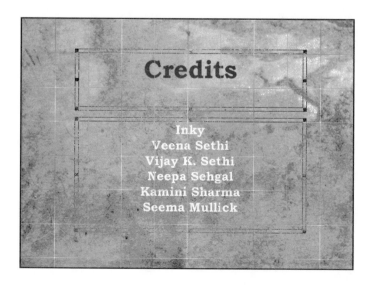

121

In this step, you are simply using the grid lines as guides to position the sprites. If you prefer to have the sprites snap to the grid, you can choose View > Grids > Snap To. This will make the sprites automatically jump, or snap, to the nearest grid line. Snapping sprites to the same grid line is one way you can be sure the sprites are exactly aligned.

tip *You can also set the color and spacing of the grid by choosing View > Grids > Settings. The default spacing in the grid is 64 × 64 pixels.*

7] Choose View › Grids › Show to turn off the grid.

Next you'll change the length of the sprites that make up the Credits screen. Right now the Bknd2, Credits 1, and Credits 2 sprites take up 28 frames in the score. Since the Credits screen doesn't have an animation or a sound file that requires a number of frames to play, you can conserve frames by shortening the sprites; then you can add a pause to the tempo channel so the credits stay on the screen long enough for people to read them. Note that you could leave the sprites in the score as they are, but the pause gives you more precise control over the length of time they remain on the stage because you can set a specific number of seconds for the pause.

8] Select the Bknd2, Credits 1, and Credits 2 sprites in the score and change their end frames to frame 139.

This change to the sprites' end frames makes them shorter; but there are still enough frames to set a 2-second pause in the tempo channel, then display the credits just a bit longer before returning users to the menu. Assigning three to four frames to movie segments like this one gives users time to recognize that there is new information on the stage; the tempo setting you add next will give them the time they need to read the text.

9] Double-click the tempo channel in frame 136 to open the Tempo dialog box.

You're going to set a delay for only this frame. Place the tempo setting in frame 136 instead of frame 135 where the new sprites appear. This limits the processing Director has to do to in a single frame. Once the playback head passes frame 136, the tempo will return to the one you originally set in the tempo channel: 10 fps.

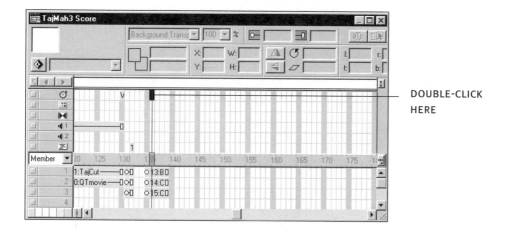

DOUBLE-CLICK HERE

10] Select Wait, use the arrow keys to set the wait time to 2 seconds, and click OK to close the dialog box.

SELECT WAIT   CLICK THE ARROW KEYS TO SET THE WAIT TIME

11] Rewind and play the movie to see what you've added.

After the digital video plays, the playback head waits in frame 130 for 2 seconds due to the tempo setting you added in the last lesson. Then the menu screen you built appears as the playback head moves through frame 131 and into 132. Then the playback head remains in frame 132 because you added a *go to the frame* script in this frame. There's no way to see the screen you've just built when the movie plays!

You want users to be able to choose to go to the Credits screen by clicking the Credits button on the menu. In the next few tasks you'll set up the navigation for the Credits button and the Quit button. Once you've finished adding the scripts to the buttons you'll be able to branch to the Credits screen by clicking the Credits button when you play the movie.

12] Save your work.

ADDING MARKERS FOR NAVIGATION

Now that you know several ways of sequencing the media for a Director movie, it's time to move on to the last two steps of the four-step process described in Lesson 1: adding interactivity to a movie and creating a projector—a way of packaging the movie for distribution. In this task, you begin to create the interaction that allows users to navigate to different parts of the movie. So far, you've created linear movies only— they play from start to end without any user interaction. With interactivity, you can provide a way for users to control how they view a movie.

In the following steps you will begin to add interactivity by identifying the frame that the playback head branches to when users click the Credits button. You'll also identify the frame to which the playback head should return after the Credits screen has been displayed. Once you've identified the frames in the score, you'll write Lingo scripts that will make the branching happen when the movie plays.

To identify a frame that Director should branch to you insert a **marker**, a small triangle that appears in the marker channel at the top of the score. After you place a marker in the score, you can type a **label** next to it. Later, when you write the Lingo script for the Credits button cast member, the script will include the marker label. The combination of a marker and a Lingo script that includes a marker makes up the simplest method of adding navigation to a movie.

In this movie, you'll first insert a marker to branch to when the Credits button is clicked. Then you'll insert another marker for the playback head to return to after displaying the Credits screen.

1] In the Marker channel at the top of the score, click frame 131.

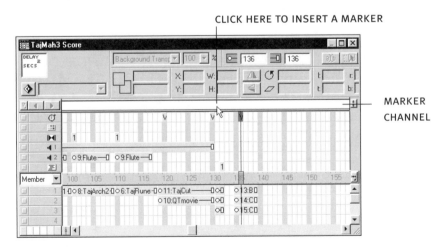

Clicking the marker channel places a marker and a highlighted label at that location.

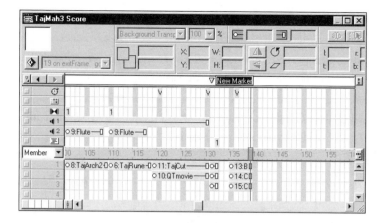

2] With the label highlighted, type *Menu* and press Enter (Windows) or Return (Macintosh) to name the marker.

Director will be able to locate this marker label when you write a Lingo script to return the playback head to this frame later in this lesson. The Menu marker identifies the screen containing the Credits and Quit buttons. Screens that contain navigation controls like these buttons often have a marker associated with them so that the playback head can return to the frame displaying the screen where users can make another selection. This is easier and more flexible than referring to frames by numbers only.

3] Insert a marker in frame 135 and name it *Credits*.

The Credits marker overlaps the Menu marker label, making it difficult to read. However, if you move the cursor over the marker, a data tip will display the marker's name.

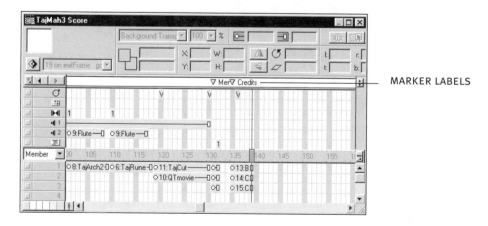

MARKER LABELS

Now you have two markers in the marker channel. In the next steps you'll add branching capability that will make the playback head move to the frames in the movie where these markers occur.

CREATING NAVIGATION SCRIPTS

In this task you create simple Lingo scripts that use the markers you just inserted in the score. Instead of using the behavior channel to write a Lingo script, you'll attach scripts directly to the Credits button and Quit button cast members.

1] Select cast member 4 (ButtonCr) in the Cast window, then click the Script button.

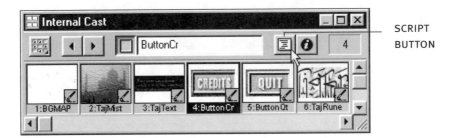

SCRIPT
BUTTON

A Script window opens that looks like the one you used to enter a script in the behavior channel. However, there is a difference. This Script window has a different default handler. The on mouseUp and end statements are the default statements for scripts created for cast members. In the next step, you will supply the instruction that should be followed once the mouse is clicked and released, for that is what on mouseUp means.

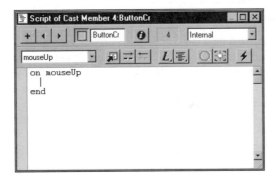

2] Type *go to frame "Credits"* in the Script window below *on mouseUp* exactly as shown here in bold:

```
on mouseUp
    go to frame "Credits"
end
```

This instruction tells Director to find a frame with a marker labeled "Credits". The label you gave the marker in frame 135 matches exactly. The marker label serves as a name of the frame in the movie. When you want to use a script to navigate to a frame where you've inserted a marker, you must include the quotation marks and spell the marker's label exactly as it appears in the marker channel.

3] Close the Script window.

Now you have a script attached to the Credits button cast member that will allow users to view the Credits screen when they click the Credits button. Next you will create a script to return users to the menu screen after the credits screen is displayed.

 You can press Enter on the numeric keypad to close the Script window.

4] Double-click frame 139 in the behavior channel to open a Script window.

This is the last frame of the credits screen. When the playback head arrives in this frame, you want the playback head to return to the menu screen. Moving the playback head back to the menu screen completes the last step of interactive branching: returning the playback head to the frame where the branching was initiated.

5] Type *go to frame "Menu"* below on *exitFrame* exactly as shown here in bold. Then close the Script window.

```
on exitFrame
    go to frame "Menu"
end
```

Remember that earlier you created a marker called Menu. Now you're using Lingo to find that marker and branch to it. After the credits screen is displayed for 2 seconds, as specified by the tempo setting in the same frame, the playback head will branch to the Menu marker and the menu screen will reappear.

Note that there's a big difference between the expression *go to frame*—which basically means stay in the current frame—and the expression *go to frame "marker label"*—which requires you to specify a marker label within the quotation marks for the playback head to branch to. In scripting Lingo, one word can make a big difference. The marker label must also be spelled inside the script's quotation marks exactly as it appears in the marker channel or Director won't be able to locate the frame.

> **tip** *Lingo is not case-sensitive, so when you use it to refer to marker labels, you don't need to be concerned with capitalization, but spelling is important. If you spell a label one way and then refer to it later with a different spelling, Director will not be able to locate the marker and will display an error message.*

Now two frames in the behavior channel have scripts assigned to them. If you move the cursor over them, the data tips display the cast member numbers of the scripts. Scripts you enter in the behavior channel are assigned as individual cast members in the Cast window.

BEHAVIOR CHANNEL INDICATORS

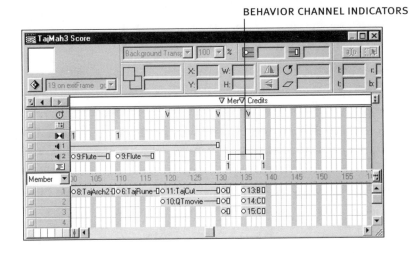

Scripts you add to cast members don't appear as individual scripts in the Cast window. Instead, a script icon appears in the thumbnail image of the cast in the Cast window.

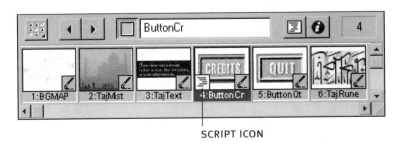

SCRIPT ICON

6] Save your work.

7] Rewind and play the movie. When you get to the menu screen, click the Credits button.

The credits screen should be displayed for 2 seconds, and then the menu screen should reappear. Why does the menu screen display again? That's right, the script in frame 139 of the behavior channel instructs Director to move the playback head to the frame labeled "Menu".

tip *If you let the movie run on the menu screen for awhile, you probably noticed that the background music stopped playing. If you look at the Score, you will notice that the Bgsound sprite in the sound channel 1 extends only to frame 130. You can change the endpoint of that sprite to 139 so that it includes all the frames used by the movie. The background music will now play when the menu screen and the credits screen are displayed.*

Now the only script left to write is a script for the Quit button on the menu screen. There is no destination screen for this button since users will quit the presentation when they click this button. This means the script statement you'll write for this button is different from the go to script statements you've written so far. Like the script for the Credits button, you'll add this script to the Quit button cast member.

8] Stop the movie. Then select cast member 5 (ButtonQt) in the Cast window, and click the Script button to open the Script window. Type *quit* below *on mouseUp* as shown here in bold:

```
on mouseUp
    quit
end
```

tip *The* quit *command closes Director and displays the Program Manager or the desktop. Note that the* quit *command closes the Director program itself, not just the movie that is open. Be sure to save your work before clicking the Quit button. An alternative to* quit *is* halt, *which stops the movie but doesn't exit Director.*

9] Close the Script window and save your work.

10] Rewind and play the movie.
The movie pauses at the menu screen.

11] Click Credits.
The credits screen is displayed for 2 seconds, and then the menu screen is displayed again.

12] When you're ready to quit, click Quit.
After you click Quit, the movie closes and Director quits. If you didn't save your work, a dialog box appears and asks you to save the movie.

CREATING A PROJECTOR

You're almost finished. You just need to package your movie so users can play it. You want people to be able to use your movie regardless of whether Director is installed on their systems.

One way to distribute a movie to users who don't own Director is to create a **projector**, which is a play-only version of a movie. Projectors play like any other program on a computer, except the projector can't be opened and edited. Projectors are actual application programs on the Macintosh and executable (.EXE) programs on Windows.

You can use the same Director movie to create a projector for either the Windows or Macintosh platform. However, to create a projector for Windows, you must use the Windows version of Director, and to create a projector for the Macintosh, you need to use the Macintosh version of Director.

note *Why do you need both Windows and Macintosh versions of Director to create projectors for both platforms? There are significant differences between these two platforms that require you to view, edit, and tweak a movie on the platform on which it will play. You may have to make changes to such things as color palettes, fonts, window locations, and Xtras.*

tip *If you use Xtras that come from developers other than Macromedia, be sure to check the documentation for each Xtra for any restrictions on distribution (some may not allow you to distribute work created with them unless you pay a fee). So that Xtras always work in the projector, create a folder and put the projector in it. In the same folder place an Xtras folder that contains any Xtras the projector uses. When the end-user runs the projector from this folder, Director will be able to locate and use the Xtras needed for the projector.*

1] Open Director.

2] Choose File › Create Projector.
The Create Projector dialog box appears.

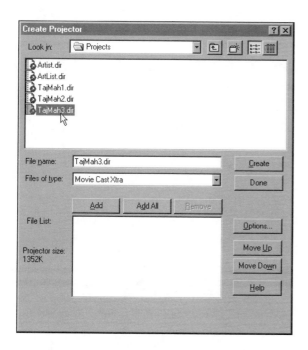

3] Open the Projects folder, if it isn't already open, and double-click TajMah3.dir.

This is the movie you have been working on in this lesson. Double-clicking the movie selects it as the movie that will become a projector.

4] Click Options. In the Projector Options dialog box, choose the Full Screen option.

This hides the desktop (any area larger than the stage is filled with the stage color, so the desktop won't be visible when the movie plays).

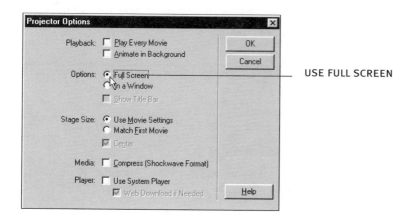

USE FULL SCREEN

5] Click OK to close the dialog box and return to the Create Projector dialog box.

6] Click Create.

A Save dialog box appears.

7] Select the Projects folder and name the file *TajMahal*. Then click Save.

A status dialog box appears while Director builds the projector. When the process is finished, look in the Projects folder. You should see a projector icon titled TajMahal. On Windows computers, the name will have an .exe extension.

TajMahal.exe

note *When you import cast members into digital movies, which tend to be large files, the cast members are generally not actually brought into the movie; instead, they are linked to the movie. The link shows Director where the cast members can be found so that Director can read them when the movie plays. In the movie you created, QTmovie is linked to a file located on the CD. When you play the projector, the CD must still be in your computer's CD drive for the movie to run properly. You can also copy the QuickTime movie into the same folder with the projector on your hard drive and the projector will be able to find it, even if the CD is not in your computer's CD drive.*

tip *You can easily create a custom icon for your projector. On the Macintosh, to replace the projector icon, copy the image you want to use onto the Clipboard. Select the projector icon in the Finder and choose File > Get Info. In the Information window, select the image of the icon and choose Edit > Paste to paste the icon from the Clipboard. After you close the Information window, the new image will appear in place of the projector icon. In Windows, you can use a third-party Xtra that lets you do this from within Director. See the Xtra list at http://www.macromedia.com/software/xtras/director*

8] When Director finishes building the projector, quit Director.

9] Locate the projector you just created and play it.

To play the projector, double-click it. This launches the play-only version of Director, which plays the movies embedded in it and then quits Director automatically.

Before distributing any projector, check your licensing agreements with any other companies whose products you may need to distribute with the projector.

132

note *Macromedia's royalty-free licensing policy means that you can distribute applications created with Director or Authorware 5 Attain to millions of end users on multiple platforms—free. The requirements are that you include the "Made with Macromedia" logo on your product's packaging and credit screen, complete the run-time distribution agreement, and register your product with Macromedia. Refer to the Made with Macromedia (MwM) folder on your Director Multimedia Studio CD for the run-time distribution agreement, logos, and logo usage guidelines. Before distributing any projector, check your licensing agreements with any other companies whose products you may need to distribute with the projector.*

You've created a mini-version of a travelog presentation in a short period of time. Of course, if you were to develop a complete interactive travelog piece, you would probably add historical facts and data, a blueprint and guide to the points of interest of the Taj Mahal, and so forth.

WHAT YOU HAVE LEARNED

In this lesson you have:

- Used the Lingo command *go to the frame* to keep the playback head in a specific frame [page 118]

- Aligned text on the stage using the grid [page 121]

- Added markers to the score [page 124]

- Used a Lingo command for navigation [page 126]

- Created a button that lets users quit the movie [page 129]

- Created a projector to distribute to end users [page 130]

techniques

more animation

LESSON 6

In this lesson you will create special effects using two animation techniques. You'll build one project using Director's Modify › Sprite › Tweening command to create a circular path animation. Then you'll build a second project in which you have Director record the path of a sprite as you drag it on the stage. The term for this type of animation is **real-time recording**.

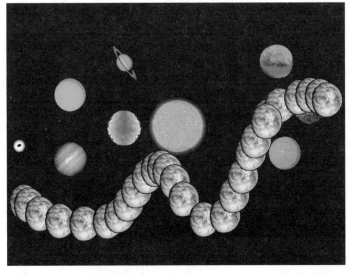

Exciting animation is in your hands when you animate a sprite with real-time recording—automatically recording a path for a sprite as you drag it on the stage. This is one of the techniques you will use to create and apply special effects in this lesson.

The 415 Productions Web site was created by Jeff Southard, 415 Productions.

The Modify › Sprite › Tweening command allows you to modify the in-betweened path that Director has already created for a sprite. This command enables Director to interpolate more than a simple change in position, however. You can use it when you want a sprite to move in a curved path, to accelerate or decelerate across the stage, or to change color or blend.

You use real-time recording to move a sprite around the stage with the mouse. When you use real-time recording, Director automatically records the movements in the score.

If you would like to view the final results of this lesson, open the Complete folder in the Lesson06 folder and play Orbit1.dir and Orbit2.dir.

WHAT YOU WILL LEARN

In this lesson you will:

- Create a circular animation
- Record mouse movements in real-time
- Leave a trail of sprites on the stage

APPROXIMATE TIME

It should take about 1 hour to complete this lesson.

LESSON FILES

Media File:
Dir7\Lessons\Lesson06\Media

Starting Files:
Dir7\Lessons\Lesson06\Start\Start1.dir
Dir7\Lessons\Lesson06\Start\Start2.dir

Completed Project:
Dir7\Lessons\Lesson06\Complete\Orbit1.dir
Dir7\Lessons\Lesson06\Complete\Orbit2.dir

SETTING MOVIE PROPERTIES

In your first project in this lesson, you use Modify > Sprite > Tweening to create animation along a circular path to make an image of the earth move in a circle around the sun. Your first task is to import an image of the earth.

1] Choose File > Open and select the Start1.dir movie in the Start folder for Lesson 6 (Windows Ctrl+O, Macintosh Command+O).

This movie includes an image of the sun that has already been placed in the score. You will import an image of the earth and sequence it in the score so that it orbits the sun.

2] Choose File > Save As and save the movie as *Orbit1.dir* (Windows Ctrl+S, Macintosh Command+S).

3] Choose File > Import and select the earth.pct file in the Media folder on the CD (Windows Ctrl+R, Macintosh Command+R). Click Add and then click Import.

Because the graphic is a 32-bit image and the stage is set to 8-bit color depth, the Image Options dialog box is displayed. Remember, if your system's color depth is set higher than 8-bit, the Stage setting will also be higher.

4] In the Image Options dialog box, click Stage (8 bits) and then click OK.

Thumbnails of the sun and the earth now appear in the cast.

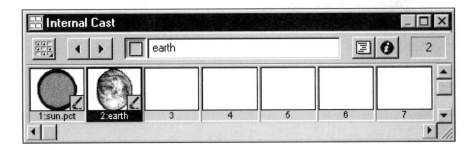

SETTING KEYFRAMES

Now you'll place the earth image in the score and set the keyframes for the earth's movement around the sun.

1] Drag the earth from the Cast window to channel 2, frame 1.

You know by now that a keyframe is a key position in an animation where a change takes place. You're going to animate the earth in this task by moving it around the stage, creating keyframes, and allowing Director to automatically tween the frames between the keyframes.

136

The animations you've created so far are linear animations. The sprites moved in a straight line onto the stage and off the stage along the same path. In this lesson the animations you'll create follow a curved path that Director automatically defines between the keyframes you set in a sprite. To make your sprite follow a curved path, you must set the sprite in at least three positions on the stage in different keyframes.

2] Click frame 1, channel 2, and then drag the earth to the lower-left area of the stage.
This is the first keyframe of the animation you're about to create.

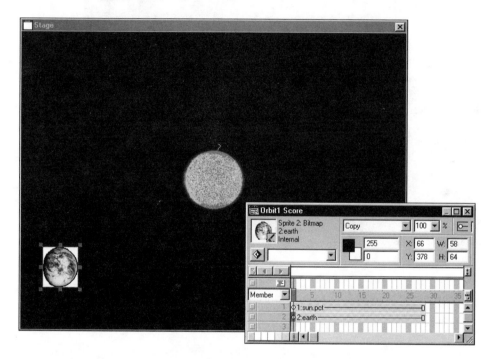

You need to set three more keyframes for the earth image to complete the animation. Choose locations for the image in the keyframes that will create an elliptical path to imitate the earth's orbit around the sun.

3] In the score, click frame 7 in channel 2 and choose Insert › Keyframe (Windows Ctrl+Alt+K, Macintosh Command+Option+K). Then drag the earth to the lower-right area of the stage.

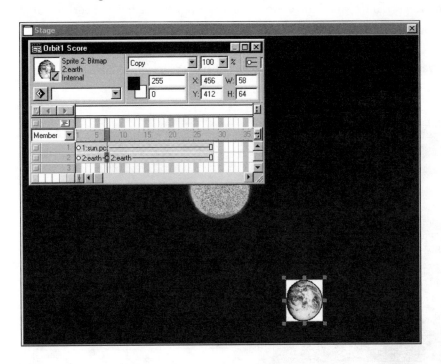

4] Insert a keyframe in frame 14, channel 2. Drag the earth to the upper-right area of the stage.

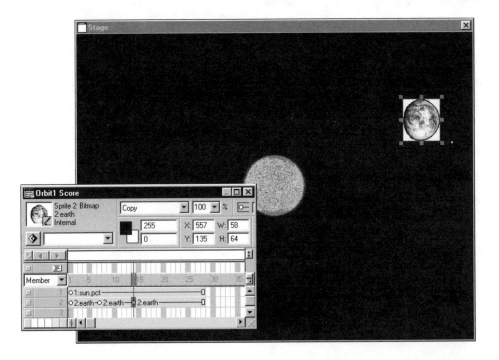

138

5] Insert another keyframe in frame 21, channel 2. Drag the earth just over the top edge of the sun image on the stage to complete the last keyframe position of the elliptical path.

On this part of its orbit, the earth should be on the far side of the sun.

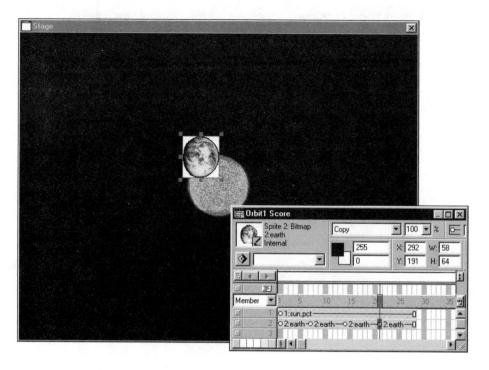

You now have defined a few points of the circular path the earth image will follow for the animation. You have a few more steps to complete to make the animation begin and end in the same position to create a truly circular effect.

6] Save your work.

7] Rewind and play the movie.

When you watch the animation, you see that Director automatically tweened the frames between the keyframes you identified. The path is somewhat circular, but it is jerky. Also, the earth passes in front of the sun instead of behind it. In the next task, you'll smooth the animation using the Modify > Sprite > Tweening feature. You'll also arrange the sprites so the earth passes behind the sun in its orbit.

CREATING A CIRCULAR PATH ANIMATION

Now you'll use Modify > Sprite > Tweening to make the earth orbit around the sun in a smooth, circular path.

1] With the entire sprite in channel 2 selected, choose Modify › Sprite › Tweening (Windows Ctrl+Shift+B, Macintosh Command+Shift+B).

The Sprite Tweening dialog box appears with a few boxes pre-selected. The Path box is checked and causes Director to create the curved paths between keyframes you defined in the previous task. The other options in the dialog box allow you to make sprites circle, speed up, or slow down. You can also make a sprite change size, shape, orientation, or color, or you can blend a sprite to make it fade in or fade out as Director tweens the sprite between keyframes.

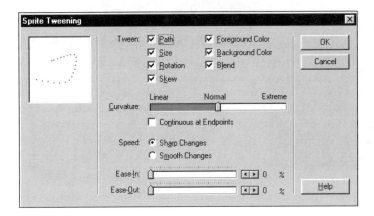

2] Check the Continuous at Endpoints box, and move the Curvature slider a little toward the right side of the scale.

Checking the Continuous at Endpoints box makes the sprites in an animation begin and end at the same point. If this box is checked, the sprite will follow a smooth, circular path around the stage. Notice as you move the slider that the animation path preview in the upper left of the dialog box changes: the path becomes rounder.

3] Click OK to apply your selections and close the dialog box.

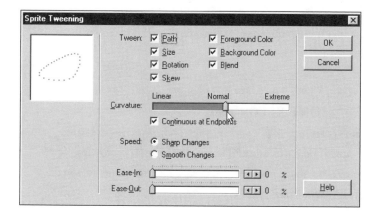

4] Play the movie.

Now the earth orbits the sun in a much smoother manner. Try using this same sprite and vary your selections in the dialog box. If you leave the sprite selected, you can choose Modify > Sprite > Tweening again and choose slightly different parameters. Experiment to see which effect you like best. Then rewind and play the movie.

You have two problems to solve: The white background for the earth sprite shows and the earth doesn't pass behind the sun image in a true orbit pattern. Let's fix these.

5] With the sprite in channel 2 selected, set the ink effect to Background Transparent.

6] With the sprite in channel 2 still selected, choose Modify › Arrange › Move Backward (Windows Ctrl+Down Arrow, Macintosh Command+Down Arrow).

The sun and the earth sprites exchange positions in the score. Moving a sprite backward in the score means moving it to a sprite channel just beneath its original position, in this case from channel 2 to channel 1. No matter what sprite you select to move backward, this command moves the sprite back one channel and places it beneath sprites in higher-numbered channels.

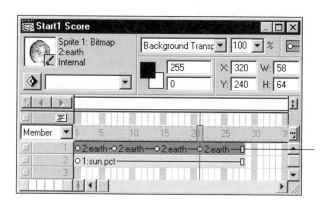

THE MODIFY › ARRANGE › MOVE BACKWARD COMMAND MOVES SELECTED SPRITES BACKWARD ONE CHANNEL

With the earth sprite moved backward, it now orbits behind the sun as it should because the sun sprite is in a higher-numbered channel than the earth sprite.

7] Save your work.

ANIMATING WITH REAL-TIME RECORDING

In this second project in this lesson, you'll use another technique for creating animation. Real-time recording creates animation by recording the movement of a sprite as you drag it across the stage. Here you'll create an animation on top of a graphic by recording your mouse movements.

> **tip** *This real-time recording technique is especially good for simulating the movement of a cursor. For example, you can use it to move a cursor across the screen as part of a demonstration or training program.*

1] Open the Start2.dir movie in the Start folder of the Lesson06 folder. Then save this movie as *Orbit2.dir*.

An image of the sun and all the planets and an image of the earth make up the cast members of this movie.

2] Drag the earth image from the Cast window to frame 1, channel 2, in the score. Then apply the Background Transparent ink effect.

Later you're going to place the sun and planets image in channel 1 as a background for the earth animation you'll create in this task. For now, the earth image is in the center of the stage in channel 2. In the next few steps, you'll define a path for the image through real-time recording.

3] Click channel 2, frame 1, and position the sprite on the lower left of the stage where you want the image to begin its animation.

This step identifies the start keyframe just as in other types of animation. You want the sprite's path you'll define by real-time recording to begin at this location.

Next you'll select the frames in the score that you want the animation to occupy. For this animation, you'll select 28 frames, the default length of the sprite.

4] Click to the left of the channel number in channel 2.

All the cells in the score between frames 1 and 28 are now highlighted and the playback head remains in frame 1.

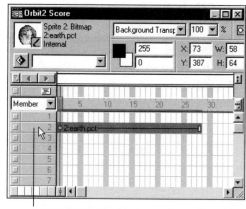

CLICK HERE TO SELECT CHANNEL 2

5] Open the Control Panel. Click the Tempo control to select it and then change the tempo to 5 fps.

The Tempo display indicates the preset tempo at which the current frame should play, in frames per second. If a tempo setting has been entered in the tempo channel of the score at a certain frame, that setting takes precedence over a tempo you set in the Control Panel. That setting will also display in the Tempo control field of the Control Panel.

CLICK THE TEMPO CONTROL FIELD
AND ENTER A NEW VALUE

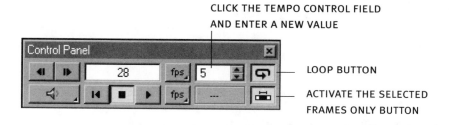

LOOP BUTTON

ACTIVATE THE SELECTED
FRAMES ONLY BUTTON

You've just reset the tempo to 5 fps for the selected frames. You set the tempo for a selection of frames with the Tempo control on the Control Panel by entering a new fps value in the field or using the arrow keys to increase or decrease the fps setting. Changing this target tempo to a lower fps lessens Director's sensitivity to your mouse movements as you record. This gives you better control when you're recording in real time and ultimately results in a smoother animation. Any time you want to create a real-time recording, decrease the tempo to record at a speed that's slower than normal. Once recorded, you can reset the tempo value to its higher rate.

6] In the Control Panel, click Selected Frames Only to turn on this option.

Clicking the Selected Frames Only button activates the tempo setting for just the frames you've selected in the score. Clicking this button also keeps the real-time recording you're about to do limited to these frames.

7] Click Loop to turn off this feature.

If the Loop feature is on in the Control Panel, Director will keep playing the animation after you finish recording it.

8] Choose Control › Real-Time Recording.

Recording begins as soon as you drag the sprite onto the stage, so be prepared to move the mouse. The real-time recording indicator appears next to the channel for the sprite being recorded.

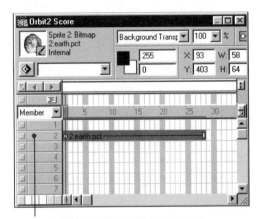

REAL-TIME RECORDING INDICATOR

9] Drag the earth sprite in a desired path on the stage to a new position.

You have 28 frames to define a path for the sprite, so watch the playback head in the score as you drag the sprite through its path. Try to position the sprite halfway through the path you want it to follow by the time the playback head is at frame 14. Finish dragging the sprite to its end position just as the playback head enters frame 28.

As you drag, you will see the sprite move across the stage. The sprite and its movements will be recorded in the score. Release the mouse button to stop recording.

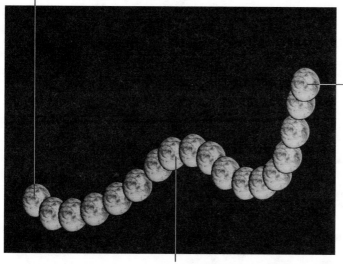

IF THE ANIMATION STARTS HERE...

...AND HERE
BY FRAME 28

...THE SPRITE SHOULD
BE HERE BY FRAME 14...

This procedure is known as **real-time recording** because Director records your mouse movements directly in the score as you work. Once Director has recorded the sprite's movement in all 28 frames, it will place an image of the sprite on the stage in the last location it recorded. If you don't like where the animation ends, you can repeat the recording process. To do this, select the frames in the score again and then choose Control > Real-Time Recording and drag the sprite through the 28 frames.

In your first attempts at real-time recording, the playback head may arrive at the end of the recording (frame 28) before you have finished moving the sprite to the place where you want it to end. Be sure to plan the path before you begin. Check the playback head as you record in real time to control the animation paths you want to record.

10] Drag cast member 1 to frame 1, channel 1, to give your animation a background image.

11] Click Loop in the Control Panel to turn on this feature.
With Loop on you can see your animation play over and over.

12] Rewind and play the movie.

Earth takes its own path through the universe, as you can see.

Now add even more interest to the animation by adding trails to the sprite.

13] Stop the movie, and then select the sprite in channel 2 and click the Trails box on the sprite toolbar.

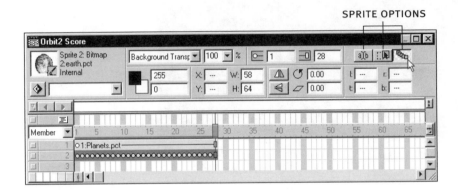

Trails is one of the sprite options you find in the sprite toolbar. Checking this box when you have selected a sprite makes the sprite leave behind a trail of images as it moves around the stage. The other two options, Moveable and Editable, also apply to sprites but allow users to interact with the sprites. When the Moveable option is applied to a sprite, users can drag it on the stage while the movie is actually playing. The Editable option applies only to sprites that are **fields**. Field sprites allow users to select and edit the text of a field while the movie is playing. Field sprites are added to a movie through a selection on the Tool Palette window.

Now the earth will leave a trail of its image as it moves along its animated path. You can apply trails to any sprite you've animated by clicking the sprite in the score and then checking the Trails box.

LINGO EQUIVALENT

   (sprite 2).trails = TRUE

tip   *Using Trails is a great way to simulate handwriting, since a trace is left wherever a cast member happens to move. Emulate the path of a pen or pencil by creating a small circle in the Paint window using the Filled Ellipse tool; then create a real-time recording that uses this cast member. The filled circle takes the place of the pen or pencil tip.*

14] Rewind and play the movie to see your work.

Great effect! With real-time recording and the Trails options, you can create many animated special effects.

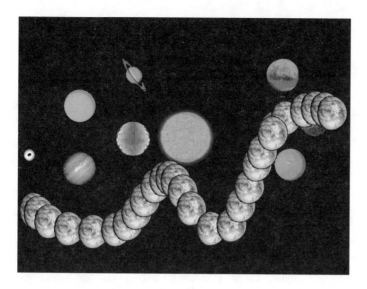

15] Save your work.

WHAT YOU HAVE LEARNED

In this lesson you have:

• Created a circular animation with Modify > Sprite > Tweening [page 140]

• Used real-time recording to record mouse movements [page 142]

• Used the Trails option to leave a trail of sprites on the stage [page 146]

and layers

keyframes

LESSON 7

One basic method of creating animation is to define the keyframes of the animation and then tween the keyframes to show movement. In this lesson you will use tweening to create an animation of a piece of paper floating from one folder to another. In this animation, multiple cast members combine to create the effect. As you build the animation, you will change the layering in the score to make the paper appear to come out of one folder and move into another folder.

If you would like to view the final result of this lesson, open the Complete folder in the Lesson07 folder and play Paper.dir.

By establishing just a few keyframes, you can create effective animations that use multiple cast members, such as a piece of paper floating into and out of a folder. You can then add sound for further impact.

Artist, Merlyn Holmes

WHAT YOU WILL LEARN

In this lesson you will:

- Create a custom stage size

- Practice applying ink

- Copy and move multiple cells simultaneously in the score

- Practice creating key positions for an animation

- Practice constraining the movement of sprites horizontally and vertically

- Practice tweening keyframes to show movement

- Play selected frames only

- Practice layering sprites below and above each other

- Practice swapping cast members

- Make a sound file play continuously

APPROXIMATE TIME

It should take about 1 hour to complete this lesson.

LESSON FILES

Media Files:

Dir7\Lessons\Lesson07\Media

Starting Files:

None

Completed Project:

Dir7\Lessons\Lesson07\Complete\Paper.dir

CREATING A CUSTOM STAGE

First you will set a custom stage size by using the Movie Properties dialog box. This stage size is smaller than the one Director uses by default. Movies with smaller stage sizes are best for creating Shockwave movies. To speed up downloading over the Web, you want to keep the size of your movie small, and a smaller stage helps create a smaller file.

1] Choose File › New › Movie to open a new movie (Windows Ctrl+N, Macintosh Command+N).

An empty stage appears.

2] Choose Modify › Movie › Properties to open the Movie Properties dialog box. Then from the Stage Size menu, choose Custom, type *304* in the Width field, and type *230* in the Height field. Click OK to close the dialog box.

You now have a custom-sized stage, 304 by 230 pixels.

LINGO EQUIVALENT

(the stage).rect = rect(left, top, right, bottom)

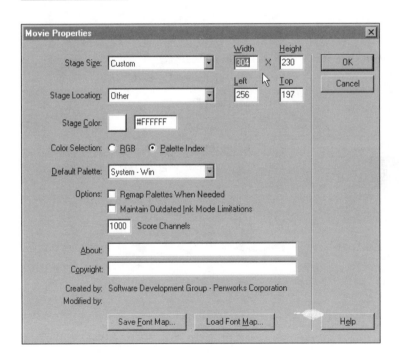

3] Save your work as *Paper.dir* (Windows Ctrl+S, Macintosh Command+S) in your Projects folder.

IMPORTING THE MEDIA

Next you need to import the media you'll use in this animation.

1] Choose File › Import (Windows Ctrl+R, Macintosh Command+R).

The Import dialog box opens.

2] Windows only: From the Files of Type menu, choose PICT. Macintosh only: From the Show menu, choose PICT.

Selecting this file type causes Director to display only graphics files in the list box. For the moment, you don't want to import any other types of files.

3] Locate and open the Media folder in the Lesson07 folder, click Add All, and then click Import.

This adds all the graphics files in the Media folder to the list and begins the import process.

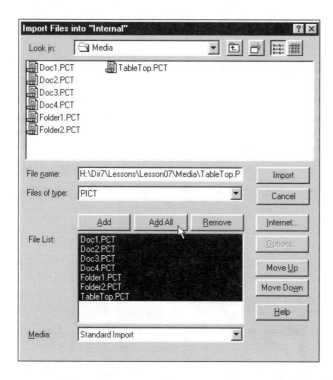

The Image Options dialog box opens.

4] In the Image Options dialog box, select Stage (8 bits). Then check the Same Settings for Remaining Images box at the bottom of the dialog box. Windows only: Select Remap To, and then choose System-Win from the menu. Click OK to close the dialog box.

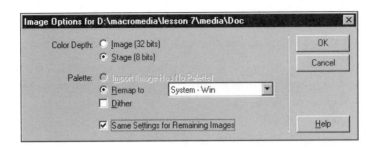

The images were created on a Macintosh using the colors in the Macintosh system palette. By remapping the images to the Windows system palette, you can be sure that the colors you see will display well in Windows-based movies.

By checking Same Settings for Remaining Images, you determine that all the graphics will be imported with this same settings and that this dialog box won't be displayed as each graphic is imported.

tip *Windows only: You'll occasionally want to use Macintosh graphics that use the Macintosh system palette. In this case, you would choose Remap to System-Mac in the Palette area of the Image Options dialog box. When you do this, however, Director elements such as the toolbar and score appear in black and white when your system is in 8-bit color mode, indicating that the movie contains a palette that does not observe Windows color palette conventions. This color change affects the Director user interface only; it does not affect the movie itself.*

Seven cast members have been imported.

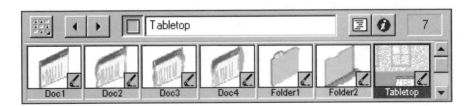

SETTING THE MOVIE TEMPO

Now you will set the speed of the movie by setting its tempo.

1] Open the score (Windows Ctrl+4, Macintosh Command+4).

2] Toggle the Hide/Show Effects Channel button, if necessary, so that the tempo channel is visible.

3] Double-click frame 1 of the tempo channel to open the Tempo dialog box and drag the tempo slider to 10 fps.

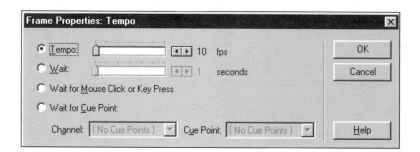

The frame rate you set in the Tempo dialog box is a requested rate only, not an absolute rate. If the computer is capable of playing the movie at the requested rate, it will. However, slower machines may not be able to achieve the faster tempo settings that can be specified in the Tempo dialog box.

4] Toggle the Hide/Show Effects Channel button off so the effects channels are hidden and there is more room in the score to see the sprite channels.

PLACING THE GRAPHICS ON THE STAGE

Now that the basic movie properties are set, you'll place the graphics on the stage.

1] With the Cast window open, drag cast member 7 (the tabletop background) from the cast to channel 1, frame 1, in the score.

The background sprite fills frames 1 through 28 in the score. You want to make your movie 30 frames long.

2] In channel 1 of the score, drag the end frame indicator to extend the length of sprite 1 to frame 30.

3] Drag cast member 5 (Folder1) from the cast to channel 2, frame 1, in the score.

The folder sprite fills frames 1 through 28 in the score and is centered on the stage.

Next you will apply some ink effects to make the sprites look better on the stage.

4] With the Folder1 sprite still selected, choose Matte from the Ink menu in the score.

If you don't see the Ink list menu at the top of the score, choose View > Sprite Toolbar to make it available.

You need to make the white areas around the edges of the Folder1 image transparent without making the white areas within the image also transparent. The Matte ink retains the white areas inside the image and makes the areas outside the image transparent.

LINGO EQUIVALENT

(sprite 2).ink = 8

Ink numbers can be found in Help under "Ink of Sprite property."

5] On the stage, select the Folder1 sprite and drag it to the lower-left part of the stage.

This sprite will be the folder from which the paper flies.

6] Click frame 1, channel 3 in the score. Then drag cast member 1 (Doc1) to the stage so it covers the folder. If necessary, use the arrow keys to nudge it into place.

tip   *When a sprite is selected in the score, you can use the arrow keys on the keyboard to nudge the sprite 1 pixel at a time on the stage.*

When you drag sprites to the stage, Director adds them in the next available channel. Director also adds the sprites to the score starting at the current frame. Clicking channel 3, frame 1 causes the sprite to be placed in that position.

The Doc1 sprite is the piece of paper that will fly out of the folder.

You can see the white background around the paper, so change the ink effect.

7] With the Doc1 sprite selected, choose Matte from the Ink menu in the score.

8] Click frame 1, channel 4. Then drag cast member 6 (Folder2) to the stage and place it on top of the folder and paper sprites. Again, choose Matte ink.
This is the top flap of the folder. Director places this cast member in channel 4. If necessary, use the arrow keys to move the sprite to cover the other two.

9] Save your work.

COPYING SPRITES TO A NEW LOCATION
Now you'll make a copy of the layered sprites to create the folder to which the paper will fly. In previous lessons you copied and pasted sprites to new locations using the Edit menu. Here you'll learn a quicker method.

1] Select channels 2 through 4.

2] Position the pointer over the selected sprites, hold down the Alt key (Windows) or Option key (Macintosh), and drag the selection to channel 5. Then release the mouse button.

When you drag while holding down the Alt or Option key, the pointer shows a plus sign (+) to indicate that you are copying rather than moving the sprites.

Release the mouse and the sprites are copied to channels 5, 6, and 7.

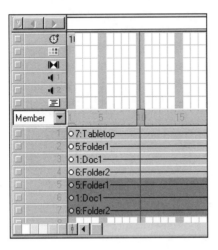

3] With the duplicate folder and paper (channels 5 through 7) still selected, drag them to the right side of the stage. Hold down Shift as you drag horizontally.

As you will recall, holding down Shift as you drag selected sprites constrains the movement of the sprites horizontally or vertically.

4] In the score, select the sprite in channel 6 and delete it.

This is the second piece of paper in the second folder. You don't need it because you're going to work with the piece of paper in channel 3.

5] Extend sprites 2, 3, 4, 5, and 7 to frame 30 by dragging their end frame indicators.

This keeps the folders and paper on the stage through all 30 frames of the movie.

CREATING THE ANIMATION WITH KEYFRAMES

Now you will create the paper animation. You will create keyframes for channel 3 (the paper) in frames 10, 20, and 30. A keyframe already exists in frame 1. In frame 1 you will leave the paper inside the folder at the left side of the stage, and in frame 10 you will place the paper sprite up and out of that folder. In frame 20 you will place the paper sprite above the folder at the right side of the stage, and in frame 30 you will place the sprite inside of that folder. Director will automatically tween the sprite positions so the paper will move smoothly between the positions you have chosen for each keyframe.

1] In the score, click frame 1, channel 3.

You will leave the paper sprite where it is already placed because this is where you want the animation to begin.

On the stage, you will see that a sprite is selected by the frame and handles that appear. The selected object is the paper, but you can't see the paper because it's layered below the top of the folder.

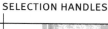
SELECTION HANDLES

SELECTION RECTANGLE

The paper is in channel 3, and the top of the folder is in channel 4. Because sprites in lower-numbered channels are behind sprites in higher-numbered channels, the paper sprite is behind the top of the folder.

2] In the score, click frame 10 of the sprite in channel 3 (the paper) and choose Insert › Keyframe.

This sets the second keyframe.

Now you need to move the paper sheet up and out of the folder.

3] With the keyframe in frame 10, channel 3, still selected, use the Up Arrow key to move the paper straight up. When it's above the folder, hold down the Shift key and use the mouse to drag it up farther.

While the paper sprite is inside the folder graphics, it can be hard to reposition using the mouse. You can use the arrow keys to move it up far enough to be selected by the mouse. Holding down the Shift key while you drag ensures that you move the sprite in a straight line.

4] In the score, click frame 20 of the sprite in channel 3 (the paper) and choose Insert › Keyframe.

This sets the third keyframe. Here you want the paper directly above the folder at the right side of the stage.

5] On the stage, hold down Shift and drag the selection (the paper) across the stage so it is directly above the destination folder.

158

6] In the score, click frame 30 of the sprite in channel 3 (the paper) and choose Insert › Keyframe.

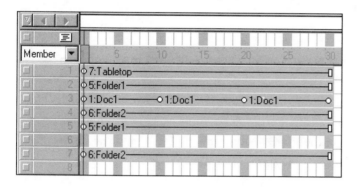

This sets the fourth and final keyframe. Here you want the paper inside the destination folder at the right side of the stage.

7] Hold down Shift and drag the selection (the paper) downward so it is behind the destination folders. Use the arrow keys, if necessary, to position the sprite.

Later, when you move the sprite layers, the paper will be between the folders.

8] Save your work.

159

PLAYING SELECTED FRAMES ONLY

Sometimes it is useful to look at only a part of your movie. Rather than playing the whole movie to view a selected part of an animation, you can select just the frames on which you want to concentrate. Playing selected frames of the movie is an effective troubleshooting technique you can use to pinpoint the frames of an animation that do not appear as you'd like them to during movie playback.

On the Control Panel, you can click the Selected Frames Only button to play back only a range of frames that you have selected in the score. You can then also select Loop Playback, so the playback head automatically loops back to the beginning of the selection after it gets to the last selected frame.

LOOP PLAYBACK

SELECTED FRAMES ONLY

1] Click the Score window to make it active. Choose Edit › Select All, and then choose Edit › Edit Sprite Frames.

Choosing the Edit > Select All command highlights all the sprites in the score. Then choosing the command Edit > Edit Sprite Frames turns on a feature that allows you to select individual frames of the sprites that you highlighted. In the next step you will work with selected frames of the sprite in channel 1.

2] In channel 1, select frames 15 through 30.

First click frame 15 and then hold down the Shift key and click frame 30. Before you performed step 1 above, clicking in any frame of the sprite selected the entire sprite. Now you can select specific frames of the sprite.

3] Open the Control Panel (Windows Ctrl+2, Macintosh Command+2) and click Selected Frames Only and Loop Playback.

When Director is set to play only selected frames, a green line appears below the frame channel in the score to indicate these frames.

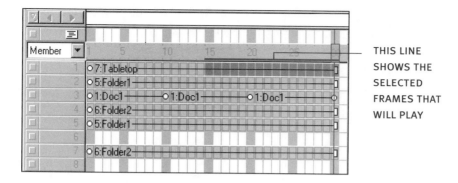

THIS LINE
SHOWS THE
SELECTED
FRAMES THAT
WILL PLAY

4] Click Play on the Control Panel.

Only part of the animation plays because you chose Selected Frames Only. In addition, because you also chose Loop Playback, the selected frames play over and over. If you were having trouble with the way the animation plays in these particular frames, you could focus on these frames to discover the problem.

5] Click Selected Frames Only to remove the green line. Then use the Control Panel to rewind and play the whole movie.

Great! Establishing keyframes and tweening them really makes the animation work. It's not quite what you want yet, but the problems are easy to fix.

6] Save your work.

FINISHING THE BASIC ANIMATION

The animation you created has several problems. First, the paper follows a curious curving path. Second, when the paper animates to the second folder, it goes behind the folder entirely, not between the folder flaps. You'll fix the curving path first.

When Director performs automatic tweening, it is guided by a set of defaults. You can change these default values if you wish. For example, the default path a tweened sprite follows on the stage has a set curvature. You will reduce this curvature to make the path appear more natural.

1] In the score, select all the sprites in channel 3 by clicking frame 1 in channel 3, holding down the Shift key, and clicking frame 30 in channel 3.

In the previous task you made it possible to select and work with a sprites in each frame. To fine-tune the animation, you want to smooth out the path the sprites travel throughout the movie, so you need to be sure to select all **30** frames.

2] Choose Modify › Sprite › Tweening to open the Sprite Tweening dialog box. Drag the Curvature slider bar at least halfway toward Linear and click OK.

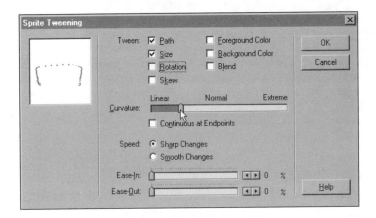

3] Rewind and play the movie again.

Now the path of the paper looks more natural.

4] Stop the movie.

The paper is still going behind the destination folder. The problem is the layering of the channels: The paper is in channel 3, but the top of the second folder is in channel 7 and the bottom of the folder is in channel 5. Because both folder sprites are in higher-numbered channels than the paper sprite, the paper looks as though it is going completely behind the folder. You need to move some of the sprites to different channels.

If you could not see this problem clearly, watch the stage while you drag the playback head back and forth between frames 25 and 30 in the score. You should be able to see that the paper falls entirely behind the folder.

Now you need to make some changes to the layers.

LAYERING THE SPRITES

In Lesson 2, you learned that sprites in higher-numbered channels appear to be in front of sprites in lower-numbered channels. Conversely, sprites in lower-numbered channels appear behind sprites in higher-numbered channels. Therefore, a sprite in channel 1000, the potentially highest numbered channel in the score, would appear at the very front of the stage, and a sprite in channel 1 would appear at the very back. In this animation, the paper should look as though it falls between the two folder flaps. To create this effect, you need to move the paper sprite so that it is between the two folder sprites at the right side of the stage.

162

You can move sprites in the score in several ways. The simplest way is to drag a selected sprite to its new location. You can do this, however, only if the destination channel is empty. Dragging, when you can do it, has the advantage of leaving the other sprites undisturbed. Although you could use dragging in this project, you will use another, more flexible method.

To rearrange the sprites in the score even when no empty channels are available, choose the Modify > Arrange command. This command gives you the option of moving the selected sprite forward or backward on the stage. In doing this, however, you will also be moving sprites in other, intermediate channels.

You can also use the Up and Down Arrow keys to achieve the same results. Ctrl+Up Arrow (Windows) or Command+Up Arrow (Macintosh) moves the selected sprites forward on the stage (or to a higher-numbered channel in the score). Ctrl+Down Arrow (Windows) or Command+Down Arrow (Macintosh) moves them backward on the stage (or to a lower-numbered channel in the score).

LINGO EQUIVALENT

(sprite 4).locz = (sprite 4).locz + 2   --Move up 2 levels

Sprites can change their display order dynamically at runtime via the ZLoc property. This property defines the sprites' positions on the Z axis, effectively allowing you to specify which sprite is on top. This setting affects playback only; it is not visible in the score.

1] **In the score, select frames 21 through 30 in channel 3.**

To select this range, click frame 21 and then Shift+click frame 30.

2] **Press Ctrl+Up Arrow (Windows) or Command+Up Arrow (Macintosh) repeatedly until the selected frames are in channel 6.**

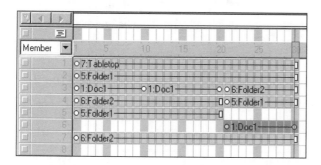

When you try to move the sprites in channel 3 "through" the sprites in channels 4 and 5, Director displays a warning message stating this operation will split sprites. Click OK to proceed.

163

3] Click Play on the Control Panel.

The paper is layered correctly and falls into the folder as it should.

You can see how channel order affects the way sprites are layered. By placing the last part of the paper animation in channel 6 instead of keeping it in channel 3, you make the paper appear to fall in between the top and bottom parts of the folder.

Did you notice that as you move the sprites down, the sprites in the next channel move up? This did not affect your animation, but it's always a good idea to keep things tidy, so you should move the other sprites back to their original locations.

4] In the score, select the sprites in channels 3 and 4, frames 21 through 30.

To select both rows, click channel 3, frame 21, and then Shift+click channel 4, frame 30.

5] Move the selected sprites to channels 4 and 5, frames 21 through 30, using Ctrl+Up Arrow (Windows) or Command+Up Arrow (Macintosh). Then save your work.

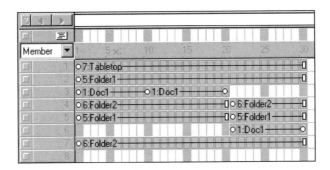

EXCHANGING CAST MEMBERS

This animation could be improved by adding different versions of the paper so that it looks as if it's flapping as it animates across the stage. You'll exchange cast members to add this enhancement.

1] In the score, select channel 3, frame 2. In the cast, select cast member 2 (Doc2). Then click the Exchange Cast Members button on the toolbar.

EXCHANGE CAST MEMBERS

Now cast member 1 is replaced with cast member 2 in channel 3, frame 2. This is a slightly altered version of the paper. You should see the number 2 in this cell. If you do not see this number, choose View > Sprite Labels > Changes Only. This will cause the sprite number to appear each time it changes. You should choose View > Zoom > 200% to enlarge the score display so that each sprite number is visible and the following steps will be easier for you to complete. Also, placing the mouse pointer over the cell will cause data tips to display the sprite number and name.

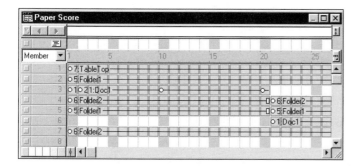

2] In the score, select channel 3, frame 3. In the cast, select cast member 3 (Doc3). Then click the Exchange Cast Members button.

This is another version of the paper. Cast member 3 replaces cast member 1 in this cell.

3] In the score, select channel 3, frame 4. In the cast, select cast member 4 (Doc4). Then click the Exchange Cast Members button.

This is the last altered version of the paper. Now cast member 4 follows 1, 2, and 3.

4] Repeat this exchange process until you have exchanged the sequence 1, 2, 3, 4 for all the sprites in channel 3.

5] Swap the cast members in channel 6, frames 21 through 30.

These are the last parts of the paper animation.

EXCHANGE THE SPRITES IN CHANNEL 3, FRAMES 1 THROUGH 20

THEN EXCHANGE THE SPRITES IN CHANNEL 6, FRAMES 21 THROUGH 30

6] Rewind and play the animation.

You should now see the paper flap and fly from one folder to another. This animation looks much better now that it uses different versions of the paper.

7] Save your work.

ADDING BACKGROUND MUSIC

Sound can add a great deal to your animation, setting a soothing mood or generating excitement. In this task you will add background music that will play while the animation runs.

1] Choose File › Import to open the Import dialog box.

2] Windows only: From the Files of Type menu, choose All files. Macintosh only: From the Show menu, choose All Files. From the list of files in the Media folder, select Boiling.aif. Then click Add, and click Import.

The sound is imported into the Cast window as a cast member.

3] Select the sound cast member and click the Cast Member Properties button in the Cast window.

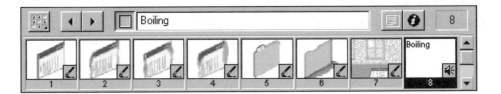

4] In the dialog box that appears, check the Options: Loop box and then click OK to close the dialog box.

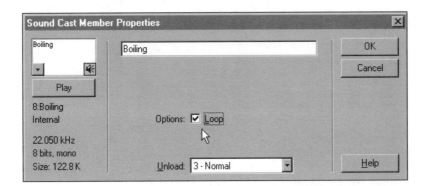

This makes the sound loop back to the beginning when it reaches the end of the sound file. Looping sounds gives the impression of a longer, continuous sound. This is a great option, especially if you need to keep file size to a minimum. Also, if you are developing custom music, you can spend less time and money on shorter sound files. Then you can loop them to make them seem longer.

tip *Keep sound files small and loop them to give the impression of longer sounds. This helps reduce download time for Shockwave movies.*

5] Drag the sound cast member to sound channel 1, frame 1, and extend it though frame 30 by dragging its end frame indicator.

Now the sound will play throughout the animation

LINGO EQUIVALENT

```
(member "boiling").loop = TRUE
puppetSound 1, "boiling"
```

6] Save your work. Then rewind and play the movie.

What a difference a sound makes!

WHAT YOU HAVE LEARNED

In this lesson you have:

- Used the Movie Properties dialog box to create a custom stage [page 150]

- Copied and moved cells with the drag and copy method [page 153]

- Created keyframes with the Insert Keyframes command [page 157]

- Used the Control Panel to play selected frames only [page 160]

- Adjusted the tweening of a sprite to produce a more natural animation [page 162]

- Moved sprites to place them in different layers [page 163]

- Exchanged cast members [page 164]

- Imported and looped a sound file [page 166]

and buttons

film loops

LESSON 8

In the previous lesson you created animation by defining keyframes and then tweening the keyframes to show movement. As part of that lesson, you exchanged cast members numerous times to display different versions of a piece of paper that floats from one file folder to another. That procedure was time-consuming. In this lesson, you will create the same animation using a quicker, more efficient technique: a **film loop.** A film loop encapsulates several cast members as a single cast member. You can use a film loop cast member anywhere you would use a regular cast member; the difference is that, as the playback head moves through the score, the film loop cast member

In this lesson you will begin by creating an animation using a sequence of several cast members, and you will then transform this sequence into a single cast member, called a film loop. A film loop encapsulates a sequence of cast members as a single cast member. This cast member then is an entire animation, and like any other cast member, it can be moved across the stage within another animation, enabling you to create complex motion.

displays each cast member it contains. Using a film loop, you can easily fine-tune complex animations by focusing just on the movement of an animated object (for example, a bird flying or a person walking) without having to worry about continually switching cast members in the score.

If you did not complete the previous lessons, you will still be able to complete this lesson. If you would like to view the final result of this lesson, open the Complete folder in the Lesson08 folder and play Loop.dir.

To give you a jump-start, the media elements have been assembled in the cast and sequenced in the score in Start.dir. You completed this same task in the previous lesson, so you don't need to repeat it here.

WHAT YOU WILL LEARN

In this lesson you will:

• Practice exchanging cast members

• Encapsulate several cast members in one cast member

• Create keyframes for a film loop cast member

• Practice tweening keyframes to show movement

• Create a copy of an animation and reverse it

• Add interactivity to a movie by creating buttons that the user can click

APPROXIMATE TIME

It should take about 1 hour to complete this lesson.

LESSON FILES

Media Files:
None

Starting Files:
Dir7\Lessons\Lesson08\Start\Start.dir

Completed Project:
Dir7\Lessons\Lesson08\Complete\Loop.dir

EXCHANGING CAST MEMBERS

First you need to open the start file. Then you will incorporate the alternative versions of the paper cast members.

1] Open Start.dir in the Start folder in the Lesson08 folder and save it as *Loop.dir* in your Projects folder.

The folders and paper are already set up on the stage and in the score. You will recognize this movie; it is the same movie you created in Lesson 7, just before you introduced the sequence Doc1, Doc2, Doc3, Doc4, Doc1, . . . to make the paper flap as it crosses the stage.

Next you will work in channel 3 to start setting up the film loop. You will set up a sequence of four frames in which each version of the four paper sprites (Doc1, Doc2, Doc3, and Doc4) appear once. This is different than what you did in the previous lesson, where you exchanged cast members after you tweened the keyframes. In this task, you will exchange cast members before you create the keyframes.

2] Delete the sprite in channel 6.

This is the part of the animation in which the paper slides into the folder on the right side of the stage. In a later task, you will re-create this sequence using the film loop cast member.

3] With both the cast and the score open, choose File > Preferences > Cast, select Number from the Label list box, and click OK. Select channels 1 through 7 and choose View > Sprite Labels > Changes Only.

With these viewing options selected, you will see only the sprite numbers in the score, and you will see the sprite number in a cell only when the sprite is different from the sprite in the previous cell. Now, for example, you see the number 1 in frame 1 of channel 3 because cast member 1 appears onstage in frame 1 and does not change during its entire duration of 20 frames.

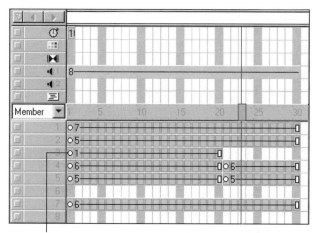

THE SCORE NOW SHOWS ONLY THE CAST MEMBER NUMBER OF EACH SPRITE

In the illustration, notice that the sprite in channel 3 is a series of individual cells. If your score does not look like this, select channel 3 and Choose Edit > Edit Sprite Frames so you can select individual cells. As you learned in Lesson 7, you will need to edit individual cells to change the cast members to create the animation.

4] Select channel 3, frame 2, in the score; select cast member 2 in the Cast window; and click Exchange Cast Members on the toolbar (Windows Ctrl+E, Macintosh Command+E).

EXCHANGE CAST MEMBERS

This is an alternative version of the paper. You now see the number 2 in channel 3, frame 2, because you set up Director to show you when a cast member changes.

5] Select channel 3, frame 3, in the score, select cast member 3 in the Cast window, and click Exchange Cast Members on the toolbar.

This is another version of the paper. You now see the number 3 in channel 3, frame 3.

6] Select channel 3, frame 4; select cast member 4; and click Exchange Cast Members on the toolbar.

You now see the number 4 in channel 3, frame 4; the number 1 should remain in channel 3, frame 5.

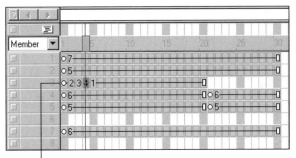

A DIFFERENT VERSION OF THE PAPER CAST MEMBER NOW
OCCUPIES EACH OF THE FIRST FOUR FRAMES OF CHANNEL 3

7] Save your work.

CREATING A FILM LOOP

To create a film loop, you use both the score and the cast. The film loop you will create will contain the four alternative versions of the paper encapsulated in a single cast member.

1] In the score, select channel 3, frames 1 through 5, and then choose Edit › Copy Sprites.

Click frame 1 and Shift+click frame 5 to select frames 1 through 5.

These cells will make up the pieces of the film loop. You need to include cast member 1 in frame 5 so that the film loop returns to its beginning.

Now you will create the film loop.

2] In the Cast window, select cast member 9, an empty cast member, and choose Edit › Paste Sprites.

A dialog box prompts you to name the film loop.

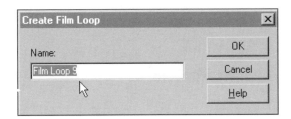

172

3] Type *Paper Loop* and then click OK to close the dialog box.

Now the film loop is a new cast member in the Cast window. This one cast member contains all the versions of the paper cast members, sequenced as an animation.

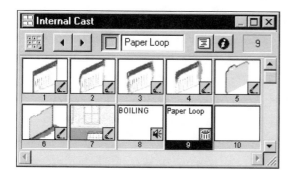

Now you will set the film loop's properties.

4] With cast member 9 still selected, click the Cast Member Properties button, uncheck the Options: Play Sound box, and then click OK to close the dialog box.

Director has two sound channels in the score. When Director encounters a film loop and the Play Sound box is checked, Director reserves the first sound channel and attempts to play a film loop sound for the duration of the film loop, even if the film loop has no sound in it. If the Play Sound box is checked and the film loop does not have a sound, you will hear only silence while the film loop is playing, even if you have a sound in sound channel 1, as you do in this movie. As a precaution, then, it's wise to uncheck this box in the first place and enable sound in the film loop only when you have a sound in the film loop that you want to play.

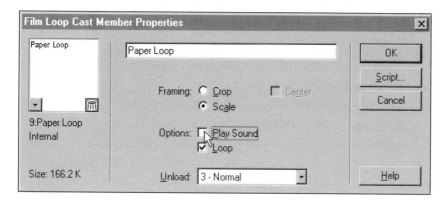

5] Delete the sprites in channel 3.

You no longer need these sprites because they've been encapsulated in the film loop as cast member 9.

173

CREATING KEY FRAMES WITH A FILM LOOP

In this task, you will add the Paper Loop sprite to your movie and then define keyframes for the Paper Loop animation.

1] Drag the paper loop (cast member 9) from the cast to channel 3, frame 1, in the score. Extend the length of the sprite to frame 30.

This is the starting point of the animation.

2] Make sure all of channel 3 is selected. On the stage, position the paper loop sprite so it fits inside the folder on the left.

Just as you did in Lesson 7, you want to start the animation with the paper inside the folder. As you move the paper loop sprite into position, you will notice that it seems to disappear inside the folder. Remember that in Lesson 7 you set up the folder sprite to be layered on top of the paper sprite. Once you drag the paper loop sprite into position and release the mouse, you may need to use the arrow keys to tweak its position slightly.

3] With channel 3 selected, choose Edit > Edit Sprite Frames.

You will be selecting individual frames as you create the animation.

4] In the score, select channel 3 (the Paper Loop sprite) and place the playback head in frame 1. Choose Insert > Keyframe.

This sets the first keyframe of the paper animation. You will leave the Paper Loop sprite in the folder where it is already placed because this is where you want the animation to begin.

On the stage, you will see a selection box. The selected object is the Paper Loop sprite, but you can't see it because it's layered below the top of the folder.

5] In the score, select channel 3 (the Paper Loop sprite) and place the playback head in frame 10. Choose Insert > Keyframe.

This sets the second keyframe. Here you want the Paper Loop sprite up and out of the folder. Make sure that channel 3, and only channel 3, is still selected. This is the Paper Loop sprite, and you need to drag it up and out of the folder.

6] With the keyframe in frame 10, channel 3, still selected, use the Up Arrow key to move the Paper Loop sprite straight up. When it's above the folder, hold down the Shift key and use the mouse to drag it up farther.

While the Paper Loop sprite is sandwiched inside the folder graphics, it can be hard to reposition using the mouse without accidentally selecting a different sprite. You can use the arrow keys to move the sprite up far enough to be selected by the mouse. Holding down the Shift key while you drag ensures that you move the sprite in a straight line.

7] In the score, select channel 3 and place the playback head in frame 20. Choose Insert › Keyframe.

This sets the third keyframe. Here you want the Paper Loop sprite to be directly above the folder at the right side of the stage.

8] In the score, make sure that the keyframe at frame 20, channel 3, is still selected. On the stage, drag the selection (the Paper Loop sprite) across the stage so it is directly above the destination folder.

Again, constrain the movement of the sprite with the Shift key.

9] In the score, select channel 3 and place the playback head in frame 30. Choose Insert › Keyframe.

This sets the fourth and final keyframe. Here you want the Paper Loop sprite inside the destination folder at the right side of the stage.

10] In the score, make sure that the keyframe at frame 30, channel 3, is still selected. On the stage, drag the selection downward so it is covered by the destination folder.

Later, when the sprites have been moved to different layers, the Paper Loop sprite will be between the folders. Again, constrain the movement of the sprite with the Shift key.

11] Rewind and play the movie.

The animation plays. It's the same animation you created in the previous lesson, but you didn't need to exchange the cast members over 30 frames to incorporate the different versions of the paper. By creating a film loop, you encapsulated four different cast members in a single cast member and then tweened that one cast member to create movement. This procedure is a great time-saver.

Notice that again the animation path is curved. You need to change it to a linear path. Although you changed the default curvature in Lesson 7, Director did not accept this as a permanent change.

12] In the score, select channel 3. Choose Modify › Sprite › Tweening to open the Sprite Tweening dialog box. Drag the Curvature slider bar to halfway between Normal and Linear and click OK.

13] Play the movie again.

Now the path of the paper looks more natural.

14] Save your work.

LAYERING THE SPRITES

Did you notice that the paper falls behind both of the flaps of the destination folder on the right, just as it did in the previous lesson? You need to move the last sequence of Paper Loop sprites down in the layering order so they are sandwiched between the sprites that make up the flaps of the folder. Since the destination channel (channel 6) is empty, you can simply drag the selected sprites to that channel.

1] In the score, select channel 3, frames 21 through 30, and then drag the selected cells to channel 6.

To make the selection, click frame 21 and Shift+click frame 30.

2] Play the movie again.

The paper is layered correctly and falls into the folder as it should.

3] Save your work.

176

REVERSING AN ANIMATION

In this task you will add a second animation that is the reverse of the one you just created. You will copy the animation you created earlier and then reverse its sequence.

1] With the score open, choose Edit › Select All. Then choose Edit › Copy Sprites.

All the sprites in the score are copied.

2] Select the tempo channel, frame 41, and then choose Edit › Paste Sprites.

You should see the entire set of sprites duplicated in frames 41 through 70, including the sound file and the tempo setting.

COPY EVERYTHING IN FRAMES 1 THROUGH 30

PASTE STARTING AT FRAME 41

The sprites you copied included a tempo setting in frame 1 of the tempo channel. That's why you placed the insertion point in the tempo channel at frame 41.

Now you will reverse the order of the sprites you just pasted.

3] Select channel 3, frames 41 through 60, and channel 6, frames 61 through 70. Choose Modify › Reverse Sequence.

To select these channels simultaneously, click channel 3, frame 41, and Shift+click channel 6, frame 70. This will also select channels 4 and 5, but that doesn't matter; since these channels are not animated, reversing them has no effect.

Now the second version of the animation, in frames 41 through 70, runs backward— that is, the paper floats from the folder on the right to the folder on the left.

177

4] Play the movie.

The animation now alternates: first you see the paper float from the folder on the left to the folder on the right, and then you see the paper float from the folder on the right to the folder on the left. Watch the playback head move in the score as you view the animation on the stage.

Notice the problem? You can see that the two pieces of the reversed animation occur in the wrong sequence: The paper first appears above the folder on the right, floats to the folder on the left, and then unexpectedly appears back in the folder on the right, where it floats directly up from the folder. You will fix this sequencing problem by adjusting the frames in which the two pieces of reversed animation occur.

5] Select channel 3, frames 41 through 60, and move them to frames 51 through 70 in the same channel. Similarly, move channel 6, frames 61 through 70, to frames 41 through 50.

6] Play the movie again.

The reverse animation is now working correctly. The paper floats back and forth between the two folders.

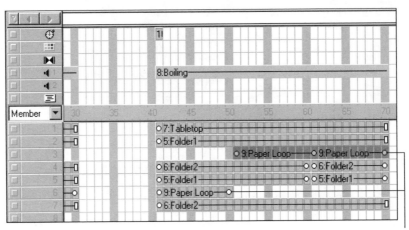

SWITCHING THE POSITIONS OF THE SPRITES IN CHANNELS
3 AND 6 MAKES THE ANIMATION RUN AS IT SHOULD

7] Save your work.

CREATING BUTTONS

In this task you will add buttons so you can select which of the two animations you view: forward or backward.

1] In the score, place the playback head in frame 1. Choose Insert › Control › Push Button.

An empty button will appear with a flashing insertion point where you can type a label.

2] Type *Forward* in the button.

3] Click the stage outside the button, and then click the button itself to select it.

Clicking outside the button deselects the button for text entry. When you reselect the button, you can alter its size and drag it to a new position on the stage.

4] Drag one of the button's handles to resize the button to your satisfaction. Then drag the button to the bottom of the stage, just left of center.

The Forward button becomes cast member 10 and is automatically placed in channel 8 of the score with the default length of 28 frames.

5] Repeat steps 1 through 4 to place a button labeled *Backward* to the right of the Forward button.

The Backward button becomes cast member 11 in channel 9 of the score.

179

6] In the score, drag the end frame indicators of the button sprites in channels 8 and 9 to channel 70.

Now the button sprites span all the frames in the movie. The two buttons will remain on the stage throughout the entire movie.

ADDING INTERACTIVITY WITH THE BEHAVIOR INSPECTOR

In Lesson 5, you learned how to add interactivity by writing Lingo scripts and assigning those scripts to buttons. When users clicked a button, the script instructed Director to branch to a specific marker in the score.

In this task you will learn an even faster way to create interactivity. You will use the **Behavior Inspector**, which lets you create scripts without having to type the Lingo commands yourself.

The scripts you create with the Behavior Inspector are called **behaviors**, because they are mostly used to define the behavior of elements in your movie—for example, the way a button responds when clicked or the actions that occur when the playback head enters or leaves a specific frame in the score.

Once you've created the behaviors using the Behavior Inspector, you can assign them to sprites in the score or to frames in the score. (In this case, you'll assign them to the Forward and Backward buttons.) You'll learn two different methods for assigning behaviors to a button.

When you complete this task, clicking the Forward button will cause the playback head to move to frame 1, where the original animation begins. Similarly, clicking the Backward button will cause the playback head to move to frame 41, where the reversed animation begins.

1] Right-click (Windows) or Ctrl+click (Macintosh) the sprite in channel 8 (the Forward button). From the menu, choose Behaviors to open the Behavior Inspector.

In Lesson 5, you assigned a script to the button cast member itself. Doing so ensured that, no matter where that button appeared in the movie, its script would always run when a user clicked that button. In this case, by clicking on the Forward button sprite in the score to open the Behavior Inspector, you are assigning a script just to that sprite. If you add the Forward button somewhere else in the movie, it will not have the script you are about to create.

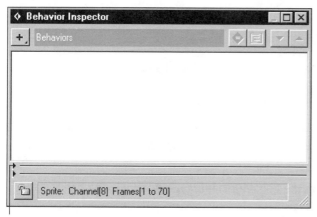

CLICK HERE TO OPEN THE EVENTS AND ACTIONS PANELS

2] If the Events and Actions panels are not visible in the Behavior Inspector, click the uppermost of the two expansion arrows.

The Events and Actions panels now appear side by side at the bottom of the Behavior Inspector.

BEHAVIOR MENU

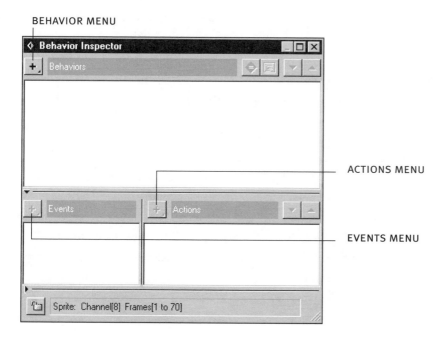

ACTIONS MENU

EVENTS MENU

A behavior consists of three basic elements:

The **behavior name** helps you identify the behavior.

The **event** is the occurrence in the movie that triggers the behavior.

The **action** is the script that Director runs in response to an event.

For example, in the following steps, you will create a behavior named Normal that responds to a user click (event) by branching to a specific frame in the score (action).

3] Choose New Behavior from the Behavior menu, type *Normal* in the Name Behavior dialog box, and click OK.

The first step in creating a behavior is giving it a name. When you finish creating the behavior, Director will add it to the cast. The name helps you identify the behavior in the Cast window.

4] From the Events menu, choose Mouse Down.

A **mouse down** event occurs when you press the mouse button (a **mouse up** event occurs when you release the mouse button). By choosing this event, you are telling Director that you want the Forward button to run a script immediately whenever the button is clicked. In the next step, you will set up the script (action) that runs.

> **tip** *You will often see these events written as* mouseDown *and* mouseUp, *which are the actual Lingo commands you would type when writing the script yourself.*

5] From the Actions menu, choose Navigation › Go to Frame.

Now you are setting up the script that runs when Director detects a mouse down event on the Forward button. You will remember the go to frame command from Lesson 4, where you used it to branch to another location in the movie.

6] Enter *1* in the Specify Frame dialog box. Then click OK to close the dialog box.

Now when the mouse button is clicked on the Forward button, the playback head will branch to frame 1, the beginning of the first animation. The Behavior Inspector shows you a description of the behavior.

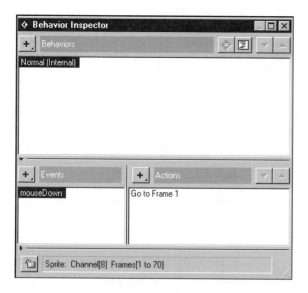

7] Play the movie and click the Forward button at random times.

You see the animation restart, with the paper coming out of the left folder each time you click the Forward button.

Examine the cast. You will see a new cast member named Normal.

BEHAVIOR NAME

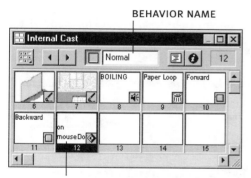

THE BEHAVIOR WAS ADDED TO THE CAST

On the stage, if you right-click (Windows) or Ctrl+click (Macintosh) the Forward button and select Script from the menu that appears, you will see that a script is attached to the button sprite even though you did not write the script yourself. The Behavior Inspector did it for you!

8] Stop the movie and save your work.

183

ADDING A SECOND BUTTON

Now you will use the Behavior Inspector to set up the Backward button. You will use a different method than you did for the Forward button, so you can see another way to use the Behavior Inspector.

1] Click anywhere in the score where there is no sprite. Then choose Window › Inspectors › Behavior.

If a sprite had been selected, any behavior created in the Behavior Inspector would be attached to that sprite. At the moment, you want to create a behavior that is not associated with any sprite, so you selected an unoccupied cell in the score before opening the Behavior Inspector.

2] If the Events and Actions panes are not visible in the Behavior Inspector, click the uppermost of the two expansion arrows at the bottom left of the window.

3] Choose New Behavior from the Behavior menu, type _Reverse_ in the Name Behavior dialog box, and click OK.

As you did in the previous task, you start by giving the new behavior a name so you can identify it in the Cast window.

4] Choose Mouse Down from the Events menu.

As with the Normal behavior you created in the previous task, you are telling Director that you want to trigger a script immediately when a user clicks the Backward button.

5] Choose Navigation › Go to Frame from the Actions menu. Type _41_ in the Specify Frame dialog box. Then click OK to close the dialog box.

Now when this script runs in response to a mouse click, the playback head will branch to frame 41, the beginning of the reversed animation.

Examine the cast. Cast member number 13 is the behavior you just created. At the moment, it is not attached to any other cast member because, when you created it, you made sure no sprites were selected in the score. Now you will learn a quick way to assign a behavior to a sprite.

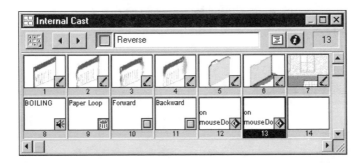

6] Drag the Reverse cast member from the cast to the Backward button on the stage.

You have just assigned the Reverse behavior to the Backward button. You could have achieved the same result by dragging the Reverse cast member to sprite 11 (the Backward button) in the score.

7] Right-click (Windows) or Ctrl+click (Macintosh) channel 9 (the Backward button) in the score and select Behaviors from the popup menu.

The Behavior Inspector opens, and you should see the Reverse behavior attached to channel 9, the Backward button.

8] Play the movie and click the Backward button at random times.

You should see the reverse animation begin each time you click the button.

9] Stop the movie and save your work.

CREATING A BEHAVIOR TO PAUSE THE MOVIE

There is still something you need to do. Watch the playback head when you click one of the buttons; it branches to the appropriate frame and then continues through the score. Thus, when you click Forward, it branches to frame 1 and then moves left to right until it reaches the end of the score—that is, it also plays the Backward sequence. To prevent this, you will create a behavior named Pause and attach it to the end of each animation. Then the animations will play once through and stop to wait for another click on the Forward or Backward button before resuming.

1] Click anywhere in the score where there is no sprite. Then choose Window › Inspectors › Behavior.

If a sprite had been selected, any behavior created in the Behavior Inspector would be assigned to that sprite. At the moment, you want to create a behavior that is not assigned to any sprite, so you selected an unoccupied cell in the score before opening the Behavior Inspector.

tip   *Whenever you use the Behavior Inspector, select an unoccupied cell first, unless you want to assign the behavior to specific sprites. Creating behaviors when sprites are inadvertently selected will assign the behavior to those sprites even though you did not intend to.*

2] Choose New Behavior from the Behavior menu, type *Pause* in the Name Behavior dialog box, and click OK.

This will create a new behavior cast member named Pause. Now that you have named the behavior, you will set up its Events and Actions.

3] Choose Exit Frame from the Events menu.

In Lesson 5, you learned how to make the playback head stay in a frame using a *go to the frame* command. The *go to the frame* command ran each time the playback head exited the frame, and it returned the playback head to the same frame. The behavior you are creating uses the same Lingo—but this time you used the Behavior Inspector instead of typing the command, as you did in Lesson 5.

4] Choose Wait › On Current Frame from the Actions menu.

Now when the playback head exits the current frame, it will be instructed to go to the current frame.

If you examine the cast, you will see a new cast member named Pause in cast location 14. As in the previous task, this new cast member is not assigned to anything because you made sure that no sprites were selected in the score before you created the behavior.

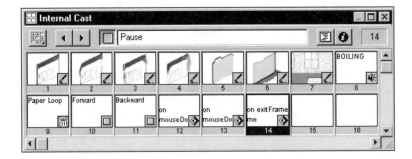

5] Drag the Pause cast member to frame 30 in the behavior channel. Then repeat the process, this time dragging the Pause cast member to frame 70.

Frames 30 and 70 are the end points of the two animations. When the playback head reaches these two points, the papers will have completed their journey from one folder to another.

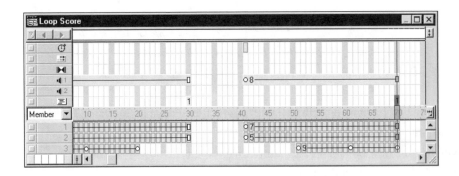

6] Play the movie. Click on the Forward and Backward buttons several times.

Watch the playback head. When you click Forward, it branches to frame 1 and then moves from frame to frame until it reaches frame 30, where it pauses because of the behavior you just added. When you click Backward, the playback head branches to frame 41 and moves from frame to frame until it reaches frame 70, where it also pauses. Each time you click a button, the chosen animation plays once. Then nothing happens until you click a button again.

WHAT YOU HAVE LEARNED

In this lesson you have:

- Created a film loop [page 172]
- Created keyframes with a film loop [page 174]
- Created a copy of an animation and reversed it [page 177]
- Practiced adding buttons [page 179]
- Used the Behavior Inspector to add interactivity to the buttons [page 185]

behaviors

built-in

Although the score lets you create extensive presentations with ease, Director offers much more power than can be found in the score alone. As you learned in Lesson 8, you can attach behaviors to your movies to facilitate powerful custom actions. Director 7 includes a library of useful behaviors that can easily be dragged and dropped onto your sprites and frames to create instant customized behaviors. These behaviors range from everyday useful actions, such as controlling video, to elaborate actions, such as permanently rotating sprites or interacting with the Internet.

LESSON 9

By exploring Director's extensive Library Palette, you can easily give your sprites custom behaviors, such as making plaid man's eyes rotate and follow the cursor's movements on the screen.

In this lesson, you will create two sprites by placing a cast member on stage twice. You will then use the behavior library to select a behavior and apply it to the sprites one at a time and see the effect. Then you'll learn how you can apply additional behaviors and change those already assigned behaviors in a project.

If you would like to review the final result of this lesson, open the Complete folder in the Lesson09 folder and play CrazyEye.dir.

WHAT YOU WILL LEARN

In this lesson you will:

- Create two sprites from a single cast member
- Explore the Library Palette and available behaviors
- Apply a behavior that controls one sprite differently than another
- Use a behavior to reduce a movie to one frame
- Use the Behavior Inspector to modify a behavior
- Animate by using behaviors only

APPROXIMATE TIME

It should take about 1 hour to complete this lesson.

LESSON FILES

Media Files:
None

Starting Files:
Lesson09\Start\Start.dir

Completed Project:
Lesson09\Complete\CrazyEye.dir

PLACING THE GRAPHICS

In this lesson, you'll open the file and create an image on the stage. The image, called "plaid man," is made of two cast members: one for the body and the other for both eyes. You'll place the eyeball graphic on stage twice (to give plaid man two eyes), making two sprite instances from a single graphic.

1] Choose File › Open and select Start.dir in the Start folder for Lesson09, and then save it as *CrazyEye.dir* in your Projects folder. Then open the Cast window.

The Cast window contains two cast members: plaid man (cast member 1) and an eyeball (cast member 2).

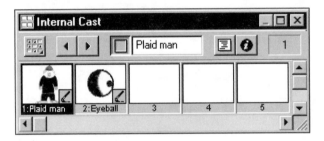

2] Drag the plaid man cast member onto the stage. Choose Background Transparent from the drop-down list of ink effects on the Sprite toolbar at the top of the Score window.

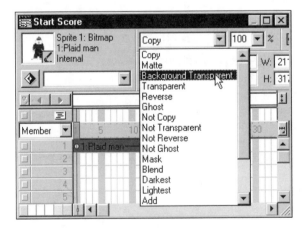

3] Drag the eyeball cast member onto the stage twice to add both a left and a right eye to plaid man.

You've created two sprites from the same cast member. Because each sprite can have its own set of behaviors, each sprite can be made to behave independently of the other or both can behave in the same way.

In the image above, notice that the white corners of the eyeball bitmaps block out part of plaid man's face. Although the eyeball itself is a non-rectangular shape, sprites, by default, display the complete rectangular shape of the bitmap. To display only the eyeball's round shape, you'll use Matte ink to make transparent the surrounding background color of the bitmap while maintaining the white color of the eyeball image.

4] Choose Window › Score to open the Score window (Windows Ctrl+4, Macintosh Command+4).

5] Select the two eyeball sprites (channels 2 and 3), and then choose Matte from the drop-down list of ink effects on the Sprite toolbar at the top of the Score window.

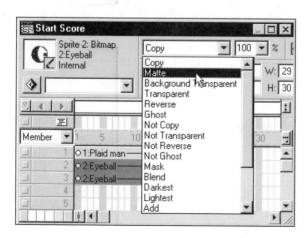

6] Choose Window > Control Panel (Windows Control+2, Macintosh Command+2) to open the Control Panel. Click the Play button to play the movie; or you can click the Play button on the Sprite toolbar to start playing the movie.

Although the movie is playing, nothing happens on screen. Three sprites currently appear on the stage, but because they don't relocate or change in any way, they don't appear to move. In earlier lessons, you learned how to animate sprites by tweening and using keyframes. You can also animate sprites by using behaviors, which you'll do in the next procedure.

7] Save your work.

ADDING BEHAVIORS

In this lesson you'll add a behavior to animate a sprite by selecting a behavior from the Library Palette and dragging it onto the sprite or sprite channel.

1] Choose Window > Library Palette to open the Library Palette.

The Library Palette window appears.

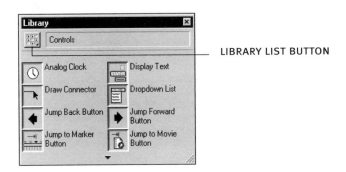

LIBRARY LIST BUTTON

In the Library Palette, you can choose from among many categories of available behaviors. Some, such as Animation, also have subcategories. For this lesson, you will need to select the Interactive subcategory.

2] Click the Library List button in the Library Palette window.

The menu of available behavior groups appears.

3] Choose Animation › Interactive from the menu.

The Interactive Library window appears.

4] Click the scroll down arrow at the bottom of the Library window until the Turn Towards Mouse behavior is visible.

TURN TOWARDS
MOUSE BEHAVIOR

SCROLL DOWN ARROW

5] Click the Turn Towards Mouse behavior icon and drag it onto one of the eyeball sprites.

You can drag the icon either to the sprite itself on the stage or to the sprite channel on the Score window.

When you release the mouse after dragging the behavior icon onto the sprite, the Parameters dialog box appears. Most behaviors let you specify custom settings for the behavior, which allows you to tailor behaviors for individual sprites.

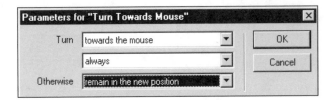

6] Select "towards the mouse," "always," and "remain in the new position." Click OK.

This behavior will make the eyeball sprite rotate and "look" at the mouse when the mouse is moved on the screen. If you don't set the behavior to "remain in the new position," the eyeball image will revert to its original state when the mouse stops moving.

This new sprite behavior is placed as a new cast member, cast member 3, in the Cast window, as shown below. The name of the cast is shown (if you have names turned on for the cast) as "Turn Towards" (short for "Turn Towards Mouse"). Notice the icon in the lower right corner of the cast member, which indicates that the cast member is a behavior.

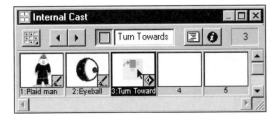

7] In the Control Panel, make sure Looping is turned off. Click the Play button to play the movie, and then move the mouse cursor around the screen.

The eyeball with the behavior follows the mouse, but only for a second or so. Then the movie stops because the sprites last for only 28 frames, and you are not animating by tweening or anything else. The other eyeball does not follow the mouse on screen, even though it is a sprite made from the same cast member as the eyeball with the behavior attached. This is because the "Turn Towards Mouse" behavior is attached to the eyeball sprite rather than to the eyeball cast member.

8] Save your work.

By just looking at the score, without sprite 2 selected, you can't tell that sprite 2 has a behavior attached to it. If you want to display the behaviors attached to the sprites in the score, you can do so by using the Display pop-up menu in the score, as shown in image that follows the next step.

9] In the Display pop-up menu, select Behavior.

In the score, channel 2 now shows the behavior that is attached to the sprite in that channel. Because no other sprites have behaviors attached, no other behaviors are shown.

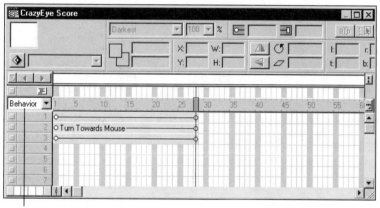

DISPLAY POP-UP MENU

You can easily switch between different displays by choosing from the Display pop-up menu to show information appropriate to whatever task you are performing.

USING THE BEHAVIOR INSPECTOR

With behaviors, you can animate within a single frame just as easily as you can animate within 28 frames. If this animation were a portion of a larger project, you could make the project easier to work with by keeping the score as compact as possible.

195

1] Open the Score window again and compact all three sprites into a single frame.

To do this, click the sprite in channel 1 and then Shift-click the sprite in channel 3 to select all three sprites. Then enter *1* in the end frame box of the Sprite toolbar.

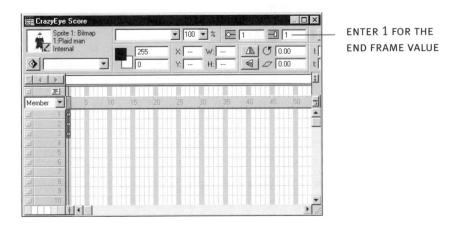

ENTER 1 FOR THE
END FRAME VALUE

Now if you play the movie, it will finish playing in only a fraction of a second. You can use a behavior to keep the movie playing in the one frame.

2] Click on any unoccupied cell in the score. Open the Behavior Inspector by choosing Window › Inspectors › Behavior (Windows Ctrl+Alt+; [semicolon], Macintosh Command+option+; [semicolon])

An empty Behavior Inspector window opens. Selecting an unused cell in the score before opening the Behavior Inspector informs the Inspector that a score behavior is being created rather than a sprite behavior. If the Behavior Inspector window does not look similar to the figure below, click the Expand Editing Pane arrow to open the lower panes.

BEHAVIOR POP-UP BUTTON

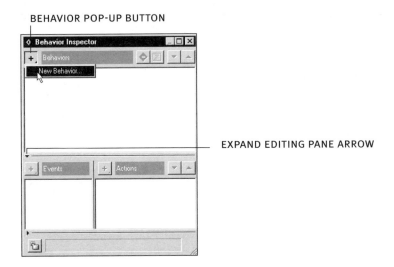

EXPAND EDITING PANE ARROW

196

3] Click the Behavior pop-up button and select New Behavior. In the New Behavior window, name the new behavior *Hold* and then click OK.

The Behavior Inspector window reflects that a new score behavior is being created and that the new behavior is placed in the cast as cast member 4.

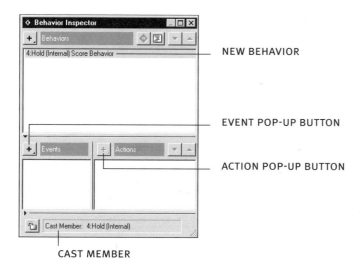

NEW BEHAVIOR

EVENT POP-UP BUTTON

ACTION POP-UP BUTTON

CAST MEMBER

4] Click the Event pop-up button and select Exit Frame. Click the Action pop-up button and select Wait › On Current Frame. The Behavior Inspector reflects your selections.

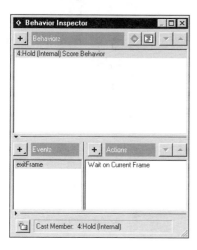

The behavior is created and placed as cast member 4.

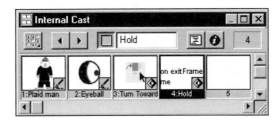

Unlike some other behaviors, the Wait on Current Frame behavior does not need to prompt you to create any customizable properties. Its only action is to keep the playback head from moving past that frame, effectively forcing an indefinite loop on the frame in which it is used.

5] In the Cast window, select the new behavior cast member and drag it to the Score window in frame 1 of the behavior channel.

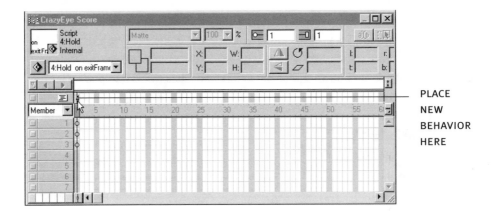

PLACE
NEW
BEHAVIOR
HERE

LINGO EQUIVALENT

go to the frame

6] In the Control Panel, make sure that Looping is turned off. Play the movie. Move the mouse cursor around on the screen.

This time the movie keeps playing because the behavior keeps the movie in a continuous loop on frame 1. As you move the mouse around on the screen, the eyeball sprite with the Turn Towards Mouse behavior rotates the sprite to follow the mouse cursor on the screen. The eyeball without the special behavior remains stationary, since it has no instructions to the contrary.

7] Save your work.

MODIFYING BEHAVIORS

The Behavior Inspector is useful for creating, modifying, and inspecting behaviors. In this task, we will use it in all three ways to view the current behaviors, to add a behavior to the second eyeball, and to modify the properties of the second eyeball's behavior.

1] In the Score, make sure the Sprite Toolbar is displayed. Choosing View › Sprite Toolbar will make it visible if it is not.

The Sprite Toolbar includes a button for invoking the Behavior Inspector as well as a drop-down menu that shows a list of behaviors for a selected sprite.

INVOKE BEHAVIOR INSPECTOR

BEHAVIOR LIST

2] Click on each of the sprites in turn, including the sprite in the behavior channel.

For the sprites that have attached behaviors, each behavior's cast number and name
are shown in the Behavior List window.

3] Select the sprite in the behavior channel and click the Behavior Inspector button.

The Behavior Inspector window appears, looking just as it did when you created the
Hold behavior earlier.

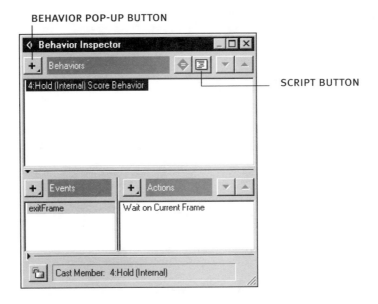

4] Click the Script button in the Behavior Inspector.

A Script window is displayed containing the Lingo code for the behavior. In this
case, the code is only a few lines long and contains the *go to the frame* line that you have
seen before. For other behaviors, hundreds of lines of Lingo script may appear here.

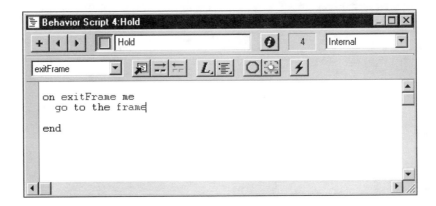

5] Close the Script window and the Behavior Inspector. Then select the sprite in channel 3, the eyeball sprite that does not have and attached behavior. Open the Behavior Inspector again.

No behavior is displayed because no behavior is attached to the selected sprite.

6] Click the Behavior pop-up button and select Turn Towards Mouse.

You've now attached the behavior to the sprite in channel 3.

PARAMETERS BUTTON

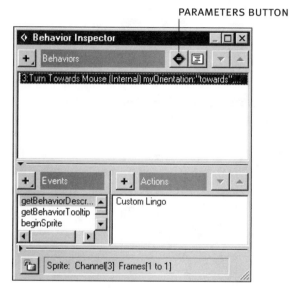

7] Close the Behavior Inspector and play the movie. Is it what you expected?

The eyeball with the new behavior attached still does not follow the mouse. But try holding down the mouse button while you move the mouse. The eyeball follows. Release the mouse button and the eyeball returns to its original position.

Although the second eyeball does have the Turn Towards Mouse behavior attached, its parameters are different than those of the other eyeball. Remember that you set the "always" and "remain in the new position" parameters when you used the Library Palette to attach the behavior to the first eyeball.

A behavior parameter applies only to the sprite or frame to which it is attached. You can apply a different set of parameters to the same behavior attached to a different sprite.

8] With the sprite in channel 3 still selected, display the Behavior Inspector again. Click the Parameters button next to the Script button.

The Parameters dialog box appears and shows the current parameters for the behavior as applied to this particular sprite. They reflect how the eyeball will behave.

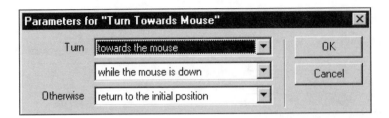

9] Use the pop-up menus in the dialog box to set the parameters to "towards the mouse," "always," and "remain in the new position." Click OK.

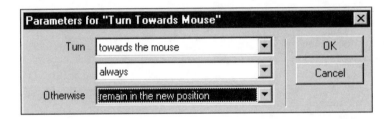

10] Save your work and play the movie.

The two eyeballs now behave identically. They follow the mouse wherever it is moved on the screen, whether or not the mouse button is pressed.

WHAT YOU HAVE LEARNED

In this lesson you have:

• Created two sprites from a single cast member [page 190]

• Explored the Library Palette and explored available behaviors [page 192]

• Used the Library Palette to create animation [page 193]

• Used the Behavior Inspector to create a behavior [page 197]

• Used the Behavior Inspector to create animation [page 199]

• Modified a behavior's parameters [page 199]

cursors

custom

Almost everyone who works with computers these days is familiar with the standard arrow-shaped cursor that moves on screen as the mouse moves. And the "busy" cursor— an hourglass in Windows or a watch on the Macintosh—plus editing cursors and others are also familiar to most computer users. Most of these are **static** (nonmoving) cursors that usually appear in black and white.

Using Director's Cursor Properties Editor, you can make animated cursors, like this Magic Wand cursor, and have them automatically appear when you roll over a sprite.

In this lesson, you will change the appearance of the cursor to respond to an event. You will also create your own custom cursor for use in your movie. Finally, you will create an **animated color cursor,** not just a static black-and-white one. You will use the Cursor Properties Editor to build your cursor and modify the cursor's animation and active hot-spot area.

To review the final result of this lesson, go to the Lesson10 folder, open the Complete folder, and then open Cursor.dir.

WHAT YOU WILL LEARN

In this lesson you will:

- Change cursors based on user actions
- Change a sprite based on the cursor location
- Create a custom animated cursor
- Adjust a cursor's hotspot area
- Modify the frame rate of a cursor

APPROXIMATE TIME

It should take about 1 hour to complete this lesson.

LESSON FILES

Media Files:

None

Starting Files:

Lesson10\Start\Start.dir

Completed Project:

Lesson10\Complete\Cursor.dir

CHANGING A CURSOR

Computer operating systems such as Windows and Macintosh use a graphical user interface and a pointing device, usually a mouse, that allow the user to work with the computer in a visually oriented manner. The mouse cursor, by default a small arrow-shaped pointer, indicates to the user where some action will take place. For example, when the cursor is over an on-screen button, the user understands that pressing and releasing the mouse button will initiate the action for which the button is supplied. In many applications, however, clickable objects don't always look like traditional buttons—especially on Web pages. They can look like a picture or text, for example. One of the ways a user knows that a location is clickable is that the cursor image changes whenever it passes over the location.

In this task, you will add information to make a cursor change how it looks whenever it passes over a sprite you have placed on the stage.

1] Open Start.dir in the Start folder and save it as *Cursor.dir*.

The Cast window shows four cast members that you will use later in this lesson.

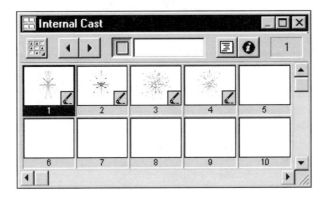

2] In the Cast window, click cast member 5 and then choose Window › Paint to open the Paint window (Windows Ctrl+5, Macintosh Command+5).

3] Create a filled rectangle about 2-inches wide by 1-inch high. Fill this rectangle with the color red. Then name it *Background*, and close the Paint window.

Although the color you choose is up to you, in this lesson we'll use a red rectangle. The graphic you created appears as cast member 5 in the Cast window.

NAME THE GRAPHIC

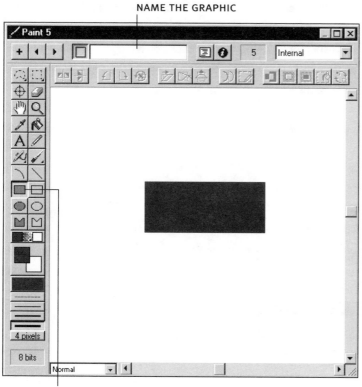

FILLED RECTANGLE TOOL

4] Drag the Background cast member from the Cast window to frame 1 of channel 1 in the score.

The sprite automatically occupies the first 28 frames in the score.

BEHAVIOR INSPECTOR BUTTON

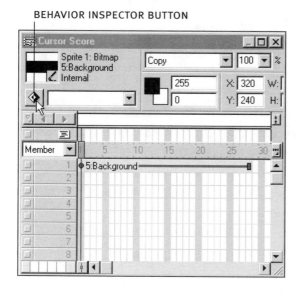

5] With the Background sprite selected, click the Behavior Inspector button in the Score window.

You used the Behavior Inspector in Lesson 9 to create behaviors. Now you will create a behavior to change the mouse cursor as it passes over the Background sprite on the stage.

note   *Because the sprite in channel 1 was selected when the Behavior Inspector was opened, the new behavior is automatically attached to the sprite.*

6] Click the Behavior button and select New Behavior. Name the new behavior *Cursor In* and click OK.

The Behavior Inspector window reflects the name of the new behavior and shows that the behavior is placed in the cast as member 6.

BEHAVIOR BUTTON

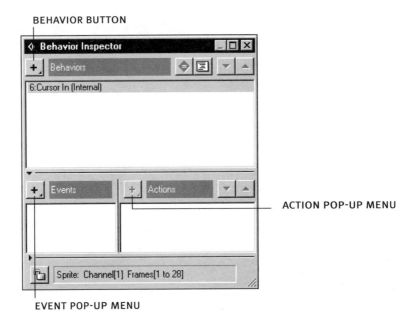

ACTION POP-UP MENU

EVENT POP-UP MENU

7] Open the Event pop-up menu and select mouseEnter. Click the Action pop-up menu and select Cursor › Change cursor. In the Specify Cursor window that appears, use the pop-up menu to choose Hand, and then click OK.

The Behavior Inspector window reflects these choices. The Hand cursor is a built-in cursor and assigned the number 260, so the Actions window shows "Change Cursor to 260."

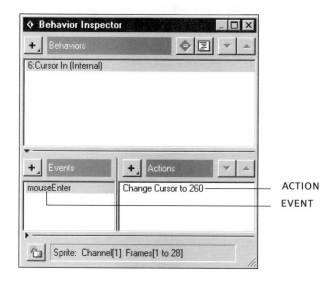

8] Choose Control › Loop Playback (Windows Ctrl+Alt+L, Macintosh Command+Alt+L), or make sure that Looping is turned on in the Control Panel so that the movie will play continuously. Then play the movie.

The mouse cursor is originally an arrow, the default cursor. Move the cursor over the sprite on the stage, and the cursor changes to the shape of a hand.

You probably have already noticed a problem: the cursor stays in the shape of a hand even when it is no longer over the sprite. To correctly impart information to the user, you will want the cursor to revert back to a pointer when it moves off the rectangle.

9] Stop the movie.

10] Select the sprite in channel 1 and open the Behavior Inspector. Create another new behavior and name it _Cursor Out_. For the Event, choose mouseLeave. For the Action choose Cursor › Change Cursor as you did before. In the Specify Cursor window that appears, use the pop-up menu to choose Arrow, and then click OK.

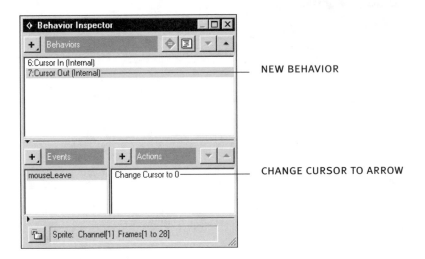

11] Run the movie.

The cursor works correctly now. On stage, when it moves over the sprite it changes to the shape of a hand. When it moves off of the sprite it changes back to the arrow cursor.

12] Stop the movie and save your work.

SPRITE BOUNDING AREAS

In most applications, objects on the screen are "regularly" shaped; they're often rectangles and occasionally circles or ovals. When you begin creating more complex graphics as clickable objects, you need to consider how their visible shapes relate to what the computer considers to be their shapes and sizes—or their **bounding areas**. In this task you will place an irregularly shaped object on the screen and investigate the object's clickable bounding area.

1] In the Cast window, double-click cast member 5, the Background cast member you created.

Double-clicking a graphic cast member brings up the Paint window that shows the selected cast member.

2] Using the filled rectangle tool, create another rectangle that's perpendicular to the original. Close the Paint window.

This change in the graphic is reflected in the Background cast member. You have simply changed the cast member; you haven't created a new one.

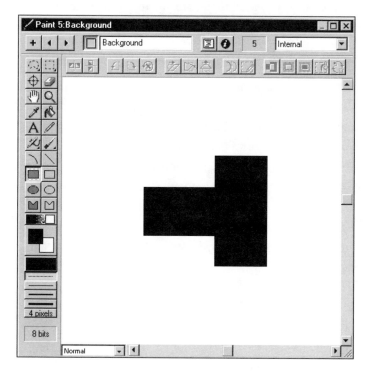

3] Choose Modify › Movie › Properties and set the Stage Color to black. Click OK.

Notice that your sprite appears on the stage with its white background area, or bounding area, showing.

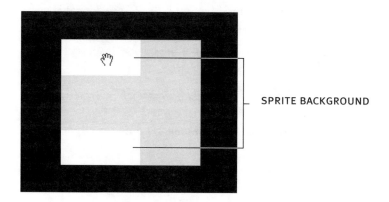

SPRITE BACKGROUND

4] Play the movie.

When you move the mouse cursor over any part of the sprite, including the white background area, the cursor changes to a hand shape.

5] Stop the movie. Select the sprite again in the score and set the Ink Effect to Background Transparent. Play the movie again.

The cursor still behaves in the same way, even though to you (or to any other user), the cursor doesn't always seem to be located over an actual object.

6] Save your work.

When you are creating interactive projects that include clickable objects, you should keep in mind the sprite's bounding area. For small objects, the user will probably never notice that the clickable area extends outside the visible area of the object. Such extra clickable space can provide the user with a more easily clicked area. If a bounding area is too large or if you'd like to remove it, you can eliminate the effect with Lingo script or by placing "invisible" sprites over portions of your clickable area.

> **tip** *If you set the Ink Effects to Matte, the transparent area around a graphic won't trigger the mouse events. Only the actual shape of the graphic will be "hot."*

CHANGING THE SPRITE

Another way to indicate that an object is clickable is to make the onscreen graphical object change in some way when the mouse cursor passes over it or clicks on it. A button, for example, can change its color when the cursor passes over it, and then it can change to a depressed button image when the mouse button is clicked on it. These kinds of actions improve the user interface of an application, making it more simple to use, even though the script that makes up the complete interface can be quite complicated.

In this task you will see how some complex sprite actions can be accomplished. You will create two new graphics by copying and modifying the Background graphic you already created. Then you will use the Library Palette to attach a behavior that modifies the sprite on the stage based on the position of the cursor.

1] In the Cast window click the Background cast member to select it.

2] Choose Edit › Copy Cast Members to copy the cast member onto the clipboard.

3] In the Cast window, select the first empty cast location: cast member number 8.

4] Choose Edit › Paste to place a copy of the cast member into the cast member 8 frame.

5] Paste another copy of the cast member into cast member 9.

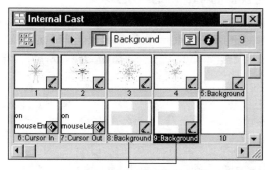

TWO NEW CAST MEMBERS

6] Double-click cast member number 8 to open the Paint window.

NEXT BITMAP

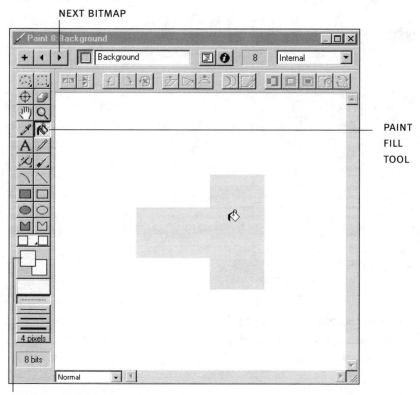

PAINT
FILL
TOOL

FOREGROUND COLOR

7] Choose a new foreground color and use the Paint Fill tool to color the graphic to a new color. Change the name of the cast member to *Mouse Over*.

8] Use the Next Cast Member button to edit cast member 9. Repeat step 7 to make this third bitmap a third color. Change the cast member's name to *Mouse Down*. Close the Paint window.

You now have three cast members of the same shape, with different colors and different names.

Now you will use the Library Palette to create the behavior that changes the sprite according to the mouse's actions. This behavior will simulate the action of a push button. The two new cast members will be used as the different button states: mouse over and mouse down.

9] Choose Window › Library Palette. Use the Library List button to select Controls.

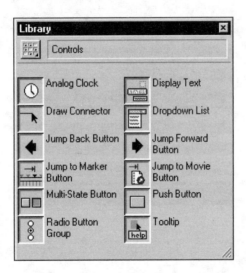

10] Make sure that the entire sprite is selected in channel 1 of the score and then drag the Push Button behavior from the Library to the sprite in the score.

The Parameters dialog box opens.

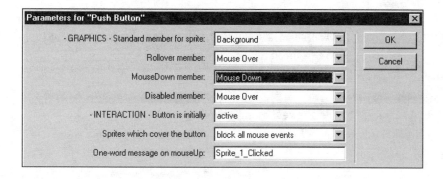

11] Use the pop-up menus to set the Standard member to Background, the Rollover member to Mouse Over, and the MouseDown member to Mouse Down. Then click OK. Close the Library window.

The Push Button behavior is now included as cast member 10. It is also attached to the sprite in channel 1 of the score.

12] Play the movie.

It's not perfect, but much of the user interface for a button is included. The sprite changes when you move the mouse over it and changes again when you hold down the mouse button while moving the mouse over it. By substituting three button graphics for our rectangles, you could make a very nice-looking and -acting button.

13] Save your work.

MAKING A NEW AND ANIMATED CURSOR

Your next task is to make a new cursor instead of using one of the cursors supplied with the computer. Director can use only 8-bit bitmap graphics for cursors, and only a limited number of colors may be used. Only the first 10 or the last 10 colors of the standard Windows palette, System - Win, can be used in Director, unless you plan to distribute your movie to run "full screen" (with the desktop hidden). You can choose the full screen option when you begin building your projector, as demonstrated in Lesson 5. Otherwise, some colors might not display correctly or might appear differently on other platforms. For your movie cursor, you will use a graphic that was already created for this purpose.

1] From the Director menu, choose Insert › Media Element › Cursor.

The Cursor Properties Editor opens. Cast member 1 should be displayed; this is the graphic we will be using. If you wanted to use a different cast member, you could select it using the arrow keys.

2] Click the Add button to add the cast member you chose.

This step is included because, as you will see, you can use more than one cast member in an animated cursor.

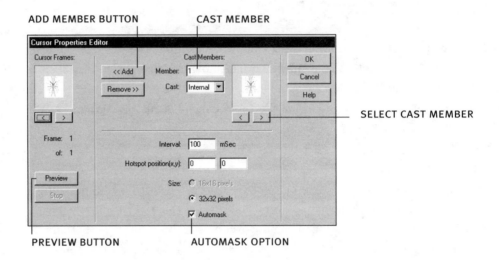

ADD MEMBER BUTTON   CAST MEMBER

SELECT CAST MEMBER

PREVIEW BUTTON   AUTOMASK OPTION

3] Click the Preview button to see how the cursor will look. If a white square appears around the cursor, make sure that the Automask option is checked.

While previewing, the cursor will move around as you move the mouse. Automask removes the bitmap's white background.

4] Center the cursor over the Stop button just below the Preview button and click the mouse. What happens?

If the cursor is really centered on the button, nothing will happen when you click the mouse. This is because the hotspot is set at the upper left corner of the cursor. If you placed the mouse cursor somewhat off center when you clicked, you might have managed to stop the preview.

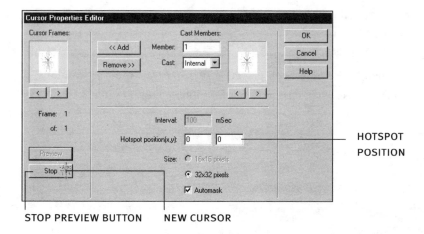

HOTSPOT
POSITION

STOP PREVIEW BUTTON   NEW CURSOR

5] Position the cursor with the upper left corner over the Stop button, and then click the mouse.

The preview will stop and the cursor will return to the shape of the standard arrow.

When you're using the standard arrow cursor, it makes sense for you to set the hotspot at the point of the arrow. For a symmetrical cursor, like the one you just created, it makes more sense to center the hotspot in the cursor. Your new cursor is a 32-by-32 pixel square. To center the hotspot, use the coordinates (16, 16). The upper left of the cursor, where the hotspot was set before, has coordinates of (0,0).

6] In each of the Hotspot Position fields in the Cursor Properties Editor, enter *16*.

This sets the hotspot to the approximate center of the cursor.

7] In the Cursor Properties Editor window use the arrow keys to display cast member 2 and then click the Add button again.

This adds a second bitmap to the cursor.

ADD BUTTON   CAST MEMBER

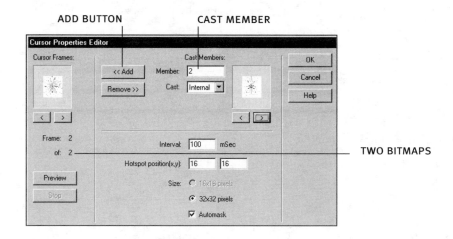

TWO BITMAPS

8] Repeat step 7 with cast members 3 and 4, and then close the Cursor Properties Editor by clicking OK.

The cast member is now complete and consists of four different bitmaps. The cursor is now a new cast member and has been placed in position 11 of the Cast window. The icon in the lower right of the cast member thumbnail identifies it as a cursor.

9] In the Cast window, name the new cast member *Magic Wand*.

You have successfully created an animated custom cursor.

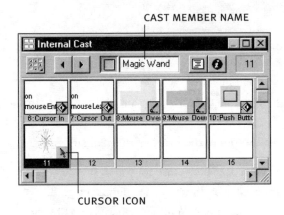

CAST MEMBER NAME

CURSOR ICON

10] Save your work.

APPLYING THE CURSOR

Earlier in this lesson, when you used the Behavior Inspector to attach cursors using behaviors, you were able to select only from among those cursors that are currently installed on your system. Although it is possible to install new and different cursors and then choose from among them, there is no way to tell whether the same cursor will be installed on another user's system. A better way is to create a custom cursor, as you have done above, since you can guarantee that the new cursor is available to any user who plays your project on any system.

You must, however, use a bit of Lingo script to make your custom cursor usable. Although you cannot choose your custom cursor with the Behavior Inspector, you can let the Behavior Inspector write most of the code for you and then slightly modify it. In this task, you will modify the *Cursor In* behavior you already created so that your custom cursor is displayed when the mouse moves over the sprite on the stage.

1] **In the Score window, make sure that the sprite in channel 1 is selected. Click the Behavior button to open the Behavior Inspector window.**

SCRIPT BUTTON

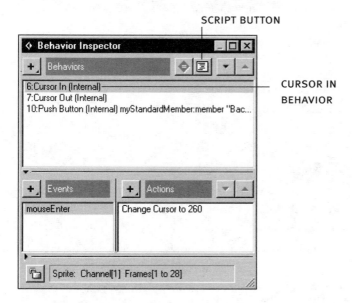

CURSOR IN
BEHAVIOR

2] **Make sure that the *Cursor In* behavior is selected, and then click the Script button.**

The script window for the behavior appears with the script displayed. Fortunately, the script is short and you can easily modify it.

CHANGE THIS LINE

3] Change the center line of the Lingo script to read *cursor member "Magic Wand"*.
Then close the Script window.

Be sure to include the quotation marks. They specify that your custom cursor, *Magic Wand*, is the cursor that will be displayed.

4] Play the movie.

When the cursor passes over the sprite on the stage, the cursor changes to the animated cursor you have created. When the cursor leaves the sprite, it appears as the arrow cursor again.

MODIFYING THE FRAME RATE

The cursor you created is animated by cycling through the four bitmap images that you used to create it. The **frame rate** for the cursor is the length of time, or interval, that each image is displayed. You can set the frame rate in the Cursor Properties Editor. You can set the frame rate for the entire cursor only; separate rates for each image are not allowed. When you set a cursor's frame rate, that rate is independent of the movie's frame rate. Setting different tempos for the movie does not effect the speed at which the images in the cursor change.

1] In the Cast window, double-click the Magic Wand cursor, cast member number 11.

This opens the Cursor Properties Editor, the window in which your custom cursor was created. Changes you make here will be applied to the Magic Wand cursor.

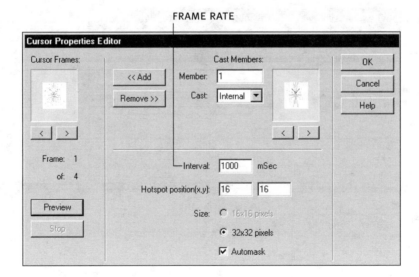

2] In the Interval field, set the frame rate to *1000*.

The interval is calculated in milliseconds, so a rate of 1000 means that the images of the cursor will each last for an entire second. This setting is a bit slow for the Magic Wand cursor, but it would be appropriate for some other cursors.

3] Click the Preview button to view the effect.

The cursor cycles very slowly—much too slowly for the twinkle effect you would like to use for the Magic Wand cursor.

4] Stop the preview and set the frame rate to *10* to speed up the cursor cycle.

Now the Magic Wand looks even better.

5] Close the Cursor Properties window and save your work.

WHAT YOU HAVE LEARNED

In this lesson you have:

• Changed cursors based on user actions [page 206]

• Changed a sprite based on the cursor location [page 212]

• Created a custom animated cursor from multiple cast members [page 215]

• Adjusted a cursor's hotspot area [page 217]

• Modified a cursor's frame rate [page 220]

channels
alpha

In the previous lessons you have worked with some of Director's sprite inks. Background Transparent, which you used as far back as in Lesson 1, is a particularly useful ink. A sprite's ink property establishes how Director will display that sprite's image against that of other sprites below it. Copy ink, the default, means that the image is copied completely. Background Transparent makes a sprite's background color invisible by allowing the sprites on stage beneath it to show through the background area. Other inks may give you special color effects or, like Blend, blend the whole image with the images below.

For this project, you'll use inks and Alpha masks to blend a text object with an image object in a dramatic animation sequence featuring the Taj Mahal.

Blend is a useful ink. You can set the blend for the whole sprite with values ranging from 0%, no blend, to 100%, blend completely. Sometimes, however, you might need even finer control. For instance, you might want different sections of the image to have different blend values. You might not want the image's center to blend at all, and you might want its edges to fully blend in. To create such an effect, you'd need to define a **mask** and use a special ink called **Mask ink**. Mask ink lets you simulate what is known as an **Alpha channel**, which is discussed on the following page.

WHAT YOU WILL LEARN

In this lesson you will:

- Create the basic animation
- Apply different inks
- Create an Alpha mask
- Layer the mask

APPROXIMATE TIME

It should take about 1 hour to complete this lesson.

LESSON FILES

Media Files:

None

Starting File:

Lesson11\Start\Start.dir

Completed Project:

Lesson11\Complete\Alpha.dir

DEFINING THE ALPHA CHANNEL

To understand the Alpha channel, you need to understand how bitmapped graphics are colored. A complete 24-bit bitmap image has three full channels of color: an 8-bit Red component, an 8-bit Green component, and an 8-bit Blue component. These three components define the RGB (Red-Green-Blue) values of an image. Each pixel in the image includes a value for each of the three RGB color channels. Each RGB value can range from 0 to 255. When all three of a pixel's channels are set at 255, the pixel's color is white, because Red, Green, and Blue are all at full strength. If only one channel is 255—Blue, for example—and the rest are 0, the color is Blue for that pixel because only the Blue channel includes a value. Since each of the Red, Green, and Blue components can be assigned values between 0 and 255, a wide range of colors is available—literally millions of colors.

tip *Don't try this at home with your old cans of paint. Colors of paint and colors of light are determined in different ways. Mixing dark red, green, and blue paints will make a black, not white. This is because the light from paint is a reflective light, which means that the light you see is reflected by the object that has been painted. The paint is actually absorbing the all the red, green, and blue, leaving black. A red paint, then, is actually absorbing all the colors except red, so that you see the reflected red. This is also known as the* subtractive color method. *On you computer or television screen, the light is shining at you, not reflecting. Imagine a friend standing half a mile away pointing red, green, and blue flashlights at you; you would see a white light (in theory, at least). In high school you may have seen a demonstration of a spinning disc with Red, Green, and Blue colors painted on it. As the disc spun, the colors blended and made white. This demonstrates the* additive color method; *computers and televisions use the RGB additive method.*

A pixel can also have a fourth component, the Alpha channel, which uses an additional 8-bits (for an image total of 32-bits). This channel can also be thought of as the **blending channel**. Again, each pixel can have a value between 0 and 255. The value determines the amount of blending that should be applied for that pixel when compositing, or merging, with another image.

Director 7 supports the Mask ink, which allows you to associate an 8-bit blending mask with a bitmap. When a sprite is drawn on screen, the pixels in the mask bitmap determine how the corresponding pixel in the image bitmap will be shown.

CREATING THE BASIC ANIMATION

Your first task is to create the basic animation effect, without inks.

1] Open Start.dir in the Start folder of the Lesson11 folder and save it in your Practice folder as *Alpha.dir*.

This movie has no score yet and contains only the a single image: the TajMist image from Lesson 3.

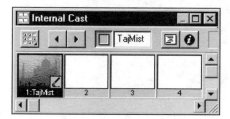

2] Open the Score window. Make sure that frame 1 of channel 1 is selected. From the Cast window, drag the TajMist cast member to the center of the stage.

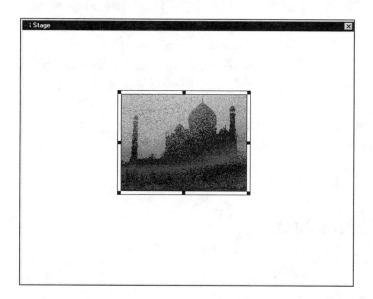

Using the techniques you learned in Lessons 2 and later, you will create some text to move from stage left to stage right.

3] Choose Window › Text to open the Text Editor window (Windows Ctrl+6, Macintosh Command+6).

The Text Editor window appears. The window title, Text 2, indicates that the text cast member you are creating will be stored as cast element 2. As you did in Lessons 1 and 2 you will use the Text Editor to create cast members of type Text.

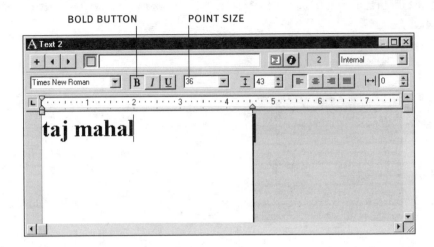

4] **In the Text Editor window, change the point size to 36, select Bold, and then type** *taj mahal* **in the text window.**

As an alternative, you could type the text, select all the text, and then adjust the point size. By changing the point size before you type, however, any text you type will appear in your selected point size.

5] **Close the text window. Select member 2 in the cast and name it** *TajText*.

Cast member 2 now contains a cast member of type Text, which is named TajText and contains the text *taj mahal*.

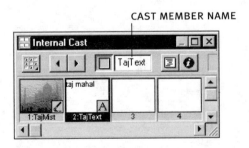

6] **Drag member 2, TajText, from the Cast window to the left side of the stage.**

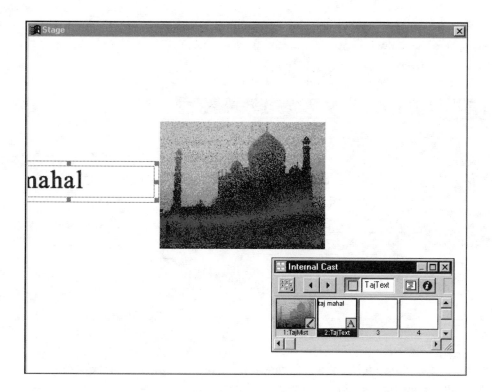

The Score window now shows the two sprites in frames 1 through 28. The TajMist sprite is located in channel 1 and the TajText sprite is in channel 2. Now you'll add a keyframe, as you learned in Lesson 2, to the TajText sprite to prepare for animating the text across the stage.

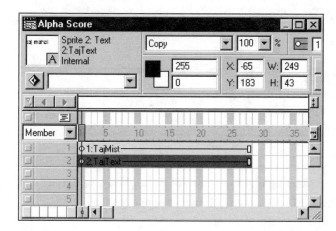

7] Prepare your keyframe by clicking sprite 2 in frame 28 of the score.

Make sure that only the last frame of the sprite is selected. This prepares the sprite for tweening. Frame 28 is the endframe of the sprite.

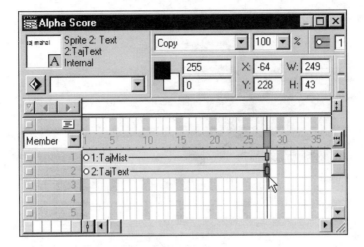

8] Hold down the shift key and drag the sprite to the far right side of the stage, to the end location for the sprite.

The sprite moves in a straight line to the right because by pressing the Shift key while you drag, you constrain its movement in one direction only. This places the sprite in the opposite tween position. Look carefully at the endframe of the sprite in channel 2. Notice that the endframe symbol has changed to a keyframe symbol. By selecting the endframe of a sprite and then moving the sprite's position on the stage, Director knows that you are preparing the sprite for tweening. In fact, it has already taken care of tweening for you.

9] Open the Control Panel by choosing Window › Control Panel. Make sure that Loop Playback is enabled and set the Tempo to 10 frames per second.

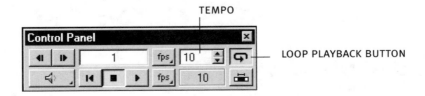

10] Rewind and play the movie.

The text *taj mahal* moves across the stage, blocking the image of the Taj Mahal as it passes over it.

11] Save your work.

APPLYING DIFFERENT INKS

Now that the basic animation is built, you can experiment with applying different inks. Inks affect how a sprite is drawn, or rendered, against the images below it. Since Director builds each image from the lowest numbered sprite channel up, the ink of the higher numbered channels determines how those sprites appear against the complete image of all the sprites and the stage below them.

When two sprites—a text sprite and an image—are involved, ink can be applied to one or both sprites. If the text is on top, as is the case with the current score, the ink we choose for sprite channel 2, the sprite for the text, will impact the way the text is rendered on the image. We could reverse the channels to place the image in a higher numbered channel and then modify the image ink, which would affect how the image renders against everything below it, text and all.

1] In the Score window, select sprite 2 and change the ink to Background Transparent. Make sure to select all of sprite 2, not just one of the endpoints.

This makes the background color of the sprite transparent, so the image below will show through.

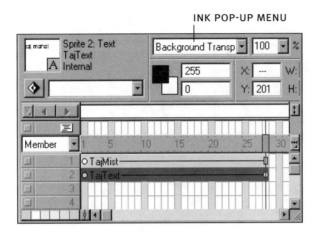

2] Play the movie.

The movie plays as before, except this time the text sprite does not obscure the image of the Taj Mahal.

This is an improvement, but it's not very interesting. Now try changing the sprite's ink to Blend.

3] In the Score window, select sprite 2 and change its ink to Blend. Then change the Blend percentage to 50%.

The blend percentage determines how much of the sprite is rendered as opposed to rendering the image below. In other words, for example, a blend of 100% will mean that the sprite commands 100% of the foreground, making the background essentially transparent. A blend of 50% means that half of the foreground sprite retains its own color, and half is blended with the color of the underlying sprite. A blend of 0% means that none of the foreground sprite appears and the image shows just the underlying sprite—the new sprite simply doesn't appear.

BLEND POP-UP MENU

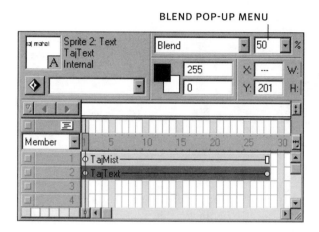

4] Play the movie.

You can see that blending is occurring, and the taj mahal text appears to lighten when it moves over the white stage. This is because the text is blended against the stage's white background.

Now try moving the Taj Mahal image on top of the text.

5] In the Score window, select sprite 1, TajMist, and drag it to channel 3.

The image will now render after the text does. Any inks applied now would affect how much the TajMist image allows the stage and images below it to show through.

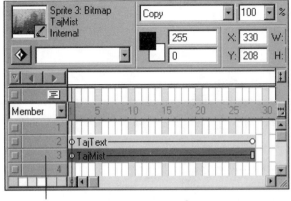

DRAG TAJMIST TO CHANNEL 3

6] Play the movie.

Now the text isn't visible as it slides beneath the image. The copy ink of the TajMist image obscures the text sprite.

7] In the Score window, select sprite 3, TajMist, and change the ink to Blend and the percentage to 50%.

Immediately you can see the image lighten on the stage.

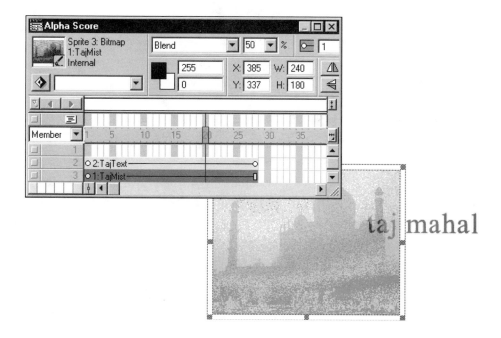

8] Play the movie.

The text appears much as before, but the TajMist image is now lighter.

9] Save your work.

tip *You can use the Display pop-up menu in the Score window to show which inks are applied to sprites in the score. Change the menu selection from Member to Ink. The ink applied to a sprite will show in place of the name of the cast member used for the sprite.*

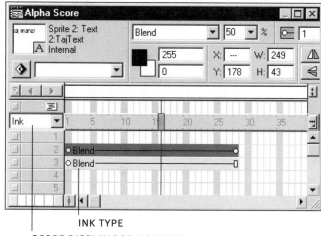

INK TYPE

SCORE DISPLAY POP-UP MENU

The background transparent and blend ink effects, although useful, affect either the whole text or the whole image, but it is not possible to use these inks to affect select portions of a sprite. In the next task, you will learn how masks can provide control over specific blend values.

CREATING AN ALPHA MASK

Director 7 offers the Mask ink, which causes a bitmap to blend with the image below it pixel by pixel according to a separate reference map. That map can be a separate 8-bit image or it can be the fourth 8-bit channel of a 32-bit image. As we discussed earlier in this lesson, the fourth channel is often called the Alpha channel. The Alpha channel is accessible using image editing programs such as Macromedia xRes and Adobe Photoshop. In this task, we will be using an 8-bit mask rather than the 8-bit channel of a 32-bit image.

The Mask ink, combined with a mask image, determines exactly which pixels of a sprite are transparent and which are opaque. In its simplest form, the mask is a black-and-white only image. The black areas of the mask make the corresponding pixels of the image opaque. The white areas make the image transparent.

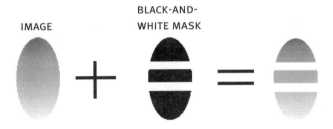

IMAGE
BLACK-AND-WHITE MASK

If a mask contains colors other than black or white, the corresponding pixels in the image become more opaque depending on the darkness of the corresponding area of the mask.

In the next task, you will create a rough mask from the source TajMist cast member. Then you'll modify it for some special effects.

1] Open the Cast window and move TajText from member 2 to member 7.

The Mask ink requires that the masked image have the mask bitmap in the very next member slot in the cast. Since the next member slot is currently occupied by the TajText member, you need to relocate that cast member elsewhere to free up slot 2.

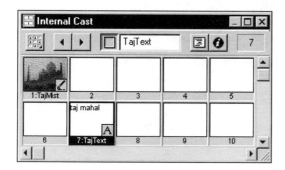

Director automatically adjusts all score references to TajText to reflect its new location.

2] Select member 1, TajMist, in the Cast window and then choose Edit › Duplicate (Windows Ctrl+D, Macintosh Command+D).

This duplicates the Taj Mahal image, TajMist, placing the duplicated cast member in slot 2 of the cast.

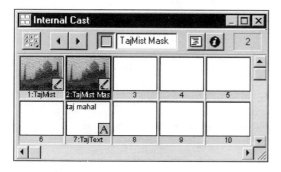

3] Change the name field for member 2 from *TajMist* to *TajMist Mask*. Click on member 2 again to make the new name take effect.

This changes the name of the cast member to reflect that it will be used as a mask.

Next you will take steps to turn the TajMist Mask cast member into a bitmap for a mask. First you'll convert the image to use the grayscale palette, and then you'll convert the image to a 1-bit color depth.

4] With cast member 2 still selected, choose Modify › Transform bitmap.

The Transform Bitmap dialog appears.

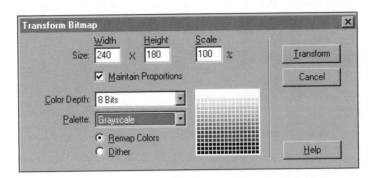

5] Select the Grayscale palette and click Remap Colors to select it. Click the Transform button and then click OK in the warning dialog box that appears.

All the colors will be remapped onto the grayscale palette, so that the darkest colors have a higher palette index and the lighter colors have a lower palette index.

Reordering the colors from lightest to darkest in the palette is an important step. The Mask ink will use this bitmap as a reference and will refer to each pixel's palette index as the indicator of how much blending to apply. The lower the index, the greater the image's transparency. The higher the index, the more the original image (that you are applying) will assert itself. Using a color with an index of 255, the last position, will cause a full copy of the image to appear for that pixel.

In theory, you can use any 256-color palette you want. The actual colors do not matter; only their index position in the palette is relevant. As a practical matter, though, anything other than a clean light-to-dark ordered palette is simply confusing to work with. The Grayscale palette lends itself very well to the Mask ink effects because it is a light-to-dark ordered palette.

> **note**   *Windows only: If your system color depth is set to 256 colors (as it should be), you will notice that Director takes on a black-and-white appearance after changing the cast member's palette. This indicates that Director knows that the movie includes elements that use the non-standard palette. Although this black-and-white appearance can be disconcerting to work with, it does not affect the playing of the movie or the functioning of Director. Try rewinding the movie: when Director's focus is shifted from the cast member with the grayscale palette, Director returns to its normal color scheme.*

6] In the Score window, select sprite 3, TajMist. Restore the Blend percentage to 100% and then change the sprite ink to Mask.

This applies the Mask ink to the TajMist sprite. The sprite will be rendered against the background according to its associated mask.

MASK INK   100% BLEND

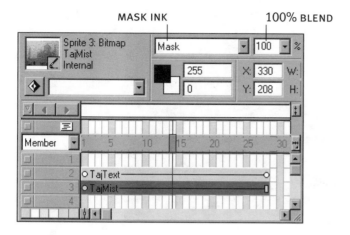

7] Play the movie.

If you watch carefully, you can see some subtle changes in blending—but they are subtle indeed. This is because your grayscale mask is still dark overall. You'll need to increase the differences between light and dark in the mask to better see the blending.

8] Select the mask in the Cast window. Choose Modify › Transform Bitmap. Change the color depth to a 1-bit depth. Select Transform and click OK in the warning dialog box that appears.

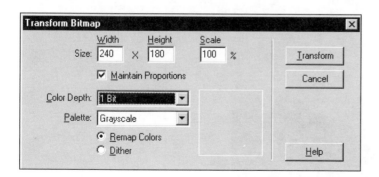

The 1-bit color depth forces the near-white colors to all-white and the near-black to all-black. The mask image is now black-and-white. Next you will touch up the mask a little in the Paint window.

237

9] Play the movie.

Now you can clearly see where the text goes behind the image. However, the masking has also affected how the TajMist image itself appears against the background. You will fix this after modifying the mask.

10] Double-click member 2 in the Cast window, or select it and choose Window › Paint (Windows Ctrl-5, Macintosh Command+5). Then press the letter E on your keyboard to activate the eraser tool.

The Paint window opens so you can edit the bitmap mask member directly. Using the eraser tool, you will better define the mask.

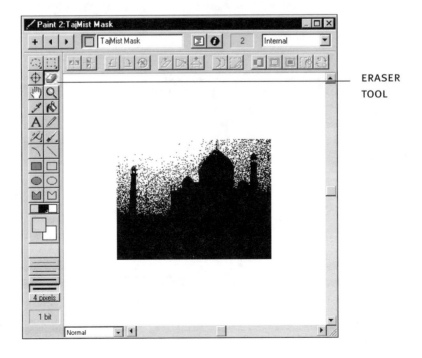

ERASER
TOOL

11] Use the eraser to roughly remove the "sky" areas and spaces between the buildings. Make a point to remove the tower on the left.

Do not worry too much at this point about being too precise. This is a rough mask.

12] Close the Paint window and replay the movie.

The text appears behind part of the image and over where the tower used to appear, but the rough masking has taken its toll on the TajMist image.

13] Save your work.

You're almost done! In the next step, you'll layer the mask and make the TajMist image look as good as new.

LAYERING THE MASK

To get the effect of the text moving behind the Taj Mahal but on top of the background, it is necessary to have two copies of the TajMist image on stage: one in the background, fully rendered with Copy ink, and a second on top with a mask applied. This will give the text something to move behind and something else to move in front of.

In this task, you will make a duplicate of TajMist, put it in the background, and then apply the Copy ink. This way the image won't look ragged when it appears on stage.

1] In the Score window, select sprite channel 3, TajMist, and choose Edit › Copy Sprites to copy the sprite to the clipboard (Windows Ctrl+C, Macintosh Command+C).

2] Select sprite channel 1, frame 1. Choose Edit › Paste Sprites to paste the copied sprite into channel 1 (Windows Ctrl+V, Macintosh Command+V).

The TajMist cast member now appears on stage twice in the same location. Note that that a copy of TajMist appears both below and above the sprite channel that holds the text.

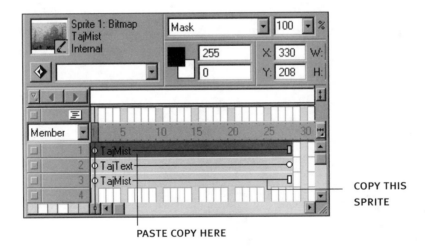

Now you'll apply copy ink to the lower channel sprite instance so it displays in full (not masked).

4] Change the ink of sprite 1 to Copy ink.

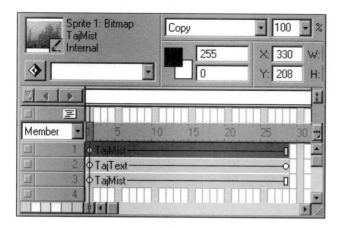

The TajMist image should now appear normally on the stage. No masking is evident because the TajMist sprite with the Copy ink shows everything that the TajMist sprite with the Mask ink has masked.

Although the TajMist image on the stage looks as it did originally, two copies of the image appear at the same location. The lowest channel (sprite channel 1) image has Copy ink, effectively making it a background image. The *taj mahal* text is in the next channel up, and then a masked version of TajMist appears on top of that. The net effect is that the masked version lets the text appear in certain areas (open sky) but not in others (the Taj Mahal building).

5] Play the movie.

The text moves behind the Taj Mahal but in front of the left tower.

The masking in this lesson used a 1-bit mask, but by using a paint program such as Macromedia's xRes and an 8-bit image, you can exactly define an object's blending areas. By carefully blending and masking, you have created the effect of text rising out of the mist.

6] Save your work.

ON YOUR OWN

Have some fun. You can do more than just control text; you can use masking to create interesting effects, such as merged images. Put the eyes of a cat on the face of a human by using a custom mask to control the blending. Use gradient blends on a grayscale-palette mask to fade out to the edges, or use the Paint window or a paint program for precise control. Make an image rise out of the sea by adjusting the blend where the image or text meets the sea. Using masking, you can control how the appearances of images interact, even when they're moving on screen.

WHAT YOU HAVE LEARNED

In this lesson you have:

- Created a basic animation [page 225]
- Applied different inks [page 229]
- Created an Alpha mask [page 234]
- Layered the mask [page 240]

and palettes

sprite properties

LESSON 12

Multimedia programs let you present any kind of information in a multitude of creative ways. Interactive multimedia is an especially effective means of presenting the creative work of artists, musicians, and other artisans whose work appeals to the senses since these presentations incorporate images and sounds. In this lesson you will build the introduction and menu for an interactive art gallery with some unique navigation controls.

Many multimedia projects are constructed to showcase creative work by artists. In this lesson you'll create an introduction and a menu screen with unexpected interactive elements, such as menu options that begin as dim selections and change to clear selections when you move the cursor over them.

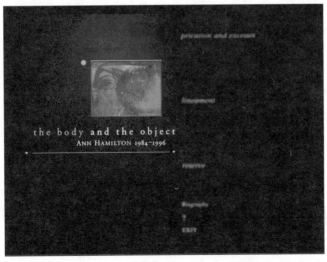

The images and sounds you'll use for this project are taken from the body and the object, *a multimedia presentation produced by Michael Polivka of* resource, *and features the art of Ann Hamilton as exhibited by the Wexner Center for the Arts at Ohio State University.*

If you would like to view the final result of this lesson, open the Complete folder in the Lesson12 folder and play Gallery1.dir.

WHAT YOU WILL LEARN

In this lesson you will:

• Set a movie palette

• Change the default length of new sprites

• Set the locations of sprites

• Use grid settings to align objects

• Use the tool palette to add color to sprites

• Identify the index number of a color in a color palette

• Modify the dimensions of a sprite

• Practice adding a sound and setting a tempo

APPROXIMATE TIME

It should take about 2 hours to complete this lesson.

LESSON FILES

Media Files:

Lesson12\Media

Starting Files:

None

Completed Project:

Lesson12\Complete\Gallery1.dir

IMPORTING MEDIA ELEMENTS

After your media elements are developed, the first step in creating a multimedia presentation is to import the media into Director and set some movie properties. Finished versions of graphics and sound files are included on the CD for use in this lesson.

1] Open a new file (Windows Ctrl+N, Macintosh Command+N).

An empty stage appears.

2] Choose File › Import to open the Import dialog box (Windows Ctrl+R, Macintosh Command+R).

You're now going to import the media elements.

3] Locate the Media folder in the Lesson12 folder and click Add All.

All the file names appear in the file list.

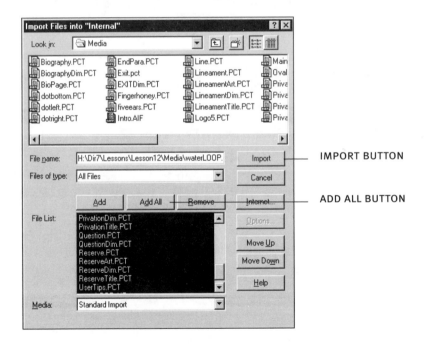

4] Click Import.

The Image Options dialog box appears.

5] In the Image Options dialog box, choose Stage (8 bits).

The graphics for this project were created on a computer whose monitor was set to "millions of colors." Depending on the type of monitor and computer you are using, a "millions of colors" setting could be either 24-bit or 32-bit. This **bit depth** (also called **color depth**) refers to the number of bits of memory used to store information about the color of a single pixel in a graphic. With 24 bits for each pixel, there are 16,777,216 possible color combinations ("millions of colors"), which is sufficient to produce any shade imaginable for **true-color** graphics.

Although true-color graphics are aesthetically appealing, 24- and 32-bit graphics require lots of disk space, and because of their size, they can slow down your movie's performance, particularly when large images or large quantities of images are transferred from CD-ROM or the Internet. Also, many end users either do not have the type of sophisticated computer monitor required to display true-color graphics or simply keep their settings at 256-colors (often a manufacturer default). For these reasons, most Director movies use a color depth of 8 bits, which allows for 256 separate colors. That may sound like a huge drop in quality from millions of colors, but in fact, 256 colors are generally sufficient for most projects.

The Image Options dialog box appears when you start to import graphics that have a higher color depth than your monitor is currently set to. The monitor's current setting determines the color depth for the movie, as shown (in parentheses) next to the Stage option in the Image Options dialog box. This dialog box asks whether you want to retain the graphics' current color depth (in this case, keeping them at 32 bits) or to convert them to match the stage's color depth (in this case, 8 bits). In this project, you are reducing the graphics to match the stage's color depth so you can learn more about the requirements for this very common scenario.

note   *If you do not see the Image Options dialog box, your computer monitor is probably set to display "millions of colors." Before going any further, delete the image you just imported, and then reset your computer monitor to display 256 colors and then redo the previous steps in this task back to this point.*

247

6] For the Palette option, click Remap To and make sure the system palette for your type of computer is selected from the menu. (If the palette is already correct for your system, the Remap To option may be grayed out.) Then select Dither.

When you selected Stage for the Color Depth option, the Palette option became available. A **color palette** is a collection of discrete colors. When your movie is running on a computer that can display only 256 colors at one time, it is essential that all graphics appearing on the stage in a single frame contain exactly the same set of 256 colors— that is, the graphics must use the same color palette. In addition, the color palette of all graphics appearing together in a single frame must match the color palette assigned to the frame. Later in this task you will set the movie's default color palette, which controls the palette assigned to the frames in your movie. In this step, you are making sure that all the graphics you are importing use the same color palette.

When you select Remap To in the Image Options dialog box, Director will analyze the colors in each image and then replace those colors with the nearest matching color contained in the palette that you choose from the menu. When Director can't find a match for a graphic's color, the Dither option tells Director to approximate the color by using a pattern of similarly colored pixels. Dithering produces best results for photographic images or complex artwork. In your own projects, always be sure to experiment by importing images with and without dithering to see which produces the best results.

By default, Director chooses the correct system palette for your type of computer, but it never hurts to double-check. If you are using Windows, make sure System - Win is selected as the palette you want to use for the graphics you are importing. If you are using a Macintosh, make sure System - Mac is selected. These are default system palettes—the palettes that the operating system uses. The default system palette for your computer's operating system is a safe choice because it ensures that, while your movie is running, it will not change the colors used by other elements of the operating system's user interface, such as icons on your desktop.

SELECT A COLOR PALETTE FOR THE
GRAPHICS YOU ARE IMPORTING

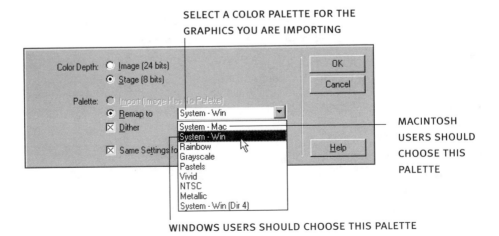

MACINTOSH USERS SHOULD CHOOSE THIS PALETTE

WINDOWS USERS SHOULD CHOOSE THIS PALETTE

In this lesson, you are choosing your computer's default system palette because this is a good way to start learning about palettes. However, you are not required to use your computer's system palette. You can choose any of the other built-in palettes in the menu, or even create your own. For projects that will be distributed both on Windows and the Macintosh, you can even use the same system palette. For example, you can use the Windows system palette for a project that you are creating on the Macintosh. This is a very common practice for cross-platform projects, because it allows you to use the same set of graphics on both platforms. Otherwise, you would have to have two sets of graphics—one set with the Windows system palette and one set with the Macintosh system palette.

note   *On Windows systems, using a palette other than the default System - Win palette can give a funny black-and-white appearance to the Director interface. This odd appearance simply indicates that a nonstandard palette is being used and does not affect the function of Director. You may, however, find Director more difficult to use and so should avoid using nonstandard palettes whenever possible.*

7] Check Same Settings for Remaining Images and click OK to close the dialog box.
For this lesson, you want all graphics to share the same palette. Selecting the Same Settings for Remaining Images option applies the options you've selected in this dialog box to all graphics you are importing. If you do not select this option, Director displays this dialog box for every image that you're importing.

8] Save the movie as *Gallery1.dir* in your Projects folder.
Your Cast window now contains all the media elements you need for this lesson and for Lessons 13 and 14 as well. You won't need some of the media elements until you reach Lesson 14, so don't worry if you don't use all the cast members in this lesson.

SETTING A MOVIE'S STAGE SIZE, BACKGROUND COLOR, AND DEFAULT PALETTE

In the previous task, you applied the same palette to all the graphics in your movie. To make sure these graphics are displayed correctly in your movie, you must also make sure that the same palette is assigned to the frames in which the graphics appear. The palette channel in the score allows you to assign a palette to any frame of the movie. To keep this project simple, however, you will set a default palette for all frames of the movie. Unless you use the palette channel to override the palette assigned to a specific frame, the default palette will always be assigned to every frame of the movie. In this task, you will also set the stage size and the background color for the stage.

1] Choose Modify > Movie > Properties.

The Movie Properties dialog box opens.

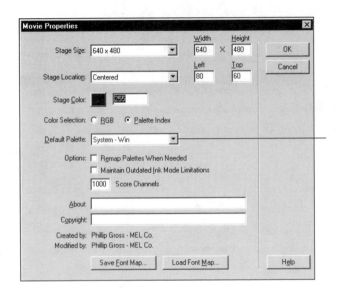

THIS IS THE CORRECT
PALETTE FOR WINDOWS
USERS; MACINTOSH USERS
SHOULD CHOOSE THE
SYSTEM - MAC PALETTE

2] Make sure the system palette for your type of computer is selected from the Default Palette menu.

By default, Director selects the System - Win palette for Windows computers and the System - Mac palette for Macintosh computers. When you're starting a project, however, it doesn't hurt to double-check these settings.

You have now ensured that all the graphics in your project will be displayed correctly, no matter where you use them. The graphics share the same palette, and that palette is also assigned as the movie's default. A **palette conflict** occurs when a graphic does not have the same palette as the frame in which it appears. This causes Director to display the graphic using the colors from the frame's palette, and frequently the colors are completely wrong for the graphic, leading to some psychedelic effects.

A related problem is **palette flash**, which occurs when a movie branches to a frame with a different palette. For a split second before the new frame appears, the new frame's palette becomes active, and the graphics on the current frame change color. One way to minimize palette flash is to first change to a frame using only colors shared by both palettes, such as black. Some developers prefer to reserve a common set of colors among all palettes for their background artwork to avoid this problem.

3] Set the movie background color to black.

To do this, click the Stage Color chip and select black from the palette. The black background was chosen because it works well with the art prepared for this project.

250

4] Set the stage to 640 x 480.

To do this, select the size from the Stage Size pop-up menu. This common stage size matches the dimensions of the typical end user's monitor.

5] Set the stage location to Centered.

To do this, select Centered from the Stage Location pop-up menu. A centered stage location ensures that the stage appears in the center of the user's screen independent of the size of that monitor. Other stage locations may work fine on some monitors, but the stage may be partially hidden on small monitors.

6] Click OK to close the Movie Properties dialog box.

SETTING CAST AND SPRITE PREFERENCES

When you drag a cast member into the score or onto the stage, Director is preset to create a sprite that spans 28 frames of the score. This 28-frame duration was chosen as a good starting point, but as you've seen in previous lessons, you frequently need to change the sprite's duration to fit the needs of the individual project. For this project, you will create a series of static screens; that is, there will be no animation. In projects such as these, the duration you choose for a sprite is largely a matter of convenience. A good rule of thumb is to choose a duration that is long enough to allow you to see the names of the cast members in the Score window.

In this task, you will set up Director to show the names of cast members in the score and then set up a new default duration that better suits this project. As you will see while you work through the rest of the tasks in this lesson, these preferences will speed up your work (because you won't have to adjust the length of sprites in the score) and will make it easier for you to see what's going on in the score.

1] Choose File > Preferences > Cast to open the Cast Window Preferences dialog box. Choose Number:Name from the Label menu and then click OK to close the dialog box.

Selecting Number:Name in the Label field allows you to see both the cast member's number and name in the Score window. This is the most helpful label for cast members when you are working with large casts.

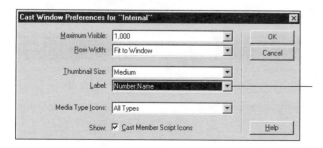

SELECT NUMBER:NAME FOR THE CAST MEMBER LABEL TO DISPLAY BOTH FOR EACH MEMBER IN THE CAST

**2] Choose File › Preferences › Sprite to open the Sprite Preferences dialog box. Type
13 in the Span Duration field and click OK to close the dialog box.**

The 13-frame duration was chosen simply because it is long enough to allow you to
see the cast member's names in the Score window. In your own projects, you may want
to specify a different duration. You can also permanently set a default duration from
the Sprite Preferences menu (File > Preferences > Sprite).

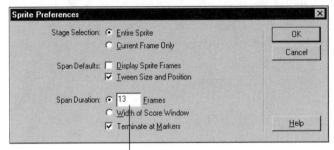

TYPE *13* AS THE DEFAULT SPAN DURATION
FOR THE SPRITES IN THE SCORE

ORGANIZING THE CAST

Next you'll organize the cast so all related cast members are in a logical order. This will
help you easily locate cast members. Devising a scheme for the cast is not a necessary
step for Director development, but it will help you keep organized, especially if you
are working with many cast members.

1] In the Cast window, drag the cast members into a logical order.

As you drag a cast member, notice that Director highlights the divider between cast
members, to show you where the cast member you're dragging will appear when you
release the mouse button. You can select a contiguous range of cast members by
clicking the first cast member, holding down the Shift key, and clicking the last
member. You can select non-adjacent members by holding down the Ctrl key
(Windows) or the Command key (Macintosh) while you click cast members.

The following list is a suggested order for the cast members you've imported. When
you used the File > Import command, the cast members filled the movie's cast in
alphabetical order according to the file names. This order doesn't give any indication
of whether cast members will be used as buttons, as the elements of a menu, and so
forth. The suggested order is more useful; it groups cast members according to their
use on the screens you'll create in this lesson and the next lesson.

Suggested cast member order:

1: Intro
2: Logo5
3: MainMenu
4: Fingerhoney
5: Line
6: QuestionDim
7: Question
8: BiographyDim
9: Biography
10: EXITDim
11: EXIT
12: LineamentDim
13: Lineament
14: PrivationDim
15: Privation
16: ReserveDim

17: Reserve
18: LineamentArt
19: ReserveArt
20: PrivationArt
21: LineamentTitle
22: PrivationTitle
23: ReserveTitle
24: dotleft
25: dotright
26: dotbottom
27: UserTips
28: BioPage
29: fiveears
30: waterLoop
31: EndPara
32: Oval

tip   *Sometimes the name of a cast member is too long to appear in full beneath the cast member thumbnail. For example, all the cast members with names beginning with Lineament appear to have the same name in the Cast window. To see the entire name of a cast member, click the cast member and its name will appear in the Cast window Name field. This will allow you to choose the correct cast member to move.*

Using this suggested cast member order will also make it easier for you to follow the rest of this lesson, because this order is used in the steps and illustrations of the Cast and Score windows. If you followed this order, your Cast window will look like this:

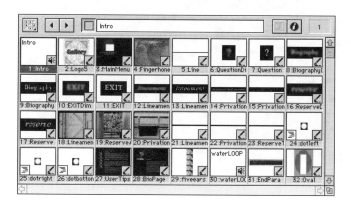

When you start designing your own movies, you'll have your own ideas about how to group the images for a movie.

253

2] Save your work (you don't want to have to reorder the cast again).

SETTING THE LOCATION OF A SPRITE

Next you'll start adding elements to the stage. In this task, you will set the location of some sprites on the stage by defining exact locations using the Sprite Overlay and the Sprite Properties dialog box, which both help you set sprite properties. To begin defining the menu screen for this presentation, you'll first center the image for the main menu in the score by dragging it from the cast to the score, just as you've done in previous lessons. Then you'll use other Director features to position the remaining sprites you add to the score.

1] Drag cast member 3, MainMenu, from the cast to channel 1, frame 15.

Start building this main menu in frame 15 so there is room at the beginning of the score to place a logo and sound for the introduction to the movie. The MainMenu image contains a title for the multimedia art gallery you're going to create. The white rectangle marks the location where you'll soon place the next sprite.

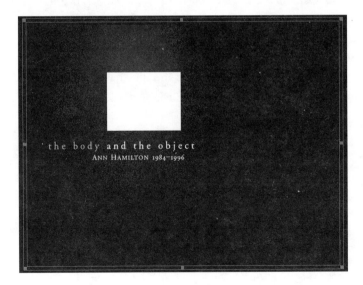

When you dragged the MainMenu cast member to the score, Director centered it on the stage. While the cast member is still selected, you can see that it does not completely cover the stage.

In the score, Director added the MainMenu sprite with a 13-frame duration, which you specified earlier as your sprite preference. Notice also that you can see the cast member number and name in the score, which you specified as your cast preference.

2] Drag cast member 4, Fingerhoney, onto the stage so it appears in the lower-right corner of the stage.

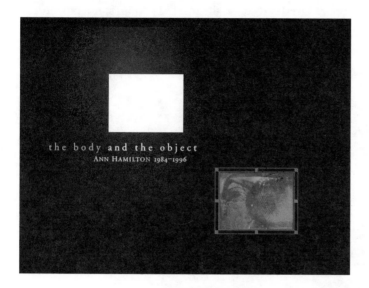

In the score, a 13-frame sprite is inserted into channel 2, frame 15, just beneath the 13-frame sprite in channel 1. Director placed the playback head in frame 15 when you dragged the MainMenu cast member to this frame in channel 1; Director then placed the start frame of the sprite you dragged onto the stage in the current frame—frame 15—of the next available channel.

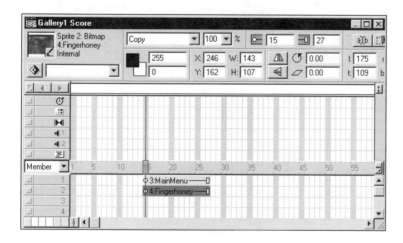

255

In the following steps you'll use a new feature to move this sprite into position on the stage. When you're finished, this sprite will appear over the white rectangle.

3] Choose View› Sprite Overlay› Show Info (Windows Ctrl+Shift+Alt+O, Macintosh Control+Shift+Command+O).

On the stage a gray box containing information about the selected sprite appears. This is the **Sprite Overlay**. The Sprite Overlay displays the most important sprite properties directly on the stage. The information displayed in this panel consolidates information about the sprite that you would normally see only by opening various dialog boxes or choosing menu commands.

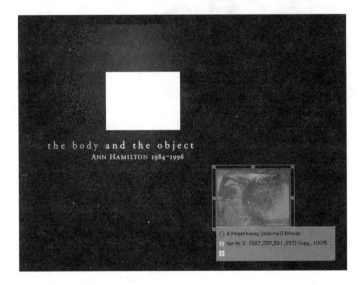

The Sprite Overlay panel is now active for the selected sprite. By default, the Sprite Overlay feature displays a panel only for the selected sprites. By choosing View > Sprite Overlay > Settings, you can select a setting that displays sprite information for all sprites on the stage or only when you move the cursor over a sprite.

ROLL OVER DISPLAYS THE SPRITE OVERLAY WHEN
YOU MOVE THE CURSOR OVER THE SPRITE

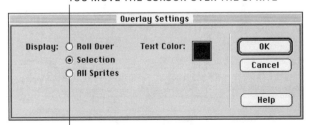

ALL SPRITES DISPLAYS SPRITE OVERLAYS FOR ALL
SPRITES ON THE STAGE AT THE SAME TIME

The three icons along the left of the Sprite Overlay panel can be clicked to open dialog boxes. You can then edit the properties associated with the sprite. The information that appears to the right of the icon at the top of the Sprite Overlay describes the cast member properties for the sprite's cast member. In previous lessons, you clicked the Cast Member Properties icon in the Cast window to see this information for a cast member.

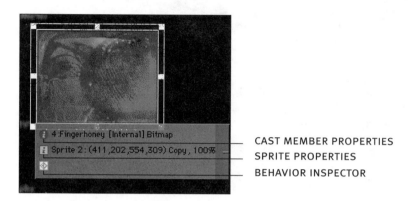

CAST MEMBER PROPERTIES
SPRITE PROPERTIES
BEHAVIOR INSPECTOR

The information associated with the second icon describes the channel number where the sprite is located and the sprite's location coordinates, ink setting, and blend setting (the percent of opacity of the image). Information associated with the third icon defines any behavior that has been assigned to the sprite.

4] Click the Sprite Properties icon to open the Sprite Properties dialog box. Set Location Left to *175* and Top to *109* and then click OK to close the dialog box.

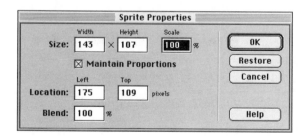

The Location fields set the location of the sprite relative to the upper-left corner of the stage. This location positions the sprite over the white rectangle of the MainMenu sprite. The artist who designed these graphics and who divided them into separate cast members kept notes about the coordinates where each element should be positioned. This sort of pixel-perfect placement is common in well-designed Director projects.

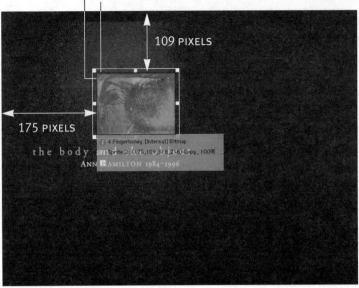

THE LEFT COORDINATE IS 175 PIXELS FROM THE LEFT EDGE OF THE STAGE

THE TOP COORDINATE IS 109 PIXELS FROM THE TOP EDGE OF THE STAGE

109 PIXELS

175 PIXELS

Remember that the stage size is not necessarily the same size as the screen. Recall that you set the stage size in the Modify > Movie > Properties dialog box. The Location boxes set the location of the sprite relative to the upper-left corner of the *stage*, not the upper-left corner of the *screen*.

tip *You can also display the Sprite Properties dialog box by choosing Modify > Sprite > Properties (Windows Ctrl+Shift+I, Macintosh Command+Shift+I).*

SNAPPING TO THE GRID

In this task you will add several elements to the stage at one time. Then you'll use the grid to align these elements quickly and easily.

1] Drag these cast members to frame 15 in the score, starting in channel 5.

PrivationDim	Channel 5
12: LineamentDim	Channel 6
16: ReserveDim	Channel 7
8: BiographyDim	Channel 8
6: QuestionDim	Channel 9
10: EXITDim	Channel 10

These cast members represent the selections users will be able to make from the main menu when they view the presentation. They will appear on the right side of the stage after you position them in the following steps. For now, they are all centered on the stage, and the Sprite Overlay panel you see contains properties that belong to the last sprite you placed in the score.

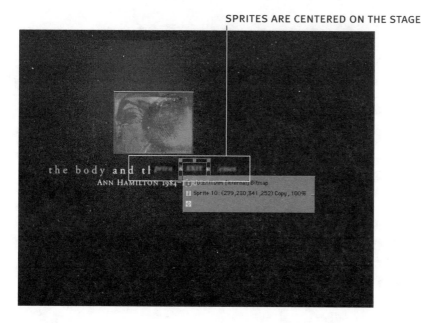

SPRITES ARE CENTERED ON THE STAGE

Notice that you're leaving two channels empty in the score. There are two reasons for this. First, you'll be filling in one of the empty channels with another sprite in the next task. Second, leaving space in the score like this makes the score easier to read. The space helps you visually group the types of sprites that will be on the stage. The sprites currently in channels 1 and 2 make up the overall background of the main menu, while the sprites in channels 5 through 10 make up the menu selections.

In the Score window, you can now begin to see the advantage of having set your cast and sprite preferences earlier. The 13-frame duration is just long enough to let you read the cast member number and name in the score, and you did not have to devote additional time to adjusting the length of the sprites.

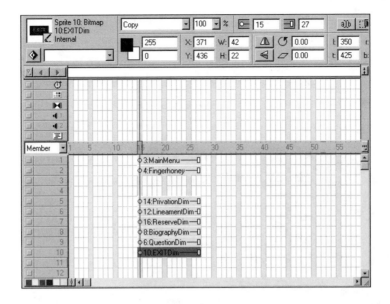

2] In the score, select the sprite in channel 5 and click the Sprite Properties icon in the Sprite Overlay. Then set the sprite's location to Left *350*, Top *50*. Click OK.

After you select the sprite in the score, the Sprite Overlay you see on the stage identifies the sprite you selected. Clicking the Sprite Properties icon in the Sprite Overlay panel then opens the Sprite Properties dialog box for the selected sprite.

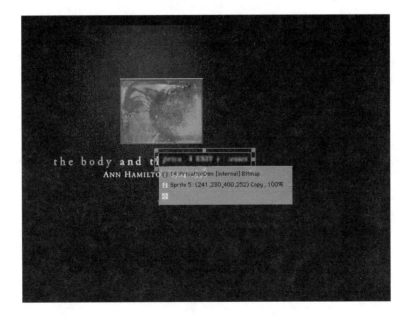

Setting the left and top location of a sprite is easy to do when, as in this project, you know the position in pixels where the sprite must appear. Depending on the project, you may be able to drag a sprite to a location on the stage that is simply pleasing to the eye. You would probably prefer that method, but here you have selected a sprite that is below all the sprites in channels 6 through 10, and clicking the center of the stage would likely select one of the other sprites. When you're working with a sprite in a lower-numbered channel that is at the same screen location as other sprites, the best way to isolate the sprite is to use the Sprite Overlay panel to make changes to the sprite properties.

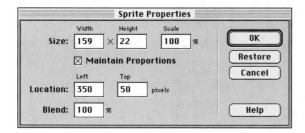

This sprite now appears in the location where it will appear as a menu option on this screen, which is the main menu for the multimedia art gallery. The other sprites you dragged to the score in step 1 will appear in a column below this sprite at the right of the stage. The sprites in channels 5, 6, and 7 will be spaced at 125-pixel intervals from each other, and the remaining sprites will be spaced at 25-pixel intervals from the sprites above them. A quick way to place the sprites precisely is to use the grid.

3] Choose View › Grids › Settings, type *50* in the Width field and *25* in the Height field, and then click OK to close the dialog box.

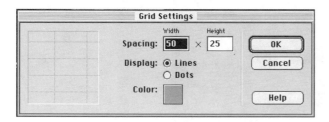

This creates a grid with boxes that are 50 pixels wide by 25 pixels high. After you finish the next step, you'll be able to see these boxes.

4] Choose View › Grids › Snap To to turn on grid snapping (Windows Ctrl+Alt+G, Macintosh Command+Option+G). Then choose View › Grids › Show (Windows Ctrl+Shift+Alt+G, Macintosh Command+Option+Shift+G).

Now you can see the grid. **Grid snapping** ensures that anything you drag near a grid line will automatically be aligned with the grid line.

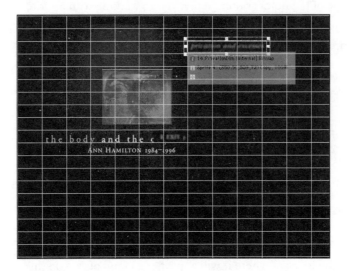

5] Using the following illustration as your guide, click each sprite that remains at the center of the stage and drag it to the right side of the stage.

Because grid snapping is turned on, the graphics jump to the grid lines, which makes aligning them much easier. The Sprite Overlay panels for each sprite tell you which cast member relates to the selected sprite so you can identify which sprite you are moving. This is helpful since the sprites contain blurred text and are difficult to identify otherwise.

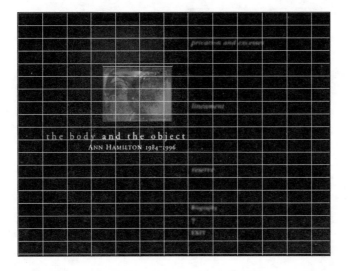

6] Turn off the grid and grid snapping.

To do this, choose View > Grids > Show and View > Snap To to uncheck those options.

Next you'll change the end frames of the sprites that make up the main menu.

CREATING A BEHAVIOR FOR NAVIGATIONAL ELEMENTS

In this task you will create a new behavior that you'll assign to the menu options you've just aligned with the grid. These menu options will be the navigational elements that users click to see the artwork. Later you'll assign scripts to these sprites that will move users to other screens in the multimedia art gallery. When you finish this task, the dimmed text in each sprite you have already placed on the stage will change to a readable selection when you move the cursor over it.

1] Double-click frame 27 in the behavior channel. In the Script window, type *go to the frame*. Then close the Script window.

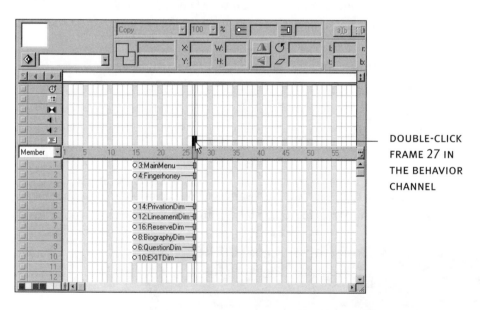

DOUBLE-CLICK
FRAME 27 IN
THE BEHAVIOR
CHANNEL

From your experience with Lingo scripts in Lesson 5, you know this script makes the playback head stay in the frame where it encounters the script. For users to be able to see the result of the behavior you're going to create, the playback head needs to stay in one place. When you assign a script to a cell in the behavior channel, you create a **frame script**. These scripts are different from other scripts you've created for sprites and cast members. Frame scripts do not require that users do anything. Director carries out the instructions in the script when the playback head is in the frame that contains the script.

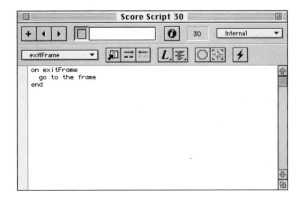

```
Score Script 30

+ ◄ ►  □          ❶  30  Internal  ▼

exitFrame  ▼    🗗 ⇄ ⇤  L ≣  ○   ⚡

on exitFrame
   go to the frame
end
```

You should not put the script in frame 15, because later you will add a transition to this frame in the transition channel. When a transition and a *go to the frame* script occur in the same frame, Director keeps playing the transition over and over. Otherwise, where you place the frame script is largely a matter of preference. Because no animation or transitions occur in frames 16 through 27, you can pause the playback head in any of those frames and achieve the same effect. One standard convention, however, is to place the script at the end of the sprite's duration, which is why frame 27 was chosen here.

With the script in frame 27, the transition occurs and then the playback head moves into frame 27, where the script holds the playback head in place. This makes the menu remain on display for your viewers so they can choose one of the menu options.

2] On the stage, click the 14:privationDim sprite you placed near the top of the stage. Then click the Behavior Inspector icon in the Sprite Overlay for the selected sprite.

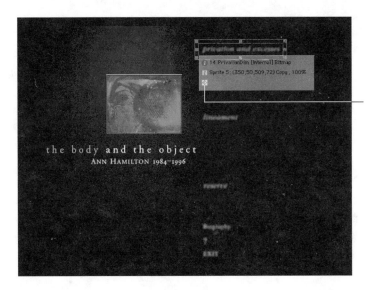

CLICK THE BEHAVIOR INSPECTOR ICON IN THE SPRITE OVERLAY PANEL TO OPEN THE BEHAVIOR INSPECTOR

The Behavior Inspector opens. If the Events and Actions panels aren't already visible, click the arrow to expand the Behavior Inspector's editing panels, so that the Behavior Inspector window looks like this:

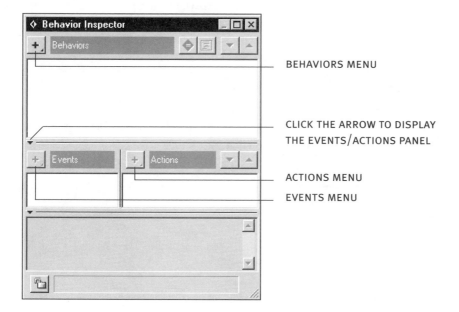

BEHAVIORS MENU

CLICK THE ARROW TO DISPLAY
THE EVENTS/ACTIONS PANEL

ACTIONS MENU

EVENTS MENU

3] In the Behavior Inspector, choose New Behavior from the Behaviors menu. In the Name Behavior dialog box that appears, name the new behavior *Button1*. Then click OK to close the dialog box.

Once you name the behavior, it appears in the Behaviors panel of the Behavior Inspector.

265

4] Open the Events menu and choose Mouse Within.

The *mouseWithin* event occurs repeatedly while the user's mouse cursor is inside the boundaries of the sprite. The boundaries are those lines and handles you can see when the sprite is selected on the stage. Next you'll define the action Director should take when the *mouseWithin* event occurs.

> **tip** *The Events menu shows event names in a generic form, such as Mouse Within. The Events list shows the event as it would be referred to in a Lingo script, such as* mouseWithin.

5] Open the Actions menu and choose Sprite › Change Cast Member. Then select the Privation cast member from the menu and click OK.

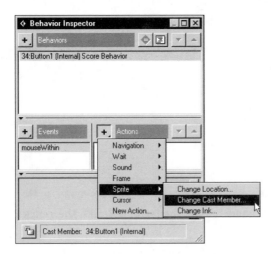

This action you're pairing with the *mouseWithin* event allows you to select a cast member that will be used to replace the currently selected sprite. A sprite of the cast member you select will appear in place of the original sprite when the *mouseWithin* event occurs. By selecting the Privation cast member, you're selecting the clear text version of the sprite.

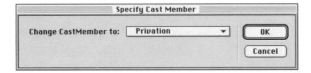

Now you've created one event and action combination for a behavior that applies to the sprite you selected in step 1. When users move the cursor within the boundaries of the sprite on the stage, the dimmed text sprite will be exchanged for a clearer version of itself.

266

Now you will add an event and action to the behavior that will redisplay the dimmed text sprite when a user moves the cursor off the sprite.

6] With the Button1 behavior still selected in the Behaviors panel, choose Mouse Leave from the Events menu. Choose Sprite › Change Cast Member to member from the Actions menu, select the PrivationDim cast member, and click OK.

Now two events are assigned to the Button1 behavior: *mouseWithin* and *mouseLeave*. Director detects a *mouseLeave* event when the cursor leaves the boundaries of the sprite to which that behavior applies.

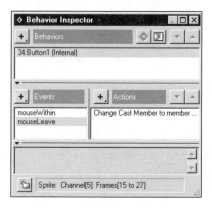

You can assign as many events as you like to a behavior and then apply the behavior to any sprite. Director can detect the differences between the events you assign to a behavior and then perform one or more actions in response.

The Sprite Overlay for the selected sprite now displays its Button1 behavior assignment next to the Behavior Inspector icon.

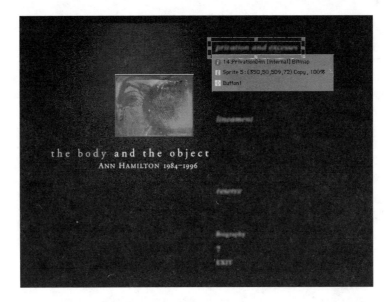

7] Save your work.

8] Rewind and play the movie. Move the cursor over the sprite to which you assigned the Button1 behavior and then move the cursor off the sprite.

You can read the menu option when you move the cursor over the sprite, because of the *mouseWithin* behavior you defined. Then when you move the cursor off the sprite, the text returns to its original, dimmed state, because of the *mouseLeave* behavior you defined. In the next steps, you'll create behaviors for the other two works of art in the multimedia art gallery: *lineament* and *reserve*.

9] On the stage, click the 12:LineamentDim sprite. With the Behavior Inspector still open, create a new Button2 behavior with a *mouseWithin* event and a Sprite › Exchange Cast Member action that exchanges the sprite with the Lineament cast member. Then add a *mouseLeave* event and an action that exchanges the sprite with the LineamentDim cast member.

10] Click the 16:ReserveDim sprite and create a Button3 behavior. Assign *mouseWithin* and *mouseLeave* events to the Button3 behavior that exchange the sprite with the Reserve and ReserveDim cast members, respectively.

Now all three of the menu options that represent works of art have similar, but separate, behaviors assigned to them. In Lesson 13, you will define the actions that occur when these menu options are clicked.

For now, the behaviors you've assigned change only the way these navigational elements appear when users explore the main menu.

11] Close the Behavior Inspector and save your work.

ON YOUR OWN

To complete the assignment of behaviors to the navigational elements you've placed on the stage, create new behaviors for the 8:BiographyDim, 6:QuestionDim, and 10:EXITDim sprites. This gives you more practice using the Behavior Inspector to create similar behaviors.

Separate behaviors are needed for each of the sprites because the desired effect for each sprite is unique to the sprite. Creating one behavior for all the sprites would be feasible if the same cast member appeared for the same event. For instance, if you wanted your viewers to see a particular image of the artist every time they moved the mouse over the sprites, you could create a behavior that included a *mouseWithin* event and a Sprite > Exchange Cast Member action for which you select that particular image.

REDUCING THE FILE SIZE OF A BITMAP

You will frequently be concerned with keeping file size to a minimum to help reduce download time for Shockwave files or to ensure that your final product will fit the disk on which it will be shipped. Many graphical cast members—both those you import and those you create in Director's Paint window—take up unnecessary space in your movie as 8-bit cast members. The simpler graphical images that are only one or two colors can easily be reduced to lower bit sizes. In this task, you'll use one technique for reducing the size of a graphical cast member.

1] Select the cast member 5, Line, in the cast.
This slim line will appear under the title on the main menu of the presentation. In the following steps and tasks, you'll reduce the size of this cast member, work with its color information, and place it in the score.

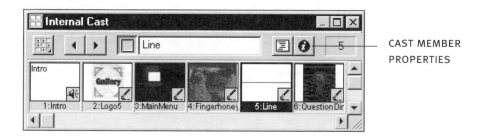

CAST MEMBER
PROPERTIES

2] Click the Cast Member Properties button.

Notice the size of the graphic in the lower-left corner of the dialog box.

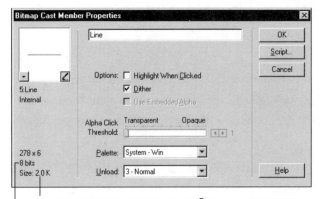

FILE SIZE OF THE BITMAP AT AN 8-BIT COLOR DEPTH

CURRENT COLOR BIT DEPTH OF THE LINE CAST MEMBER

3] Close the dialog box.

4] With the Line cast member still selected, choose Modify › Transform Bitmap.

The Transform Bitmap dialog box opens. The following illustration shows the dialog box that Windows users see. Macintosh users will see a dialog box with System - Mac selected as the Palette option for the graphic.

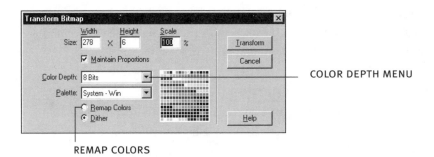

COLOR DEPTH MENU

REMAP COLORS

5] From the Color Depth menu, choose 1 Bit. Then choose Remap Colors and click Transform.

A warning appears; the change you are about to make cannot be undone.

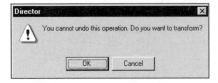

6] Click OK to transform the 8-bit cast member to 1-bit color depth.

This reduces the size of the graphic. The original graphic was 8 bits. An 8-bit graphic stores more color information and therefore takes more disk space than a 1-bit graphic. Transforming images to 1-bit color means creating a black-and-white image from the original color information in the image. For the line graphic, this color choice will be fine.

The Line cast member is now black. Clicking Transform changes to black all the pixels in an image that are closer to black than white; likewise, all the pixels that are closer to white become white.

7] Select the Line cast member in the cast again. Then click the Cast Member Properties button to check the size of the graphic.

Notice the size of the graphic in the lower-left corner of the dialog box. The graphic is much smaller than before.

FILE SIZE OF THE BITMAP IMAGE AT A 1-BIT COLOR DEPTH

NEW COLOR BIT DEPTH OF THE LINE CAST MEMBER

tip   *Most users browsing the Internet are using modems with speeds of 28.8 Kbps or 33.6 Kbps. When you are creating Shockwave movies embedded in Web pages, you need to keep your movies as small as possible for these modems to download the pages in an acceptable amount of time. Transforming graphics from 8 bits to 1 bit reduces the amount of storage space the bitmap needs and also enables faster downloading. Also, Web pages now see users from many different countries, and in some of those countries users pay dearly for telephone connectivity and greatly appreciate quick-loading pages.*

271

8] Drag the Line cast member to channel 3, frame 15, and position it under the title on the stage. Set the ink to Background Transparent.

You can see that the Line sprite is black and too close in color to the MainMenu sprite to show up well. You'll fix this in the next task.

9] With the line sprite still selected, choose Window › Tool Palette (Windows Ctrl+7, Macintosh Command+7) to open the tool palette.

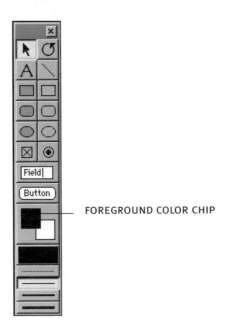

FOREGROUND COLOR CHIP

10] From the foreground color chip on the tool palette, choose an orange color that matches as closely as possible the orange used for the type.

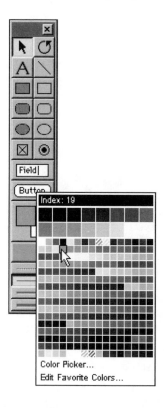

Even though the cast member itself is just black and white, you can display a color version of it on the stage by applying a foreground color to its sprite. The foreground color takes the place of the black pixels in the cast member while it is on the stage. This technique lets you keep the size of a cast member very small while not losing the ability to display it in color.

11] Choose View › Sprite Overlay › Show Info to turn off the Sprite Overlay (Windows Ctrl+Shift+Alt+O, Macintosh Control+ Shift+Command+O).

Turning off the Sprite Overlay helps you see the elements of the screen you're building.

12] Save your work.

273

FINDING AN INDEX COLOR NUMBER

Index color numbers are associated with each color in a color palette. These numbers help you identify colors. Index color 0 is always at the top left of the palette. Index color 255 is always at the bottom right of the palette (assuming that the palette contains 256 colors). Colors are numbered from left to right, top to bottom.

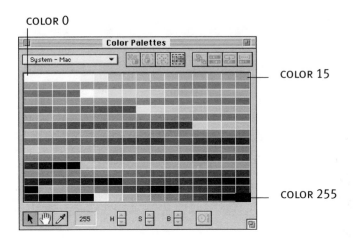

If you know the exact location of a color in the color palette (by determining its index color number), you can verify that you have assigned the same color to another object for which you want to use the same color. Also, if another person is working on a graphic that requires a specific color in a palette, you can specify the index color number to use. Of course, you could simply look closely at the color palette and describe the location of the color: for example, "it's 2 over and 9 down." However, identifying a color in a particular palette by its index color number helps you communicate the exact color you want applied to an image. You'll need to identify colors in this manner for graphic designers and others who are developing images for your Director movies. The Color Picker identifies color position at the top of the dialog box.

1] Double-click cast member 4 to open the Paint window. Choose Window › Color Palettes (Windows Ctrl+Alt+7, Macintosh Command+Option+7) to open the Color Palettes window. Arrange the two windows side by side.

2] Select a color from the foreground color chip in the Paint window's tool panel.
Notice that the same color is selected in the Color Palettes window. The index color of the selected color is shown in the small window at the bottom of the Color Palettes window.

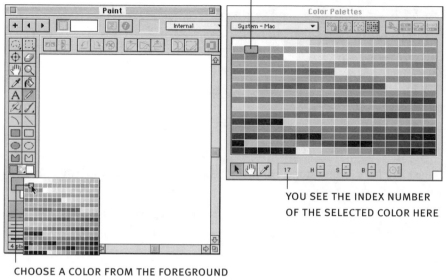

WHEN YOU CHOOSE A COLOR IN THE PAINT WINDOW, THE SAME COLOR IS SELECTED HERE IN THE COLOR PALETTE WINDOW

YOU SEE THE INDEX NUMBER OF THE SELECTED COLOR HERE

CHOOSE A COLOR FROM THE FOREGROUND COLOR CHIP IN THE PAINT WINDOW

The palette that is open in the Paint window and that appears in the Color Palettes window is the default palette you chose in an earlier task. The palette you see depends on the type of computer you are using. Macintosh users will see the Macintosh system palette (as shown in this illustration); Windows users will see the Windows system palette.

In the Color Palettes window, you can see the difference between the two system palettes by choosing one or the other from the menu at the top of the window. For example, choose color number 17, as shown in the illustration. When the System - Win palette is selected in the Color Palettes window, you'll see a pink color. When the System - Mac palette is selected, you'll see an orange color.

3] Close the Paint and Color Palettes windows.

MODIFYING SPRITE PROPERTIES

You've seen that you can set the location of sprites by opening the Sprite Properties dialog box and entering values for the sprite's Left and Top coordinates. In that same dialog box, you can change the width and height of a sprite. In the next task, you'll make the Line sprite thinner.

275

1] Select the sprite in channel 3 and then choose Modify › Sprite › Properties.

The Sprite Properties dialog box appears.

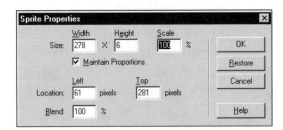

2] Uncheck Maintain Proportions. For the height of the Line sprite, specify *1*. Then click OK to close the dialog box.

Be sure Maintain Proportions is unchecked; otherwise, the width of the sprite will be scaled proportionately. Uncheck Maintain Proportions first, before you type in the Height field.

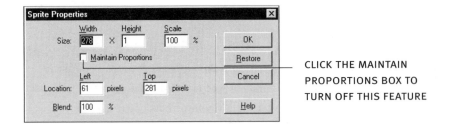

CLICK THE MAINTAIN PROPORTIONS BOX TO TURN OFF THIS FEATURE

The Line sprite is resized.

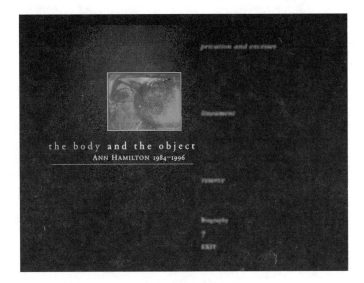

In the remaining steps of this task, you'll create a new cast member right on the stage. Then you'll use the Sprite Properties dialog box to change the location and size of other sprites you place in the score using this single cast member.

3] Click frame 15 in the frame channel to move the playback head to frame 15.
This ensures that the new sprite you want to create will appear in the correct frames.

4] Click the Filled Ellipse tool in the tool palette and then create a small circle on the stage at the left end of the line. Use the following illustration as a guide for the location of this new element.

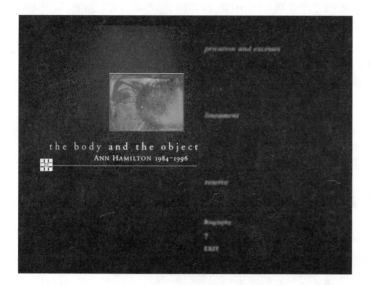

You'll use this small circle as a design element on the stage. The filled ellipse is added to the cast when you create it. The icon in the lower-right corner of the thumbnail image is the icon for a shape cast member. Shape cast members are created using the tools on the tool palette.

5] In the cast, select the filled ellipse cast member you just created. Then type *Dot* in the Cast window's name field and press Enter (Windows) or Return (Macintosh).

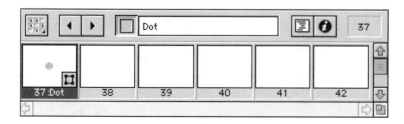

277

Naming cast members is a good habit to get into so you or someone else can easily locate them later.

6] Reselect the Dot sprite on the stage, choose Modify › Sprite › Properties, and note the top coordinate of the sprite.

You're going to add another Dot sprite at the other end of the Line sprite. Knowing this top coordinate will help you align the two sprites in the next steps. Write this number down for later reference. Then click Cancel to close the Sprite Properties window.

7] Drag the Dot cast member from the Cast window into channel 12, frame 15. Then drag the sprite to a position on the stage at the right end of the Line sprite.

8] With the sprite still selected, choose Modify › Sprite › Properties and enter the same top coordinate you noted in step 6. Click OK to close the Sprite Properties window.

Now the two Dot sprites are aligned horizontally.

9] Drag the Dot cast member to channel 13, frame 15. Choose Modify › Sprite › Properties and set the width and height to *10* and *10*. Then set the location to *155, 105*.

Look at the stage to see where you have placed this new Dot sprite, which is a different size than the others.

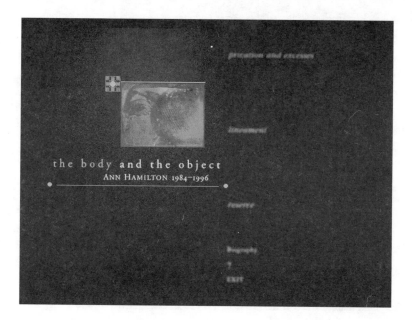

Entering these new properties resizes and relocates the sprite. As you can see, the Sprite Properties dialog box is very useful. You will be using it frequently in your Director development.

tip   *All objects created with the tool palette tools can be modified as sprites on the stage without affecting the parent cast member. Note that Director can much more quickly display resized objects that are created using the tools in the tool palette than it can resize imported graphics or ones created with the paint tools. Reusing the same cast member also saves storage space. Once the cast member is on the stage, you can resize the sprite or change any of its attributes, and it will look like a different cast member entirely.*

All the sprites that make up the main menu are now on the stage and sequenced in the score.

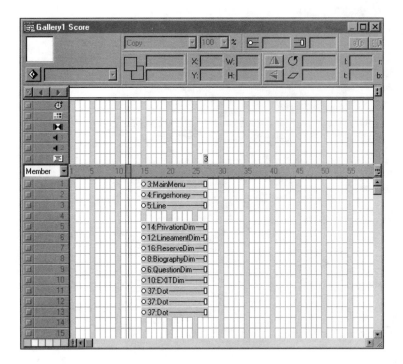

To complement the front-end of the multimedia art gallery, you'll next create a beginning for the movie using a logo and a sound. In the next two lessons you'll create the screens and navigation scripts that will allow your viewers to see what's in the presentation.

ADDING A BACKGROUND SOUND

Now you'll add a sound and logo to the beginning of the presentation. These movie elements will serve as a sort of advertisement that users will see as the presentation begins. In this task you'll add these elements along with some transitions that will present the main menu to users after the sound finishes playing.

1] Drag the Intro cast member to sound channel 1, frame 1, in the score.
As with all the other sprites you've created for this lesson, Director adds the sound sprite with a 13-frame duration. You can now see why you have earlier been creating your main menu at frame 15. The sprites for the opening sequence will span frames 1 through 13. Frame 14 is left blank to improve the readability of the score. The main menu section starts at frame 15.

Next you'll create a tempo setting that signals Director to play the whole sound before letting the playback head advance.

tip *Instead of dragging a sound from the Cast window, you can double-click the sound channel to display a dialog box that lists available sounds. Choosing Modify > Frame > Sound opens the same dialog box.*

tip *If you have sound in only one frame, occasionally it won't play smoothly. To avoid this problem, always extend sounds so they're at least two frames long.*

2] Double-click frame 13 of the tempo channel. In the dialog box, click Wait for Cue Point, select {End} in the Cue Point field, and then click OK.

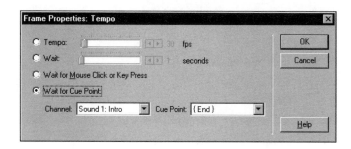

Cue points are fixed points within a sound file; they are similar to markers in a Director score. By default, every sound file in the cast has a start cue point and an end cue point. You can add additional cue points to a sound file using a sound editing program like Macromedia's SoundEdit 16.

As a sound plays, Director looks for cue points in the sound files, and you can use those cue points to control the movement of the playback head. In this case, you have instructed Director to keep the playback head in frame 13 until it encounters the end cue point—that is, until the sound finishes playing. Without this tempo setting, you would hear only a few notes of the sound as the playback head traveled quickly through frames 1 through 13 and then immediately continued on.

Next you'll place the logo in the score so users have something to view while they hear the sound play.

3] Drag the Logo5 cast member to frame 1, channel 1.

Your score should now look like this:

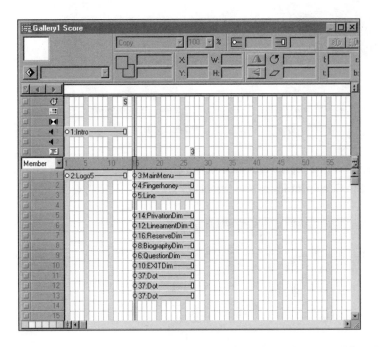

The presentation begins with a nice sound and a logo, but the logo just disappears when the playback head reaches the blank stage in frame 14, and the menu appears quickly after that. In the next step you'll add two transitions that will make the appearance of the menu much more dramatic.

4] Double-click frame 14 of the transition channel, select an Edges In, Square transition, and click OK.

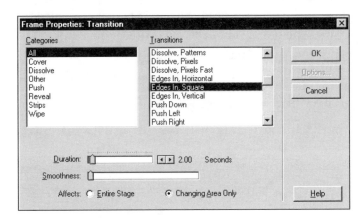

5] Double-click frame 15 of the transition channel, select Center Out, Square, and click OK.

The two transitions will make the logo seem to collapse into the middle of the screen. This focuses the user's eyes on the center of the stage, and from that point, your main menu appears. Very dramatic!

6] Save your work and play the movie.

Now the logo begins the movie as the sound plays. Then the transitions you just added reveal the main menu. The playback head pauses so users can begin to get the feel of the presentation they will be exploring.

So far, you've been concentrating on creating the layout of the presentation's opening. You'll be adding more frames to this movie in the next two lessons.

WHAT YOU HAVE LEARNED

In this lesson you have:

• Set a movie palette [page 249]

• Changed the default length of new sprites [page 251]

• Organized cast members in a logical sequence [page 252]

• Used the Sprite Overlay and Sprite Properties dialog boxes to set locations of sprites [page 256]

• Used grid settings and snapping to align objects [page 258]

• Created behaviors for navigational elements [page 263]

• Transformed a sprite from 8 bits to 1 bit to reduce file size [page 269]

• Used the tool palette to color sprites [page 272]

• Determined a color's index color number [page 274]

• Modified the dimensions of a sprite [page 275]

• Added a background sound [page 280]

navigation
markers and

In the previous lesson you created the introduction and main menu for a multimedia art gallery by adding sound, graphics, and menu options that change into other images when you move the mouse over them. In this lesson, you will add scripts to these menu options that will allow users to go to the corresponding work of art in the gallery when they click a menu option.

You will also create the destination screens that contain the artwork and the markers that identify the locations of the artwork in the score. Finally, you'll use relative markers to allow users to navigate backward and forward through a series of screens in the presentation.

LESSON 13

privation and excesses Capp Street Project, San Francisco, 1989

Director allows you to mark any part of your movie so you can go to it with a mouse click. In this lesson, you'll create the screens that contain the artworks in the multimedia art gallery. Then you'll insert markers in the score and assign each of the works a location in the presentation so you'll be able to navigate to each work with a click of the mouse. Using markers and creating your own navigation controls for presentations are skills you'll rely on in all the Director projects you'll build on your own.

If you would like to view the final result of this lesson, open the Complete folder in the Lesson13 folder and play Gallery2.dir.

WHAT YOU WILL LEARN

In this lesson you will:

• Practice inserting and using markers

• Build screens you can reuse in a presentation

• Practice exchanging cast members

• Practice navigating to markers

• Navigate relative to the playback head

APPROXIMATE TIME

It should take about 1½ hours to complete this lesson

LESSON FILES

Media Files:

None

Starting Files:

Lesson13\Start.dir

Completed Project:

Lesson13\Complete\Gallery2.dir

INSERTING MARKERS

You'll start by inserting markers for the frames that will display the artworks in the gallery. Just as in Lesson 5, you will use markers to indicate where certain sections of the movie are located so Director can navigate to those sections when users click a menu option. After you insert the markers, you'll set up navigation scripts for the menu options you created on the main menu so users will be able to see the artwork.

1] Open Start.dir in the Start folder within the Lesson13 folder and save it as *Gallery2.dir* in your Projects folder.

This is the prebuilt file that contains the introduction and the main menu. If you completed the last lesson, you can use the movie you created there instead. Save it as *Gallery2.dir* in your Projects folder.

2] Choose File › Preferences › Sprite to open the Sprite Preferences dialog box. Type *13* for the Span Duration and click OK.

Just as you did in the previous lesson, you set up Director to add sprites to the score with a 13-frame duration. This duration is long enough so you can see the cast member names in the score, making the score easier for you to work with.

3] Click frame 15 in the marker channel and type *Main* as the marker name. Then press Enter (Windows) or Return (Macintosh).

CLICK FRAME 15 IN THE MARKER CHANNEL

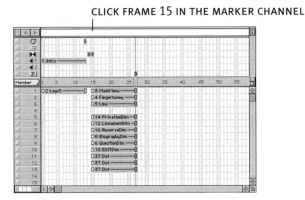

This marker indicates the location of the main menu frame, as shown below. You'll need a marker for the main menu so you can write a Lingo script that returns users to the main menu from the destination screens. After you insert the markers, you'll build these screens. The destination screens will contain the artwork and other content relevant to the presentation.

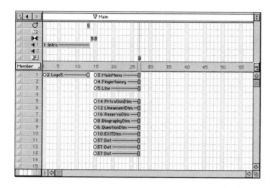

4] Insert markers in frames 30, 45, and 60 and name them *Priv*, *Line*, and *Res*, respectively.

These markers indicate the locations of the destination screens that will display the different works of art in the gallery. The names you've given them are just long enough to identify the artwork they refer to.

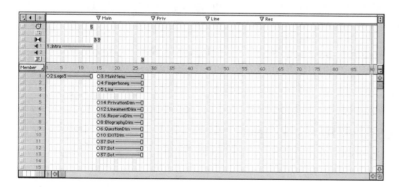

There's no magic formula for selecting the frames where markers appear. Placing these markers 15 frames apart makes sense because this spacing puts some empty frames between each of the markers so they can be viewed as distinct pieces of the presentation. Since you changed the default sprite length to 13 frames—and no more than 13 frames will be needed to display the sprites that make up the destination screens—there will still be nice spaces between each destination screen in the presentation.

5] Insert a marker in frame 75 and name it _Bio_. Then insert another marker in frame 90 and name it _?_.

Now you have all the markers you'll need to display the art, biographical information about the artist, and navigation tips for this presentation.

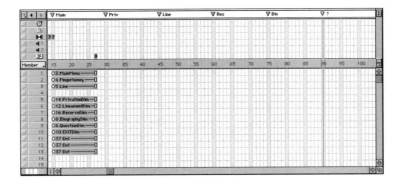

The markers _Priv, Line_, and _Res_ refer to the titles of the artwork that will be included on the destination screens associated with these markers. The _Bio_ marker refers to a screen of biographical information you'll create, and the _?_ marker refers to a screen of user tips for moving around in the presentation. When you look over the sprites that make up the menu options on the main menu screen, it is easy to determine which menu options will be used to move users to the markers. Good planning like this helps you (and others who may be working on your project) easily understand how the project works.

Don't worry about creating the _Exit_ marker—you'll do that in the next lesson.

6] Save your work.

BUILDING A DESTINATION SCREEN

Now you'll start adding sprites to the frame where you placed the _Priv_ marker. This destination screen will display the _privation and excesses_ art.

The screen you create in this task will contain elements you can reuse for the other screens. Presenting the same navigation controls from screen to screen gives viewers confidence as they explore your presentations.

288

1] **Drag the 20:PrivationArt cast member from the cast to channel 1, frame 30, in the score.**

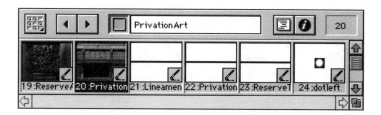

This is the artwork named *privation and excesses*. Notice that the sprite appears in frames 30 through 42 only. This is because you changed the default length of the sprite to 13 frames.

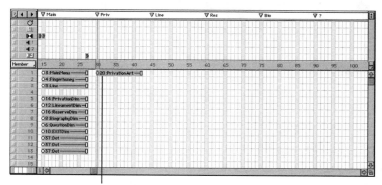

THE DEFAULT SPRITE DURATION IS 13 FRAMES

2] **Drag the following cast members to the channels and frames listed.**

These are the remaining elements for the screen that contains the *privation and excesses* art. One is a title identifying the art, and the other three elements are bitmap images that will be used as navigation controls.

22:PrivationTitle	Channel 2, frame 30
24:dotleft	Channel 3, frame 30
25:dotright	Channel 4, frame 30
26:dotbottom	Channel 5, frame 30

The PrivationArt image is centered on the stage by default because you dragged the cast member to the score to create this sprite. This is exactly where it should appear.

The sprites you moved to the score in this step are all stacked at the center of the stage, too. Next you'll place these elements where they should appear on the stage.

3] Hold down Shift and drag the sprite selected in the center of the stage to a position near the bottom of the stage.

This sprite is 26:dotbottom, a simple bitmap image of a white dot on a black background. Later you'll transform this image into a navigational control that sends users back to the main menu when they click it.

290

Two more sprites on the stage look just like the dotbottom sprite. You'll place these at the sides of the stage so users can click them to navigate to the next screen in the presentation or return to the previous screen.

4] Click the white dot at the center of the stage to select it, hold down the Shift key, and drag the white dot to the right edge of the stage. Then select the dot remaining at the stage's center and Shift-drag it to the left edge of the stage.

The dots should appear on the stage as shown in the following illustration. With three white dots as sprites on the stage, how can you be certain you have placed the dotright sprite on the right edge of the stage, the dotleft sprite at the left, and dotbottom at the bottom? That's right: use the View > Sprite Overlay > Show Info command and click each of the dot sprites on the stage to view its name in the panel.

In the previous lesson you created an orange dot as a cast member and then used that single dot to create two others on the stage. Here you have three separate white dot cast members. Why can't you use just one white dot cast member to create the other two? The answer lies in the way the white dots will be used. The orange dots are design elements placed on the stage for visual interest. The white dots will be navigational controls, and each dot will have a separate, unique Lingo script attached to it.

The scripts you'll write will enable users to click the white dots and navigate to different parts of the presentation. Because individual cast members can have only one script, you need three cast members to hold the three different scripts.

The only sprite left to place is the title of the artwork. You'll move that to the top of the stage in the next step.

5] Select the title sprite at the center of the stage and then Shift-drag the sprite to the top edge of the stage.

Each of the screens that displays artwork will look like the screen you've just composed. The only elements you'll need to change will be the title at the top of the stage and the art itself.

In the next few steps you'll copy the sprites associated with the *Priv* marker and paste them into the frames where the *Line* and *Res* markers appear. Then you'll use the Exchange Cast Member command to swap the necessary elements.

6] In the score, drag to select the sprites in frame 30, channels 1 through 5.
Be sure you begin dragging with the mouse in an empty cell of the score and not in the frame channel. If you begin to drag the sprites with the mouse in the frame channel, the playback head will move to the frame you click. If you begin to drag the sprites with the mouse in an occupied cell, the sprite in that cell will be affected.

CLICK AN EMPTY CELL TO BEGIN DRAGGING

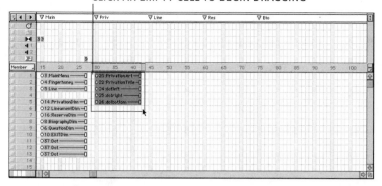

7] Copy the sprites (Windows Control+C, Macintosh Command+C) and then click channel 1, frame 45, and paste the sprites (Windows Control+V, Macintosh Control+V).

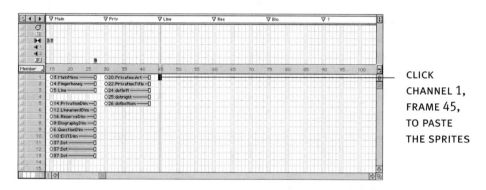

CLICK
CHANNEL 1,
FRAME 45,
TO PASTE
THE SPRITES

Copies of the sprites now appear beneath the *Line* marker. You'll continue pasting these sprites beneath the remaining markers.

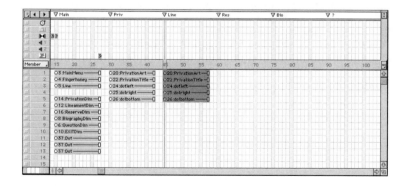

8] Paste the sprites in channel 1, frames 60, 75, and 90.

As you would expect, the score contains the same destination screen for each of the markers you inserted. Now it's time to use the Exchange Cast Member command to exchange the titles and artwork that go with the *Line* and *Res* markers.

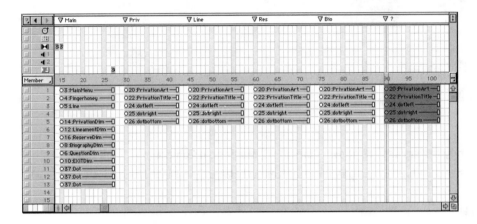

9] Save your work.

At this point, you have one of the destination screens built and copies of it distributed throughout the score where the other destination screens will appear. Using the Exchange Cast Member command, you can quickly insert the correct sprites in the copied screens so they display the correct images and titles.

EXCHANGING CAST MEMBERS

You've used the Exchange Cast Member command in earlier lessons. This Director feature allows you to swap images easily without having to place new images in the score or on the stage. This is the perfect feature for quickly exchanging the artwork that should appear in the frames that contain the *Line*, *Res*, *Bio*, and *?* markers.

1] Select the 20:PrivationArt sprite in frame 45, channel 1. Then select the 18:LineamentArt cast member in the Cast window and click Exchange Cast Member on the toolbar.

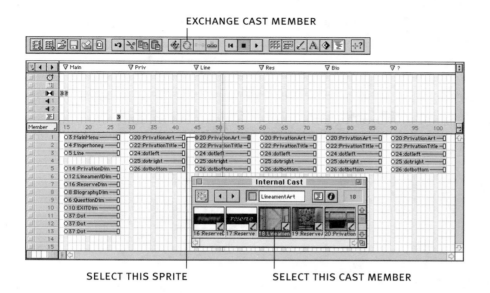

SELECT THIS SPRITE   SELECT THIS CAST MEMBER

In frame 45, the *privation and excesses* art is replaced with the *lineament* art. When users navigate to the *Line* marker, they will see this artwork. Now the title above the *lineament* art must be exchanged with the *privation and excesses* title so the artwork can be correctly identified.

EXCHANGE THIS TITLE WITH THE APPROPRIATE TITLE FOR THIS PANEL

privation and excesses Capp Street Project, San Francisco, 1989

2] Select the 22:PrivationTitle sprite in frame 45, channel 2. Exchange it for cast member 21:LineamentTitle.

The title above the image you exchanged now correctly identifies it.

THIS PANEL NOW DISPLAYS THE CORRECT TITLE

3] Use Exchange Cast Member to display the correct image and title for the *reserve* art that should appear in frame 60 for the *Res* marker.

In just a few keystrokes, you have created three destination screens for the *Priv*, *Line*, and *Res* markers you inserted for this presentation. You can check the sprite labels to make sure you have exchanged the correct cast members.

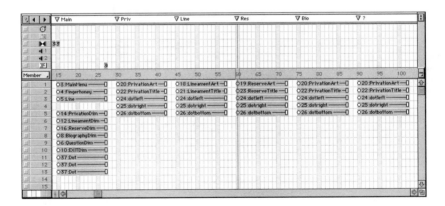

You have two destination screens to complete. These screens will be displayed when users click the Biography and ? menu options. Each needs a new image to replace the 20:PrivationArt sprite, but they don't need titles, so the 22:PrivationTitle sprites can be deleted from these groups of sprites.

4] Use the Exchange Cast Member command to display the 28:BioPage image in channel 1, frame 75. Then select the 22:PrivationTitle sprite in channel 2 beneath it and press Delete.

This page contains biographical information about the artist and does not need a title. For the next screen, you'll also exchange an image and delete the title.

5] Use Exchange Cast Member to display the 27:UserTips image in channel 1, frame 90. Then delete the 22:PrivationTitle sprite beneath it in channel 2.

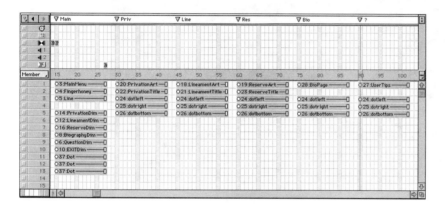

All the destinations screens now contain the elements that your viewers will see when they navigate to them.

6] Save your work.

Now there are screens to navigate to from the main menu. Next you'll return to the main menu to work on the navigation controls that will display the new screens.

NAVIGATING TO A MARKER

When the movie plays, you want to be able to get to the frames with the *Priv, Line,* and *Res* markers from the main menu by clicking the corresponding menu options. To make that happen, you will add to the behaviors you created for the first three menu options on the main menu.

1] In the score, click frame 15 in the frame channel.

On the stage you can see the main menu you created in the preceding lesson.

2] Choose View > Sprite Overlay > Show Info (Windows Ctrl+Shift+Alt+O, Macintosh Command+Shift+Option+O).

This turns on the Sprite Overlay feature so you can see the behaviors already assigned to the sprites when they're selected on the stage.

3] Click the 14:PrivationDim sprite in the upper-right corner of the stage.

The Sprite Overlay panel for this sprite appears.

4] Click the Behaviors icon in the Sprite Overlay panel.

If the other panels of the Behavior Inspector are not open, click the arrows to open them.

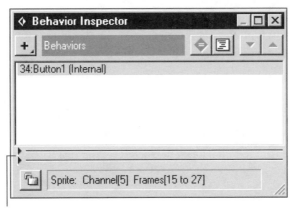

EXPANSION ARROWS

298

The Behavior Inspector appears, and the Button1 behavior is listed in the Behaviors panel. Next you'll add another type of event and action combination.

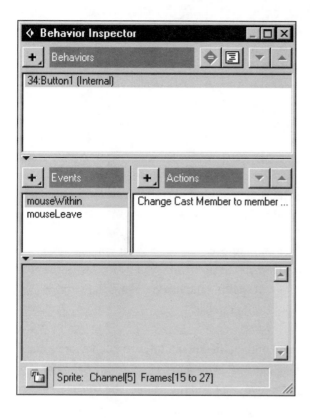

5] From the Events menu, choose mouseDown. Then from the Actions menu, choose Navigation › Go to Marker.

A dialog box asks you to chose the marker you want to go to.

6] From the menu in the dialog box, select the *Priv* marker. Then click OK.

Now when the *privation and excesses* sprite is clicked, a *mouseDown* event message is sent to Director, which branches the playback head to the *Priv* marker. This new event is now one of three that you've assigned to this sprite in the Button1 behavior you created in the previous lesson. As this example shows you, many Lingo instructions can be executed from a single behavior that applies to one sprite.

When you were introduced to navigation scripts in Lesson 5, great emphasis was placed on spelling the marker name correctly in the scripts you wrote. Using the Behavior Inspector takes the worry out of spelling the marker name correctly because you can simply select a marker from the list.

7] Select the sprite for the next menu option, lineament. Click the Behaviors icon in the Sprite Overlay panel and add a *mouseDown* event to its Button2 behavior. For the action, choose Navigation › Go to Marker and then select the *Line* marker. Now Director will move the playback head to the *Line* marker in the score when users click the lineament menu option on the main menu.

8] Add a *mouseDown* event to the Button3 behavior assigned to the reserve menu option. Make sure the action you select moves the playback head to the *Res* marker in the score.

9] Save your work.

10] Rewind and play the movie.
After the introduction, the playback head is held on frame 27, because of the *go to the frame* script you added to the behavior channel in the previous lesson. The playback head will not move forward until the user makes a selection from the menu.

11] Click the privations and excesses menu option and watch the playback head.
The playback head branches to the *Priv* marker because of the *mouseDown* event you added to the sprite's Button1 behavior. Then the playback head continues on to the

end of the presentation because no other instructions control the playback head. To keep the playback head on this frame, you can loop on the frame. You will do that in the next task.

12] Add a *mouseDown* event to the Button4 and Button5 behaviors assigned to the Biography and Question menu options, respectively. Make sure you choose the correct markers to go to. The Exit menu option does not get a *mouseDown* behavior just yet.

13] Stop the movie and close the Behavior Inspector.

Good work! You've just built some destination frames and added navigation to them using the Behavior Inspector.

LOOPING ON A FRAME

One way to keep the playback head from advancing in the score is to create a script that instructs Director to go back to a particular frame. Then every time the playback head arrives in the frame where the script occurs, the playback head will be moved back to the designated frame. The frame the playback head moves to may be the frame in which the script occurs or it may be any other frame in the score.

1] Double-click the behavior channel, frame 30. Type *go to frame "Priv"* below *on exitFrame*. Then press Enter on the numeric keypad to close the Script window.

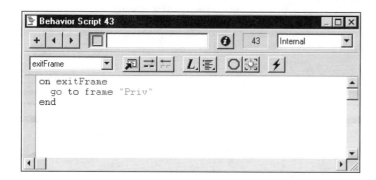

When you open the Script window, it already displays *on exitFrame* and *end*. The *on exitFrame* command is the default event for frame scripts. Remember that when you double-click the behavior channel, you create a frame script.

Now when the playback head moves to frame 30, it will stay in that frame because it will keep looping to frame "Priv" (frame 30). You need not worry that the playback head will never travel through frames 31 to 42. No action occurs in those frames, so you can place this frame script anywhere from frame 30 to 42 and still achieve the same effect.

Did you notice that the script you wrote was *go to frame "MarkerName"* and not *go to marker "MarkerName"*? Director interprets this instruction as "go to a frame with a marker named *MarkerName*" and does not need to differentiate between a frame and a marker since they are the same to Director. You can use either *go to frame* or *go to marker*.

You may have been wondering what the difference is between scripts created by double-clicking the behavior channel and the sprite scripts you've put together in the Behavior Inspector or the cast member scripts you've assigned to cast members. Unlike sprite and cast member scripts, frame scripts don't require user input to be activated. You use frame scripts when you want Lingo instructions to be activated when the playback head is within a certain frame. In frame scripts, two events that are commonly specified are *on exitFrame* and *on enterFrame*. So far, you have used frame scripts to handle the *exitFrame* event. You need to add frame scripts in frames 45 and 60 to hold the playback head on the artwork destination screens.

2] Add a *go to frame "Line"* script to frame 45 in the behavior channel. Then add a *go to frame "Res"* script to frame 60 in the behavior channel.

Now the destination screens will stay on the stage as they should. The remaining destination screens will need the same script to hold the playback head in the frame.

3] Add scripts that will keep the playback head from moving past the *Bio* and *?* markers when the playback head is in the same frame as the marker.

When you've written all the scripts, you'll see numbers in the script channel. These numbers correspond to the cast member numbers because each script is now a cast member. You can reuse a script by dragging the script cast member to a frame in the behavior channel.

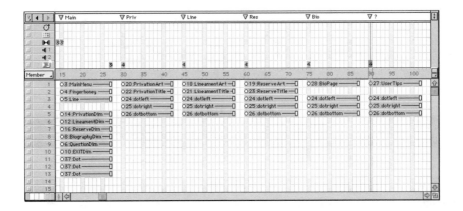

4] Save your work. Then rewind and play the movie several times to navigate to each of the destination screens and test your frame scripts.

You've added much more control to the presentation, and now users can choose any menu option and arrive at a destination screen. Watch the playback head as you click the menu options. The playback head stops and waits on these screens because you've inserted frame scripts that loop the playback head—but where can users go from there? These screens contain the white dot navigation controls. You'll set up navigation for them in the next task.

The UserTips destination explains how to navigate through the presentation. Read the information on this page to understand how the original designer supplied some creative ideas in the professionally produced CD-ROM of Ann Hamilton's work, *the body and the object*. You have reproduced some of the effects presented on the CD-ROM; now you know how to produce some of the other effects mentioned in the text on this screen.

USING RELATIVE MARKERS

If you want navigation controls to display the previous screen or the next screen in a series, it is best to use **relative markers**. As you know, when you play a movie, the playback head moves left to right across the score, and markers can appear anywhere in the score. So far, you've been referring to markers by their names (as in *go to frame* "*Priv*"). However, you can also refer to a marker by its position relative to the playback head. To identify a marker without using its name, you use a numbering scheme.

As the playback head moves, marker(0) is the marker in the current frame or the marker the playback head has most recently passed. The first marker to the right of marker(0) is marker(1), and so on; the first marker to the left of marker(0) is marker(–1), and so on. These markers are numbered *relative* to the position of the playback head, and they always refer to a destination based on the current position of the playback head, not to a destination in a specific frame.

Study the following two illustrations of the score. They're the same except that the position of the playback head is different. Notice how the relative marker locations change based on the location of the playback head.

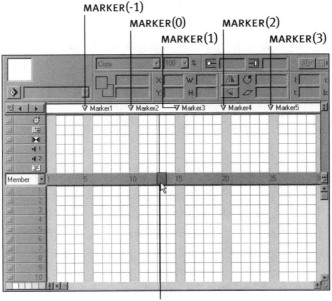

MARKER(-1)
MARKER(0)
MARKER(1)
MARKER(2)
MARKER(3)

PLAYBACK HEAD IN FRAME 13

Marker(0) is the marker in the current frame or the marker the playback head has most recently passed. In the above illustration, the playback head is in frame 13, which has no marker. The marker the playback head has most recently passed is in frame 10, so marker(0) is the marker named *Marker2*.

The markers in the next illustration are exactly the same as the ones in the above illustration. The difference here is that the playback head is now in frame 15. This frame contains a marker, so marker(0) is the marker in this frame, named *Marker3*.

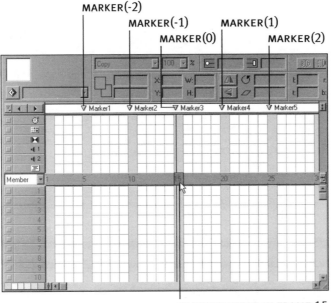

MARKER(-2)
MARKER(-1)
MARKER(0)
MARKER(1)
MARKER(2)

PLAYBACK HEAD IN FRAME 15

In this task, you'll add relative markers to scripts. When you want your viewers to navigate to a previous or next screen in a series, it is best to use relative markers. Instead of creating separate scripts to go to each marker in the presentation, you need to create only two scripts to go to the next and previous markers. You'll create cast member scripts using relative markers for the dotright and dotleft cast members. Then you'll create a cast member script for the dotbottom cast member that always returns your viewers to the main menu.

1] In the cast, select the 25:dotright cast member. Then click the Script icon in the Cast window to open the Script window.

SCRIPT ICON

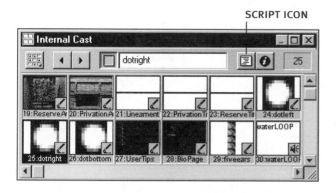

You are assigning a script to a cast member, so the instructions you add to the cast member will apply to all the sprites in the score that relate to this cast member. This way you have to write the script only once, and automatically all the dotright sprites on the destination screens you've created will use the script.

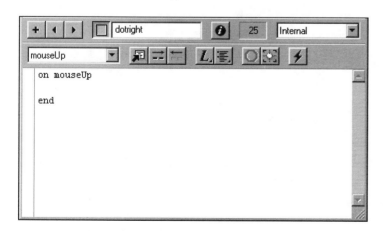

2] In the Script window for the 25:dotright cast member, type *go to marker (1)* below *on mouseUp* and then close the window.

When the user releases the mouse button, the playback head will branch to the next marker to the right in the score. If there is no marker to navigate to, the playback head remains in place. This would be the case when users click the dotright sprite on the screen that displays the user tips since there are no more markers in the score after frame 90.

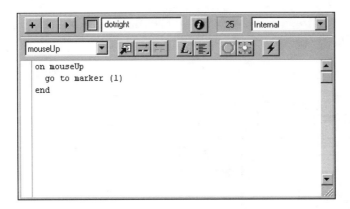

3] Select the 24:dotleft cast member in the cast and then click the Script icon to add a cast member script. In the Script window, type *go to marker (–1)* below *on mouseUp* and then close the window.

When users click the dot at the left edge of the stage, the playback head will branch to the first marker to the left of the playback head.

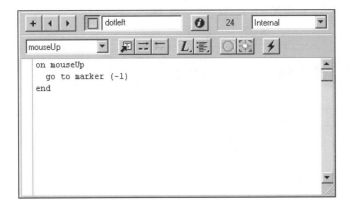

One more cast member needs a script assigned to it: the dotbottom cast member. This cast member doesn't need a reference to a relative marker since it always returns the playback head to the main menu.

4] Select the 26:dotbottom cast member and then click Script. In the Script window, type *go frame "Main"* below *on mouseUp* and then close the window.

This script will branch the playback head to the frame with the *"Main"* marker.

> **tip** *You can also type* go to frame *"Main"* or go *"Main"* *and everything will still work the same.*

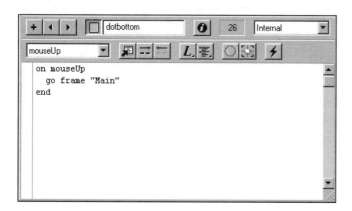

5] Rewind and play the movie. Click a menu item and then use the dots to return to the menu.

Now you can select a menu item and see a destination screen, and you can use the dots to navigate backward and forward.

SIMPLIFYING SCRIPTS USING RELATIVE MARKERS

In the next task you'll use relative markers in another way.

1] Select the behavior channel, frame 30, and delete the script by pressing Delete. Also delete the scripts in frames 45, 60, 75, and 90 of the behavior channel.

The scripts in these frames were *go to frame "MarkerName"* scripts. You placed these scripts here to keep the playback head on these frames so users could make another selection on the screen. You still need to keep the playback head from moving past all the frames of the destination screens, but you're going to refer to a relative marker instead.

The *go to frame "MarkerName"* script would still work, of course, but with relative markers, you can write just one script and have it work effectively in many sections.

2] Double-click the behavior channel, frame 31, to open the Script window. Type
go marker(0) **below** *on exitFrame* **and then close the window.**

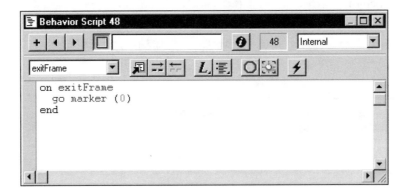

This script returns the playback head to frame 30, which is the closest frame to the left that contains a marker.

tip   *It is best to leave the* go frame *script in frame 27 of the behavior channel because looping the playback head to frame 15 would trigger the transition in frame 15 of the transition channel. That would make the transition play over and over again, annoying users. The* go frame *script keeps the playback head in one place so users can make a selection from the main menu.*

3] Click frame 31 in the behavior channel and then copy and paste the script into frames 46, 61, 76, and 91 in the behavior channel.

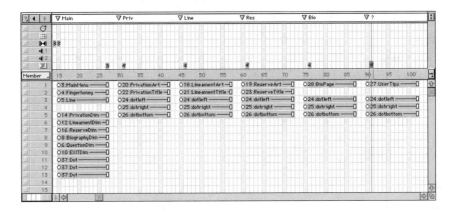

Now when you click the menu options on the main screen, the playback head will branch to the frames you assigned to these options through the Behavior Inspector and then move to the next frame (just as before). As the playback head begins to exit the frame after the marker, it will encounter the command *go marker(0)*. At this time, marker(0) (the marker the playback head has passed most recently) is the marker in the previous frame, so the playback head goes back to the previous frame. When it moves to the next frame, Director instructs it to go to marker(0) again. Thus, the playback head will loop between the frame where the marker occurs and the following frame continuously until the user makes another selection.

Remember that marker(0) is *relative* to the position of the playback head. Relative markers always refer to a marker based on the current position of the playback head, not to a marker in a specific frame.

4] Rewind and play the movie. Click the privations and excesses menu option.
Everything still works as it did before, but now the script refers to a relative marker instead of a marker name. Look at the playback head and notice that it is looping between frames 30 and 31.

5] Click the dotbottom navigation control to return to the main menu. Click another menu option to display one of the destination screens you've built.
The playback loops between the frame that contains the script and the frame that precedes it. You'll frequently use this technique in your own Director development. As you've seen in this task, you have to write the script only once and then just copy and paste, and it will work!

6] Stop the movie and save your work.

WHAT YOU HAVE LEARNED

In this lesson you have:

• Added markers and named them [page 286]

• Reused your work to create other screens in the presentation [page 288]

• Added navigation scripts to sprite behaviors [page 297]

• Paused the playback head with the *go to* command [page 301]

• Created score scripts containing relative markers [page 303]

and blends

color cycling

Color cycling and blends are techniques used to create animation without having to create different images. With color cycling, you tell Director to repeatedly change some or all of the colors used in an image, creating the illusion that the image is shimmering or glowing. With blending, you can make an image appear to fade in or out of the background. Both techniques add great visual impact and attract attention quickly.

To finish the multimedia Gallery project you've been developing in the previous two lessons, you will build a screen that users will see when they click the Exit option on the main menu. To create a memorable closing sequence when the user exits the presentation, you'll incorporate color cycling and a fade-out blend.

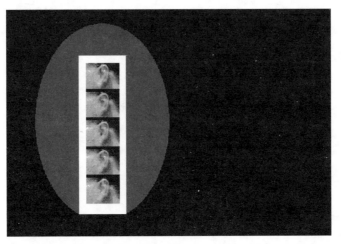

The last screen your viewers see in a presentation should be like your signature, something unique and distinctive that identifies the project. Rather than have your movie abruptly end when users click an Exit button, you can ease them out of the experience they've been enjoying with a striking closing sequence that uses color cycling and blends.

If you would like to see the final result of this lesson, open the Complete folder in the Lesson14 folder and play Gallery3.dir.

WHAT YOU WILL LEARN

In this lesson you will:

• Change the background transparent color of a sprite

• Use an animation technique to cycle colors

• Apply blends to a sprite to fade out an image

• Define a color gradient

APPROXIMATE TIME

It should take about 1½ hours to complete this lesson.

LESSON FILES

Media Files:
None

Starting Files:
Lesson14\Start\Start.dir

Completed Project:
Lesson14\Complete\Gallery3.dir

ADDING A MARKER FOR THE CLOSING SEQUENCE

To start building your closing sequence, you need to add a marker where the sequence starts in the score and then position an image in the score. First, however, you'll open the starting file and check your preferences.

1] Open Start.dir in the Start folder within the Lesson14 folder and save it as *Gallery3.dir* in your Projects folder.

This is the prebuilt file. Alternatively, if you completed the last lesson, you can use the movie you worked on there. Save it as *Gallery3.dir* in your Projects folder.

note *Windows users: The cast members in the prebuilt Start.dir file use the Macintosh system palette. If you use this prebuilt file and your monitor is set to display only 256 colors, Director will switch to a black-and-white interface (for example, the score window will appear in black and white, without shades of gray). Only Director windows, dialog boxes, and other interface elements are affected; the colors of the cast members are not affected. If you completed Lesson 13 and you use the movie you created there, the Director interface will not change because the cast members use the Windows system palette.*

2] Choose File › Preferences › Sprite to open the Sprite Preferences dialog box. Type *13* in the Span Duration field and click OK.

If you completed Lessons 12 and 13, your sprite preferences are probably already correctly set, but it doesn't hurt to check. The tasks in this lesson assume that Director is adding sprites to the score with a 13-frame duration, and you will find it easier to follow the illustrations in this lesson if you use the 13-frame preference setting. There is nothing special about this sprite duration. It was chosen because it is long enough so you can see the cast member names in the score, making the score easier for you to work with.

3] Insert a marker in frame 105 of the marker channel and label it *Exit*.

This is the marker that the playback head will branch to when users click the Exit option on the main menu.

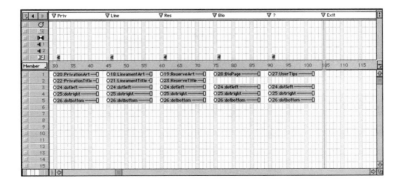

4] Drag cast member 32, Oval, to frame 105, channel 1. If you do not see the Sprite Overlay for the Oval sprite on the stage, choose View › Sprite Overlay › Show Info.

The Oval cast member is the first of two images you need to build the closing sequence. When you drag it to the score, it is automatically selected, and you should be able to see the Sprite Overlay for it. If you don't see the Sprite Overlay, you need to turn it on so you can set some properties for the Oval sprite.

tip *If the text in the Sprite Overlay is difficult to read, choose View > Sprite Overlay > Settings. In the Overlay Settings dialog box, click the Text Color chip and choose a lighter color.*

5] Click the Sprite Properties button in the Sprite Overlay panel to open the Sprite Properties dialog box, and then set the location of the sprite to 50, 25.

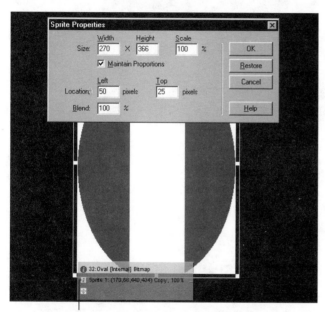

CLICK THE SPRITE PROPERTIES BUTTON TO
OPEN THE SPRITE PROPERTIES DIALOG BOX

To set the location, enter *50* in the Left Location box and *25* in the Top Location box.

313

6] Click OK to close the dialog box.

Now the gray oval image with the white background appears at the left side of the stage.

This image will frame the 29:fiveears cast member you'll place in the vertical white rectangle inside the oval. In the following steps, you'll learn how to manipulate the white background of the oval image so that the edges around the oval become transparent while the white vertical space remains white.

CHANGING THE BACKGROUND TRANSPARENT COLOR

As you have seen in earlier lessons, you can apply the Background Transparent ink effect to an image so that the white background-color pixels in the image become transparent, allowing the background to show through. The Matte ink has a similar effect, turning all the adjacent white pixels around the edge of an image transparent; white pixels that are inside the image but are not adjacent to any of the white pixels around the edge remain white. The gray oval you just added to the stage is surrounded by white pixels, and the white inside the oval is connected to the white area surrounding the oval. In this task, you will first experiment with Ink effects, and then you will learn how to turn the white area surrounding the oval transparent while leaving the area inside the image white.

1] In the score, select the Oval sprite and apply the Background Transparent ink.

See how all the large white areas of the image become transparent?

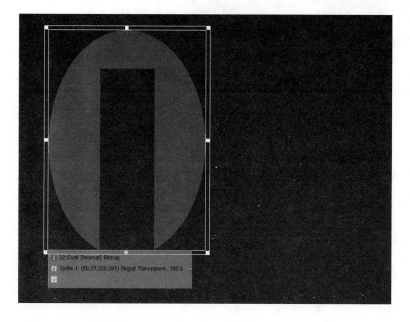

2] With the Oval sprite still selected, apply the Matte ink.

You don't see any change; the white areas of the image remain transparent, even the white inside the image. The reason is that the white inside the image touches the white surrounding the image. The matte ink effect spreads to all connected white pixels.

The solution to this problem is to use a color other than white around the edges of the graphic and then make that color transparent instead.

3] Select the Copy ink to return the sprite to its original state.

With the sprite in its original state, you can see that there are four white areas surrounding the oval and one rectangular white area inside the oval. In the next steps, you'll change the color around the outside of the oval and leave the area inside the oval white.

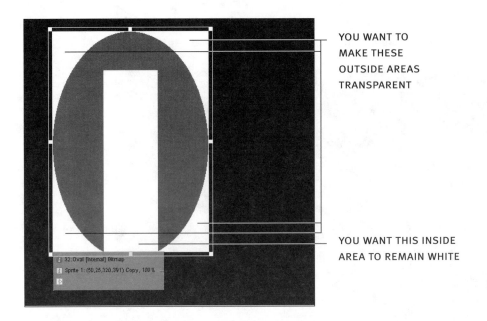

YOU WANT TO MAKE THESE OUTSIDE AREAS TRANSPARENT

YOU WANT THIS INSIDE AREA TO REMAIN WHITE

4] Double-click the Oval sprite to open the Paint window. In the Paint window, click the foreground color chip and choose a bright pink from the color palette.

PAINT BUCKET TOOL

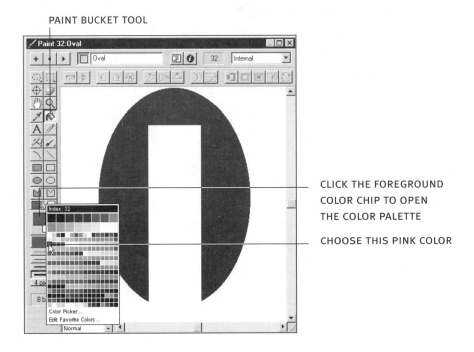

CLICK THE FOREGROUND COLOR CHIP TO OPEN THE COLOR PALETTE

CHOOSE THIS PINK COLOR

316

Changing the foreground color chip to pink allows you to use the Paint Bucket tool to fill all the white area around the oval with pink. There is nothing special about this pink color; it was chosen only because it does not appear anywhere else in the image. When using these technique, remember that the color you use will become transparent, so be careful about where else this color appears in your image.

note *Although the illustration shows a Macintosh color palette, the selected color is pink in the Windows color palette as well.*

5] Select the Paint Bucket tool and click any white area in the image.

All the white turns pink.

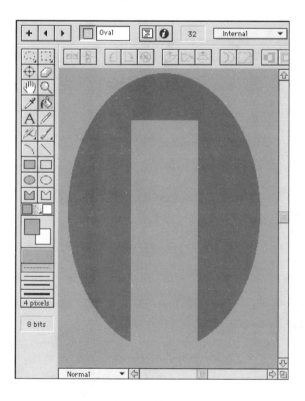

Now you need to restore the white area inside the oval. The simplest way to do so is to draw a rectangle filled with white.

6] Click the foreground color chip and choose white. Then select the Filled Rectangle tool and draw a white rectangle inside the oval.

Position the cross-hair pointer in the upper-left corner of the pink area inside the oval and then drag down and to the right. Make sure the right edge of the rectangle you're drawing just covers the pink area and that the bottom edge is even with the bottom of the oval. Make sure not to leave any pink areas inside the oval; use the other paint tools to clean up the rectangle if necessary. If you make a mistake, you can immediately undo it and try again. Edit > Undo Bitmap (Windows Control+Z, Macintosh Command+Z) will undo your last action.

7] Close the Paint window.

On the stage, the sprite is surrounded by pink, and the white rectangle appears inside the oval shape. You can now make the pink areas transparent without affecting the white rectangle inside the oval.

However, you can't select Background Transparent yet to make the pink areas transparent because white is still the color that is made transparent with the Background Transparent ink. In the next step, you'll change the background color Director makes transparent.

8] With the Oval sprite on the stage still selected, click the background color chip in the tool palette. Change the background color chip to the same pink that you used to fill the area around the oval.

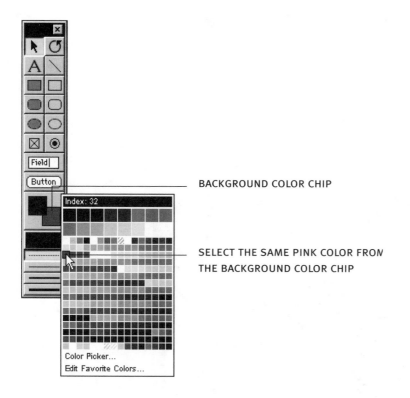

BACKGROUND COLOR CHIP

SELECT THE SAME PINK COLOR FROM
THE BACKGROUND COLOR CHIP

9] In the score, set the ink for the Oval sprite to Background Transparent.

On the stage, the graphic should now have a transparent background so you can see
through to the black background.

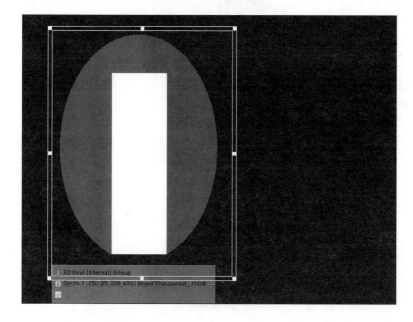

If the background is not transparent, you have selected the wrong color from the tool palette's background color chip. Make sure that the color you used to fill around the edges of the oval in the Paint window is the same color you choose from the background color chip in the tool palette.

tip *To double-check the location of the pink color used in the cast member, open the Oval cast member in the Paint window. Select the Eyedropper tool and click the pink color. Click the foreground color chip, and you will see the exact color highlighted in the color palette.*

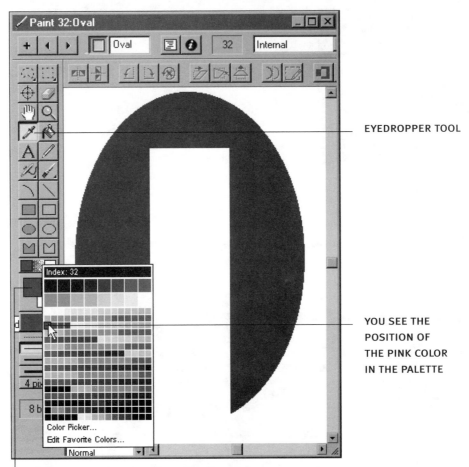

EYEDROPPER TOOL

YOU SEE THE
POSITION OF
THE PINK COLOR
IN THE PALETTE

AFTER CLICKING THE PINK COLOR WITH THE EYEDROPPER
TOOL, CLICK THE FOREGROUND COLOR CHIP

Now you can complete this closing scene by adding one more cast member.

10] Drag the 29:fiveears cast member to frame 105, channel 2, in the Score window. Then, on the stage, center it inside the white rectangle.

The white rectangle makes a nice frame for this image.

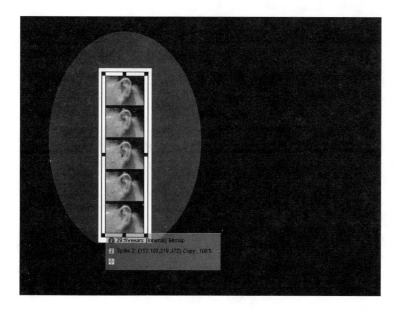

11] Choose View › Sprite Overlay › Show Info to turn off the Sprite Overlay feature. Then close the tool palette and save your work.

The Sprite Overlay panel is a great help when you want a shortcut for editing sprite properties or behaviors. Turning it off when you've finished working with sprite properties gives you a better look at the screen you're building. You won't need the tool palette for the rest of this lesson, so closing it frees up more screen space, which also allows you to see your work better.

ANIMATING WITH COLOR CYCLING

The animation technique known as **color cycling** gives the illusion of animation by rotating colors through a selected color range in a palette. For example, you may have seen animations that show a fire blazing in a fireplace by using colors that pulse through a series of reds, yellows, and oranges to create the effect of a fire. Color cycling is an excellent way to create simple movement in a movie without doing any real animation or taxing system resources.

In the following task, you'll select a range of colors from the color palette for the fiveears image. At the end of this task, you'll see the colors in the fiveears image move through a cycle, with one color changing to another in the order in which the colors appear in the color palette.

Color cycling offers you the chance to use the palette channel, the only special effects channel you haven't used yet in this book. After you activate color cycling, you'll add a sound and set up navigation to the Exit marker so you can move from the main menu to the Exit screen and watch the color cycling animation.

1] In the palette channel, drag to select frames 105 through 117.

PALETTE CHANNEL

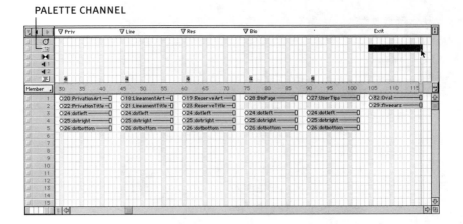

These are the frames in which the fiveears graphic appears on the stage. The color cycling effect will occur in all the frames that you have selected.

2] Choose Modify › Frame › Palette to open the Palette dialog box. Click Color Cycling.

In the Palette dialog box, you must select Color Cycling before you can select a range of colors to cycle.

3] In the palette on the left side of the Palette dialog box, drag to select the range of colors you want to cycle. Click Between Frames and then set the rate as shown in the proper illustration, as determined by your computer type.

The colors and rate you select depend on the type of computer you are using.

WINDOWS USERS: DRAG TO SELECT THESE COLORS

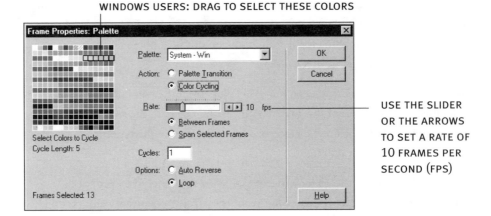

USE THE SLIDER OR THE ARROWS TO SET A RATE OF 10 FRAMES PER SECOND (FPS)

```
┌─────────────────────────────────────────────────────────────┐
│            ═══ Frame Properties: Palette ═══                  │
│  ┌──────────────┐  Palette:  ┌─ System – Mac ──▼┐  ┌───────┐  │
│  │              │                                  │  OK   │  │
│  │              │  Action: ○ Palette Transition   └───────┘  │
│  │              │          ● Color Cycling       ┌───────┐   │
│  │              │                                 │Cancel │   │
│  │              │   Rate: ▭──────▭ ◄ ► 20  fps    └───────┘   │
│  │              │         ● Between Frames                    │
│  │              │         ○ Span Selected Frames              │
│  │ Select Colors│                                             │
│  │ to Cycle     │  Cycles: │1    │                            │
│  │ Cycle Length:│                                             │
│  │ 10           │  Options: ○ Auto Reverse                    │
│  │              │           ● Loop                            │
│  │ Frames       │                              ┌───────┐      │
│  │ Selected: 12 │                              │ Help  │      │
│  └──────────────┘                              └───────┘      │
└─────────────────────────────────────────────────────────────┘
```

USE THE SLIDER
OR THE ARROWS
TO SET A RATE
OF 20 FRAMES
PER SECOND

In the fiveears graphic, some of the colors in the man's temple fall within the range of colors you selected in the Palette dialog box. As the playback head moves through the selected frames, Director will cycle the colors in the selected range. The man's temple will appear to shimmer, as if water were running down his face.

The Between Frames option tells Director that, in each of the 13 selected frames, you want to cycle once through the selected colors. You will see 13 color cycles, one in each frame. (In comparison, if you choose Span Selected Frames, Director will cycle through the colors only once, stretching the single color cycle throughout the 13 selected frames.)

Each cycle will play at a rate of 10 frames per second (Windows) or 20 frames per second (Macintosh). The difference between the Windows and Macintosh rates is that Macintosh users selected 10 colors to cycle whereas Windows users selected five, or half as many as the Macintosh users. The difference in the number of colors selected simply reflects artistic differences between the Windows and Macintosh color palettes.

tip   *If any other sprites in the frames that are cycling use any of the colors in the range you selected, they will start cycling, too, so unless you want that effect, make sure that only the item to which you want to apply color cycling uses the colors you select.*

note   *The color cycling method used in this lesson will work only if the monitors are set to 256 colors. But the new color cycling behavior will work at any color depth because of the new RGB colors in Director 7.*

4] Click OK to close the dialog box.

Next you'll add a sound that will enhance the effect of the color cycling you've added.

5] Drag the 30:waterLOOP cast member to frame 105 of sound channel 1.

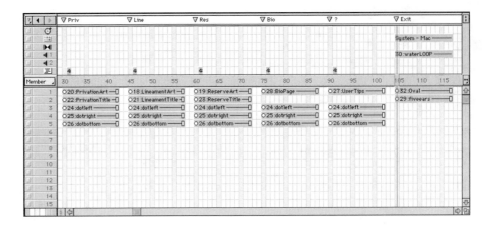

In the next step, you'll add the navigation script to the main menu's Exit option.

6] Click frame 15 in the frame channel to move the playback head to the main menu. On the stage, click the Exit option near the bottom of the screen.

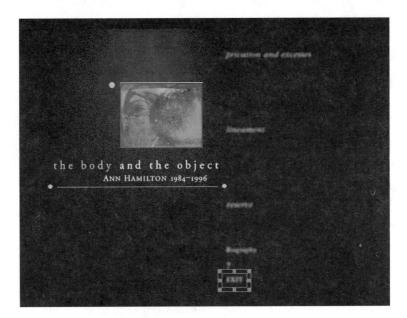

Next you'll open the Behavior Inspector and assign a script to this sprite by using a *mouseDown* event and by choosing Navigation > Go to Marker.

7] In the score, click the Behavior Inspector button.

BEHAVIOR INSPECTOR BUTTON

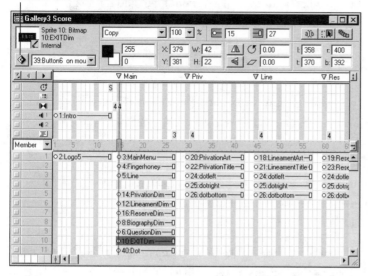

8] Add a *mouseDown* event to the Button6 behavior. Then from the Actions menu, choose Navigation › Go to Marker. Choose Exit as the marker name and click OK.

Now when users click the Exit option, Director will branch to the frame with the *Exit* marker.

Once you add the new event and action to the Button6 behavior, the Behavior Inspector shows your additions in the Events and Actions panels. This adds the needed navigation to the Exit screen from the main menu.

325

9] Rewind and play the movie and click the Exit option on the main menu.

Watch the fiveears image closely! The range of colors you selected for this animation cycles through the white pixel areas in the image, seeming to add motion to the water drops on the faces. This technique makes the screen come alive by cycling colors across one sprite.

10] Save your work.

As you can see, color cycling is a great way to simulate motion without creating different artwork. Before you finish this lesson, you'll use color cycling one more time.

TWEENING A BLEND OF SPRITES

You use blending along with tweening to make sprites fade in or out of a background. Fading images out is a common way of creating endings for presentations, like a fade-out in film.

In this task you will set up a blend that makes the fiveears image gradually fade out into the background. To fade the fiveears image to black, you'll set keyframes in the image and add Blend to the types of tweening that Director automatically performs.

1] In the score, select the fiveears sprite. Then change the end frame of the sprite to frame 132.

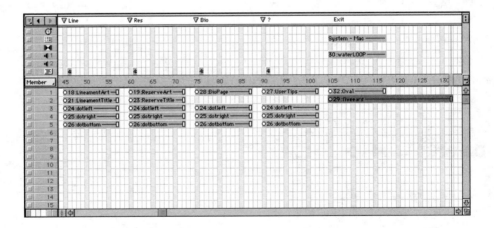

You need the additional frames so you can add the fade-out. In frame 118, the Oval sprite will leave the stage, and the fiveears image will be on the stage alone from frames 118 to 132. The image will fade out within these frames.

2] With the fiveears sprite still selected, choose Modify › Sprite › Tweening (Windows Ctrl+Shift+B, Macintosh Command+Shift+B).

The Sprite Tweening dialog box appears.

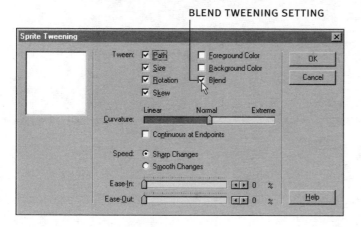

BLEND TWEENING SETTING

3] Make sure the Blend box is selected.

Now Director will automatically tween **blend values** that are set for the keyframes of a sprite. A blend value controls a sprite's transparency—that is, the degree to which the background shows through the sprite. For example, when a sprite's blend value is 80%, you see 20% of the background showing through the sprite.

When a sprite's blend value is 100%, no background is showing through; when a sprite's blend value is 0%, the sprite is no longer visible, and you see just the background. By starting a sprite's blend value at 100% and tweening it over a range of frames to 0%, you make the sprite appear to fade into the background.

In the next steps, you'll insert keyframes in the sprite and set blend values for the keyframes to produce the fade-out effect.

4] Click frame 118 of the fiveears sprite and then choose Insert › Keyframe (Windows Ctrl+Alt+K, Macintosh Command+Option+K).

This is the first frame in which the fiveears sprite is on the stage by itself. In the sprite toolbar at the top of the score, notice the blend percentage in the menu next to the Ink menu. It shows 100% as the blend value for the sprite in the keyframe.

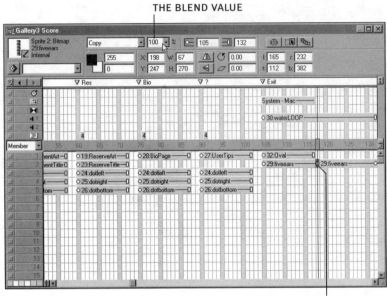

THE BLEND VALUE

THE KEYFRAME AT FRAME 118 IS THE
START OF THE FADE-OUT EFFECT

To complete the fade-out, you need to create a keyframe with a blend value of 0%.

5] Click frame 132 of the sprite and insert a keyframe. On the sprite toolbar, select the blend percentage value, type *0*, and press Enter (Windows) or Return (Macintosh).

In frame 132, the last frame of the sprite, the sprite will fade out entirely. Note that the menu has no 0% blend setting to choose, so you must type *0* to completely fade out the image.

Now between frames 118 and 132, Director automatically assigns various blend percentages to each frame of the sprite to create the fade-out effect. To see these percentages, click any frame in the sprite between the keyframes you've inserted and use the Sprite Overlay panel to view the blend percentage assigned through automatic tweening of the blend values. In the following illustration, the blend of the sprite in frame 122 is 72%.

328

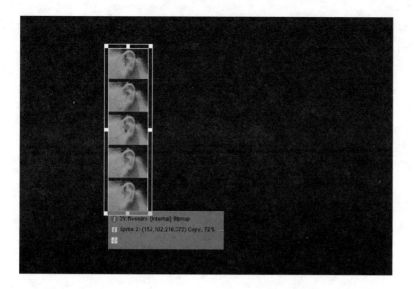

Next you'll extend the waterLOOP sound so it continues as the fiveears image fades out.

6] Select the waterLOOP sound sprite and change the end frame to frame 132.

Frame 132 is the last frame of the fiveears sprite. You introduced this image with a sound, and you should continue the sound until the image leaves the stage.

7] In the score, click frame 105 in the frame channel and then play the movie.

This moves the playback head to the frame where the Exit screen is located in the presentation. You can play the movie from this frame onward to see the effects you've created.

The fade-out effect follows the color cycling nicely. Fade-out effects ease viewers out of the presentation and satisfy their expectations when they click Exit on the main menu. However, blending can be a processor-intensive operation and should be used sparingly.

Director builds each frame as the playback head moves through the movie. This means that each time you run the movie, Director needs to determine the requirements for each frame. If you use blending, Director must also determine the amount of blend, the color depth, and other color information for each frame. Because Director is busy with all these calculations, less processing power is available for other work, which slows down animation or anything else you've added to the frames where the blend is being tweened. The frames of the Exit screen that involve blending, however, contain only the one image that you've blended, so blending will not noticeably slow the display of the frames.

A good technique for handling this problem is to apply the blend and then export the frames from Director to PICT images or to QuickTime movies. Then you can reimport the images and replace the sprites you originally blended with the pictures of the blend. Director can display pictures much more quickly than it can display sprites with blend values.

8] Save your work.

SETTING A GRADIENT

Now you'll add the finishing touch to the Exit screen. After the fiveears image fades out, you'll present the EndPara sprite, which contains a paragraph of text about the sponsor of the art project used in this lesson. Text like this that appears at the end of presentations is often necessary to credit a sponsor or to comply with regulations that pertain to the use of images or other media elements in the presentation.

Along with the EndPara sprite, you'll define a color gradient for a line sprite, to apply a blend of colors to the line. Then you will cycle through the range of the gradient's colors to create animation.

1] In the score, drag the 31:EndPara cast member to channel 2, frame 133.
This sprite contains text that you want viewers to have time to read. The 13-frame sprite will not stay on the screen long enough, so you'll set up a color cycling animation that will play at a slow enough rate to allow the text to be read.

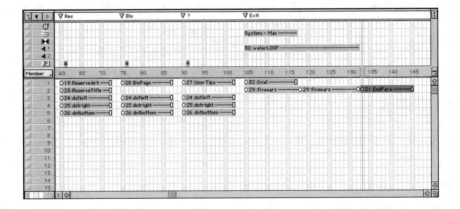

First you'll create a paint cast member to use as an accent around this text. Then you'll assign a color gradient to it and cycle the colors in the gradient.

2] On the stage, double-click the 31:EndPara sprite.

The Paint window opens for you to edit this sprite.

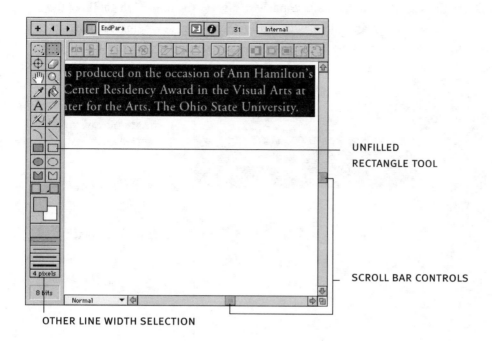

UNFILLED
RECTANGLE TOOL

SCROLL BAR CONTROLS

OTHER LINE WIDTH SELECTION

3] Click the Unfilled Rectangle tool and then double-click the Other Line Width selection at the bottom of the Paint window's tool palette.

This opens the Paint Window Preferences dialog box.

4] In the dialog box, set the "Other" Line Width slider to 12 pixels and then click OK.

Now the unfilled rectangle you will draw around the 31:EndPara sprite will be created with a wide line.

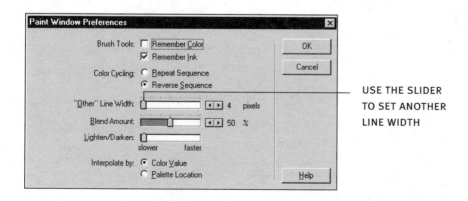

USE THE SLIDER
TO SET ANOTHER
LINE WIDTH

5] Use the Foreground color chip to set the foreground color to black.

6] Use the scroll bars in the Paint window to display the upper-left corner of the 31:EndPara bitmap image. Then, with the Rectangle tool still selected, draw a rectangle that surrounds the bitmap of the paragraph already in the Paint window.

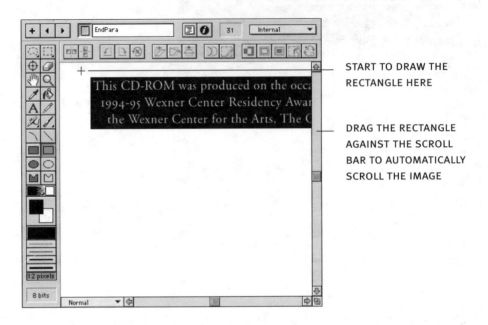

START TO DRAW THE
RECTANGLE HERE

DRAG THE RECTANGLE
AGAINST THE SCROLL
BAR TO AUTOMATICALLY
SCROLL THE IMAGE

The Paint window will automatically scroll as you drag the rectangle against the scroll bar. Use the following illustration as a guide to place the rectangle. Make sure there is some white space between the rectangle you are drawing and the original graphic. If the rectangle doesn't look right to you, stop and undo it using Edit > Undo Bitmap (Windows Ctrl+Z, Macintosh Command+Z) and then try again.

332

PAINT BUCKET TOOL

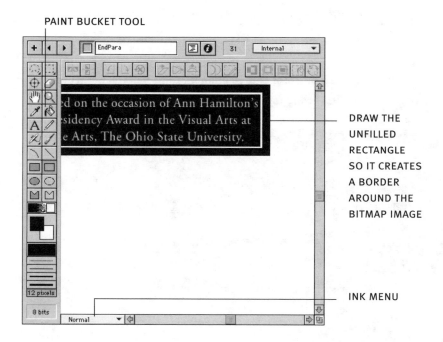

DRAW THE
UNFILLED
RECTANGLE
SO IT CREATES
A BORDER
AROUND THE
BITMAP IMAGE

INK MENU

7] Select the Paint Bucket tool and choose Gradient from the Ink menu.

This selection sets up the Paint Bucket tool to paint a gradient color instead of a solid one. When you paint with Normal ink set, one solid color is applied to an object. When you paint with a gradient, a blend of colors will be applied, often shading from light to dark. For example, a gradient color could go from light purple to dark red. In this task, you'll paint the line of the rectangle with a gradient color.

8] Double-click the Paint Bucket tool to open the Gradient Settings dialog box.

ENDING GRADIENT COLOR CHIP

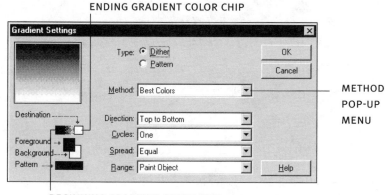

METHOD
POP-UP
MENU

BEGINNING GRADIENT COLOR CHIP

333

COLOR CYCLING AND BLENDS

Next you will set the beginning and ending gradient colors that the Paint Bucket tool will use to paint the gradient.

9] Select the beginning gradient color chip to open its color palette. Select the color at the beginning of the second row (orange) as the beginning color.

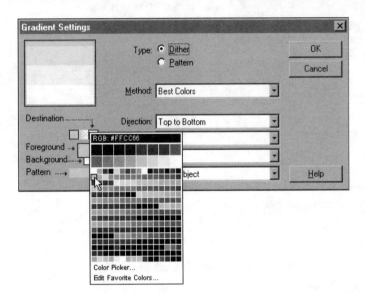

In the next step you'll select the destination, or ending, color for the gradient. The destination color will be the dark pink that is at the end of the row on which your beginning color selection appears.

note *Although the illustration shows a Windows color palette, the same steps work equally well with the Macintosh color palette. The starting color (orange) and ending color (pink) look similar. Getting the exact colors is not critical to this task. The second row of colors in the palette was chosen for ease in demonstrating the technique. Once you learn this technique, you can use any range of colors you wish.*

10] Select the destination gradient color chip and select the color at the end of the second row (pink).

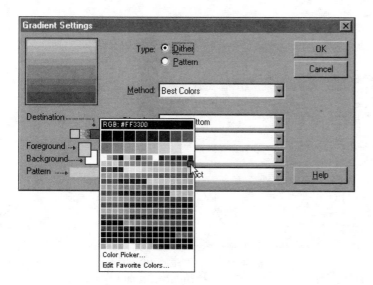

You've selected index colors 16 and 31 for the gradient that the Paint Bucket tool will apply. In the next step, you'll include the colors in between your selections so they are also applied to objects painted with this tool.

INDEX COLOR 16

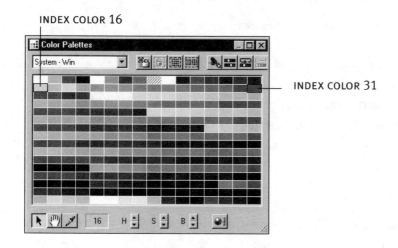

INDEX COLOR 31

11] From the Method menu, choose Adjacent Colors. From the Direction menu, choose Right to Left. Leave the other settings as they appear and then click OK to close the dialog box.

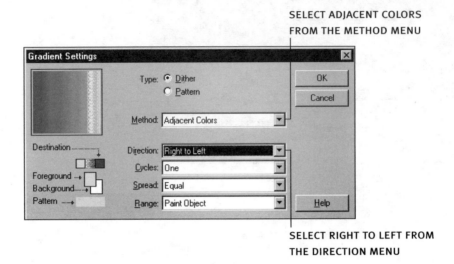

SELECT ADJACENT COLORS
FROM THE METHOD MENU

SELECT RIGHT TO LEFT FROM
THE DIRECTION MENU

You are setting a color gradient from one shade to another. Choosing Adjacent Colors means that the gradient between the two colors you just selected will be created using the colors that lie between them in the color palette.

The Direction menu selection determines the way the gradient fills an area in the Paint window. Right to Left puts the starting color on the right and the destination color on the left.

12] With the Paint Bucket tool, click the line of the rectangle.

The gradient with the colors you just defined fills the line of the rectangle. If you accidentally filled the center of the rectangle, choose Edit > Undo Bitmap (Windows Ctrl+Z, Macintosh Command+Z) and then click the line with the Paint Bucket tool again.

13] Close the Paint window and save your work.

You've just added a rectangle to the paragraph text sprite by editing the cast member in the Paint window. This image now appears on the stage.

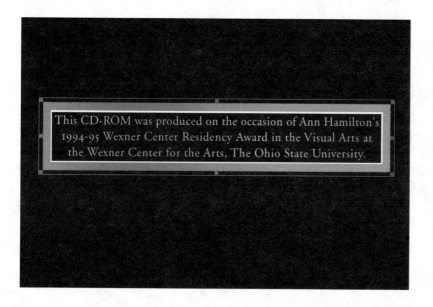

This CD-ROM was produced on the occasion of Ann Hamilton's 1994-95 Wexner Center Residency Award in the Visual Arts at the Wexner Center for the Arts, The Ohio State University.

In the next task you'll add color cycling to this rectangle.

CYCLING GRADIENT COLORS

Now that you have a specific gradient color range applied to the rectangle you created around the paragraph text, you can make the colors cycle. This creates a marquee-like effect around the text.

1] Double-click frame 133 in the palette channel to open the Palette dialog box.

This is the frame where the 31:EndPara sprite first appears on the stage.

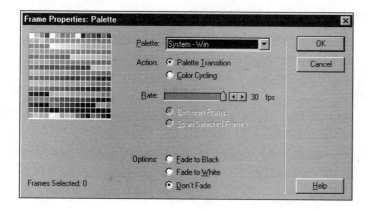

2] Next to Action, click Color Cycling and drag the Rate slider to 20 fps. In the color palette, drag to select the colors in the second row that you just used in the gradient and click OK to close the dialog box.

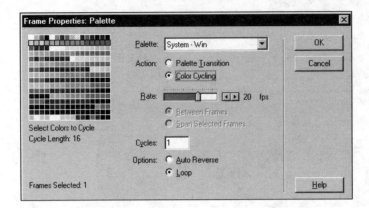

The Rate slider controls the speed at which the colors cycle. The colors you selected are the ones that will cycle. In this case, you selected the range of colors you used to create the gradient. You must be precise when you select these colors or the color cycling effect will not work.

3] In the palette channel, select frame 133. Then hold down Alt (Windows) or Option (Macintosh) and drag the end frame of the palette channel sprite to frame 145.
This extends the color cycling effect to the same end frame as for the 31:EndPara sprite.

4] Click frame 118 in the frame channel and play the movie.
From frames 118 to 132 you see the fiveears image fade out, and then in the closing frames the paragraph appears surrounded by the rectangle with the color cycling. The rapidly changing colors draw attention to the text in a dramatic way. Then the movie ends. In the next step, you'll add a script that quits the Director application and truly ends the presentation. Then your multimedia art gallery will be complete.

5] Double-click frame 145 in the behavior channel. Then type *halt* below *on exitFrame* and close the Script window.

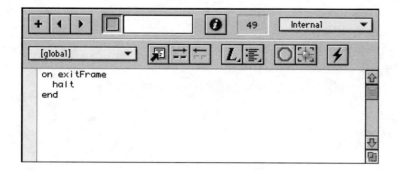

When the playback head leaves this frame, Director stops the movie. This action is similar to clicking the Stop button on the toolbar. There is also a *quit* command, which actually quits the Director application. However, while you're authoring a movie, the *halt* command is preferable because it is too time-consuming to test the ending sequence by actually quitting Director. In a projector of your movie, the *halt* command actually quits the project. Therefore, the *halt* command is the best all-around choice.

6] Save your work. Then rewind and play the movie. Click the Exit option on the main menu.

After the last frame in which the 31:EndPara sprite appears, the movie stops.

You can use the techniques you've learned while building the last screen of this presentation to add more visual interest to the endings of your own presentations.

WHAT YOU HAVE LEARNED

In this lesson you have:

• Changed the background transparent color of a sprite [page 314]

• Used the palette channel to define color cycling for an illustration [page 321]

• Created a fade-out effect using sprite blend values and tweening [page 326]

• Defined gradient settings in the Paint window [page 333]

• Used the palette channel to define color cycling for a gradient [page 337]

director

shockwave for

LESSON 15

Shockwave is the name for the playback version of Director that works with Internet browsers. Developers can use Shockwave to prepare multimedia for the World Wide Web, and Web users can interact with the multimedia production once it's posted on the Web. Your operating system, Web browser, or other software products may include Shockwave, or you can download it from the Macromedia Web site. Shockwave can be applied to almost all Macromedia products; in this lesson, you'll learn about Shockwave Director.

Shockwave is the latest in Web technology for delivering interactive multimedia and large sound files over intranets and the Internet. As you will see in this lesson, you can easily shock a Director movie and then embed it in an HTML document—a file created to play on the Web—for playback over the Internet. The movie you'll work with is the finished version of the project you created in Lesson 8.

When used to create multimedia for the World Wide Web, Shockwave Director delivers high-impact Director movies—with interactivity, graphics, sound, and animation. When you use Director to save a movie for Shockwave, or **shock** it, the movie's data is compressed to the smallest possible size for downloading. This compression converts the movie to the DCR file format, designed specifically for the Web. When a user views a Web page that includes a Shockwave movie, the data from the movie begins downloading to the user's disk. Shockwave decompresses the data and plays the movie in the user's Web browser. If the movie was created for **streaming**, the movie begins playing almost immediately. The difference between movies created for streaming and those that are not is only in the timing of when the movie begins to play. Movies that have not been prepared to stream play only after the entire movie has been downloaded and decompressed. Movies prepared to stream can begin to play as the data arrives for the first frame of the movie (or any number of frames that you specify). The rest of the movie's data continues to download in the background while the movie is playing.

You create a Director movie for use with Shockwave and the World Wide Web the same way you create any other Director movie. A Web page can contain a regular DIR-format Director movie. Since space and download time is at a premium, however, Director also lets you save your movie in Shockwave, or **compressed**, format. Another advantage of the Shockwave format is that the files can only be played, not edited, so the end user cannot view or change your source media, score, or scripts. Movies for the Web can include almost any effect that any other Director movie can include: interactivity, animation, and so on. This lesson guides you through the steps of shocking a Director movie. You'll see how to include a shocked Director movie in a Web page and then test the Web page to see how the shocked version will look when Web users view it. You'll also prepare a Director movie for streaming and then navigate to a shocked movie through Macromedia's Web site to see how shocked movies stream over the Internet to play on your own computer.

As you begin to create movies intended for use on a Web site, keep these considerations in mind:

• Delete cast members that are not used in the movie to reduce file size.

• Use stage sizes smaller than 640 x 480 pixels as not all browsers have 640 x 480 pixels of available window space. Keep movies small by using small cast members, changing images to 8 bits or smaller and, where possible, using shapes on the tool palette to create cast members instead of using the Paint window.

• To reduce file size, create animations that use as few cast members as possible and use Director's automatic tweening to move single cast members around the stage.

If you would like to see the final result of this lesson, open the Complete folder in the Lesson15 folder and play Loop.dir (or, if you finished Lesson 8, use your own version of Loop.dir). Click the Forward and Backward buttons to make the document sail back and forth between the file folders.

WHAT YOU WILL LEARN

In this lesson you will:

• Explore Shockwave and how you can use it

• Prepare a Director movie for distribution over the Internet

APPROXIMATE TIME

It should take about 1 hour to complete this lesson.

LESSON FILES

Media Files:

None

Starting Files:

Lesson15\Start\Start.dir

Completed Project:

Lesson15\Complete\Loop.dir

Lesson15\Complete\Loop.dcr

Lesson15\Complete\Loop2.dir

Lesson15\Complete\Loop2.dcr

OBTAINING SHOCKWAVE PLUG-INS AND THE BROWSER SOFTWARE

To view a Director movie in a browser, you'll need to save it as a Shockwave movie and you'll need the latest Shockwave Director player for your Web browser. If you are using Microsoft Internet Explorer with Windows, you will need the ActiveX version of the Shockwave Director player. If you are using Netscape Navigator or any browser that supports Netscape plug-ins, you will need the plug-in version of the Shockwave Director player; different plug-in versions are used for Windows and the Macintosh. The most up-to-date version of the Shockwave Director player can be downloaded for free from Macromedia's Web site. The Macromedia Web site also has a wealth of technical support information, tips, and other resources for those developing Shockwave movies. Shockwave in Director 7 has a lot of built-in features that allow Shockwave to update itself with the most current version and to repair incomplete installations automatically.

note   *Before using Shockwave, you should visit Macromedia's Web site to be sure you have the latest version of the Shockwave plug-in for Director.*

1] If you don't already have a Web browser that supports the Shockwave plug-in, download that now.

A Web browser is software that is used to navigate around the World Wide Web and view files published there. The Shockwave Director player is available for Netscape Navigator versions 3.0 and later (both Windows and Macintosh) and Microsoft Internet Explorer version 3.0 and later for Windows. Both are available for downloading from the Web. To download Netscape Navigator, go to *http://www.netscape.com*. To download Internet Explorer, go to *http://www.microsoft.com*.

Since Shockwave comes preinstalled on most major browsers these days, you may already have all the files you need. If you can successfully play the examples given here, you do not need to download additional files yourself. Shockwave will automatically take you to the Macromedia site to download Director 7 Shockwave components if necessary.

2] If you don't already have the Shockwave plug-in on your computer, download it now.

For the most up-to-date version of the Shockwave Director player, go to Macromedia's Web site and download it now. The location is *http://www.macromedia.com*. Find the Shockwave download page and follow the instructions for downloading and installing the software. You will not be able to follow the steps for the following tasks if you do not have this software installed on your computer. To see if your browser is set to use Shockwave correctly, go to *http://www.macromedia.com/shockwave/welcome*. If your installation is correct, you will see Director Shockwave animation running at the site.

CREATING AND PLAYING A SHOCKWAVE MOVIE

Earlier in this book you created a projector to distribute a play-only version of a movie. Another way to distribute movies is to create Shockwave versions of them for playback on the World Wide Web. With the Director Shockwave player installed in a Web browser, Director movies will play on any Web page. Movies playing in Web browsers can range from simple animated banners to online games and presentations. Thousands of exciting Shockwave movies are already in use on the Web.

Preparing a movie for Web browsers is even simpler than creating a projector for your Director movie. In the next task, you'll open the Start.dir movie and shock it for playback in a Web browser. This movie contains both sound and exciting interactive animation. To view the shocked version of the movie, you will use your Web browser to open an **HTML** document containing a reference to the name of the shocked version of this Director movie. HTML, or hypertext markup language, is the programming language used to create Web pages. This book does not cover HTML, but Director 7 can build an HTML file for you that you can load in your browser.

1] Open the Start.dir movie in the Start folder within the Lesson15 folder. Save this movie as *Loop.dir* in your Projects folder.

If you finished Lesson 8, you can instead use the version of Loop.dir that you created for that lesson.

Movies with .dir extensions are editable, meaning you can make changes to the score and cast members as you have been doing in the movies you've created throughout this book. When you shock a movie, Director creates a copy of the movie with the extension .dcr, which indicates a compressed, uneditable version of the movie ready for playback in a Web page.

2] Play the movie and click the Forward and Backward buttons. When you finish getting reacquainted with the way the movie works, stop the movie.

The Forward and Backward buttons make the document sail back and forth between the two file folders. As the movie plays, you hear a sound playing in the background. After you shock this movie, it will work exactly the same way. The only difference will be that the movie plays in a Web browser.

3] Choose Xtras › Shockwave for Audio Settings to open the Shockwave for Audio Settings dialog box.

Shockwave Audio is a technology that makes sounds smaller and plays them faster from a disc or over the Internet. Because this movie contains a sound cast member, you need to use the Shockwave Audio Settings Xtra to specify compression settings for the sound. You can choose compression settings for the sound at any time before you shock the movie. The options you select in this dialog box apply to all internal sounds in a movie; you cannot set separate options for each sound.

It's important that you understand the distinction between the sound in the Loop.dir movie, which is stored as a cast member in the movie file, and Shockwave Audio files (commonly called SWA files) that are stored externally from the movie. External SWA files can stream from an Internet site or a disk; the sound begins to play almost immediately while the rest of the sound file is still downloading. External SWA files are ideally suited for long sounds—for example, extended music or long sequences of narration. In the Loop.dir movie, however, a relatively short sound is included as a cast member. Like all other cast members in a Shockwave movie (streaming or otherwise), the entire sound cast member must download before the Director movie can use it.

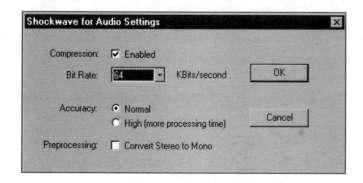

4] Check the Enabled box to enable compression for the audio embedded in the movie. Then click OK to close the dialog box.

The options in this dialog box allow you to set a bit rate for the sound and convert stereo to monaural sound. The default settings in this dialog box are fine for the movie you are working on, but you'll want to be aware of what the bit rate option represents. In general terms, the bit rate determines the speed at which the sound plays. However, this option has different effects depending on whether you are using an internal sound or an external SWA file.

In the case of the Loop.dir movie, where the sound is stored internally, the bit rate represents a trade-off between file size and output quality. A low bit rate reduces the size of the sound file substantially for the quickest possible download time, but it can result in the loss of sound quality. A high bit rate produces higher quality but larger sound files. Note that the Shockwave for Audio bit rate settings are not related to sampling rate settings used in some sound recording and editing programs.

The bit rate setting would have an additional impact if you were using an external SWA file. In that case, the bit rate also determines the speed at which the sound streams from the Internet or a disk to the end user's computer. When you start to work with external SWA files, be sure to see Director's online Help (see "About compression quality in Shockwave audio") for a table that compares bit rates for different types of delivery systems (Internet, CD-ROM, and so on) and the resulting quality of the sound.

Now you'll shock the movie.

5] Save your movie and then choose File › Save as Shockwave Movie.

If you have not saved changes to your movie, Director will prompt you to save it before it will save the movie as a Shockwave movie. A Save Shockwave Movie As dialog box appears for you to name your Shockwave movie.

346

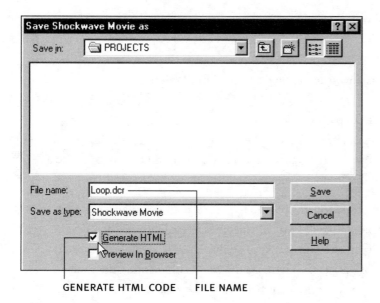

GENERATE HTML CODE   FILE NAME

Director can generate the HTML code for you automatically.

6] Select the Generate HTML option and then save the file as *Loop.dcr* in your Projects folder.

Director opens the Save As dialog box with a suggested file name by changing the .dir extension to .dcr. For this lesson, make sure you name the file *Loop.dcr*. The Web page that will play the movie will look for the movie under this name.

You can name the Shockwave version of a movie anything you want, but always use the .dcr extension. Most Web browsers depend on this extension to identify the file type, and the extension also helps you recognize shocked files from the file name alone. In general, it's also a good practice to leave the main portion of the file name the same. You can then easily recognize which uneditable, shocked version of a Director movie (for example, Loop.dcr) corresponds to the editable version (for example, Loop.dir).

Once you click Save, Director compresses the file so that it's ready for playback on a Web page. The result is a file with a .dcr extension, indicating a shocked file. You now have an icon that looks like this in your Projects folder:

Loop.dcr

The HTML file is saved as Loop.htm.

7] Close Director.

The shocked movie is now ready to be embedded in a Web page.

8] View the HTML file Loop.htm.

The Loop.htm file is a pure text file and can be opened in any text editor or word processor. When you created the Shockwave movie, you told Director to create an HTML file as well as the Loop.dcr movie.

The text you see is scripted in HTML, the hypertext markup language used to create Web pages. This simple HTML file includes a few lines that describe the document to the browser, one line of text to be displayed in the browser window, and the HTML <EMBED> tag, which tells the browser to include the shocked movie. This same line tells the browser to display the movie at 304 by 230 pixels (the size of this movie's stage).

This HTML code includes references to Loop.dcr. Be sure you've given your movie the same name or this file won't work. The Loop.dcr file must be in the same folder with the HTML file.

THIS TEXT WILL BE DISPLAYED AT
THE TOP OF THE BROWSER WINDOW

```
<head>
<title>Loop.dcr</title>
</head>

<body>
<center>
<h1>Loop.dcr</h1>
<br> <object classid="clsid:166B1BCA-3F9C-11CF-8075-444553540000"
codebase="http://active.macromedia.com/director/cabs/sw.cab#version=7,0,0,0" width="304"
height="230">
    <param name="src" value="Loop.dcr">
 <embed src="Loop.dcr" pluginspage="http://www.macromedia.com/shockwave/download/" width="304"
height="230"></embed>
 </object>
</center>
</body>
</html>
```

1. THIS SHOCKED MOVIE...

2. WILL PLAY AT THIS WIDTH...

3. AND AT THIS HEIGHT

9] Drag the HTML file, Loop.htm, from your Projects folder to a browser that supports Shockwave.

Your browser will support Shockwave so long as the Shockwave plug-in is installed. When you drop the document icon on the icon for your browser, the file will open in the browser.

If the file does not open, use the browser's File > Open command to locate and open the file. In this case, make sure that you first open a file that does not contain a Shockwave movie.

When the file opens in the browser, you'll see the "Loop.dcr" text at the top of the browser window, and the movie will begin to play.

That's it! You've just shocked a Director movie and seen how the browser's plug-in places the movie in the Web page. The movie is now ready for Internet or intranet distribution.

note *When you view this Web page using your Web browser, you are simply testing it on your local hard drive. To view the page on the Internet, you need to place the HTML page and your Shockwave movie on a Web server.*

PREPARING A MOVIE FOR STREAMING SHOCKWAVE

Streaming movies provide a much more satisfying experience to users, so long as the movie is prepared to stream properly. When streaming a movie from the Internet or over an intranet, Shockwave first downloads all the score data as well as scripts, shapes, and the size of each cast member's bounding rectangle to determine the size of the cast members included in the movie. Shockwave then downloads cast members in the order they appear in the score. When all the cast members needed to start the movie have arrived, the movie begins playing.

While the movie plays on the user's screen, Shockwave continues to download cast members. If the movie jumps ahead in the score, a cast member might not be available yet. If cast members are not available, the movie will ignore them or display a placeholder where they should appear, depending on how you set the streaming options for the movie before you shock it. In the next task, you'll prepare a movie for streaming playback so cast members will appear as they should on the stage when the movie is streamed to a user's computer.

1] Open Director and then open the Start.dir movie in the Start folder within the Lesson15 folder. Save the movie as *Loop2.dir* in your Projects folder.
You'll use the same movie you shocked in the previous task.

2] Choose Modify › Movie › Playback.
A dialog box opens so you can choose the way you want the movie to stream.

STREAMING OPTIONS

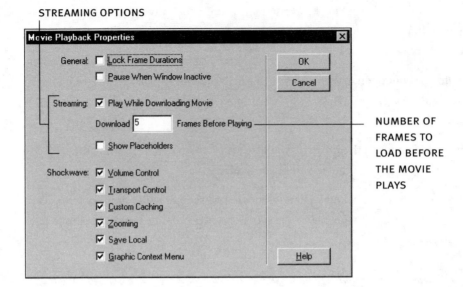

NUMBER OF
FRAMES TO
LOAD BEFORE
THE MOVIE
PLAYS

3] Select the Play While Downloading Movie option for streaming.

This is the standard option for streaming movies. This option turns on streaming playback and makes the streaming movie ignore cast members that have not yet downloaded when the frame in which they appear is played. Once cast members are downloaded, they appear in the movie and function as usual.

4] In the Download X Frames Before Playing box, enter 5 as the number of frames you want to download before playing begins. Then click OK.

It's a good idea to download about five frames before a movie starts to play to make sure all the cast members for the first few frames are available before the movie starts. If most cast members do not appear in the first five frames of the movie, increase the number of frames downloaded before streaming starts.

You're almost ready to shock the movie, but first you need to choose some audio settings.

5] Choose Xtras › Shockwave for Audio Settings. Check the Enabled box and then click OK to close the dialog box.

For any movie that includes sound, you must select compression settings for the audio. This compresses the sounds when you shock the movie.

6] Save your work.

You must save the changes you made in the last few steps before you can shock the movie.

7] Choose File › Save as Shockwave Movie. As you did before, click Generate HTML and then save the file as *Loop2.dcr* in your Projects folder.

Just as before, Director compresses the file so that it's ready for playback on a Web page, only this shocked movie is ready to begin playing as soon as five frames of the score have been downloaded. The new file for playing the shocked movie, *Loop2.htm*, is also created.

You now have two shocked movies in your Projects folder. Both of them can be used in Web pages, but Loop.dcr must download completely before users can interact with the movie, whereas Loop2.dcr allows users to interact with it after five frames of the movie have streamed to their computers.

8] Close Director.

ON YOUR OWN

If you have established a connection to the Internet and the ability to create a Web page, you can see for yourself how the movie you prepared for streaming downloads to your computer. Upload both the HTML file and your DCR file and then visit that page with your browser. You'll have posted your own streaming Shockwave movie on the Web. Perhaps you'll soon find your work included in the Macromedia Shockwave Gallery among other great examples of shocked multimedia being produced today. You can see examples of Shockwave movies in the Macromedia Shockwave Gallery at *http://www.macromedia.com/shockzone*.

WHAT YOU HAVE LEARNED

In this lesson you have:

• Shocked a Director movie for playback on the Internet [page 344]

• Generated an HTML document for a Shockwave movie [page 347]

• Prepared a movie for streaming playback [page 349]

lingo
learning

LESSON 16

No matter what kind of Lingo script you write, you'll use the same basic tools in Director and the same basic procedure: You decide what kind of script to create, create the script in the Script window, test the script by running it, and find and fix any problems. This lesson introduces you to those basic tools and procedures and to the different types of Lingo scripts. It describes how Lingo works and shows you how you can use the Message window to look under Director's hood and see Lingo in action.

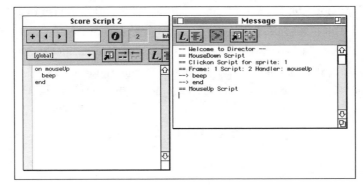

The Script window and Message window are basic tools for writing the Lingo commands that convey instructions to Director.

WHAT YOU WILL LEARN

In this lesson you will:

• Learn the difference between a script and a behavior

• Write a Lingo script

• Use the Message window to watch a script perform

• Learn how Lingo communicates

• Learn about the Lingo elements

• Learn about the different kinds of Lingo scripts

• Create Lingo scripts to see how Director passes information to different types of scripts

APPROXIMATE TIME

It should take about 1 hour to complete this lesson.

LESSON FILES

None

CHOOSING BETWEEN A SCRIPT AND A BEHAVIOR

A **script** is a series of instructions written in **Lingo**, Director's scripting language. A script can describe a simple action, such as sounding a beep when a user clicks a button, or it can describe a complex series of actions, such as how a character in an interactive game moves around the stage. Lingo is the most powerful of all Director's tools for creating rich, interactive experiences for users.

Behaviors are prebuilt scripts that provide common Lingo functionality. You can drag and drop behaviors into sprite channels as a quick alternative to writing Lingo yourself. Using the **Behavior Inspector**, you can create simple scripts (for example, one that sounds a beep) by choosing from menus. Director also comes with a variety of ready-made behaviors you can access through the Library Palette.

Here is an example of the Beep behavior provided with Director 7:

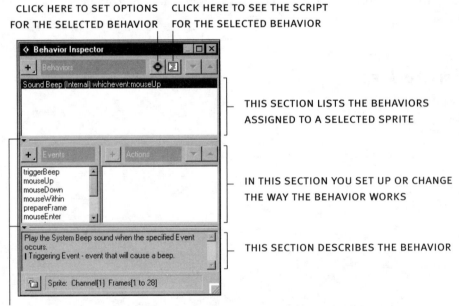

CLICK HERE TO SET OPTIONS FOR THE SELECTED BEHAVIOR

CLICK HERE TO SEE THE SCRIPT FOR THE SELECTED BEHAVIOR

THIS SECTION LISTS THE BEHAVIORS ASSIGNED TO A SELECTED SPRITE

IN THIS SECTION YOU SET UP OR CHANGE THE WAY THE BEHAVIOR WORKS

THIS SECTION DESCRIBES THE BEHAVIOR

CLICK THESE ARROWS TO SHOW OR HIDE A SECTION OF THE BEHAVIOR INSPECTOR

The Behavior Inspector stores each new behavior you create in the cast; you can drag the behavior from the cast and drop it on the score or the stage.

In some of these initial Lingo lessons, many of the scripts you will write would be even easier to create with the Behavior Inspector. But you're reading these chapters because you want to learn the basics of Lingo scripting, so it's best for you to start at the beginning, by learning how to write simple scripts. Also, as you will find out, there is much more you can do, or may want to do, than is provided by Behaviors. Learning scripting techniques gives you the ultimate control over your Director movies.

354

CREATING A SIMPLE LINGO SCRIPT

Every Lingo script is attached to an element of a Director movie: a sprite on the stage, a member of the cast, a frame of the score, or the movie itself. In this task, you'll create a movie with a button cast member and then attach a script to that button.

1] Choose File › New › Movie (Windows Ctrl+N, Macintosh Command+N).

This opens a new Director movie. You need to do this only if you already have another movie open.

2] Choose Modify › Movie › Properties.

In the Movie Properties window, make sure that the stage size is set to 640 × 480 pixels and the stage location is set to Centered. Also make sure that the default palette is set to the system palette for your system: System - Win for Windows and System - Mac for the Macintosh. In previous lessons, the settings may have been different; using these settings will help you to follow the steps and the illustrations in this lesson.

STAGE LOCATION: CENTERED

STAGE SIZE: 640 x 480 PIXELS

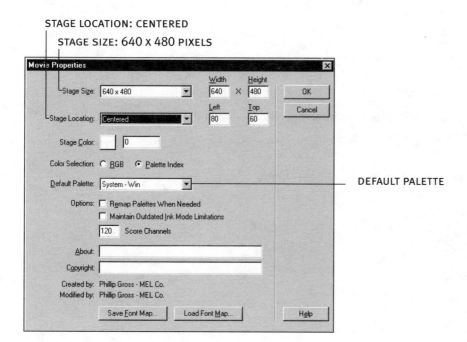

DEFAULT PALETTE

3] Click OK to close the Movie Properties dialog box.

4] Choose Control › Loop Playback to make sure the Loop Playback command is checked (Windows Ctrl+Alt+L, Macintosh Command+Option+L).

When the Loop Playback command is checked, the playback head returns to frame 1 when it reaches the end of the last sprite in the score. The movie will continue to loop until you stop it.

5] Open the score and select channel 1, frame 1.

SPRITE TOOLBAR

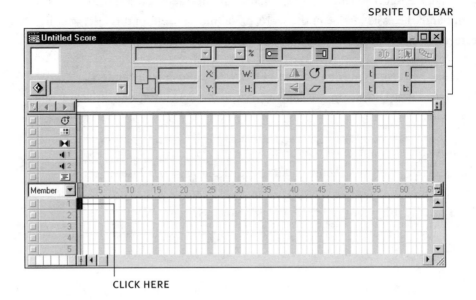

CLICK HERE

If you don't see the sprite toolbar at the top of the Score window, choose View > Sprite Toolbar (Windows Ctrl+Shift+H, Macintosh Shift+Command+H).

6] Open the tool palette by choosing Window › Tool Palette (Windows Ctrl+7, Macintosh Command+7).

7] Click the Button tool in the tool palette

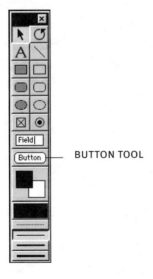

BUTTON TOOL

8] Click on the stage where you want to place the button.

A button appears where you click, with a blinking insertion point indicating where you can type the button name. Remember that you can reposition the button sprite later if you want.

9] Type *Beep* in the Button text field.

This names the button.

note *Director is preset to add new sprites to the score with a duration of 28 frames. The length of the sprite isn't important in this task, so you need not worry if your button spans a different number of frames. If you want to have your score look the same as the illustrations, choose File > Preferences > Sprite and set the span duration to 28 frames.*

10] Select the button sprite in channel 1 of the score and choose New Behavior from the Script pop-up menu in the sprite toolbar.

You're creating a **sprite script**, which affects only this sprite. You'll learn about the various script types later in this lesson.

CHOOSE NEW BEHAVIOR

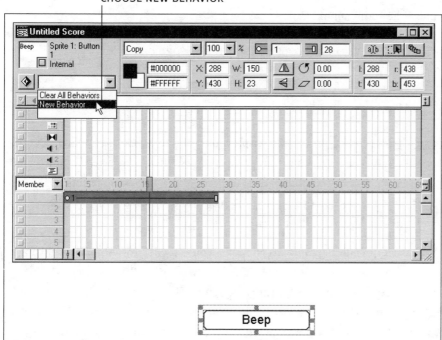

The Script window appears, already containing the Lingo commands *on mouseUp* and *end*. Whenever you create a sprite script, these lines will already be entered in the Script window by default.

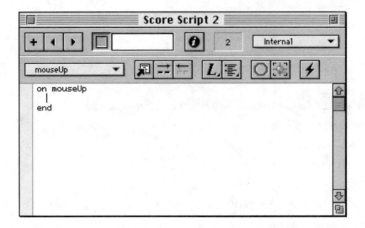

11] Type *beep* in the Script window, at the insertion point, below *on mouseUp*.

Beep is a Lingo command that sounds a system beep on the computer.

This is how the script should look:

on mouseUp ———— EVERY HANDLER STARTS WITH THE WORD *ON*
  beep
end ———————— EVERY HANDLER ENDS WITH THE WORD *END*

Here, and wherever you type a Lingo script, you'll want to check the spelling carefully. Director can't interpret Lingo commands that are misspelled or incorrectly punctuated. You can, however, use any combination of uppercase and lowercase letters in your commands. Director does not pay attention to case and would understand this command typed as *beep*, *BEEP*, or *Beep*.

To make it easier to enter commands correctly, you can click the Alphabetical Lingo button or Categorized Lingo button in the Script window and choose from the lists that are displayed. The Alphabetical Lingo button displays a list of all Lingo commands in alphabetical order. The Categorized Lingo button displays the commands organized in categories. When you select a command, it is pasted into the Script window at the insertion point. Because you don't need to type the command, you are less likely to make typing and syntax errors.

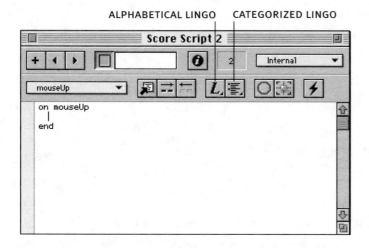

12] Close the Script window by pressing Enter on the numeric keypad or by clicking the close box (in the upper-right corner of the Script window on Windows systems or in the upper-left corner of the Script window on the Macintosh).

note   *Macintosh users: Although pressing Return usually does the same thing as pressing Enter, this is not the case in the Script window. Here, Return starts a new line, just as it does in a word processing application.*

tip   *Pressing Enter on the numeric keypad enters a script only when the Script window is open. When the Script window is closed, pressing Enter on the numeric keypad plays the current movie.*

13] Save your work as *Button1* in your Projects folder.

TESTING A SCRIPT

Any scripting language has certain elements you must use and rules you must follow. If you follow the rules and use the elements correctly, you are rewarded when the script performs as you expect. If the script does not work, you perform **debugging** to correct the syntax or change the elements to satisfy Lingo's rules. In this task, you will test the script you just created.

1] On the toolbar, click the Rewind and Play buttons to rewind and play the movie.
The movie loops because you turned on looping with the Control > Loop Playback command.

2] Click the button you created.

You should hear a beep. If you don't hear a beep, repeat the steps for creating the script in the preceding task. Make sure you type *beep* correctly and close the window when you're done. Also, make sure your speakers are turned on.

3] Stop the movie.

USING THE MESSAGE WINDOW

Now that you know what a script is and how it's created, it's time to delve a little deeper into the way Director and Lingo work together.

Director sends out **messages** whenever some event occurs in a movie. For instance, when the user presses the mouse button to click something, this is a *mouseDown* event, and Director responds to that event by sending a *mouseDown* message. The message is then available for a while for use in Lingo scripts. (You will learn more about how long messages are available in the task "Examining Types of Lingo Scripts" later in this lesson.) When the user releases the mouse button, this is a *mouseUp* event, and Director sends a *mouseUp* message. All actions performed through Lingo are triggered by events.

Lingo scripts can be thought of as a series of instructions to Director to execute specific actions in response to events in a movie. Groups of instructions that relate to a specific event are called **handlers**, because they handle messages issued as the result of events. For instance, in the script you just wrote, you created a handler for the *mouseUp* event associated with the Beep button. When the handler receives the *mouseUp* message, it handles that message by sounding a beep.

In a Lingo script, every handler:
• Begins with the word *on* followed by a message name
• Includes the series of actions to be taken when that event occurs
• Ends with the word *end*

If a script includes several instructions, Director executes the first instruction, then the next one, and so on, until it reaches the end of the handler. Here again is the script you just created:

```
on mouseUp
  beep
end
```

Director automatically sends built-in message names for most common events that occur in a movie. For example, Director sends a *mouseDown* message when you click the mouse button, a *mouseUp* message when you release the mouse button, a *keyDown* message when you press a key on the keyboard, and an *enterFrame* message when the playback head enters a frame. In Lesson 21, you will learn how to define your own messages and corresponding handler names.

You can watch this event-occurrence and message-sending process in action by using the Message window.

1] Choose Window › Message (Windows Ctrl+M, Macintosh Command+M).

The Message window appears.

2] Turn on the Trace function by clicking the Trace button.

When Trace is on, the Message window displays messages and scripts as the movie plays.

TRACE BUTTON

3] Rewind and play the movie. Then click the Beep button you created.

When you click the button on the stage, the Message window displays the messages Director sends and the lines of script it executes. The lines in the Message window preceded by == indicate Director messages that are generated automatically. The lines preceded by --> are the lines in the *mouseUp* handler you created. The actual content in your Message window may differ from what is shown here, but it should include *Handler: mouseUp*, *beep*, and *end*.

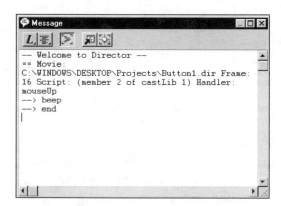

4] Click the Trace button to turn off tracing.

When left on, the Trace feature dramatically slows the speed of the movie.

In addition to seeing the messages Director is sending, you can use the Message window to "talk" to Director yourself, using Lingo. You can test commands by typing them directly in the Message window; Director will run them immediately. You will use the Message window often for creating, testing, and debugging your Lingo scripts.

EXAMINING LINGO ELEMENTS

The instructions included in a Lingo handler consist of a combination of **elements** that are like words in an English sentence. The elements can be categorized according to what they do, and rules determine how they can be combined. All Lingo elements are defined in the "Lingo Dictionary" section of Director's online Help.

Lingo elements are grouped into the following categories:

- **Commands** tell a movie to do something. For example, *go to* instructs the playback head to branch to a specified frame.

- **Functions** return a value. For example, *date* returns the current date as set in the computer.

- **Keywords** are reserved words that have a special meaning in Lingo. For example, all Lingo properties and many sprite properties and functions require that the keyword *the* precede the property name. This keyword distinguishes the property name from a variable or object name.

- **Properties** are attributes of an object. For example, *the colorDepth* is a property of the computer's monitor. Properties may also be expressed with **dot syntax**, as in *sprite (4).visible*, where the property is associated with the object by a period, or dot.

- **Operators** are terms that change or compare one or more values. For example, the > operator compares greater and lesser values, and the + operator adds values.

- **Constants** are elements that don't change. For example, TRUE always has the same meaning. (In Lingo, you can also use numbers to represent the values of TRUE and FALSE. The value of TRUE is 1, and the value of FALSE is 0.)

During editing, the script editor automatically assigns different colors to different Lingo elements, so you can distinguish between reserved keywords and variable names and simple comments.

Now you'll use the Message window to see how some of the Lingo elements work.

The *put* command tells Director to display any results in the Message window. For example, the *the date* function returns the current date according to the computer's system clock. When you string these two elements together, the result is the date displayed in the Message window. In this task, you will use *put* to examine Lingo elements.

362

1] In the Message window, type *put the date* and then press Enter:

You should see the date displayed in the Message window.

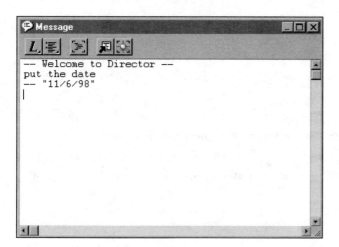

The *the time* function returns the current time according to the computer's system clock. Check it out.

2] Type *put the time* in the Message window and then press Enter:

You should see the time displayed in the Message window.

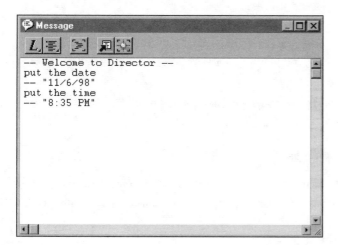

Properties return information about specific items. For instance, you can use properties to get information about the background color of a sprite, the cast member number of a sprite in a particular channel, or the last frame of a movie. You will next try using the *the colorDepth* property of the computer monitor, which returns the current color depth setting.

3] Type *put the colorDepth* in the Message window and then press Enter.

The result should be *8* (assuming your monitor is set to 8-bit color).

The *the loc of sprite* property determines the coordinates (*loc* is short for location) of the specified sprite. The coordinate value is returned as a point (X,Y), where X is the horizontal location and Y is the vertical location. Earlier you created a button called Beep and placed it in channel 1, frame 1. You can use the *the loc of sprite* property to get that button's location.

4] Type *put the loc of sprite 1* in the Message window and then press Enter.

The result is the horizontal and vertical coordinates of the button—for example, the point (181,293). (Your result will likely be different because your button is probably in a different location.)

Operators compare or change values. The + operator adds two numbers together, as you will see next.

5] Type *put 5 + 5* in the Message window and then press Enter.

The result should be *10*. Try another operator.

6] Type *put 5 ‹ 9* in the Message window and then press Enter.

The result is *1*, or TRUE. Remember that 1 represents TRUE and 0 represents FALSE.

7] Type *put 5 › 9* in the Message window and then press Enter.

The result is *0*, or FALSE. Remember that TRUE and FALSE are constants, and their values never change.

8] Type *put TRUE* in the Message window and then press Enter.

The result is *1* because TRUE is a constant value and always equals 1.

9] Close the Message window.

You've just used the Message window to see how various Lingo elements work. This window is a great tool for testing Lingo commands and functions to see how they work before you add them to your scripts.

EXAMINING TYPES OF LINGO SCRIPTS

You can write several types of Lingo scripts. The type of script you choose to write depends on a combination of factors:

• Where you store the script

• The object (for example, a sprite or a cast member) to which you assign the script

• Where you want the script to be available (for example, within a single frame or throughout the movie)

Here's a brief overview of the types of scripts you can write:

• **Primary event scripts** (more often called **primary event handlers**) are overriding, "assume control" scripts. A primary event script can be established to be the first, or primary, receiver of an event. A primary event handler can intercept the event generated when a user clicks the mouse or presses a key, or when a specified amount of time elapses since the last mouse click or key press.

• **Score scripts** (also called **behaviors**) can be invoked only by objects in the score. You can assign a score script to a sprite or to a frame, and it is available only when the sprite or frame is active in the movie.

• **Cast member scripts** are associated with a specific cast member. A cast member script runs in response to an action affecting the cast member.

• **Movie scripts** are assigned to the entire movie.

• **Parent scripts** are the code framework, or class, for a Lingo object.

With the exception of cast member scripts, all scripts take up a slot in the Cast window. Multiple sprites and frames can use the same score script. Cast member scripts, on the other hand, cannot be shared among different cast members—they are stored with each cast member and are editable either through the cast member's script icon or through the Script option from the cast member's Properties window. You will learn how to edit a cast member script in later lessons.

You will use score scripts, cast member scripts, and movie scripts while developing the projects in this book. The rest of this section describes these script types in greater detail. For more information about primary event handlers and parent scripts, see the *Learning Lingo* manual included with Director.

There are two types of score scripts: **sprite scripts** and **frame scripts**.

Sprite scripts, like the one you created earlier for the Beep button, are assigned to a sprite in the score. If you need to control a cast member's actions for only a short time, or only in a particular section of the score, or only in one particular instance of that cast member on the stage, create a sprite script. A single sprite can have multiple sprite scripts.

Frame scripts are assigned to a specific frame in the score. Use frame scripts to create handlers that you want to always be available for an individual frame or to control the playback head without requiring input from the user. A frequent use of a frame script is to keep the playback head paused in a frame until a specific event (such as a button click) occurs.

Cast member scripts are assigned to a cast member. Assigning a script to a cast member is useful when you want the cast member to always execute the same Lingo code, regardless of where the cast member appears in the score. If you are creating something like a Return to Main Menu button that always performs the same action, create a cast member script.

Movie scripts are available to the entire movie while the movie plays. Movie scripts can control what happens when a movie starts, stops, or pauses. If you want to access a script from anywhere in a movie, place it in a movie script. If every cast member or frame needs access to the functionality of a handler, place the handler in a movie script. For example, a handler in a movie script might run when the movie starts in order to check the color depth of the user's monitor.

When an event (such as a mouse click) occurs, Director responds by issuing a message of the same name. For example, when a user releases the mouse button, a *mouseUp* event is generated. Director responds to the *mouseUp* event by issuing a *mouseUp* message. A message travels, in order, through sprite scripts, cast member scripts, frame scripts, and movie scripts, looking for a handler by the same name. In most cases (including all the scripts you will write for the projects in this book), a message runs the first matching handler it encounters, and then the message stops. An exception occurs at the sprite level. A sprite can have more than one script, and a message always looks at all of a sprite's scripts and runs any matching handlers it finds before stopping. For example, a sprite can have two or more *on mouseUp* handlers; a *mouseUp* message that reaches the sprite runs both handlers in the order in which you assigned the *mouseUp* scripts to the sprite, and only then does the message stop.

The following illustration shows the message order for the types of Lingo scripts you will create in this book.

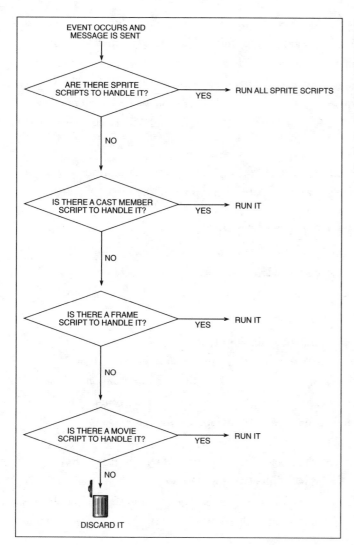

```
            EVENT OCCURS AND
            MESSAGE IS SENT
                   │
                   ▼
         ┌─────────────────────┐
         │   ARE THERE SPRITE   │  YES
         │ SCRIPTS TO HANDLE IT?│ ──────▶  RUN ALL SPRITE SCRIPTS
         └─────────────────────┘
                   │ NO
                   ▼
         ┌─────────────────────┐
         │ IS THERE A CAST MEMBER│  YES
         │ SCRIPT TO HANDLE IT?  │ ──────▶  RUN IT
         └─────────────────────┘
                   │ NO
                   ▼
         ┌─────────────────────┐
         │   IS THERE A FRAME   │  YES
         │ SCRIPT TO HANDLE IT? │ ──────▶  RUN IT
         └─────────────────────┘
                   │ NO
                   ▼
         ┌─────────────────────┐
         │   IS THERE A MOVIE   │  YES
         │ SCRIPT TO HANDLE IT? │ ──────▶  RUN IT
         └─────────────────────┘
                   │ NO
                   ▼
               DISCARD IT
```

Messages travel in a specific order through the scripts in a movie, looking for a handler with a matching name. If Director does not find any handler for the message, it simply discards the message, and nothing happens.

This illustration does not show all the intricacies of Director's message order. For example, Lingo is a flexible language, and it provides a way (through the *pass* and *stopEvent* commands) for you to override the message order illustrated here. Also, even though you will not be creating primary event handlers in this book, you should keep in mind that they are first in the message order. Finally, parent scripts for objects, also not covered in this book, are not a part of the message order. Consult the *Learning Lingo* manual that comes with Director for a comprehensive discussion of messages and message order.

For beginning Lingo programmers, it's important to understand that a movie can contain many handlers with the same name. Your project design—how you assign scripts—determines which version of a handler runs. For example, it is common for a movie to have many different *on mouseUp* handlers. Each *on mouseUp* handler might be attached to a different sprite in the score, and other *on mouseUp* handlers might be assigned to cast members. Which *on mouseUp* handler actually runs depends on when and where a user clicks.

The next task will help you understand how the message order determines which script runs. You will also learn how to create each type of script.

CREATING DIFFERENT TYPES OF SCRIPTS

In this task, you will continue work on the Beep button you started earlier by creating four types of scripts: a sprite script, cast member script, frame script, and movie script. You will then test these scripts to observe how the message order affects which script runs.

As you work through these steps, you will notice that Director sometimes gives you a head start by opening the Script window with a handler for the most common message already partially entered for you. For a sprite script, Director enters *on mouseUp* and *end* commands; for a frame script, Director enters *on exitFrame* and *end* commands. You are not restricted to these handlers only; Director defaults to them to be helpful.

1] Select the Beep button on the stage. Then choose Modify › Sprite › Script (Windows Ctrl+Shift+', Macintosh Shift+Command+').
You already assigned this sprite a script that sounds a beep when the Beep button is clicked. You will now change the script to do something else.

The *alert* command sounds a beep and displays a dialog box containing a message you specify. Replace the *beep* command with the *alert* command now.

tip *Here and in the following steps, notice that the Script window's title bar identifies the script type. If you're ever unsure of the type of script being displayed, check the title bar.*

2] Make the change shown here in bold and then close the Script window.

```
on mouseUp
    alert "This is the sprite script"
end
```

The quotation marks tell Director that this is the text of the message you want to display. Now when you click the Beep button, a dialog box displays *This is the sprite script*.

3] Play the movie and click the Beep button.

You should see a dialog box with your message and an OK button.

4] Click OK to dismiss the dialog box.

5] Stop the movie.

Now you're going to create a cast script for the Beep button.

6] In the Cast window, select the Beep button (cast member 1). Then click the Cast Member Script button.

SCRIPT BUTTON

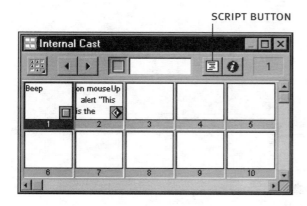

The Script window appears, already containing the Lingo commands *on mouseUp* and *end*. Whenever you create a cast script, these lines appear in the Script window. (Recall that these lines are also displayed whenever you create a sprite script.)

tip *With a cast member selected, you can also create a cast member script by choosing Modify > Cast Member > Script (Windows Ctrl+', Macintosh Command+') or by clicking the Script button on the toolbar.*

7] **Create the handler shown here and then close the Script window.**

```
on mouseUp
    alert "This is the cast script"
end
```

Now you have a *mouseUp* handler in both the sprite script attached to the Beep button and the cast script attached to the Beep button. According to the message order listed previously, the *mouseUp* handler in the sprite script should take precedence, and the *mouseUp* handler in the cast script should not be executed. Try out the button now.

8] **Play the movie and click the Beep button.**

As expected, you see the dialog box with the sprite script message. This is because sprite scripts take precedence over cast scripts.

9] **Click OK to dismiss the dialog box and then stop the movie.**

Next you'll remove the sprite script to see how the *mouseUp* message passes through the sprite level to the cast member level.

10] **Select the Beep button on the stage. Then choose Clear All Behaviors from the Behaviors menu in the score.**

CLEAR ALL BEHAVIORS

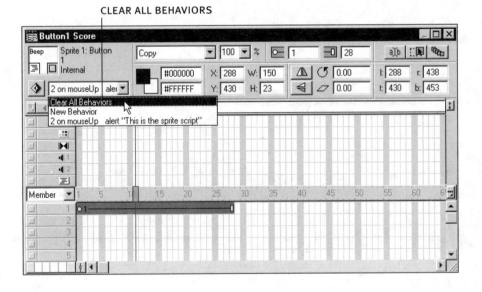

This removes the sprite script from the button sprite. However, the cast script still remains intact.

11] Play the movie and click the Beep button.

Now an alert box appears with the cast script message. This is because there is no *mouseUp* handler at the sprite script level, so the message was sent to the next level in the message order.

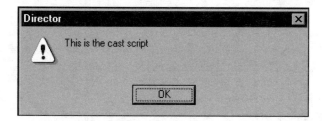

12] Click OK to dismiss the dialog box and then stop the movie.

Next you'll add a frame script to the movie, but you need to make a minor adjustment first.

13] If the button sprite in your score spans more than one frame, adjust the sprite's duration so that the sprite occupies only frame 1.

As the previous steps demonstrated, when you select a sprite and assign a script to it, that script is active for the sprite's entire duration, regardless of the number of frames the sprite spans. Frame scripts, however, are active only within the frame to which they are assigned. The following steps will be easier if you reduce the sprite to a single frame; you can then attach a frame script to this single frame, rather than assigning it to every frame within the button sprite's duration.

14] Double-click the script channel, frame 1.

DOUBLE-CLICK HERE

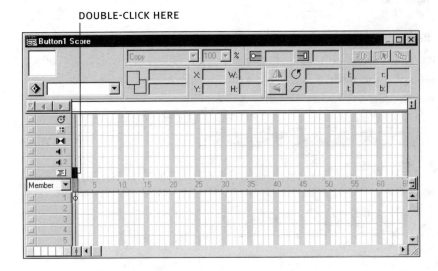

The Script window appears, already containing the Lingo commands *on exitFrame* and *end*. To see how the message order works in this task, you need to change the default handler name from *on exitFrame* to *on mouseUp*.

15] Select all the text in the Script window and delete it. Type the following and then close the window:

```
on mouseUp
  alert "This is the frame script"
end
```

You now have a *mouseUp* handler in the cast member script attached to the Beep button that displays an alert message when the Beep button is clicked. You also have a *mouseUp* handler in the frame script attached to frame 1 that displays an alert message whenever the mouse is clicked. For the frame script to go into action, the mouse doesn't have to be clicked on any particular area because the frame script isn't attached to any particular object (such as a button). Try it out.

16] Play the movie and click the Beep button.
Because the cast script takes precedence over the frame script, you see a dialog box with the cast script message, and the *mouseUp* handler in the frame script is not executed.

17] Click OK to dismiss the dialog box and then click anywhere except on the Beep button.

You see a dialog box with the frame script message. This is because a *mouseUp* message was generated by the mouse click. Even though the Beep button contains a handler for the *mouseUp* message, you did not click the Beep button itself, so that cast script is not executed because it never received the *mouseUp* message. Sprites (and casts) receive the *mouseUp* message only if the sprite (or cast member) is the object being clicked. Because Director can't find a sprite or cast script to handle the *mouseUp* message, the message is sent up to the next level in the message order, the frame script level. Because you have a *mouseUp* handler in the frame script, that handler is executed here.

18] Click OK to dismiss the dialog box and then stop the movie.

19] Press Ctrl+Shift+U (Windows) or Command+Shift+U (Macintosh) to open the movie script.

In this case, the Script window contains no default Lingo commands. This is different than when you create a sprite script, cast script, or frame script.

20] Type the following and then close the window:

```
on mouseUp
    alert "This is the movie script"
end
```

You now have a *mouseUp* handler in the cast member script attached to the Beep button. You have a *mouseUp* handler in the frame script attached to frame 1. You also have a *mouseUp* handler in the movie script. Test the handlers.

21] Play the movie and click the Beep button.

As expected, the cast script message is displayed in the dialog box.

22] Click OK to dismiss the dialog box and then click anywhere except on the Beep button.

According to the message order, the frame script takes precedence over the movie script, so the frame script message is displayed in the dialog box, and the *mouseUp* handler in the movie script is not executed.

23] Stop the movie.

You're going to clear the frame script to see how the *mouseUp* message is forwarded to the movie script.

24] Select the behavior channel, frame 1. Then choose Clear All Behaviors from the Behaviors menu in the score.

This removes the script attached to the frame. However, a *mouseUp* handler still remains in the movie script.

25] Play the movie and click the Beep button.

The cast script message is displayed in the dialog box.

26] Click OK to dismiss the dialog box and then click anywhere except on the Beep button.

Because you removed the frame script, the *mouseUp* message is sent to the next level in the message order, and you see the movie script message.

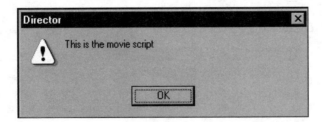

27] Stop the movie.

As you can probably guess, if a script is not working correctly, you can track the message through the message order, and you may be able to find the problem that way. Understanding message order can be very important when you are debugging scripts. It's also useful for creating scripts that temporarily override other scripts, as you've just seen in this task. (For example, you could create a cast member script for a button that usually performs one action and also create a sprite script for the button so it performs differently in some cases.)

WHAT YOU HAVE LEARNED

In this lesson you have:

• Written and tested a simple Lingo script [page 355]

• Used the Message window to watch a script perform [page 360]

• Examined types of Lingo scripts: sprite, cast member, frame, and movie scripts [page 365]

• Learned how Lingo communicates using messages and handlers [page 366]

• Created Lingo scripts to test the message order [page 368]

and events

handlers

LESSON 17

Lingo is a full-featured scripting language designed primarily to respond to events in the Director environment. When a movie plays, Director generates messages for various milestones in the playback process. Just as an actor called onto the stage may work from a script, so too a sprite can work from a script when Director calls it onto the stage or when any significant event occurs.

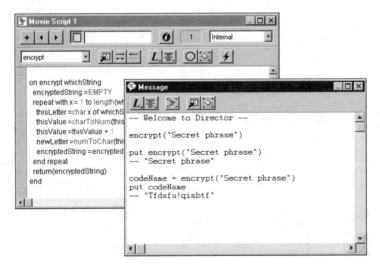

```
Movie Script 1                                    _ □ ×
+ ◄ ►  □                          ❶   1   Internal   ▼
encrypt          ▼   🗗 ⇄ ⊟ L ☰  ○ 🖵 ⚡
                                                    ▲
  on encrypt whichString
    encryptedString =EMPTY        🗨 Message                        _ □ ×
    repeat with x = 1 to length(wh
      thisLetter =char x of whichS    L ☰  ☲ 🗗 🖵
      thisValue =charToNum(this
      thisValue =thisValue + 1    -- Welcome to Director --              ▲
      newLetter =numToChar(this
      encryptedString =encrypted   encrypt("Secret phrase")
    end repeat
    return(encryptedString)        put encrypt("Secret phrase")
  end                              -- "Secret phrase"

                                   codeName = encrypt("Secret phrase")
                                   put codeName
                                   -- "Tfdsfu!qisbtf"

                                                                        ▼
  ◄                                ◄                                   ►
```

Director issues notifications of nearly every event in a movie. You can intercept these event messages and write handlers to take control of Director, perform common services, encrypt passwords and encode messages, and more—all using Lingo.

Practically every action in Director can be scripted to the point at which the score is literally optional. Although most of the examples in this book use the score, it is possible to avoid the score altogether and use Lingo scripts for everything, just by creating scripts to respond to events. Even if you don't want to completely abandon the score, the capability to write scripts to respond to events in the Director environment gives you a powerful, efficient way to add interaction and other features to your Director movies.

In this lesson, you'll learn in detail about the various events that Director can generate, how event handlers work, and how to create your own event handlers using Lingo.

WHAT YOU WILL LEARN

In this lesson you will:

- Learn about events and messages
- Learn how to detect events
- Learn how to log events
- Learn about handlers and handler hierarchy
- Learn about parameters and return values
- Create a handler that accepts a parameter and returns a value

APPROXIMATE TIME

It should take about 1 hour to complete this lesson.

LESSON FILES

Media Files:

None

Starting Files:

Lesson17\Start\Start.dir

Completed Files:

Lesson17\Complete\Events.dir
Lesson17\Complete\Crypt.dir

WHAT EVENTS ARE

If Lingo didn't exist, Director would play your movies, starting at frame 1, and continue until the end unless some instruction in the tempo channel intervened, such as an instruction to wait for a mouse click. Neither the Behavior Inspector nor the Library Palette would exist—behaviors are just Lingo scripts packaged for your convenience—so you could not use behaviors to add interactivity and other features. The display of your movies would be essentially linear.

Of course, Director is capable of much more than just linear play. Games, training software, presentations, and much more have been written with Director, and most of these applications use interactivity, branching, and other types of nonlinear execution achieved using Lingo scripts or behaviors that respond to **events**. Nearly everything that occurs in a Director movie is an event, and as a Director movie plays, Director issues notifications internally that specific events have occurred. These notifications are called **messages**. When the user presses the mouse button, for example, that is a *mouseDown* event, and Director responds by sending a *mouseDown* message.

Because nearly every action results in an event, you have the ability to intercede in a Director movie at nearly any point. You can intercede when Director is launching a projector, preparing a movie, starting a movie, or preparing a frame; you can intercede after Director draws a frame, exits a frame, starts using a sprite, or stops using a sprite; you can intercede when the mouse cursor enters a region, is within a region, or exits a region. Director sends a message when any event occurs and gives you the opportunity to respond to the event using Lingo.

WATCHING EVENTS

In this task, you'll take an initial look at some of the common events for which Director generates messages. A good way to do this is to set up **handlers** to catch particular messages and display them on the screen as they occur. A handler is a group of Lingo instructions designed to handle a particular message. (For a detailed discussion of handlers, see "Handlers and Handler Hierarchy" later in this lesson.)

1] Open Start.dir in the Lesson17 folder and save it as *Events.dir*.
Start.dir contains the basic framework for detecting events.

2] Choose Window › Score (Windows Ctrl+4, Macintosh Command+4) to open the Score window.

Only one sprite, Status, appears in the score. This sprite (cast member 2) is a text field on the stage.

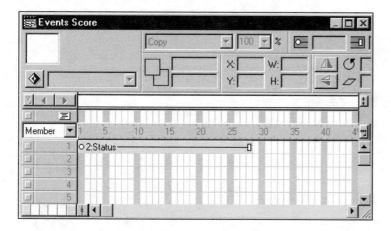

3] Close the Score window (Windows Ctrl+4, Macintosh Command+4).

Now look at the cast.

4] Choose Window › Cast (Windows Ctrl+3, Macintosh Command+3) to open the Cast window.

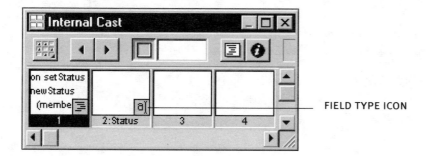

FIELD TYPE ICON

Two cast members are visible. Cast member 2 is the Status text field, a field type cast member. You use field cast members when you want the user to be able to enter or modify text on the stage. You can also use Lingo to enter text into a text field, as you will do in this lesson. Notice the icon for the field type in the cast window: a letter *a* with the editing cursor next to it.

Cast member 1 is a movie script that contains the following Lingo script:

```
on setStatus newStatus
  (member "status").text = newStatus
end

on prepareMovie
  setStatus("PrepareMovie")
end

on startMovie
  setStatus("StartMovie")
end

on prepareFrame
  setStatus("PrepareFrame")
end

on enterFrame
  setStatus("EnterFrame")
end

on exitFrame
  setStatus("ExitFrame")
end

on stepFrame
  setStatus("StepFrame")
end

on stopMovie
  setStatus("StopMovie")
end

on mouseDown
  setStatus("MouseDown")
end

on mouseUp
  setStatus("MouseUp")
end

on keyDown
  setStatus("KeyDown")
end

on keyUp
  setStatus("KeyUp")
end
```

This script consists of a number of handlers, each beginning with the keyword *on* and ending with the keyword *end*. The script essentially has two parts. The first part is the first handler, *setStatus*.

```
on setStatus newStatus
  (member "status").text = newStatus
end
```

The *setStatus* handler takes a parameter, *newStatus*, and updates the contents of the text field, *"status"* (cast member 2). A **parameter** is an additional piece of information that can be passed to a handler. In this case, the handler takes the information, stored locally in a variable called *newStatus*, and uses it to update the *text* property of the Status cast member. You will use variables extensively in later lessons, but for now, you can consider a **variable** to be like a container that you can put things into for storage—like a cup or a box. Using Lingo, you can create variables and place **values** (names and numbers, for example) into them. You can also use Lingo to retrieve the values (or change the values) of variables as needed.

Each type of cast member has various attributes that are specific to that type. These attributes are called **properties**. A bitmap cast member, for instance, has a palette property that denotes what palette is assigned to the bitmap. A sprite has location properties that are determined by the sprite's location on the stage. In this case, the Status cast member is a field type, and field cast members have a property called *text*, which means that the field content is a string of characters. You can set this content through Lingo, which gives you the power to change the information stored in the field cast member.

note *For a list of other properties of field cast members, open Director Help and type* Field *in the index entry box. Under Field Cast Member Properties and Field Properties, you will see entries such as* autoTab of member *and* font of member. *The documentation indicates whether you can set the property to a new value or simply view the existing value.*

The second part of the script contains handlers that all perform a similar function: They catch, or handle, different messages and call on the *setStatus* handler to describe the messages they are handling. Look at two of these handlers:

```
on prepareMovie
  setStatus("PrepareMovie")
end

on startMovie
  setStatus("StartMovie")
end
```

These two instructions are similar except for the handler names and the text that gets placed in the Status cast member. You can see that when the *prepareMovie* handler is called, it sets the Status text to "PrepareMovie", and when the *startMovie* handler is called, it sets the Status text to "StartMovie". In other words, the *setStatus* function updates the Status field every time one of these handlers is invoked. As the movie runs, you can watch the Status field as it changes to report the last executed event.

5] In the Score window, double-click frame 1 of the tempo channel. Use the slider to set the tempo to 1 frame per second (fps) and then click OK.

This slower tempo will allow you to see the changes in the Status field without their overwriting themselves too quickly to be read.

USE THE SLIDER TO SET THE TEMPO TO 1 FRAME PER SECOND

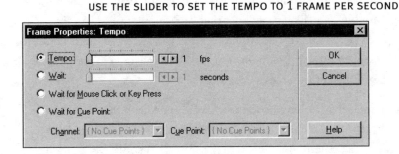

6] Bring the stage to the front by choosing Window › Stage (Windows Ctrl+1, Macintosh Command+1) and then click Play on the control panel or choose Control › Play (Windows Ctrl+Alt+P, Macintosh Command+Alt+P).

The movie plays, and you see the Status field updating in response to each of the messages received by the handlers in the movie script. Even at this slow tempo, many messages are being displayed too quickly for you to read them.

7] Try generating messages of your own: Press the mouse button, release the mouse button, or type on the keyboard.

Your actions generate *mouseDown*, *mouseUp*, *keyDown*, and *keyUp* events that cause Director to send their respective messages.

8] Stop the movie by clicking the Stop button on the control panel or choosing Control › Stop (Windows Ctrl+Alt+. [period], Macintosh Command+Alt+. [period]).

The playback stops, and "StopMovie" should appear in the Status field.

The *stopMovie* event is the last event that Director generates; you can use it to exercise some control over the movie at the time of its completion. For example, you can use this event to perform various cleanup tasks, such as closing any files you may have opened.

The Status field undoubtedly updated too quickly for you to see each event as it happened. What you really need is a printed log of events. Your next task will be to log the events to the Message window.

LOGGING EVENTS

You used Director's Message window in Lesson 16 to receive trace output and test simple equations. In fact, you can use the Message window to test many of Lingo's commands. You can use Lingo's *put* command to direct output (results) from a function to the Message window. This feature allows you to log information as you work.

1] Open the Cast window if it is not already open. Double-click cast member 1 to open the Movie Script window for editing.

The *setStatus* handler is at the top of the script. It currently sets the text of the Status field; however, because Director is constantly generating events, no sooner is one event displayed than another appears to take its place. You don't have time to read the text before it disappears from the screen.

2] **Click the Script window and modify the *setStatus* handler by adding the line shown here in bold:**

```
on setStatus newStatus
  put newStatus
  (member "status").text = newStatus
end
```

Now when this handler is called, it will not only update the Status field, but it will also write the information in the Message window so you can read it even after new output arrives. (Eventually, though, the oldest messages will be discarded if there are a lot of messages; the Message window does not have sufficient memory to record all messages indefinitely.)

3] **Close the Script window and play the movie again. Let it run for a few seconds and then stop it.**

As before, the status display changes very rapidly. However, the status information now appears in the Message window as well.

4] **Choose Window › Message to open the Message window (Windows Ctrl+M, Macintosh Command+M).**

The Message window appears, and the last few messages are visible. If you scroll back, you can see the previous messages as well.

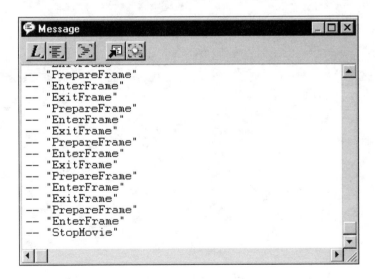

By studying the messages, you can see what is happening: Director generates a *prepareFrame* message when it prepares to draw a frame and then an *enterFrame* message when it has actually drawn the frame. At that point, Director reports an *exitFrame* event to indicate that it is about to leave the current frame. Then the cycle repeats. Even if Director were looping on a single frame, the sequence would be the same.

5] Save your work.

ON YOUR OWN

You can leave the Message window open while you run the Events movie. As each event occurs, it is logged in the Message window by the *setStatus* handler. Watch the playback head as it moves to see when events are reported. Use the keyboard and mouse to generate more messages.

HANDLERS AND HANDLER HIERARCHY

You can think of handlers as instruction sheets for various tasks. Each handler can perform one or more instructions, in a specified order, and can return information to wherever the handler was called from. Handlers can optionally take **arguments**, also known as **parameters**, which are additional values passed to the handler when it is called and that provide additional information the handler needs to complete its task. For example, the *setStatus* handler you used earlier in the lesson took one parameter: *newStatus*. By itself, *setStatus* doesn't know what to change the Status text to, but by passing in the *newStatus* value, you give it the information it needs.

Each handler has a name that is used to invoke it. In the script, the name is preceded by the keyword *on*. The Events movie, for example, contains a handler to handle the *mouseUp* message. That handler is called the *mouseUp* handler or the *on mouseUp* handler. You can name a handler almost anything you want, so long as the name conforms to the language rules, which specify that the name must start with a letter and can include only letters, numbers, and underscore (_) characters. Some names, however, already have assigned uses. When Director events occur, Director tries to invoke handlers with certain names for each event. For instance, when a movie starts, Director calls a *startMovie* handler, which may or may not exist. If you have written a handler called *startMovie* and it is available in a movie script, then Director will invoke that handler automatically when the movie starts. If no such handler exists, nothing special happens; Director tries to call handlers, but you aren't required to have a handler for every event.

When certain events occur, Director automatically calls various handler names, such as those listed here; you can write scripts for these handlers to respond to the events that triggered the calls. Director programmers commonly write handlers with the following names automatically invoked by Director:

- *prepareMovie* is called after cast members are loaded but before the first frame is drawn or any behaviors are assigned.
- *startMovie* is called just before the playback head enters the first frame.
- *stopMovie* is called when the movie ends.
- *prepareFrame* is called before the current frame is drawn.
- *enterFrame* is called after the current frame is drawn and before Director leaves the frame.
- *exitFrame* is called when the playback head is about to exit the current frame and move on.
- *mouseDown* is called when the mouse button is pushed down (a *rightMouseDown* handler is also available).
- *mouseUp* is called when the mouse button is released (a *rightMouseUp* handler is also available).
- *mouseEnter* is called when the mouse cursor enters a sprite's boundary region from another sprite or the stage.
- *mouseWithin* is called repeatedly while the mouse cursor is over a sprite.
- *mouseLeave* is called when the mouse cursor leaves a sprite's boundary region.
- *keyDown* is called when a key on the keyboard is pressed down (modifier keys such as Ctrl, Alt, and Shift do not trigger this handler).
- *keyUp* is called when a key on the keyboard is released.
- *beginSprite* is called when the playback head encounters the first frame of a sprite span.
- *endSprite* is called when the playback head reaches the last frame of a sprite.
- *idle* is called when Director is just waiting between frames.

Director calls many other handlers as well.

The Events movie shows an example of how a handler is invoked in response to a statement in another handler. All the handlers in that script except the first one are invoked in response to one of Director's built-in messages. Each of these handlers contains a line such as:

```
setStatus("StartMovie")
```

Director recognizes this as a **call** to another handler named *setStatus*. When a command in Lingo (or some other programming language) invokes a handler, it is said to call the handler. Using Lingo, one handler can call another, or you can call a handler from the Message window. If Director finds a handler with the called name, the handler is invoked and the instructions in that handler are executed. When the called handler finishes, execution returns to the handler that did the calling. If the handler contains additional instruction, they have the chance to be executed. For example, the *on startMovie* handler could have been written like this:

```
on startMovie
    put the date
    setStatus("StartMovie")
    beep
end
```

When the *on startMovie* handler is invoked, execution begins with the first statement: *put the date*. This causes the current date to be displayed in the Message window. The next statement calls the *setStatus* handler. This causes execution to switch to the statements in that handler. When *setStatus* finishes, as indicated by the *end* statement, execution returns to the *startMovie* handler and continues with the statement following the call to *startMovie*. In the example, the *beep* statement is executed. If any other statements followed, they too would be executed until the *end* statement is reached in the *startMovie* handler.

As discussed in Lesson 16, Director attempts to call a handler according to a hierarchial sequence. For events that could apply to an individual sprite, such as a *mouseEnter* event (because the mouse cursor goes over the sprite), a *mouseDown* event (because the mouse can click a sprite), or a *beginSprite* event, Director attempts to call a handler by that name in a script attached directly to the sprite involved. If the sprite does not have a handler for the event, Director gives the original cast member for that sprite an opportunity to respond. This order of response lets a cast member provide a handler that supports all sprites created from it, but a single sprite can override the cast member's handlers by providing its own handlers. This works, because the sprite is given the opportunity to respond to the call first.

When a script is available for the whole movie, it is called a movie script. When you choose Window > Script while in an empty cast member, Director automatically makes the script a movie script. If you double-click a frame script channel (the behavior channel) or select the script icon for a cast member or sprite, then Director automatically creates a score script, or behavior.

Director makes a distinction between movie-level handlers and behaviors assigned to score objects (such as frames, sprites, or cast members). This is because sprites, cast members, and frames can all respond to the same kind of message with the same name, such as a *mouseDown* message, when it is directed to them. However, Director recognizes only one handler of a given name within movie scripts. If a movie contains two movie scripts, for example, and each contains a handler with the same name, then only the first handler Director finds will be executed. The other handler with the same name will be ignored.

A movie script is identified in the title bar of the Script window when you edit it.

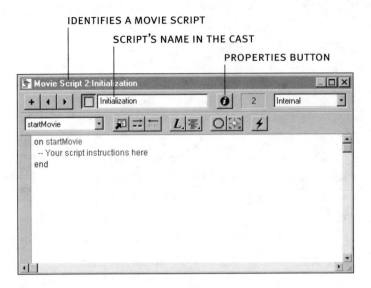

IDENTIFIES A MOVIE SCRIPT

SCRIPT'S NAME IN THE CAST

PROPERTIES BUTTON

You can change a movie script to a behavior script by clicking the Properties button in the Movie Script window and choosing Type > Behavior in the Script Cast Member Properties dialog box.

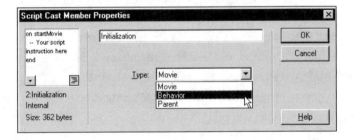

A handler in a behavior script is invoked only when the script is attached to a sprite or frame and that sprite or frame is asked to invoke that handler.

A handler in a movie script is invoked only if no sprite, cast member, or frame behavior script accepts the message first. Some events, such as *startMovie*, are sent only to movie handlers, because they apply to the whole movie, not just a specific sprite or frame.

tip *A common mistake is to write a* startMovie *handler and then place it in a behavior for the frame script for the first frame. Although this seems like a reasonable place for the handler, the* startMovie *event in fact occurs before the playback head reaches the first frame, and so the* startMovie *handler will not be called. Instead,* startMovie *must be placed in a movie script in order for it to be called.*

388

PARAMETERS AND RETURN VALUES

Handlers can return values to the caller. That is, they can perform an action and return information, as if to say, "and the result was. . . ." Most of the handlers for Director events do not need to return values to Director. If they did, Director would just ignore the return values anyway. However, you will often find it useful to write handlers that return values to you.

In this next task, you will write a handler to encrypt a string of characters. The encryption technique will be simple: You will just shift each letter up or down a certain number of characters in the alphabet. You will need to pass in the string to encrypt (a parameter) and get an encrypted string back (the return value).

1] Choose File › New › Movie to start a new movie (Windows Ctrl+N, Macintosh Command+N).

2] Choose Window › Script to open a movie script (Windows Ctrl+0, Macintosh Command+0).

A blank Script window appears. Unlike behavior scripts, a movie script does not assume default handlers and does not provide a default framework.

3] Type the following handler in the script editor:

```
on encrypt whichString
  return(whichString)
end
```

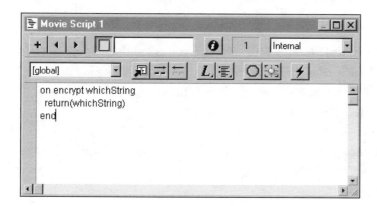

This handler takes one parameter, the variable *whichString*, and returns it to you; nothing has happened between the call and the return, so you get back exactly what you put in. You can see this by calling the handler from the Message window.

4] Close the script editor and choose Window › Message to open the Message window.

5] In the Message window, type

encrypt("Secret phrase")

and press Enter (Windows) or Return (Macintosh) on the main keyboard.

tip   *You may still have many lines in the Message window from previous tasks. You can delete them if you want. An easy method is to select all the text (Windows Ctrl+A, Macintosh Command+A) and then press the Delete key. If you make mistakes in a line you enter in the Message window, you can edit the text using the same techniques you would use in any simple text editor.*

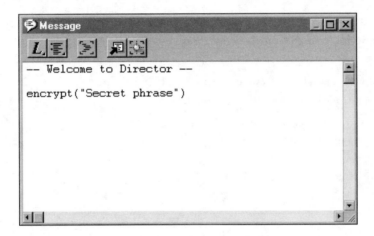

Nothing seemed to happen. This is because, although you called the *encrypt* handler and the handler sent back a value, there was no way to see the result. One solution is to use the *put* command to put the result in the window. You saw how the *put* command can be used with the Message window in the previous lesson.

6] In the Message window, type

put encrypt("Secret phrase")

and press Enter (Windows) or Return (Macintosh) on the main keyboard.
This time you can see the string that was returned.

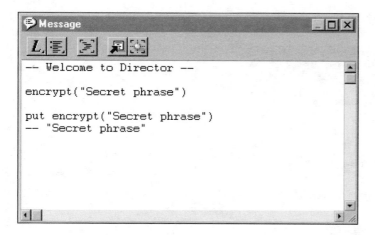

It is the same string that you passed in, but that was to be expected since as yet the *encrypt* handler contains no Lingo script for performing the actual encryption. You have just passed in a value, a string of characters, to a handler and received a result. Although this procedure demonstrates the mechanics of passing values, the handler still needs to modify or evaluate or act on the value to be of any use. Your next task will be to write the Lingo statements to encrypt the string.

7] Choose Window › Script to open the Script window again.

You can now modify the script.

8] Replace the existing script instructions with the ones shown here in bold:

```
on encrypt whichString
    encryptedString = EMPTY
    repeat with x = 1 to length(whichString)
        thisLetter = char x of whichString
        thisValue = charToNum(thisLetter)
        thisValue = thisValue + 1
        newLetter = numToChar(thisValue)
        encryptedString = encryptedString & newLetter
    end repeat
    return(encryptedString)
end
```

The Script window should look like this:

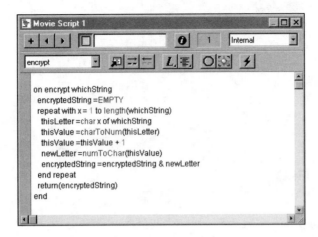

This handler starts by assigning the variable *encryptedString* a value of *EMPTY* (because nothing has been added yet). In Lingo, a variable such as *encryptedString* is created just by using it. If you have worked in other programming languages, you know that some require you to declare a variable before you can use it. This is not the case in Lingo. In the sample script, the variable *encryptedString* is created at the same time that it is assigned a value. Values can be assigned in many ways using Lingo; this example uses the equal sign and has the form:

variable = value

One type of value that can be assigned to a variable is a **string**. A string is a sequence of letters enclosed in quotation marks, such as the string you asked the handler to encrypt: "Secret phrase". The quotation marks tell Director that the text is a string and not a variable name or some other element.

Next the script repeats a body of instructions a certain number of times: once for each letter in the parameter that the handler received. These are the lines beginning with *repeat* and ending with *end repeat*. This is called a **loop**, because the movie loops through the code repeatedly. The Lingo in the loop contains a number of statements, some of which may seem obvious to you, but most probably will not. All of them will be discussed in later lessons. Here's what's going on:

- A variable *x* keeps track of the number of times the movie goes through the loop: once for each letter in the string contained in the variable *whichString*.

- Each time the movie goes though the loop, Director processes a single letter of the *whichString* string converting it to a number, adding 1 to that number, and converting it back to a letter again.

- The converted letter is placed in a string (in the variable *encryptedString*) along with the letters from the previous passes through the loop.

This script has the effect of shifting an A to a B, a Q to an R, and so on. After each letter is shifted, it is added to the originally empty *encryptedString*. This builds an encrypted string from a nonencrypted one, one letter at a time. After Director executes the *repeat* loop the appropriate number of times, it executes the following statement: *return(encryptedString)*. The *return* command causes the return value to be sent back to the handler (or Message window) that called the *encrypt* handler.

9] Close the Script window. Open the Message window if it is not already open.

10] Again call the *encrypt( )* function using the Message window. This time, rather than using the *put* command, assign the result to the variable *codeName*. Type the following and press Enter (Windows) or Return (Macintosh):

```
codeName = encrypt("Secret phrase")
```

Nothing appears in the Message window to indicate that anything happened, but the encrypted string was returned and was placed in the variable *codeName*.

11] To see that something did occur, type the following and press Enter (Windows) or Return (Macintosh):

```
put codeName
```

This time, the result displayed is actually encrypted.

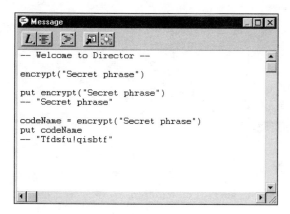

All the letters are shifted. Note that the seventh character is an exclamation point. If you look at the source string, "Secret phrase," you see that the seventh letter is actually the space character. That, too, was encrypted and returned as an exclamation mark. To a computer, the alphabet and other characters all are in an order. In that order, "T"

follows "S," "f" follows "e," and the exclamation point follows the space character. That is how the encryption was performed: each letter was shifted to the next letter in the computer's character order.

Now you can return encrypted messages; to read them, though, you need to create a decryption handler. You will do that next. You will start by creating a second copy of the handler script you just finished.

12] Open the Cast window.

Cast member 1 (the script) should be selected. If it is not, select it now.

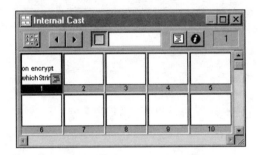

13] Choose Edit › Duplicate (Windows Ctrl+D, Macintosh Command+D).

The script is duplicated in cast member 2. You now have two identical scripts, one of which you can edit without having to type it all in again. When you start writing many handlers, this type of editing can save you a lot of time.

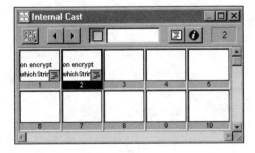

You will edit this second script to create the decryption handler.

14] Choose Window › Script to open the script in cast member 2 for editing.

The script is written for encryption, so the first thing you need to do is to change the variable names to minimize confusion. You will change all occurrences of *encrypt* to *decrypt*.

15] Choose Edit > Find > Text to open the Find Text window (Windows Ctrl+F, Macintosh Command+F).

16] Enter *encrypt* in the Find field. Then enter *decrypt* in the Replace field. Make sure the search is limited to cast member 2.

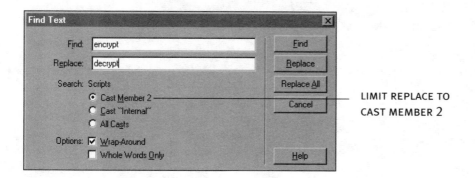

LIMIT REPLACE TO
CAST MEMBER 2

17] Click Replace All and click OK when the warning dialog box appears.

All occurrences of *encrypt* are now changed to *decrypt* in cast member 2—quick and easy editing!

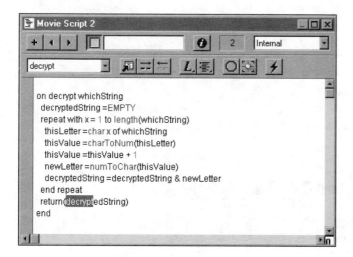

Although the names have been changed, the function of the *decrypt* handler is still the same as that of the *encrypt* handler. You need to make it shift letters down, instead of up, to decrypt a coded string; where *encrypt* shifted an "A" to a "B", the *decrypt* handler needs to shift a "B" to an "A".

18] Find this line:

thisValue = thisValue + 1

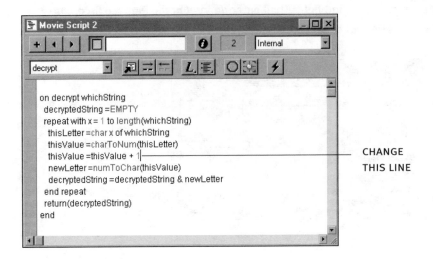

CHANGE
THIS LINE

This is the line that adjusts the letter value upward and reassigns the new higher value to the variable. You will change it so that instead it adjusts the value downward.

19] Change the line so that it reads like this:

thisValue = thisValue − 1

That is, subtract 1 instead of adding 1. This will cause the letter value to shift back down instead of up.

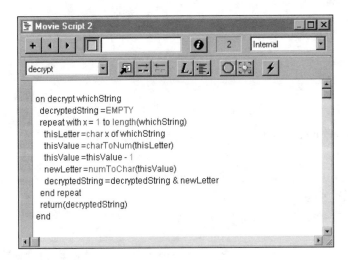

20] Close the Script window and open the Message window if it is not already open.

With the change in place, you will try decrypting again.

21] Type the following and press Enter (Windows) or Return (Macintosh) on the main keyboard.

```
put decrypt(codeName)
```

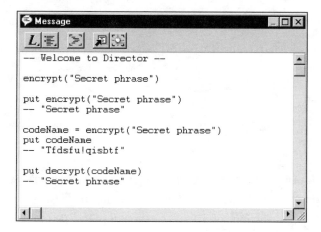

This time the phrase successfully reverted back to its original form.

22] Save your work as *Crypt.dir*.

You have successfully created a handler that takes a parameter and uses that information to create a special return value. Because you placed the encryption and decryption code in handlers, you can now easily invoke these actions as often as necessary to encode or decode strings.

WHAT YOU HAVE LEARNED

In this lesson you have:

- Learned about events and messages [page 378]
- Learned how to watch events [page 378]
- Learned how to log events [page 383]
- Learned about handlers and handler hierarchy [page 385]
- Learned about parameters and return values [page 389]
- Created a handler that accepts a parameter and returns a value [page 389]

navigating with lingo

One of the most common uses for Lingo is to navigate within a movie's score. Lingo's navigational tools include the *go* command and markers. In this lesson, you will use all of these tools to branch to different sections of the score in response to user input.

This menu for a Fine Dining application prototype provides access to three other panels: a Restaurants panel, which lets users search for specific restaurants; a Locations panel, which lets users search for restaurants based on their location; and an Order panel, which lets users place orders through the Internet. In this lesson, you will provide users with a way to navigate to and from those three panels and to quit the application.

Graphics for the Fine Dining project were designed by Ming Lau, BlueWaters.

If you would like to review the final result of this lesson, open the Complete folder in the Lesson18 folder and play Menu.dir.

WHAT YOU WILL LEARN

In this lesson you will:

- Check the movie properties and create the basic structure for the score
- Set up the main menu to wait for user interaction
- Create markers within the score and use those markers to control user navigation
- Branch to another movie
- Implement a Quit button

APPROXIMATE TIME

It should take about 1½ hours to complete this lesson.

LESSON FILES

Media Files:
None

Starting Files:
Lesson18\Start\Start1.dir
Lesson18\Start\Start2.dir
Lesson18\Start\Start3.dir

Complete Files:
Lesson18\Complete\Menu.dir
Lesson18\Complete\Order.dir

SETTING UP FOR THIS LESSON

To give you a jump-start on the Fine Dining application, the cast has been assembled for you.

1] Choose File › Open and locate and open Start1.dir in the Lesson18 folder.

2] Save this file as *Menu.dir* in your Projects folder.

Don't play the movie yet. First you need to make some additions.

3] Open the Cast window and familiarize yourself with the project assets it contains.

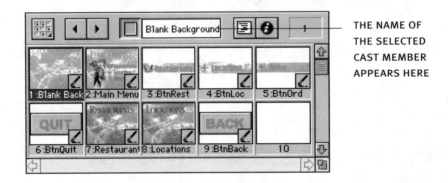

THE NAME OF
THE SELECTED
CAST MEMBER
APPEARS HERE

The cast members are grouped in the order in which you will add them to the score. Arranging a cast of more than a few members into logical groups saves time by making it easier for you to locate the cast members you need. The cast members have also been given names to make it easier for you to identify them as you work through the tasks in this lesson.

Now you're ready to get started on your project.

CHECKING MOVIE PROPERTIES AND FILLING IN THE SCORE

To begin, you will check the movie properties and set the tempo—two steps that you should complete before starting any movie file. Then you will build the basic structure of the Fine Dining application.

1] Choose Modify › Movie › Properties to display the Movie Properties dialog box.

With each new project, it's always a good idea to check the movie properties as the first step. Notice that some important options have already been set up for you: Stage Size, Stage Location, Stage Color, and Default Palette.

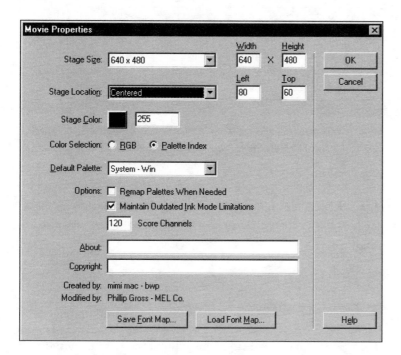

When you start a new project in the other lessons in this book, be sure to open the Movie Properties dialog box so you can get an idea of the movie's basic setup. When you start work on a new movie (File > New > Movie) without quitting Director first, Director remembers some settings from your previous project. These may not necessarily be the settings you want.

2] Click OK to close the Movie Properties dialog box.

Now you will start adding sprites to the score.

3] Drag the Blank Background graphic (cast member 1) to channel 1, frame 1, of the score.

Director centers the Blank Background cast member on the stage.

4] If necessary, adjust the duration of the background sprite so it spans frames 1 to 9.

By default, Director adds new sprites to the score with a duration of 28 frames. To adjust the background sprite's duration, drag the last frame of the sprite to frame 9.

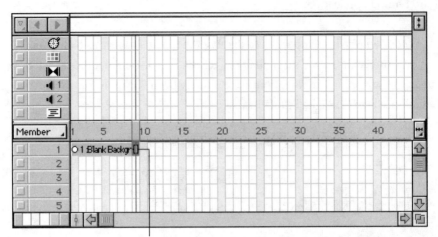

TO ADJUST A CAST MEMBER'S DURATION, DRAG ITS END FRAME
TO THE FRAME WHERE YOU WANT THE SPRITE TO END

5] In the Score window, click channel 1, frame 10. Click the Main Menu graphic (cast member 2). Then choose Modify › Cast to Time and adjust the sprite's duration so it spans frames 10 through 18.

tip *To modify the length of a sprite that spans only a single cell, hold down the Alt (Windows) or Option (Macintosh) key while you drag the sprite.*

The blank background is a version of the main menu without the heading or the buttons. When the movie starts, the blank background will appear momentarily and then is replaced by the main menu. You will add a transition to make the change less abrupt between the blank background in frame 9 and the main menu in frame 10.

As you will see in later tasks, the scripts that you write will be the same regardless of the sprites' durations. The durations chosen for the sprites in this project are long enough for the cast member names to be readable in the score.

6] Double-click the transition channel, frame 10, to open the Transition dialog box. Select Edges In, Square, set the duration to .5 seconds, select Changing Area only, and click OK.

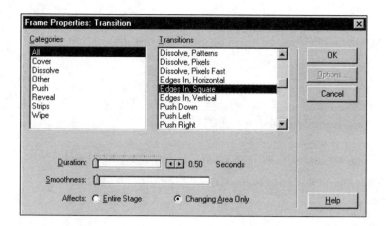

The other elements you need are the cast members that act as buttons in the menu. Once these are on the stage, you will attach scripts to them to monitor user action.

7] Click channel 2, frame 10, and then drag the Restaurants button (cast member 3, BtnRest) onto the stage. Position the sprite exactly over the word "Restaurants" on the Fine Dining background.

tip *To make sure the button precisely covers the one on the main menu, place the button where you think it should be and then choose Edit > Cut Sprites to cut the button. If you see any screen jumping immediately after you cut the button, then the button was not positioned exactly. Choose Edit > Undo and use the arrow keys to move the button into place. Continue with this cut-and-undo procedure until the screen doesn't jump any more.*

403

8] Click channel 3, frame 10, and then drag the Locations button (cast member 4, BtnLoc) onto the stage. Position the sprite exactly over the Locations button on the Fine Dining background.

tip   *With the Cast window selected, you can type a cast member number, and Director will scroll to that part of the window and highlight the cast member.*

9] Click channel 4, frame 10, and then drag the Order button (cast member 5, BtnOrd) onto the stage. Position the sprite exactly over the Order button on the Fine Dining background.

10] Click channel 5, frame 10, and then drag the Quit button (cast member 6, BtnQuit) onto the stage. Position the sprite exactly over the Quit button on the Fine Dining background.

11] If necessary, adjust the duration of the four button cast members so they all span frames 10 through 18.

With the two background graphics and the four cast members now on the stage, your score should look like this:

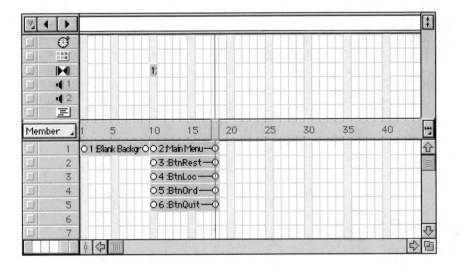

12] Drag the Restaurants graphic (cast member 7) to channel 1, frame 20, in the score. Adjust the endpoint to frame 28.

The Restaurants graphic is the background for the first of the three sections that will be available through the Fine Dining main menu. In later tasks, you will learn how to set up the Restaurants button on the main menu to branch to this section of the score.

13] Drag the Locations graphic (cast member 8) to channel 1, frame 30, in the score. Adjust the endpoint to frame 38.

The Locations graphic is the background for the second of the three sections that will be available through the Fine Dining main menu. Don't worry that you didn't add a panel for Order, the third section. You'll handle the Order function in a different way later in the lesson.

Your score should now look like this:

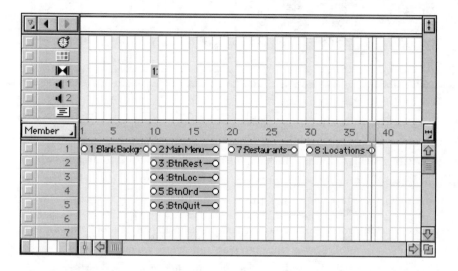

14] Save your work.

The raw materials for your Fine Dining application are now mostly in place. You are ready to start creating the navigation using Lingo.

USING LINGO TO WAIT AT THE MAIN MENU

The score lays out events in linear fashion. Without any instructions to the contrary, Director will play the frames you've set up in consecutive order.

To see this, rewind the movie now and play it. You see the blank background, a transition to the Fine Dining main menu, a blank stage, the Restaurants panel, a blank stage, and the Locations panel in quick succession. The only information Director has at the moment is the score you created, and so it sends the playback head forward starting at frame 1 and plays every frame in sequence.

THE PLAYBACK HEAD TRAVELS THROUGH
ALL THE FRAMES IN SEQUENCE

When the playback head reaches the last frame that contains a sprite (frame 38 in this case), it will go back to frame 1 if the Control > Loop Playback command (which you used in Lesson 16) is checked; otherwise, Director stops when it reaches the last frame. If the movie is still playing, click the Stop button.

As you can see, like any good application, Director does exactly as it's told and nothing more. It's up to you to tell Director where to stop and where to go in response to user actions such as button clicks. You will now create a simple script to make the playback head stop at the Fine Dining main menu and wait for a user action.

1] Double-click the Behavior channel, frame 18, to display the Script window.

DOUBLE-CLICK IN THE BEHAVIOR CHANNEL
TO CREATE A NEW SCRIPT FOR A FRAME

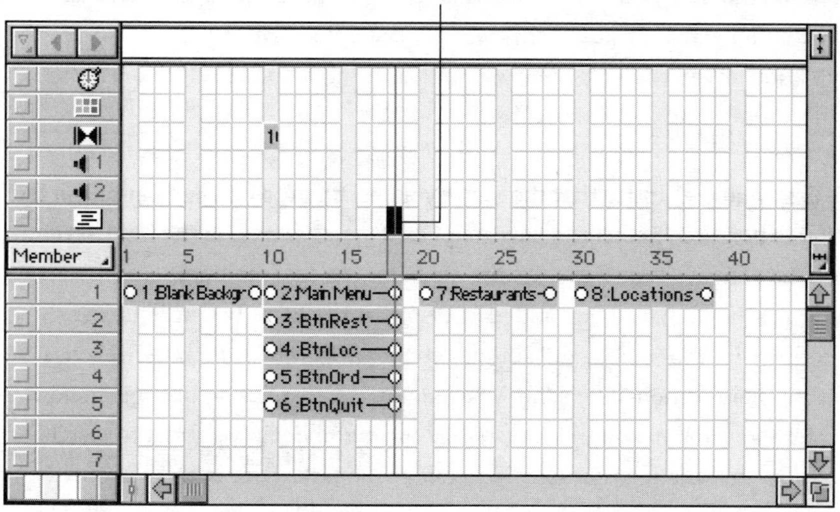

As you saw in Lesson 16, Director opens the Script window with the most common
frame script—an *exitFrame* handler in this case—already started for you.

2] Modify the *exitFrame* handler as shown here in bold:

```
on exitFrame
    go to the frame
end
```

You have just created a frame script, which you learned about in Lesson 16. When
the playback head reaches frame 18 and begins to exit that frame, Director generates
an *exitFrame* message. The message searches for an *exitFrame* handler by first looking
in the sprite scripts and the cast member scripts. The message then passes to the frame
script, where it finds an *exitFrame* handler. The *go to the frame* command brings the
playback head to a standstill. The *the frame* part of the statement represents the current
frame number, so *go to the frame* tells Director to reposition the playback head on the
frame it just exited, causing it to loop, or hold, on that frame. When this happens, the
movie is effectively paused. The playback head is no longer moving, which means that
no action occurs on the stage. Some other event—such as a mouse click—is needed to
start the movie going again.

You may be wondering why you don't see frame 19 (a blank stage without any sprites). After all, hasn't the playback head exited frame 18? Look closely at the script and remember that Director executes scripts one line at a time. After the *on exitFrame* command, Director ran the *go to the frame* command and looped back to the same frame. Director never reached frame 19.

3] In the Cast window, notice that the script you just created has been added in the next available position. Select the new script cast member and, in the field at the top of the Cast window, type *Pause* as the name for the cast member.

The new script should have been added as cast member 11. If you have been experimenting with the project and adding other cast members, your frame script may be in another position. The script's position in the cast has no bearing on how it works. However, you may want to rearrange the members in your cast to match the illustration, to make it easier for you to follow the tasks later in this lesson. To rearrange cast members, simply drag them to the desired location in the cast.

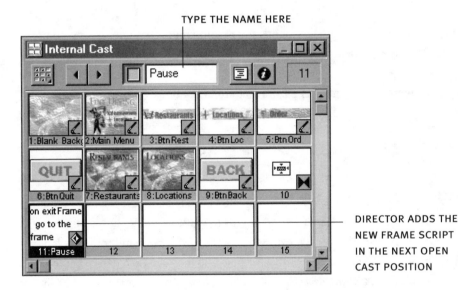

4] Close the Cast window and save your work. Rewind and play the movie.

The movie now stops at frame 18, awaiting further instructions.

With the movie paused on the Fine Dining main menu, users can now click one of the buttons. You then want the movie to branch, or jump, to the appropriate section in the score. In the next task, you will lay the groundwork so you can tell Director to branch to different frames in the score depending on the buttons users click.

USING MARKERS TO LABEL FRAMES

When movie actors enter a scene, they move to the spot the director has specified for them. This is often a chalk mark on the floor, unseen by the movie camera but of vital importance to the actor, who must "hit the mark" to make the scene work according to the director's wishes.

Director also uses markers—in this case, to designate locations in the score to which the playback head can branch. Each marker has a name that identifies the frame containing the marker. Once you've named a particular frame, you can use Lingo to tell the playback head to go to that frame. In fact, the syntax of the Lingo command is *go to frame "name"*. You replace *name* with a frame name, surrounded by quotation marks.

Like the movie director's chalk marks, the frame names aren't visible to the audience—the users of your application. They're a tool you use behind the scenes to control the flow of action.

In this task, you will set up markers for each section of the score and then use the Message window to experiment and see how they work.

1] In the marker channel of the score, click frame 10.

Director adds a triangle icon at frame 10 to show the marker's location. You can now type a marker name, which replaces the highlighted text.

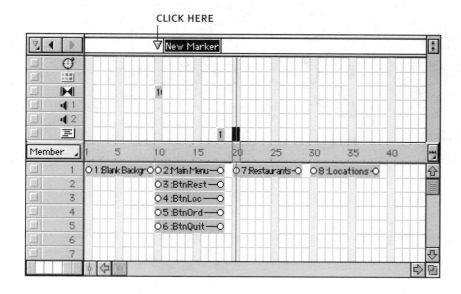

2] Type *Main* as the frame name.

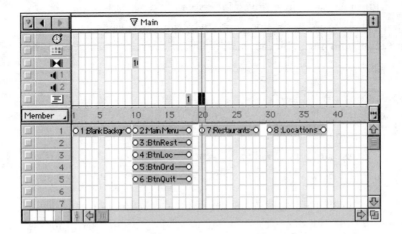

3] In the marker channel, click frame 20 and type *Restaurants*.

4] In the marker channel, click frame 30 and type *Locations*.

Your score should now look like this:

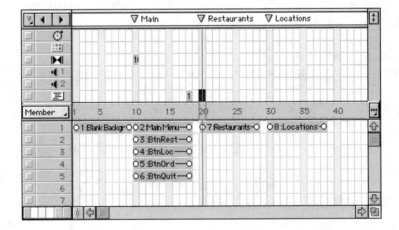

5] Save your work.

Again, don't worry that there isn't a marker for the Order button. You'll handle the Order feature in a different way later in this lesson.

You can get a good idea of how markers work by experimenting with the Message window.

6] Click anywhere in frame 10 to move the playback head there.

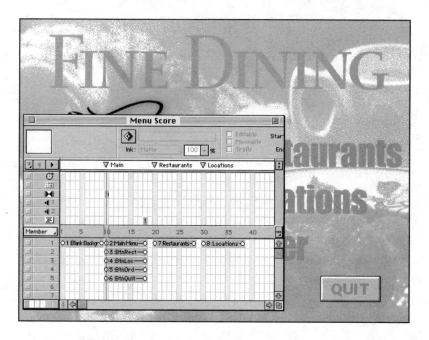

7] Choose Window › Message to open the Message window (Windows Ctrl+M, Macintosh Command+M).

8] Type *put the framelabel* and press Enter (Windows) or Return (Macintosh).
You see the marker named *Main*.

9] Type *put the frame* and press Enter (Windows) or Return (Macintosh).
As you know from Lesson 16, the *put* command evaluates expressions and displays the results in the Message window. Functions return values. The *the framelabel* function returns the name assigned to the marker in the current frame, and the

the frame function returns the number of the current frame. The results in the Message window should look something like this:

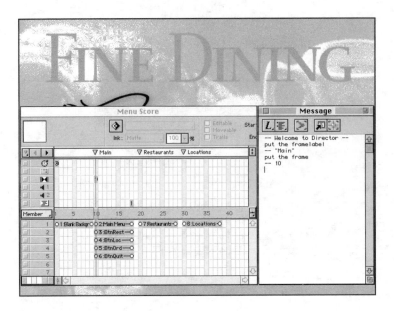

These two *put* commands show that you can refer to a specific frame in two ways: by its frame number or by its marker name.

10] Type *go to frame "Restaurants"* and press Enter (Windows) or Return (Macintosh).
You now see the Restaurants panel on the stage. In the score, notice that the playback head is at frame 20, where you placed the *Restaurants* marker.

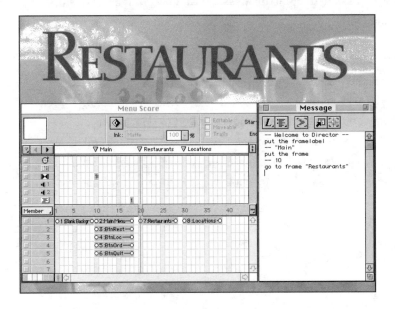

412

The *go to frame "Restaurants"* command instructed Director to position the playback head at the frame whose name is *Restaurants*. The quotation marks around *Restaurants* told Director that you were referring to the frame by its name rather than by its number.

11] Type *put the frame* and press Enter (Windows) or Return (Macintosh).

The Message window confirms that you are now at frame 20.

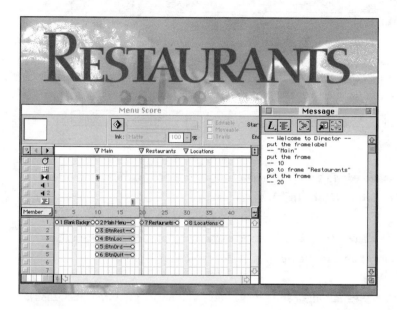

From these experiments, you see that you can refer to a frame by either the name you assigned to its marker or its frame number.

Now you will see why it's best to navigate by referring to frame names instead of frame numbers.

12] Click the Score window to make it active and then click frame 19. Press Ctrl+] (Windows) or Command+] (Macintosh).

This adds a frame to the score.

413

ADD THE NEW FRAME HERE

13] Click the Message window and, on a new line, type _go to frame 20_ and press Enter (Windows) or Return (Macintosh).

The playback head is now on frame 20, but the stage is blank. As you can see by looking at the score, that's because adding the extra frame pushed the Restaurants section one additional frame to the right.

14] Type _go to frame "Restaurants"_ and press Enter (Windows) or Return (Macintosh).

Now you see the Restaurants panel again.

Again, by looking at the score, you will notice that the _Restaurants_ marker also moved one frame to the right when you inserted the extra frame at frame 19. This is one of the most important advantages of navigating using markers instead of fixed frame numbers: When you add or delete frames (which is quite common while you are developing a movie), the frame numbers spanned by existing sprites will change, but the markers also slide right or left, remaining with the frame to which you originally assigned them.

15] Click frame 19 again and choose Insert › Remove Frame (Windows Ctrl+[, Macintosh Command+[).

This restores the score to its correct state.

16] Save your work.

Now that you understand how markers work, you will add scripts that use markers to provide navigation.

BRANCHING TO A MARKER

As you learned in Lessons 16 and 17, Director responds to events—for example, mouse clicks—by sending out a message of the same name. The message travels through a specific path, searching for a handler with a name that matches the message.

For example, when you click the mouse, Director first sends a *mouseDown* message followed (when you release the mouse button) by a *mouseUp* message. For the *mouseUp* message, Director looks for any *mouseUp* handlers assigned to the sprite you just clicked. If Director can't find a *mouseUp* handler among the sprite's scripts, it searches through the scripts assigned to the cast member associated with that sprite, to the frame in the movie that contains the sprite, and finally to the movie itself. If it can't find a *mouseUp* handler anywhere, Director discards the *mouseUp* message.

note *This is a simplified account of Director's message order. For a full review, see "Examining Types of Lingo Scripts" in Lesson 16.*

In this task, you'll set up the Restaurant button with a *mouseUp* handler that tells Director to branch to the *Restaurants* marker.

1] In the Cast window, click the Restaurants button (cast member 3, BtnRest) and click the Script button to open the Script window.

CLICK THE SCRIPT BUTTON TO ADD A
SCRIPT TO THE SELECTED CAST MEMBER

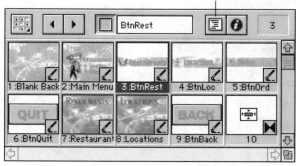

The Restaurants button appears only on the main menu. No matter what the circumstance, you always want a click on the Restaurants button to branch to the Restaurants section of the score. Therefore, you are creating a cast member script. As you learned in Lesson 16, you use a cast member script whenever you want a cast member to act in the same way no matter where it appears in the score.

Director gives you a head start by opening the Script window with the most common type of cast member script—a *mouseUp* handler—already started for you.

2] Complete the *mouseUp* handler as shown here in bold and then close the Script window.

```
on mouseUp
  go to frame "Restaurants"
end
```

note   *In the* go to frame *command, the words* to *and* frame *are optional. For example, the commands* go frame "Restaurants", go to "Restaurants", *and* go "Restaurants" *all work equally well.*

You've enabled Director to branch to another section of the score, but you have one additional step to perform. Once the playback head branches to the *Restaurants* marker at frame 20, what happens then? The playback head will continue through the score, and just as you saw earlier in this lesson, it will continue to the end of the movie because you have not provided any other instructions. Just as you paused the playback head at frame 18, the end of the Main section, you need to pause the playback head at frame 28, the end of the Restaurants section. You could write a new frame script for frame 28, giving it an *exitFrame* handler containing a *go to the frame* command. However, you already have exactly the same frame script stored in the cast, where Director placed it when you created it for frame 10.

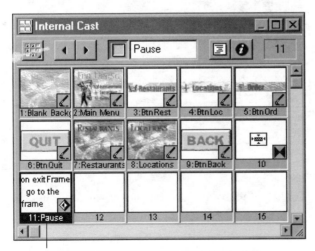

DIRECTOR STORED THE FRAME SCRIPT YOU
CREATED EARLIER AS MEMBER 11 IN THE CAST

Instead of creating a new frame script, you can reuse the existing frame script by assigning it to frame 28 as well.

3] Click the Behavior channel, frame 28, and then choose the frame script (cast member 11) from the bottom of the Behavior menu in the sprite toolbar.

THE SCRIPT'S CAST NUMBER AND NAME APPEAR
FIRST IN THE MENU TO HELP YOU IDENTIFY IT

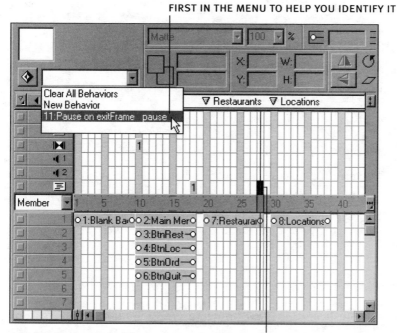

MAKE SURE YOU'VE SELECTED THE FRAME TO
WHICH YOU WANT TO ASSIGN THE EXISTING SCRIPT

It's a good idea to reuse scripts whenever practical. Writing separate, identical scripts soon clutters up your cast and makes it difficult to understand how your movie is designed. Most important, however, is that reusing scripts gives you the power to make changes quickly. Say that you did write separate *exitFrame* handlers for frames 18 and 28, and then you later decide to also sound a beep when the playback head reaches the end of a section. You would have to add the *beep* command to both scripts. However, since you reused the script, you need to make the change in only one place. The advantages of reusing scripts increase as your project grows more sophisticated.

tip   *You can also assign the* pause *script (cast member 11) by dragging it from the cast and dropping it in the Behavior channel at frame 28. Dragging it from the cast or choosing it from the menu in the sprite toolbar have the same effect.*

4] Rewind and play the movie. Click the Restaurants button.

Director branches to the Restaurants panel!

Watch the playback head as you test the movie. You see it travel from frame 1 to frame 18, where it pauses. When you click the Restaurants button, the playback head branches to frame 20 and continues to frame 28, when it pauses again.

5] Stop the movie and save your work.

ADDING A BACK BUTTON

As your movie becomes more complex, it becomes increasingly important to visualize your navigational structure. It may help to draw a diagram. So far, your structure is pretty simple:

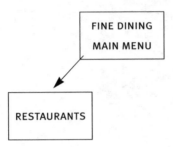

But something is obviously missing in this structure. Once your users have navigated to the Restaurants panel, how do they get back to the main menu? You need a structure that looks like this:

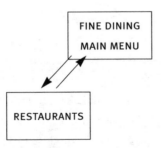

In this next task, you'll add a Back button so users can move between the Restaurants panel and the main menu.

1] In the Score window, click channel 6, frame 20.

2] From the Cast window, drag the Back button (cast member 9, BtnBack) to the stage and position it in the lower-right corner of the Restaurants panel. Adjust the button sprite's duration so it spans frames 20 through 28.

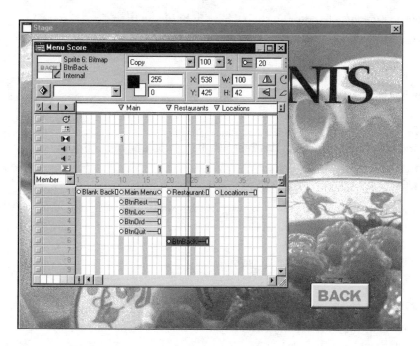

3] In the Cast window, click the Back button (cast member 9, BtnBack) and then click the Script button to open the Script window.

CLICK THE SCRIPT BUTTON TO ADD A
SCRIPT TO THE SELECTED CAST MEMBER

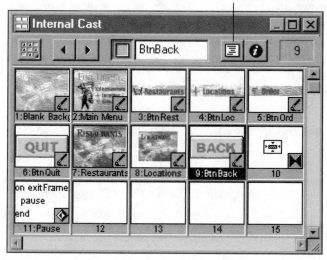

419

Just as you did for the Restaurants button, you will create a cast member script for the Back button. No matter where the Back button appears in this movie, you always want it to return you to the main menu.

Director has already started a *mouseUp* handler for you.

4] Complete the *mouseUp* handler as shown here in bold and then close the Script window.

```
on mouseUp
   go to frame "Main"
end
```

5] Rewind and play the movie. Click the Restaurants button and then click the Back button.

You should be able to branch back and forth now between the two panels. Again, watching the playback head in the score as you click back and forth will help reinforce what you've learned about navigating in the score.

6] Save your work.

ON YOUR OWN

Using the techniques described in the two preceding tasks ("Branching to a Marker" and "Adding a Back Button"), add the navigation between the Fine Dining main menu and the Locations panel.

Here are a few tips to help you make short work of this task:

• The cast member script you need for the Locations button is nearly identical to the cast member script you've already created for the Restaurants button. Open the cast member script for the Restaurants button, copy it, create a cast member script for the Locations button, and paste. Then change the *go to frame "Restaurants"* command *to go to frame "Locations"*.

• You need to pause the playback head at the end of the Locations section, frame 38. Just as you assigned the same *pause* script in similar circumstances at frames 18 and 28, you can assign that *pause* script at frame 38 as well. One simple method: Click the Behavior channel at frame 18, copy the script, click the frame channel at frame 38, and paste.

• You can quickly place the Back button on the Locations panel by copying it from channel 6, frames 20 through 28, and pasting it in the Locations section at channel 6, frames 30 through 38. That's all you need to do: The Back button's cast member script ensures that clicking the Back button on the Locations panel returns you to the main menu.

420

BRANCHING TO ANOTHER MOVIE

Imagine a children's storybook on a CD-ROM. The storybook may have 50 pages (or scenes), each with several frames of animation. Imagine how complex and difficult to follow the score would become if you tried to create all that content in a single movie.

For efficiency, many Director producers break their projects into a series of bite-sized movies. The entire project is then easier to create, revise, and maintain. An additional benefit is that many authors can work on the project at once, each with his or her own movie file.

In this task, you will see how to set up a modular project by implementing the Order panel as a separate movie. To do so, you will use the *go to movie* command instead of the *go to frame* command. The *go to movie* command tells Director to close the current movie and branch to the first frame of another movie. Your Back button in the Order movie will also use the *go to movie* command, and you will specify a marker to return to (the *Main* marker).

note *If you didn't finish the previous tasks, you can open the Start2.dir movie to follow along from this point.*

1] In the Cast window, click the Order button (cast member 5, BtnOrd) and then click the Script button to open the Script window.

As with the other buttons in this project, you want a user's click on the Order button to always result in the same action. Therefore, you create a cast member script.

Director has already started a *mouseUp* handler for you.

2] Finish the *mouseUp* handler as shown here in bold and then close the Script window.

```
on mouseUp
  go to movie "Order.dir"
end
```

The *go to movie* command instructs Director to close the current movie and play the movie you specify in quotation marks. The Order.dir movie will begin playing from frame 1.

3] Save your work.

If you used the Start2.dir movie, make sure to save the movie as *Menu.dir* in your Projects folder.

You're now ready to start setting up the Order.dir movie to which the Order button branches.

4] Open the movie Start3.dir in the Lesson18 folder on the CD and save it as *Order.dir* in your Projects folder.

This prebuilt movie file has already been set up with some of the essential elements you'll need to finish this project. In the next several steps, you will get acquainted with the elements the movie contains and then create a button that branches back to the main Menu.dir movie.

5] Open the Score window.

The Order background panel in channel 1, frames 1 through 8, and the Back button in channel 6, frames 1 through 8, have already been added for you.

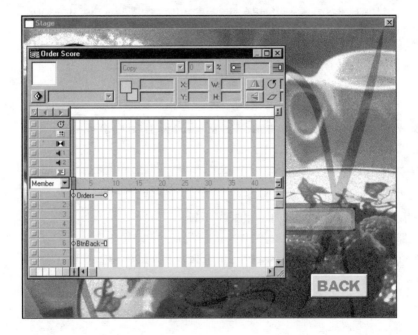

6] Open the Cast window, click the Back button (cast member 2, BtnBack), and then click the Script button to open the Script window.

Director has already started a *mouseUp* handler for you.

7] Finish the *mouseUp* handler as shown here in bold and then close the Script window.

```
on mouseUp
  go to frame "Main" of movie "Menu.dir"
end
```

If you use just *go to movie "Menu.dir"* here, Director branches back to frame 1 of the Menu.dir movie. At that point, you'll see the opening sequence that plays before the playback head reaches the *Main* marker. Instead, you can instruct Director to open Menu.dir and branch directly to the *Main* marker.

As before, you need to make sure the playback head pauses at the end of the Order section.

8] Double-click the Behavior channel, frame 8, to open the Script window.

To pause the playback head, you need to create a frame script. Director starts an *exitFrame* handler for you.

9] Finish the *exitFrame* handler as shown here in bold and then close the Script window.

```
on exitFrame
    go to the frame
end
```

Previously in this lesson, you reused an existing script for several frames in which you needed to pause the playback head. Why can't you do so here? Remember that the *exitFrame* handler you created previously is in the Menu.dir movie. You need to create a new handler in the Order.dir movie.

10] Save your work.

11] Open the Menu.dir movie again, play the movie, and click the Order button.

You branch to the Order movie.

Watch the playback head in the score as you test your Order button. Notice how the score changes to show that the Order.dir movie is now open.

12] Click the Back button.

You branch back to the Fine Dining main menu in Menu.dir!

Director will find the Order.dir movie so long as you keep it in the same folder with Menu.dir. If you move Order.dir to another folder elsewhere on your system, try playing Menu.dir and then clicking the Order button; Director will display a dialog box asking you to locate the missing movie. Try it for yourself.

tip You're actually better off omitting the .dir extension from your movie files. If you specify Menu.dir, Director will accept only a file by that name. However, if you specify simply Menu, Director will accept all files named Menu, whether they be .dir (source), .dxr (protected), or .dcr (Shockwave) files. This approach allows you to distribute your movie in a number of different formats without having to reauthor it each time to match.

You have tremendous flexibility in where you ultimately place the Order.dir movie. In Lesson 20, you will learn some additional rules for placing the components of a modular Director project in different locations. In Lesson 27, you will even discover that Order.dir can be located on any computer in the world, so long as your movie has access to the Internet!

You're almost done. You've created a complete navigation system between all the panels in your project. Only one thing remains: As fascinating as you know your project will be to users, they will inevitably want a way to quit.

IMPLEMENTING A QUIT BUTTON

The main menu has a Quit button that users can click when they're finished using your application. As you did with other buttons, you need to create a cast member script with a *mouseUp* handler, because you always want a click on this button to produce the same action.

Lingo provides a *quit* command that you would think is the perfect tool for this situation. However, there is one problem with using *quit* while your Fine Dining application is under construction: The *quit* command actually quits Director itself, just as if you chose File > Exit (Windows) or File > Quit (Macintosh). It would be too time consuming to test the Quit button by actually quitting Director itself.

The best choice then, is the *halt* command. While you are creating the movie, the *halt* command simply stops the movie so you can continue working. It has the same effect as clicking the Stop button on the toolbar: The playback head stops at the current frame. In a projector of your movie, the *halt* command actually quits the movie. That makes the *halt* command the best all-around choice for your Quit button.

1] In the Cast window, click the Quit button (cast member 6, BtnQuit) and click the Script button to display the Script window.

Director has started a *mouseUp* handler for you.

2] Complete the *mouseUp* handler as shown here in bold and then close the Script window.

```
on mouseUp
   halt
end
```

3] Save your work.

4] Rewind and play the movie. Click the Quit button.

The movie stops, but Director stays open.

WHAT YOU HAVE LEARNED

In this lesson you have:

• Checked the movie properties and created the basic structure for the score [page 401]

• Used the *go to the frame* command to stop the playback head at the main menu [page 406]

• Created markers within the score for navigation [page 409]

• Used marker names and the *go to frame* command to control user navigation [page 415]

• Branched to another movie using the *go to movie* command [page 421]

• Implemented a Quit button using the *halt* command [page 424]

navigation
advanced

LESSON 19

In Lesson 18 you created the basic navigational structure for a Fine Dining application prototype. Users can now click buttons to move from the main menu to the Restaurants, Locations, and Order panels. On each of these three panels, a Back button lets users return to the main menu. The coding itself is rock-solid, but the navigational design is still weak because users have no feedback to guide them through the application. In

In this lesson you will add animation and sound to provide user feedback and enhance the Fine Dining application prototype you started in Lesson 18.

Graphics for the Fine Dining project were designed by Ming Lau, BlueWaters. Sound files were provided by Jeff Essex, Audiosyncrasy.

this lesson, you will enhance the Fine Dining application with visual and audio feedback—and, in the process, you'll learn some advanced techniques for navigating with Lingo.

If you would like to review the final result of this lesson, open the Complete folder in the Lesson19 folder and play Menu.dir.

WHAT YOU WILL LEARN

In this lesson you will:

• Create visual feedback by branching to different sections of the score

• Add audio feedback

• Keep the playback head in a specific frame

• Branch to frames in the movie relative to the position of the playback head

APPROXIMATE TIME

It should take about 2 hours to complete this lesson.

LESSON FILES

Media Files:
None

Starting Files:
Lesson19\Start\Start1.dir
Lesson19\Start\Start2.dir
Lesson19\Start\Order.dir

Complete Files:
Lesson19\Complete\Menu.dir
Lesson19\Complete\Order.dir

SETTING UP FOR THIS LESSON

To give you a jump-start on the second part of the Fine Dining application, the cast has been assembled for you and sections of the score have been filled in.

1] Choose File › Open and locate and open Start1.dir in the Lesson19 folder on the CD.

You must use the Start1.dir movie file in the Lesson19 folder. Even though this lesson is a continuation of Lesson 18, the Menu.dir file you completed in Lesson 18 is not the same as the Start1.dir file for Lesson 19. The Start1.dir file for Lesson 19 contains additional material that was not needed for Lesson 18.

2] Save this file as *Menu.dir* in your Projects folder on your hard drive.

Don't play the movie yet. First you need to add to the movie.

3] From the Lesson19 folder on the CD, copy the Order.dir file into your Projects folder on your hard drive.

This is the movie you completed in Lesson 18. You will need this movie if you want to test the Order button during this project. If you finished Lesson 18, you can use your own copy of Order.dir instead.

4] Open the Cast window and familiarize yourself with the project assets it contains.

THE NAME OF THE SELECTED CAST MEMBER APPEARS HERE

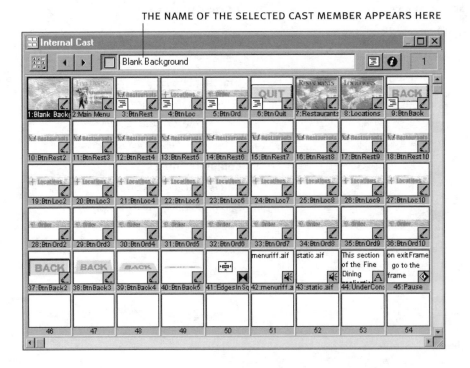

In addition to the elements you started with for Lesson 18, the cast for Lesson 19 contains graphics and audio files that you will need to add feedback to the Fine Dining application's user interface. Similar elements are grouped together to make them easier for you to locate: graphics are first, in the order they are used in the score; the transition from Lesson 18 is next; sounds come after the transition; text is next; and scripts are last. The scripts that you add to this project will be added starting with the first empty position, cast member 46.

5] Open the Score window and familiarize yourself with the project flow.

The first 38 frames of the score are just as you laid them out in Lesson 18. The movie begins with a simple background (in channel 1, frames 1 through 9), followed by an edges-in transition (in frame 10) into the main menu. The Restaurants and Locations panels are also where you placed them in Lesson 18. Play the movie and click the buttons to refresh your memory of how the navigation currently works.

The score also contains four additional sections, labeled with the markers *BtnRest*, *BtnLoc*, *BtnOrd*, and *Back*. These sections contain a series of one-frame sprites that, when played, animate the Restaurants (BtnLoc), Locations (BtnLoc), Orders (BtnOrd) and Back (Back) buttons. The busywork of placing the individuals button sprites on the stage has already been done for you so you can get right to work creating the Lingo that will make these animations spring to life. Drag the playback head through these sections to familiarize yourself with the look of these animations.

Now you're ready to get started on your project.

ADDING VISUAL FEEDBACK USING *MOUSEENTER*

The Fine Dining main menu has a variety of elements. Yet only the Quit button has the traditional sculptured look that says "I'm a button—click me!" The design of the three icons implies that you can click them as well—but can you click the type next to them? Can you click the large logo on the left and expect something to happen? Ideally, as you move the mouse pointer around the main menu, you should get some visual feedback that lets you know which of these items you can click.

In this project, you want to provide visual feedback this way: When a user moves the mouse pointer over the Restaurants button in the main menu, you want the playback head to branch to the BtnRest section of the score so that the button animation plays. You want the animation to keep playing over and over until the user moves the mouse pointer off the Restaurants button. The animation provides a visual clue to users that they can click the Restaurants button to trigger some action.

As you know from Lesson 18, you have set up the movie to pause at the main menu. Even though the playback head is no longer moving forward, Director is still awake and waiting for an event—such as a mouse click or key press—to trigger an action. In this task, you will use another event, *mouseEnter*, to implement visual feedback.

A sprite's outer edges—its borders—define its bounding rectangle. Director sends a *mouseEnter* message every time the mouse pointer enters the bounding rectangle of a sprite. While the pointer stays inside the sprite, Director sends a continuous stream of *mouseWithin* messages. When the pointer leaves the sprite's bounding rectangle, Director sends a *mouseLeave* message.

A SPRITE'S EDGES DEFINE ITS BOUNDING RECTANGLE

tip *If you set a bitmap cast member's ink effect to Matte, Director will send* mouseEnter, mouseWithin, *and* mouseLeave *messages only when the pointer is over or at the edge of the actual graphic. Any transparent areas around the graphic won't trigger one of these mouse events; only the actual shape of the graphic will be "hot."*

You will begin creating the visual feedback by writing a *mouseEnter* handler for the Restaurants button. When the mouse "enters" the button (that is, when the pointer first moves into the button's bounding rectangle), Director will generate a *mouseEnter* event. Your *mouseEnter* handler will tell the playback head to branch to the *BtnRest* marker, using the *go to* command you learned in Lesson 18.

First, however, you need to set the movie's tempo and make sure that the button animation plays continuously.

1] Double-click the tempo channel, frame 1, to open the Tempo dialog box. Drag the tempo slider to 30 frames per second (fps). Then click OK to close the dialog box.
If you don't set the tempo, Director will use the default setting, 15 frames per second, which is a little slower than you need for this project.

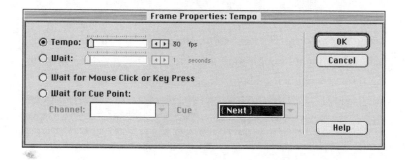

2] In the score, double-click the behavior channel, frame 48, to open the Behavior Script window.

Frame 48 is the last frame of the BtnRest animation section of the score. When the playback head reaches this frame, you want the playback head to return to the start of the animation at frame 40. You will now write a frame script that tells the playback head where to go when it leaves this frame.

Director gives you a head start by opening the Script window with the most common type of frame script—an *exitframe* handler—already started for you.

3] Complete the *exitframe* handler as shown here in bold and then close the Script window.

```
on exitframe
    go loop
end
```

The *go loop* command sends the playback head back to the nearest marker to its left. Now when the playback head exits frame 48, it will loop back to the nearest marker on the left, which is the *BtnRest* marker at frame 40. The playback head will keep looping through this section of the score until some other event interrupts it.

WHEN THE PLAYBACK HEAD REACHES THE
GO LOOP COMMAND IN THIS FRAME...
...IT RETURNS TO THE PREVIOUS MARKER

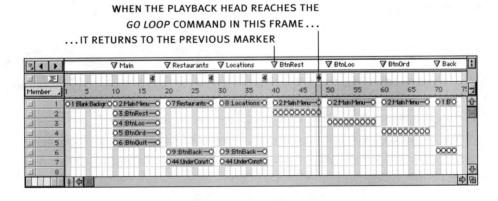

You could also have used a *go to frame "BtnRest"* command, as you learned in Lesson 18. In this case, the *go loop* command is a bit more flexible because you don't need to know the name of the frame to which the playback head should branch.

You are now ready to write a script to implement the animation for the Restaurants button.

4] In the cast, click the Restaurants button (cast member 3, BtnRest) and click the Script button to open the Script window.

The cast member script for the Restaurants button already contains the *mouseUp* handler you wrote in Lesson 18. The cast member script is also the correct location for the *mouseEnter* handler you need to write, because you want the Restaurants button to always display the animation when the mouse enters its bounding rectangle.

5] Enter the *mouseEnter* handler as shown here in bold and then close the Script window.

```
on mouseUp
  go to frame "Restaurants"
end
on mouseEnter
  go to frame "BtnRest"
end
```

Now when the mouse pointer enters the bounding rectangle of the Restaurants button, Director will branch to the frame labeled with the *BtnRest* marker. The playback head will continue to move forward, playing a short, nine-frame sequence that animates the button.

6] Save your work. Then rewind and play the movie. Move the pointer over the Restaurants button.

Keep the Score window open as you play the movie. Notice how the playback head jumps from frame 18 to frame 40 when you move the pointer over the Restaurants button and then keeps looping between frames 40 and 48.

Of course, your work has just begun. You'll notice that the Restaurants button continues to animate even after you move the pointer off the button. You haven't yet implemented a way to stop the animation and return the playback head to the main menu. That's what you'll do next.

COMPLETING THE FEEDBACK SEQUENCE USING *MOUSELEAVE*

You used *mouseEnter* to branch to the animation sequence in frames 40 through 48, and so, logically enough, you will use *mouseLeave* to leave the animation sequence and branch back to the main menu once the mouse pointer is no longer over the Restaurants button.

There's one complication, however. Until now, you have been creating navigation by attaching scripts to cast members. The cast member scripts are appropriate because you always want the cast members to react in the same way no matter where they occur within the score. Another important feature of cast member scripts is that they tend to be unique: The actions in the script are specific to the cast member.

The animation sequence for the Restaurants button consists of nine separate cast members, each occupying a single frame. No matter which of these nine sprites is actually under the pointer when it leaves the bounding rectangle, you want to achieve the same result: to return the playback head to the main menu. Not only do you want to avoid writing nine individual cast member scripts, you want to avoid writing the same script nine times!

The solution is to write a single script that you can assign to all nine sprites in the animation. This calls for a sprite script, which you learned about in Lesson 16.

1] Click the first sprite in the animation loop, in channel 2, frame 40. Hold down the Shift key and click the last sprite in the animation loop, in channel 2, frame 48.
All the button sprites in the animation sequence are now selected.

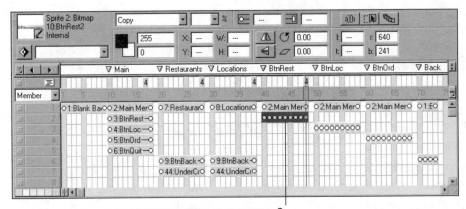

MAKE SURE ALL THE BUTTON SPRITES IN CHANNEL 2,
FRAMES 40 THROUGH 48, ARE SELECTED

2] Choose New Behavior from the Behavior menu in the sprite toolbar to open the Script window.

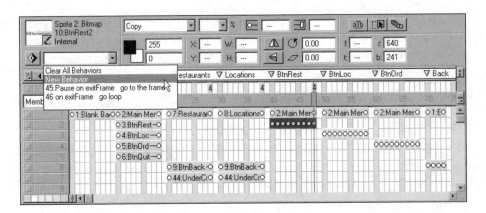

434

This action creates a single sprite script that is assigned to all nine selected sprites. In contrast to the cast member scripts that you wrote earlier, a sprite script specifies the way the associated cast members behave only within the sprite's duration. If you placed any of those nine button cast members as a separate sprite elsewhere in the score, it would not be affected by the sprite script you are writing here.

Director opened the Behavior Script window with the most common sprite script—a *mouseUp* handler—already started for you.

3] Delete the *mouseUp* script and replace it with the following script:

```
on mouseLeave
    go to frame "Main"
end
```

Now, when the mouse pointer leaves the bounding rectangle of the Restaurants button any time during the animation, the playback head will branch back to the *Main* marker in frame 10.

4] Close the Script window and save your work.

Notice that Director stored the sprite script in the cast in the next available position, cast member 47. Go ahead and give the sprite script a name, such as GoMain, so you can identify it later.

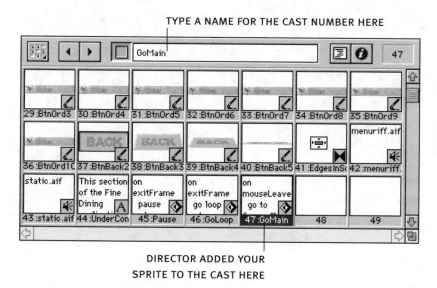

TYPE A NAME FOR THE CAST NUMBER HERE

DIRECTOR ADDED YOUR
SPRITE TO THE CAST HERE

5] Rewind and play the movie. Move the pointer back and forth over the Restaurants button.

If you keep the Score window open as you test your button, you can see how the playback head branches back and forth between the button animation section and the main menu section. The *mouseEnter* script you assigned to the Restaurants cast member spanning frames 10 through 18 sends the playback head to the animation sequence. The *mouseLeave* script you assigned to the sprites in frames 40 through 48 returns the playback head to the main menu section.

Occasionally when you work with Lingo, enhancing one feature causes problems with another feature. Try clicking the Restaurants button and you'll see that you've lost the ability to branch to the Restaurants panel. What happened and how can you fix it?

ASSIGNING ADDITIONAL SCRIPTS TO A SPRITE

Think for a moment why clicking the Restaurants button no longer branches to the Restaurants section. Recall from Lesson 18 that you implemented the branching by assigning a *mouseUp* script to the Restaurants button cast member (cast member 3, BtnRest). When this cast member is clicked anywhere within the movie, the playback head branches to the Restaurants section of the score. The problem now is that this cast member never stays on the stage long enough for you to click it.

THE RESTAURANTS BUTTON
CONTAINS A *MOUSEENTER*
SCRIPT AND A *MOUSEUP* SCRIPT

THE *MOUSEENTER* SCRIPT BRANCHES
TO THIS SECTION OF THE SCORE

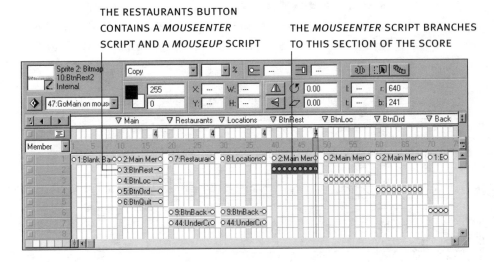

Here's the current sequence: At the main menu in frames 10 through 18, you pass the mouse pointer over the Restaurants button. Instantly, Director branches to the animation in frames 40 through 48. When you click to navigate to the Restaurants panel, you're actually clicking one of the cast members in the animation sequence— your original Restaurants button with the *mouseUp* script has been left behind in frames 10 through 18.

436

Thus, you need to relocate the *mouseUp* script that is currently attached to the Restaurants button cast member so that it can be triggered anywhere within the animation sequence in frames 40 through 48. You could assign a copy of this script to every cast member in the sequence, but as you learned in the previous task, it is more efficient to assign a single sprite script to the button sprites in the animation sequence.

Of course, the sprites in the animation sequence already have a sprite script assigned—the *mouseLeave* handler you wrote in the previous task. You could modify that sprite script to include a *mouseUp* handler as well. However, that would give you a single sprite script with handlers that send the playback head to two different locations (the *mouseLeave* handler sends the playback head to the main menu section, and the *mouseUp* handler sends the playback head to the Restaurants section). This would severely limit your ability to reuse the script (which you will, in fact, do in a later task). Therefore, you will take advantage of Director's ability to assign multiple scripts to a sprite.

1] In the cast, click the Restaurants button (cast member 3, BtnRest) and click the Script button to open the Script window.

The Script window contains the *mouseUp* handler you wrote in lesson 18 and the *mouseEnter* handler you wrote earlier in this lesson.

```
on mouseUp
  go to frame "Restaurants"
end

on mouseEnter
  go to frame "BtnRest"
end
```

2] Select the mouseUp handler, cut it (not copy it) to the clipboard, and close the Script window.

Since the *mouseUp* handler never has a chance to run, you could leave it where it is, but it's better to remove unused scripts; doing so makes it easier for you to understand a project when you return to it later.

3] Click the first sprite in the button animation, in channel 2, frame 40. Hold down the Shift key and click the last sprite in the loop, in channel 2, frame 48.

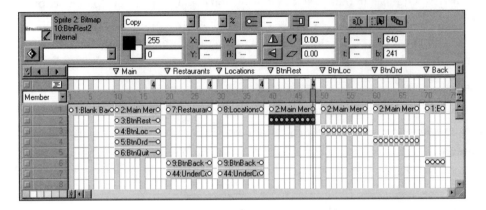

All the button sprites in the animation sequence are now selected.

4] Choose New Behavior from the Behavior menu in the sprite toolbar to open the Script window.

Director has already started a *mouseUp* script for you.

5] Remove the existing *mouseUp* script and paste the *mouseUp* script on the clipboard into the Script window.

Your script should look like this:

```
on mouseUp
  go to frame "Restaurants"
end
```

Now, any time you click the Restaurants button while it is animating, the playback head will branch to the Restaurants section of the score.

6] Close the Script window and save your work.

Once again, Director saved your sprite script in the score in the next open position, cast member 48. Go ahead and give the cast member a name, such as *GoRestaurants*, so you can identify it later.

7] Confirm that the button animation sprites have two sprite scripts assigned by clicking any of the sprites in channel 2, frames 40 through 48.

438

You should see the word "Multiple" in the Behavior menu in the sprite toolbar. Click the Behavior button to display the Behavior Inspector. The Behavior Inspector lists the scripts attached to the selected sprite.

CLICK HERE TO SEE THE SCRIPTS
ATTACHED TO THE SELECTED SPRITE

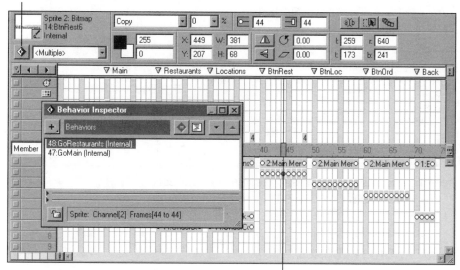

MAKE SURE TO SELECT ONE OF THE BUTTON SPRITES

8] Rewind and play the movie. Test the Restaurants button.

You should now be able to move the mouse pointer on and off the Restaurants button to start and stop the animation. You should also be able to click the Restaurants button at any time to branch to the Restaurants panel. If your movie isn't working as it should, go back through the preceding steps until the button works properly.

ON YOUR OWN

Following the instructions in the preceding tasks, implement the *mouseEnter*, *mouseLeave*, and *mouseUp* scripts you need to add animation and restore the branching to the Locations and Order buttons. As you do, remember these points:

• The *mouseUp* script that branches to the Order feature should use the *go to movie "Order.dir"* command instead of the *go to frame* command.

• You can assign the *mouseLeave* sprite script that you created for the BtnRest animation sequence to the sprites in the BtnLoc and BtnOrd animation sequences as well. This is one reason why, in the previous task, you left the *mouseLeave* script as a separate script and didn't add the *mouseUp* script to the end of it. All you need to do is select all the sprites in the animation sequence and then choose the existing script from the Behavior menu in the sprite toolbar.

SELECT THIS ENTIRE RANGE OF SPRITES AND THEN CHOOSE
THE *MOUSELEAVE* SCRIPT FROM THE SCRIPT MENU

ADDING AUDIO FEEDBACK

Next you'll add some background music that will play while the main menu is
displayed and some music that will play when the mouse is over the buttons.

> **tip** *If you did not complete the preceding tasks, you can use the Start2.dir file in the
> Lesson19 folder on the CD. Remember to save it as Menu.dir in your Projects folder.*

1] Select cast member menuriff.aif and click the Cast Member Properties button.

> **tip** *To quickly search for a cast member, you can click the binoculars (Find Cast Member
> button) on the toolbar or choose Edit > Find > Cast Member.*

CAST MEMBER PROPERTIES

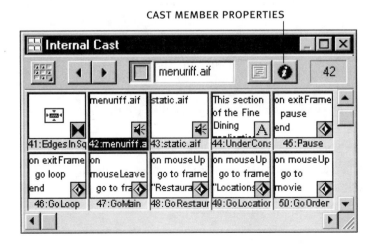

The Sound Cast Member Properties dialog box opens.

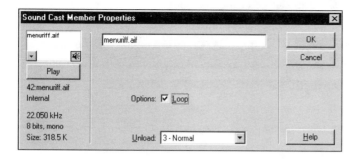

2] Check the Options Loop box to make the music loop when Director reaches the end of the sound file. Then click OK to close the dialog box.

When the Loop option is not selected, the sound plays once and then stops. With Loop selected, the sound plays over and over again.

3] Drag menuriff.aif to sound channel 1, frame 10, and adjust its duration so that it spans frames 10 through 18

By spanning menuriff.aif from frames 10 through 18, you are telling Director that you want to hear the music playing when those frames are displayed.

Next you'll add a different sound that will play when the mouse pointer is over the Restaurants button (that is, while the button animation sequence is playing in frames 40 through 48).

4] Select cast member static.aif, turn on the Loop option (click the Cast Member Properties button and check the Loop box), and drag this cast member to sound channel 2, frame 40 and adjust its duration to span frames 40 through 48.

By spanning static.aif from frames 40 through 48, you are telling Director that you want to hear the music playing when those frames are displayed.

5] Save your work. Rewind and play the movie.

Music plays while the main menu is displayed, and when the mouse is over the Restaurants button, different music plays.

The music sounds great, but there is still a problem. Listen carefully, and you will notice that, as you move the mouse over the Restaurants button, the menuriff.aif music continues to play until Director reaches the end of the sound file. Similarly, when you move the mouse off the Restaurants button, the static.aif music continues to play until Director reaches the end of that sound file. It would be better if the two music files did not overlap one another. You'll fix that next.

USING *SOUNDBUSY* TO CHECK THE SOUND CHANNEL

Using *if* with the elements *then* and *else*, you can have Lingo test whether a condition exists and respond accordingly. An everyday example of a condition you could test for is whether to turn a light bulb on or off: If it is dark, then turn on the light; otherwise, turn off the light. Here's how the *if-then-else* block would look if you could actually write Lingo to turn a light on or off:

```
if (dark) then
    turn on the light
else
    turn off the light
end if
```

Between the keywords *if* and *then* is an expression that Director tests for TRUE or FALSE. If the condition exists (TRUE), Lingo executes all the commands after the *then* keyword; if the condition doesn't exist (FALSE), Lingo executes the commands after the *else* statement. You finish the *if-then-else* block of statements with an *end if* statement. The *else* statement is optional. In this task, you will use just *if-then* to see whether a sound is playing and, if it is playing, you will then turn it off.

You will also use a new Lingo function, *soundBusy*. This function allows you to test a sound channel to determine whether a sound is playing. If a sound is playing, *soundBusy* returns TRUE; otherwise, it returns FALSE. The syntax for this function is *soundBusy(whichChannel)*. You will also use the *sound stop* command, which stops the sound playing in the specified channel. The syntax for this command is *sound stop whichChannel*.

The *enterFrame* handler is used to contain statements that you want executed each time the playback head enters a specific frame. You want the sound to stop immediately when the playback head enters frame 10, so you will write an *enterFrame* handler instead of the *exitFrame* handlers that you have employed previously.

1] Double-click the behavior channel, frame 10. Delete the *exitFrame* handler that Director started and type this handler:

```
on enterFrame
    if soundBusy(2) = TRUE then
        sound stop 2
    end if
end
```

You are creating a frame script that will run every time the playback head enters frame 10. Remember that the button animation sequences all branch the playback head back to the *Main* marker at frame 10 when the mouse is no longer over one of their sprites. The sound in those animation sequences plays in sound channel 2. Now, with this new script, when the playback head enters frame 10, Director checks whether a sound is currently playing in sound channel 2. If a sound is playing, Director shuts off the sound.

2] Double-click the behavior channel, frame 40. Delete the *exitFrame* handler that Director started and type this handler:

```
on enterFrame
  if soundBusy(1) = TRUE then
    sound stop 1
  end if
end
```

This frame script is the flip side of one you just wrote in the previous step. The sound in the main menu section plays in sound channel 1. Now, when the playback head branches to the Restaurant button animation sequence starting at frame 40, Director checks whether a sound is currently playing in sound channel 1. If a sound is playing, Director shuts off the sound.

3] Save your work. Rewind and play the movie.
Now the sounds play only where they should.

USING A *REPEAT* STRUCTURE

Your Fine Dining application is looking pretty good. You've added animating buttons and music, and your navigation between panels is solidly in place. It's now time to enhance the Restaurants and Locations panels by adding some animation to the Back button. In the score, drag the playback head through frames 70 to 73 to see the animation that is already set up for you.

You want a click on the Back button to clear the screen, trigger the button animation, and then branch back to the main menu. You can provide a two-step feedback sequence by clearing the screen when the user presses down on the mouse button and triggering the button animation when the mouse button is released.

A close cousin of the *mouseUp* event you have used many times already is the *mouseDown* event. You will use a *mouseDown* handler to branch to a background screen without any text or graphics. You don't know how long users will keep pressing on the mouse, so you need a way to hold the playback head on this frame until the mouse button is released. You can test whether the mouse button is still down using the *the stilldown* function, which returns TRUE if the mouse is still down and FALSE if it is not.

To make the playback head pause, you will create a *repeat* structure. There are different forms of *repeat* structures. Here, you will use *repeat while*. The syntax for this structure is

```
repeat while testCondition
   {statements}
end repeat
```

This type of *repeat* structure tests whether a given condition is TRUE or FALSE. If the condition is TRUE, Director runs the statements between the *repeat while* and the *end repeat* commands. When it reaches the *end repeat* command, Director goes back up to the *repeat while* command and evaluates the test condition again. Director keeps evaluating the test condition and running the statements in the repeat loop for as long as the test condition is TRUE. If at any time Director discovers that the test condition is FALSE, Director skips all the statements in the *repeat* structure and continues at the line following the *end repeat* command.

Inside the *repeat* structure you will use a rather unusual Lingo command: *nothing*. The *nothing* command does exactly what it says: nothing. Although the *repeat* command does not require any statements inside the loop, it is unusual to omit them. If an empty loop is used, it's because it is the test condition itself that is the purpose of the loop. Specifying *nothing* indicates to you or others that the loop body was left empty on purpose. Its use is purely optional, though.

1] Double-click the behavior channel, frame 70, and create the following script:

```
on exitFrame
   repeat while the stilldown = TRUE
      nothing
   end repeat
end
```

This frame script keeps the playback head in this frame as long as the mouse button is held down. Once the mouse button is released, the playback head resumes its journey. When the playback head reaches frame 74, which is the last frame in the Back button animation sequence, it needs to branch back to the main menu. For this, you need a frame script with an *exitFrame* handler.

2] Double-click the behavior channel, frame 74, and add the line shown here in bold:

```
on exitFrame
   go to frame "Main"
end
```

Now when the playback head exits frame 74, it will branch back to the main menu.

3] In the cast, click the Back button (cast member 9, BtnBack) and click the Script button.

The Script window shows the cast member script (a *mouseUp* handler) currently assigned to this cast member.

4] Delete the *mouseUp* handler and enter this handler:

```
on mouseDown
  go to frame "Back"
end
```

The *mouseUp* handler that you deleted sent the playback head directly to the main menu. Now you want to first play the animation that begins at frame 70, where the Back marker is located. Remember that your goal is to hold the playback head in frame 70 for as long as the mouse button is down. Therefore, you must use a *mouseDown* handler to branch the playback head to frame 70. If you use a *mouseUp* handler, the mouse button will already be up by the time the playback head arrives in frame 70.

5] Close the Script window and save your work.

6] Rewind and play the movie. Click Restaurants and then click the Back button.

Watch the playback head in the score when you first click the Back button. It branches to the Back section, starting at frame 70, because of the *mouseDown* handler you placed in its cast member script. The *repeat* structure in the frame script you wrote for frame 70 keeps the playback head in that frame for as long as the mouse button is held down. When you release the mouse button, the playback head continues. When it reaches the frame script you just added at frame 74, the playback head branches to the frame named Main.

7] Click the Locations button on the main menu. Then click the Back button.

This button works just like the Back button in the Restaurants section. That's because the script that sends the playback head to the Back button animation is a cast member script. A cast member script is active from any part of the score.

You're very close to being done. But maybe you've noticed something just a bit odd about the way the Restaurants, Locations, and Orders button animations look when you move the mouse off of them. As the animation stops (because the playback head has branched back to the main menu), the buttons sometimes seem to "snap" back into place.

445

NAVIGATING RELATIVE TO MARKERS

In Lesson 18 you used markers and their frame names in conjunction with the *go* command to send the playback head to different frames in the score. In this lesson you learned how to use the *go loop* command to return the playback head to the marker immediately to the left of the playback head. Both of these techniques are useful, but there is another way you can control the playback head without referring to specific frame numbers or frame names.

The *marker* function returns the frame number of markers that are placed before, on, or after the current marker. The current marker is considered to be the one in the current frame (where the playback head is) or the one closest to the left of the playback head. (This function is useful for implementing a Next or Previous button or for setting up an animation loop.) If you use *go marker(0)*, for example, the playback head goes to the current frame if the current frame contains a marker. If the current frame has no marker, the playback head goes to the previous marker to the left. If you use *go marker(1)*, the playback head will go to the first marker after the current frame. If you use *go marker(–2)*, the playback head will go to the second marker before the current frame. Any positive or negative integer or 0 can be used with the *marker* function.

The *marker* function provides a way of referring to relative markers—markers that refer to locations relative to the playback head instead of to specific frame names or frame numbers. As the playback head moves through the score, the value of the *marker* function will change, and so will the locations specified by relative markers.

To get a feel for relative markers, you will experiment using the Message window.

1] In the score, click frame 27.

2] Choose Window › Message to open the Message window (Windows Ctrl+M, Macintosh Command+M).

3] Type *put marker(0)* and press Enter (Windows) or Return (Macintosh). Type *put marker("Restaurants")* and press Enter (Windows) or Return (Macintosh).

Your Message window and score should look something like this:

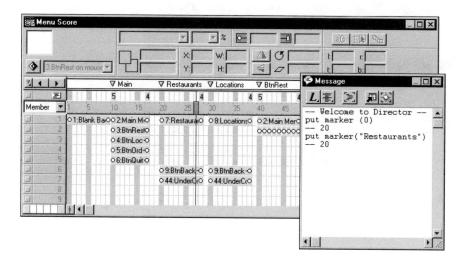

Remember that *marker(0)* returns the frame number of the current marker based on the location of the playback head. Because there was no marker in frame 27, *marker(0)* returned 20, the number of the marker to the immediate left. The *marker("Restaurants")* function shows you another way you can use the *marker* function to find a frame number.

4] Type *go to marker(−1)* and press Enter (Windows) or Return (Macintosh).

The playback head branches to frame 10, the marker (named *Main*) to the immediate left of the current marker.

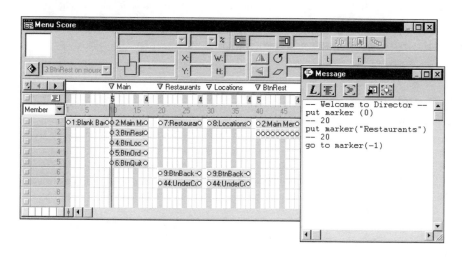

447

5] Type *go to marker(1) + 3* and press Enter (Windows) or Return (Macintosh).

The playback head branches to frame 23, which is the third frame beyond the next marker in frame 20 (named *BtnRest*). This should give you an idea of how to navigate from the Back button animation to two frames before the *Main* marker, which will include the transition in frame 10.

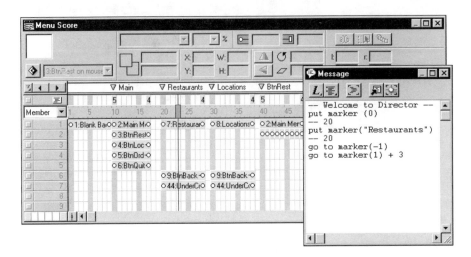

6] Type *go to "Main" – 2* and press Enter (Windows) or Return (Macintosh).

Oops. Director doesn't do anything because you can't add a number (*2*) to a name (*Main*). You need to use the marker function, which returns the frame number of a specified marker.

7] Close the Message window. Double-click the behavior channel, frame 74, to open the Script window.

The Script window contains the *exitFrame* handler you wrote in a previous task.

8] Revise the *exitFrame* handler as shown here in bold:

```
on exitFrame
  go to marker("Main") – 2
end
```

MARKER("MAIN") -2

MARKER("MAIN")

Member	▽ Main	▽ Restaurants	▽ Locations	▽ BtnRest	▽ BtnLoc	▽ BtnOrd
	5	4	4 5	4 5	4 5	4
1 5 10 15	20 25	30 35	40 45	50 55	60 65	
1	O1:BlankBackgr O O2:MainMenu O	O7:Restaurants O	O8:Locations O	O2:MainMenu O	O2:MainMenu O	O2:MainMenu O
2	O3:BtnRest O			OOOOOOOOO		
3	O4:BtnLoc O				OOOOOOOO	
4	O5:BtnOrd O					OOOOOOOO
5	O6:BtnQuit O					
6		O9:BtnBack O	O9:BtnBack O			
7		O44:UnderConst O	O44:UnderConst O			
8						

The *marker* function returns the frame number of the marker named *Main*. Your script will now work because Director can subtract 2 from the frame number.

When you are returning from another section of the movie, you want the playback head to land just a few frames short of the *Main* marker, so that you see a few frames of the blank background (frames 8 and 9) before the transition into the main menu at frame 10.

9] Save your work. Rewind and play the movie. Click Restaurants and then click Back.
After the Back button animation ends, the transition in frame 10 now provides a classy transition back into the main menu.

Of course, you could have just added another marker in frame 8 instead of using a relative marker. However, your markers channel can easily become cluttered, and you will find relative markers a handy technique—especially, as you saw here, to branch a frame or two ahead of a marker to include a transition or to branch a frame or two after a marker to avoid a transition.

Congratulations. You've just created the infrastructure for a professional application!

WHAT YOU HAVE LEARNED

In this lesson you have:

- Used the *mouseEnter* and *mouseLeave* event handlers to branch to different sections of the score [page 430]
- Added audio feedback and fine-tuned it using the *soundBusy* function [page 440]
- Used a *repeat* structure to keep the playback head in a specific frame [page 443]
- Created additional navigation using relative markers [page 446]

digital video

synchronizing with

One of the most striking types of media you can use in a Director movie is a digital video clip. Director lets you combine digital video with text, animation, and other effects to create exciting multimedia movies, and special Lingo functions let you synchronize the media to make sure everything works together smoothly. In this lesson, you'll be creating a multimedia advertisement for a Star Trek® movie.

Coming soon to a store near you!

Get Movie Time

This multimedia advertisement synchronizes animated text created in Director with different sections of a QuickTime digital video. Using Lingo, you can make sure that animations and digital video work together to produce a single, striking movie.

Star Trek: The Next Generation Interactive Technical Manual ® and © 1994 Paramount Pictures. ALL RIGHTS RESERVED. STAR TREK: THE NEXT GENERATION is a Registered Trademark of Paramount Pictures. Interactive Prototype Design and Programming by The Imergists, Inc.

LESSON 20

You'll use both cue points and the movie time to synchronize animations and digital video to produce a striking presentation.

If you would like to review the final result of this lesson, open the Complete folder in the Lesson20 folder and play StarTrek.dir.

WHAT YOU WILL LEARN

In this lesson you will:

- Import a digital video as an external cast member
- Play back a digital video in Director
- Use cue points to synchronize a digital video with score events
- Create a custom development tool to get timing information from a digital video and use this timing information to synchronize the digital video with score events
- Use comments and variables
- Practice moving channels in the score
- Create a transition to a digital video

APPROXIMATE TIME

It should take about 3 hours to complete this lesson.

LESSON FILES

Media Files:

Lesson20\Media

Starting Files:

Lesson20\Start\Start1.dir
Lesson20\Start\Start2.dir

Complete Files:

Lesson20\Complete\StarTrek.dir

SETTING UP FOR THIS LESSON

To give you a jump-start, the cast for the Star Trek application has been assembled for you.

1] Open the Start1.dir movie in the Lesson20 folder on the CD and save it as *StarTrek.dir* in your Projects folder.

2] Open the Cast window and familiarize yourself with the project assets it contains.

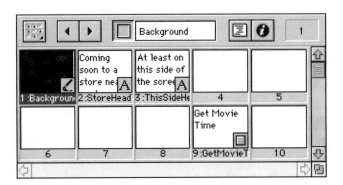

The cast contains a background for your production, two headlines that will move on and off the stage at different times during the movie, and a button for a development tool you will create. The empty positions are for scripts that you will write during this lesson and for the digital video you will work with.

You will start by importing the digital video into the cast.

IMPORTING A DIGITAL VIDEO

The first step in creating this multimedia advertisement is importing the digital video that includes the footage of the spaceship and the soundtrack.

You can import digital video just as you can other types of media, but unlike other media, digital video files are imported as *external* files. This means that the Director movie includes only a reference to the digital video file; it does not include the file itself. Thus, you must provide the digital video file along with the Director file when you distribute the movie as a projector. Note that when the finished Director movie is played, Director looks for the digital video in the same relative place it was when you imported it; if you move it to a different location, users will not be able to play your movie.

Suppose the digital video is in a folder called Videos that is in the same folder (called MyDemo) as the Director movie. Director will be able to find the digital video so long as you keep all the files in those relative locations, in folders with the same names. Director will even find the digital video file if you move the MyDemo folder to a different folder, disk drive, or CD. However, if you move the digital video file to a folder other than a Videos folder in the same folder as the Director movie, Director won't be able to find the digital video, and users will see an error message when they try to run the Director movie.

If you do want to move a Director movie or digital video file after you import the digital video, just place all files in the locations where you want them and play the Director movie. A dialog box will appear prompting you for the location of the digital video file. Just select the new location from the dialog box and then save the movie. Now the Director movie will know where to find the digital video in its new location.

tip   *For more information on how Director handles external file references and ways to ensure successful use of external files, see the Macromedia Tech Notes on these issues. Macromedia Tech Notes can be found at the Macromedia Web site at* http://www.macromedia.com/support/director/

In this task, you will import a QuickTime digital video.

1] Choose File › Import to open the Import dialog box (Windows Ctrl+R, Macintosh Command+R).

2] Choose Files of Type: QuickTime (Windows) or Show: QuickTime (Macintosh).
You now see only digital video files in the list box, making it easier to find the file you want.

3] Select StarTrek.mov from the Complete folder in the Lesson20 folder on the CD, click Add, and then click Import.
Director adds the digital video at the next available position, cast member 4.

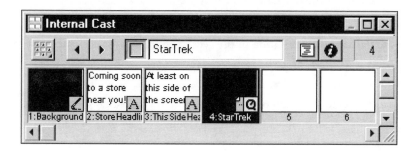

4] Double-click the new cast member to open the QuickTime digital video and then play the video. Close the window when you're done.

CLICK HERE TO PLAY THE VIDEO

This window allows you to preview a digital video.

The palette used for the Star Trek digital video is Thousands of Colors, so the movie looks best with the monitor display set to 16-bit or Thousands of Colors. QuickTime digital videos are frequently set to this color depth to display the digital video at its best color. If your monitor is set to 8-bit color depth, the digital video will look grainy.

PLAYING A DIGITAL VIDEO CAST MEMBER

Like a sound file, a digital video cast member will play only as long as the playback head is in the frame that contains it. For example, if the digital video sprite is in just one frame of the score and the playback head is moving at 15 frames per second, you will see only ¹⁄₁₅ of a second of the digital video when the playback head passes through that frame. To play more of the digital video, you can use three techniques:

• You can extend the video sprite's duration in the score. The video plays as long as the playback head is moving through the frames that contain the digital video sprite. This technique alone is usually impractical, because it is difficult to match the length of the digital video exactly to the length of the digital video sprite in the score, especially when you do not know the capabilities of the user's system.

- You can use Lingo to keep the playback head looping in a frame that contains the digital video sprite. The video continues to play while the playback head loops. In this case, the duration of the sprite in the score is not significant. The sprite can span one frame or many frames, so long as the last (or only) frame keeps the playback looping (in most cases, with an *exitFrame* handler containing a *go to the frame* command).

- Use cue points to synchronize the video playback with other elements or continue playing the video to its end.

Most projects use a combination of these techniques. The score is arranged so that other actions in the project—for example, headlines that move across the screen—are working correctly. The digital video sprite is then placed in the score to span the entire length of the action.

> **tip**   *Even if the digital video is the only element on the stage, it is still a good idea to span the digital video sprite over several frames of the score. Doing so makes the score much more readable because you can see the name of the digital video cast member in the score.*

In this task you will use the first two of these techniques: You'll play the digital video through the series of frames that will contain the rest of this Director movie sequence and then tell Director to loop on the last frame to finish the video.

You will begin building your project by adding the digital video sprite to the score.

1] Drag the StarTrek digital video (cast member 4) to the upper-right part of the stage.

By default, Director adds new sprites to the score with a duration of 28 frames. If the digital video sprite in your score is some other duration, adjust it so that its end point is in frame 28. Your score should look like this:

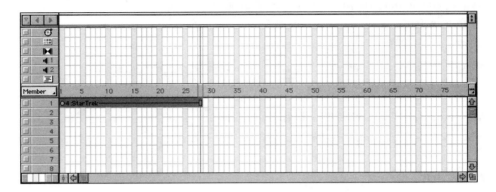

This is just a convenient duration to start working with. For now, the duration of the digital video sprite is not important.

2] Make sure Control › Loop Playback is not selected. Play the movie.

Watch the playback head in the score as well. You don't see much because the digital video doesn't really begin for a second or so, and the playback head quickly reaches frame 28. At frame 28, the movie stops, and so does the playback head.

If Control > Loop Playback had been selected, the playback head would have returned to frame 1, and the video would have continued to play until it finished. Give it a try to see for yourself and watch the playback head in the score.

As you saw if you played the completed project, the advertisement plays once in a linear fashion, so looping the playback head back to frame 1 isn't appropriate. Instead, you need to loop in the last frame of the movie.

3] Double-click the behavior channel, frame 28, to open the Behavior Script window. Type the script shown here in bold and then close the window.

```
on exitFrame
  go to the frame
end
```

You're creating a frame script that causes the Director movie to loop on frame 28. (Recall from Lesson 16 that frame scripts are generally used to control the playback head without involving user interaction.) Now the digital video will play until you stop the Director movie.

4] If Looping is on, turn it off. Rewind and play the Director movie.

The digital video now plays through to completion. By watching the playback head, you can see that it travels through the first 28 frames of the score and then loops on frame 28, giving the digital video the time it needs to finish playing.

5] Stop the movie and save your work.

CREATING ANIMATED TEXT

In the finished movie, you want headlines to move on and off the stage at specific points while the digital video is playing. In this task, you will start setting up the first of the two headlines. This headline appears at the left edge of the screen and moves horizontally to the center of the screen.

1] Select channel 3, frame 11, and then drag cast member 2 (which contains the headline "*Coming soon to a store near you!*") onto the stage.

Notice that you have skipped channel 2. You will use channel 2 for another element later in this lesson.

2] Adjust the duration of the text sprite so it spans frames 11 through 31.

This will be the first phase of the animation, when the headline appears at the left edge of the screen and moves to the center of the screen. This duration is long enough to make the text animate smoothly across the screen.

3] Select the entire sprite in channel 3. Set the ink for the text sprite to Background Transparent.

Now the white pixels around the text are transparent.

Your score should now look like this:

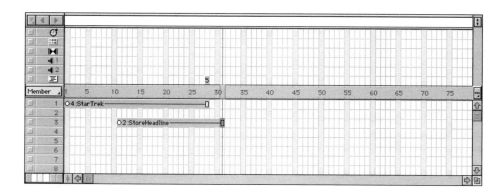

4] Position the text sprite where you want it vertically on stage and then move the text to the left so it's off the stage.

Your screen should look similar to this:

This represents the starting point of the animation, when the text first appears at the left edge of the screen.

note *When you play the digital video, the last frame of the video to be displayed (when the movie finishes or you've stopped the movie) remains on the screen even when you start to work in other frames. Therefore, the frame of the digital video that you see on your screen will likely be different from the one shown in the illustrations throughout this lesson.*

5] Click channel 3, frame 31, and choose Insert › Keyframe (Windows Ctrl+Alt+K, Macintosh Command+Option+K).

This keyframe indicates the stopping point for the text when it reaches the center of the stage.

6] With the keyframe at frame 31 still selected, move the text sprite on the stage until it's centered. Hold down the Shift key as you drag to constrain the sprite to the same vertical position.

This is the final position for the text in the first phase of its animation. You have set the starting point (frame 11) and ending point (frame 31) for the animation, and Director does all the work of calculating the position of the text in the in-between frames, 12 through 30.

7] Select the frame script sprite in the behavior channel, frame 28, and move it to frame 31.

Remember that this script keeps the playback head in the last frame of the Director movie so the digital video can play through in its entirety.

8] Extend the duration of the digital video sprite in channel 1 from frame 28 through frame 31.

The digital video sprite needs to span the entire duration of the movie. Your score should now look like this:

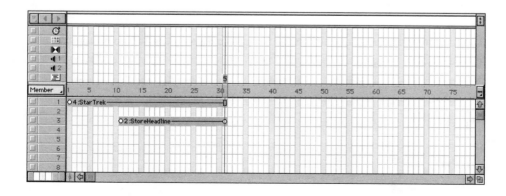

459

9] Play the movie again.

You see the text slide onto the stage from the left and then stop in the center of the screen. The digital video plays until it finishes.

Unfortunately, the text animation isn't synchronized with the video. The text appears on the screen as soon as the playback head reaches frame 11, when the digital video has barely begun to play. You need a way to make the text appear when the starship begins to make its first turn. In the next two tasks, you will use two different methods to tie the beginning of the text animation to a specific moment in the digital video.

USING CUE POINTS IN THE QUICKTIME MOVIE

The easiest and most precise method for synchronizing events in the score—such as type moving across the stage—with a digital video is to use cue points. Cue points can be added to QuickTime digital videos using a separate editing program, such as Macromedia's SoundEdit on the Macintosh. But once those digital videos are imported into a Director cast, you can work with their cue points in the Windows version of Director equally well.

Cue points are labels that you assign at specific points in the movie's timeline, similar to the markers in a Director score. Once you add cue points to a QuickTime digital video, you can refer to them using Lingo or the tempo channel. Cue points are also a power tool for synchronizing score events with SoundEdit 16 sound files and Shockwave Audio files. The cue point techniques discussed in the following tasks apply equally to synchronizing sound (such as voice-over narration) with score events as well. Two cue points have already been added to the StarTrek digital video: StoreOn andStoreOff. In the next two tasks, you will learn different methods of synchronizing the text animation with the cue points in the digital video.

SYNCHRONIZING THE ANIMATION USING THE TEMPO CHANNEL

The easiest way to learn how cue points work is by using Director's tempo channel to control the text animation.

1] In the tempo channel, double-click frame 10 to display the Tempo dialog box.

The text animation begins in frame 11. Therefore, you need a way to make the playback head loop in frame 10 until the digital video reaches the first cue point, StoreOn. When the video reaches the StoreOn cue point, you want to let the playback head continue, starting the text animation in frame 11.

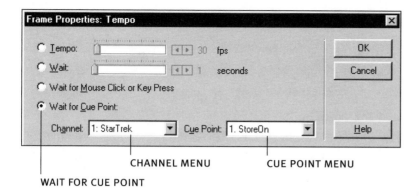

CHANNEL MENU   CUE POINT MENU

WAIT FOR CUE POINT

2] Select Wait for Cue Point.

The Wait for Cue Point option tells Director to keep looping the playback head in the current frame until a cue point that you specify has passed. The Channel list contains the name of every sprite that is capable of using cue points. In this case, only the digital video sprite has cue points, so this is the only item you will see in the Channel list.

3] Click the Cue Point menu to see the choices.

This menu contains the StoreOn and StoreOff cue points that are already in the video. Director also includes two built-in cue points: Next (which tells the playback head to loop in the current frame until the next cue point passes) and End (which tells the playback head to loop in the current frame until the media finishes playing).

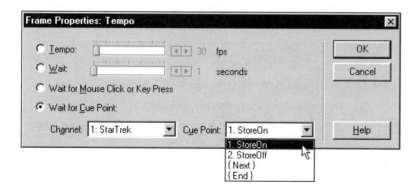

The numbers in front of the cue point names identify each cue point's position within the digital video's timeline. In this case, the StoreOn cue point is first, and the StoreOff cue point is second. Make a note of these numbers, because you will use them in a later task.

4] Choose StoreOn from the Cue Point menu. Then click OK.

This tells Director to loop the playback head at the current frame until the StoreOn cue point is reached. Once the StoreOn cue point passes, the playback head will start to move again.

5] Rewind and play the movie.

Watch the playback head in the score. The playback head moves quickly until it reaches frame 10, where it loops to continue playing the movie. When the StoreOn cue point passes, the playback head moves forward, playing frames 11 through 31. You see the headline glide onto the screen.

THE TEMPO INSTRUCTION YOU SET HERE KEEPS THE PLAYBACK HEAD
LOOPING IN FRAME 10 UNTIL THE STOREON CUE POINT PASSES

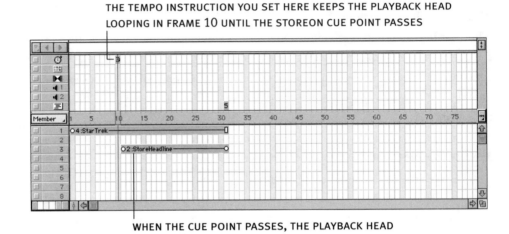

WHEN THE CUE POINT PASSES, THE PLAYBACK HEAD
CONTINUES, AND THIS TEXT ANIMATION BEGINS

Now that you see how cue points work, you're ready to use Lingo to track them.

SYNCHRONIZING THE ANIMATION USING LINGO

Using cue points and the tempo channel to synchronize digital video with events in the score is so easy that it may be the only technique you ever need. However, there may be times when you need to use Lingo instead. For example, you may want to synchronize a digital video with an animation that you have created using Lingo (as you will do in Lesson 21). In this case, the Lingo that is doing the animation also needs to be able to monitor the cue points, because the tempo channel can control events only in the score, not events generated by Lingo. Or you may have a digital video playing with a separate sound file for narration, each with its own set of cue points. The Tempo dialog box lets you set only one cue point per frame, and therefore you will need to monitor both cue points simultaneously with Lingo.

As the digital video plays, Director keeps track of cue points as they occur in the movie. You will use the *the mostRecentCuePoint* property to ask Director for the number of the last cue point it encountered. The numbers returned by this property correspond to the order of the cue points within the digital video; these are the numbers you wrote down earlier when you were in the Tempo dialog box.

The syntax for this property is *sprite(whichChannel).mostRecentCuePoint*. You replace *whichChannel* with the channel that the digital video occupies in the score.

In this task, you will write a handler that keeps the playback head looping in frame 10 until the first cue point in the digital video passes.

1] Delete the sprite in the tempo channel, frame 10.

You're going to replace this functionality with a Lingo script.

2] Double-click the behavior channel, frame 10, to open the Script window.

As you learned in Lesson 16, you need a frame script to control the playback head. Director has started the most common type of frame script—an *exitFrame* handler.

3] Complete the *exitframe* handler as shown here in bold and then close the Script window:

```
on exitFrame
    if sprite (1).mostRecentCuePoint = 0 then
        go to the frame
    end if
end
```

Until the first cue point in the QuickTime digital video passes, the *the mostRecentCuePoint* property returns 0. So long as the *the mostRecentCuePoint* is 0, the *if-then* statement keeps the playback head looping in the current frame. Only after the first cue point passes and the *the mostRecentCuePoint* property returns 1 will the *if-then* statement be bypassed, so the playback head can travel past frame 10.

4] Close the Script window, save your work, and play the movie.

Now you are controlling the synchronization through Lingo!

note *As this book went to press, the pre-release version of Director 7 encountered a problem relating to* mostRecentCuePoint. *When you rewind and start the movie, the* mostRecentCuePoint *property is not being reset to zero. Thus, when you replay the movie, the test* if sprite(1).mostRecentCuePoint=0 *is always false and the movie does not pause at frame 10. This affects authoring with Director only and has no effect on projectors or Shockwave movies. If you experience this problem, you can save your movie and then re-open it. The movie will then play correctly. You will need to re-open the movie each time you need to test it.*

Before you complete the rest of the text synchronization, you need to improve your scripts so they will be easier and more flexible to work with.

USING VARIABLES

As you build the next section of the multimedia advertisement, you will use one of Lingo's most powerful features: variables. First, however, you need to understand how this feature works.

A **variable** is a container, like a cup, that can hold different values, such as a name or a number. You can assign a value to a variable with the *set* or *put into* commands or the equal (=) operator. A variable is created the first time you assign a value to it, which is also called **initializing** the variable.

Variables can hold different types of data: numbers, character strings (such as "Mary"), or Boolean values (either TRUE or FALSE), as well as member specifications (*member 3 of castlib 2*), lists of information, and more. In the following example, the items to the left of the equal sign are examples of variable names, and the items to the right are variable values. Notice that the word "Mowgli" is enclosed in quotation marks. The quotation marks let Director know that the characters are a string and should be treated as characters and not as a variable or handler name.

```
myAge = 33
catName = "Mowgli"
fuzzy = TRUE
```

You can use any name for a variable, so long as it follows the rules described here.

Variable names must:

- Start with a letter: *upSideDown* and *Stickball* are acceptable; *4UrHealth* and *2X2* are not.

- Include alphanumeric characters only: *Twinky45* and *Route66* are acceptable; *T@#$%* and *old/new* are not. One exception is the underscore (_) character, which you can use to simulate_spaces_between_words.

- Consist of only one word (no spaces): *thirtysomething* and *TenLittleIndians* are acceptable; *thirty something* and *Ten Little Indians* are not.

- Not be the same as the name of a Lingo element: *myTRUE* and *repeatTwice* are acceptable; *TRUE* and *repeat* are not because they are existing Lingo keywords.

The following steps show how to declare and initialize a variable in the Message window.

1] In the Message window, type *put myAge* and then press Enter (Windows) or Return (Macintosh).

The window displays <Void> because you haven't declared the variable *myAge* yet; it has no value, and Director doesn't know what *myAge* is.

2] Type *myAge = 30* and then press Enter (Windows) or Return (Macintosh).

This entry declares that *myAge* is a variable and initializes the variable to 30. Optionally, you can type *set myAge =30*. The *set* keyword was required in previous versions of Director, but is optional in Director 7. In either case, the variable that appears on the left of the equal sign is assigned the value of whatever appears on the right side of the equal sign.

3] Type *put myAge* and then press Enter (Windows) or Return (Macintosh).

Now the Message window returns the value 30 because you assigned a value to *myAge*.

That's great, you may be saying, but why bother? Isn't it just as easy to type *30* in a Lingo script as it is to type *MyAge*?

465

The problem that variables solve for you is that many times you don't know what specific data value you need to work with; you know only what type of value you need. For example, say you want your application to start by greeting users with a message that tells them how many more days it is until January 1, 2000. When you're writing this script, you don't know what future date users will run your program. You only know that you need to get the date from the computer's operating system, perform some calculations on it, and display the result. In your script, you represent the current date with a variable. When your script runs, it asks the computer's operating system for the current date, assigns that date to the variable you've set up to hold it, and then does the necessary math using the value in the variable. As you will soon learn in your real-world projects, variables are among the most common tools you'll use in your Lingo scripts.

Another reason for using variables is that as you prepare more involved programs, you will find that it is much easier to understand a script that refers to, say, the *quitButton* sprite rather than sprite 30. By using named variables instead of only numbers, you make your scripts more readable. Further, when you use named variables, you have to set *quitButton =30* in only one place in your movie. If you need to relocate the button to another sprite channel, you need merely change one line. If you did not use named variables, you would have to hunt down every use of *30* in your scripts and change them all.

In the following task, you will see how using a variable can make updating your Lingo scripts easier.

ADDING COMMENTS AND A GLOBAL VARIABLE TO A MOVIE SCRIPT

In this task, you're going to create a variable that holds the channel number of the digital video. Then you will use this variable to refer to the digital video channel in every script that needs it. You will also add comments to your scripts to make them more understandable to humans.

A **comment** is an explanation in the script itself, provided to help humans reading the script understand how each part works. Special characters preceding each comment— two hyphens—tell Director to ignore this text as it runs the script; comments provide information to you and whoever else reads your script, not to Director. Comments are not required in any script, but including them is good programming practice and will make your work much easier to follow. You should include comments in all of your handlers as you write them. The comments can be as long as you wish; Director skips over them, so they won't slow down your scripts when they run. You'll see good examples of comments throughout this book.

A variable can be either local or global. A **local variable** is available for use only so long as the handler in which it is created is running. A **global variable** can be used anywhere in the movie where it is declared. To use a global variable, you enter the word *global* before the variable name.

tip *It's a good idea to use different naming conventions for each type of Lingo element so you can clearly see what is a local variable, global variable, or handler name, for instance. For variable names, a good practice is to start with a lowercase letter and then capitalize the beginning of each new word in the name. For global variables, a good practice is to begin each name with a lowercase "g." For example, you might use the name* theCharacter *for a local variable and* gTheCharacter *for a global variable.*

To better understand the difference between local and global variables, look at how the value of the variable *myAge* is set in the following script:

```
on startMovie
   global myAge          --myAge is declared as a global variable.
   myAge = 33            --Here, myAge is initialized to 33.
   Gym()                 --This line calls the Gym handler below.
                         --After the Gym handler runs, myAge is still 33.
   Home()                --This line calls the Home handler below.
                         --After the Home handler runs, myAge equals 43.
end

on Gym
   myAge = 23            --Here, myAge is a local variable, so its scope
end                      --is limited to this handler. Changing the value
                         --of myAge here doesn't affect the global
                         --variable myAge in the startMovie handler.

on Home
   global myAge          --Because myAge is declared as a global variable
   myAge = myAge + 10    --in this handler, its scope is program-wide.
end                      --Now myAge equals 33 + 10, or 43.
```

Remember that lines in handlers run in the order they're placed in the handler, so the first line is executed first, the second line next, and so on. In this example, the *startMovie* handler runs first and declares *myAge* as a global variable. In the second line, it sets the value of *myAge* to 33. The *startMovie* handler then refers to the *Gym* handler. (Referring to a handler is known as calling a handler.) The *Gym* handler then goes into action and creates a local variable with the same name, *myAge*, and sets its value to 23. After the *Gym* handler finishes executing, control returns to the *startMovie* handler, which calls the *Home* handler in the next line. The *Home* handler declares the global variable *myAge* and sets its value to 43. Then control returns to the *startMovie*

467

handler. However, when the *startMovie* handler completes its work, control returns to Director; it does not go to the *Gym( )* or *Home( )* handler, because these handlers must be explicitly called to be executed. Read the comments next to the script lines to see how the value of *myAge* changes as this script runs.

Now it's time to use a global variable in your project. You will also use comments to document the script as you write it.

Once you've set up the global variable, you will see how it can save you lots of time as you develop your movie. Using a variable to hold a value like the number of the channel that contains the digital video allows you to easily move the digital video into other channels. When you move the digital video into a different channel, you can just reset the value of the variable, and every script that uses that variable will automatically use the correct value.

1] Click cast member 7, which is empty, and open a Movie Script window by pressing Ctrl+Shift+U (Windows) or Command+Shift+U (Macintosh).

So far, you've created sprite scripts to control events that apply to specific sprites, cast member scripts to control events that apply to cast members, and frame scripts to control the action that occurs when the playback head enters or leaves a frame. Now you will create a movie script. You use a movie script when you need to control what happens when a Director movie starts, stops, or pauses. You also use a movie script to hold handlers that need to be available from anywhere in the movie.

You may recall from Lesson 16 that no default script lines are displayed when you open a new movie script; the Movie Script window is completely empty.

2] Create a global variable and a comment by typing the following:

```
global gQTChannel        --Declare gQTChannel as a global variable.
                         --It contains the channel number of the digital video.
```

As you can see, creating a global variable is easy: You just type *global* and then a name for the variable. Now you can refer to the variable in a handler in the movie script.

3] On the next line of the script, type the lines shown here in bold:

```
global gQTChannel        --Declare gQTChannel as a global variable.
                         --It contains the channel number of the digital video.
on startMovie            --When the movie starts,
   gQTChannel = 1        --set the value of gQTChannel to 1.
end
```

The *startMovie* message is a built-in message that Director sends at the beginning of every movie. The line *gQTChannel=1* initializes the value of the global variable to 1, which is the channel currently occupied by the digital video sprite. Initializing global variables in the *startMovie* handler ensures that they're available to any script in the movie as soon as the movie starts.

Now you will change the scripts that refer to the channel number of the digital video so they refer to the global variable you just created instead of to the specific channel number in the score.

4] Double-click the behavior channel, frame 10. Then change the script as shown here in bold:

```
global gQTChannel         --Declare gQTChannel as a global variable.
                          --It contains the channel number of the digital video.


on exitFrame
  if sprite (gQTChannel).mostRecentCuePoint = 0 then
                          --If the first cue point in the movie
                          --in channel gQTChannel hasn't
                          --passed, then
      go to the frame     --loop in the current frame.
  end if                  --When the first cue point passes,
                          --the playback head will continue.
end
```

This is the frame script you created in an earlier task to synchronize the appearance of the text with a point in the digital video. You've added comments and substituted the hard-coded reference to sprite 1 with the more flexible sprite *gQTChannel*.

5] Close the Script window, save your work, and play the movie.

It should work exactly as it did before, except this time you're using a global variable instead of the number 1. You'll be glad you did this a little later, when you need to make some changes to the score.

MOVING TEXT OFF THE STAGE

Now you're ready to finish the text animation. So far, you have a dramatic opening sequence: The spaceship flies into one corner of the screen accompanied by music in the digital video, and as the spaceship turns, text animates onto the stage. Now you will animate the text off the stage, once again synchronizing its movement with a specific spot in the digital video.

1] Select the text sprite in channel 3 that extends from frame 11 through frame 31 and choose Edit › Copy (Windows Ctrl+C, Macintosh Command+C).

To animate the text off the screen, you can simply use a reverse sequence of the animation that moves the text onto the screen.

2] Click channel 3, frame 32, and choose Edit › Paste (Windows Ctrl+V, Macintosh Command+V). Then choose Modify › Reverse Sequence.

This command was introduced in Lesson 8. It reverses the order of the selected cells. In this case, the text will animate off the stage in the exact reverse order it animated onto the stage.

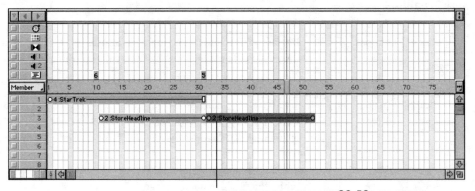

THIS SPRITE IN FRAMES 32-53 IS A COPY
OF THE SPRITE IN FRAMES 11-31, EXCEPT
THAT THE SEQUENCE HAS BEEN REVERSED

3] Move the script in the behavior channel, frame 31, so that it is in frame 52.

RELOCATE THIS FRAME SCRIPT
FROM FRAME 31 TO FRAME 52

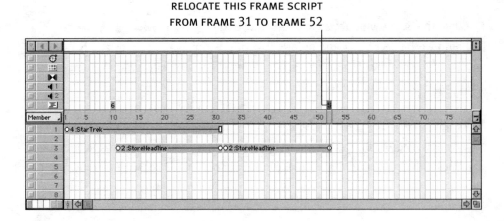

Remember: That's the *go to the frame* script you need at the end of the movie so that the digital video plays through in its entirety.

Now you'll set the synchronization time, as you did earlier in frame 10, by adding a new frame script at frame 31, the point where the text begins to slide back off the screen.

4] Double-click the behavior channel, frame 31, to open the Script window. Enter the script shown here in bold:

```
global gQTChannel
                        --Declare gQTChannel as a global variable.
                        --It contains the channel number of the digital video.

on exitFrame
   if sprite (gQTChannel).mostRecentCuePoint = 1 then
                        --If the second cue point in the movie
                        --in channel gQTChannel hasn't
                        --passed, then
      go to the frame   --loop in the current frame.
   end if               --When the second cue point passes,
                        --the playback head will continue.
end
```

This is similar to the score script you wrote at frame 10, only this time you are waiting for cue point 2, StoreOff, to arrive before allowing the playback head to continue.

5] Extend the duration of the digital video sprite in channel 1 to span frames 1 through 52.

This adds the digital video to the new frames. The score should look like this:

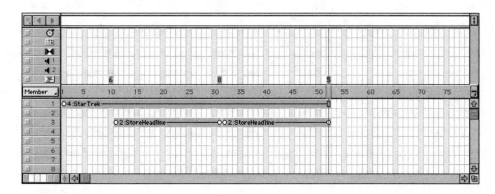

6] Play the movie.

Watch the playback head. Now the text begins to move off the screen after the second cue point, StoreOff, is passed.

THE FRAME SCRIPT YOU ADDED HERE KEEPS
THE PLAYBACK HEAD LOOPING IN FRAME 31
UNTIL THE SECOND CUE POINT PASSES

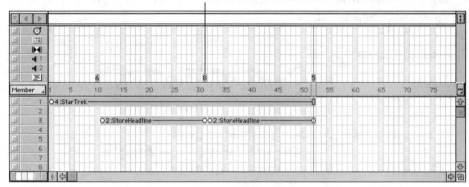

7] Save your work.

GETTING TIMING INFORMATION FROM A DIGITAL VIDEO

If don't have an editing program like SoundEdit 16 to add cue points to QuickTime digital videos, you can still synchronize the digital video with score events. In this task you will learn how to use Lingo to get timing information.

note *If you did not complete the preceding tasks, you can open Start2.dir in the Lesson20 folder to continue with this lesson.*

Time-based media such as digital video and sound files include timing information. Director developers commonly create custom tools to use during the authoring process, and that's what you'll do here: create a development tool that gets the timing information from a digital video as it's playing. You're going to create a button that you can click to record the timing information at key points in the digital video as the digital video plays. To do this, you will use a Lingo sprite property created especially for monitoring a digital video's timing information: *movieTime*. The syntax of this property is *sprite (channelNumber).movieTime*.

This sprite property is an internal counter that keeps track of the current position in the digital video movie. It's similar to *the frame* in Director movies, which instructs Director to track the position of the playback head.

You're going to create a handler to get the timing information from the digital video while it's playing. This handler will need the number of the channel where the movie is located.

1] Drag cast member 9 to channel 2, frame 1.

This is a button cast member that has been created for you. The button text reads "Get Movie Time."

2] Position the button at the lower right part of the stage.

3] Select cast member 9 (the button) in the Cast window. Then click the Script button to open the Script window.

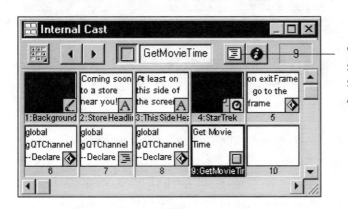

WITH CAST MEMBER 9 SELECTED, CLICK THE SCRIPT BUTTON TO ADD A CAST MEMBER SCRIPT

473

The Get Movie Time button will always perform the same action, so you're going to create a cast member script for this button. In the Script window, Director has started a *mouseUp* handler for you.

4] Modify the script as shown in bold and then close the Script window.

global gQTChannel

```
on mouseUp
  put sprite (gQTChannel).movieTime
end
```

When the button is clicked, this script causes the Message window to display the current time within the digital video. Notice that the digital video is identified using the global variable that you set up for that purpose in an earlier task.

5] Extend the button sprite's duration in channel 2 from frame 1 to frame 52.
You want the button to be visible throughout the movie. Your score should now look like this:

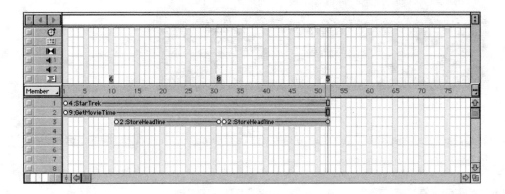

6] Choose Window › Message to open the Message window.
You will use the Message window to see the results of the *put sprite (gQTChannel).movieTime* command.

7] Play the movie. Then click the Get Movie Time button several times.
As you click the button, you should see numbers appear in the Message window. These numbers represent the digital video time at the point at which you clicked the button. The numbers you see refer to **ticks**, the timing measurement digital video uses. There are 60 ticks per second, so "60" is 1 second into the movie, "120" is 2 seconds into the movie, and so on.

You will see the usefulness of this information a bit later.

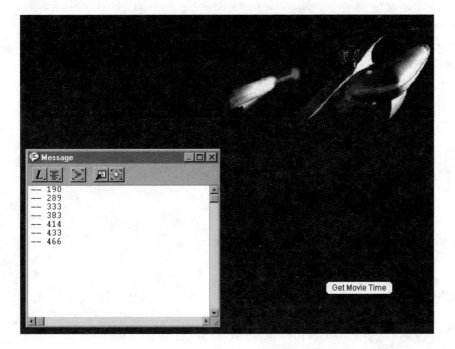

8] Save your work.

SYNCHRONIZING WITH A VOICE-OVER IN A MOVIE

Now you will add and synchronize the second text animation. This headline appears from the bottom of the screen, moves up to the middle of the screen, and then immediately moves back off the bottom of the screen. This headline repeats a phrase that's used in the voice-over narration of the digital video, so you want to make sure it appears on the screen at the same time that the voice-over speaks those words.

1] Play the movie. When the voice-over begins to say, "At least on this side of the screen," click the Get Movie Time button.

Remember: To select a time, play the movie and click the button you created. To see the movie time, you must have the Message window open. For the example here, you should get a movie time of approximately 1180. That's when the narration begins, and that's when you'll begin the animation of the text onto the stage.

2] Select channel 4, frame 53, and then drag cast member 3 (which contains the headline "*At least on this side of the screen*") onto the stage. Adjust its duration so it spans frames 53 through 70.

The first text animation ends at frame 52. You don't want the two text animations to be on the screen at the same time, so you start working at frame 53. Like the duration you chose for the first text animation, the duration for this sprite is long enough to make the animation appear smooth. Your score should look like this:

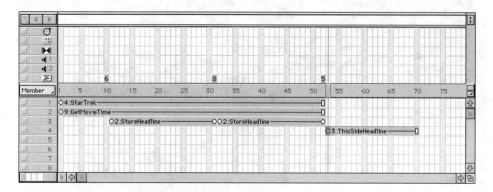

3] Set the ink to Background Transparent.

4] Position the text, centered, at the bottom of the stage so it's just off the screen.

This represents the starting point of the first phase of the animation.

5] Click frame 70 and choose Insert › Keyframe.

This is the point where you want the text to reach the center of the screen.

6] With the keyframe still selected, center the text in the middle of the stage, just below the digital video.

This takes care of getting the text onto the stage. Next you will reverse the sequence to move the text off the stage.

7] Copy the sprite in channel 4. Click frame 71 and then paste.

8] Select the sprite in channel 4, frames 71 through 88. Then choose Modify › Reverse Sequence.

The text will now move onto the stage and then off again in the same way. Your score should look something like this:

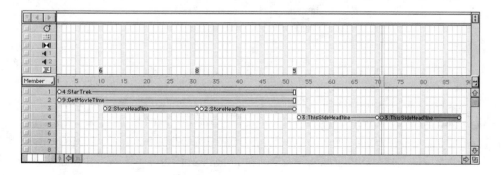

9] Extend the sprites in channels 1 and 2 to frame 88.

You need to make sure the digital video (in channel 1) and the button for your development tool (channel 2) appear throughout the movie. The text animation in channel 3 is finished and does not need to be extended.

477

10] Select frame 52 in the behavior channel and move it to frame 88.

Remember: This is the *go to the frame* script you need at the end of the movie so the digital video plays through to the end. Your score should now look something like this:

REPOSITION THE FRAME SCRIPT IN FRAME 52 TO FRAME 88

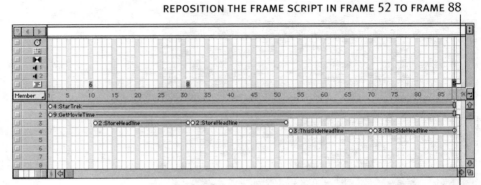

EXTEND THE SPRITES IN CHANNELS 1 AND 2 TO END AT FRAME 88

Now you'll set the synchronization time, as you did earlier, by adding a new script.

11] Double-click the behavior channel, frame 52, to open the Script window. Enter the script shown here:

```
global gQTChannel          --Declare gQTChannel as a global variable.
                           --It contains the channel number of the
                           --digital video.

on exitFrame
   if sprite (gQTChannel).movieTime ‹ 1180 then go to the frame
                           --If movieTime is less than 1180,
                           --stay in this frame.
   end
```

The first text animation finishes at frame 52. You now need to keep the playback head looping in frame 52 until it's time for the second text animation to start in frame 53. Therefore, you are writing a frame script to control the playback head. The script tells Director to keep looping in the current frame if the *movieTime* function returns a value that is less than 1180. When the *movieTime* function returns a value greater than 1180 (when the voice-over begins the words, "At least on this side of the screen"), the playback head can continue to frame 53, and the second text animation begins.

If the Lingo commands get too long to fit on one line in the Script window, you must use a second line to complete your typing. You do this by inserting a special character, called a **continuation symbol**, to tell Director to ignore the Return and read the two lines as one. You enter the continuation symbol (¬) by pressing Alt+Enter (Windows) or Option+Return (Macintosh) when you reach the end of a line. In the example here, you might type the *exitFrame* handler like this:

```
on exitFrame
  if sprite (gQTChannel).movieTime ‹ 1180 ¬
    then go to the frame
                                      --If movieTime is less than 1180,
                                      --stay in this frame.
  end
```

tip *You may have noticed that there is no* end if *statement in the* on exitFrame *handler even though the handler contains an* if *statement. If the entire* if-then *construct fits on a single line (or continued line), then an* end if *statement is not required.*

12] Play the movie. Watch the playback head as the movie plays.

It works!

THE FRAME SCRIPT IN FRAME 53 KEEPS THE
PLAYBACK HEAD LOOPING UNTIL THE *MOVIETIME*
OF THE DIGITAL VIDEO IS 1180 OR GREATER

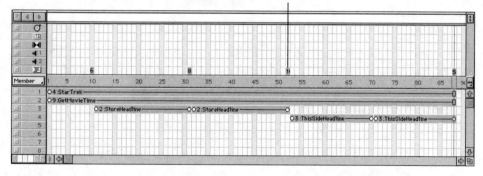

13] Save your work.

ADDING A BACKGROUND BY MOVING CHANNELS

A background graphic for the movie will tie all the elements together. Remember, though, that Director displays each channel on top of the previous one, so if you want a graphic to be displayed as a background, underneath all the other elements, you will need to place it in channel 1. In this Director movie, though, channels 1 through 4 are already filled up. One way to reorder the channels is to use the Arrange command on the Modify menu.

1] Click channel 1 on the left side of the score to select all the cells in this channel. Then hold down the Shift key and click channel 4 to select all the filled cells in the score.

CLICK HERE...

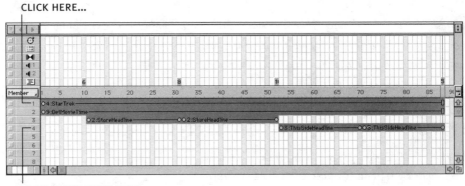

THEN SHIFT-CLICK HERE

You can now move the selection down a channel. You can also drag the selection, if you prefer.

2] Choose Modify › Arrange › Move Forward.

The entire selection moves forward one channel, freeing channel 1 for the background image you will add next.

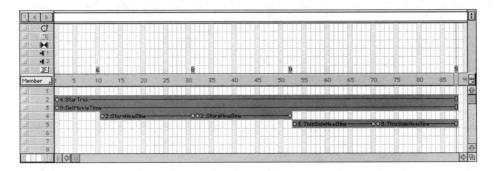

3] Click channel 1, frame 1. Then click cast member 1 (Background) and choose Modify › Cast to Time.

The Cast to Time command centers a cast member on the stage. This is quick way to place a full-screen background so that it exactly covers the stage. This cast member provides a more interesting space background than the plain black background you've been working with up until now.

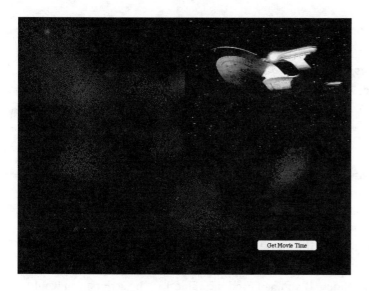

4] Extend the duration of the bitmap sprite in channel 1 through frame 88.

Your score should now look like this:

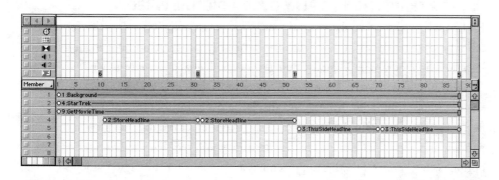

tip *To extend a sprite that is only one frame, hold down Alt (Windows) or Option (Macintosh) while you drag.*

481

5] Rewind and play the movie.

The script in frame 10 no longer works, and the text doesn't animate onto the stage. Why? The channel that contained the digital video (channel 1) now contains the background graphic. Your movie script doesn't work any more because the *gQTChannel* global variable is initialized to 1, but the digital video movie is now in channel 2. You need to reinitialize the global variable to a new number.

6] Open the movie script.

7] Change the *value assigned to the gQTChannel variable* in the *startMovie* handler as shown here in bold:

```
global gQTChannel          --Declare gQTChannel as a global variable.
                           --It contains the channel number of the digital video.

on startMovie              --When the movie starts,
  gQTChannel = 2           --set the value of gQTChannel to 2.
end
```

8] Close the window and play the movie.

With one simple change, the movie plays correctly. The script can now find the channel that contains the digital video. If you had used the value 1 in the scripts, you would have had to find all the locations where you used 1 and in each case change the value to 2. Now you can see the value of variables.

USING A TRANSITION TO PLAY OVER A DIGITAL VIDEO

Earlier in this lesson you discovered that Director treats digital video differently than other types of media by adding it as an external file rather than importing it directly into the Director movie. Digital video gets other special treatment as well. To ensure that digital video plays back smoothly and quickly, Director places it directly on the stage, without running it through the analysis it performs for other elements to determine their place in the score's layers. (If you select the digital video in the Cast window and click the Cast Information button, you'll see that the Direct to Stage option is checked.) While this approach has advantages for the digital video's performance, it means that you can't control the placement of a digital video among a Director movie's layers, and it causes complications when you want to apply a special effect, such as a screen transition, only to the digital video. In this task, you will work around these problems by applying a screen transition to a separate element that takes the place of the digital video for the duration of the screen transition.

1] Move the start of the digital video in channel 2 from frame 1 to frame 2.

You want the background to appear in frame 1 without the digital video or the placeholder you will be creating.

2] Double-click the transition channel, frame 2. In the dialog box, choose Center Out, Square, set the duration to 1 second, and select Changing Area Only. Then close the dialog box.

You will apply the transition to the placeholder that you will create next.

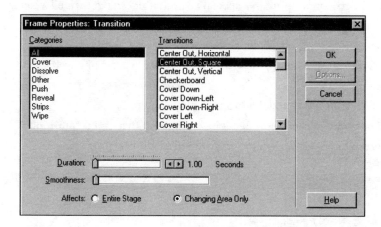

3] Select channel 5, frame 2. Then open the tool palette and draw a filled black rectangle that completely covers the digital video.

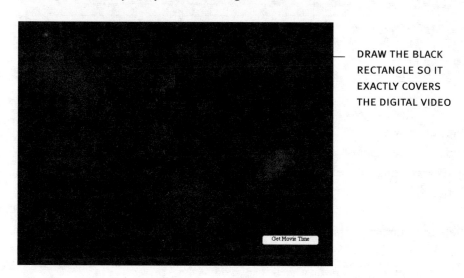

DRAW THE BLACK RECTANGLE SO IT EXACTLY COVERS THE DIGITAL VIDEO

You can estimate the size of the rectangle, or you can set the exact dimensions by selecting the digital video sprite and then choosing Modify > Sprite > Properties. The Properties dialog box will show you the exact height and width of the digital video. Then you can select the rectangle sprite, choose Modify > Sprite > Properties, and type the same height and width in the Properties dialog box.

4] With the rectangle selected, check the Trails button in the sprite toolbar at the top of the Score window.

Selecting Trails puts the rectangle sprite in a special layer that doesn't get wiped away immediately as the playback head leaves the frame. The black rectangle will stay on the stage until it is completely wiped away by the transition, which takes 1 second to complete. As the box disappears, the digital video in channel 2 will be uncovered.

5] Adjust the rectangle sprite in channel 5 to span frames 2 and 3.

This ensures that the rectangle is on the stage long enough for the screen transition to start animating through it. Your completed score should look like this:

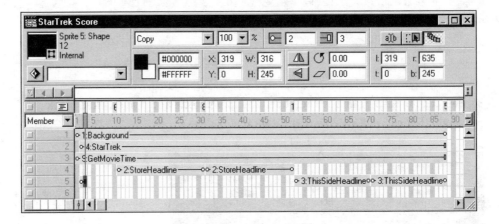

6] Play the movie.

It works! You just applied a screen transition over a digital video by using a special technique: creating a placeholder for the digital video and then applying the transition to it.

7] Delete the timing information button.

Your movie is complete, so you can delete the timing information button you added as a development tool; you won't need it anymore.

8] Save your work.

WHAT YOU HAVE LEARNED

In this lesson you have:

- Imported a digital video cast member [page 452]
- Learned how to distribute movies with externally stored cast members [page 452]
- Played back digital video from Director [page 454]
- Used the *the mostRecentCuePoint* property to synchronize the digital video with score events [page 462]
- Used comments and variables [page 464]
- Created a custom development tool to get timing information from a digital video [page 472]
- Used the *movieTime* property to synchronize the digital video with score events [page 475]
- Used the Move Forward command to move channels in the score [page 480]
- Created a transition to a digital video [page 482]

with lingo

controlling sprites

Until now, you have always determined which sprites appear on the stage and where they appear by arranging the sprites in channels of the score. In this lesson, you will learn how to control sprites directly with Lingo, which is often the easiest way to achieve an effect that would otherwise require a very complex score. Because you are already manipulating the sprites through Lingo, you can also more easily add actions that are triggered by user input or some other movie event.

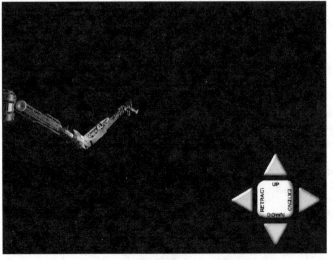

In the Iron Helix game from Pulse Entertainment, players move a robot arm across the stage to gather DNA samples. The game extensively uses the Lingo techniques taught in this lesson to control the movement of the arm.

LESSON 21

Graphics from Iron Helix © Copyright 1993 Pulse Entertainment, Inc. All Rights Reserved. Pulse Entertainment, the Pulse Entertainment logo, and Iron Helix are either registered trademarks or trademarks of Pulse Entertainment, Inc., in the United States and/or other countries.

If you would like to review the final result of this exercise, open the Complete folder in the Lesson21 folder and play Robot.dir.

WHAT YOU WILL LEARN

In this lesson you will:

• Switch the cast member assigned to a sprite using Lingo

• Control button states based on mouse position

• Create animation using Lingo

• Practice creating a *repeat* structure

• Constrain the movement of sprites

• Alter the speed of an animation

• Simplify scripts by creating custom messages

APPROXIMATE TIME

It should take about 3 hours to complete this lesson.

LESSON FILES

Media Files:
None

Starting Files:
Lesson21\Start\Start1.dir
Lesson21\Start\Start2.dir

Completed Files:
Lesson21\Complete\Robot.dir

SETTING UP FOR THIS LESSON

To give you a jump-start, the cast for the robot arm movie has been assembled for you.

1] Open the Start1.dir movie in the Lesson21 folder and save it as *Robot.dir* in your Projects folder.

2] Display the Cast window and familiarize yourself with the project assets it contains.

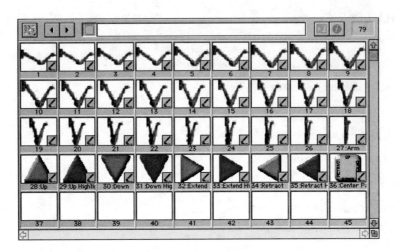

The first 27 cast members provide the animated sequence for the robot arm. You will use cast members 28 through 36 to construct a control panel with buttons that users can click to move the robot arm up and down and to extend and retract the arm.

USING THE SCORE TO ANIMATE THE ARM

Before you start controlling sprites through Lingo, you will first create an animation using the score. Your score-based animation will provide a point of comparison when you create an animation with Lingo later in this lesson.

1] Drag cast member 27 (Arm) to channel 1, frame 1. Then drag the arm to the far left edge of the stage and center it vertically.

This cast member is the robot arm in its most retracted state. You're going to place the arm in different positions on the stage to animate it.

2] Choose Background Transparent from the Ink menu in the score.

This will remove the white background surrounding the robot arm.

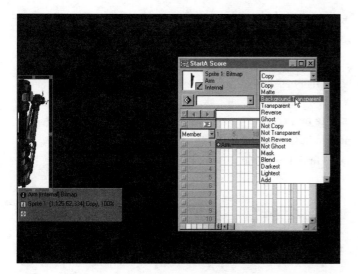

3] Make sure the sprite in channel 1 spans frames 1 to 30.

Director is preset to add new sprites with a duration of 28 frames. Just how much you have to move the sprite's end frame depends on how you previously set the Span Duration option in the Sprite Preferences dialog box (File > Preferences > Sprite).

tip *If the sprite is only a single frame in channel 1, frame 1, click the sprite; Shift-click channel 1, frame 30; and then choose Modify > Extend Sprite (Windows Ctrl+B, Macintosh Command+B).*

4] Click frame 10 of the sprite and choose Insert › Keyframe to establish a new keyframe (Windows Ctrl+Alt+K, Macintosh Option+Command+K). Move the robot arm in this keyframe to the upper edge of the stage.

The robot arm doesn't need to be in any particular location. It just needs to be in a different position than in frame 1. This 30-frame sprite now has two keyframes: one at frame 1 and one at frame 10.

5] Click frame 20 of the sprite and choose Insert › Keyframe to establish a new keyframe. Move the robot arm in this keyframe to the right edge of the stage.

Again, the robot arm in this third keyframe doesn't need to be in any particular location. It just needs to be in a different position than in the keyframes at frames 1 and 10.

6] Click frame 30 of the sprite and choose Insert › Keyframe to establish a new keyframe. Move the robot arm in this keyframe to the bottom edge of the stage.

Once again, the sprite in this final keyframe doesn't need to be in any particular location, just in a different position than in the keyframes at frames 1, 10, and 20.

7] Rewind and play the movie.

The arm moves around the stage.

This animation is nothing new to you. By now, you should be very familiar with the use of keyframes to set up animations.

ADDING SPRITES TO THE STAGE

Next you'll set up the movie and place the remaining sprites on the stage. The additional sprites you need are buttons that users can click to move the robot arm.

1] Double-click the tempo channel in frame 1 to open the Tempo dialog box. Then set the tempo to 10 frames per second (fps).

The actual tempo setting used in this task isn't very important because all animation is going to be performed through Lingo. However, it's a good habit to set the tempo at the beginning of every project, even if it is changed later. If no tempo is set, the default tempo is 30 fps, which is a little faster than what's needed here.

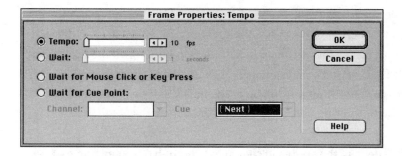

2] Delete the sprite in channel 1. Drag cast member 27 (Arm) to channel 1, frame 1. Then drag the arm to the far left edge of the stage and center it vertically, as you did in the previous task. Set its ink effect to Background Transparent.

The Arm sprite that you added to channel 1 in the previous task has several keyframes. You don't need those keyframes now, because you're going to control the movement of the arm through Lingo. It's easier to delete the existing sprite and add it to the stage again than it is to delete the keyframes.

3] Drag cast members 28, 30, 32, 34, and 36 to the lower-right part of the stage as in the following illustration. Set their ink effect to Matte.

These cast members are the Up (cast member 28), Down (30), Extend (32), and Retract (34) buttons with which the user will be able to control the robot arm. Cast member 36 is a panel on which you can place the buttons.

Matte ink is useful for irregularly shaped cast members; it makes the white edges around the graphic transparent, while any white inside the graphic remains white. Your buttons should look something like this:

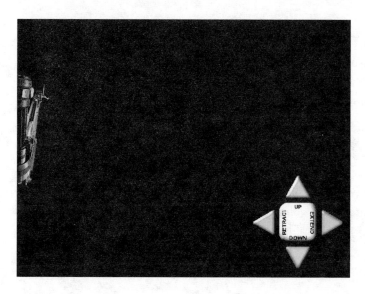

As always, after channel 1 is occupied by a cast member, Director automatically fills in each channel in numerical order with subsequent cast members that are dragged onto the stage. This means that cast member 28 (the Up button) will be in channel 2, cast member 30 (Down) will be in channel 3, cast member 32 (Extend) will be in channel 4, cast member 34 (Retract) will be in channel 5, and cast member 36 (Center Panel) will be in channel 6.

4] Adjust the durations of the sprites in channels 1 through 6 to span frames 1 through 10.

The duration of these sprites is not important because you will control all action using Lingo. This duration was chosen because it is long enough to allow the cast member names to be readable in the score. Your score should now look like this:

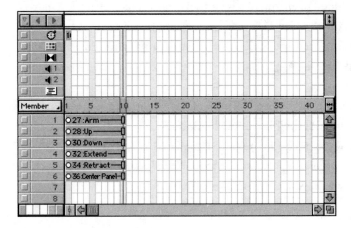

5] Save your work.

USING *ROLLOVER* TO CONTROL BUTTON STATES

As you learned in Lesson 19, user feedback is an important feature of any interactive movie. In this task, you will learn some new techniques to provide visual cues to users when they click a button. You will use Lingo to switch between two different states of a button: a normal state and a highlighted state.

While you are holding down the mouse button, a properly constructed button remains highlighted only as long as the pointer is directly over the button. If you slide the pointer off the button (while keeping the mouse button pressed), the button should revert to its normal state. When you release the mouse button, the button should trigger its associated action only if the mouse pointer is actually over the button itself.

To accomplish this functionality, you will use the *rollOver* function to determine whether the pointer is currently over a specific sprite. The syntax is *sprite (whichChannel).rollOver*, which returns TRUE when the pointer is over the sprite in *whichChannel*, and which returns FALSE when it is not. An alternative syntax is *rollOver(whichChannel)*.

To switch between the normal and highlighted states of the buttons, you will use the *memberNum* sprite property. The syntax is *sprite (whichChannel).memberNum*. This sprite property determines the number of the cast member associated with the sprite currently occupying *whichChannel*. Setting this property lets you switch the cast member assigned to a sprite.

In this task you will use the Message window to see how to replace the normal version of a button with its highlighted version, and then you will use what you learned to write a Lingo script to do the same thing.

1] Open the Cast window.

Look at the buttons Up (cast member 28), Down (30), Extend (32), and Retract (34); these represent the normal state of each button. Notice that there is a highlighted version of the cast member next to each of the four buttons.

2] Choose Window › Message to open the Message window (Windows Ctrl+M, Macintosh Command+M).

3] Type the following and press Enter (Windows) or Return (Macintosh):

```
sprite (2).memberNum = 29
```

This command sets the cast member number for sprite 2 to 29, the new Up button you just created. Nothing happens on the stage because you first must redraw the stage with the *updateStage* command.

Notice that the *memberNum* command refers to sprite 2. This is shorthand for "the sprite in channel 2." It is important to remember that the *memberNum* sprite property refers to a channel number in the score, not to the number of the cast member in that channel. It is, however, a number of the cast that is being assigned to the *memberNum* sprite property.

4] Type the following and press Enter (Windows) or Return (Macintosh). Watch the stage carefully.

updateStage

THE HIGHLIGHTED
VERSION OF THE
UP BUTTON (CAST
MEMBER 29) IS
NOW ON THE
STAGE

You see the new button state! You changed the cast member number of sprite 2 from 28, the original Up button, to 29, the highlighted state of the Up button, and you did it using Lingo, without changing the score. Now you will use this technique in a script.

5] In the Cast window, select cast member 28 and then click the Script button.
Because the Up button will always do the same thing, you will create a cast member script for it.

6] Delete the default *mouseUp* handler and enter the following *mouseDown* handler. Then close the Script window.

```
on mouseDown
  repeat while the mouseDown          --While the mouse button is held down
    if rollOver(2) = TRUE then        --and the mouse is over the Up button (sprite 2),
      sprite(2).memberNum = 29        --display the highlighted button state.
    else                              --Otherwise,
      sprite(2).memberNum = 28        --display the normal button state.
    end if
    updateStage                       --Update the stage to show changes.
  end repeat                          --The mouse button is no longer down,
  sprite(2).memberNum = 28            --so return to the normal button state.
  updateStage                         --Update the stage to show changes.
end
```

Now if the mouse button is clicked and held down on the Up button, the highlighted state of the button is displayed. When the mouse button is released, the normal state is redisplayed.

The comments in the script explain how each line works. When the mouse button is pressed, the *mouseDown* handler checks to see whether the mouse pointer is over the Up button (the sprite in channel 2), and if it is, it sets sprite 2 to cast member 29 (the highlighted state of the button). If it's not, it sets sprite 2 to cast member 28 (the normal state of the button). Then it updates the stage to show the change. When the mouse button is released, the *repeat while the mouseDown* loop is exited, and the sprite is set to the normal state for the button.

WHEN THE SPRITE IN CHANNEL 2 IS CLICKED, THE
NORMAL STATE OF THE BUTTON (CAST MEMBER 28) . . .

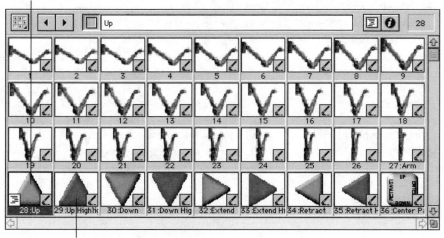

. . . IS REPLACED WITH THE
HIGHLIGHTED STATE OF THE
BUTTON (CAST MEMBER 29)

7] Double-click the behavior channel, frame 10, and in the Script window type *go to the frame*, as shown here in bold:

```
on exitFrame
    go to the frame
end
```

This *exitFrame* handler pauses the playback head once the frame is drawn on the stage. Why are you pausing the playback head here? Because from this point on, all the actions are performed using Lingo, so the playback head doesn't need to move. Because you need to control the playback head without relying on user interaction, you're creating a frame script.

8] Rewind and play the movie. Then click the Up button to see what happens.

Now when you click and hold the mouse on the Up button, the highlighted state is displayed. When you release the mouse button, the normal state is displayed again.

9] Repeat steps 5 and 6, this time for the Down button.

What will be different about the *mouseUp* and *mouseDown* handlers for the Down button? When you set the highlighted state of the button, you will use cast member 31. When you set the button back to its normal state, you will use cast member 30. You also need to change the channel number; the Down button is the sprite in channel 3. This is what the handler for cast member 30 should look like when you're through:

```
on mouseDown
   repeat while the mouseDown          --While the mouse button is held down
      if rollOver(3) = TRUE then       --and the mouse is over the Down button (sprite 3),
         sprite(3).memberNum = 31      --display the highlighted button state.
      else                             --Otherwise,
         sprite(3).memberNum = 30      --display the normal button state.
      end if
      updateStage                      --Update the stage to show changes.
   end repeat                          --The mouse button is no longer down,
   sprite(3).memberNum = 30            --so return to the normal button state.
   updateStage                         --Update the stage to show changes.
end
```

10] Save your work.

11] Rewind and play the movie. Click the Down button to see the different states of the button.

It works! You now see a normal state and a highlighted state when you click the button.

ON YOUR OWN

Create cast member scripts for the Extend and Retract buttons to display the normal and highlighted states when the buttons are clicked.

USING *LOCH* AND *LOCV* TO MOVE THE ARM

Your next task is to make the robot arm react in response to the user's clicks on the buttons you just created, moving the arm up or down according to which button is clicked. The tools for this task are the sprite properties *locH* and *locV*, which return the horizontal and vertical positions, respectively, of the specified sprite in terms of pixels (the individual dots that make up an image on the screen). You can find and set a sprite's location using *locH* and *locV*. The syntax of these properties are *sprite (whichChannel).locH* (or *the locH of sprite whichChannel*) and *sprite (whichChannel).locV* (or *the locV of sprite whichChannel*).

Sprite coordinates are relative to the upper-left corner of the stage. The (0,0) origin is at the upper-left corner of the stage. The first 0 represents the horizontal value, and the second 0 represents the vertical value. As you progress toward the right of the stage, the horizontal value increases; as you progress toward the bottom of the stage, the vertical value increases.

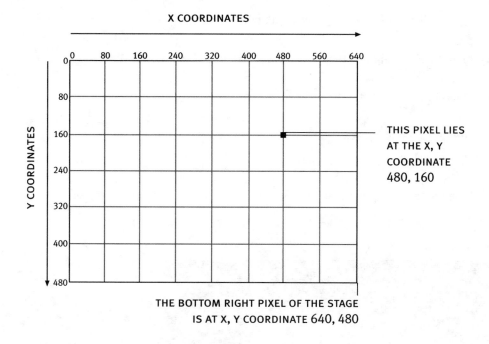

As you did in the preceding task, you will test the commands in the Message window before you build a script with them.

1] Rewind and play the movie. Don't click any buttons—just play the movie. Then stop the movie.

This ensures that all the scripts are read into memory so the following steps using the Message window work correctly.

2] Choose Window › Message to open the Message window.

3] Type the following and then press Enter (Windows) or Return (Macintosh):

    put sprite (1).locV

The value returned depends on exactly where you placed the sprite on the stage. In the movie used to create this task, 141 is returned. Remember that sprite 1 contains the robot arm, and the *locV* value of sprite 1 is the vertical location of the top of the sprite's bounding rectangle.

Now you will see how you can control the position of the arm.

4] Type the following and then press Enter (Windows) or Return (Macintosh):

    sprite (1).locV = sprite (1).locV - 40

Nothing is returned because you are only setting a value. You need to put the value in the Message window.

5] Type the following and then press Enter (Windows) or Return (Macintosh):

    put sprite (1).locV

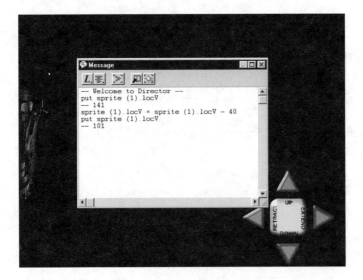

This time, 101 is returned. You have set the location of the arm 40 pixels above the current location of the arm on the stage, but nothing has changed on the stage. To see the change on the stage, you must update the stage.

6] Type the following and then press Enter (Windows) or Return (Macintosh). Watch the arm on the stage.

updateStage

The arm moves up 40 pixels. (Compare the preceding illustration with the illustration in step 5; you can see how the arm has moved up in relation to the Message window, for example.)

Now you can apply what you've just practiced to your own scripts.

7] In the Cast window, select cast member 28 (the Up button) and then click the Script button.

This cast member script contains the handler that you wrote in the previous task to set the button states when the button is clicked.

You're going to add lines to the script to move the arm up when the Up button is clicked. You want users to be able to keep holding down the mouse button to keep the movement going, so you will use the *stillDown* function, which indicates whether the user is still pressing the mouse button. When the user is pressing the mouse button, the *stillDown* property is TRUE; when the user is not pressing the mouse button, the *stillDown* property is FALSE.

8] Add the lines shown here in bold; then close the window.

```
on mouseDown
   repeat while the mouseDown        --While the mouse button is held down
      if rollOver(2) = TRUE then     --and the mouse is over the Up button (sprite 2),
         sprite(2).memberNum = 29    --display the highlighted button state.
         repeat while the stillDown  --While the mouse button is held down,
            sprite (1).locV = sprite (1).locV – 1
                                     --move the arm up 1 pixel.
            updateStage              --Update the stage to show changes.
         end repeat
      else                          --Otherwise,
         sprite(2).memberNum = 28    --display the normal button state.
      end if
      updateStage                   --Update the stage to show changes.
   end repeat                       --The mouse button is no longer down,
   sprite(2).memberNum = 28         --so return to the normal button state.
   updateStage                      --Update the stage to show changes.
end
```

These additional lines direct the arm to move up. Once again, the comments describe the purpose of each line. The repeat loop runs so long as the mouse button is pressed down. Each time Director sends the *stillDown* message, the handler subtracts 1 pixel from the vertical location of the sprite and then updates the stage.

Thus, the final result of this handler is that the sprite is moved up by 1 pixel at a time on the stage. Remember that in the coordinate system, (0,0) is at the top left of the stage, so subtracting 1 moves the sprite up.

Notice that you placed these lines in the *mouseDown* handler. If you had put them in a *mouseUp* handler, the robot arm would move up only after you release the mouse button. If you wanted to move the arm up for a great distance, you would need to click the button repeatedly. However, with *mouseDown*, all you need to do is click and hold down the mouse button, and the arm will move so long as the mouse button remains pressed.

9] In the Cast window, select cast member 30 (the Down button) and then click the Cast Member Script button.

This cast member script contains the handlers that exchange the button states when the button is clicked.

10] Add the lines shown here in bold; then close the window.

```
on mouseDown
  repeat while the mouseDown         --While the mouse button is held down
    if rollOver(3) = TRUE then        --and the mouse is over the Down button (sprite 3),
      sprite(3).memberNum = 31        --display the highlighted button state.
      repeat while the stillDown      --While the mouse button is held down,
        sprite (1).locV = sprite (1).locV + 1
                                       --move the arm down 1 pixel.
        updateStage                   --Update the stage to show changes.
      end repeat
    else                              --Otherwise,
      sprite(3).memberNum = 30        --display the normal button state.
    end if
    updateStage                       --Update the stage to show changes.
  end repeat                          --The mouse button is no longer down,
  sprite(3).memberNum = 30            --so return to the normal button state.
  updateStage                         --Update the stage to show changes.
end
```

These lines make the Down button react exactly the way the Up button does, except instead of subtracting 1 pixel from the *locV* value each time the *stillDown* property is TRUE, this handler adds 1 pixel, which moves the sprite down 1 pixel. Because in the coordinate system, (0,0) is at the top left of the stage, adding 1 moves the sprite down.

Last, you update the stage to show the results (*updateStage*).

11] Close the Script window, save your work, and play the movie. Click the Up and Down buttons.

Great! The arm moves up and down, and the different buttons states are displayed when you click the buttons.

The features you have implemented in this lesson are fundamentally different from those in the previous lessons. In this lesson, you used Lingo instead of the score to control the movie's actions. It would be very difficult and time consuming to create this arm movement in the score. You would need different sections in the score to display the arm at every vertical location possible, and you would need to write numerous scripts to branch to the various sections. Using Lingo to control sprites for this type of animation is quite advantageous, as you can see.

How do you decide whether to use Lingo or to create the animation in the score? There is no single right answer. For each project, you need to consider the requirements and use the best approach to satisfy those requirements. For example, you can easily create a simple linear presentation in the score without having to use Lingo. On the other hand, suppose you have a more complex situation: a movie that has a frame with five check boxes on it, and you want different pictures displayed according to the combination of boxes that are selected. Numerous combinations can be created with five check boxes, and creating each combination in the score would be tedious and difficult. It's much easier to use Lingo to perform this task.

CREATING CUSTOM MESSAGES AND HANDLERS

The *mouseDown* handlers for both the Up and Down buttons are getting very large and cumbersome. You can both reduce the size of these handlers and make them easier to read by instead creating three handlers: one handler to move the arm up, a second to move the arm down, and a third to display the normal and highlighted states of the button. Placing pieces of functionality in separate handlers makes your Lingo scripts modular and therefore easier to maintain.

Just as Director sends messages in response to events in a movie, you can create custom messages to trigger handlers that you write. As you know from previous lessons, when Director sends a *mouseDown* message, the message travels through the scripts in the movie, looking for a *mouseDown* handler to execute. In the same way, you can send a custom *MoveArmUp()* message:

```
on mouseDown
  MoveArmUp( )
end
```

Somewhere else in the movie, you must write a corresponding handler:

```
on MoveArmUp
  [commands that move the arm up]
end
```

When Director encounters your *MoveArmUp()* message in the *mouseDown* handler, it finds the corresponding *MoveArmUp* handler, executes the code it finds there, and then returns to the *mouseDown* handler at the line immediately following the *MoveArmUp()* message.

*The empty parentheses () mean that you are not supplying additional information (**parameters**) to the handler. They also help to remind you that* MoveArmUp() *is a handler and not the name of a variable. They are used only when calling the handler, not when defining it.*

A custom message or handler name must

• Be a single word—that is, it cannot contain spaces, although it could contain an underscore (_)

• Start with a letter

• Contain only alphanumeric characters

• Not be the same as a Lingo element name

A good naming convention to follow is to begin a custom message or handler name with a capital letter so you won't confuse it with a local variable name. (Recall that Lesson 20 suggested starting a local variable name with a lowercase letter.) Using these conventions will enable you to easily distinguish between custom handlers and local variables when looking at a script. Another good coding convention is to capitalize each word in a handler name for easier reading: *MoveArmUp*, for example.

Now you're ready to create *MoveArmUp* and *MoveArmDown* handlers for your movie.

1] In the Cast window, select cast number 38, the first empty cast member. Choose Window › Script to open the Script window (Windows Ctrl+0, Macintosh Command+0).

You are now going to create a movie script. As you learned in Lesson 16, a movie script contains handlers that need to be available from anywhere in the movie. The two handlers that will handle your custom messages will be called from either the Up or Down button, and therefore you need to place them in a movie script.

2] Type the following for the movie script:

```
on MoveArmUp
   repeat while the stillDown        --While the mouse button is held down,
      sprite (1).locV = sprite (1).locV– 1   --move the arm up 1 pixel.
      updateStage                    --Update the stage to show changes.
   end repeat
end


on MoveArmDown
   repeat while the stillDown        --While the mouse button is held down,
      sprite (1).locV = sprite (1).locV + 1  --move the arm down 1 pixel.
      updateStage                    --Update the stage to show changes.
   end repeat
end
```

You should recognize the functionality in these handlers—you put the same functionality in the Up and Down buttons. Here, though, these handlers handle two new messages that you've defined: *MoveArmUp* and *MoveArmDown*. You will see how to call these handlers in the next task.

3] Close the Script window and save your work.

Don't play the movie yet. You've created the handlers that move the arm up and down, but you still need to replace the functionality in the button scripts with a message to call the new handlers instead.

CALLING A MOVIE HANDLER FROM A CAST MEMBER SCRIPT

Now you'll add the custom messages that will call the handlers you just added to the movie script.

1] In the Cast window, click cast member 28 (the Up button). Then click the Script button to open the Script window.

You're going to add a line that calls the *MoveArmUp* handler you just created in the movie script.

2] Replace the lines that move the arm up with the line shown here in bold:

```
on mouseDown
  repeat while the mouseDown        --While the mouse button is held down
    if rollOver(2) = TRUE then      --and the mouse is over the Up button (sprite 2),
      sprite(2).memberNum = 29      --display the highlighted button state.
      MoveArmUp()                   --Call the MoveArmUp handler
                                    --in the movie script.
    else                            --Otherwise,
      sprite(2).memberNum = 28      --display the normal button state.
    end if
    updateStage                     --Update the stage to show changes.
  end repeat                        --The mouse button is no longer down,
  sprite(2).memberNum = 28          --so return to the normal button state.
  updateStage                       --Update the stage to show changes.
end
```

Now when the Up button is clicked and the *mouseDown* handler runs, the handler calls the *MoveArmUp* handler in the movie script. After the *MoveArmUp* handler runs in the movie script, control returns to the *mouseDown* handler at the next line, which is *else*. However, because the *if* section of the handler has been executed, the *else* section of the handler is ignored. The next line to be executed, *then*, is the *updateStage* command. This redraws the stage to show the changes.

Now this cast member script contains only functionality for the button itself; it displays the highlighted or normal state of the button. The functionality that moves the arm up is in the movie script. If you ever need to modify the way the arm moves up, you can make the changes in the *MoveArmUp* handler in the movie script—that is, you don't need to search through the cast to find the button that contains that functionality; you need to look only in the movie script. (This advantage will become quite apparent when you begin building larger movies with numerous cast members.) Also, if other elements in your movie require the functionality contained in the *MoveArmUp* handler, you can use the handler again by calling it from another script. This practice of centralizing functionality in the movie script, where it is available to any handler, can save lots of maintenance time.

3] Close the Script window.

Now you'll add a call to the *MoveArmDown* handler to the Down button.

4] In the Cast window, click cast member 30. Then click the Script button to open the Script window.

You're going to add a similar line to the Down button.

5] Replace the lines that moved the arm down with the lines shown here in bold:

```
on mouseDown
   repeat while the mouseDown      --While the mouse button is held down
      if rollOver(3) = TRUE then   --and the mouse is over the Down button (sprite 3),
         sprite(3).memberNum = 31  --display the highlighted button state.
         MoveArmDown( )            --Call the MoveArmDown handler
                                   --in the movie script.
      else                         --Otherwise,
         sprite(3).memberNum = 30  --display the normal button state.
      end if
      updateStage                  --Update the stage to show changes.
   end repeat                      --The mouse button is no longer down,
   sprite(3).memberNum = 30        --so return to the normal button state.
   updateStage                     --Update the stage to show changes.
end
```

6] Close the Script window and save your work.

Now you have a movie script that contains the *MoveArmUp* and *MoveArmDown* handlers. You also have a cast script attached to the Up button that calls the *MoveArmUp* handler in the movie script, and you have a similar cast script attached to the Down button that calls the *MoveArmDown* handler in the movie script.

7] Rewind and play the movie. Click the Up and Down buttons. Stop the movie when you're done.

It still works!

There's no visible difference in the functionality of the buttons (well, almost none—more on this later). However, you have just made the handlers easier to read and more modular.

USING *IF-THEN* TO SET LIMITS

Did you notice that the arm moves off the stage when it reaches the top or bottom? You can fix this problem by adding limits to the arm movement. You'll do that now by using the Lingo construct *if-then*. You used this in a previous lesson.

note *If you did not complete the preceding tasks, open Start2.dir in the Lesson6 folder to continue with this lesson.*

1] Open the movie script and modify the script as shown here in bold:

```
on MoveArmUp
   repeat while the stillDown        --While the mouse button is held down,
      if sprite (1).locV > 0 then    --if the vertical location of the
                                     --sprite is greater than the top of the stage,
         sprite (1).locV = sprite (1).locV – 1
                                     --move the arm up 1 pixel.
            updateStage              --Update the stage to show changes.
      end if
   end repeat
end

on MoveArmDown
   repeat while the stillDown        --While the mouse button is held down,
      if sprite (1).locV < 270 then  --if the vertical location of the
                                     --sprite is less than 270,
         sprite (1).locV = sprite (1).locV + 1
                                     --move the arm down 1 pixel.
            updateStage              --Update the stage to show changes.
      end if
   end repeat
end
```

Where did the numbers 0 and 270 come from? First consider what happens when the robot arm reaches the top of the stage.

THE TOP OF THE STAGE IS AT VERTICAL (Y) COORDINATE 0. AS LONG AS THE TOP OF THE SPRITE IS AT Y COORDINATE 0 OR GREATER, YOU CAN CONTINUE TO MOVE THE SPRITE UP THE STAGE.

Any Y coordinate less than 0 (that is, a negative value) will be located above the stage and will not be visible; any Y coordinate that is 0 or greater will be on the stage and visible. Thus, if the robot arm's vertical position (which is measured from the top of the sprite) is greater than 0 and the *MoveArmUp* handler is running, you want the arm to continue moving. If the arm is at the top of the stage already, the vertical coordinate will be 0, so the arm shouldn't move any more. By adding the Lingo statement if *sprite (1).locV > 0*, you compare the value of the *locV* property of sprite 1 (which is the current location of the sprite) to the limit of 0. Note that you are not actually moving the sprite; you are only comparing the value. So long as the *locV* property of sprite 1 is greater than 0, the sprite moves up the stage. The sprite is actually moved by the next line, *sprite (1).locV = sprite (1).locV - 1*, just as it always has been. The *if-then* structure merely determines whether to execute that line.

Conversely, if the robot arm is at the bottom of the screen, you don't want to move it down any more.

THE BOTTOM OF THE STAGE IS AT VERTICAL (Y) COORDINATE 480. AS LONG AS THE SPRITE'S Y COORDINATE, PLUS ITS HEIGHT, IS LESS THAN 480, YOU CAN CONTINUE TO MOVE THE SPRITE DOWN THE STAGE.

In this case, you don't want to move the arm down if the value of the *locV* property of sprite 1 is already 270. The value 270 is found by subtracting the height of cast member 27 (the tallest of all the robot arm cast members), which is 209 (found by using the Sprite Properties dialog box), from the bottom vertical coordinate of the stage, which is 480. The result is 271. By limiting movement to 270, you prevent the bottom of the arm sprite from going off the bottom of the stage. Note that you are not actually moving the sprite; you are only comparing the value. So long as the *locV* property of sprite 1 is less than 270, the sprite moves down the stage.

2] Close the Script window, save your work, and play the movie. Click the buttons.
Now the arm movement is limited to the stage.

INCREASING THE ARM SPEED

Everything is working pretty well, but the speed of the robot arm's movement seems a little slow. You can't make it move faster by changing the movie tempo because that controls the rate at which the playback head moves from frame to frame. Because the playback head is paused, changing the tempo has no effect on the speed of the robot arm.

In this task, you will edit the *MoveArmUp* and *MoveArmDown* handlers to increase the arm's speed by subtracting and adding a greater number of pixels to its *locH* and *locV* values. (Currently, the arm moves 1 pixel at a time.)

1] Double-click cast member 38 to open the movie script.

2] In the *MoveArmUp* handler, replace 1 with 3, as shown here in bold:

```
on MoveArmUp
   repeat while the stillDown        --While the mouse button is held down,
      if sprite (1).locV › 3 then    --if the vertical location of the
                                     --sprite - 3 is greater than the top of the stage,
         sprite (1).locV = sprite (1).locV – 3
                                     --move the arm up 3 pixels.
         updateStage                 --Update the stage to show changes.
      end if
   end repeat
end
```

Subtracting 3 causes the arm to move 3 pixels at a time instead of 1.

3] In the *MoveArmDown* handler, replace 1 with 3, as shown here in bold:

```
on MoveArmDown
   repeat while the stillDown        --While the mouse button is held down,
      if sprite (1).locV ‹ 268 then  --if the vertical location of the
                                     --sprite + 3 is less than 271,
         sprite (1).locV = sprite (1).locV + 3
                                     --move the arm down 3 pixels.
         updateStage                 --Update the stage to show changes.
      end if
   end repeat
end
```

Adding 3 causes the arm to move 3 pixels at a time instead of 1 pixel.

4] Close the Script window, save your work, and play the movie. Click the Up and Down buttons.

The robot arm should move much faster now. Your changes do not alter the actual speed of the movie; they merely adjust the number of pixels the arm moves each time the mouse is clicked.

SWAPPING CAST MEMBERS

Now you're going to create a set of custom handlers that will direct the robot arm to extend or retract. Your handlers will be called *ExtendArm* and *RetractArm*. While the up and down movement was created by changing the location of one sprite on the stage (by subtracting and adding to the *locV* sprite property), the extend and retract movement will be created by displaying different cast members to show the different positions of the arm. In this case, you will subtract and add to the *memberNum* sprite property, which you've used before. (Recall that the syntax of this property is *sprite (whichChannel).memberNum* or *the memberNum of sprite whichChannel*.)

To make this technique work, you have to create a logical sequence for the cast members. If you open the Cast window and look at cast members 1 through 27, you'll see that the different states of the robot arm are organized in a logical order, from most extended (cast member 1) to least extended (cast member 27).

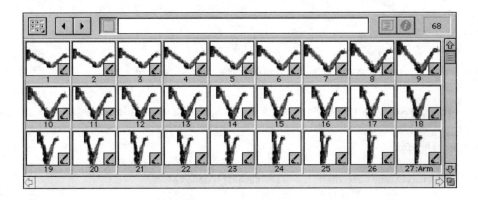

You'll see why this organization is important as you complete this task.

1] Choose Window › Message to open the Message window.

Just as you did earlier, you're going to test some commands in the Message window before adding them to your scripts.

2] Type the following and then press Enter (Windows) or Return (Macintosh):

put sprite (1).memberNum

This entry returns 27, the cast member number of the sprite currently in channel 1, frame 1.

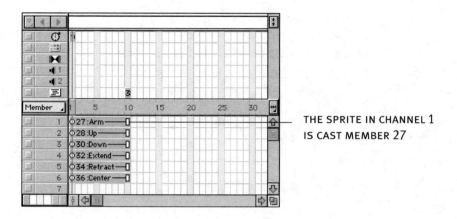

THE SPRITE IN CHANNEL 1
IS CAST MEMBER 27

Now you're going to replace this cast member with the one to its left in the cast (a slightly more extended position) by subtracting from the *memberNum* value of sprite 1.

3] Type the following and then press Enter (Windows) or Return (Macintosh):

```
put sprite (1).memberNum - 1
```

This entry returns 26, which is 27 (the number of the last arm cast member in the cast) minus 1. Cast member 26 is another version of the robot arm, only slightly extended.

Next you will make this cast member change and display the change on the stage.

4] Type the following and then press Enter (Windows) or Return (Macintosh):

```
sprite (1).memberNum = sprite (1).memberNum - 1
```

This changes the cast member number in sprite 1 from 27 to 26, but nothing happens on the stage. You must update the stage to see the effect of this command.

5] Type the following and then press Enter (Windows) or Return (Macintosh). Watch the stage carefully.

```
updateStage
```

Cast member 26 is now displayed on the stage. You will use this technique of adding and subtracting cast member numbers to display different versions of the arm.

27 IS THE MEMBERNUM VALUE OF SPRITE 1
AND IS INITIALLY DISPLAYED ON THE STAGE

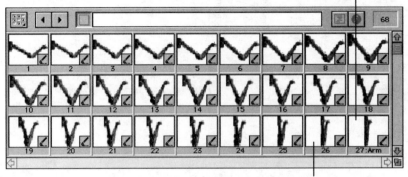

WHEN YOU SUBTRACT 1 FROM THE MEMBERNUM
OF SPRITE 1, YOU GET 26; THUS, CAST MEMBER
26 IS DISPLAYED ON THE STAGE

6] Close the Message window. Open the movie script. Below all the other handlers, type the lines shown here.

Instead of first adding lines to the cast scripts and then moving the functionality into handlers in the movie script (as you did with the up and down movements), you're going to save a step and write the handlers directly in the movie script.

```
on ExtendArm
    repeat while the stillDown          --While the mouse button is held down,
        if sprite (1).memberNum › 1 then    --if the cast member in channel 1 is greater than 1,
            sprite (1).memberNum = sprite (1).memberNum - 1
                                        --subtract 1 from the current cast member number
                                        --to extend the arm.
        end if
        updateStage                     --Update the stage to show changes.
    end repeat
end
```

```
on RetractArm
   repeat while the stillDown           --While the mouse button is held down,
      if sprite (1).memberNum ‹ 27 then --if the cast member in channel 1 is less than 27,
       sprite (1).memberNum = sprite (1).memberNum + 1
                                        --add 1 to the current cast member number
                                        --to retract the arm.
      end if
      updateStage                       --Update the stage to show changes.
   end repeat
end
```

These two handlers direct the arm to extend or retract.

The comments describe the action of each line. In the *ExtendArm* handler, you use an *if-then* structure to determine whether the current cast member is already the most extended version (cast member 1). If it's not, you subtract 1 from the *memberNum* sprite property each time the *stillDown* message is received. (Director continues sending the *stillDown* message so long as the user keeps the mouse button pressed down.) This has the effect of swapping the cast member for the one just to its left in the Cast window (a slightly more extended position). For example, if the sprite in channel 1 started out as cast member 21, at the end of this handler, it would be cast member 20, which is the arm in a more extended position than it was as cast member 21. The *updateStage* command makes the effect of the actions visible on the stage.

CAST MEMBER 1 IS THE ARM IN ITS MOST EXTENDED POSITION

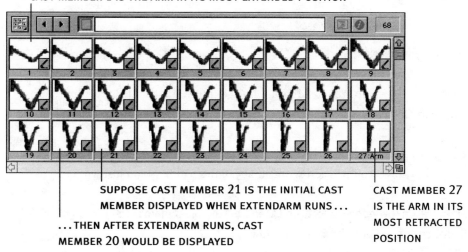

SUPPOSE CAST MEMBER 21 IS THE INITIAL CAST MEMBER DISPLAYED WHEN EXTENDARM RUNS...

...THEN AFTER EXTENDARM RUNS, CAST MEMBER 20 WOULD BE DISPLAYED

CAST MEMBER 27 IS THE ARM IN ITS MOST RETRACTED POSITION

The *RetractArm* handler works in a similar way. Instead of checking whether the arm is at its most extended state, though, the *if-then* structure determines whether the arm is at its most retracted state. If it's not, you add 1 to the *memberNum* sprite property to replace the cast member with the one directly to its right in the cast. For example, if the sprite in channel 1 started out as cast member 2, at the end of this handler, it would be cast member 3, which is the arm in a more retracted position than it was as cast member 2. Last, the *updateStage* command makes the effect of the actions visible on the stage.

SUPPOSE CAST MEMBER 2 IS THE INITIAL CAST
MEMBER DISPLAYED WHEN RETRACTARM RUNS...

...THEN AFTER RETRACTARM RUNS,
CAST MEMBER 3 WOULD BE DISPLAYED

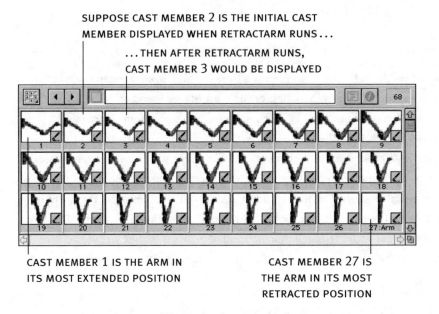

CAST MEMBER 1 IS THE ARM IN
ITS MOST EXTENDED POSITION

CAST MEMBER 27 IS
THE ARM IN ITS MOST
RETRACTED POSITION

7] Save your work.

You now have handlers available to extend and retract the arms, but you don't call them from anywhere. You need to add lines to the Extend and Retract button cast scripts so they call these handlers.

CALLING THE HANDLERS

In this next task, you will add scripts that call the handlers you just wrote.

1] In the Cast window, select the Extend button (cast member 32). Then click the Script button to open the Script window.

This script already contains the handlers that display the normal and highlighted states of the button.

2] Add the line shown here in bold and then close the window.

```
on mouseDown
  repeat while the mouseDown        --While the mouse button is held down
    if rollOver(4) = TRUE then      --and the mouse is over the EXTEND button (sprite 4),
      sprite(4).memberNum = 33      --display the highlighted button state.
      ExtendArm()                   --Call the ExtendArm handler in the movie script.
    else                            --Otherwise,
      sprite(4).memberNum = 32      --display the normal button state.
    end if
    updateStage                     --Update the stage to show changes.
  end repeat                        --The mouse button is no longer down,
  sprite(4).memberNum = 32          --so return to the normal button state..
  updateStage                       --Update the stage to show changes.
end
```

3] In the Cast window, select the Retract button (cast member 34). Then click the Script button to open the Script window.

This script already contains the handlers that display the normal and highlighted states of the button.

4] Add the line shown here in bold and then close the window.

```
on mouseDown
  repeat while the mouseDown        --While the mouse button is held down
    if rollOver(5) = TRUE then      --and the mouse is over the RETRACT button (sprite 5),
      sprite(5).memberNum = 35      --display the highlighted button state.
      RetractArm()                  --Call the RetractArm handler in the movie script.
    else                            --Otherwise,
      sprite(5).memberNum = 34      --display the normal button state.
    end if
    updateStage                     --Update the stage to show changes.
  end repeat                        --The mouse button is no longer down,
  sprite(5).memberNum = 34          --so return to the normal button state.
  updateStage                       --Update the stage to show changes.
end
```

5] Save your work.

Now you have a movie script that contains the *ExtendArm* and *RetractArm* handlers. You also have a cast script attached to the Extend button that calls the *ExtendArm* handler in the movie script, and you have a similar cast script attached to the Retract button that calls the *RetractArm* handler in the movie script.

6] Play the movie and click all the buttons. Stop the movie when you're done.

Good work! All the buttons should now be active and working correctly.

Swapping sprites like this is a great technique for displaying different versions of cast members. Remember that the cast has been arranged so that the fully extended arm is at one end of the sequence and the fully retracted arm is at the other end. Planning ahead and arranging the cast makes this type of animation using Lingo easier.

Think about how you might create this project in the score only. Consider a simplified example: Suppose the arm can move up only 4 pixels and can extend using only four cast members. Identify these as pixel1, pixel2, pixel3, pixel4, cast1, cast2, cast3, and cast4, respectively. Assume that the arm starts at location pixel1 using cast1. This means you would need a frame in the score to display this instance of cast1 at location pixel1. If you were to click the Up button, cast1 would move to pixel2. That means you would need to create a frame in the score showing cast1 at location pixel2. Suppose you then click the Extend button; you would need a frame in the score showing cast2 at location pixel2. Suppose you click the Extend button again; you would need a frame in the score showing cast3 at location pixel2.

As you can see, the potential combinations are staggering, even for this small example, and developing handlers to deal with each and every situation would be quite difficult. Using Lingo instead of the score is often a much simpler solution than trying to develop handlers for all instances of possible combinations in the score that your project might require.

ON YOUR OWN

As so often happens when you develop your Lingo scripts, a change you made to one feature has affected another. You may have noticed in the last few tasks in this lesson that the normal and highlighted states you implemented for the Up, Down, Extend, and Retract buttons early in this lesson no longer work exactly as you originally designed them. Rewind and play the movie. Click and hold down the mouse on the Up button and then, with the mouse button still down, move the mouse pointer off the button. The Up button remains in its highlighted state, and the robot arm continues to move up. When you first implemented the Up button, "rolling off" the button (as it is often called) with the mouse button depressed returned the button to its normal state, and rolling back on displayed the highlighted state.

There is nothing wrong with the way the Up button works currently. In any project, a design decision like this—whether the button action should continue when users roll off the button—is largely a matter of taste or a subject for usability testing (when you're lucky enough to have the time or resources to do it). Still, it's instructive to examine your scripts to see if you can discover what happened.

The best way to start is by examining the code that changes from one button state to another. The scripts for the four buttons are essentially the same; look at one example, the script for the Up button:

```
on mouseDown
    repeat while the mouseDown          --While the mouse button is held down
        if rollOver(2) = TRUE then      --and the mouse is over the Up button (sprite 2),
            sprite(2).memberNum = 29    --display the highlighted button state.
            MoveArmUp()                 --Call the MoveArmUp handler
                                        --in the movie script.
        else                            --Otherwise,
            sprite(2).memberNum = 28    --display the normal button state.
        end if
        updateStage                     --Update the stage to show changes.
    end repeat                          --The mouse button is no longer down,
    sprite(2).memberNum = 28            --so return to the normal button state..
    updateStage                         --Update the stage to show changes.
end
```

You originally designed the *if sprite (2).rollOver = TRUE* section to set the normal or highlighted state of the Up button, depending on the mouse pointer's location. For some reason, the highlighted state is being set by the *sprite(2).memberNum = 29* command, but after the pointer rolls off the button, the *sprite (2).memberNum = 28* command in the *else* clause is never being executed. The only instruction that intervenes between these two is the custom *MoveArmUp* message, and so your analysis should focus there:

```
on MoveArmUp
    repeat while the stillDown               --While the mouse button is held down,
        if sprite (1).locV > 3 then          --if the vertical location of the
                                             --sprite - 3 is greater than the top of the stage,
            sprite (1).locV = sprite (1).locV – 3   --move the arm up 3 pixels.
            updateStage                      --Update the stage to show changes.
        end if
    end repeat
end
```

Aha! When control passes to the *MoveArmUp* handler, the *repeat* loop keeps moving the robot arm up, and it won't stop until the *stillDown* function returns FALSE. Therefore, this handler can be interrupted only when the user releases the mouse button. That's the culprit: The *repeat* loop in this handler never takes into account whether the pointer is still over the Up button, and it won't give the *mouseDown* handler a chance to check either.

If you want to restore the Up button to its original functionality, how would you do so? Since the *MoveArmUp* handler is the one that disregards the position of the mouse pointer, it's natural to look for a way to modify it with a rollover check. Here's one way, with modifications shown in bold:

```
on MoveArmUp
    repeat while sprite (2).rollOver = TRUE    --While the pointer is over the Up button,
        if sprite (1).locV › 3 then            --if the vertical location of the
                                               --sprite - 3 is greater than the top of the stage,
            sprite (1).locV = sprite (1).locV – 3   --move the arm up 3 pixels.
            updateStage                        --Update the stage to show changes.
        end if
    end repeat
end
```

Now the *MoveArmUp* handler will relinquish control when the user rolls the mouse pointer off the Up button. Unfortunately, control is not relinquished when the user releases the mouse button while the pointer is still over the Up button. The arm will continue to move, and the Up button will remain in its highlighted state. You need to check for both the *stillDown* and *rollOver* states.

```
on MoveArmUp
    repeat while (the stillDown and sprite (2).rollOver = TRUE)
                                               --While the pointer is over the Up button,
        if sprite (1).locV › 3 then            --if the vertical location of the
                                               --sprite - 3 is greater than the top of the stage,
            sprite (1).locV = sprite (1).locV – 3   --move the arm up 3 pixels.
            updateStage                        --Update the stage to show changes.
        end if
    end repeat
end
```

The *and* logical operator requires both conditions to be *TRUE* for the *repeat* loop to continue looping. Otherwise, control passes back to the *mouseDown* handler, whose *repeat while the mouseDown* command continues looping so long as the mouse button remains down. At the moment when the user rolls the pointer back over the Up button, the *if sprite (2).rollOver = TRUE* command once again passes control to the *MoveArmUp* handler. Give it a try yourself.

This on-your-own task is just for exploration. Lesson 22 is a continuation of this lesson, and it assumes that you have not used the rollover check in the four handlers that move the robot arm.

WHAT YOU HAVE LEARNED

In this lesson you have:

• Used the *rollOver* function to control button states [page 492]

• Used the *memberNum* property to switch the cast member assigned to a sprite [page 493]

• Used the *locV* and *locH* properties to move sprites on the stage [page 497]

• Created custom messages and their associated handlers [page 502]

• Constrained the movement of sprites with an *if-then* statement [page 506]

• Altered animation speed by increasing or decreasing the number of pixels a sprite moves [page 508]

• Created animation by swapping cast members with the *memberNum* property [page 510]

scripts

optimizing

LESSON 22

Now that you have put together the robot arm project in Lesson 21, it's time to optimize the scripts you just created. In this lesson, you will use variables, make statements easier to read, and add final touches, including incorporating sound and preloading information into memory to speed up the playback of the project.

If you would like to view the final result of this lesson, open the Complete folder in the Lesson22 folder and play Robot2.dir.

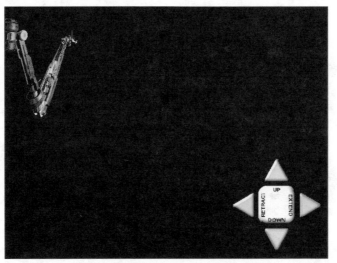

The Lingo code in the final version of this project is optimized to make the program more flexible, easier to read, and faster.

WHAT YOU WILL LEARN

In this lesson you will:

- Replace hard-coded values with variables

- Replace an *if-then* structure with a simpler *case* structure

- Make statements easier to read by self-documenting them

- Use Lingo to play sounds

- Use techniques to improve playback consistency

APPROXIMATE TIME

It should take about 3 hours to complete this lesson.

LESSON FILES

Media Files:

None

Starting Files:

Lesson22\Start\Start1.dir

Lesson22\Start\Start2.dir

Completed Project:

Lesson22\Complete\Robot2.dir

USING A LOCAL VARIABLE

You can use a local variable to represent a repeated value in the *ExtendArm* and *RetractArm* handlers. As you discovered earlier, using a variable also provides more flexibility. In Lesson 20, for instance, you learned that using a variable to refer to a sprite in a specific channel gave you the flexibility to change the sprite location without having to rewrite every script that referred to that sprite.

1] Open the Start1.dir movie in the Lesson22 folder and save it as *Robot2.dir* in your Projects folder.

This is the finished version of the Robot.dir project from Lesson 21. If you completed Lesson 21, you can use your own Robot.dir movie instead. Just be sure to save it as Robot2.dir so that you still have your copy of Robot.dir.

2] Double-click cast member 38 to open the movie script and look at the *ExtendArm* and *RetractArm* handlers.

Notice that *sprite (1).memberNum* is repeated throughout each handler. Each time you need to refer to this line, you must type it in its entirety—a process that is cumbersome and can easily lead to typing mistakes. You can make your life easier by using a local variable that represents the value *sprite (1).memberNum*. You will now change these handlers by creating a local variable, *currCast*, to represent *sprite (1).memberNum* throughout the handlers.

3] Make the changes shown here in bold:

```
on ExtendArm
   repeat while the stillDown      --While the mouse button is held down,
      currCast = sprite (1).memberNum
                                    --Initialize currCast to the cast
                                    --member number of the sprite in channel 1.
      if currCast › 1 then         --If the cast member in channel 1 is greater than 1,
         currCast = currCast - 1   --subtract 1 from the variable to extend the arm
         sprite (1).memberNum = currCast
                                    --and set the cast member number of
                                    --the sprite in channel 1 to the new value of currCast.
      end if
      updateStage                  --Update the stage to show changes.
   end repeat
end
```

```
on RetractArm
    repeat while the stillDown         --While the mouse button is held down,
        currCast = sprite (1).memberNum
                                       --initialize currCast to the cast
                                       --member number of the sprite in channel 1.
        if currCast < 27 then          --If the cast member in channel 1 is less than 27,
            currCast = currCast + 1     --add 1 to the variable
            sprite (1).memberNum = currCast
                                       --and set the cast member number of the
                                       --sprite in channel 1 to the new value
                                       --of currCast to retract the arm.
        end if
        updateStage                    --Update the stage to show changes.
    end repeat
end
```

These two handlers work exactly as they did before. In these lines you first create and initialize a new variable, *currCast*, giving it the value of *sprite (1).memberNum*. Then you replace most of the occurrences of *sprite (1).memberNum* with *currCast*. Notice that you cannot replace the occurrence of *sprite (1).memberNum* used to set the new value of *currCast*.

Because *currCast* is a local variable, you need to reinitialize it in every handler that uses it.

4] Close the Script window, save your work, and play the movie.

Everything works just as it did before, but the new script is clearer and easier to maintain than the older version.

Next you will use a local variable to represent a repeated value in the *MoveArmUp* and *MoveArmDown* handlers.

5] Double-click cast member 38 to open the movie script and look at the *MoveArmUp* and *MoveArmDown* handlers.

```
on MoveArmUp
    repeat while the stillDown         --While the mouse button is held down,
        if sprite (1).locV > 3 then    --if the vertical location of the
                                       --sprite - 3 is greater than the top of the stage,
            sprite (1).locV = sprite (1).locV – 3
                                       --move the arm up 3 pixels.
            updateStage                --Update the stage to show changes.
        end if
    end repeat
end
```

```
on MoveArmDown
    repeat while the stillDown                --While the mouse button is held down,
        if sprite (1).locV < 268 then        --if the vertical location of the
                                             --sprite + 3 is less than 271,
            sprite (1).locV = sprite (1).locV + 3    --move the arm down 3 pixels.
            updateStage                      --Update the stage to show changes.
        end if
    end repeat
end
```

Notice that *sprite (1).locV* is repeated throughout each handler. Each time you need to refer to it, you must type the entire line. Instead, you can use a local variable that represents the value of *sprite (1).locV*. You will create a local variable, *currVert*, to represent *sprite (1).locV* throughout the handlers.

6] Make the changes shown here in bold and then close the window:

```
on MoveArmUp
    repeat while the stillDown                --While the mouse button is held down,
        currVert = sprite (1).locV           --initialize currVert to the vertical
                                             --location of sprite 1.

        if currVert > 3 then                 --If currVert - 3 is greater than the stage top,
            sprite (1).locV = currVert – 3   --move the arm up 3 pixels.
            updateStage                      --Update the stage to show changes.
        end if
    end repeat
end


on MoveArmDown
    repeat while the stillDown                --While the mouse button is held down,
        currVert = sprite (1).locV           --initialize currVert to the vertical
                                             --location of sprite 1.

        if currVert < 268 then               --If currVert + 3 is less than 271,
            sprite (1).locV = currVert + 3   --move the arm down 3 pixels.
            updateStage                      --Update the stage to show changes.
        end if
    end repeat
end
```

You have created and initialized the *currVert* variable by setting it to the value of *sprite (1).locV* and then replaced most of the occurrences of *sprite (1).locV* with the new variable. Notice that you cannot replace the occurrence of *sprite (1).locV* used to set the value of *currVert+3*.

7] Close the Script window, save your work, and play the movie.

Everything works just as it did before. You have simply cleaned up the code by using a local variable.

USING A *CASE* STATEMENT

You have now created four handlers that control the movement of the robot arm on the stage through Lingo, and you have streamlined the code in each of them by using variables. In this task you'll see how you can streamline the code even more by using a **conditional** structure, which enables you to create a script that chooses among two or more actions according to the condition that exists at that time.

You have already used simple conditional structures in the form of *if-then-else* statements. The conditional structure you will use in this task, the *case* statement, uses the same basic idea as *if-then-else* statements, but it streamlines the code when you are testing for multiple conditions.

Suppose you want to create a script that takes different actions depending on which sprite a user clicks. For example, you might say, "If the user clicks the sprite in channel 1, then show picture 1; otherwise, show picture 2." In Lingo, this statement might look like this:

```
on mouseDown
  if the clickOn = 1 then
    go to picture1
  else
    go to picture2
  end if
end
```

The *clickOn* function returns the number of the sprite that was just clicked.

If there are several conditions, you may have to use several *if* statements, like this:

```
on mouseDown
  if the clickOn = 1 then
    go to picture1
  end if
  if the clickOn = 2 then
    go to picture2
  end if
  if the clickOn = 3 then
    go to picture3
  end if
end
```

The *case* statement is a shorthand alternative to repeating *if-then* statements. Instead of repeating *then* and *end if*, the *case* statement lists the possible responses to the condition. Using a *case* statement, the preceding example looks like this:

```
on mouseDown
  case (the clickOn) of
    1: go to picture1
    2: go to picture2
    3: go to picture3
  end case
end
```

In this example, numbers are used (1, 2, 3), but you could use other expressions, such as variables or strings, instead.

As part of this task, you will also need to use an **argument**. An argument enables a single handler to use different information or values in much the same way as an algebraic formula uses a letter to represent an unknown value, where numbers can be plugged in for different results.

For example, a handler for adding two numbers together might look like this:

```
on AddNumbers a, b
  c = a + b
  return c
end
```

The handler name is *AddNumbers*, and the two arguments are *a* and *b*. To use this handler, you would type *AddNumbers (3, 4)*, for example. The values being passed as the arguments—in this case, 3 and 4—are called **parameters**. Director will substitute 3 in place of argument *a* and 4 in place of argument *b* and set *c* t to 7. The line *return c* will then return the value 7 to the location where the *AddNumbers* handler is being called.

Now you will see how to apply this to your movie script.

tip   *If you did not complete the preceding tasks, you can open and use Start2.dir in the Lesson22 folder to continue with this lesson.*

1] Double-click cast member 38 to open the movie script. Replace the four handlers that move the arm with the single handler shown here. You can cut and paste as necessary, but be very careful as you replace text.

```
on MoveArm direction
   repeat while the stillDown              --While the mouse button is held down,
      case (direction) of                  --if the direction is
         1:                                --1: Move the arm up.
            currVert = sprite (1).locV – 3 --Set currVert to the vertical
                                           --location of (sprite 1) - 3.

            if currVert › 0 then           --If the sprite is not at the top of the
               sprite (1).locV = currVert  --stage, then move the arm up 3 pixels.
            end if
         2:                                --2: Move the arm down.
            currVert = sprite (1).locV + 3 --Set currVert to the vertical
                                           --location of (sprite 1) + .3.

            if currVert ‹ 271 then         --If the sprite is not at the bottom of the
               sprite (1).locV = currVert  --stage, then move the arm down 3 pixels.
            end if
         3:                                --3: Extend the arm.
            currCast = sprite (1).memberNum --Initialize currCast to the cast
                                            --member number of sprite 1.

            if currCast › 1 then            --If the arm is not already fully extended,
               currCast = currCast – 1      --subtract 1 from the variable
               sprite (1).memberNum = currCast --and set the cast member number
                                            --of sprite 1 to the new value of currCast.

            end if
         4:                                --4: Retract the arm.
            currCast = sprite (1).memberNum --Initialize currCast to the cast
                                            --member number of sprite 1.

            if currCast ‹ 27 then           --If the arm is not already fully retracted,
               currCast = currCast + 1      --add 1 to the variable
               sprite (1).memberNum = currCast --and set the cast member number
                                            --of sprite 1 to the new value of currCast.

            end if
      end case
      updateStage
   end repeat
end
```

What's going on in this script? You have simply combined all the code that handled the arm movement into a single handler with a *case* statement. This new handler handles a message called *MoveArm*, which has one argument, *direction*. The case that is executed depends on the value of *direction*, which indicates which button (Up, Down, Extend, or Retract) was clicked. *MoveArm* is a message that you have defined yourself (it is not built in to Director). You send the *MoveArm* message by calling the *MoveArm* handler from another script, which you will set up in the next task.

The other change in this handler is that the *updateStage* command is moved outside the *case* statement (below *end case*). This was done because the screen needs to be redrawn only after the arm is moved, so this command doesn't need to be repeated in each section.

2] Save your work.
Don't play the movie yet. You have changed the movie script, but you haven't changed the cast scripts for the buttons. You need to change the cast scripts so they use the new structure in the movie script.

USING PARAMETERS

To work with the *case* structure you just built, you need to change the button scripts to call the *MoveArm* handler and send along information about what button was clicked. The call to the *MoveArm* handler will replace the code in each button script previously used to move the arm.

1] In the Cast window, select cast member 28. Then click the Script button. Make the changes shown here in bold:

```
on mouseDown
  repeat while the mouseDown         --While the mouse button is held down
    if rollOver(2) = TRUE then       --and the mouse is over the Up button (sprite 2),
      sprite(2).memberNum = 29       --display the highlighted button state.
      MoveArm(1)                     --Call the MoveArm handler in the movie script
                                     --and send parameter 1.

    else                             --Otherwise,
      sprite(2).memberNum = 28       --display the normal button state.
    end if
    updateStage                      --Update the stage to show changes.
  end repeat                         --The mouse button is no longer down,
  sprite(2).memberNum = 28           --so return to the normal button state.
  updateStage                        --Update the stage to show changes.
end
```

Now when this button is clicked, this script calls the *MoveArm* handler and sends a parameter of 1 to tell the *MoveArm* handler which case it should execute.

2] In the Cast window, select cast member 30. Then click the Script button. Make the changes shown here in bold:

```
on mouseDown
  repeat while the mouseDown        --While the mouse button is held down
    if rollOver(3) = TRUE then      --and the mouse is over the Down button (sprite 3),
      sprite(3).memberNum = 31      --display the highlighted button state.
      MoveArm(2)                    --Call the MoveArm handler in the movie script
                                    --and send parameter 2.
    else                            --Otherwise,
      sprite(3).memberNum = 30      --display the normal button state.
    end if
    updateStage                     --Update the stage to show changes.
  end repeat                        --The mouse button is no longer down,
  sprite(3).memberNum = 30          --so return to the normal button state.
  updateStage                       --Update the stage to show changes.
end
```

When this button is clicked, it calls the *MoveArm* handler and sends a parameter of 2 to tell the *MoveArm* handler to execute case 2.

3] In the Cast window, select cast member 32. Then click the Script button. Make the changes shown here in bold:

```
on mouseDown
  repeat while the mouseDown        --While the mouse button is held down
    if rollOver(4) = TRUE then      --and the mouse is over the Extend button (sprite 4),
      sprite(4).memberNum = 33      --display the highlighted button state.
      MoveArm(3)                    --Call the MoveArm handler in the movie script
                                    --and send parameter 3.
    else                            --Otherwise,
      sprite(4).memberNum = 32      --display the normal button state.
    end if
    updateStage                     --Update the stage to show changes.
  end repeat                        --The mouse button is no longer down,
  sprite(4).memberNum = 32          --so return to the normal button state.
  updateStage                       --Update the stage to show changes.
end
```

4] In the Cast window, select cast member 34. Then click the Script button. Make the changes shown here in bold:

```
on mouseDown
  repeat while the mouseDown          --While the mouse button is held down
    if rollOver(5) = TRUE then        --and the mouse is over the Retract button (sprite 5),
      sprite(5).memberNum = 35        --display the highlighted button state.
      MoveArm(4)                      --Call the MoveArm handler in the movie script
                                      --and send parameter 4.

    else                              --Otherwise,
      sprite(5).memberNum = 34        --display the normal button state.
    end if

    updateStage                       --Update the stage to show changes.
  end repeat                          --The mouse button is no longer down,
  sprite(5).memberNum = 34            --so return to the normal button state.
  updateStage                         --Update the stage to show changes.
end
```

5] Close the Script window, save your work, and play the movie.

It works! All the buttons should still be active and working correctly.

USING A GLOBAL VARIABLE

In the previous lesson you experimented with some different speeds for the robot arm's up and down movements. First you moved the arm 1 pixel for each *stillDown* event, and then you sped it up by moving it 3 pixels for each *stillDown* event. When you made those changes, you had to edit each handler separately. In that case, the process wasn't so difficult because only two handlers were affected, but imagine a case in which you have several objects whose speed you want to change, or suppose you want to experiment with different speeds before settling on a final one. As you have probably guessed by now, you can streamline your work by creating a variable for this value. That's what you will do in this task.

1] Double-click cast member 38 to open the movie script. At the top, add the lines shown here in bold:

```
global gArmSpeed        --This global variable will specify the number of
                        --pixels the arm should move.
on startMovie
  set gArmSpeed = 3     --This will move the arm 3 pixels at a time.
end
```

The *startMovie* message is a built-in message that Director sends just before the playback head enters the first frame of a movie. Therefore, a *startMovie* handler is a good place to include any commands that do any necessary preparation before any action takes place in the score. For example, a *startMovie* handler might include Lingo commands that find out whether the movie is running on a Windows or Macintosh system and then, depending on the results, branch to a different frame of the movie. A *startMovie* handler is also a good place to initialize global variables, and that is what you have done in this case. In this script, you initialized the global variable *gArmSpeed* and set its initial value to 3. Recall from Lesson 20 that you must declare a global variable at the top of the script, and that it is customary to start a global variable name with the letter *g*. This convention is helpful because it enables you to determine whether a variable is global or local simply by looking at it.

2] In the *MoveArm* handler later in the movie script, replace 3 with *gArmSpeed* and update the comments as shown here in bold:

```
on MoveArm direction
   repeat while the stillDown              --While the mouse button is held down,
      case (direction) of                  --if the direction is
         1:                                --1: Move the arm up.
            currVert = sprite (1).locV – gArmSpeed
                                           --Set currVert to the vertical
                                           --location of (sprite 1)  - gArmSpeed.
            if currVert › 0 then           --If the sprite is not at the top of the
               sprite (1).locV = currVert  --stage, then move the arm up gArmSpeed pixels.
            end if
         2:                                --2: Move the arm down.
            currVert = sprite (1).locV + gArmSpeed
                                           --Set currVert to the vertical
                                           --location of (sprite 1) + gArmSpeed.
            if currVert ‹ 271 then         --If the sprite is not at the bottom of the
               sprite (1).locV = currVert  --stage, then move the arm down gArmSpeed pixels.
            end if
         3:                                --3: Extend the arm.
            currCast = sprite (1).memberNum
                                           --Initialize currCast to the cast
                                           --member number of sprite 1.
            if currCast › 1 then           --If the arm is not already fully extended,
               currCast = currCast – 1     --subtract 1 from the variable
               sprite (1).memberNum = currCast
                                           --and set the cast member number
                                           --of sprite 1 to the new value of currCast.
            end if
```

```
        4:                            --4: Retract the arm.
           currCast = sprite (1).memberNum
                                       --Initialize currCast to the cast
                                       --member number of sprite 1.
           if currCast ‹ 27 then       --If the arm is not already fully retracted,
              currCast = currCast + 1   --add 1 to the variable
              sprite (1).memberNum = currCast
                                       --and set the cast member number
                                       --of sprite 1 to the new value of currCast.
           end if
        end case
        updateStage
     end repeat
   end
```

3] Close the Script window, save your work, and play the movie. Click the Up and Down buttons.

Everything works just as it did before. What's the advantage? You'll see in the next few steps when you change the speed of the arm again, this time to 10.

4] Double-click cast member 38 to open the movie script. Make the changes shown here in bold:

```
   global gArmSpeed        --This global variable will specify the number of
                           --pixels the arm should move.


   on startMovie
      gArmSpeed = 10       --This will move the arm 10 pixels at a time.
   end
```

5] Close the Script window, save your work, and play the movie. Click the Up and Down buttons.

Now the arm moves much faster, and you had to make a change in only one location.

6] Double-click cast member 38 to open the movie script. Change the speed back to 3 as shown here in bold:

```
   global gArmSpeed        --This global variable will specify the number of
                           --pixels the arm should move.

   on startMovie
      gArmSpeed = 3        --This will move the arm 3 pixels at a time.
   end
```

Now changing the speed is fast and easy.

You may be wondering why you created some variables locally and others globally. Look carefully at the movie script. You use three variables: *currCast*, *currVert*, and *gArmSpeed*.

You set the value of *currCast* to *sprite (1).memberNum* twice in the *case* statement, and you could have made it a global variable and initialized it in the *startMovie* handler.

For *currVert*, however, you set the variable to different values in the *case* statement, by either adding or subtracting the value of *gArmSpeed*. In this situation, it's better to keep the variable local because you need to assign it different values depending on the case.

Last, you created *gArmSpeed*. You could have made this a local variable and defined and initialized it in two different places in the *case* statement, and everything would still work. Here, however, the value of *gArmSpeed* will be constant throughout the movie; it will not change, regardless of the value of any other variable. Using a global variable to represent a constant value is a more sophisticated programming technique than creating a local variable whose value will never change as the movie runs.

USING SYMBOLS IN A *CASE* STATEMENT

A *case* structure is an efficient means of handling situations in which multiple actions can occur, depending on changing conditions, but when reading the script you just wrote, it's hard to remember just what the differences are among cases 1, 2, 3, and 4. Lingo offers an easy way to make your code more readable. Instead of case numbers, you can use **symbols**, a special kind of Lingo data type, analogous to a string, number, or other value.

All symbol names must begin with a pound sign (#) for Lingo to recognize them as symbols. Symbols can be used as variable names and can be compared to other data (for example, using =). Symbols can also be passed as parameters to handlers, and handlers can return them as values.

In this task, you will replace the numbers 1, 2, 3, and 4 with symbols. Why? Essentially, symbols have the speed and memory advantages of integers but give you the descriptive power of strings.

1] Double-click cast member 38 to open the movie script and replace the numbers with symbols. Use *#Up* for 1, *#Down* for 2, *#Extend* for 3, and *#Retract* for 4. Make the changes shown here in bold:

```
on MoveArm direction
   repeat while the stillDown          --While the mouse button is held down,
      case (direction) of              --if the direction is
         #Up:                          --#Up: Move the arm up.
            currVert = sprite (1).locV – gArmSpeed
                                       --Set currVert to the vertical
                                       --location of (sprite 1) - gArmSpeed.
            if currVert › 0 then       --If the sprite is not at the top of the
               sprite (1).locV = currVert --stage, then move the arm up gArmSpeed pixels.
            end if
         #Down:                        --#Down: Move the arm down.
            currVert = sprite (1).locV + gArmSpeed
                                       --Set currVert to the vertical
                                       --location of (sprite 1) + gArmSpeed.
            if currVert ‹ 271 then      --If the sprite is not at the bottom of the
               sprite (1).locV = currVert --stage, then move the arm down gArmSpeed pixels.
            end if
         #Extend:                      --#Extend: Extend the arm.
            currCast = sprite (1).memberNum
                                       --Initialize currCast to the cast
                                       --member number of sprite 1.
            if currCast › 1 then       --If the arm is not already fully extended,
               currCast = currCast – 1 --subtract 1 from the variable
               sprite (1).memberNum = currCast
                                       --and set the cast member number
                                       --of sprite 1 to the new value of currCast.
            end if
         #Retract:                     --#Retract: Retract the arm.
            currCast = sprite (1).memberNum
                                       --Initialize currCast to the cast
                                       --member number of sprite 1.
            if currCast ‹ 27 then       --If the arm is not already fully retracted,
               currCast = currCast + 1 --add 1 to the variable
               sprite (1).memberNum = currCast
                                       --and set the cast member number
                                       --of sprite 1 to the new value of currCast.
            end if
      end case
      updateStage
   end repeat
end
```

2] Save your work.

Don't play the movie yet. You have changed the movie script, but you haven't changed the cast scripts for the buttons. You need to change the cast scripts so they use the new structure in the movie script.

USING SYMBOLS AS PARAMETERS

Now you must change the cast scripts for all the buttons to send the new parameters.

1] In the Cast window, select the Up button (cast member 28) and then click the Script button. Make the changes shown here in bold:

```
on mouseDown
  repeat while the mouseDown          --While the mouse button is held down
    if rollOver(2) = TRUE then        --and the mouse is over the Up button (sprite 2),
      sprite(2).memberNum = 29        --display the highlighted button state.
      MoveArm(#Up)                    --Call the MoveArm handler in the movie script
                                      --and send the parameter #Up.
    else                              --Otherwise,
      sprite(2).memberNum = 28        --display the normal button state.
    end if
    updateStage                       --Update the stage to show changes.
  end repeat                          --The mouse button is no longer down,
  sprite(2).memberNum = 28            --so return to the normal button state.
  updateStage                         --Update the stage to show changes.
end
```

2] In the Cast window, select the Down button (cast member 30) and then click the Script button. Make the changes shown here in bold:

```
on mouseDown
  repeat while the mouseDown          --While the mouse button is held down
    if rollOver(3) = TRUE then        --and the mouse is over the Down button (sprite 3),
      sprite(3).memberNum = 31        --display the highlighted button state.
      MoveArm(#Down)                  --Call the MoveArm handler in the movie script
                                      --and send the parameter #Down.
    else                              --Otherwise,
      sprite(3).memberNum = 30        --display the normal button state.
    end if
    updateStage                       --Update the stage to show changes.
  end repeat                          --The mouse button is no longer down,
  sprite(3).memberNum = 30            --so return to the normal button state.
  updateStage                         --Update the stage to show changes.
end
```

3] In the Cast window, select the Extend button (cast member 32) and then click the Script button. Make the changes shown here in bold:

```
on mouseDown
   repeat while the mouseDown        --While the mouse button is held down
      if rollOver(4) = TRUE then     --and the mouse is over the Extend button (sprite 4),
         sprite(4).memberNum = 33    --display the highlighted button state.
         MoveArm(#Extend)            --Call the MoveArm handler in the movie script
                                     --and send the parameter #Extend.
      else                           --Otherwise,
         sprite(4).memberNum = 32    --display the normal button state.
      end if
      updateStage                    --Update the stage to show changes.
   end repeat                        --The mouse button is no longer down,
   sprite(4).memberNum = 32          --so return to the normal button state.
   updateStage                       --Update the stage to show changes.
end
```

4] In the Cast window, select the Retract button (cast member 34) and then click the Script button. Make the changes shown here in bold:

```
on mouseDown
   repeat while the mouseDown        --While the mouse button is held down
      if rollOver(5) = TRUE then     --and the mouse is over the Retract button (sprite 5),
         sprite(5).memberNum = 35    --display the highlighted button state.
         MoveArm(#Retract)           --Call the MoveArm handler in the movie script
                                     --and send the parameter #Retract.
      else                           --Otherwise,
         sprite(5).memberNum = 34    --display the normal button state.
      end if
      updateStage                    --Update the stage to show changes.
   end repeat                        --The mouse button is no longer down,
   sprite(5).memberNum = 34          --so return to the normal button state.
   updateStage                       --Update the stage to show changes.
end
```

5] Close the Script window, save your work, and play the movie. Click all the buttons.
Nothing has changed, and everything still works as before. However, now if you ever need to return to this movie script, you will be able to understand it a lot more easily than before.

USING LINGO TO PLAY SOUNDS

Next you'll add sound that will play while the arm moves. This sound has already been imported into the cast (as cast member 40, armSound). In this task you will play the sound using Lingo, without bringing it into the sound channel in the score. This approach is known as **puppeting** a sound. In a sense, the sound becomes a puppet, and Lingo is pulling the strings.

Playing sound through Lingo gives you more control over when the sound plays because you can turn a sound off and on regardless of what is set in the score's sound channels. This approach might be useful in a game, for example, where you have a sound in sound channel 1 that loops while the opening graphic is displayed. You can use puppeting to play a different sound in the sound channel when the user clicks a button to start the game.

To complete this task, you need to use the *puppetSound* command. The syntax of this command is *puppetSound whichChannel, "whichCastMember"*. Puppeted sounds play in sound channel 1 by default, so if the first sound channel already contains something, a puppeted sound will interrupt it.

You're also going to use *soundBusy*, which you used in Lesson 19 to turn sound off and on when the mouse is over a button. Recall that this command determines whether a sound is currently playing in a particular channel. You're going to check sound channel 1 because if it's busy, you don't want the puppeted sound to interrupt it.

1] Double-click cast member 38 to open the movie script.

2] In the *MoveArm* handler, add the lines shown here in bold:

```
on MoveArm direction
  repeat while the stillDown          --While the mouse button is held down,
    if not soundBusy(1) then puppetSound 1, "armSound"
                                      --if sound channel 1
                                      --isn't playing anything, play the file armSound.
    case (direction) of               --If the direction is
      #Up:                            --#Up: Move the arm up.
        currVert = sprite (1).locV – gArmSpeed
                                      --Set currVert to the vertical
                                      --location of (sprite 1) – gArmSpeed.
        if currVert › 0 then          --If the sprite is not at the top of the
          sprite (1).locV = currVert  --stage, then move the arm up gArmSpeed pixels.
        end if
```

```
        #Down:                          --#Down: Move the arm down.
          currVert = sprite (1).locV + gArmSpeed
                                        --Set currVert to the vertical
                                        --location of (sprite 1) + gArmSpeed.
          if currVert ‹ 271 then        --If the sprite is not at the bottom of the
            sprite (1).locV = currVert  --stage, then move the arm down gArmSpeed pixels.
          end if
        #Extend:                        --#Extend: Extend the arm.
          currCast = sprite (1).memberNum
                                        --Initialize currCast to the cast
                                        --member number of sprite 1.
          if currCast › 1 then          --If the arm is not already fully extended,
            currCast = currCast − 1      --subtract 1 from the variable
            sprite (1).memberNum = currCast
                                        --and set the cast member number
                                        --of sprite 1 to the new value of currCast.
          end if
        #Retract:                       --#Retract: Retract the arm.
          currCast = sprite (1).memberNum
                                        --Initialize currCast to the cast
                                        --member number of sprite 1.
          if currCast ‹ 27 then         --If the arm is not already fully retracted,
            currCast = currCast + 1      --add 1 to the variable
            sprite (1).memberNum = currCast
                                        --and set the cast member number
                                        --of sprite 1 to the new value of currCast.
          end if
      end case
      updateStage
    end repeat
  end
```

Notice that, when you place both the *if* and *then* statements on a single line, you do not need to include the *end if* statement.

3] Close the Script window and play the movie. Click the buttons.

As you click the buttons, the sound plays. However, it does not stop when you release the mouse button. To make the sound stop, you must add another *puppetSound* command to the movie script: *puppetSound 1, 0.* Using 0 (zero) for *whichCastMember* tells Director to stop playing the puppeted sound and return control of the sound channel to the score.

4] Double-click cast member 38 to open the movie script. Type the text shown here in bold above the last line of the *MoveArm* handler:

```
on MoveArm direction
  repeat while the stillDown          --While the mouse button is held down,
    if not soundBusy(1) then puppetSound 1, "armSound"
                                      --if sound channel 1
                                      --isn't playing anything, play the file armSound.
    case (direction) of               --If the direction is
      #Up:                            --#Up: Move the arm up.
        currVert = sprite (1).locV – gArmSpeed
                                      --Set currVert to the vertical
                                      --location of (sprite 1) - gArmSpeed.
        if currVert › 0 then          --If the sprite is not at the top of the
          sprite (1).locV = currVert  --stage, then move the arm up gArmSpeed pixels.
        end if
      #Down:                          --#Down: Move the arm down.
        currVert = sprite (1).locV + gArmSpeed
                                      --Set currVert to the vertical
                                      --location of (sprite 1) + gArmSpeed.
        if currVert ‹ 271 then        --If the sprite is not at the bottom of the
          sprite (1).locV = currVert  --stage, then move the arm down gArmSpeed pixels.
        end if
      #Extend:                        --#Extend: Extend the arm.
        currCast = sprite (1).memberNum
                                      --Initialize currCast to the cast
                                      --member number of sprite 1.
        if currCast › 1 then          --If the arm is not already fully extended,
          currCast = currCast – 1     --subtract 1 from the variable
          sprite (1).memberNum = currCast
                                      --and set the cast member number
                                      --of sprite 1 to the new value of currCast.
        end if
      #Retract:                       --#Retract: Retract the arm.
        currCast = sprite (1).memberNum
                                      --Initialize currCast to the cast
                                      --member number of sprite 1.
        if currCast ‹ 27 then         --If the arm is not already fully retracted,
          currCast = currCast + 1     --add 1 to the variable
          sprite (1).memberNum = currCast
                                      --and set the cast member number
                                      --of sprite 1 to the new value of currCast.
        end if
    end case
    updateStage
  end repeat
  if soundBusy(1) then puppetSound 1, 0
end
```

If sound channel 1 is playing sound, then this command will ensure that the sound stops when the mouse button is released and the *repeat* loop stops executing.

5] Close the Script window, save your work, and play the movie. Click all the buttons.
This time the sound plays only while the arm is moving. When you release the mouse button, the sound stops.

> **tip** *If you are using a combination of puppeted sounds and sounds in the score, be sure to issue the* puppetSound 0 *command when you're finished puppeting a sound and want to return control to the score. This command releases the sound channel from the control of Lingo and lets the score take over again. Once the sound channel has been puppeted, the score sounds won't be heard until a* puppetSound 0 *command is issued to turn the puppet off.*

USING THE MEMORY INSPECTOR AND PRELOADING CAST MEMBERS

So far, you have focused on ways to optimize your scripts to make them easier to read, write, and edit. But optimization has another important meaning for programmers: You can optimize performance by making the animations and user responses execute as quickly as possible.

If you pay close attention to the arm movement when you first run the movie and extend the robot arm, you will notice that the arm moves slowest the first time you play the movie. That's because Director has to load each cast member into memory the first time it uses it; after the movie has played once, the cast members are already in memory and are quickly available. In this task, you will optimize movie performance by preloading cast members into memory.

1] Choose Window › Inspectors › Memory. Then click Purge to clear the current memory contents.
The Memory inspector is a graphical representation of some of your system's memory. Clicking Purge clears the current memory contents. In this case, you are unloading the cast members from memory.

2] Move the Memory Inspector window to the side, still keeping it visible, and play the movie.
When you click the Extend button, you will see the Cast & Score and the Total Used values in the Memory Inspector increase, indicating that memory is being used.

3] Click the Purge button to clear the memory again. Then click the Extend and Retract buttons.

When you play the movie, you'll see the arm extend slowly the first time and then more quickly on subsequent plays. Note the differences in performance.

Notice how the listing in the Memory Inspector that represents the Cast & Score changes after you click Purge.

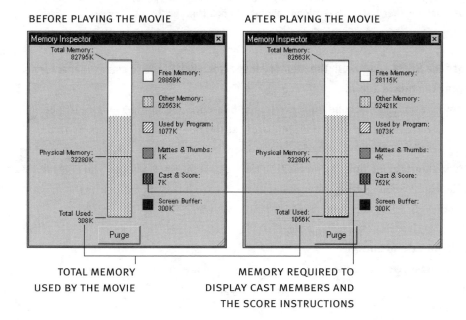

BEFORE PLAYING THE MOVIE   AFTER PLAYING THE MOVIE

TOTAL MEMORY   MEMORY REQUIRED TO
USED BY THE MOVIE   DISPLAY CAST MEMBERS AND
                      THE SCORE INSTRUCTIONS

note   *The numbers you see in the Memory Inspector will vary depending on the type of computer you have.*

It's important to understand why you see the memory requirements go up when you click the Extend and Retract buttons but not when you click the Up and Down buttons. Remember that the Up and Down buttons merely move the cast members already on the stage. When you click the Extend and Retract buttons, your script is loading other cast members from the cast for display on the stage.

Now you're going to add a command to the movie script to improve performance. You'll use the command *preLoadMember fromCastmember, toCastmember*. This command loads into memory a range of cast members, starting with the cast member specified by *fromCastmember* and ending with the cast member specified by *toCastmember*.

4] Double-click cast member 38 to open the movie script. Modify the *startMovie* handler by adding the line shown here in bold:

```
global gArmSpeed          --This global variable will specify the number of
                          --pixels the arm should move.


on startMovie
   gArmSpeed = 3          --This will move the arm 3 pixels at a time.
   preLoadMember 1, 27    --Preload cast members 1 through 27.
end
```

5] Close the Script window. In the Memory Inspector, click Purge to clear the memory. Then play the movie again.

The movie takes a split second longer to begin, but you'll see in the Memory Inspector that the cast members are loaded immediately at the beginning of the movie. In fact, no more time is needed to load the cast members into memory in this way than it is needed without preloading. By preloading the cast members, however, you control when they are loaded, getting the task out of the way so it doesn't happen as the movie is being played, when the delay would be more visible.

6] Click the Extend button.

Now performance is better and is more consistent each time you play the movie. Preloading is extremely useful for getting the maximum performance and consistency out of a movie.

7] Save your work.

The degree of added performance you realize from preloading depends on the situation. In the case of the simple movie you just completed, the performance difference is slight, though still welcome (and on some extremely fast machines, you may not be able to see much difference at all). In other situations, the performance difference can be dramatic. For example, the performance of a graphics-rich movie that plays from a CD-ROM will benefit tremendously from a judicious use of preloading.

ON YOUR OWN

Many values in your scripts, such as the starting cast member number in the extend-retract range and the upper and lower limits on the range of motion, can be changed to global variables for more sophisticated scripting. Once you have done so, if you later want to change the way the arm is used or to add cast members, you will need to change only the variables instead of having to find all the locations with the hard-coded values and change each instance. Experiment with global variables by making these changes to your movie.

If you would like to view more advanced techniques in the actual environment of the Iron Helix game, open and play Robot3.dir in the Complete folder. To move the arm in this movie, click and drag the mouse in the gray area at the upper left of the movie. The arm will appear as you click and drag.

WHAT YOU HAVE LEARNED

In this lesson you have:

• Used variables instead of hard-coded values [page 522]

• Replaced *if-then* statements with a *case* structure [page 525]

• Used symbols instead of numbers in a *case* structure [page 533]

• Used symbols in the calling handler [page 535]

• Played sounds using the *puppetSound* command [page 537]

• Checked memory with the Memory Inspector [page 540]

• Used the *preLoadMember* command to improve performance [page 541]

control

keyboard

LESSON 23

So far, you have developed projects that let users control the actions of a movie based on mouse movements or mouse clicks on the stage. In this lesson, you will give users a way to control actions using the keyboard. Keyboard control is useful in a wide variety of projects. For example, in some games it may be faster and easier to control events using the keyboard rather than a mouse. Keyboard control can even be essential in projects such as kiosk applications, where a mouse is not available.

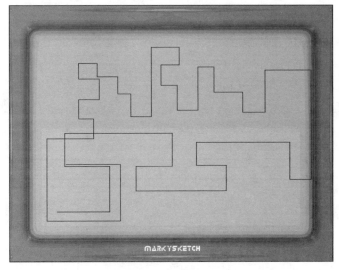

This "Markysketch" is an electronic version of a sketch toy. You draw lines using the keyboard's arrow keys to move the drawing dot up, down, right, and left. You will use Lingo to make the arrow keys draw on the screen.

Graphics and programming by Mark Castle, Castle Productions.

If you would like to review the final result of this lesson, open the Complete folder in the Lesson23 folder and play Sketch.dir.

WHAT YOU WILL LEARN

In this lesson you will:

• Determine what key has been pressed on the keyboard

• Practice setting the vertical and horizontal locations of a sprite

• Turn trails on and off using Lingo instead of the score

• Limit the movement of a sprite to the borders of another sprite

• Control the speed that a sprite moves on the stage

• Determine whether any key is held down

• Set the stage color using Lingo

APPROXIMATE TIME

It should take about 3 hours to complete this lesson.

LESSON FILES

Media Files:
None

Starting Files:
Lesson23\Start\Start1.dir
Lesson23\Start\Start2.dir
Lesson23\Start\Keyinput.dir

Completed Project:
Lesson23\Complete\Sketch.dir

DETERMINING KEY CODES

The sketch toy you will develop in this lesson is designed to let the user create drawings using the arrow keys on the keyboard. To accept input from the keyboard, Director needs some way to understand, through Lingo, what key is being pressed. To solve that problem, Lingo uses **key codes**, which are unique numeric values assigned to each key.

This task shows you a special Director movie, Keyinput.dir, that you can use to determine the code for any key on the keyboard. Keyinput.dir is located in the Lesson23 folder.

1] Open Keyinput.dir and play it. Click the anywhere on the stage. Type any key to see its key code.

In authoring mode, you need to make sure the stage is the frontmost window. Otherwise, Director will not be able to detect when you press a key on the keyboard. That's why you need to click the stage before pressing a key. If you create a projector of this movie and run the projector, the projector will be the current application, and you will not need to click it before pressing a key.

As you press keys, notice how the key codes differ from the ASCII codes. There is a single key code for each key on the keyboard. For example, when you press W and Shift+W, you get the same key code: 13. Each separate character, however, has a different ASCII code: W is 119, while Shift+W is 87.

2] Get the key code for the left, right, up, and down arrow keys.

Keyinput.dir provides other pieces of information about a keystroke in addition to the key code, but for now you can ignore everything except the second box in the movie. As you will see, the key code for the left arrow is 123, the right arrow is 124, the down arrow is 125, and the up arrow is 126.

If you're curious how this movie works, take a look through its scripts. Director's online help also includes an excellent sample movie that illustrates keyboard input.

Now that you know the necessary key codes, you can open a new movie and start the project.

SETTING UP FOR THIS LESSON

To give you a jump-start, the score and the essential cast members have already been set up for you.

1] Open the Start1.dir movie in the Lesson23 folder. Double-click the behavior channel, frame 10, and note the *exitFrame* handler:

```
on exitFrame
   go to the frame
end
```

This script keeps the playback head from moving. You're going to control the action using Lingo, as you did in Lessons 21 and 22, so you need to pause the playback head and wait for the user to press a key.

2] Save this movie as *Sketch.dir* in your Projects folder.

CREATING THE DRAWING DOT

The sketch toy graphic is already in place on the stage. You need to create the other part of the user interface: the dot that draws the lines on the screen.

1] In the score, click frame 1 in channel 2. Open the tool palette (Windows Ctrl+7, Macintosh Command+7), select the Filled Rectangle tool, set the foreground color to black, and then draw a small square on the stage within the bounds of the gray drawing area.

This square—called the drawing dot—should be in channel 2, spanning frames 1 through 10. You can draw the dot any size because you're going to resize it in the next step. The sprite's duration isn't important either, since you're going to control it using Lingo and not the score. The 10-frame duration chosen for the sprites in this project is long enough for the cast member names to be readable in the score.

2] Choose Modify › Sprite › Properties to open the Sprite Properties dialog box.

You're going to use this dialog box to adjust the size of the sprite.

3] Uncheck the Maintain Proportions box. Set both the height and width to 1. Then close the dialog box.

If Maintain Proportions is checked, the height and width will always adjust when one of those fields is altered. You need to uncheck the box to make independent adjustments to each field.

4] Save your work.

You now have a drawing dot that is 1-pixel square. This is the tool the user will move to draw lines on the screen.

USING KEY CODES TO CONTROL ACTION USING THE KEYBOARD

Now you use the key codes you found earlier to create a handler that moves the drawing dot around the stage. As part of this script, you will use the Lingo elements *keyDown*, *the keyCode*, and *the locH*.

The *keyDown* event is a standard Lingo message that is sent when a key is pressed. The *the keyCode* system function returns the numerical code for the last key pressed. For example, the key code for the left arrow key is 123. Note that key codes are automatically generated by the computer's operating system and cannot be controlled or set by you.

Recall from Lesson 21 that *the locH* returns the horizontal position of the specified sprite, and *the locV* returns the vertical position of the specified sprite. (Remember that sprite coordinates are relative to the upper-left corner of the stage.)

1] Open a new Movie Script window (Windows Ctrl+Shift+U, Macintosh Command+Shift+U) and type the following script:

```
on keyDown                                  --When a key is pressed,
  if the keyCode = 123 then                 --if the key is the left arrow,
    sprite (2).locH = sprite (2).locH – 1   --move the dot 1 pixel left.
  else if the keyCode = 124 then            --If the key is the right arrow,
    sprite (2).locH = sprite (2).locH + 1   --move the dot 1 pixel right.
  end if
  updateStage                               --Update the stage to show changes.
end
```

Some of the statements in this script are already familiar to you, but some are new. Let's take a look at how this script works.

You created a movie script because the *keyDown* event message does not depend on user interaction with the sprites on the stage or on the playback head. (To handle event messages generated by those dependencies, you would usually create sprite, cast, or frame scripts.) Therefore, a movie script is the best location for this handler.

The *keyDown* handler contains an *if-then* structure that checks whether the key code matches either of the key codes for the left and right arrow keys, which are 123 and 124, respectively. If the key code is 123 or 124, the script moves the sprite using the same techniques you used to move the robot arm in Lessons 21 and 22. When the left arrow key is pressed (key code 123), the script subtracts 1 pixel from the current horizontal location of sprite 2 (the dot). When the right arrow key is pressed (key code 124), it adds 1 pixel. Then it updates the stage to show the changes.

2] Play the movie and press the left and right arrow keys.

When you press the left or right arrow key, the dot moves left or right.

You may need to click the stage to make it active so the arrow keys work. If the score or cast is active, the arrow keys will be active in the score or cast, and the dot on the stage won't move. Also, a 1-pixel object on the stage is very small; you will have to look very carefully to see it move across the stage.

Now that you've learned the principles involved in controlling action from the keyboard, you're ready to create ways to move the drawing dot up and down, too. First, however, you will improve the efficiency of your scripts using the techniques introduced in Lesson 22.

USING A *CASE* STATEMENT INSTEAD OF *IF-THEN-ELSE*

Now, just as you did in Lesson 22, you will turn this *if-then-else* structure into a *case* structure. This will make it easier to add conditions to the *keyDown* handler for the up and down arrow keys.

1] Open the movie script and make the changes shown here in bold.

```
on keyDown                              --When a key is pressed,
   case (the keyCode) of
      123:                              --if the key code represents the left arrow,
         sprite (2).locH = sprite (2).locH – 1    --move the dot 1 pixel left.
      124:                              --If the key code represents the right arrow,
         sprite (2).locH = sprite (2).locH + 1    --move the dot 1 pixel right.
   end case
   updateStage                          --Update the stage to show changes.
end
```

Recall the *case* structure you created in Lesson 22. It combines multiple *if-then* statements into a single structure. This *case* structure sets up different actions for different values returned by *the keyCode*, the function that returns the numerical code for the last key pressed. Unlike in Lesson 22, you do not send a parameter to the *case* structure yourself. The value for *the keyCode* is automatically generated by the system when the user presses a key.

2] Rewind and play the movie.

Remember that you may need to click the stage to make it active so the arrow keys work. Everything should still work as before.

USING TRAILS

Now your drawing dot moves in response to pressing the left and right arrow keys, but no drawing takes place. The previous location of the dot is erased each time the stage is updated.

Setting the *trails* property for a sprite causes Director *not* to erase the sprite in the current frame before the playback head moves on to the next frame, as Director normally would do. The result is that the sprite remains on the stage instead of being erased. Here you will use trails to leave a line behind the dot as it moves across the stage.

In this task, you will use Lingo to turn on the *trails* property. The syntax of this property is *sprite (whichSprite).trails = TrueOrFalse*. Setting *trails* to FALSE turns trails off, and setting *trails* to TRUE turns trails on. You must use Lingo (instead of the score) to turn trails on because while you are using Lingo to move the drawing dot around the stage, Director ignores any score instructions for that sprite.

note *If you did not complete the previous tasks, you can open and use Start2.dir in the Lesson23 folder to complete this lesson.*

1] Open the movie script, add the lines shown here in bold, and then close the window.

```
on startMovie
   sprite (2).trails = TRUE              --Turn on trails for the dot (sprite 2).
end

on keyDown                              --When a key is pressed,
   case (the keyCode) of
      123:                              --if the key code represents the left arrow,
         sprite (2).locH = sprite (2).locH – 1    --move the dot 1 pixel left.
      124:                              --If the key code represents the right arrow,
         sprite (2).locH = sprite (2).locH + 1    --move the dot 1 pixel right.
   end case
   updateStage                          --Update the stage to show changes.
end
```

As you learned in Lesson 22, the *startMovie* handler runs before the first frame of a movie. It is the best place to set any options that affect the entire movie. Here you are using it to execute the command that turns trails on for sprite 2 (the drawing dot that is in channel 2).

2] Play the movie and press the left and right arrow keys.

Remember that you may need to click the stage first to make it active.

It works! The trails feature draws a line behind the dot as you move it.

CREATING A BOUNDING RECTANGLE

Currently, you can use the arrow keys to move the dot entirely off the screen. However, the dot should be limited to the red boundaries of the sketch graphic. In Lesson 21, you kept a sprite from moving off the stage by making sure it didn't go beyond a vertical location by using an *if-then* structure and the *the locV* sprite property. Here you will use a different technique, creating an invisible rectangle around the area within which the dot is constrained.

1] Open the tool palette and select the Unfilled Rectangle tool.

2] Click the dotted line near the bottom of the tool palette.

This setting controls the border width of the rectangle; in this case, the rectangle's border will be invisible.

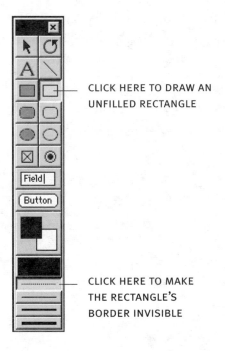

CLICK HERE TO DRAW AN
UNFILLED RECTANGLE

CLICK HERE TO MAKE
THE RECTANGLE'S
BORDER INVISIBLE

3] Draw a rectangle inside the red borders of the background graphic.

This new sprite should be in channel 3, frames 1 through 10 (if Director added the dot's sprite over more frames of the score, drag the sprite's end frame back to frame 10). In the next task, you will modify the *keyDown* handler to make the rectangle act as a constraining fence beyond which the dot will not be able to travel.

YOU WILL CREATE A
SCRIPT THAT PREVENTS
THE DRAWING DOT FROM
MOVING BEYOND THE
BORDERS OF THIS SPRITE

4] Save your work.

USING *THE CONSTRAINT OF SPRITE* TO LIMIT MOVEMENT

Next you need to update the movie script to use the new boundary that you just created. Lingo has a built-in command to do just that: *the constraint of sprite.* The syntax of this command is *sprite(whichSprite).constraint* or *the constraint of sprite whichSprite.*

This sprite property limits the position of the sprite specified by *whichSprite* by constraining it to the bounding rectangle of another sprite. The constrained sprite cannot be moved outside the bounding rectangle of the constraining sprite.

Now you'll see how this works.

1] Open the movie script and make the changes shown here in bold.

```
on startMovie
    sprite (2).trails = TRUE        --Turn on trails for the dot (sprite 2).
    sprite (2).constraint = 3       --Constrain the dot (sprite 2) to
                                    --the boundaries of the rectangle (sprite 3).
end
```

```
on keyDown                                --When a key is pressed,
  case (the keyCode) of
    123:                                  --if the key code represents the left arrow,
       sprite (2).locH = sprite (2).locH – 1    --move the dot 1 pixel left.
    124:                                  --If the key code represents the right arrow,
       sprite (2).locH = sprite (2).locH + 1    --move the dot 1 pixel right.
  end case
  updateStage                             --Update the stage to show changes.
end
```

This new line constrains the dot (sprite 2) to the bounding rectangle you created (sprite 3).

2] Play the movie and press the left and right arrow keys until you reach a border of the rectangle.

The dot movement is now limited to the bounding rectangle.

USING THE *WIDTH OF SPRITE* TO INCREASE DRAWING SPEED

A pixel is a tiny dot, and moving 1 pixel at a time is a pretty slow rate. In Lesson 21, you changed the speed of a sprite's movement by changing the number of pixels it moved. In this task, you will use a similar technique. However, in this case, there is a slight complication.

Suppose you set the dot to move 5 pixels at a time instead of 1, using the 1-pixel by 1-pixel dot that you created. When you pressed the arrow key, you would see a dot, then 4 empty pixels, and then the next dot. The trail would be a dotted line.

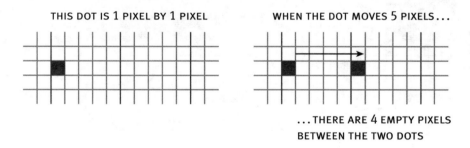

THIS DOT IS 1 PIXEL BY 1 PIXEL   WHEN THE DOT MOVES 5 PIXELS...

...THERE ARE 4 EMPTY PIXELS
BETWEEN THE TWO DOTS

On the other hand, suppose you set the width and height of the dot to 5 pixels by 5 pixels. If you continue to use the same script, you will be moving the dot 1 pixel at a time. That means the 5-pixel dot will move 1 pixel per key press, and the trail will be covered by 4 pixels of the new dot. This would make drawing a large dot very, very slow and inefficient.

THIS DOT IS 5 PIXELS BY 5 PIXELS

WHEN THE DOT MOVES 1 PIXEL...

...THE TWO DOTS OVERLAP
4 PIXELS (AS SHOWN BY
THE CROSS-HATCHING)

To create a smooth line, you need a drawing dot that is the same width as the number of pixels the dot moves. For a 5-pixel movement, you need a 5-pixel-wide dot. In this task, you will use variables to tie the width of the dot to the number of pixels the dot moves with each key press.

THIS DOT IS 5 PIXELS BY 5 PIXELS

WHEN THE DOT MOVES 5 PIXELS...

...THERE IS AN UNBROKEN LINE
WITH NO OVERLAP

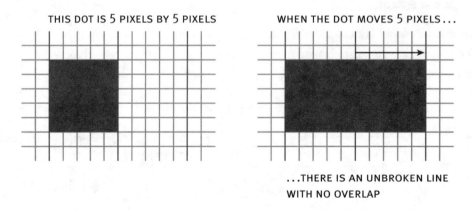

As part of this task, you will use *the width of sprite*, a sprite property that determines the horizontal size (in pixels) of a specified sprite. The syntax of this property is *sprite(whichSprite).width* (or *the width of sprite whichSprite*). You're going to increase the speed at which the dot moves by first creating a global variable to hold the width of the dot sprite. Then instead of moving the dot 1 pixel to either the left or right, you'll move the dot as many pixels as the dot is wide.

1] Open the movie script and make the changes shown here in bold.

```
global gDrawSpeed

on startMovie
    sprite (2).trails = TRUE            --Turn on trails for the dot (sprite 2).
    sprite (2).constraint = 3           --Constrain the dot (sprite 2) to
                                        --the boundaries of the rectangle (sprite 3).
    gDrawSpeed = sprite (2).width       --Tie the drawing speed to the width of the dot.
end

on keyDown                             --When a key is pressed,
    case (the keyCode) of
        123:                           --if the key code represents the left arrow,
        sprite (2).locH = sprite (2).locH – gDrawSpeed
                                        --move the dot left by
                                        --the number of pixels that the dot is wide.
        124:                           --If the key code represents the right arrow,
        sprite (2).locH = sprite (2).locH + gDrawSpeed
                                        --move the dot right by
                                        --the number of pixels that the dot is wide.
    end case
    updateStage                        --Update the stage to show changes.
end
```

This handler now uses the width of the drawing dot as the speed at which the dot moves. The global variable *gDrawSpeed* holds the number of pixels that the dot moves with each key press. Next, you used the *the width of sprite* property to set the value of *gDrawSpeed* to the width of sprite 2. This ties the two values together, changing the value of *gDrawSpeed* (the number of pixels the dot travels) to the width of the sprite; when the width changes, so will the drawing speed. Last, you edited the lines that change the location of the dot by replacing the absolute number with the new variable, *gDrawSpeed*.

Now if you change the size of the dot, the speed it moves will also change automatically. To see the result, you'll need to resize the drawing dot. You'll do that next.

2] Select the dot sprite in channel 2 of the score. Then choose Modify › Sprite › Properties and set the height and width to 3.

3] Play the movie and press the left and right arrow keys.
Not only is the dot larger, but the distance it moves is now exactly the same as its width.

4] Set the dot back to 1 pixel square using Modify › Sprite › Properties.

5] Save your work.

ADDING KEY CODES FOR THE UP AND DOWN ARROWS

Now that your coding is optimized, it's time to add controls for the other two keys. To do this, you need to change only the case structure so it includes the key codes for the up and down arrows, which, as you discovered earlier, are 125 and 126, respectively.

1] Open the movie script and add the two new key codes to the *case* structure, as shown here in bold.

```
global gDrawSpeed

on startMovie
    sprite (2).trails = TRUE         --Turn on trails for the dot (sprite 2).
    sprite (2).constraint = 3        --Constrain the dot (sprite 2) to
                                     --the boundaries of the rectangle (sprite 3).

    gDrawSpeed = sprite (2).width    --Tie the drawing speed to the width of the dot.
end

on keyDown                           --When a key is pressed,
    case (the keyCode) of
        123:                         --if the key code represents the left arrow,
            sprite (2).locH = sprite (2).locH – gDrawSpeed
                                     --move the dot left by
                                     --the number of pixels that the dot is wide.
        124:                         --If the key code represents the right arrow,
            sprite (2).locH = sprite (2).locH + gDrawSpeed
                                     --move the dot right by
                                     --the number of pixels that the dot is wide.
        125:                         --If the key code represents the down arrow,
            sprite (2).locV = sprite (2).locV + gDrawSpeed
                                     --move the dot down by
                                     --the number of pixels that the dot is wide.
        126:                         --If the key code represents the up arrow,
            sprite (2).locV = sprite (2).locV - gDrawSpeed
                                     --move the dot up by
                                     --the number of pixels that the dot is wide.
    end case
    updateStage                      --Update the stage to show changes.
end
```

The existing sections for key codes 123 and 124 use the *the locH* property to move the drawing dot side to side. The sections you just added for key codes 125 (the down arrow) and 126 (the up arrow) use the *the locV* property to move the dot up and down.

2] Play the movie and press the arrow keys.

It works! Now all the arrow keys draw as they should.

3] Save your work.

USING *THE KEYPRESSED*

Although the basic functionality of the movie is complete, you can speed up the drawing and add some keyboard functionality to improve the movie.

Do you remember how you created the script to move the robot arm in Lesson 21? There you used *the stillDown* to track whether the mouse button was pressed and held down. A similar property, *the keyPressed*, is available for tracking whether a key is pressed and held down. You can also use *the keyPressed* so users can simply hold the key down to rapidly move the dot.

The *the keyPressed* property returns the character assigned to the key being pressed or, if no key is pressed, it returns the value *empty*. If you use the *keyPressed( )* function and specify a key letter (such as *A*) or key code, it will return TRUE if that key is actively being held down. To keep the dot moving as long as an arrow key is pressed, you will enclose part of the *keyDown* handler inside a *repeat* loop that executes until the value of *the keyPressed* is empty (until the key is no longer held down).

1] Open the movie script and add the lines shown in bold.

```
global gDrawSpeed

on startMovie
  sprite (2).trails = TRUE          --Turn on trails for the dot (sprite 2).
  sprite (2).constraint = 3         --Constrain the dot (sprite 2) to
                                    --the boundaries of the rectangle (sprite 3).
  gDrawSpeed = sprite (2).width     --Tie the drawing speed to the width of the dot.
end
```

```
on keyDown                            --When a key is pressed,
    keySave = the keyCode             --Retrieve and save keyCode.
    repeat while not (the keyPressed = EMPTY)
                                      --Repeat as long as a key is held down.
        case (keySave) of
            123:                      --If the key code represents the left arrow,
                sprite (2).locH = sprite (2).locH – gDrawSpeed
                                      --move the dot left by
                                      --the number of pixels that the dot is wide.
            124:                      --If the key code represents the right arrow,
                sprite (2).locH = sprite (2).locH + gDrawSpeed
                                      --move the dot right by
                                      --the number of pixels that the dot is wide.
            125:                      --If the key code represents the down arrow,
                sprite (2).locV = sprite (2).locV + gDrawSpeed
                                      --move the dot down by
                                      --the number of pixels that the dot is wide.
            126:                      --If the key code represents the up arrow,
                sprite (2).locV = sprite (2).locV - gDrawSpeed
                                      --move the dot up by
                                      --the number of pixels that the dot is wide.
        end case
        updateStage                   --Update the stage to show changes.
    end repeat
end
```

Be careful to place the *repeat* and *end repeat* statements at the correct locations in the handler.

note *You are testing only one result of* the keyPressed: *whether it's empty. You don't need to use its ability to report which key is being pressed because that is taken care of by the* case *structure and the* the keyCode *function.*

note *The form of this* repeat *structure is a little different from that of the one you used before. Here, you want the handler to repeat while the value is not the named one, so the form of the command is* repeat while not.

2] Play the movie.

You should notice a dramatic improvement when you play the movie. The drawing action may even be too fast on some systems. Making changes like these, which don't alter the functionality but instead improve performance, increase execution speed, or improve the readability of the code, are excellent ways to optimize performance.

USING *THE OPTIONDOWN* AND *THE STAGECOLOR* TO ADD FEATURES

In the last task of this lesson, you will experiment with some Lingo elements that add new features to the project—and can come in handy for lots of other uses as well. The first is *the optionDown*, a function that determines whether the user has pressed the Alt key (Windows) or the Option key (Macintosh) and returns TRUE or FALSE. In this example, you will use *the optionDown* to let users press the Alt or Option key to move the drawing dot without drawing a line (by turning trails off).

The other feature you will experiment with is *the stageColor*, which acts as both a function and a command. As a function, it returns the current color of the stage; as a command, it sets the stage color to a particular value. In this example, you will use *the stageColor* to add an erase feature to the sketch toy: The user will be able to press Backspace (Windows) or Delete (Macintosh) to erase the stage.

1] Open the movie script and add the changes shown here in bold.

```
global gDrawSpeed

on startMovie
   sprite (2).trails = TRUE              --Turn on trails for the dot (sprite 2).
   sprite (2).constraint = 3             --Constrain the dot (sprite 2) to
                                         --the boundaries of the rectangle (sprite 3).
   gDrawSpeed = sprite (2).width         --Tie the drawing speed to the width of the dot.
end

on keyDown                              --When a key is pressed,
   if the optionDown = TRUE then sprite (2).trails = FALSE
                                         --if Alt or Option is pressed, turn off the dot trail.
   keySave = the keyCode                 --Retrieve and save keyCode.
   repeat while not (the keyPressed = EMPTY)
                                         --Repeat as long as a key is held down.
     case (keySave) of
       51:                               --If the key code represents Backspace or Delete,
         the stageColor = the stageColor
                                         --erase all lines on the stage.
       123:                              --If the key code represents the left arrow,
         sprite (2).locH = sprite (2).locH – gDrawSpeed
                                         --move the dot left by
                                         --the number of pixels that the dot is wide.
       124:                              --If the key code represents the right arrow,
         sprite (2).locH = sprite (2).locH + gDrawSpeed
                                         --move the dot right by
                                         --the number of pixels that the dot is wide.
       125:                              --If the key code represents the down arrow,
         sprite (2).locV = sprite (2).locV + gDrawSpeed
                                         --move the dot down by
                                         --the number of pixels that the dot is wide.
```

```
    126:                                    --If the key code represents the up arrow,
        sprite (2).locV = sprite (2).locV - gDrawSpeed
                                            --move the dot up by
                                            --the number of pixels that the dot is wide.
      end case
      updateStage                           --Update the stage to show changes.
    end repeat
    sprite (2).trails = TRUE                --Turn the dot trail back on.
  end
```

With just a few simple changes you have improved the performance of the movie
and increased the available features. The first line you added is an *if-then* structure
(compressed on one line so it doesn't need an *end-if* statement) that turns off the
drawing dot trail when Alt (Windows) or Option (Macintosh) is pressed. The second
change you made resets the stage color to its current value when Backspace (Windows)
or Delete (Macintosh) is pressed, in the process erasing any trails left by earlier drawing.
(The key code for both of these keys is 51.) After the drawing function is complete,
the last line added turns the *trails* property back on so the sketch toy will work
normally the next time a key is pressed.

2] Rewind and play the movie to see the results.

Try holding down the Alt (Windows) or Option (Macintosh) key while using the arrow
keys to move the dot without leaving a trail. Press the Backspace (Windows) or Delete
(Macintosh) key to erase all the lines. You have just added two new features with
three simple lines of Lingo code.

ON YOUR OWN

Efficient as it is, this script can still use a bit more optimization. Remember how you
created variables to contain the current channel for sprites when you optimized the
scripts in Lesson 22? That feature would be useful in this script as well, to let you
move sprites easily as you add features to your toy. To add this feature, open the movie
script again and create a global variable for sprite 2. You'll need to declare it in the
startMovie handler. Then substitute the global variable for the constant value
throughout the entire script.

WHAT YOU HAVE LEARNED

In this lesson you have:

• Used *on keyDown*, *the keyCode*, *the locH*, and *the locV* to draw on the stage [page 548]

• Practiced changing an *if-then-else* structure into a *case* structure [page 549]

• Used trails to leave a line on the stage [page 550]

• Created a bounding rectangle and used *the constraint of sprite* to limit movement [page 551]

• Increased drawing speed with *the width of sprite* [page 553]

• Increased drawing speed with a *repeat* structure and *the keyPressed* [page 557]

• Added features with *the optionDown* and *the stageColor* [page 559]

multiple casts

using lists and

LESSON 24

In the movies you have created so far, you have stored the project assets (text, graphics, sounds, and other elements) in a single cast. A movie's assets can be stored in any number of casts, however. In this lesson, you will build an electronic catalog that demonstrates an especially effective use of multiple casts: Using a movie that contains only a few frames in its score, you will write Lingo scripts to dynamically change casts as users browse from one page to another in the catalog. You will set up the navigation using lists, which are one of Lingo's most powerful tools for managing information.

Using Lingo, you can create an electronic catalog that dynamically changes casts as users browse from one page to another. By using multiple casts, you can create movies that you can easily update and expand just by changing the casts.

Graphics for the electronic catalog project by Ming Lau, BlueWaters. Programming by Frank Elley, Behind the Curtain.

If you would like to review the final results of this lesson, open the Complete folder in the Lesson24 folder and play Catalog.dir.

WHAT YOU WILL LEARN

In this lesson you will:

• Learn how to plan a strategy for the use of multiple casts

• Create a new external cast

• Link an existing external cast to a movie

• Transfer assets from one cast to another

• Create a template layout for all of a movie's external casts

• Switch casts using Lingo

• Use lists to manage the appearance of different casts on the stage

• Align registration points

APPROXIMATE TIME

It should take about 3 hours to complete this lesson.

LESSON FILES

Media Files:

None

Starting Files:

Lesson24\Start\Start.dir
Lesson24\Start\FreshPpr.cst
Lesson24\Start\DriedPpr.cst
Lesson24\Start\PeprCorn.cst

Completed Project:

Lesson24\Complete\Catalog.dir

SETTING UP FOR THIS LESSON

To start, you need to copy several files from the CD to your computer.

1] Make a folder like your Projects folder, but call it your *Work* folder. Then, open the Start.dir movie in the Lesson24 folder and save it as *Catalog.dir* in your Work folder.

2] From the Lesson24 folder on the CD, also copy the FreshPpr.cst, DriedPpr.cst, and PeprCorn.cst cast files into your Work folder.

These are casts that contain assets your movie will need.

> **note** *The Lingo scripts that you will develop in this lesson assume that the cast files and movie files are in the same folder. If they are not, you will not be able to complete the project in this lesson.*

3] Choose File › Preferences › Sprite and type *13* for Span Duration.

Most of the sprites you create in this lesson will be this length. Setting this preference now will save you time in adjusting span durations during the lesson. This 13-frame duration is not important to the way the movie works; it was chosen merely because it was long enough to show the names of the cast members in the score.

PLANNING A STRATEGY FOR MULTIPLE CASTS

A movie's casts can be stored either internally or externally. **Internal casts** are stored within the movie file and cannot be shared by other movies. Director automatically creates one internal cast when you create a movie, and this default internal cast is the one you have been using throughout this book. **External casts** are stored as separate files outside the movie. An external cast must be explicitly **linked** to a movie to which it contributes assets, and a movie can have many linked external casts. A single external cast can be linked to many movies, and thus external casts often serve as libraries for commonly used movie elements. You can use Lingo to switch the external casts linked to a movie while the movie is running. You work with all cast members in the same way, regardless of whether the cast is internal or external.

External casts offer some especially powerful benefits, because you can change the contents of the cast without having to change any of the movies to which the cast is linked. Here are just a few ideas:

• When working on a large project team, you can segregate different media types into separate casts: text in one cast, graphics in another cast, sound in yet another cast, and so on. This strategy speeds project development because team members with different specialties can work on their own casts; no one has to wait for someone else to finish with the movie files in order to work.

564

- If your movie will be translated into different languages, you can segregate elements that will require translation into separate casts. Copies of these casts can be sent to translators, and the translated casts can later be integrated back into the main movie—either by creating a separate movie for each language or by creating a single movie that asks customers to choose a language and then displays its content using the appropriate cast.

- For projects that present large amounts of data or that use data that requires frequent updating, you can create a template movie with a consistent format that displays information stored in external casts. A single movie can display content from hundreds or thousands of casts. Because the casts are stored externally, you can update a cast's contents, and the updated content will appear the next time the movie is run.

When you use multiple casts, it is important that you work with a definite strategy in mind. Trying to mix strategies (for example, dividing the casts required for a database application into media types as well) can quickly produce an unmanageable number of casts.

Your strategy for multiple casts should also determine where the casts are located. The easiest, most predictable approach is to place the casts in the same folder as your movie or in a subfolder within the movie's folder. In this case, Director stores the **relative path** to the casts it needs; that is, it knows where the casts are located in relation to the movie file itself: either in the same folder or in a subfolder. When you move the folder containing the movie, the casts move along with it, and Director is still able to find them.

One of the most exciting aspects of multiple casts, however, is that they can be located literally anywhere in the world. You can link a movie to a cast elsewhere on the same computer, on a network server, and even on the Internet. As long as the network or Internet connection is active when the movie opens, Director will find the linked cast. Such a movie can reside on a user's computer, but this scenario is especially attractive for Shockwave movies, which are created for use within a Web browser that is already connected to the Internet.

While you are creating a movie, you also do not need to have the casts located on your computer. From within Director, you can open or link to casts on a network or on the Internet. Project teams can be truly global. For example, from an office in San Francisco you can create a Shockwave movie with links to graphics casts in Singapore, music casts in Buenos Aires, and text casts in London!

In this lesson you will work with both internal and external casts and use Lingo to dynamically swap external casts to display different cast members within a single movie. You will work with casts stored in the same folder as the movie file, but as you work, keep in mind that the electronic catalog you are creating would be an ideal candidate for a Shockwave movie linked to casts stored at various locations on the Internet.

CREATING A NEW EXTERNAL CAST

For this lesson, imagine that you're one of many team members working on an electronic catalog of fruits and vegetables. The project leader assigns you to create a section on peppers, and this section contains three "pages" (this lesson refers to pages instead of screens): one each for fresh peppers, dried peppers, and peppercorns. Information about each of the three pepper types is stored in a separate cast. You will first set up a flexible cast structure by moving the movie's existing assets into a new external cast and then linking another, existing cast to the movie.

In this task you will create a new, external cast to hold all assets that will be common to every page of the catalog. Placing these assets in an external cast enables you to update the content of the movie just by updating the cast, without re-creating the projector (you will see this demonstrated later in the lesson).

1] Choose Modify › Movie › Casts (Windows Ctrl+Shift+C, Macintosh Shift+ Command+C) to open the Movie Casts dialog box.

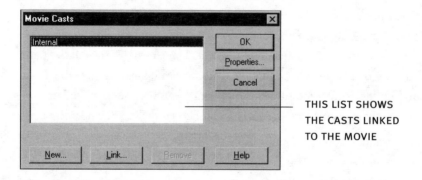

THIS LIST SHOWS
THE CASTS LINKED
TO THE MOVIE

You use the Movie Casts dialog box to create new casts, link casts to movies, and remove links.

note *You can also create, link to, and remove, casts at runtime through Lingo, but to do so requires a third-party Xtra. See the Xtra list at http://www.macromedia.com/software/ xtras/director.*

2] Click New to open the New Cast dialog box.

566

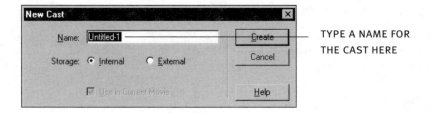

TYPE A NAME FOR
THE CAST HERE

The dialog box asks you for information on the cast you want to create.

3] Type *Main.cst* in the Name field and click External. Make sure Use in Current Movie is selected and then click Create.

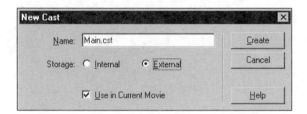

The new external cast you created will be saved as a separate file called Main.cst. (Windows uses the .cst filename extension to identify the file as a Director cast. Even if you are working on a Macintosh, it is a good idea to use this filename extension, since it makes your project easier to work with on a Windows system later.) By selecting External, you're telling Director to save the cast as a separate file instead of storing it in the movie file. The Use in Current Movie option links the new cast to the current movie. If this option is not selected, Director still creates the cast as a separate file, but the cast is not available from within the current movie.

When the New Cast dialog box closes, you see that the Movie Casts dialog box now lists the cast you just created.

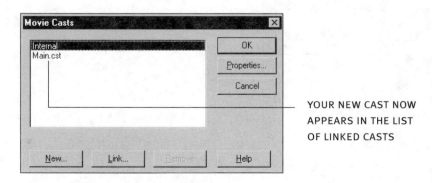

YOUR NEW CAST NOW
APPEARS IN THE LIST
OF LINKED CASTS

567

4] Click OK to close the Movie Casts dialog box.

5] Choose Window › Cast; do not select a specific cast.

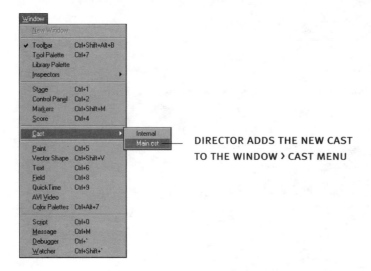

DIRECTOR ADDS THE NEW CAST
TO THE WINDOW › CAST MENU

The Main cast is available on the menu because it is now linked to the movie. On the Window > Casts menu, you see only the casts actually linked to the movie. When you choose a cast from this menu, the cast opens in its own window.

6] Choose Window › Cast › Internal to open the Internal cast. Click the button at the upper-left corner of the window.

Notice that Main.cst is available from this menu as well.

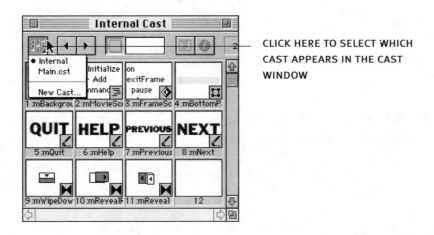

CLICK HERE TO SELECT WHICH
CAST APPEARS IN THE CAST
WINDOW

When you choose a cast name from the menu in the Cast window, that cast replaces the contents of the window.

You now know two ways to view a cast. From the Window > Cast menu, you can open a cast in a separate window. From a Cast window, you can switch to another linked cast. As you switch between the multiple casts in the following tasks, you can use the method that best suits your working style.

MOVING ASSETS TO AN EXTERNAL CAST

Now that you've created the Main external cast, you will move the movie's prebuilt assets there. Doing so will enable you to update the movie's contents without having to update the movie file itself. This task will also help you understand how such an updating scheme works.

1] Open the score to familiarize yourself with its layout. Click the sprite in channel 1 and note that the upper-left area of the sprite toolbar indicates the cast in which the sprite's cast member is stored.

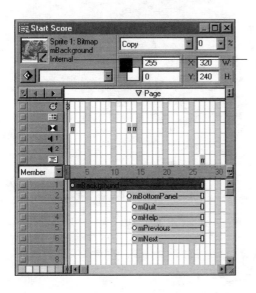

THIS PREVIEW IDENTIFIES THE CAST IN WHICH THE SELECTED SPRITE IS STORED

tip   *If you don't see the sprite toolbar in your score, make sure the score is the active window and then choose View > Sprite Toolbar (Windows Ctrl+Shift+H, Macintosh Shift+Command+H).*

If you click the sprites one by one, you'll see that the score consists entirely of cast members currently stored in the Internal cast.

2] Play the movie.
Notice the different elements: The background appears first, then a transition to a navigation panel, followed by another transition to show labels for the navigation

569

buttons (you will add the actual buttons later). A frame script in frame 27 pauses the playback head.

3] Choose Window › Cast › Internal to open the Internal Cast window.

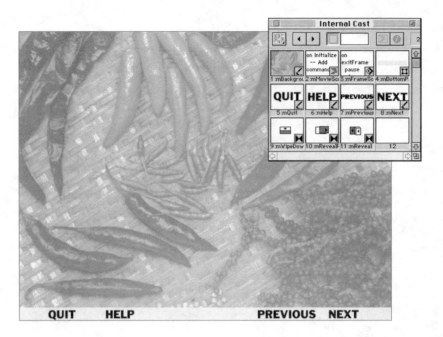

Once again, notice that the Internal cast contains all the movie's assets. Remember that the cast stores not only the elements you see on the stage but also the scripts and transitions that make up the action.

4] Choose Window › Cast › Main to open the Main cast in its own window. Then arrange the Internal and Main Cast windows side by side.

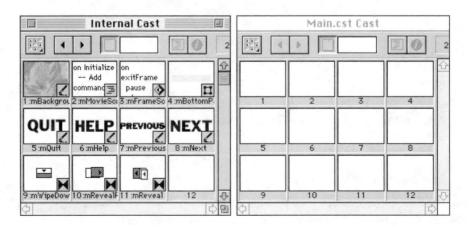

You will now move the contents of the Internal cast to the Main cast.

5] In the Internal cast, click cast member 1, Shift-click cast member 11 to select all the cast members in the Internal cast, and drag the cast members to the Main Cast window.

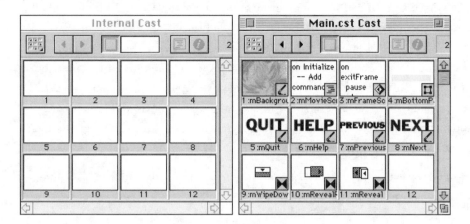

Make sure your mouse pointer is over cast member 1 in the Main Cast window when you release the mouse button. If the cast members drop into the Main Cast window in another position, drag them into the position shown here. Repositioning the cast members will make it easier for you to compare your work with the illustrations shown later in this lesson.

6] In the score, click channel 1 and note that the sprite toolbar now indicates that the cast member is stored in the Main cast.

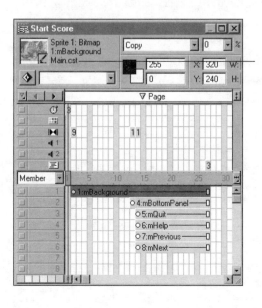

THE PREVIEW NOW SHOWS
THAT THE SELECTED SPRITE
IS STORED IN THE MAIN CAST

If you click the sprites one by one, you'll see that the score now consists entirely of cast members currently stored in the Main cast.

7] Choose File › Save All. When Director asks you to choose a location for the Main cast, select your Projects folder (not the new Work folder) and then click OK.

Your movie consists of two separate files now: the movie file, Catalog.dir in the Work folder, and the linked external cast, Main.cst in the Projects folder. Choosing Save All ensures that changes you made to both files are saved. Because this is the first time you've saved since creating the Main cast, Director wants you to confirm where the cast should be stored before it creates the actual physical file on your computer's hard drive. Be sure to save the cast in your Projects folder. Your movie will remember the location where you saved the cast, and your movie will look for the cast in that location whenever it runs in the future.

You will now see how this external cast setup allows you to update the movie's content without actually changing the movie file.

8] Choose File › New › Movie (Windows Ctrl+N, Macintosh Command+N).

To prove the point of the following exercise, you don't want the Catalog.dir movie to be active during the next steps, because you want to see how you can edit an external cast separately from the movie to which it is linked. Creating a new, blank file closes the Catalog.dir movie (the File > Close command is not available for a movie file; to stop using a movie file, you create a new file, open another file, or quit Director).

9] On your computer's desktop, make a copy of the Main.cst file and place it in your Work folder. Leave the original Main.cst file in your Projects folder.

You're going to edit the version of Main.cst in your Projects folder. The copy in the Work folder is a backup you will need to restore the cast to its correct form later.

10] Back in Director, choose File › Open to display the Open dialog box. Select the Main.cst file in the Projects folder and click Open.

Notice that the window's background is a darker gray than usual, which is Director's way of reminding you that the cast is not linked to the current movie.

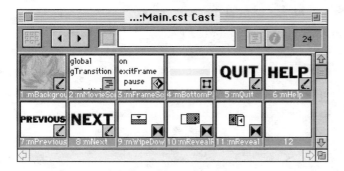

You're going to edit the Main cast file separately from the movie it's attached to.

11] Double-click cast member 1, the background graphic, to open it in the Paint window. Make any change you like.

You're going to discard this changed version of the Main cast later, so have fun. In the illustration shown here, a circle with a line drawn through it was added to the graphic.

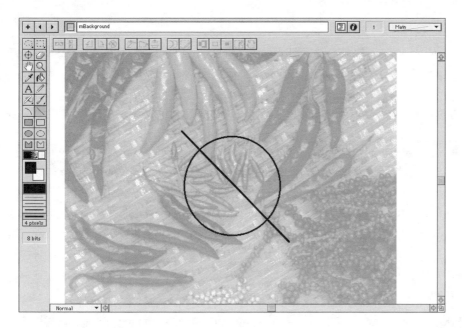

12] Choose File › Save and then close the Main Cast window.

You need to save the changes so that when you open the Catalog.dir movie, those changes will be available to it.

13] Open and play your Catalog.dir movie from the Work folder.

Now you see the revised version of the background graphic.

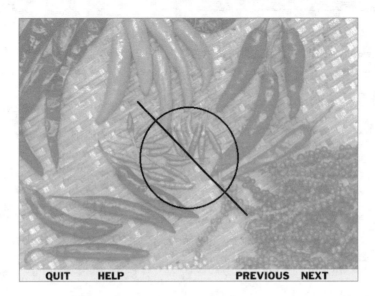

By editing the Main cast separately from the movie, you have actually changed the movie's content. Now you want to restore the correct version of the background graphic.

14] Close the Catalog movie file again by choosing File › New.

15] On your computer's desktop, remove the edited version of Main.cst from your Projects folder. Then drag your backup copy of Main.cst from your Work folder into your Projects folder.

To be on the safe side, don't delete the unneeded version of Main.cst until you're sure you've switched the two versions of the casts correctly.

16] Open and play your Catalog.dir movie again.

The original background graphic is now back in place.

From this exercise you see how you can change the movie's background graphic without actually changing the movie file itself. You merely edited the graphic in the movie's linked, external cast, and the movie automatically reflected those changes the next time it ran. With all the graphics, scripts, and transitions stored in an external cast, you can change the entire look and feel of the movie just by editing the cast members.

Your movie contains the basic layout for the electronic catalog: a generic background and navigation buttons. Now it's time to start adding the elements you need for the pages in the catalog.

LINKING AN EXISTING EXTERNAL CAST TO A MOVIE

The assets for the three pages of your pepper catalog are stored in the three cast files you copied to your Projects folder earlier. Although the movie's assets are stored externally, the movie's score remains in the movie file itself. Therefore, your strategy for external casts is to set up your movie so that a single section of the score works equally well with all the external casts linked to the movie. For this project, you can think of the movie score as a template for all the external casts. To create the template section of the score, you will use the elements from one of those casts. Then, using Lingo, you can link the other casts as needed.

In this task you will link one of the pepper casts to the movie. To get started, you'll take a look at all the casts to see what they have in common.

1] Choose File › Open and open the FreshPpr.cst cast file. Then open the DriedPpr.cst and PeprCorn.cst files and arrange all three so you can compare their contents.
Notice that all three casts contain similar elements in the same order: background, heading, Quit button graphic, Help button graphic, Previous button graphic, Next button graphic, and a picture. Inspect the cast properties of corresponding elements in each cast: Select a cast member and click the Info button at the top of the Cast window and then look at the properties for the corresponding elements in the other two casts. Although the look of the corresponding elements in each cast is different, the dimensions are identical. For example, the headings (cast member 2) in all three casts are exactly 570 by 97 pixels.

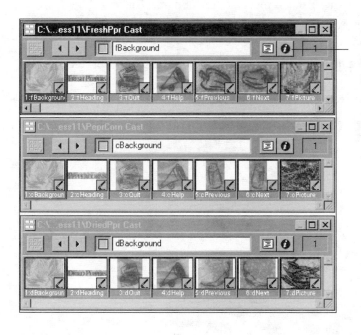

TO SEE THE PROPERTIES OF THE SELECTED CAST MEMBER, CLICK HERE

Director has darkened the gray window background to show that these are external casts that are not linked to the movie that is currently open.

2] Close the FreshPpr.cst, DriedPpr.cst, and PeprCorn.cst Cast windows without saving any changes.

You will now link the FreshPpr cast to your movie. It doesn't matter which cast you choose to link. The FreshPpr cast was chosen because it will also be the first page of the catalog, but this choice is not required for the project to work.

3] Choose Modify › Movie Casts to open the Movie Casts dialog box (Windows Ctrl+Shift+D, Macintosh Command+Shift+D).

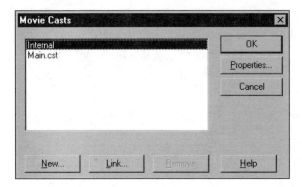

The dialog box shows the Internal cast that all Director movies have and the Main cast you created in the previous task.

4] Click Link to display a dialog box where you can choose a cast file. Select FreshPpr.cst.

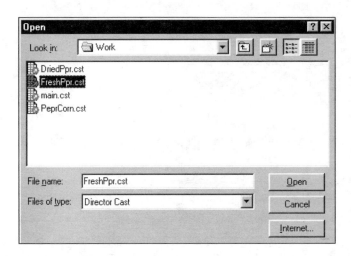

5] Click Open.

The Movie Casts dialog box now shows the FreshPpr cast added to the bottom of the list.

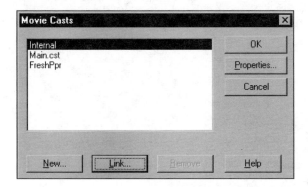

As you will learn in more detail later, Lingo uses numbers to keep track of casts; these numbers correspond to the casts' positions in the Movie Casts dialog box. The Internal cast is always listed first, and it is cast 1. The external casts are listed next, in the order in which you linked them to the movie. Thus, the Main cast is number 2, and the FreshPpr cast is number 3. Remember that FreshPpr is cast 3, because you will use this number in a later task.

6] Click OK to close the Movie Casts dialog box.

7] Save your work.

With the FreshPpr cast now linked to your movie, you're ready to start laying out the elements of your electronic catalog.

CREATING A TEMPLATE LAYOUT IN THE SCORE

Your next step is to create a basic layout—a **template**—for the page elements: a background, a headline, a picture of the peppers, and navigation buttons. You will create only a single section of the score using the FreshPpr cast.

1] Open the score and the Main cast. Click frame 27 to see all the basic elements that are already in place for you.

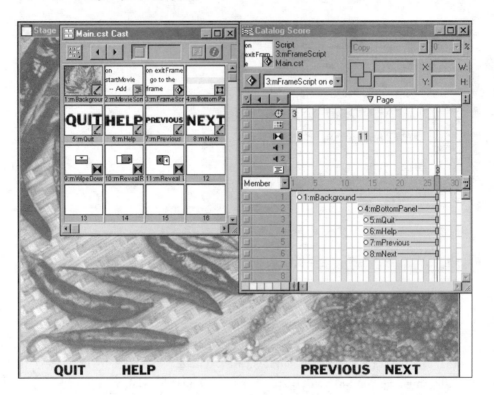

This cast includes a background image (cast member 1) covering the entire stage, a navigation panel that appears along the bottom of the page (cast member 4), and four button labels: Quit (cast member 5), Help (cast member 6), Previous (cast member 7), and Next (cast member 8). The Main cast contains a movie script (in cast member 2), which you will need later; it also contains the frame script (cast member 3) for frame 27, which contains an *exitFrame* handler with a *go to the frame* command to keep the playback head looping in this frame.

2] In the score, adjust the duration of the background sprite in channel 1 so it ends at frame 11 instead of frame 27.

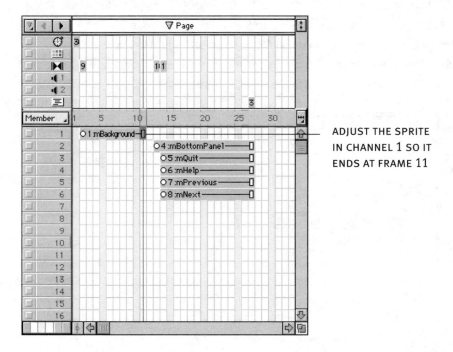

ADJUST THE SPRITE IN CHANNEL 1 SO IT ENDS AT FRAME 11

This change makes room for a background that will come from the FreshPpr cast.

3] Open the FreshPpr cast.

4] Click channel 1, frame 12. In the FreshPpr cast, click cast member 1 (fBackground) and choose Modify › Cast to Time.

This command centers the background graphic from the FreshPpr cast on the stage.

5] If necessary, adjust the duration of the fBackground sprite so it ends in frame 27.

Now you have a background in frames 2 through 11 that comes from the Main cast and a background in frames 12 through 27 that comes from the FreshPpr cast. In this case, the background graphics are identical, so users will not notice any difference as the playback head moves from one background to the next. However, this score structure gives you the flexibility to change the background for individual pages in the catalog if you so desire.

Notice that the background in the Main cast is named mBackground (for Main Background), and the background in the FreshPpr cast is named fBackground (for FreshPpr Background). Also notice the same naming convention has been applied to the other cast members. This convention helps you quickly identify where a cast member came from just by looking at its name in the score.

6] Drag the Fresh Peppers heading (cast member 2) to the score and place it in channel 7, frame 15. If necessary, adjust its duration to span frames 15 through 27.

Make sure to drag the cast member into the score, not onto the stage. The cast member has been set up so that dragging it into the score automatically positions it correctly. (This positioning works because of the cast member's registration point, which you will learn about in a task later in this lesson.)

Why start at frame 15? Notice in the score that the elements are appearing on the stage in phases: first the background in frame 12, then the navigation panel in frame

13, and then the button labels in frame 14. The elements that make up each page of the pepper catalog will appear last, at frame 15. Your score should look like this:

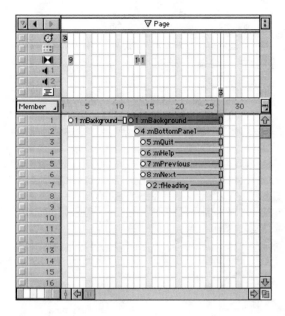

tip *If you don't have the headline positioned correctly, you can position it precisely by selecting the sprite on the stage and pressing Shift+Ctrl+I (Windows) or Shift+Command+I (Macintosh) to open the Sprite Properties dialog box. Type 22 for the Left coordinate and 13 for the Top coordinate of the sprite and click OK.*

As you saw when you examined the casts earlier, all the corresponding elements are exactly the same size. Later, using Lingo, you will switch the elements from the FreshPpr cast with elements from the DriedPpr and PeprCorn casts. The precise alignment ensures that, when the new cast members appear on the stage, there will be no screen jumping.

7] Drag the rest of the elements from the FreshPpr cast into the score, starting at frame 15 and extending to frame 27:

Channel 8: cast member 7, fPicture

Channel 9: cast member 3, fQuit

Channel 10: cast member 4, fHelp

Channel 11: cast member 5, fPrevious

Channel 12: cast member 6, fNext

581

Again, make sure to drag the cast members into the score, not onto the stage. The cast members have been set up so that dragging them into the score automatically positions them correctly.

tip *If you don't have the cast members positioned so that they blend in with the background, you can position them precisely using the Sprite Properties dialog box, as explained in the tip for step 6. Use the following top and left coordinates: channel 8, fPicture (165, 115); channel 9, fQuit (42, 378); channel 10, fHelp (136, 379); channel 11, fPrevious (414, 383); and channel 12, fNext (512, 384).*

When you're finished, the stage and score should look like this:

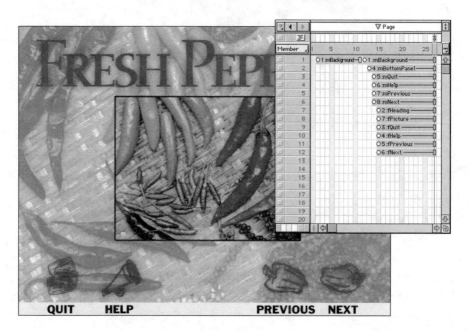

8] Save your work. Then rewind and play the movie.
Watch the playback head. You now see the elements from the FreshPpr cast appear on the stage at frame 15.

So far, so good: You have a basic layout that works well for the elements stored in the FreshPpr external cast. If you had some way to replace those elements with the corresponding elements from the DriedPpr or PeprCorn cast, the new elements would drop right into place, because as you saw, they are stored in the same slots within their cast and are the same size as their cousins in the FreshPpr cast. This is a job for Lingo!

USING LINGO TO SWITCH CASTS

As the playback head encounters a sprite in the score, the sprite's properties tell Director which cast member the sprite represents, where to display the sprite on the stage, and so on. One of those sprite properties is the cast where the cast member is stored—for example, the Internal cast or, as in this project, the Main or FreshPpr external cast.

Each cast is identified by a number that corresponds to the order in which the cast is listed in the Movie Casts dialog box (Modify > Movie > Cast). As you saw in a previous task, the FreshPpr cast is cast 3; it appears third in the list in the Movie Casts dialog box. To switch casts, all you need to do is tell Director that cast 3 should be some other file. You can do this using the property *castlib (whichCast).filename*, where *whichCast* is the number or name of the cast. (The keyword *castlib* stands for **cast library**, which is another term for cast. The tasks in this lesson only use the term *cast*, not *cast library*, but the meaning is the same. The correct Lingo term, however, is *castlib*.)

You will see how cast switching works using the Message window. Then you will use what you learn to create a simple button to switch casts.

1] Click frame 27.

This is one of the frames where you see all the elements on the stage.

2] In the Message window, type *put Sprite (7).castLibNum* and press Enter (Windows) or Return (Macintosh).

The message window should look like this:

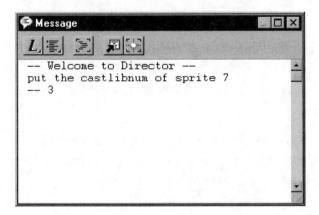

The *Sprite(whichSprite).castLibNum* property returns the number of the cast where a sprite is stored. Sprite 7 (that is, the sprite in channel 7) is the Heading cast member in the FreshPpr cast, so Director returns 3, the number of the FreshPpr cast. This demonstrates that cast assignment is part of a sprite's properties: Sprite 7 comes from cast 3.

3] Type *put the filename of castlib 3* and press Enter (Windows) or Return (Macintosh).

The Message window should look like this:

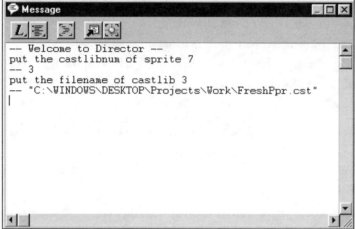

Director returns the path of the FreshPpr cast; the path you see on your computer may be different. This demonstrates that a cast number is associated with a specific file name, which implies that you can assign a new file name to a cast. You'll do that now.

4] Type *set the filename of castlib 3 = "DriedPpr.cst"* and press Enter (Windows) or Return (Macintosh).

The stage is updated with new cast members from the DriedPpr cast. (If the stage isn't updated, try entering an *updateStage* command.)

When you entered the *put castLib (3).fileName* command in the Message window, Director returned the complete path of the cast file. However, as long as the cast file is in the same folder as its associated movie, you need only give the file name when setting the *castLib(whichCast).fileName* property.

Now you'll use what you've learned to set up your movie for multiple casts and to create a button that switches casts.

5] Close the Message window and open the Main cast.

6] Double-click cast member 2 (mMovieScript) to display the Script window. Replace the comment in the *startMovie* handler with the lines shown here in bold and then close the Script window.

```
on startMovie
   castlib (3).filename = "FreshPpr.cst"
                     --Link the FreshPpr cast to the movie as cast number 3.
end
```

This movie script was already set up for you in the prebuilt file. Delete the existing comment before adding the new line.

The *castlib (3).filename* command tells the *startMovie* handler to always reset the file name of the external cast to its default setting, FreshPpr.cst, which is cast 3. From now on, you will be using Lingo to change the file assigned to cast 3. Depending on where you stop a movie while testing, the file assigned to cast 3 may be any of the three pepper casts. It's a good idea to make sure that the movie always starts with the proper default setting.

7] In the score, click frame 15.

8] Open the tool palette (Windows Ctrl+7, Macintosh Command+7), select the Unfilled Rectangle tool, and select a line width of 0.

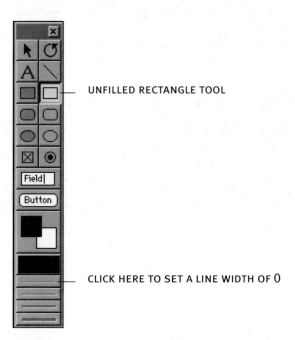

UNFILLED RECTANGLE TOOL

CLICK HERE TO SET A LINE WIDTH OF 0

You're going to create a button by drawing an unfilled, borderless rectangle. You must be sure, however, that the cast member is created in the correct cast.

585

9] Click the next open position in the Main cast (which should be cast member 12).
When using multiple casts, remember that Director places new cast members in the first position available in the current cast, so you must first always make sure that the cast where you want to store new cast members is currently active. One way to do this is to close all Cast windows except the one that contains the cast you want to work with. Here, be careful to create the new cast member in position number 12 as well, so your project will match the illustrations in this book.

10] Draw a box around the Next button graphic and the word *NEXT* in the lower-right corner of the stage.

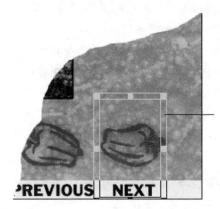

DRAW A BORDERLESS BOX AROUND
THE GRAPHIC AND THE TYPE

An unfilled, borderless rectangle is an effective way to create a button that encompasses several sprites—in this case, the button graphic and the button text.

11] In the Main cast, name the rectangle sprite *mBtn-Next* so that it will be easy to identify later.
The lowercase *m* follows the convention of identifying the cast (Main) in which the cast member is stored. Naming cast members is a good idea in general. When you have selected either Name or Number:Name for the Label setting in the Cast Window Preferences dialog box (File > Preferences > Cast), the cast member name appears in the score, making it easier for you to understand how a movie is constructed. In this case, naming the cast member will also make it easier for you to follow later tasks.

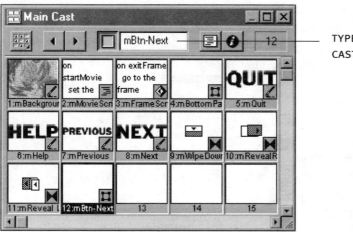

TYPE A NAME FOR THE
CAST MEMBER HERE

12] In the score, adjust the rectangle sprite so it spans frames 15 through 27.

When you drew the rectangle, Director added its sprite in the next available channel (channel 13 in this case). Your score should now look like this:

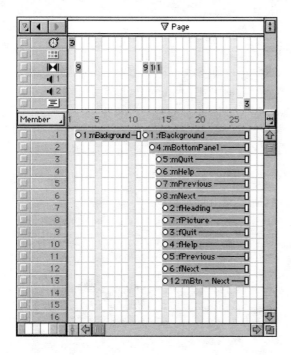

13] Click the new rectangle cast member (cast member 12) in the Main cast and then click the Script button to display the Script window. Revise the *mouseUp* script (which Director started for you) as shown here in bold:

```
on mouseUp
  castLib (3).fileName = "DriedPpr.cst"
end
```

This is the script for the Next button you created in the previous steps. You are creating a cast member script because you always want the Next button to do the same thing: display the next page of the catalog.

The *castLib (3).fileName* command tells Director to use elements from the DriedPpr cast instead of the FreshPpr cast. For the moment, your are hard-coding the command: that is, you are typing a specific cast's file name rather than using a variable. In later tasks you will substitute a variable to make the script more flexible.

14] Close the Script window. Rewind and play the movie. Click the Next button.
You see the cast members from the DriedPpr cast!

15] Stop the movie and save your work.
At this point, your movie is set up to take advantage of multiple casts, and you know how to switch casts using Lingo. In the next tasks you will implement a flexible mechanism for moving back and forth through the pages of your catalog.

CONTROLLING NAVIGATION WITH AN *IF-THEN* OR *CASE* STRUCTURE
Imagine your electronic catalog as a linear sequence of pages:

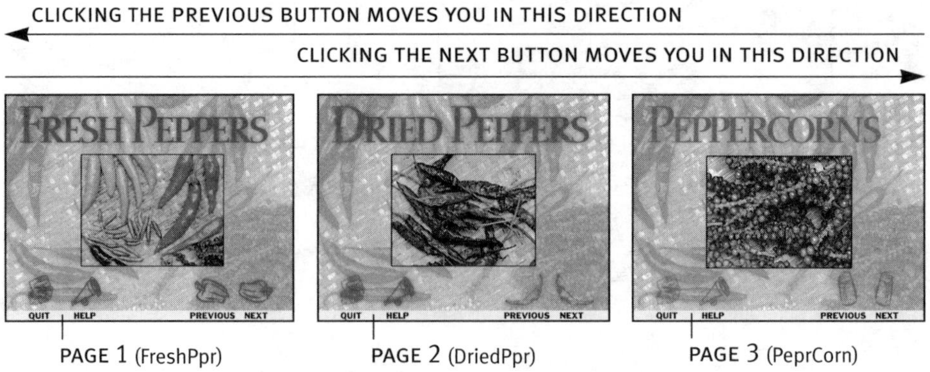

CLICKING THE PREVIOUS BUTTON MOVES YOU IN THIS DIRECTION

CLICKING THE NEXT BUTTON MOVES YOU IN THIS DIRECTION

PAGE 1 (FreshPpr)   PAGE 2 (DriedPpr)   PAGE 3 (PeprCorn)

Clearly, the Next button can't remain hard-coded as you implemented it in the previous task. How, then, do you ensure that the Next button displays the right page?

When planning your Lingo scripts, it helps to begin by describing your goal in general terms, without worrying about the exact Lingo commands needed to achieve that goal. In this project,

• Clicking the Next button displays the next page in the sequence.

• Clicking the Previous button displays the previous page in the sequence.

• At the first page in the sequence, clicking the Previous button displays the last page in the sequence (that is, at page 1, clicking Previous displays page 3).

• At the last page in the sequence, clicking the Next button displays the first page in the sequence (that is, at page 3, clicking Next displays page 1).

Reading this description, you might notice that, for every page, there is a clearly defined next and previous page. That predictability suggests an *if-then* structure: If the user is at page 2, then a click on the Next button displays page 3; if the user is at page 1, then a click on the Previous button displays page 3; and so on.

In Lesson 22 you learned about the *case* statement, which provides a more efficient way to handle multiple *if* conditions, such as those in this project. Here's how you might create the script for the Next button with a *case* statement:

```
on mouseUp
  case (castlib (3).filename) of
    "FreshPpr.cst":
      castlib (3).filename = "DriedPpr.cst"
    "DriedPpr.cst":
      castlib (3).filename = "PeprCorn.cst"
    "PeprCorn.cst":
      castlib (3).filename = "FreshPpr.cst"
  end case
end
```

The *case* statement evaluates which cast is currently linked to the movie as cast 3 (as determined by the *castlib (3).filename* property). For every possible cast, it specifies the cast that represents the next page in the catalog.

In a project such as this, which consists of just three cast files, this *mouseUp* handler with the *case* statement would work just fine—but what if the electronic catalog had 10 pages instead? How about 100 pages, or 1,000? What if you wanted to rearrange the pages in the catalog? Would you really want to do all that time-consuming and error-prone typing? Of course not.

The solution to this design challenge is to use one of Lingo's most powerful tools: lists.

CREATING A NAVIGATION LIST

Until now, you have used variables to hold a single value. For example, the following command assigns a single value to a variable called *page*:

    page = "FreshPpr.cst"

If you set the value of the *page* variable again, like this,

    page = "DriedPpr.cst"

the initial value of *page*, "FreshPpr.cst", is lost because the value "DriedPpr.cst" takes its place. A variable such as this can hold only one value at a time.

A **list** is a variable that can contain multiple values at once. The list of values is enclosed by brackets, and each value is separated by a comma. For example, the following command assigns three values to a list variable called *pageList*:

    pageList = ["FreshPpr.cst","DriedPpr.cst","PeprCorn.cst"]

Each value in a list is an **item**, and each item is identified by its order within the list. The *pageList* variable has three items: "FreshPpr.cst" is item 1 (because it is first), "DriedPpr.cst" is item 2, and "PeprCorn.cst" is item 3.

The quotation marks around the items in the *pageList* list variable tell Director that these items are **strings** of text. A string is any series of characters—letters, numbers, spaces, and punctuation—that is treated simply as text. In Lingo, all file names are handled as strings.

A list can store many types of data, including strings, numbers, and variables. Here are some examples; the comments explain what type of data each list contains:

    names = ["Joan","Leslie","Chae","Howard"]
                        --This list stores strings of text. The quotation marks
                        --tell Director to treat the information as a string.
    ages = [31, 43, 29, 57]   --This list stores numbers.
    calculations = [departmentCode, EmployeeNo]
                        --This list stores variables. Because there are no
                        --quotation marks around the list items, Director treats
                        --them as variables rather than as strings.
    employeeData = ["Joan", 31, departmentCode, EmployeeNo]
                        --This list stores a variety of data types. The first item,
                        --"Joan", is a string. The second item, 31, is a number.
                        --The remaining two items are variables.

Director provides two types of lists, **linear lists** and **property lists**. The preceding examples are all linear lists, which are lists in which each item consists of a single value. In Lesson 25, you will learn about property lists, which are lists in which each item consists of two parts: a name (called a property) and a corresponding value. In this lesson, you will work with a linear list of text strings that holds the file names of the project's external casts.

Lingo provides several functions to help you work with the data stored in lists. For example, the *count* function counts the number of items in a list, the *getAt* function returns the value at a specific location in a list, and the *getPos* function finds the position of a value within a list. In this task you will use the Message window to learn about the Lingo functions you'll need to build a list that you can use to navigate within your electronic catalog.

1] Open the Message window. Type *put pageList* and press Enter (Windows) or Return (Macintosh).

Director returns <Void> because you have not yet initialized the *pageList* variable by assigning any values it.

2] Type *pageList = [ ]* and press Enter (Windows) or Return (Macintosh).

This command initializes *pageList* as a list variable that does not contain any items. You don't see anything because you have simply made the assignment; you have not told Director to display anything.

3] Type *put pageList* and press Enter (Windows) or Return (Macintosh).

Now Director returns [ ] to show that *pageList* is a list variable (as indicated by the brackets) that does not have any values stored in it.

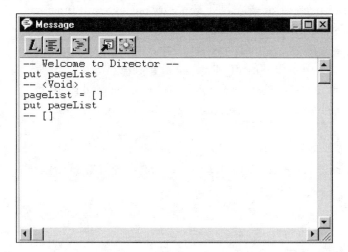

591

4] Type *pageList = ["FreshPpr.cst", "DriedPpr.cst", "PeprCorn.cst"]* **and press Enter (Windows) or Return (Macintosh).**

The quotation marks tell Director to treat the values as strings of text. Lingo scripts always treat file names as strings.

You have now placed values in the *pageList* list variable, but you still need to display those values.

5] Type *put pageList* **and press Enter (Windows) or Return (Macintosh).**

Director returns ["FreshPpr.cst", "DriedPpr.cst", "PeprCorn.cst"]. Your Message window should now look like this:

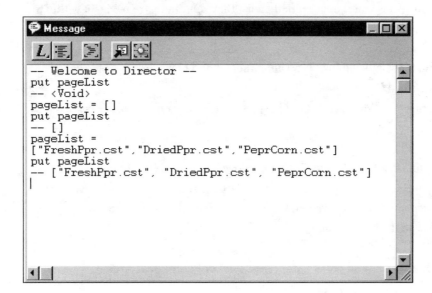

Now that you have your cast names stored in a list, you'll try out some list functions that you'll need later when you write your scripts.

6] Type *put count(pageList)* **and press Enter (Windows) or Return (Macintosh).**

The *count* function accepts the name of a list variable as an argument and then returns the number of items in the list. Director returns 3, the number of items in *pageList*.

7] Type *put getAt(pageList,2)* **and press Enter (Windows) or Return (Macintosh).**

The *getAt* function accepts the name of a list variable and a number as arguments. Director returns the item that is at the position specified by the number; in this case, you see "DriedPpr.cst" in the Message window because it is the item in position 2 within *pageList*.

8] Type *put getPos(pageList,"PeprCorn.cst")* and press Enter (Windows) or Return (Macintosh).

The *getPos* function accepts the name of a list variable and a value as arguments. It looks for the specified value within the list and, if it finds that value, returns the position of that item within the list. If *getPos* can't find the value in the list, it returns 0.

tip   *The* getPos *function performs a case-sensitive search for string values. If you had typed* getPos(pageList, "peprCorn.cst") *instead, Director would have returned 0, because it sees "peprCorn.cst" as a different string value from "PeprCorn.cst". This case sensitivity applies only to strings, not to the function name (*getPos *could be* getpos*) and to variable names (*pageList *could be* Pagelist*).*

In this case, Director returns 3, the position of the value "PeprCorn.cst" within *pageList*. Your Message window should look like this:

```
-- Welcome to Director --
put pageList
-- <Void>
pageList = []
put pageList
-- []
pageList =
["FreshPpr.cst","DriedPpr.cst","PeprCorn.cst"]
put pageList
-- ["FreshPpr.cst", "DriedPpr.cst", "PeprCorn.cst"]
put count(pageList)
-- 3
put getAt(pageList, 2)
-- "DriedPpr.cst"
put getPos(pageList, "PeprCorn.cst")
-- 3
```

Now you're ready to put these functions to use in a navigation script for the Next button.

WRITING A NAVIGATION SCRIPT

Now visualize the flow of pages in the electronic catalog as a list variable. You can use the file name of an external cast to represent the corresponding page in the electronic catalog.

For example, the dried peppers page needs to be page 2 in the catalog, and so its file name is item 2 in the navigation list. From the previous tasks, you know how to create a list of casts and how to determine the current cast and its position within the list. All you need now is to create a script that takes this information, decides which is the next page number to be displayed, and then switches to the cast that matches that page number.

Again, before worrying about the specific Lingo commands you need, it helps to first develop a general description of the logic the Next button uses when it is clicked. Sometimes it helps to sketch an informal flow chart. The following chart shows the logic for the Next button script, with sample data to illustrate what happens at each step.

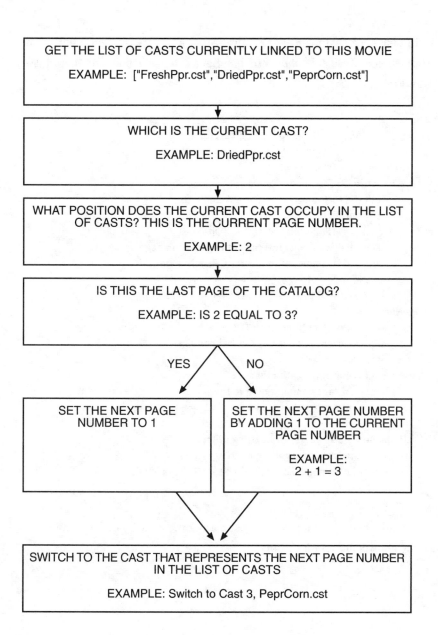

GET THE LIST OF CASTS CURRENTLY LINKED TO THIS MOVIE

EXAMPLE: ["FreshPpr.cst","DriedPpr.cst","PeprCorn.cst"]

WHICH IS THE CURRENT CAST?

EXAMPLE: DriedPpr.cst

WHAT POSITION DOES THE CURRENT CAST OCCUPY IN THE LIST OF CASTS? THIS IS THE CURRENT PAGE NUMBER.

EXAMPLE: 2

IS THIS THE LAST PAGE OF THE CATALOG?

EXAMPLE: IS 2 EQUAL TO 3?

YES   NO

SET THE NEXT PAGE NUMBER TO 1

SET THE NEXT PAGE NUMBER BY ADDING 1 TO THE CURRENT PAGE NUMBER

EXAMPLE:
2 + 1 = 3

SWITCH TO THE CAST THAT REPRESENTS THE NEXT PAGE NUMBER IN THE LIST OF CASTS

EXAMPLE: Switch to Cast 3, PeprCorn.cst

With this general outline for your script clearly in mind, filling in the Lingo commands is easy.

1] In the Main cast, click cast member 12 (mBtn-Next) and click the Script button to open the Script window. Revise the *mouseUp* handler as shown in bold and then close the Script window.

```
on mouseUp
   pageList = ["FreshPpr.cst","DriedPpr.cst","PeprCorn.cst"]
                  --Initialize pageList with the file names of the
                  --pepper casts.
   currentPage = castlib (3).filename
                  --Put the file name of the current cast into
                  --currentPage.
   currentPageNumber = getPos(pageList,currentPage)
                  --Find the position of the current page within pageList
                  --and put this number into currentPageNumber.
   if currentPageNumber = count(pageList) then
                  --If the current page is the last page in the catalog,
      nextPageNumber = 1
                  --reset nextPageNumber to 1.
   else           --If the current page is not the last page in
                  --the catalog,
      nextPageNumber = currentPageNumber + 1
                  --set nextPageNumber equal to the
                  --currentPageNumber plus 1.
   end if
   castlib (3).filename = getAt(pageList,nextPageNumber)
                  --Get the cast that is at the nextPageNumber
                  --position in pageList and switch cast 3 to that cast.
end
```

You can understand what this script does by comparing the actual Lingo commands with the informal flowchart you developed.

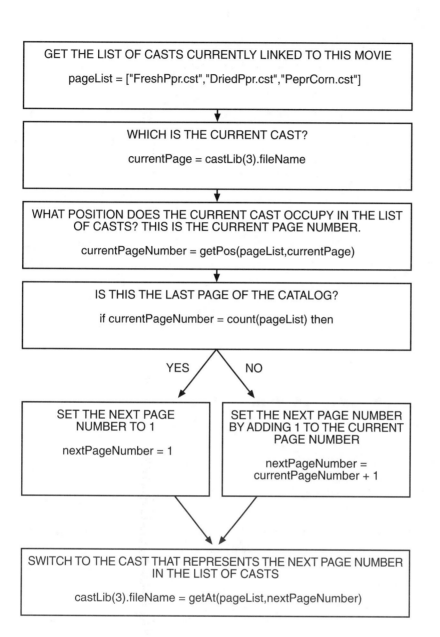

GET THE LIST OF CASTS CURRENTLY LINKED TO THIS MOVIE

pageList = ["FreshPpr.cst","DriedPpr.cst","PeprCorn.cst"]

WHICH IS THE CURRENT CAST?

currentPage = castLib(3).fileName

WHAT POSITION DOES THE CURRENT CAST OCCUPY IN THE LIST OF CASTS? THIS IS THE CURRENT PAGE NUMBER.

currentPageNumber = getPos(pageList,currentPage)

IS THIS THE LAST PAGE OF THE CATALOG?

if currentPageNumber = count(pageList) then

YES / NO

SET THE NEXT PAGE NUMBER TO 1

nextPageNumber = 1

SET THE NEXT PAGE NUMBER BY ADDING 1 TO THE CURRENT PAGE NUMBER

nextPageNumber = currentPageNumber + 1

SWITCH TO THE CAST THAT REPRESENTS THE NEXT PAGE NUMBER IN THE LIST OF CASTS

castLib(3).fileName = getAt(pageList,nextPageNumber)

The first three commands set up some variables to hold the information that the rest of the handler needs to work with. First the list of casts is stored in the list variable *pageList*. (Remember to type the file names exactly as you see them here. Later, you will use the *getPos* function on the *pageList* variable, and *getPos* will perform a case-sensitive search. Any difference in capitalization between the entries you type in *pageList* and the actual file names will cause your script to fail.) In the second command, *castlib (3).fileName,* the *fileName* property is used to get the file name of the currently displayed cast and to store that file name in the *currentPage* variable. Once you have the list of pages and the current page, you can use the *getPos* function to find the position of the current page within the list of pages, and you can store that number in the *currentPageNumber* variable.

The *if-then* structure is responsible for determining what page is displayed next and for setting the *nextPageNumber* variable accordingly. The *count* function returns the number of items in the *pageList* list variable. If that number (3 in this case) is equal to *currentPageNumber*, you know you're at the end of the list and you need to set *nextPageNumber* to 1 (that is, you want to display the first cast in the list). Otherwise, you set *nextPageNumber* by adding 1 to *currentPageNumber*.

Once the *if-then* structure has set the *nextPageNumber* variable, your script can use the *filename* property to switch to the cast that occupies the position equal to *nextPageNumber* in *pageList*.

2] Save your work, but don't play the movie yet.

If you try to test the Next button now, you'll find that it still doesn't work. That's because your script needs one more line to function properly.

DELETING A PORTION OF A STRING

The problem lies in the first three commands in the Next button script:

```
pageList = ["FreshPpr.cst","DriedPpr.cst","PeprCorn.cst"]
currentPage = castlib (3).filename
currentPageNumber = getPos(pageList,currentPage)
```

Recall from an earlier task that the *castlib (3).filename* property returns the entire path name of cast 3. On a Windows system, for example, on the first page of the catalog, the command

```
currentPage = castlib (3).filename
```

in the Next button script might set the *currentPage* variable to

```
"C:\Work\FreshPpr.cst"
```

Therefore, when Lingo substitutes the value in the *currentPage* variable in the following command, the results are something like this:

```
currentPageNumber = getPos(pageList, "C:\Work\FreshPpr.cst")
```

The value assigned to the *currentPageNumber* variable won't be accurate because the value "C:\WorkProjects\FreshPpr.cst" does not occur in the *pageList* list variable (when the *getPos* function can't find a value in the specified list, it returns 0). You need a way to delete the path information from the string returned by the *filename* property so that you are left with a string containing just the file name, "FreshPpr.cst". You have three Lingo tools at your service: the *the moviePath* property, which returns the current path of the movie file; the *length* function, which returns the number of characters in a string; and the *delete* command, which specifies a portion of a string variable to delete. In the following task, you will use the Message window to become familiar with these Lingo commands, and then you will use what you've learned to revise the script for the Next button.

note   *The following steps work only if you have stored the Catalog.dir file and the external cast files in the same folder. If you have not done so, you can read this task and the following "On Your Own" section for general information.*

1] Rewind and play the movie. When the movie pauses on the first page of the catalog, Fresh Peppers, stop the movie.

If you have been testing your movie, some other page may currently be displayed. This step ensures that the FreshPpr cast is the current cast, making it easier for you to follow the next steps.

2] In the Message window, type *currentPage = castLib (3).fileName* and press Enter (Windows) or Return (Macintosh).

This is the same command you used in the Next button script to determine which page of the catalog you are currently on. This command places the full path of the current cast (FreshPpr.cst) in the *currentPage* variable. You don't see the value of *currentPage* because you haven't asked Director to display it yet.

3] Type *put currentPage* and press Enter (Windows) or Return (Macintosh).

Director returns the full path of the cast that is currently displayed on the stage, surrounded in quotation marks to indicate that it is a string. Your Message window should look something like this:

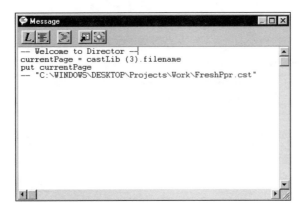

In this example, the full path is "C:\WINDOWS\DESKTOP\Projects\Work\FreshPpr.cst". The actual path name you see preceding the file name may be different, depending on where you stored the Catalog.dir and FreshPpr cast and the type of computer you're using. However, the final portion of the string should be the file name FreshPpr.cst.

4] Type *put the moviePath* and press Enter (Windows) or Return (Macintosh).

Director returns the path name where the movie is currently stored. Your Message window should look something like this:

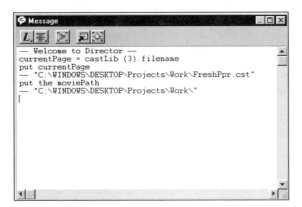

In this example, the full path is "C:\WINDOWS\DESKTOP\Projects\Work\". Again, the path name you see may vary, depending on where you stored your files and the type of computer you are using. Here's the important thing to note: Compare the value in the *currentPage* variable (as displayed in step 3) with the path name returned by Director in this step. You will see that the two are identical, except that the *currentPage* variable also contains the file name FreshPpr.cst at the end. Your goal is to delete the path name from the *currentPage* variable so that all you have left is FreshPpr.cst.

5] Type *put length(the moviePath)* and press Enter (Windows) or Return (Macintosh).
In this example, Director returns 33, which is the number of characters in the string containing the current path. Once again, the number you see may differ; it will match the number of characters in the path name on your computer. Knowing the length of the path name gives you all the information you need to delete the path name from the *currentPage* variable.

6] Type *delete char 1 to length(the moviePath) of currentPage* and press Enter (Windows) or Return (Macintosh).
This *delete* command tells Director to delete everything from character 1 to character 33 (the length of the path name, which you saw in the previous step) from the *currentPage* variable. This command makes the deletion, but you don't see anything because you have not told Director to display the value yet.

7] Type *put currentPage* and press Enter (Windows) or Return (Macintosh).
Director returns "FreshPpr.cst". Your Message window should look something like this:

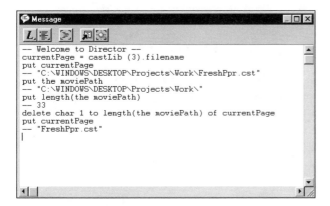

Although your path name information may be different, the value on the final line, "FreshPpr.cst", will be the same. As long as you always keep the movie file and cast files in the same folder (so they share the same path), these Lingo commands will work correctly.

You now know enough to revise the Next button script.

8] In the Main cast, click cast member 12 (mBtn - Next) and click the Script button to open the Script window. Revise the following lines of the cast member script as shown in bold then close the Script window.

```
on mouseUp
  pageList = ["FreshPpr.cst","DriedPpr.cst","PeprCorn.cst"]
                --Initialize pageList with the file names of the
                --pepper casts.
  currentPage = castlib (3).filename
                --Put the file name of the current cast into
                --currentPage.
  delete char 1 to length(the moviePath) of currentPage
                --Delete the path name from currentPage.
  currentPageNumber = getPos(pageList,currentPage)
                --Find the position of the current page within pageList
                --and put this number into currentPageNumber.
  if currentPageNumber = count(pageList) then
                --If the current page is the last page in the catalog,
    nextPageNumber = 1
                --reset nextPageNumber to 1.
  else          --If the current page is not the last page in
                --the catalog,
    nextPageNumber = currentPageNumber + 1
                --set nextPageNumber equal to the
                --currentPageNumber plus 1.
  end if
  castlib (3).filename = getAt(pageList,nextPageNumber)
                --Get the cast that is at the nextPageNumber
                --position in pageList and switch cast 3 to that cast.
end
```

This new line takes the contents of the *currentPage* variable, which has been assigned the full path name of cast 3, and deletes everything from character 1 up through the number of characters in the path name.

9] Rewind and play the movie. Click the Next button repeatedly to cycle through the pages.

It works! As you click the Next button, you see the pages in the order they are listed in the *pageList* list variable.

10] Stop the movie and save your work.

ON YOUR OWN

Create the Previous button. Store its cast member in position 13 of the Main cast, right after the Next button, and name it *mBtn-Previous*. Place its sprite in the score in channel 12, spanning frames 17 to 27. Your completed score should look like this:

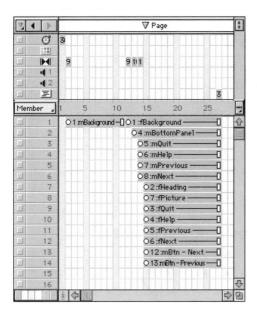

Also create the *mouseUp* cast member script for the Previous button. To start, copy the script for the Next button cast member and paste it into the script for the Previous button cast member. The script will need a few changes to work properly. Instead of checking whether you are currently on the last page in the catalog, you want Director to check whether you're on the first page. Also, you must set the cast to the previous position in the *pageList* list variable, instead of to the next position.

When you're done, compare your version of the cast member script for the Previous button with the one shown here. The changes you need to make to the script are shown in bold:

```
on mouseUp
  pageList = ["FreshPpr.cst","DriedPpr.cst","PeprCorn.cst"]
                --Initialize pageList with the file names of the pepper casts.
  currentPage = castlib (3).filename
                --Put the file name of the current cast into currentPage.
  delete char 1 to length(the moviePath) of currentPage
                --Delete the pathname from currentPage.
  currentPageNumber = getPos(pageList,currentPage)
                --Find the position of the current page within pageList
                --and put this number into currentPageNumber.
```

603

```
        if currentPageNumber = 1 then
                          --If the current page is the first page in the catalog,
             nextPageNumber = count(pageList)
                          --reset nextPageNumber to the last page of the catalog.
        else             --If the current page is not the last page in
                          --the catalog,
             nextPageNumber = currentPageNumber – 1
                          --set nextPageNumber equal to the
                          --currentPageNumber minus 1.
        end if
        castlib (3).filename = getAt(pageList,nextPageNumber)
                          --Get the cast that is at the nextPageNumber
                          --position in pageList and switch cast 3 to that cast.
    end
```

ALIGNING REGISTRATION POINTS

In Lesson 21, you learned how to switch cast members through Lingo using the *the memberNum* property of a sprite. In this lesson, you learned how to switch cast members by switching casts. In both Lesson 21 and this lesson, you learned that it is a good idea to make sure the cast members being switched are the same size, but Director does not require this. In fact, in other instances, it may not be possible or desirable for switched cast members to be exactly the same size. Imagine, for example, an animated character whose cast members shrink as it walks into the distance.

When you place the original cast member in the score, Director knows its position by its top and left coordinates. However, when you switch that cast member with another, Director places the new cast member on the stage so that its **registration point** matches the original cast member's registration point, not the original cast member's top and left coordinates. The registration point is a fixed point assigned to the cast member; the registration point can fall inside or outside the boundaries of the cast member. Thus, a cast member that takes the place of another cast member of exactly the same size still may not be aligned properly on the stage if the two cast members' registration points do not match. Such a misalignment causes screen jumping, in which a portion of the screen appears to move as the movie plays.

By default, a registration point is in the middle of the cast member, but you can change the registration point; sometimes registration points are changed inadvertently when you edit cast members as well.

In this task you will move the registration point of a cast member so you can learn to recognize and fix screen jumping if it ever occurs in one of your projects. Save your work before following the steps. This task is only an exercise, and you won't want to save any of the work you do here.

1] Open the FreshPpr cast. Then choose File › Open and open the PeprCorn.cst cast file.

You must open the PeprCorn cast from the File menu because it is not linked to the current movie.

2] Double-click the picture in cast member 7 of the FreshPpr cast to open it in the Paint window.

3] Click the Registration tool.

After you click the registration tool, two perpendicular dotted lines appear on the graphic. The intersection of these lines is the cast member's registration point. Here it's in the center of the cast member.

REGISTRATION TOOL

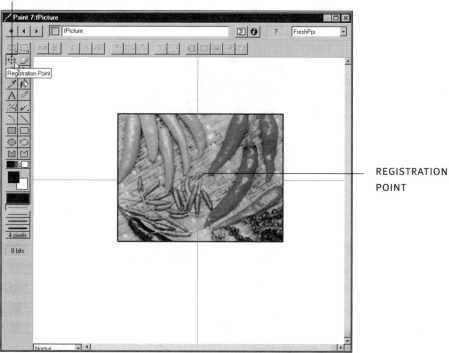

REGISTRATION
POINT

Can you guess where the registration point is set on the corresponding graphic in the PeprCorn cast?

4] Close the Paint window and double-click the picture in cast member 7 of the PeprCorn cast to open it in the Paint window.

The registration point here is also at the center of the graphic, which is why the graphics were aligned when they were switched by clicking the Next and Previous buttons.

You can move the registration point by using the Registration tool to click anywhere inside or outside the graphic. Try it.

5] Click the upper-left corner of the peppercorn picture to move the registration point.

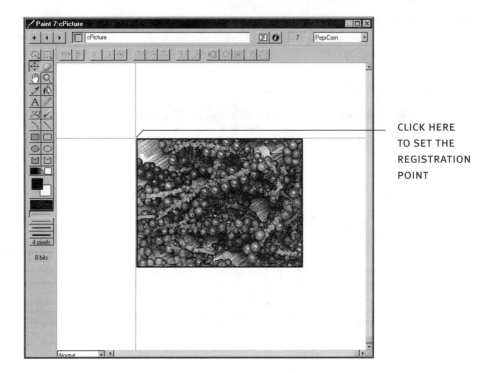

CLICK HERE
TO SET THE
REGISTRATION
POINT

Now you have two graphics in two different casts, each with a different registration point. When you play the movie, the graphics will not be aligned. See for yourself.

6] Play the movie and click the Next button until you see the Peppercorns page.

Now the picture in the Peppercorns page is not aligned correctly.

The registration point of the peppercorn picture is now in its upper-left corner. Director placed this registration point on top of the registration point of the Fresh Pepper picture, which was in the center of the picture. The misalignment here is obvious, but sometimes it may be a shift of only a few pixels. If you have trouble aligning graphics from multiple casts, you now know one avenue of investigation— registration points.

Now you will see how to fix the registration point problem.

7] Stop the movie.

8] In the Paint window with the peppercorn picture, double-click the Registration tool.

Double-clicking the Registration tool is the quickest, surest way to set the registration point to the center of the graphic.

DOUBLE-CLICK THE REGISTRATION TOOL TO CENTER THE REGISTRATION POINT

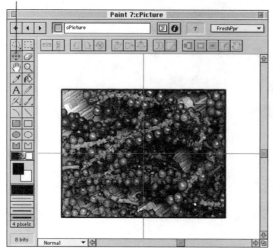

You can also try placing the point at the center by clicking the Registration tool on the graphic where you think its center is, but this method is inexact.

9] Close the Paint window.

10] Test the movie.

Everything works and is now once again aligned correctly.

Discard any changes you made to the movie during this task; it was only an exercise to help you understand registration points.

ON YOUR OWN

From a very simple score, you have created a project that can be endlessly updated. You can add any number of additional pages (or casts) just by placing them in the same folder with your projector and editing the *pageList* variables in the cast member scripts of the Next and Previous buttons (which are also stored in an external cast: Main). For more practice, here are some improvements you can make:

• Hard-coding the *pageList* variable in two places (the Next and Previous buttons) makes your project harder to update. In the *startMovie* handler, initialize a global *gPageList* variable that both the Next and Previous button scripts can use.

- Use another global variable, *gCurrentPage*, to track the current page number.

- Add transitions for visual appeal.

- Implement the Quit button using the *halt* command, as you did in Lesson 18.

The Catalog2.dir file in the Complete folder demonstrates one way to enhance your electronic catalog. Especially note the way global variables were used to simplify the scripting for the Next and Previous buttons.

WHAT YOU HAVE LEARNED

In this lesson you have:

- Created a new external cast and moved project assets to it [page 566]

- Linked an existing external cast to a movie [page 575]

- Set up the score to work with multiple casts [page 578]

- Used the *filename* property of casts to switch casts with Lingo [page 583]

- Used a list with the *getAt* and *getPos* functions to manage navigation [page 590]

- Used the *delete* command to delete a portion of a string variable [page 598]

- Used the *length* function to find the number of characters in a string variable [page 601]

- Experimented with aligning sprites using registration points [page 604]

lists

databases and

LESSON 25

Databases—electronic files used to store large amounts of information—can be used to create interactive movies as well as the mailing lists and other items usually associated with them. The Director movie you will work with in this lesson, for example, depends on a database that keeps track of the cast member name associated with each user choice.

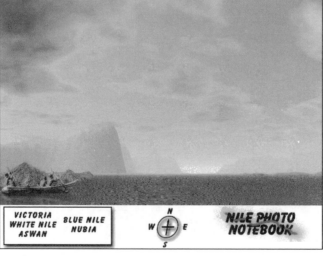

The Nile Photo Notebook is an electronic photo album featuring graphics of the Nile River. The user can click one of five locations and one of four directions (N, S, E, and W) for each location to pick a view. To determine what view to display on the stage, the movie depends on a small database that contains the names of the cast members corresponding to each view.

Nile: Passage to Egypt *was developed by Human Code for Discovery Channel Multimedia. Additional interface artwork and programming for Macromedia training was produced by Mark Castle, Castle Productions.*

To use Director as a database, you need to know how to build a database in a form Director can read. One solution is to use a property list, a special type of Lingo variable available for just that purpose. This lesson introduces you to property list variables. You will learn how to create a list by typing it in a field cast member, and you will then build a script that reads that list into a list variable.

WHAT YOU WILL LEARN

In this lesson you will:

• Create fields to store data in lists so it can be easily retrieved

• Set and retrieve values from a property list

• Watch variables update in the Watcher window

• Step through a handler using the Debugger

APPROXIMATE TIME

It should take about 2 hours to complete this lesson.

LESSON FILES

Media Files:

None

Starting Files:

Lesson25\Start\Start1.dir
Lesson25\Start\Start2.dir

Completed Project:

Lesson25\Complete\Nile.dir

LOOKING AT THE FINISHED MOVIE

In this lesson and in Lesson 26, you will be creating an electronic photo album of the Nile River. You will start with a prebuilt file that contains the graphics and some of the handlers you will need. Before you begin your work on this project, look at the finished movie to see how it works.

1] Open and play the finished version of the project, Nile2.dir, in the Complete folder within the Lesson26 folder.

Be sure you open the finished project in the Lesson26 folder, not the Lesson25 folder. The Complete folder in Lesson25 contains the part of the movie you will create in this lesson, not the completed project, and script error messages will appear if you play it and click the buttons. You will complete this project in Lesson 26.

At the bottom of the stage you see five locations: Victoria, White Nile, Aswan, Blue Nile, and Nubia. For each location, you can view four directions: north, south, east, and west.

2] Click a location name to display a picture of that location. Then click a direction on the compass to display a specific view of that location.

The view changes according to the location name and direction you choose.

FIRST CHOOSE THE LOCATION   THEN CHOOSE A COMPASS POINT TO
YOU WANT TO EXPLORE   SEE A SPECIFIC VIEW OF THAT LOCATION

SETTING UP FOR THIS LESSON

Now you are ready to start the project in this lesson. First you'll open the prebuilt file that contains the beginnings of the Nile photo album, and then you'll write a frame script that will pause the playback head.

1] Open Start1.dir in the Lesson25 folder and save it as *Nile.dir* in your Projects folder.

2] Open the Score window (Windows Ctrl+4, Macintosh Command+4).

As you can see, the cast members for the main menu are already on the stage. You will create this movie's action by using Lingo to control the sprites, so the duration of the sprites in the score is relatively unimportant here. The 18-frame duration was chosen here only because it is just long enough to ensure that all the cast member names are fully visible in the score channels.

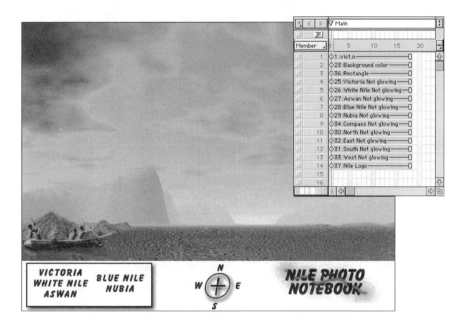

3] Double-click the behavior channel, frame 18, and create the following script:

```
on exitFrame
  go to the frame
end
```

This frame script will pause the playback head at frame 18, and Director will wait for users to click objects on the screen.

4] Open the Cast window (Windows Ctrl+3, Macintosh Command+3).

Notice that the Cast window already contains cast member scripts for most of the location names and direction letters. The script icon in the lower-left corner of the cast member tells you this (for example, see cast members 25 and 26). These scripts were created for you to give you a jump-start on the project.

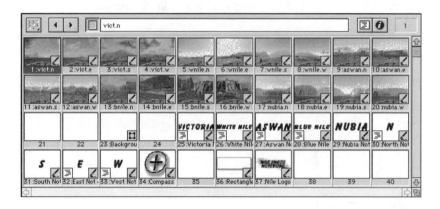

5] Select cast member 25 and then click the Cast Member Script button.

Most of the location names have prebuilt handlers, which call the *SetPlace* handler when the sprite is clicked on the stage. You will build the *SetPlace* handler in a later task.

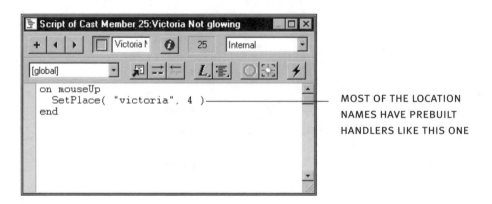

MOST OF THE LOCATION NAMES HAVE PREBUILT HANDLERS LIKE THIS ONE

6] Select cast member 30 (North Not glowing) and then click the Script button to open the Script window.

Most of the compass directions have cast member scripts with prebuilt handlers, which call the *SetDirection* handler when the sprite is clicked on the stage. You will build the *SetDirection* handler in a later task.

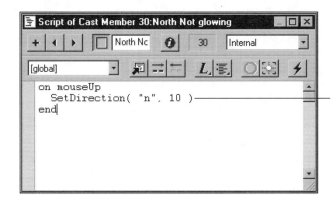

```
on mouseUp
   SetDirection( "n", 10 )
end
```

MOST OF THE COMPASS
DIRECTION LETTERS HAVE
CAST MEMBER SCRIPTS
WITH PREBUILT HANDLERS
LIKE THIS ONE

Don't play the movie yet. At this point, only part of the movie is complete. If you play the movie and click the location names or a direction, a script error message will appear because the handlers called by the cast member scripts haven't been written. You will write these handlers as part of this project.

USING A FIELD CAST MEMBER

Database programs are designed to make it easy to enter, sort, and retrieve information. They do this by using **fields** to hold each type of information. In a mailing list database, for example, you may have fields for first name, last name, street address, city, state, and zip code. Because each type of information is saved as a separate piece of data, each element can be dealt with individually.

Every database program has its own way of storing information, but most can save information in a common format called **comma-delimited text**, which saves database information in a plain text file with fields separated by commas. When you create a list database in a Director movie, you will use this format. In this task, you will quickly create a small database file for use in this project.

As part of this project, you will use text in a field cast member to create a list of graphics, and you will use this list to retrieve and display graphics on demand. This technique has much in common with the list technique you learned in Lesson 24, in which you used a simpler linear list to change the external cast linked to a movie. You use field cast members instead of text cast members because you can use Lingo to read or manipulate the text in a field cast member while a movie is playing.

tip   *Consider using field cast members instead of text cast members for text in Shockwave movies. Although text cast members usually look best on the stage, they also require more disk space than field cast members—and thus more time to download over the Internet.*

1] Choose Window › Field to open the Field window (Windows Ctrl+8, Macintosh Command+8).

2] Type the following in the field:

victoria,vict
white nile,wnile
aswan,aswan
blue nile,bnile
nubia,nubia

Don't use any capital letters and don't put spaces between the text and the commas. Each line in the field consists of the name of a location, a comma (no spaces), and an abbreviated version of the location name. This list contains the name of each location and the code that Director will use to catalog and look up the associated location. You'll see why you created this list in the next step.

3] Name this field cast member *Location codes*. Then close the window.

To do this, type *Location codes* at the top of the Field window.

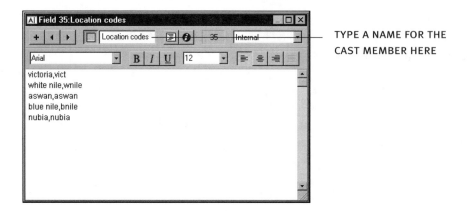

TYPE A NAME FOR THE
CAST MEMBER HERE

Now look at the cast. If you look at the names of the first 20 cast members, you'll see that each name is partly made up of the code you just entered for that location. You'll be referring to these names later and using them in your scripts, so using abbreviated cast member names is advantageous. The first part of the name is the code, and the second part is the direction of that view, with a period separating the two parts: vict.n contains the northern view of Victoria, vict.s contains the southern view of Victoria, and so on.

In creating the list in step 2, you associated a location with a code for that location. For example, you associated victoria with *vict* and white nile with *wnile*. All the cast members starting with *vict* are part of the victoria category, all the cast members starting with *wnile* are part of the white nile category, and so on.

4] Save your work.

CREATING A PROPERTY LIST FROM FIELD TEXT

In Director, you can create two types of lists: linear lists and property lists. As you learned in Lesson 24, a linear list is a single variable that can hold multiple distinct items. The items can be text, numbers, or a mixture of different data. A linear list simply lists values separated by commas.

Property lists are similar to linear lists, but they have an additional capability. They let you define properties for each list item (analogous to the field names in a database). Each property has a name that defines the kind of information it holds. For example, look at this property list variable:

PROPERTY NAME

set myList = ["first name":"Jeffrey","last name":"Smith"]

VALUE

In this example, the property list variable *myList* has two items, and each list item has two parts: the property name (for example, *"first name"*) and the assigned value (for example, *"Jeffrey"*). The two parts are separated by a colon and no spaces. An empty property list (which you will use later) is written as *[:]*.

The Lingo command *setaProp* allows you to change a list's property values from a script or even add a new property to a list. The syntax for this command is *setaProp list, property, newValue*.

You will see how to use these Lingo elements in the script you will create here. This script will insert the list you created earlier into a property list variable. Essentially, this property list will act as a database. Once you have generated a property list, you can use Lingo to retrieve the pictures from the database.

1] Open a new movie script (Windows Ctrl+Shift+U, Macintosh Command+Shift+U). Type the script shown here, but don't close the Script window yet.

> **tip** *This is a good place to use the continuation symbol (¬). Press Alt+Enter (Windows) or Option+Return (Macintosh) to insert it wherever you think a line of code is too long for you to read easily. For example, you can add the continuation symbol to a line like this:*
> *setaProp(gLocationList, item 1 of line 1 of field "Location codes", ¬*
> *item 2 of line 1 of field "Location codes")*

```
global gLocationList, gCurrentView    --Declare these as global variables.

on startMovie                         --At the start of the movie, do the following:
  CreateLocationList                  --Run this handler to create the location list.
  gCurrentView = "vict.n"             --Set the northern view of Victoria as the default.
end

on CreateLocationList                 --startMovie calls this handler.
  gLocationList = [:]                 --Declare an empty property list.
  setaProp(gLocationList, item 1 of line 1 of field "Location codes",¬
    item 2 of line 1 of field "Location codes")
                                      --Insert the first item in line 1 of the field into
                                      --the property list, gLocationList.
                                      --This is the property.
                                      --Insert the second item of
                                      --the field into the list as the data
                                      --associated with that property.
  setaProp(gLocationList, item 1 of line 2 of field "Location codes",¬
    item 2 of line 2 of field "Location codes")
                                      --Insert the first item in line 2 of the field into
                                      --the property list, gLocationList.
                                      --Insert the second item of line 2
                                      --of the field into the list as the data
                                      --associated with that property.
```

```
        setaProp(gLocationList, item 1 of line 3 of field "Location codes",¬
          item 2 of line 3 of field "Location codes")
                                          --Insert the first item in line 3 of the field into
                                          --the property list, gLocationList.
                                          --Insert the second item of line 3
                                          --of the field into the list.
        setaProp(gLocationList, item 1 of line 4 of field "Location codes",¬
          item 2 of line 4 of field "Location codes")
                                          --Insert the first item in line 4 of the field into
                                          --the property list, gLocationList.
                                          --Insert the second item of line 4
                                          --of the field into the list.
        setaProp(gLocationList, item 1 of line 5 of field "Location codes",¬
          item 2 of line 5 of field "Location codes")
                                          --Insert the first item in line 5 of the field
                                          --the property list, gLocationList.
                                          --Insert the second item of line 5
                                          --of the field into the list.
    end
```

This is a pretty complicated script, and some of the concepts it uses are new to you, but it should become clearer if you work through it step by step. (In the next tasks, you will also use other methods to see just how the script performs.)

The first line of this script declares two global variables: *gLocationList* and *gCurrentView*. You used *List* as part of the first variable name to identify it as a list variable. (This is a convention, like using *g* in the names of global variables, that makes scripts easier to read.) You use these variables in the lines that follow.

The *startMovie* handler calls *CreateLocationList*, a handler (which you then defined after the *startMovie* handler) that pulls information from the field cast member you created in the previous task into the *gLocationList* variable. The other line that is executed when the movie starts initializes the *gCurrentView* variable with a value of *"vict.n"*—the northern view of Victoria will be the default view whenever the movie starts.

The *CreateLocationList* handler, called from the *startMovie* handler, adds values from the Location codes field to the *gLocationList* variable. The first command initializes the *gLocationList* variable as an empty property list; the variable is initialized, but no properties or data are associated with the properties yet.

The next five lines (not counting the comments) add the data from the field you created earlier to the *gLocationList* variable. Remember that the syntax of this command is *setaProp list, property, newValue*. In your script, the first *setaProp* command inserts the first item of line 1 of the field into the variable *gLocationList*; this is the property. (If you look at the field you created, you'll see that the first item in line 1 is *victoria*. In this comma-delimited format, the first item is everything up to, but not including, the first comma.) The next part of the command inserts the second item of line 1 of the field into the variable *gLocationList*; this is the data associated with that property. (If you look at the field, you'll see that the second item in line 1 is *vict*.) At this point in the script, *gLocationList* contains this: *["victoria":"vict"]*.

The second *setaProp* command inserts the first item of line 2 of the field into the variable *gLocationList*; this is the property. The next part of the command inserts the second item of line 2 of the field into the variable *gLocationList*; this is the data associated with that property. At this point in the script, *gLocationList* contains this: *["victoria":"vict","white nile":"wnile"]*. A comma separates each item in the list; within each item, a colon separates the property from its associated value.

The remaining three *setaProp* lines accomplish similar actions. When this script finishes running, *gLocationList* will contain all the location names (the properties) and their codes (the data associated with each property) that are in the Location codes field.

note *You'll notice a lot of repetition in the* CreateLocationList *handler. This handler could have been written more compactly by using variables and incorporating a* repeat *structure.*

2] Save your work.
If you didn't follow all this, don't despair. The next tasks, using Director's Watcher and Debugger windows, should help.

USING THE WATCHER

The Watcher window allows you to track variables and simple expressions and view their contents while a movie runs. In this task, you will use the Watcher window to view the contents of the property list you just created.

1] If you have run the movie, re-open it again (File › Open). This clears any variables that had been set while the movie was running and will make it easier for you to follow along with the next steps.

2] Choose Window › Watcher (Windows Ctrl+Shift+', Macintosh Command+Shift+').
The Watcher window opens.

3] Copy the text *gLocationList* from your script and then paste it into the box at the top of the Watcher window.

To ensure that the variable name is exactly the same in the Watcher window as it is in your script, you should copy it from the script and paste it into the window. If the spelling of the variable name differs in these two places, the Watcher won't be able to track it.

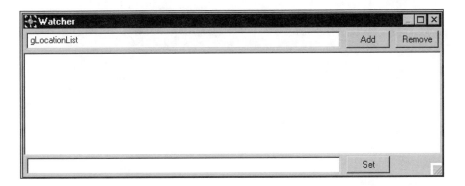

4] Click the Add button to add the variable to the Watcher list.

The variable currently has no value, so <Void> is returned.

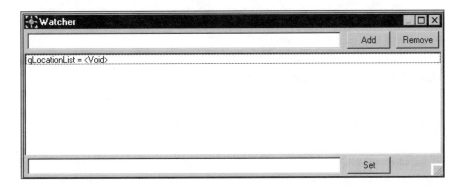

5] Close the Script window.

6] Play the movie. Don't click any of the buttons on the stage—just click Play to play the movie.

Playing the movie ensures that the new script is read into memory. Now you can see that your script works. In the Watcher window, you can see that the global variable contains all the names and code information from the Location codes field. With this information in memory, Director now has access to this information and can use it throughout the movie.

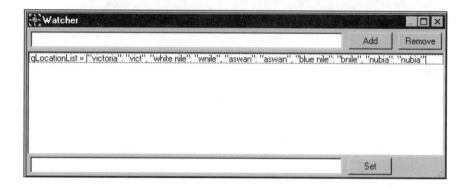

Using the Watcher is a good way to make sure that a variable or simple expression holds the value you expect.

7] Stop the movie and save your work.

WATCHING THE SCRIPT IN THE DEBUGGER

In this section you will use the Debugger to further understand what's going on in the *CreateLocationList* handler. You saw the result of this handler already: The global property list variable *gLocationList* contains a value after you play the movie. Now you'll use the Debugger to watch Director execute Lingo statements. If you're having trouble with a script, the Debugger can help you find the problem. It also helps clarify why a script does work, because you can use it to step slowly through a script as the movie runs.

note *If you did not complete the previous tasks, you can open and use Start2.dir in the Lesson25 folder to complete this lesson.*

1] Open the Message window (Ctrl + M Windows, Command + M Macintosh). Type *clearglobals* and press Enter (Windows) or Return (Macintosh). Then close the Message window.

In the previous task, you ran the movie and the *startMovie* handler assigned values to the global variables. The values in those global variables remain even after you stop the movie. In this task, you will watch the movie script run step by step. The *clearglobals* command clears the values in those global variables so you can see the movie script run as if it were running for the first time.

2] Open the movie script.

3] Click to the left of *CreateLocationList* in the *startMovie* handler.

A red dot will appear next to the first statement in the handler. This tells Director that this is the point at which you want to open the Debugger when the movie runs. This location is known as a **breakpoint**. As soon as this handler reaches the breakpoint, the Debugger window will open and handler execution will stop. From that point, you can step through each statement.

CLICK IN THE MARGIN OF THE SCRIPT WINDOW TO SET A BREAKPOINT

note   *For simplicity's sake, the illustrations in this task show just the movie script and not the comments.*

4] Close the movie script and play the movie. Don't click any of the buttons on the stage—just play the movie.

The Debugger window opens. Notice the green arrow pointing to the statement where you set the breakpoint. The arrow indicates that this line is about to be executed. The upper-left area of the Debugger window now shows the current handler that is running, *startMovie*. In the upper-right part of the Debugger window is a list of all the variables used in the current handler. You can see the values in local variables as well as the current values in the global variables.

THESE VARIABLES HAVE NOT YET BEEN ASSIGNED A VALUE; WATCH THEIR VALUES CHANGE AS YOU STEP THROUGH THE SCRIPT

THE ARROW (DISPLAYED IN FRONT OF THE BREAKPOINT HERE) SHOWS THAT DIRECTOR WILL EXECUTE THIS LINE NEXT

5] Click the Step into Script button and watch the changes in the Debugger.

The *CreateLocationList* handler has been called, which causes the green arrow to move down to the first line in that handler. The upper-left area of the Debugger window now shows that the *CreateLocationList* handler is running, and that it was called from the *startMovie* handler. In the upper-right part of the Debugger window, the list of variables has not changed because no assignments have been made yet.

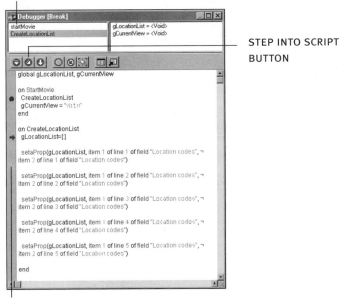

STEP INTO SCRIPT
BUTTON

THE ARROW HAS MOVED TO SHOW THE NEXT LINE TO BE EXECUTED

6] Click the Step into Script button again and watch the changes in the Debugger.

Director executes the *set gLocationList = [:]* command and moves the arrow down to
the next line. The list of variables in the upper-right area of the Debugger window
updates to show that *gLocationList* has been initialized as an empty list.

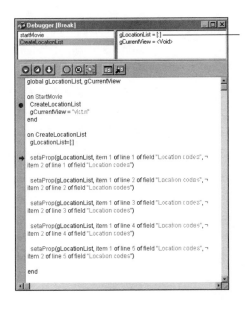

GLOCATIONLIST HAS
NOW BEEN INITIALIZED

7] Click the Step into Script button again and watch the changes in the Debugger.

Director executes the next command, which places the items in the first line of the
Location codes field in the *gLocationList* property list.

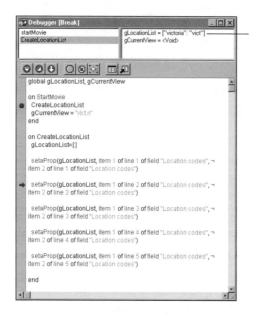

THE LIST OF VARIABLES
SHOWS THAT *GLOCATIONLIST*
HAS BEEN UPDATED

**8] Click the Step into Script button five more times, until all the commands
in the *CreateLocationList* handler have been executed, and watch the changes
in the Debugger.**

Stepping through the *CreateLocationList* handler line by line will give you an idea of
how it builds the property list from the values stored in the Location codes field. When
the last command, which is actually the *end* command, has been executed, the green
arrow moves back up to the *startMovie* handler, next to the *set gCurrentView = "vict.n"*
command. Control returns there because it is the first line immediately following the
call to the *CreateLocationList* handler, which just finished executing. The upper-left
area of the Debugger window shows that just the *startMovie* handler is now executing.

THE *GLOCATIONLIST*
PROPERTY LIST HAS NOW
BEEN COMPLETELY UPDATED

WHEN THE *CREATELOCATIONLIST* HANDLER
FINISHES EXECUTING, CONTROL RETURNS HERE

9] Click the Step into Script button again and watch the changes in the Debugger.

The list of variables in the upper-right area of the Debugger window shows that the
gCurrentView variable has now been initialized.

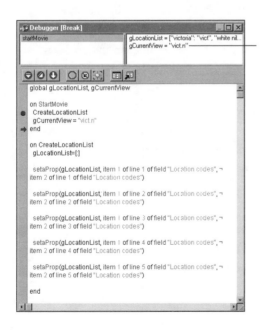

THE *GCURRENTVIEW*
VARIABLE HAS NOW
BEEN INITIALIZED

627

10] When you're done, click the breakpoint dot next to the handler to remove it. Then close the Debugger and Script windows.

If you don't remove breakpoints, the movie will always stop at them.

RETRIEVING DATA FROM THE PROPERTY LIST

In the previous task, you used the Debugger to see step by step how the property list is generated. Now you need a way to retrieve information from that property list. Director has a built-in mechanism for doing exactly that. You will use the *getaProp* command to retrieve data from the list. The syntax for this command is *getaProp(list, positionOrProperty)*.

The *getaProp* command identifies the data associated with the specified position (for a linear list) or property (for a property list) in the named list. The command returns the result <Void> when the list does not contain the specified position or property. You'll use the Message window to test this command in the next task.

1] Open the Watcher and Message windows.

2] In the Message window, type *put getaProp(gLocationList, "victoria")* and then press Enter (Windows) or Return (Macintosh):

After you press Enter or Return, you'll see the following in the Message window:

-- "vict"

Remember that vict is the code associated with victoria. You can use the Watcher window to see which properties are associated with which values in the property list variable, *gLocationList*.

3] Try these same steps with several location names, such as blue nile and nubia.

Be sure to use quotation marks and lowercase letters for the property names. This is one of the very few times that Director is case-sensitive. If you don't use lowercase letters, or if you misspell the property names, Director returns <Void> instead of the associated data.

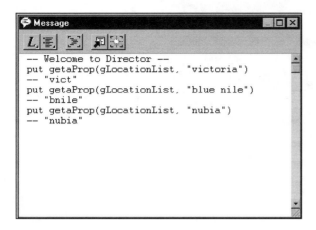

```
-- Welcome to Director --
put getaProp(gLocationList, "victoria")
-- "vict"
put getaProp(gLocationList, "blue nile")
-- "bnile"
put getaProp(gLocationList, "nubia")
-- "nubia"
```

Great; it works!

4] Close both the Watcher and Message windows.

5] Save your work.

So far, you've created a property list variable and retrieved data from it. In the next lesson, you'll apply this knowledge to show different views on the stage based on user interaction.

WHAT YOU HAVE LEARNED

In this lesson you have:

• Created a field to store data in a list [page 615]

• Inserted data into a property list with *setaProp* [page 617]

• Watched variables update in the Watcher window [page 620]

• Stepped through a handler using the Debugger [page 622]

• Set a breakpoint [page 623]

• Retrieved values from a property list with *getaProp* [page 628]

using a list database

In the last lesson, you built a property list—a variable that acts as a database—to associate name codes with the locations a user can choose from the Nile Photo Notebook menu. In this lesson you will complete the project by creating a handler to access the values of the variable and update the stage based on the user's choices.

If you would like to view the final result of this lesson, open the Complete folder in the Lesson26 folder and play Nile2.dir.

The Nile Photo Notebook offers four views of five different areas along the Nile. Clicking the name of a location calls up images from that destination. Clicking a direction on the compass shows that part of the area for the chosen location. The user's choices trigger a script that combines the direction choice with the location choice to display the correct view from the cast.

WHAT YOU WILL LEARN

In this lesson you will:

• Identify characters in an expression

• Return the count of characters in an expression

• Switch cast members with Lingo

• Combine strings

• Practice creating global and local variables

APPROXIMATE TIME

It should take about 4 hours to complete this lesson.

LESSONS FILES

Media files:
Lesson26\Media

Starting files:
Lesson26\Start\Start1.dir
Lesson26\Start\Start2.dir

Completed project:
Lesson26\Complete\Nile2.dir

CREATING A HIGHLIGHT

As you already know, part of creating any successful user interface is providing user feedback, letting the user know what parts of the screen are "live" and what option is currently selected. In this task, you will create a highlight that shows the current destination selection in the Nile Photo Notebook you began in the previous lesson.

1] Open Start1.dir in the Lesson26 folder and save it as *Nile2.dir* in your Projects folder.

This is the prebuilt file. If you completed the previous lesson, you can use the movie you worked on there and save it as *Nile2.dir*.

2] Click channel 15, frame 1.

You will place the highlight sprite here.

3] Open the tool palette (Windows Ctrl+7, Macintosh Command+7), select the Filled Rectangle tool, and then set the foreground color to blue.

4] Draw a rectangle over the word *Victoria* on the stage.

This is the first location that will be displayed when the movie opens, and it is the location on the stage right now, so it should be highlighted.

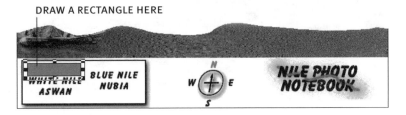

DRAW A RECTANGLE HERE

5] While the rectangle sprite is still selected, set the ink to Lightest.

Lightest ink compares the pixel colors in the foreground and background and uses whichever pixel color in the foreground or background is lightest. Now the location name looks blue.

6] In the Cast window, name the new blue rectangle you just created *Blue Highlight*.

It should be cast member number 24.

7] Save your work.

> **tip** *Using a highlight sprite over a graphic, rather than creating a separate graphic for the highlighted state of the button, as you have done before, is a great way to save disk space and download time.*

632

USING THE *THE RECT* FUNCTION TO MOVE HIGHLIGHTS

The function *the rect* returns the coordinates of the rectangle for any graphic cast member. You will use this function to move the rectangle highlight to a new location.

1] Open the Message window.

2] Type the following and then press Enter (Windows) or Return (Macintosh):

sprite (15).rect = sprite (6).rect

Nothing happens. You need to update the stage to see any results.

3] Type *updateStage* and then press Enter (Windows) or Return (Macintosh). Watch the stage carefully.

The rectangle now highlights Aswan because you moved the rectangle in sprite 15 so it covers sprite 6 (the sprite in channel 6). Notice that the rectangle not only has a new location but is resized as well. Because you set its value to *sprite (6).rect*, the rectangle has the same rectangular coordinates as sprite 6.

4] Type the following and then press Enter (Windows) or Return (Macintosh). Watch the stage carefully.

sprite (15).rect = sprite (7).rect

5] Type *updateStage* and then press Enter (Windows) or Return (Macintosh).
Now what?

YOU SEE *BLUE NILE*
HIGHLIGHTED

The rectangle highlights Blue Nile because that's sprite 7 (the sprite in channel 7). By setting the *the rect* value for the rectangle to the *the rect* value for a particular sprite, you move and resize the highlight.

RETRIEVING VALUES WITH *GETAPROP*

Now that you have created the visual cues that will help a user navigate through the options, the next step is to use Lingo to link the user's choices to the image displayed on the stage. In this task, you will use *getaProp* (which you became acquainted with at the end of the last lesson), a command designed to retrieve a value from a property list variable. You will create a handler that retrieves a value from the *gLocationList* variable based on a user's choice and assign that value to a new variable, which you will later use to control the view shown on the stage.

1] Rewind and play the movie, but don't click any buttons on the stage.

To complete the following steps, you'll need the property list, *gLocationList*, generated and in the computer's memory. Recall that the property list is created in the *startMovie* handler, which runs every time the movie plays, so playing the movie now generates the list and places it in memory.

You should see the Victoria north view.

2] Open the Message window, type the line shown below, and then press Enter (Windows) or Return (Macintosh).

You can add spaces to the command to make it more readable, as shown here.

```
put getaProp(gLocationList, "white nile")
```

This command returns "wnile".

3] Type *put getaProp(gLocationList, "victoria")* and then press Enter (Windows) or Return (Macintosh).

This command returns "vict".

These are the codes you associated with the location names in the previous lesson. Next you will create a variable to retrieve the same values.

4] Type *newView = getaProp(gLocationList, "white nile")* in the Message window and then press Enter (Windows) or Return (Macintosh).

This creates a variable called *newView* and assigns it a value based on the *getaProp* command. Nothing is returned in the Message window because you are creating a variable, not displaying its value. To get a variable value, you type *put* followed by the variable name.

5] Type *put newView* and then press Enter (Windows) or Return (Macintosh).

This command returns "wnile", the code assigned to *"white nile"* in the *gLocationList* property list.

6] Type *newView = getaProp(gLocationList, "blue nile")* and then press Enter (Windows) or Return (Macintosh).

7] Type *put newView* and then press Enter (Windows) or Return (Macintosh).

This command returns "bnile", the code assigned to *"blue nile"* in the *gLocationList* property list. Now the value of *newView* is *bnile*.

For the following steps to work correctly, you must have completed the previous steps because you've assigned new values in the Message window, and Director will need access to those values.

USING CHUNK EXPRESSIONS

The commands you have already used will get the location of a user's choice from the *gLocationList* variable and put it into the *newView* variable. However, the location name isn't enough to choose a cast member for display. The view to be displayed on the stage depends on both the location and the compass direction the user selects. In the next tasks, you will combine two values into a single value—adding "n" to "vict", for example—to arrive at a complete cast member name that reflects the user's choices for both options. To do this, you will use two Lingo expressions, *char* and *count*, designed to work with strings of text.

Chunk expressions are any character, word, or line in any text source such as field cast members or variables that hold strings. For example, the field cast member Location codes you created in the previous lesson is a chunk expression.

Char is a keyword that identifies a character or range of characters in a chunk expression. *Count* is a function that returns a count of the characters in a chunk expression, among other things. You will now use the Message window to see how these work.

1] In the Message window, type *put gCurrentView* and then press Enter (Windows) or Return (Macintosh).

This command returns "vict.n", the value you set in the *startMovie* handler in Lesson 25. This is the code for the location that is currently displayed, the northern view of Victoria.

2] Type *put ("vict.n").chars.count* **and then press Enter (Windows) or Return (Macintosh).**

Using *.chars* specifies that *count* is to count the number of characters in the string. Since *count* can also be used to count other things besides the number of characters, the *.chars* element is required.

This command returns 6 because this string contains six characters (including the period).

3] Type *put ("vict.n").char[6]* **and then press Enter (Windows) or Return (Macintosh).**

Remember that *char* is a keyword that identifies a character in a chunk expression. Note the use of the square brackets to delineate the specified character, the sixth character in this example.

This command returns "n" because *n* is the sixth character in the string "vict.n". The syntax is *textMemberExpression.char[whichCharacter]*.

4] Type *put ("vict.n").char[("vict.n").chars.count]* **and then press Enter (Windows) or Return (Macintosh).**

The value "n" is still returned because *n* is the sixth character in the string "vict.n". In step 3, though, you used a literal value (6) to get the last character of the string. In step 4, you used a function, *("vict.n").chars.count,* to get the same value. Using this technique, you can get the last character without knowing exactly how many characters are in the string. The last character of these strings is important because it tells you which direction of the view is currently displayed. If the last character is *n*, then you know that the north view is displayed. If the last character is *s*, then you know that the south view is displayed. You're going to need this value whenever the user clicks a location name. For example, if the north view of Victoria (vict.n) is displayed and the user clicks Blue Nile, you need to display the cast member with the view that faces the same direction (north) for the Blue Nile, which is bnile.n.

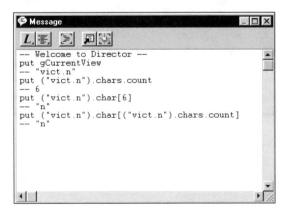

Now you will create a variable called *oldDirection* to hold this value.

5] Type *oldDirection = ("vict.n").char[("vict.n").chars.count]* and then press Enter (Windows) or Return (Macintosh).

Once again, you're only setting the value of *oldDirection*, so nothing is returned in the Message window. What is the value? To find out, you can put *oldDirection* in the Message window.

6] Type *put oldDirection* and then press Enter (Windows) or Return (Macintosh).

This command returns "n" because *n* is the last character of the string "vict.n". Try another one.

7] Type *oldDirection = ("bnile.s").char[("bnile.s").chars.count]* and then press Enter (Windows) or Return (Macintosh).

8] Type *put oldDirection* and then press Enter (Windows) or Return (Macintosh).

Now "s" is returned because *s* is the last character of the string "bnile.s".

```
-- Welcome to Director --
put gCurrentView
-- "vict.n"
put ("vict.n").chars.count
-- 6
put ("vict.n").char[6]
-- "n"
put ("vict.n").char[("vict.n").chars.count]
-- "n"
oldDirection = ("vict.n").char[("vict.n").chars.count]
put oldDirection
-- "n"
oldDirection = ("bnile.s").char[("bnile.s").chars.count]
put oldDirection
-- "s"
```

For the following steps to work correctly, you must have completed the previous steps because you've assigned new values in the Message window, and Director will need access to those values.

CONCATENATING TWO EXPRESSIONS

Now that you have a way to find what direction is displayed on the stage, you will add the direction to the location choice selected by the user to create a cast member name. Adding two expressions together is called **concatenation**, and in Lingo you perform concatenation using the & symbol. You can concatenate strings to create a new string. For example, the statement *put "abra"&"cadabra"* concatenates the strings *"abra"* and *"cadabra"*, resulting in the string *"abracadabra"*. When using a string, you surround it with quotation marks to indicate that Director should read the text as a string and not as a variable, numerical value, or Lingo element.

You can also concatenate variables. Suppose you have two variables, *myName* and *myInitials*, that are set to *"Tristen"* and *"TT"*, respectively. To concatenate these variables, you would type *put myName&myInitials* in the Message window. The result would be *"TristenTT"*. To separate the name and initials, you could use a period between the two variables. To do this, you must use quotation marks around the period to indicate that it is a literal value (that is, that it's a string and not a variable, numerical value, or Lingo element). For example, this statement concatenates *myName* and *myInitials* and places a period between the two variables: *put myName&"."&myInitials*. The result would be *"Tristen.TT"*.

You will use the Message window to see how concatenation works.

1] Type *put newView* in the Message window and then press Enter (Windows) or Return (Macintosh).

This command returns "bnile". If you followed all the steps in the previous task, *newView* should still have this value. If you see a different value, type *newView = "bnile"* in the Message window and then press Enter (Windows) or Return (Macintosh).

2] Type *put oldDirection* and then press Enter (Windows) or Return (Macintosh).

This command returns "s". If you followed all the previous steps, *oldDirection* should still have this value. If you see a different value, type *oldDirection = "s"* in the Message window and then press Enter (Windows) or Return (Macintosh).

Now you can concatenate the two variables to get a new value—one that describes the new view. You will do this by placing the new value in the variable called *gCurrentView*. (Remember that you initialized this global variable in the movie script in Lesson 25.)

638

3] Type *gCurrentView = newView & "." & oldDirection* and then press Enter (Windows) or Return (Macintosh).

As usual, because you are only setting a value, nothing is returned in the Message window. You need to put the value there.

4] Type *put gCurrentView* and then press Enter (Windows) or Return (Macintosh).

Now "bnile.s" is returned. You've concatenated the values.

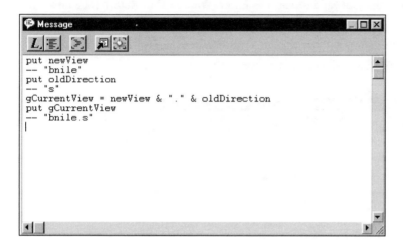

In the Message window, the quotation marks that appear around the period indicate that the period is a literal value. Try another one.

5] Type *newView = getaProp(gLocationList, "nubia")* and then press Enter (Windows) or Return (Macintosh).

6] Type *put newView* and then press Enter (Windows) or Return (Macintosh).

This command returns "nubia" because that's the code for "nubia".

7] Type *oldDirection = ("aswan.e").char[("aswan.e").chars.count]* and then press Enter (Windows) or Return (Macintosh).

8] Type *put oldDirection* and then press Enter (Windows) or Return (Macintosh).

This command returns "e" because *e* is the seventh character of "aswan.e"—*char(7)* of "aswan.e". Now combine *newView* and *oldDirection* together.

9] Type *gCurrentView = newView & "." &oldDirection* and then press Enter (Windows) or Return (Macintosh).

10] Type *put gCurrentView* and then press Enter (Windows) or Return (Macintosh).

Now "nubia.e" is returned. You concatenated the values and placed them in the variable *gCurrentView*. You will use this technique to determine what picture should be displayed after the user clicks a location or direction.

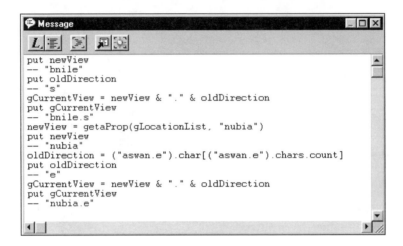

For the following steps to work correctly, you must have completed the previous steps because you've assigned new values in the Message window, and Director will need access to those values.

SETTING THE *THE MEMBERNUM* PROPERTY

Using *getaProp*, *count*, *char*, and concatenation, you now have created a variable that holds the name of the view that should be displayed in response to a user's choices. To put that view on the stage using Lingo, you will need to get the cast member number of the view based on its cast member name. In this task, you will use a new cast member property, *number*, to find the cast member number of a specified cast member. The syntax for this property is *member(whichCastmember).number*. Then you can use the *the memberNum* sprite property (which you have already used several times in this book) to assign this cast member to sprite 1: the view displayed on the stage.

In the task "Using Chunk Expressions," you typed *put gCurrentView* in the Message window and the window returned "vict.n" (Victoria north) because that was the view with which you initialized the variable at the start of the movie. In the preceding task, you changed *gCurrentView* to "nubia.e." How do you think *gCurrentView* and *the memberNum* can be used to display a new view?

1] Type the following in the Message window and then press Enter (Windows) or Return (Macintosh):

    put gCurrentView

This command returns "nubia.e". You set this value in the previous task. If you did not complete the previous task, type *gCurrentView = "nubia.e"* in the Message window and then press Enter (Windows) or Return (Macintosh).

2] Type the following and then press Enter (Windows) or Return (Macintosh):

    put member (gCurrentView).number

This command returns 18. This is the cast member number of nubia.e. You can check this by looking in the Cast window.

WITH CAST MEMBER 18 SELECTED,
YOU SEE THE MEMBER NAME HERE

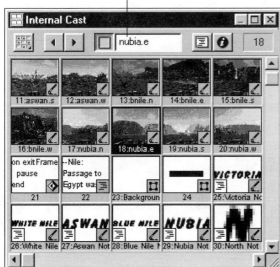

The score is set up so that the current view is in sprite 1 (channel 1). This is now cast member vict.n. To change the view on the stage, you can swap this graphic with the graphic in cast member 18, which is nubia.e. You'll do that now.

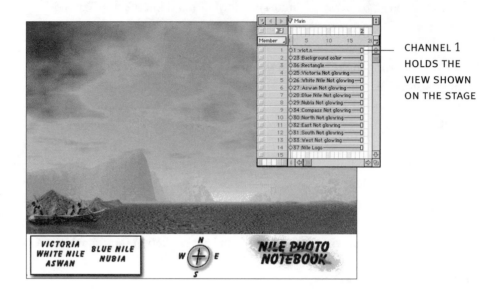

CHANNEL 1
HOLDS THE
VIEW SHOWN
ON THE STAGE

3] Type the following in the Message window and then press Enter (Windows) or Return (Macintosh):

    put sprite (1).memberNum

This command returns 1, because vict.n is cast member 1.

4] Type the following and then press Enter (Windows) or Return (Macintosh):

    sprite (1).memberNum = member (gCurrentView).number

Nothing happens. You are only setting the value of *the memberNum*. As usual, to see changes on the stage, you must update the stage.

5] Type *updateStage* and then press Enter (Windows) or Return (Macintosh). Watch the stage carefully.

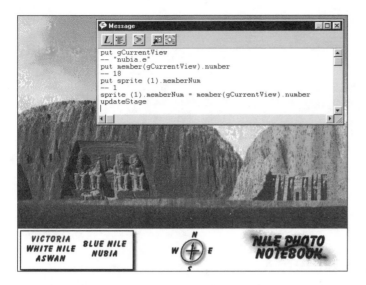

You see Nubia east! Why? If you enter *put sprite (1).memberNum* in the Message window now, you will get 18, which is the cast member named nubia.e. When you update the stage, the changed view appears.

You are ready to combine all your work into one handler. This handler will determine the current view and direction and display the new view the user has selected.

SENDING PARAMETERS

You may recall from the previous lesson that a cast member script already exists for most of the location names. These scripts were provided to give you a jump-start on this project. You will now take a look at one of those scripts to see how it works.

1] Select cast member 26. Then click the Script button.

SCRIPT
BUTTON

643

The handler looks like this:

```
on mouseUp
  SetPlace("white nile", 5)
end
```

In this handler, you send the name of the view (*"white nile"*) as the first parameter and the channel number of the sprite that was clicked (5) as the second parameter. The handler that is called, *SetPlace*, is the one that carries out the steps you just practiced in the Message window, which you are going to add to the movie script next.

2] Close the Script window.

COMBINING YOUR WORK INTO A HANDLER

Now you will use all of the Lingo elements you've been testing in the Message window, stringing them together into one handler that determines the current view and direction of the scene, sets the new view and direction, and then displays the graphic. The handler will also move the highlight to the sprite the user clicked.

1] Open the movie script and add the lines shown in bold:

```
global gLocationList, gCurrentView      --Declare these as global variables.

on startMovie  --At the start of the movie, do the following:
  CreateLocationList                     --Run this handler to create the location list.
  gCurrentView = "vict.n"                --Set the northern view of Victoria as the default.
end

on CreateLocationList                    --startMovie calls this handler.
  gLocationList = [:]                    --Declare an empty property list.
  setaProp(gLocationList, item 1 of line 1 of field "Location codes",¬
  item 2 of line 1 of field "Location codes")
                                         --Insert the first item in line 1 of the field into
                                         --the property list, gLocationList.
                                         --This is the property.
                                         --Insert the second item of
                                         --the field into the list as the data
                                         --associated with that property.
  setaProp(gLocationList, item 1 of line 2 of field "Location codes",¬
  item 2 of line 2 of field "Location codes")
                                         --Insert the first item in line 2 of the field into
                                         --the property list, gLocationList.
                                         --Insert the second item of line 2
                                         --of the field into the list as the data
                                         --associated with that property.
```

```
setaProp(gLocationList, item 1 of line 3 of field "Location codes",¬
item 2 of line 3 of field "Location codes")
                                        --Insert the first item in line 3 of the field into
                                        --the property list, gLocationList.
                                        --Insert the second item of line 3
                                        --of the field into the list.
setaProp(gLocationList, item 1 of line 4 of field "Location codes",¬
item 2 of line 4 of field "Location codes")
                                        --Insert the first item in line 4 of the field into
                                        --the property list, gLocationList.
                                        --Insert the second item of line 4
                                        --of the field into the list.
setaProp(gLocationList, item 1 of line 5 of field "Location codes",¬
item 2 of line 5 of field "Location codes")
                                        --Insert the first item in line 5 of the field into
                                        --the property list, gLocationList.
                                        --Insert the second item of line 5
                                        --of the field into the list.
end


on SetPlace thePlaceName, theSprite
                                        --When a location name is clicked, the name
                                        --of the location and the sprite number are
                                        --sent as parameters.
    newView = getaProp(gLocationList, thePlaceName)
                                        --Get the data associated with thePlaceName
                                        --in the gLocationList property list. Then set
                                        --newView to that data. The data is a code
                                        --for a particular location.
    oldDirection = (gCurrentView).char[(gCurrentView).chars.count]
                                        --Get the last character of gCurrentView. This
                                        --will be a direction letter. Then set
                                        --oldDirection to that letter.
    gCurrentView = newView&"."&oldDirection
                                        --Concatenate newView and oldDirection and
                                        --place a period between them. This results
                                        --in the name of a cast member.
                                        --Set gCurrentView to this value.
    sprite (1).memberNum = member (gCurrentView).number
                                        --Switch the cast member assigned to
                                        --sprite 1 with the cast member
                                        --assigned to gCurrentView.
    sprite (15).rect = sprite (theSprite).rect
                                        --When a location name is clicked,
                                        --the sprite number of the location
                                        --name is sent as a parameter (theSprite).
                                        --Move the highlight to the sprite that
                                        --was clicked.
    updateStage                         --Update the stage to show the new view
                                        --and the new highlight location.
end
```

Now look at the *SetPlace* handler.

In the first line, the handler defines two arguments for *SetPlace*: *thePlaceName* and *theSprite*. Recall the script you looked at earlier for cast member 26. This script calls the *SetPlace* handler and sends the parameter values *"white nile"* (for *thePlaceName*) and *5* (for *theSprite*). You will use these parameters later in the handler.

The second line, *newView = getaProp(gLocationList, thePlaceName)*, creates the *newView* variable and initializes it to hold the value retrieved from *gLocationList* by the *getaProp* command. If the user clicks White Nile, for example, that value would be *"wnile"*: *newView = (gLocationList, "white nile")*.

Next you create a variable, *oldDirection*, which is set to the last character of the name of the view currently on the stage, contained in *gCurrentView*. Here is how this line breaks down:

```
oldDirection = (gCurrentView).char[(gCurrentView).chars.count]
oldDirection = ("vict.n").char[6]
oldDirection = "n"
```

Now that you have both the code and the direction, the name of the cast member to be displayed can be determined by concatenating *newView* and *oldDirection*. The name is placed in the global variable *gCurrentView*. In the example, this is how this line breaks down:

```
gCurrentView = "wnile"&"."&"n"
gCurrentView="wnile.n"
```

Now you use *the memberNum* to switch the cast member assigned to sprite 1. Remember that sprite 1 contains the view that is displayed on the stage. In this case, you switch the image contained in channel 1 with the image contained in *gCurrentView*. This line breaks down like this:

```
sprite (1).memberNum = member ("wnile.n").number
sprite (1).memberNum = 26
```

Next you move the rectangle that highlights the location name to the location name that was just clicked: *sprite (15).rect = sprite (theSprite).rect*

The value of *theSprite* was sent as a parameter of *SetPlace* when the user clicked the White Nile option. Its value is 5. The line for this example breaks down like this:

```
sprite (15).rect = sprite (5).rect
```

646

Remember that *the rect* contains the coordinates of a rectangle. In this case, it sets the coordinates of the rectangle in sprite 15 (the default position of the rectangle over the Victoria button) to sprite 5 (the White Nile button). Thus, the blue rectangle is set to the same coordinates as White Nile.

Finally, you update the stage to show the changes.

2] Save your work.

3] Close the Script window and play the movie. Click any location except Nubia. Don't click a direction on the compass.

Now when you click a location name, the name is highlighted and the appropriate image is displayed. Every button works except Nubia, because all the other locations have scripts. You will create a script for the Nubia button next.

ADDING A SCRIPT TO A BUTTON

If you click the Nubia location name, you will discover that nothing happens. This is because there is no script for that cast member yet. You will add that script now.

note *If you did not complete the previous tasks, you can open Start2.dir in the Lesson26 folder to complete the lesson.*

1] In the Cast window, select cast member 25, Victoria Not glowing. Then click the Script button.

The handler looks like this:

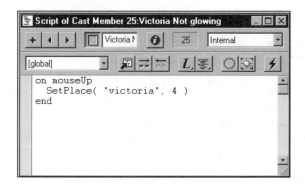

2] Select all the text in the Script window (Windows Control+A, Macintosh Command+A), choose Edit › Copy Text to copy the script, and then close the window.

You will use this handler as a starting point for the script you want to create for the Nubia location.

3] In the Cast window, select cast member 29. Then click the Cast Member Script button.

4] Select all the text in the Script window and then choose Edit › Paste Text to paste the handler you just copied.

As you've seen many times before, Director automatically fills in *on mouseUp* and *end* when a cast member script is first opened. Simply select all the text in the script and paste over it.

5] Make the change shown here in bold and then close the window.

```
on mouseUp
  SetPlace("nubia", 8)
end
```

Recall that *SetPlace* is the handler you just created. It has two arguments: *thePlaceName* and *theSprite*. When Nubia is clicked, the *SetPlace* handler runs; *"nubia"* will be plugged into *thePlaceName*, and *8* will be plugged into *theSprite* (the Nubia sprite is in channel 8).

6] Rewind and play the movie. Click any of the locations. Don't click a direction on the compass.

It works! Now when you click a location name, the background image is updated to show the new graphic.

THE CAST MEMBER SCRIPTS IN THE LOCATION
NAMES CONTAIN A CALL TO THE *SETPLACE*
HANDLER IN THE MOVIE SCRIPT

7] Stop the movie and save your work.

ADDING ANOTHER HIGHLIGHT

The interface and the scripts for choosing a location are all in place, but the interface for choosing a compass direction still doesn't work. You will fix that in the next several tasks. Your first job is to add a highlight for the compass interface to show the selected direction.

1] Select the Blue Highlight sprite in channel 15. Copy it and then paste it into channel 16. Make sure it also spans frames 1 through 18.

Channel 15 contains the rectangle used to highlight the location name. Channel 16 now contains a similar rectangle, which you can use to highlight the compass direction. The new sprite is also placed on the stage and selected.

tip *When copying sprites, make sure to select the entire sprite by clicking somewhere other than on a keyframe. Clicking a keyframe in the sprite selects just the keyframe, not the entire sprite.*

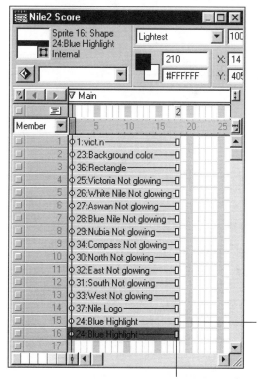

CHANNEL 15 HOLDS THE RECTANGLE THAT HIGHLIGHTS THE LOCATION NAME

CHANNEL 16 HOLDS THE RECTANGLE THAT HIGHLIGHTS THE COMPASS DIRECTION

2] On the stage, drag the new rectangle sprite to the _N_ above the compass and resize the rectangle as necessary.

You don't need to set the ink or the color because it's already been set. Now you have two rectangles that you can use to highlight the two navigation elements on the stage.

RESIZE THE RECTANGLE SO IT COVERS ONLY THE _N_

CHANGING DIRECTIONS

Clicking the direction letters still produces a script error because you haven't written the handler yet. You may recall from the previous lesson that cast member scripts already exist for most of the direction letters. These scripts were provided to give you a jump-start on this project. Now you will take a look at one of those scripts to see how it works.

1] Select cast member 30. Then click the Script button.

The handler looks like this:

```
on mouseUp
  SetDirection("n",10)
end
```

This handler sends the letter of the direction as the first parameter in the handler ("n") and the channel number of the sprite that was clicked as the second parameter (10). The script that is called, _SetDirection_, is the one you will create next in the movie script.

2] Close the Script window.

3] Open the movie script and add the lines shown in bold:

```
global gLocationList, gCurrentView     --Declare these as global variables.

on startMovie                          --At the start of the movie, do the following:
  CreateLocationList                   --Run this handler to create the location list.
  gCurrentView = "vict.n"              --Set the northern view of Victoria as the default.
end

on CreateLocationList                  --startMovie calls this handler.
  gLocationList = [:]                  --Declare an empty property list.
  setaProp(gLocationList, item 1 of line 1 of field "Location codes",¬
  item 2 of line 1 of field "Location codes")
                                       --Insert the first item in line 1 of the field into
                                       --the property list, gLocationList.
                                       --This is the property.
                                       --Insert the second item of
                                       --the field into the list as the data
                                       --associated with that property.
  setaProp(gLocationList, item 1 of line 2 of field "Location codes",¬
  item 2 of line 2 of field "Location codes")
                                       --Insert the first item in line 2 of the field into
                                       --the property list, gLocationList.
                                       --Insert the second item of line 2
                                       --of the field into the list as the data
                                       --associated with that property.
  setaProp(gLocationList, item 1 of line 3 of field "Location codes",¬
  item 2 of line 3 of field "Location codes")
                                       --Insert the first item in line 3 of the field into
                                       --the property list, gLocationList.
                                       --Insert the second item of line 3
                                       --of the field into the list.
  setaProp(gLocationList, item 1 of line 4 of field "Location codes",¬
  item 2 of line 4 of field "Location codes")
                                       --Insert the first item in line 4 of the field into
                                       --the property list, gLocationList.
                                       --Insert the second item of line 4
                                       --of the field into the list.
  setaProp(gLocationList, item 1 of line 5 of field "Location codes",¬
  item 2 of line 5 of field "Location codes")
                                       --Insert the first item in line 5 of the field into
                                       --the property list, gLocationList.
                                       --Insert the second item of line 5
                                       --of the field into the list.
end
```

```
on SetPlace thePlaceName, theSprite
                                --When a location name is clicked, the name
                                --of the location and the sprite number are
                                --sent as parameters.
   newView = getaProp(gLocationList, thePlaceName)
                                --Get the data associated with thePlaceName
                                --in the gLocationList property list. Then set
                                --newView to that data. The data is a code
                                --for a particular location.
   oldDirection = (gCurrentView).char[(gCurrentView).chars.count]
                                --Get the last character of gCurrentView. This
                                --will be a direction letter. Then set
                                --oldDirection to that letter.
   gCurrentView = newView&"."&oldDirection
                                --Concatenate newView and oldDirection and
                                --place a period between them. This results
                                --in the name of a cast member.
                                --Set gCurrentView to this value.
   sprite (1).memberNum = member (gCurrentView).number
                                --Switch the cast member assigned to
                                --sprite 1 with the cast member
                                --assigned to gCurrentView.
   sprite (15).rect = sprite (theSprite).rect
                                --When a location name is clicked,
                                --the sprite number of the location
                                --name is sent as a parameter (theSprite).
                                --Move the highlight to the sprite that
                                --was clicked.
   updateStage                  --Update the stage to show the new view
                                --and the new highlight location.
end

on SetDirection theDirectionLetter, theSprite
                                --When a direction letter is clicked, the
                                --letter and the sprite number are sent
                                --as parameters.
   put theDirectionLetter into gCurrentView.char[(gCurrentView).chars.count]
                                --Replace the last character of gCurrentView
                                --with the theDirectionLetter value that was
                                --sent as a parameter. This generates a
                                --new value for gCurrentView.
   sprite (1).memberNum = member (gCurrentView).number
                                --Switch the cast member assigned to
                                --sprite 1 with the cast member associated
                                --with the new value of gCurrentView.
```

652

```
sprite (16).rect = sprite (theSprite).rect
                                    --The sprite number of the direction letter
                                    --is sent as a parameter (theSprite).
                                    --Move the highlight to the letter that
                                    --was clicked.
         updateStage                --Update the stage to show the new view
                                    --and the new highlight location.
     end
```

tip   *This is a good place to use the continuation symbol (¬). Press Alt+Enter (Windows) or Option+Return (Macintosh) to insert it wherever you feel the line is too long for you to read.*

Now take a look at the new *SetDirection* handler that you added. As in the *SetPlace* handler, you define two arguments for the *SetDirection* handler: *theDirectionLetter* and *theSprite*. Recall the script you just looked at for cast member 30, the N button on the compass. When that script calls the *SetDirection* handler, it sends "n" for *theDirectionLetter* and 10 for *theSprite*. You will see how these are used in a moment.

The next line sets *theDirectionLetter* ("n" in the example) as the last character of *gCurrentView*. For example, if nubia.e is displayed and N is clicked on the compass, then *e* will be replaced by *n* in *gCurrentView*. This gives *gCurrentView* a new value. This line uses the *put . . . into* command, which is required when setting a character. Previously you used concatenation to combine text to create *gCurrentView*. In this case, you replaced the last letter of the existing global variable *gCurrentView*.

Next you set the *the memberNum* value of sprite 1 (the view shown on the stage) to the cast member number of *gCurrentView*, which now has a new cast member name.

In the next line you move the highlighting rectangle to cover the letter on the compass just clicked by setting the coordinates of the rectangle to the coordinates of the sprite specified by *theSprite*, the second parameter that was sent when the direction letter was clicked.

Finally, you update the stage to show changes.

4] Close the Script window.

653

5] Play the movie. Click all the direction letters on the compass except S. Also click location names.

You can now navigate to any image in the collection by clicking the location names and direction letters, except if you want to see the southern views. You'll create the handler for the southern view now.

6] In the Cast window, select the N, cast member 30. Then click the Script button.

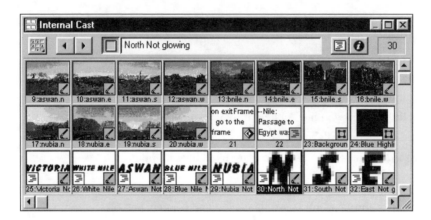

7] Copy the script. Then close the window.

You're going to use this script as the basis for the script for the S cast member.

8] In the Cast window, select the S. Then click the Script button.

9] In the Script window, paste over any text already there (Edit › Paste). Then make the change shown here in bold:

```
on mouseUp
  SetDirection("s", 12)
end
```

Be sure to use a lowercase *s* or the handler won't function properly. This handler will call the *SetDirection* handler you just created in the movie script. The arguments for the *SetDirection* handler are *theDirectionLetter* and *theSprite*. The *mouseUp* handler here plugs "s" into *theDirectionLetter* and 12 (the sprite number of the S) into *theSprite*.

10] Rewind and play the movie. Click all the locations and all the direction letters.

They all work!

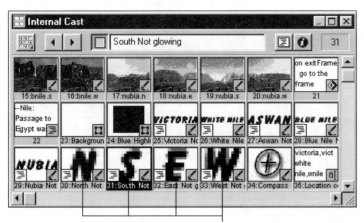

THE CAST MEMBER SCRIPTS IN THE DIRECTION
LETTERS CONTAIN A CALL TO THE *SETDIRECTION*
HANDLER IN THE MOVIE SCRIPT

11] Save your work.

Good work! The data storage and retrieval procedures you just developed can be used for a variety of information types of all sizes.

PUPPETING SOUND

The functionality for the movie is complete, but you can add one final element to make this electronic photo album more exciting: a background soundtrack that will play while the images are displayed. You'll do that now by puppeting a sound, just as you did in Lesson 22. Remember that the playback head is paused on frame 18, removing the control of the sprites from the score and giving it to Lingo. This means you need to puppet the sound as well.

1] In the Cast window select cast member 38, *Wlkabout.aif*. Click the Cast Member Properties button.

This is the sound you will use for the movie.

2] Loop the sound in the cast. Check the Loop box in the dialog box and click OK to close the dialog box.

With the Loop box checked, the sound will continue to play while the movie runs.

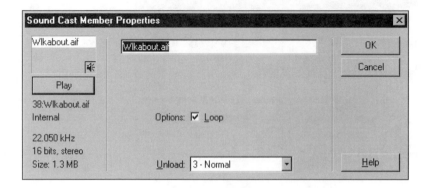

Next you will alter the *startMovie* script in cast member 22.

3] Double-click cast member 22, and make the changes shown here in bold:

```
on StartMovie              --At the start of the movie, do the following:
   CreateLocationList      --Run this handler to create the location list.
   gCurrentView = "vict.n"  --Set the northern view of Victoria as the default.
   puppetSound "Wlkabout.aif"  --Puppet this sound file.
end
```

4] Rewind and play the movie.

The music plays immediately.

5] Save your work.

Now the movie is complete!

WHAT YOU HAVE LEARNED

In this lesson you have:

• Created a highlight and used *the rect* to move highlights [page 632]

• Retrieved values with *getaProp* [page 634]

• Used *char* and *count* to get values from chunk expressions [page 635]

• Concatenated two expressions [page 638]

• Set the *the memberNum* property [page 640]

• Added a script to a cast member and sent parameters [page 647]

• Puppeted sound with *puppetSound* [page 655]

on the web

using lingo

LESSON 27

The movies you have created so far in this book (except those for Lesson 15) have been self-contained. They reside on your user's computer, and all interaction occurs within the movie itself. In this lesson you'll learn how to make your movies communicate with the exciting world of the Internet. As you will see, you can create projectors that launch Web browsers or retrieve information from Internet sites for use within your movies, and you can use Shockwave to make your movies play in Web browsers, where they can interact with other Shockwave movies and with content available anywhere on the Internet.

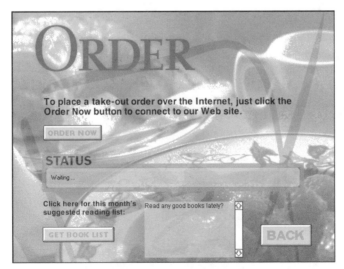

The Order screen from the prototype Fine Dining application features an Order Now button, which launches the user's Web browser and displays a Web page for placing take-out orders on the Internet. Clicking the Get Book List button downloads and displays a list of recommended readings, updated monthly by this organization.

Graphics for the Web movie project were designed by Ming Lau, BlueWaters. Programming by Frank Elley, Behind the Curtain.

For the project in this lesson, you will return to the Order.dir movie you started in Lessons 18 and 19. You will create a movie that launches a Web browser and navigates to a specific Web page. You'll also retrieve a text file from an Internet site and display its contents in your movie.

If you would like to review the final results of this lesson, open the Complete folder within the Lesson27 folder. If you have an Internet connection, play Order.dir, which retrieves sample files from the Internet. If you do not have an Internet connection, play Order2.dir, which retrieves sample files stored on the CD.

WHAT YOU WILL LEARN

In this lesson you will:

• Set up Director to work with a Web browser

• Launch a Web browser from a movie

• Set up a simple status field

• Retrieve text files from Internet sites and display them in a movie

• Create a Shockwave movie

• Embed a Shockwave movie in a Web page

APPROXIMATE TIME

It should take about 4 hours to complete this lesson.

LESSON FILES

Media Files:

None

Starting Files:

Lesson27\Start\Start.dir
Lesson27\Start\FineDine.htm
Lesson27\Start\FineLogo.dir
Lesson27\Start\FineLogo.gif
Lesson27\Start\BookList.txt

Completed Projects:

Lesson27\Complete\Order.dir
Lesson27\Complete\Order2.dir

SETTING UP FOR THIS PROJECT

To fully benefit from this lesson, you need a Web browser and a connection to the Internet, either through an Internet service provider or through your company network. You can also complete this lesson if you have access to a Web server through a company intranet. For simplicity, this lesson refers primarily to the Internet, but everything you learn applies equally to intranets as well.

Even if you have just a Web browser but no Internet or intranet connection, you can still complete many of the tasks in this lesson. Tasks that require a live connection to the Internet or an intranet are noted. If you don't have a Web browser, you can read this lesson for general information.

To start, you need to copy several files from the CD to your computer. The main starting file is a version of the Order.dir movie you worked on in Lessons 18 and 19. Recall that Order.dir is one component of the prototype Fine Dining application; it is a separate movie that is called from the Fine Dining application's main menu.

1] Open the Start.dir movie in the Start folder and save it as *Order.dir* in your Projects folder.

2] Copy the following files from the Start folder into your Projects folder on your hard drive:

FineDine.htm

FineLogo.gif

FineLogo.dir

BookList.txt (if you do not have an Internet connection)

You will need the FineDine.htm and the FineLogo.gif files for the first project in this lesson, when you will be developing a Web movie that interacts with the Internet. If you do not have an Internet connection, you will also need BookList.txt for the first project. You will need FineLogo.dir for the second project, when you create a Shockwave movie.

SELECTING A WEB BROWSER

To complete all the tasks in this lesson, you will need a Web browser. You can use either Microsoft Internet Explorer 3.0 or later on Windows, or you can use Netscape Navigator 3.0 or later on Windows or the Macintosh. You can also use any browser that supports Netscape plug-ins. Your Web browser should have the latest version of Shockwave for Director installed. Check Macromedia's Web site at http://www.macromedia.com for the most recent version.

In the first phase of this project, you will create an Order Now button that launches the Web browser on the user's computer. When a user clicks that button, Director will first search the user's computer for a Web browser. If Director can't find a browser, it will open a dialog box and ask the user to locate and select a Web browser.

When you are authoring the movie and test the Order Now button, Director will also search your computer for a Web browser. Before you start, you will follow the steps in this task to make sure Director has found the Web browser you want to use. When you are developing Web movies, you often have to test them with a variety of browsers, and you will follow the same steps to change browsers for testing purposes.

1] Choose File › Preferences › Network to display the Network Preferences dialog box.

THIS FIELD SHOWS THE LOCATION OF THE BROWSER THAT DIRECTOR WILL USE

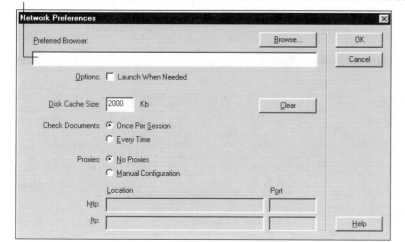

2] If the Preferred Browser field doesn't show the browser you want to use, click Browse and select the browser you want to use. Then click Open.

3] Select the Launch When Needed option. Then click OK to close the dialog box.

The Launch When Needed option applies only to authoring mode and does not affect any projectors you create. When this option is selected and you use a Lingo command that requires a Web browser, Director will launch the Web browser if it isn't already open. Deselect this option if you do not want Director to launch a Web browser when a Lingo command requires it; this is useful during testing when you don't want to wait for a browser to launch.

Now you're ready to start setting up your Web movie.

USING *GOTONETPAGE* TO LAUNCH A WEB BROWSER

You can easily provide your users with a simple, one-click way to reach your Web site for the latest product announcements, updates, or technical support. They don't need to remember or type the URL—your movie gets them where they need to go.

To connect to a Web site directly from a Director movie, you use the *gotoNetPage* command, which launches the user's Web browser and goes to a URL, or Web address, that you specify. The syntax of this command is *gotoNetPage "URL"*. You will use this command for the Order Now button on the Fine Dining application's main menu.

In this task, you will begin by setting up the button to display the FineDine.htm file you earlier copied to your Projects folder. Once you've tested the button with this local file, you'll add some features and then finally connect the button to a Web page on the Internet. Because you will need to revise the button's functionality several times, you will organize your scripts to make them easily accessible. Instead of placing all the button's functionality in a cast member script, you will set up the button to call a custom handler. You will then write the custom handler as a movie script, which is stored in the cast. That will make it easy to quickly open the custom handler for revisions by double-clicking it in the cast.

1] Choose Window › Score to open the Score window (Windows Ctrl+4, Macintosh Command+4).

Take a moment to familiarize yourself with the movie that has been constructed for you.

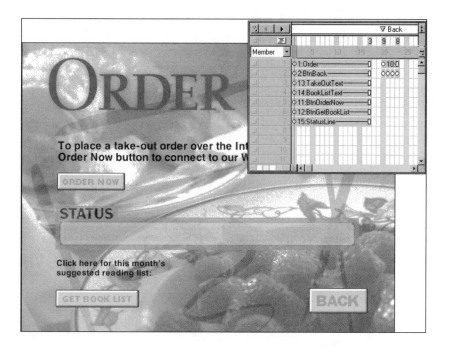

Notice the background in channel 1, the Back button in channel 2, and the Back animation sequence spanning frames 20 through 23. You completed these elements in Lessons 18 and 19 and won't be working with them in this lesson.

Also notice the two text fields (in channels 3 and 4) that describe how to use the Order panel, the Order Now button (channel 5), the Get Book List button (channel 6), and the field cast member that displays status information (channel 7). Double-click the behavior channel, frame 17; this frame script contains a simple *go to the frame* command to loop the playback head at frame 17.

The duration of the sprites in frames 1 through 17 frames is mostly a matter of taste. No animation or other action occurs in those 17 frames. This 17-frame duration was chosen because it makes the sprites long enough for their cast member names to be recognizable in the score.

Now that you understand how the movie is constructed, you can begin setting up the Order Now button.

2] In the cast, click cast member 13 (the Order Now button) and click the Script button to open the Script window.

You are creating a cast member script because no matter when or where this button is clicked in the movie, you want it to perform the same action. Director opens the Script window with a *mouseUp* handler—the most common type of cast member script—already started for you.

3] Complete the *mouseUp* handler as shown here in bold:

```
on mouseUp
  ConnectToWebSite( )
end
```

ConnectToWebSite is a custom handler that you will create in the next step. By placing this call to a custom handler here, you are now finished with the Order Now button. For the rest of this lesson, you will work on the *ConnectToWebSite* handler.

4] Press Control+Shift+U (Windows) or Command+Shift+U (Macintosh) to open the Script window.

Creating a cast member this way creates a blank movie script. As you learned in Lesson 16, any handlers that you place in a movie script will be available from anywhere in the movie.

5] Type the script for the *ConnectToWebSite* handler as shown below and close the Script window.

```
on ConnectToWebSite      --This handler is called from the Order Now button.
  gotoNetPage " "
end
```

The *gotoNetPage* command requires a parameter, surrounded by quotation marks, that specifies what should be displayed in the browser once it is launched. You could type the parameter, but for now just leave this element blank. You will learn an easier way to specify this parameter.

6] In the Cast window, give your new movie script the name *ConnectToWebSite*.

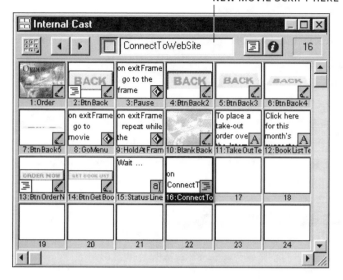

TYPE A NAME FOR THE
NEW MOVIE SCRIPT HERE

Director creates the movie script in the first open position in the cast. If your *ConnectToWebSite* script is not cast member 16, move it to position 16 to make it easier for you to follow the steps in the following tasks.

7] Save your movie, but do not play it yet.

USING A TEST FILE ON A LOCAL DRIVE

Developing a Web movie would be extremely time consuming if you could test your work in progress only by repeatedly launching your Web browser and connecting to the Internet. Fortunately, Lingo commands for creating Web movies accept URLs or file path names interchangeably. By using a file path name instead of a URL, you can greatly speed up your project development. For your initial development work, you will display a test file in the Web browser. When your scripting is complete, you'll substitute a URL that has been set up for you on Macromedia's Web site.

The test file you'll use is the FineDine.htm file you earlier copied to your hard disk. To use the FineDine.htm test page, you need to specify the file's path name in the *gotoNetPage* command that you set up in the previous task. Here's a trick that guarantees that you won't make a typing mistake when specifying the path name:

1] Launch your Web browser.

2] From the Projects folder on your computer, drag the FineDine.htm file and drop it on the browser window.

The browser displays the test file. If for some reason you can't drag and drop a file on your browser window, use the browser's File > Open command to open the FineDine.htm test page.

3] Select the path name that the browser displays and copy it to the clipboard (Windows Ctrl+C, Macintosh Command+C).

In Internet Explorer, the path name appears in the Address field. In Netscape Navigator, the path name appears in the Go To or Location field. Other browsers display the path name in different locations.

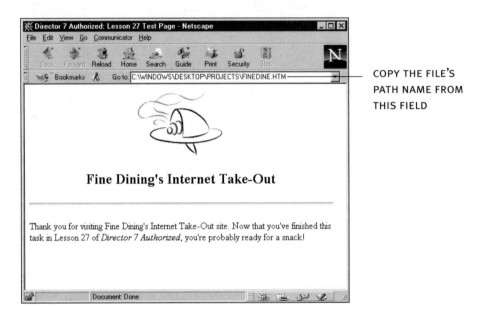

COPY THE FILE'S PATH NAME FROM THIS FIELD

4] Switch back to Director and double-click cast member 16 to open the *ConnectToWebSite* handler in the Script window.

5] Paste the path name between the quotation marks in the *gotoNetPage* command as shown here in bold and then close the Script window (Windows Ctrl+V, Macintosh Command+V).

Note that your path will probably be different than the one shown, depending on how you set up your Projects folder.

```
on ConnectToWebSite      --This handler is called from the Order Now button.
  gotoNetPage "C:\WINDOWS\DESKTOP\PROJECTS\FINEDINE.HTM"
end
```

666

This cut-and-paste method is a quick, foolproof way to specify a parameter for the *gotoNetPage* command. Although this method is used here for a file path, you could cut and paste a Web page's URL as well.

When you are displaying a file that is in the same folder with your Director movie, you do not have to specify the entire path name, as shown here. You can simply type the file's name, such as *FineDine.htm*.

note *Your path may begin with "file:///", reflecting the way Netscape Navigator sometimes displays files. Internet Explorer simply displays the path name without the "file:///" prefix.*

6] Quit your Web browser.

You want to be sure the *gotoNetPage* command launches the Web browser when requested to do so.

7] Save your movie and play it. Click the Order Now button.

Director should launch your Web browser, and the FineDine.htm test page should be displayed.

If your Order Now button doesn't work, go back over the previous steps. Especially make sure that you specified your preferred browser (by choosing File > Preferences > Network), and that the pathname for the FineDine.htm test page is correct.

8] Quit your Web browser.

Again, you'll want your browser closed so you can test your button on the Internet.

TESTING YOUR MOVIE ON THE INTERNET

Once the Order Now button is predictably launching your Web browser and opening the test file on your hard disk, it's time to put it to the test "live" on the Internet. For this task to work, you'll need an Internet or intranet connection.

If your Internet access is through a dial-up modem connection, you should configure your Web browser (if possible) to automatically dial your Internet service provider when the Web browser launches. If your Internet access is through a company network, make sure your Internet connection is active before testing your movie. Make sure your Web browser isn't running so you can be sure your movie actually launches your Web browser when requested to do so.

1] Double-click cast member 16 to open the *ConnectToWebSite* handler in the Script window. Revise the handler as shown here in bold:

```
on ConnectToWebSite      --This handler is called from the Order Now button.
   gotoNetPage "http://special.macromedia.com/lingotrng/finedine.htm"
                          --Launch a Web browser and display this Web page.
end
```

This is a special URL set up by Macromedia just for people using this book. If you don't have access to the Internet but are working on a company intranet, you can copy the FineDine.htm test page to a network server and then substitute the path to that file in the *gotoNetPage* command here.

2] Save your work. Play the movie and click the Order Now button.
Director should launch your Web browser and display a version of the FineDine.htm page retrieved from the Web site.

USING A FIELD TO DISPLAY STATUS INFORMATION

One disadvantage of the *gotoNetPage* command is that once it executes, your Director movie has no way to know whether the action succeeded. Director simply sends a message through the computer's operating system to the Web browser, telling it to launch and to navigate to a specific URL or file. Director then steps out of the picture. Many things could go wrong: The Web browser might not be present or it might not launch, the connection to the Internet might fail, the URL might not be found, and so on. Even if the Web browser launches and displays the requested Web page successfully, your Director movie has no way of knowing this.

In such a situation, there is no fully satisfactory way to provide feedback to your users. In this task, you will implement a modest form of feedback by displaying messages in the Status field on the Order panel. The initial message, which says "Waiting…", will be replaced by the message "Launching your Web browser…" when users click the Order Now button.

In this task you will learn how to change the text displayed in a field cast member using the cast member's *text* property. Beginning with Director 7, all text can be edited, either while authoring or while the movie is playing, with the use of Lingo. A field type is used in this example because field text provides the best choice for text of small size. It also provides the smallest cast member size, which is important for Internet use.

You'll want to change the text in the Status field on several occasions: when the movie starts, when users click the Order Now button, and when users click the Get Book

List button. Therefore, you will write a custom handler that you can use throughout your movie to reset the Status field.

1] Double-click cast member 15 (StatusLine) to display the Field window.

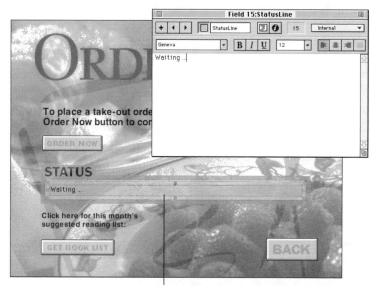

THIS TEXT FIELD WILL HOLD A STATUS MESSAGE

The StatusLine cast member has already been positioned on the stage, and the message "Waiting…" has already been entered for you. You can type any text you want here; this beginning text doesn't matter because you will control the contents of this field later through Lingo. For now, though, make no changes.

2] Close the Field window.

3] In the cast, click the next open position (cast member 17) and choose Window › Script to create a new movie script.
As you did for the *ConnectToWebSite* handler, you are creating a movie script whose contents will be available throughout the movie.

4] Type the following handler:

```
on UpdateStatusLine messagetext
                    --This handler accepts the text specified in the messagetext
                    --parameter and displays it in the Status field.
    member ("StatusLine").text = messagetext
                    --Put the message text into the StatusLine field.
end
```

669

This *UpdateStatusLine* handler accepts a parameter that specifies the message you want to display in the field named StatusLine (cast member 15).

When you call this handler from other scripts in your movie, remember that it is using the *text* property of a cast member. This places text in a field, which means the parameter it accepts must be a string. Therefore, you must remember to specify the parameter for the *UpdateStatusLine* handler using quotations marks so that Director will treat it as a string. You will see how this works in the following steps.

5] In the cast, give the new script cast member the name *UpdateStatusLine* to make it easier for you to follow along with later tasks.

You will now use your new *UpdateStatusLine* handler at key points in your program.

6] Click the New Script button in the upper-left corner of the Script window to start a new movie script.

NEW SCRIPT BUTTON

Using the New Script button is a handy way to write several movie scripts, each as a separate cast member, without opening and closing the Script window.

7] Type the following *startMovie* handler as shown and then close the Script window:

```
on startMovie
    UpdateStatusLine("Waiting...")      --Display a starting message in the Status field.
end
```

As you have seen in several previous lessons, a *startMovie* handler stored in a movie script is the place where you set initial values for any information, such as global variables or text fields, that you intend to change dynamically while your movie runs.

670

In this case, the *startMovie* handler uses the *UpdateStatusLine* handler you wrote earlier to make sure the Status field always displays the "Waiting…" message when the movie starts. You used quotation marks around the text of the message so that Director will treat it as a string when it passes it to the *UpdateStatusLine* handler.

Notice that Director created this movie script in the next available cast position, number 18.

8] In the Cast window, give the new movie script in cast position 18 the name ***startMovie.***

Naming the cast member will make the script easier to find as you continue to refine your application.

You will now use the *UpdateStatusLine* handler to provide feedback when the Order Now button is clicked.

9] Double-click cast member 16 to open the *ConnectToWebSite* handler in the Script window. Revise the handler as shown here in bold and then close the Script window:

```
on ConnectToWebSite      --This handler is called from the Order Now button.
   UpdateStatusLine("Launching your Web browser...")
                         --Display a message indicating that the Order Now
                         --button has been clicked.
   gotoNetPage "http://special.macromedia.com/lingotrng/finedine.htm"
                         --Launch a Web browser and display this Web page.
end
```

When a user clicks the Order Now button, it triggers the *ConnectToWebSite* handler. The line you just added to the handler displays a status message informing the user that an action is now in progress.

10] Rewind and play the movie. Click the Order Now button.

When you click the Order Now button, you now see the initial "Waiting…" message replaced by "Launching your Web browser…".

Unfortunately, "Launching your Web browser…" remains displayed regardless of what happens. You will learn a simple way to reset the message in the next task.

tip *When your movie launches the Web browser, the Director program is moved into the background. If you find that the Director movie stops when this happens, make sure that the movie is set to run in the background. To do this, choose File > Preferences > General and make sure that Animate in Background is checked.*

USING THE TIMER TO RESET STATUS MESSAGES

Your movie can't detect whether users successfully used their Web browsers to place an order, but you can still update the "Launching your Web browser…" message in the Status field by resetting the message back to "Waiting…" after a delay of a few seconds.

The delay serves two purposes. If nothing happens when users click the Order Now button—that is, if the Web browser doesn't launch—at least the reappearance of the "Waiting…" message will be a sign to them that, even though the Web browser isn't going to launch, at least the Director movie hasn't frozen and they can perform other tasks or even try clicking Order Now again. If the browser does launch, the status message will also reset to "Waiting…" once the user returns to your movie. The mechanism you set up for the message delay will also be of use in a later task, where more detailed feedback can be provided.

From the moment a movie starts, Director keeps track of the elapsed time in **ticks**, which are increments of $\frac{1}{60}$ second; it is as if Director has its finger on a stopwatch. You can tell Director to reset the stopwatch—that is, to set its timer back to 0—by issuing the *startTimer* command, and at any point you can use the *the timer* property to ask Director for the current elapsed time, in ticks, since the movie started or since you last issued the *startTimer* command.

The design question now becomes: How do you monitor the *the timer* property until, say, 480 ticks (8 seconds: 480 divided by 60 ticks per second) have elapsed? For this, you need a handler that executes repeatedly while no other action is occurring. One obvious choice is an *exitFrame* handler that has a *go to the frame* command, because this handler will execute over and over as the playback head enters and exits the frame. You have left the tempo for this movie at its default setting of 15 frames per second. That means that an *exitFrame* handler looping the playback head in a frame will execute 15 times per second, which is a sufficient rate for monitoring the *the timer* property.

You now have all the tools you need to reset the status message after a short delay.

1] In the Cast window, select cast member 3 (named Pause) and then click the Script button to display the Script window. Replace the contents of the *on exitFrame* handler as shown here in bold:

```
on exitFrame
    CheckConnectionStatus()    --Call a handler to check the status of the current
                               --network operation.
    go to the frame
end
```

This frame script is assigned to frame 17, where its role is to keep the playback head in the frame while the movie waits for a user action. You now need a way to monitor the status of current network operations (of both the *ConnectToWebSite* handler that you are currently implementing and the file download you will implement later in this lesson). By using a *go to the frame* command here, you make the playback head continuously loop in the frame, and every time it does, Director can call a handler that will check the status and take any necessary action.

You will now write the *CheckConnectionStatus* handler that this frame script calls.

2] In the cast, click the next open position (cast member 19) and choose Window › Script to create a new movie script.

As you have seen in several previous lessons, a movie script is the place to put any handler, such as the *CheckConnectionStatus* handler you are going to write, that can be called from anywhere in the movie.

3] Type the *CheckConnectionStatus* handler as shown and then close the Script window.

```
on CheckConnectionStatus
                    --This handler is called from the exitFrame handler
                    --in frame 17.
    if the timer › 480 then UpdateStatusLine("Waiting...")
                    --When more then 480 ticks have elapsed since the
                    --Order Now button was clicked, update the Status field
                    --with this message.
    go to the frame
end
```

Remember that this handler is being called 15 times per second as the playback head loops through the *exitFrame* handler in frame 17. The *if-then* statement checks to see if more than 480 ticks have elapsed since the *startTimer* command was last issued. When *the timer* returns a number greater than 480, a call to the *UpdateStatusLine* handler resets the message to "Waiting…". Notice that there is no need to use an *end if* statement because the *if-then* structure is on a single line.

tip   *While you are developing your movie, you might want to use an even shorter time than 480 ticks so you don't have to wait too long before the Status field is reset. Once your movie is nearing completion, you can experiment to see how long the final elapsed time should be.*

4] In the Cast window, give the new movie script in cast position 19 the name *CheckConnectionStatus***.**

Naming the cast member will make the script easier to find as you continue to refine your movie.

You've now established a way to reset the status message after 480 ticks have elapsed. The next step is to make sure the event that changed the status message in the first place—clicking the Order Now button—also resets the *the timer* property to begin the countdown to 480. To do so, you will revise the handler that is called when the Order Now button is clicked.

5] Double-click cast member 16 to open the *ConnectToWebSite* **handler in the Script window. Revise the handler as shown here in bold and then close the Script window:**

```
on ConnectToWebSite      --This handler is called from the Order Now button.
   UpdateStatusLine("Launching your Web browser...")
                         --Display a message indicating that the Order Now
                         --button has been clicked.
   gotoNetPage "http://special.macromedia.com/lingotrng/finedine.htm"
                         --Launch a Web browser and display this Web page.
   startTimer            --Reset the timer.
end
```

When users click the Order Now button, this *ConnectToWebSite* handler is called, and Director starts counting again from 0.

Now you can see the flow of the status message handling: Users open your Web movie, and the *startMovie* handler sets the status message to "Waiting…". Users click the Order Now button. Director sets the status message to "Launching your Web browser…" and resets its internal timer to 0. The playback head loops in frame 17, repeatedly calling the *CheckConnectionStatus* handler. When the *the timer* property returns a value greater than 480, the *CheckConnectionStatus* handler resets the status message to "Waiting…". The only thing that can change the message is another click on the Order Now button, which starts the process all over again.

6] Save your work and choose File › Create Projector.

It is useful to see how your movie will be seen by your users. To do this, you will create a projector. This will also let you see how the message line changes with the launching of the browser and the passing of the 480 ticks.

7] In the Create Projector dialog box, select your Order.dir movie and click Add to add it to the Playback Order list. Then click Options to open the Display Options dialog box.

8] In the Display Options dialog box, make sure the Animate in Background option is selected. Then click OK to close the Display Options dialog box.

When the Web browser launches, it will become the active application. Although Director will be able to continue keeping track of its timer while it is in the background, Director will be able to update its message line only if you select the Animate in Background option. It is especially desirable for the Director movie's message line to update when the Web browser window and your movie are positioned on the screen so that both are visible at the same time. Otherwise, the "Launching your Web browser…" message will be displayed until your movie becomes the active application again.

9] In the Create Projector dialog box, click Create, give the movie a name, and click Save.

Director creates a projector of the Order.dir movie. You will notice that many files are used in the creation of the projector, including the **Xtras** used for network operations. The "net Lingo" commands such as *gotoNetPage* and *getNetText* require several Director Xtras to work. Xtras are separate program modules that add capabilities to Director. When you use an Xtra to create a movie, you must distribute a copy of that Xtra with your projector. Director 7 now automatically includes the network Xtras when a projector needs to use network commands. Consult your Director manuals and online help for more information about Xtras.

10] Run the projector and click the Order Now button.

Your Web browser launches and displays the special Web page. You're wired!

The minimal status message you implemented for this specific task—launching a Web browser from a Director movie—would probably be only the starting point for most real-world applications. For example, a more robust application might provide users with additional instructions in case the Web browser does not start. This example using Director's internal timer was chosen because it shows you one simple, general-purpose method for displaying, maintaining, and resetting status messages within an application. In the next phase of this project, you will build upon the timing mechanism you've implemented so far to provide better status messages for operations that can be monitored more closely.

USING *GETNETTEXT* TO RETRIEVE DATA FROM THE INTERNET

Many products these days seem to be out of date only days after they are released. A Director movie, however, need never be out of date because you can update it with information retrieved remotely from the Internet, and you can entice customers to stay in touch by offering them Internet access to information that is updated more frequently than is possible through more traditional delivery methods. The Order screen that you are building employs one such device, offering customers access to a new list of suggested readings each month.

In this task you will add a script to the Get Book List button that retrieves a text file—the book list—from an Internet location. In fact, you can retrieve any type of Internet file—graphics, Shockwave movies, HTML-coded Web pages, and so on—and in addition to retrieving a specific file, you can send a query to a network database and then retrieve the results.

You will retrieve the text file in two stages. In the first stage, your movie requests the file using the *getNetText ("URL")* command. When this command is executed, your Director movie will send a request through your user's Internet connection to the location (specified by the *URL* parameter) where the file can be found. Director will then download the file from that location into the movie's memory. In the second stage, you use the *getTextResult* function to retrieve the file from memory and store it somewhere—in this case, in a field cast member that you will create.

Like the *gotoNetPage* command, the *getNetText* command doesn't have to point to a location on the Internet. For the *URL* parameter, you can also specify files stored on an intranet or even on the user's computer for retrieval.

If the *getNetText* command executes when no Internet connection is active on a user's computers, your Director movie tries to establish one using any automatic dial-up feature currently configured on the computer. This automatic-connection feature is similar to the feature that enables a user's Web browser to try to dial up or connect to the Internet when it is launched when no Internet connection is active.

In this first task you will implement the basic button script.

1] In the cast, click cast member 14 (the Get Book List button) and click the Script button to open the Script window.

You are creating a cast member script because no matter when or where this button is clicked in the movie, you want it to perform the same action. Director opens the Script window with a *mouseUp* handler—the most common type of cast member script—already started for you.

676

2] Complete the *mouseUp* handler as shown here in bold:

```
on mouseUp
  GetBookList()    --Call a handler to download the book list.
end
```

As you did for the Order Now button, you are keeping the cast member script simple by including a call to a custom handler, which you will write in the next step. You'll see an added benefit—in addition to those mentioned in the discussion of the Order Now button—a little later.

3] Click the New Script button to open the Script window for a new movie script. Enter the script shown here and then close the Script window:

```
on GetBookList
                    --This handler is called from the Get Book List button.
  UpdateStatusLine("Retrieving this month's book list...")
                    --Update the Status field to indicate that the book list
                    --is being retrieved.
  getNetText ("http://special.macromedia.com/lingotrng/BookList.txt")
                    --Download the book list into memory.
end
```

The path specified in the *getNetText* command points to a file on Macromedia's Web site created especially for readers of this book. If you don't have access to the Internet but are working on a company intranet, you can copy the BookList.txt file from the Complete folder in the Lesson27 folder on the CD to a network server and then substitute the path to that file in the *getNetText* command here. If you have neither an Internet nor intranet connection, then copy the BookList.txt file from the CD and place it on your computer in the same folder as your movie and then revise the *getNetText* command as follows:

```
getNetText ("BookList.txt")
```

The *getNetText* command will then be requesting the BookList.txt file on your hard drive. As long as the file is in the same folder as your movie, you need not specify the full path name.

This script also updates the Status field to let users know that clicking the Get Book List button has had the desired effect; later, you'll add a script to give users more feedback as the list is displayed.

Notice that Director created this movie script in the next available cast position, number 20.

4] In the Cast window, give the new movie script in cast position 20 the name *GetBookList*.

Naming the cast member will make the script easier to find as you continue to refine your application.

In the Cast window you can now see some additional benefits of organizing the handlers so that most of the functionality is stored in movie scripts instead of in cast member scripts.

USE THESE ARROW BUTTONS TO BROWSE
BACK AND FORTH THROUGH YOUR SCRIPTS

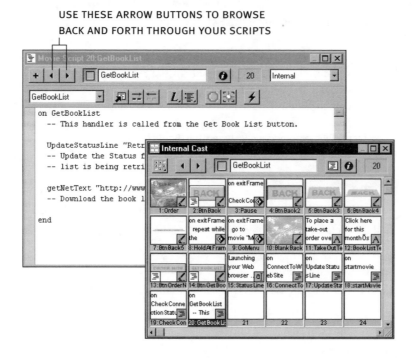

Cast members 16 through 20 now hold the basic scripts that drive your application. You've named the cast members to match the handlers in those scripts, making them easy to find. Because they are side by side, you can browse back and forth through them to get a quick sense of the entire scripting structure of your application.

CREATING A SCROLLING TEXT FIELD

The next phase in developing the features for the Get Book List button is to create a text field to display the book list once it is downloaded. Earlier in this lesson (for the status message), you used a text field whose contents you were able to change using Lingo. You will also create a field for the book list, but it will be different from previous text fields you've used.

For the status message, you knew ahead of time how much text would be displayed in the field, which made it easy to decide how big the field should be. In this project, the book list might be only a few lines long one month and several dozen lines the next month. In this task you will learn how to set up a field cast member with scroll bars so it can hold text of any length.

1] Click the Field tool in the tool palette. Drag to create a box at the bottom of the stage, centered between the Get Book List and Back buttons.

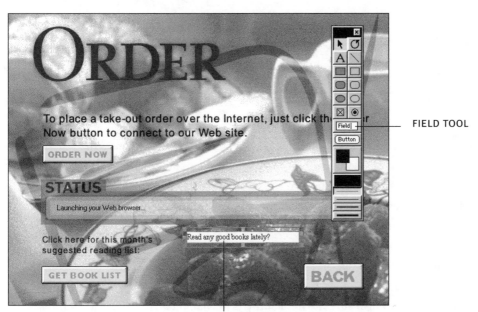

DRAW A FIELD FOR THE BOOK LIST HERE

Don't worry about the exact size and positioning of the text field. You will fine-tune it later.

2] Select Window › Field to open the field editor. Type *Read any good books lately?* in the field. Then select a font and size for the text. Close the field editor and tool palette.

Actually, you can type any text you wish, since you will set this field's contents with Lingo later.

3] In the Cast window, select the new field cast member and press Ctrl+I (Windows) or Command+I (Macintosh) to open the Field Cast Member Properties dialog box. Type *BookList* as the cast member name, select Scrolling from the Framing menu, select the Word Wrap option, and click OK.

TYPE THE CAST MEMBER NAME HERE

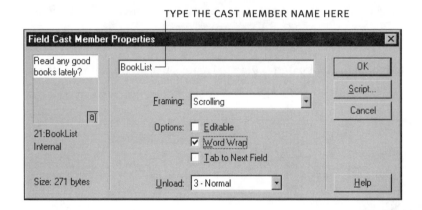

By default, once you adjust the width of a text field, Director adjusts the length automatically to fit whatever text you have typed into it. The Scrolling option will allow you to resize the text field to a specific size vertically as well, and it will add a scroll bar to allow users to view all the text when the text is too long to be viewed in the field at one time. The Word Wrap feature tells Director to wrap lines in a paragraph of text within the field's boundaries, in the same way that paragraphs wrap in a word processor.

4] In the score, make sure the field sprite is in channel 9 and adjust its duration so it spans frames 1 through 17. Set its ink to Background Transparent.

You're skipping channel 8 for the moment because you will use it for another element later.

5] On the stage, drag the book field's resizing handles so the field occupies most of the space to the right of the Get Book List button.

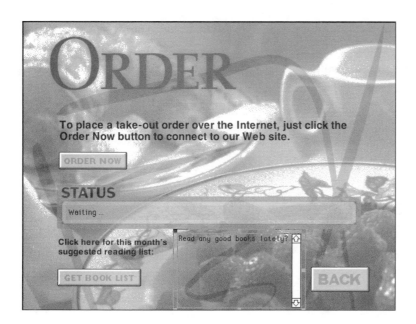

The text in the BookList field is a bit difficult to read, since the field is transparent and the panel's background is showing through. You will use a nice trick for toning down the background.

6] In the tool palette, select white as the foreground color and then, with the Filled Rectangle tool, draw a second rectangle exactly over the text field.

You will use this second rectangle to filter out some of the background, making the text in the book field easier to read.

> **tip** *If you have trouble positioning the second rectangle exactly, select the text field in the score and press Shift+Ctrl+I (Windows) or Shift+Command+I (Macintosh) to display the field sprite's properties. Note the field's Width and Height settings, plus its Left and Top coordinates, and then close the dialog box. Select the white rectangle sprite, display its sprite properties, deselect Maintain Proportions, and enter the same values for Width, Height, Left, and Top. Now the white rectangle is positioned exactly over the text field.*

7] In the score, make sure the white rectangle sprite is in channel 8.

Sprites in higher-numbered channels always sit "on top of" sprites in lower-numbered channels. With the white rectangle behind the book field, it will filter out just the background without affecting the type in the book field.

8] In the cast, select member 22, the new white rectangle, and name it *ListBackground*.

9] In the score, select the white rectangle sprite and adjust its duration so it spans frames 1 through 17. Set its ink effect to Blend and choose a blend value of 50 percent.

Your score should now look like this:

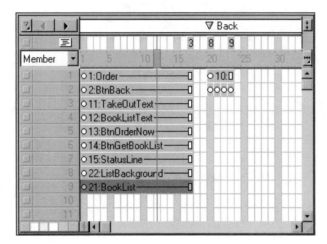

The white rectangle now allows only about half the value of the background to show through: a very classy effect!

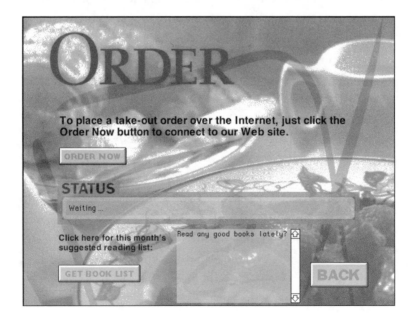

10] Save your work but do not play the movie.

Your movie now includes a button that can download the book list, and it has a place to display the list once it is downloaded. In the final phase of implementing the Get Book List button, you will learn how to display the downloaded text in the book field.

USING *NETDONE* AND *GETNETTEXT* TO DISPLAY THE DOWNLOADED TEXT

Once your movie starts a network operation such as the *getNetText* download, a whole range of factors beyond your movie's control come into play: the availability of a network connection, response time on the Internet, and so on. In addition, the download is taking place behind the scenes and out of sight: the text is being loaded into your movie's memory. Your movie needs a way to determine when the download finishes so it can display the text.

One complication is that on another user's computer, your Web movie might be only one of several applications vying for network attention. For example, a user might also be running an e-mail program that periodically sends a query to a network mail server to see if new mail has arrived. The computer's operating system manages these operations by assigning each one a unique numeric ID. Your scripts can use the numeric ID of the network operation that started when the *getNetText* command was issued.

Once you have this operation ID, you can use it with the *netDone* function to track the status of that operation. When *netDone* returns TRUE, you know that the download has finished and it is time to display the downloaded text in the book field. You can retrieve the downloaded text from memory using the *netTextResult* function. Here's an overview of the steps:

• Start downloading the data into memory with the *getNetText* function.

• Get the operation ID returned by the *getNetText* function.

• Check to see if the download is complete with the *netDone* function (using the operation ID).

• Retrieve the downloaded data from memory using the *netTextResult* function.

You have already created the *GetBookList* handler to start the download. In this task you will complete the scripting by implementing the final three steps in this process.

1] Double-click cast member 20 to open the Script window. Revise the *GetBookList* handler as shown here in bold:

```
global gOperationID      --Declare a global variable to hold the connection ID.

on GetBookList
                         --This handler is called from the Get Book List button.
    UpdateStatusLine("Retrieving this month's book list...")
                         --Update the Status field to indicate that the book list
                         --is being retrieved.
    gOperationID = getNetText ("http://special.macromedia.com/lingotrng/BookList.txt")
                         --Download the book list into memory. Place the connection ID
                         --into a global variable.
    startTimer           --Reset the timer.
end
```

You are placing the operation ID in a global variable so it can be available to other handlers throughout the movie. As you learned in Lesson 20, a global variable must be declared before you use it, which is why you placed the global *gOperationID* statement at the top of the script. Your *GetBookList* handler resets the status message to "Retrieving this month's book list…". Just in case the operation fails at this point, you include a *startTimer* command. This resets Director's internal timer back to 0. The *CheckConnectionStatus* handler will reset the status message to "Waiting…" after 480 ticks have elapsed.

Now that you've set up a way to capture the operation ID for the download, what can you do with it? You need to monitor the status of that operation, and your *CheckConnectionStatus* handler is the perfect place to do so. Before you edit your *CheckConnectionStatus* handler, however, you will make sure that the global variable you just created is initialized when the movie starts.

2] Double-click cast member 18 and revise the *startMovie* handler as shown here in bold:

```
global gOperationID              --Declare a global variable to hold the connection ID.

on startMovie
   UpdateStatusLine("Waiting...")  --Display a starting message in the Status field.
   set gOperationID = –1           --Initialize the global variable that holds
                                    --the network ID.
end
```

As you have learned in previous lessons, you must initialize a variable with a starting value before you use it in a script. For global variables, which might be used by any script in your movie, the best place to set an initial value is in the *startMovie* hander, which ensures that the global variable is initialized before any other script has a chance to use it.

Why choose an initial value of –1? The *getNetText* function always returns a positive number. By setting the initial value of the *gOperationID* global variable to –1, you give other handlers in that movie a way to check whether a *getNetText* operation is in progress. If a handler finds that the value in *gOperationID* is –1, it knows that no operation is in progress. Otherwise, the handler knows that the value in *gOperationID* represents the ID for the most recent *getNetText* download operation.

You are now ready to write the script that will actually monitor the progress of the download.

3] Double-click cast member 19 to open the Script window. Revise the *CheckConnectionStatus* handler as shown here in bold and then close the Script window:

```
global gOperationID              --Declare a global variable to hold the operation ID.

on CheckConnectionStatus          --This handler is called from the exitFrame handler
                                  --in frame 17.
   if the timer › 480 then UpdateStatusLine("Waiting...")
                                  --When more then 480 ticks have elapsed since the
                                  --Order Now button was clicked, update the Status field
                                  --with this message.
   if gOperationID ‹› –1 then     --If a download operation is in progress,
      if netDone(gOperationID) = TRUE then
                                  --and if the operation has completed then
         UpdateStatusLine("Displaying this month's book list...")
                                  --change the status message to indicate that the book list
                                  --is being displayed.
```

```
                    member ("BookList").text = netTextResult()
                                        --Put the downloaded text into the BookList field.
            startTimer                  --Reset the timer.
            set gOperationID = –1       --Reset the operation ID to indicate that there is
                                        --no current network operation.
        end if
      end if
        go to the frame
    end
```

Remember that your *CheckConnectionStatus* handler is called from the *exitFrame* handler, which keeps the playback head looping in frame 17. The movie is set at the default rate of 15 frames per second, and therefore your Web movie is checking the status of the network connection many times a second.

The comments in this handler explain what's going on. You just set up the *startMovie* handler to initialize the global variable *gOperationID* to –1. In the *CheckConnectionStatus* handler, the first step in checking the status of the *getNetText* operation is the *if-then* structure, which checks the value in the *gOperationID* global variable. If *gOperationID* is not –1, then a network operation is under way, and all the status-checking logic in the *if-then* structure is evaluated. If *gOperationID* is –1, then a status check is not necessary, and all the status-checking logic in the *if-then* clause is bypassed.

Within the *if-then* clause, the first step is to use the *netDone* function to check whether the operation specified in the *gOperationID* global variable is finished. If the operation is finished, *netDone* returns TRUE. When *netDone* returns TRUE, all the downloaded text is in the movie's memory. The *netTextResult* function will return the text downloaded into memory, and you can put that text into the BookList field.

As a final step in the *if-then* structure, the *gOperationID* global variable is reset to –1 to indicate that the network operation is done. When the *CheckConnectionStatus* handler is called again, the *if-then* clause will be skipped. The *startTimer* command also resets Director's internal clock back to 0, so the *CheckConnectionStatus* handler will reset the status message back to "Waiting…" after 480 ticks have elapsed.

4] Close the Script window and save your work.

5] Rewind and play the movie. Click the Get Book List button.
You see the status message indicate that your movie is retrieving the book list, and then you see the list appear in the BookList field!

USING *NETERROR*

If everything works as it is supposed to, the text in the BookList field will be replaced with text downloaded from the Internet—but what if something goes wrong? A well-written program will check for all possible errors and deal with each possibility. For network operations such as *getNetText*, you can use the *netError* function to check the operation results.

1] Double-click cast member 19 to open the Script window. Revise the *CheckConnectionStatus* handler as shown here in bold:

```
global gOperationID          --Declare a global variable to hold the operation ID.

on CheckConnectionStatus     --This handler is called from the exitFrame handler
                             --in frame 17.
  if the timer › 480 then UpdateStatusLine("Waiting...")
                             --When more then 480 ticks have elapsed since the
                             --Order Now button was clicked, update the Status field
                             --with this message.
  if gOperationID ‹› –1 then --If a download operation is in progress,
    if netDone(gOperationID) = TRUE then
                             --and if the operation has completed then
      put netError(gOperationID)
                             --Display error results in the Message window.
      UpdateStatusLine("Displaying this month's book list...")
                             --change the status message to indicate that the book list
                             --is being displayed.
      member ("BookList").text = netTextResult()
                             --Put the downloaded text into the BookList field.
      startTimer             --Reset the timer.
      set gOperationID = –1  --Reset the operation ID to indicate that there is
                             --no current network operation.
    end if
  end if
  go to the frame
end
```

The *netError* function returns 0 (zero) if there are no errors; otherwise, it returns a number for the particular error. Putting the error number in the Message window is educational, but in a real application, you should test the value returned and respond to any errors as appropriate. If the Internet address is incorrect, for example, you might display a dialog box to let the user enter a different Internet address. The *Lingo Dictionary* provides a list of possible error numbers returned by *netError*. If your program generates errors, you can check there to determine where the problem lies.

2] Close the Script window and save your work.

UNDERSTANDING SHOCKWAVE MOVIES

Earlier in this lesson, you set up your Order.dir movie to launch a Web browser and display the sample FineDine.htm Web page. The page that you linked to at the Internet site is the same as the FineDine.htm test page provided for testing on the CD—with one exception. In the FineDine.htm page on the Internet, the nifty logo at the top of the page is animated: The curls of steam arising from the platter change colors. That logo is actually—you guessed it—a Director movie.

What makes the movie playing within the Web browser different from a regular Director movie is Shockwave, Macromedia's technology for delivering dynamic content over the Internet. Shockwave for Director has two components. First, Shockwave provides a Director viewer engine for Web browsers in the form of an ActiveX control for Internet Explorer and a plug-in for Netscape Navigator on both Windows and Macintosh operating systems. Therefore, your Shockwave movie does not have to be a projector that binds the content of your movie files with the Director viewer engine. With the Director Shockwave movie engine residing as an ActiveX control or a plug-in within the browser, all you have to do is embed the movie files in a Web page, and the browser can play your movie.

The second component of Shockwave is a compression technology that shrinks the size of your movie files drastically to make them download more quickly over the Internet (or a company intranet). Because of this compression and the fact that the viewer engine does not have to be included, a "shocked" version of a movie is often minuscule when compared with a projector of the same movie.

Besides providing faster download times, compression has another benefit: The movie files cannot be opened again using Director, which means your project's assets are safe.

In addition, Director 7 Shockwave movies can **stream** through the Internet connection: The movie can begin to play almost immediately, while the rest of the movie continues to stream onto the user's computer in the background. Streaming drastically reduces any delays that occur when loading a Shockwave movie from the Internet, and it thus enables you to deliver far more media- and content-rich movies over the Internet.

The combination of streaming and high compression also make Shockwave movies appealing for other projects, such as CD-ROMs. Not only can you play Shockwave movies from inside a Web browser, you can also play them from projector files. (However, you can't open or play a Shockwave movie from Director in authoring mode.)

The most exciting aspect of Shockwave is that you often need to make very few, if any, modifications to an existing Director project before saving it as a Shockwave movie. Most of the projects you have created so far, including the Web movie you worked on in this lesson, can be made into Shockwave movies without modification. (Consult the Director manuals and online help for a list of features that are not available in Shockwave movies.)

When you save a movie as a Shockwave file, Director is careful to save the movie as a copy, but you should also be careful to keep backups of any movie files you are saving in Shockwave format, just to be on the safe side.

ON YOUR OWN

Put your Fine Dining application completely on the Web! Here's an overview of how to do it.

1] Create a folder called *Shocker* in your Projects folder. In this folder, place a copy of the Menu.dir file from the Complete folder in the Lesson19 folder and a copy of the Order.dir file from the Complete folder in the Lesson27 folder.

2] In Menu.dir, open the score script in cast member 50, which looks like this:

```
on mouseUp
  go to movie "Order.dir"
end
```

3] Change the script to read:

```
on mouseUp
  gotoNetMovie "Order.dcr"
end
```

4] In the Order.dir movie, open the frame script for frame 23 and change this script

```
on exitFrame
  go to movie "Menu.dir"
end
```

to read:

```
on exitFrame
  gotoNetMovie "Menu.dcr"
end
```

5] Save Menu.dir as a Shockwave movie called *Menu.dcr*, and save Order.dir as a Shockwave movie called *Order.dcr*. Drag Menu.dcr and drop it on your Navigator Web browser.

You see the menu for the Fine Dining application, working just as it did before but now playing inside a Web browser.

6] Click the Orders button.

You will see that the *gotoNetMovie* command is similar to *go to movie*, except that the movie you go to continues to play inside the Web browser, displacing the movie that was originally playing in the browser.

You can also experiment with some of the other commands that Lingo offers for working with movies that interact with the Internet. For instance, try using the *preloadNetThing* command, which resembles the *preload* command you used in Lesson 22. This command loads a file from the Internet into your Web browser's memory so the file can be displayed later without delay.

Consult the *Learning Lingo* manual for Director 7 and the online help for more information.

WHAT YOU HAVE LEARNED

In this lesson you have:

• Set up Director to work with a Web browser [page 661]

• Launched a Web browser from a movie using the *gotoNetPage* command [page 662]

• Set up a simple status field using Director's internal timer [page 672]

• Used the *getNetText* command to download a text file from the Internet [page 676]

• Created a scrolling text field [page 679]

• Monitored the status of a network operation using the operation ID and the *netDone* function [page 683]

• Created a Shockwave movie [page 688]

date conversions

There are often times when your Director movie needs to know what the current date is, or how far away a future date is, or how long ago a past date occurred. In an interactive educational movie, for example, you may need to compare dates to find the number of days since a person first set foot on the moon or the number of days until the millennium. You may need to compare dates for security or business purposes or to enable a person to use a trial version of your movie for only 30 days or only until a specific date, such as December 31.

Today's date:
Tuesday, December 01, 1998

Find difference between today and this date: 4 day(s)

Year: 1998

Month: 12

Day: 5

Find difference between these two dates   2 day(s)

Year: 1998

Month: 12

Day: 7

The DateCalc date calculator determines the number of days between two dates or a given date and the current date. To perform the calculations, the calculator must be capable of inputting and outputting information in the date *format and be able to convert date information into different forms.*

Dates can be tricky to compare, with varying days per month and leap years to be accounted for, and to complicate matters, printed date formats vary by country. In the United States, the date 11/2/98 is November 2, 1998, but it represents February 11, 1998, to someone living in Europe. As you will learn in this lesson, Director's *date* function enables you to add, subtract, and compare dates with ease and provides a standard date format, regardless of country.

If you would like to view the final results of this lesson, open the Complete folder in the Lesson28 folder and play Datecalc.dir.

WHAT YOU WILL LEARN

In this lesson you will:

• Retrieve the current date

• Compare dates and create a date calculator

• Make field sprites editable

• Prevent your movie from running after a certain date

APPROXIMATE TIME

It should take about 2 hours to complete this lesson.

LESSON FILES

Media Files:
None

Starting Files:
Lesson28\Start\Start.dir

Completed Project:
Lesson28\Complete\Datacalc.dir

RETRIEVING THE CURRENT DATE

Director can display the current date in several formats. For example, it can display the date in several types of string format. You can easily examine these formats in the Message window.

note *When a value is in string format, it is stored as a series of characters—both letter characters and digit and punctuation characters. Although string format works fine for visual presentations, the format does not lend itself to math or other internal calculations that expect values to be stored in a numeric format. Later in this lesson you will learn how to convert string values to numeric formats.*

1] Open Director or choose File › New to open a new Director movie.

2] Choose Window › Message to open the Message window (Windows Ctrl+M, Macintosh Command+M).

After the Message window opens, you can try out different date formats.

3] In the Message window, type the following and press Enter (Windows) or Return (Macintosh):

put the date

The *date* function responds by displaying the date in the form of a string. The actual format used depends on how the date is formatted on the computer. In the example shown, the date is in the form *MM/DD/YY* (month/day/year), which is December 1, 1998.

The format used to display the date depends on the regional date settings you specified in your computer's control panel preferences. On Windows systems, these

694

are specified with the Regional Settings control panel; on the Macintosh, these are specified with the Data and Time control panel.

The *date* function returns the current date from the system clock. The date is provided as a string in any of three different formats: short date, abbreviated date, and long date. The short date is the default format; it was used in the previous example. The abbreviated date is also referred to as the *abbrev* or *abbr* format.

4] In the Message window, type the following, pressing Enter (Windows) or Return (Macintosh) after each line.

    put the long date
    put the abbr date

As you can see in the Message window, the *date* function returns the date in a text format and includes the day of the week. The abbreviated format uses an abbreviation for both the day of the week and the month.

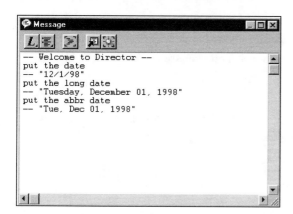

Although the *date* function is great for visually displaying dates in the user's preferred format, it is not useful for date calculations because the date format can vary from user to user and is therefore unpredictable. In fact, until now, you could perform date calculations efficiently only with the use of an Xtra.

Director 7, however, provides a date variable that makes date calculations easy.

5] Type the following in the Message window, ending the statement by pressing Enter (Windows) or Return (Macintosh):

    put the systemDate

The *systemDate* property is new to Director 7. It returns the current date in the new *date* format.

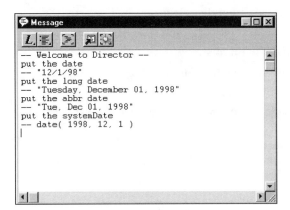

The date displayed by *systemDate* looks different from the dates displayed by the string formats. To begin with, the date is not surrounded by quotation marks. This is because the date is not returned in string format but rather in an internal format that lends itself to date calculations. A key advantage of the *systemDate* format over the string date formats is that the day, month, and year are readily identifiable; you can easily access them using date properties.

6] Type the following in the Message window, ending the statement by pressing Enter (Windows) or Return (Macintosh):

    put the systemDate.year

Using the *year* property causes Director to display only the current year instead of the entire date. The *day* and *month* properties are also available to access the day and the month, respectively.

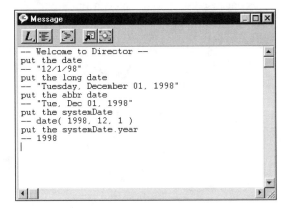

696

7] Type the following in the Message window, ending each statement by pressing Enter (Windows) or Return (Macintosh):

```
put the systemDate.day
put the systemDate.month
```

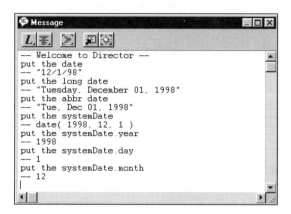

tip *If you wanted to display only the current date on the stage in your movie, you would use the* date *function in one of its formats, such as* the long date. *In general, you will use the date properties when you are using* systemDate *because they let you manipulate individual elements of the date. Another reason the* systemDate *format is preferable over the string format is that the month of the string format date is given in the machine's default language. A user running a French version of Windows, for example, would see* Janvier, *not January. If your script expects the month names to appear in a particular language, it may fail to run properly on a system configured for a different language.*

HOW TO COMPARE DATES

You can compare a date against today's date (the *systemDate* value), or you can compare two specific dates. To do either, you need to be able to enter dates as well as to retrieve them. The *systemDate* property returns the date in a standard date format or data type. Director also allows you to supply a date in the standard date data type. Three formats are available for entering such a date:

```
date(19621125)        --Date is entered as an integer.
date(1962, 11, 25)    --Date is entered in comma-separated format.
date("19621125")      --Date is entered as a string.
```

In all three forms, the year always is specified first and requires four digits, the month is second and requires two digits, and the day is third and also requires two digits. This standard convention ensures that the date will always be consistent, regardless of the country or display preferences set on the individual user's computer.

1] If the Message window is not open, choose Window › Message to display it.

2] Subtract the current date from January 3, 2000, by typing the following, ending the statement by pressing Return or Enter:

    put date("20000103") – the systemDate

Director returns a number (the number you see will be different):

    --412

By subtracting the current date from January 3, 2000, you can see how many days until (or since) "20000103", which is the year 2000, the month 01, and the day 03 (that is, January 3, 2000). You have just performed a date calculation! More commonly, you will be using dates that you store in variables so they can be saved and used elsewhere.

3] Type the following, ending each statement by pressing Return or Enter:

    lunarLanding = date(1969, 7, 16)
    put the systemDate – lunarLanding

Director returns a number indicating the number of days since the famous moon landing on July 16, 1969 (your number of days since the landing will be higher):

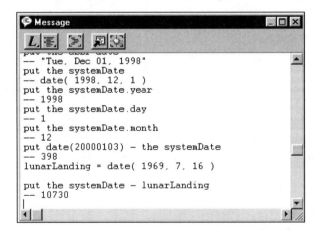

From these quick tests, you can see that you can easily compare dates, assign a date to a variable, and compare the current date to a variable. In the same manner, you can also compare two date variables to each other.

CREATING A DATE CALCULATOR

Now you'll use Director's *date* functions to create a date calculator.

1] Choose File > Open to open Start.dir from the Start folder in the Lesson28 folder (Windows Ctrl+O, Macintosh Command+O). Save this file as *Datecalc.dir* in your Projects folder.

The Start movie comes with the interface prebuilt for you, but you will need to write all of the Lingo code to make if functional.

2] If the stage is hidden, choose Window > Stage to display the stage (Windows Ctrl+1, Macintosh Command+1).

The elements are all visible except for three response fields: the current date and the calculated values that will appear to the right of the two date calculation buttons. Although they are on the stage, you can't see them yet because they use Background Transparent ink and they won't appear until they have some information stored in them.

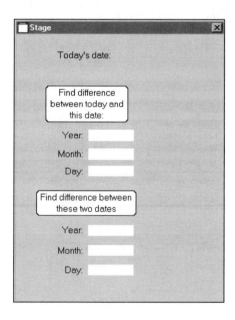

When the calculator is complete, it will display today's date when you run it. It also has two sets of fields for entering year, month, and day information, and two buttons for performing calculations. The top button will compare the current date with the date entered in the top date fields. The second button will compare the two user-supplied dates.

3] Play the movie and click each of the date calculation buttons on the calculator.

Although the movie is playing, you don't see today's date, and clicking the buttons does nothing. There are sprites on the stage, but they don't include the Lingo code necessary to support the *date* functions. This is what you need to add.

Now take a look at the cast.

4] Choose Window › Cast to display the Cast window (Windows Ctrl+3, Macintosh Command+3).

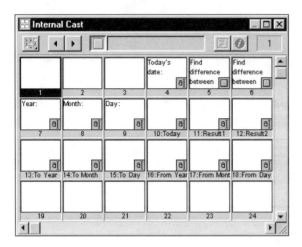

Cast members 1, 2, and 3 are empty (you will enter a script in cast member 1), and cast member 4 is the prompt for today's date. Cast members 5 and 6 are the two date calculation buttons, and cast members 7, 8, and 9 are the Year, Month, and Day prompts.

Cast members 10 through 18 are all text fields, as indicated by the text field icon at the lower right of each; these are titled Today, Result1, Result2, To Year, To Month, To Day, From Year, From Month, and From Day, respectively. The user will be entering values into some of these fields, and your scripts will have to refer to these fields by name to retrieve those values.

DISPLAYING THE CURRENT DATE

Your next task will be to initialize the Today field, which is cast member 10, with the current date.

1] Select cast member 1, which is currently an empty cast member, and choose Window › Script to open the Script editor (Windows Ctrl+0, Macintosh Command+0).

You will create a *StartMovie* handler, as discussed in Lesson 17, to initialize cast member 10, Today, with the current date.

2] Click in the Script Editor window and enter the following:

```
on startMovie                              --Do every time the movie starts.
    member ("Today").text = the long date  --Place the date in the Today text field.
end
```

As you saw in the last task, the long date is a very readable version of the date: for example, "Saturday, November 14, 1998." The actual display depends on the date format and language settings of the user's computer, but it will likely be something similar.

The Lingo instruction

```
member ("Today").text = the long date
```

assigns the long date string to the *text* property of the field cast member "Today". This changes the text of that field to the current date, so that when the movie starts, that field (which appears on the stage as a sprite) will display the current date to the user. You can see that happen now by closing the Script editor and rerunning the movie.

3] Close the Script editor (Windows Ctrl+0, Macintosh Command+0) and play the movie again. Then stop the movie.

The movie starts, and the current date appears in the Today field. You can see the date under the heading "Today's date." Every time your movie runs, this field will be updated with the current date.

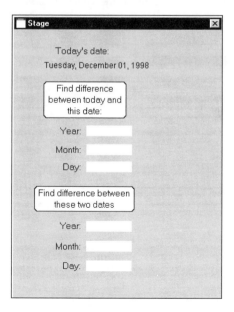

701

Unless you have Looping turned on for your movie, you probably noticed that the movie stopped at the last frame of the movie, frame 28. You need a frame behavior to keep the movie paused at that frame.

4] In the Behavior channel, double-click frame 28 to open the Script editor and modify the default script as shown in bold:

```
on exitFrame
  go to the frame
end
```

The movie now continually loops on frame 28.

MAKING FIELDS EDITABLE

Although the calculator contains text field sprites, in their current state the user cannot use them to enter information. This is because, by default, fields on the screen are not editable by the user. You must specifically designate the fields as editable. You will do that next; you need to change all of the fields in cast members 13 through 18 to make them editable.

1] Select cast member 13 in the Cast window, the To Year field. Choose Modify › Cast Member › Properties (Windows Ctrl+I, Macintosh Command+I) to display the Properties editor. The Field Cast Member Properties dialog box appears.

2] In the Options group, select the Editable and Tab to Next Editable Item options. Make sure the Word Wrap option is not selected.

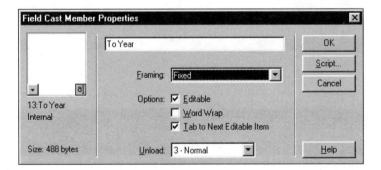

Now the field in cast member 13 can be edited by the user. In addition, the Tab to Next Editable Item option allows the user to move easily between editable fields with the Tab key, a common feature in forms with multiple data-entry fields.

3] From the Framing pull-down menu, choose Fixed.

This prevents the size of the sprite from increasing if the user enters too much text.

4] Click OK to close the dialog box. Then repeat steps 1, 2, and 3 for cast members 14 through 18.

Now all six of the date entry fields can be edited, and the user can easily tab from one to another.

5] Play the movie. Try entering dates into the fields.

You may need to click the stage to give the stage the focus. Otherwise, some other Director window that is open may receive the numbers you type.

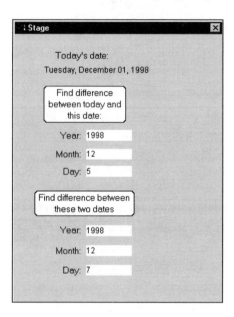

You can enter dates, but as of yet nothing is done with the values entered. They show up on the stage and are placed in the field cast members, but there is no Lingo yet to perform actions on them. You will fix that in the next task.

MAKING A DATE COMPARISON

Now you will add some instructions so that clicking the buttons will actually compare dates. You saw earlier how to compare dates. Now you need to create a date variable that uses the year, month, and day that the user enters in the Year, Month, and Day fields. Just as you were able to set the text of the Today field to the current date, you can retrieve the existing text from a field.

1] Open the Cast window. Click cast member 5 to select it and then click the Script button to edit the cast member's script.

Cast member 5 is the button that the user will click to compare today's date to the date entered. By default, Director displays the framework for an *on mouseUp* handler. This is what you need, because you want Director to calculate the date when the button is clicked.

2] Modify the *mouseUp* handler as shown here in bold:

```
on mouseUp      --Get the values entered by the user.
  toYear = member ("To Year").text
          --Place the value in the "To Year" field in the variable toYear.
  toMonth = member ("To Month").text
          --Place the value in the "To Month" field in the variable toMonth.
  toDay = member ("To Day").text
          --Place the value in the "To Day" field in the variable toDay.
end
```

You have now assigned the text of each of the fields to three variables, *toYear*, *toMonth*, and *toDay*. This is still not quite what you want. You need to create a date value from this set of values so that the date value can be compared to the current date and the results can be displayed.

There are two ways to do this. You can create a date variable providing a string in the form "*YYYYMMDD*" (for instance, "19981231") by using Lingo's concatenation operator (&). The drawback to this approach is that if the user enters single digits for the single-digit months and days (for example, 1 and 2 instead of 01 and 02), then you could end up with a string like "199812", which isn't a valid date variable because it's not clear whether the month is 12 and the day is missing or the month is 1 and the day is 2. Valid date strings must have four digits for the year, followed by two each for the month and day—eight characters in all.

One way around this problem is to add a 0 to the beginning of each date if it is only one digit long. Another option, since the date variable allows you to enter numbers for dates in comma-separated format, *date(YYYY,MM,DD)*, is to convert the dates to numbers and supply them that way. Separating the values with commas helps keep the month and day separate. Strings can be converted to numeric variables with the *integer( )* function.

note   *The only way to retrieve the contents of a text or field member is through the* text *property. The member's contents are always stored in string format, which means that even a number like 9 is treated as a letter character "9" and not as a value on which you can perform calculations. Lingo provides conversion functions such as* integer(), float(), value(), *and* string() *that allow you to convert variables from internal string format to internal numeric format and back again.*

3] Modify the script of cast member 5 as shown here in bold:

```
on mouseUp   --Get the values entered by the user.
  toYear = member ("To Year").text
           --Place the value in the "To Year" field in the variable toYear.
  toMonth = member ("To Month").text
           --Place the value in the "To Month" field in the variable toMonth.
  toDay = member ("To Day").text
           --Place the value in the "To Day" field in the variable toDay.
           --Convert the variable's string content to integers.
  toYear = integer(toYear)
  toMonth = integer(toMonth)
  toDay = integer(toDay)
end
```

Now each of the variables is converted to a number, like 1998, and is not a quoted string, like "1998". The difference is subtle but important to Lingo; it dramatically affects the way the information is treated. With the user's input saved as integers, you can now compare dates.

4] Modify the script of cast member 5 as shown here in bold:

```
on mouseUp   --Get the values entered by the user.
  toYear = member ("To Year").text
           --Place the value in the "To Year" field in the variable toYear.
  toMonth = member ("To Month").text
           --Place the value in the "To Month" field in the variable toMonth.
  toDay = member ("To Day").text
           --Place the value in the "To Day" field in the variable toDay.
           --Convert the variable's string content to integers.
  toYear = integer(toYear)
  toMonth = integer(toMonth)
  toDay = integer(toDay)
  compareDate = date(toYear, toMonth, toDay)
           --Convert the user's input to date format and save the results in compareDate.
  difference = compareDate – the systemDate
           --Subtract compareDate from the current date and
           --save the results in difference.
end
```

The first instruction builds a date variable from the year, month, and day components. The second instruction subtracts the current date and comes up with the difference between the target date and the current date. This is your objective. The only thing left to do is to update the Result1 text field with the answer.

5] Enter the lines shown here in bold:

```
on mouseUp   --Get the values entered by the user.
  toYear = member ("To Year").text
              --Place the value in the "To Year" field in the variable toYear.
  toMonth = member ("To Month").text
              --Place the value in the "To Month" field in the variable toMonth.
  toDay = member ("To Day").text
              --Place the value in the "To Day" field in the variable toDay.
              --Convert the variable's string content to integers.
  toYear = integer(toYear)
  toMonth = integer(toMonth)
  toDay = integer(toDay)
  compareDate = date(toYear, toMonth, toDay)
              --Convert the user's input to date format and save the results in compareDate.
  difference = compareDate - the systemDate
              --Subtract compareDate from the current date and save the results in difference.
  member ("Result1").text = difference && "day(s)"
              --Display the result in the Result1 field.
end
```

The double ampersand (&&) tells Director to create a string from the two components, placing a space in between. The result must be in string format to be reassigned to the *text* property, and the space in between allows the calculator to display, for instance, "42 day(s)" rather than "42day(s)". If you used just a single ampersand, Director would still have concatenated, or combined, the strings, but without inserting a space.

The handler now includes instructions to take the values from the three fields, build a date from these values, calculate the difference between the this date and the current date, and return the result in the text field. Try the calculator and see how it works.

6] Close the Script editor and play the movie. Enter values for the Year, Month, and Day fields. Then click the button that says "Find difference between today and this date."

The number of days is shown in the field to the right of the button.

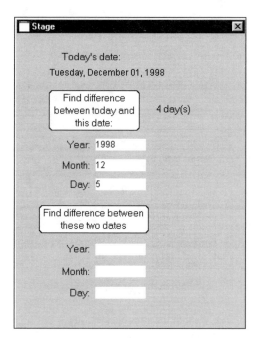

Congratulations! It works!

7] Stop the movie and save your work.

The only task left is to wire up the other button so it will compare the two user-specified dates. The method will be similar.

8] Open the Cast window and select the other button, cast member 6. Click the Script button to open the editor.

For the previous button, you added instructions to retrieve the user's entries from the fields on the screen and then you built a date variable from them. Then you compared this variable to the system date. For this button, which compares two arbitrary dates, you will need to retrieve information from both sets of fields and build two date variables. The procedure is nearly the same. In this case, the result will be displayed in Result2, not Result1.

9] Enter the following _mouseUp_ handler. This is a good place to use the cut-and-paste editing capabilities of the Script editor.

```
on mouseUp      --Get the first date.
   toYear = member ("To Year").text
                   --Place the value in the "To Year" field in the variable toYear.
   toMonth = member ("To Month").text
                   --Place the value in the "To Month" field in the variable toMonth.
   toDay = member ("To Day").text
                   --Place the value in the "To Day" field in the variable toDay.
                   --Convert the variable's string content to integers.
   toYear = integer(toYear)
   toMonth = integer(toMonth)
   toDay = integer(toDay)
                   --Get the second date.
   fromYear = member ("From Year").text
                   --Place the value in the "From Year" field in the variable fromYear.
   fromMonth = member ("From Month").text
                   --Place the value in the "From Month" field in the variable fromMonth.
   fromDay = member ("From Day").text
                   --Place the value in the "From Day" field in the variable fromDay.
                   --Convert the variable's string content to integers.
   fromYear = integer(fromYear)
   fromMonth = integer(fromMonth)
   fromDay = integer(fromDay)
                   --Convert the user's input to date format and save.
   toDate = date(toYear, toMonth, toDay)
   fromDate = date(fromYear, fromMonth, fromDay)
   difference = fromDate – toDate
                   --Subtract toDate from the fromDate and save the results in difference.
   member ("Result2").text = difference && "day(s)"
                   --Display the result in the Result2 field.
end
```

The instructions for getting the date from the first set of fields is essentially copied for the second set and the variable names changed. The two dates are then compared.

10] Close the Script editor and play the movie. Enter two dates and compare them by clicking the button labeled "Find difference between these two dates."

The difference between the two dates is displayed in the second result field.

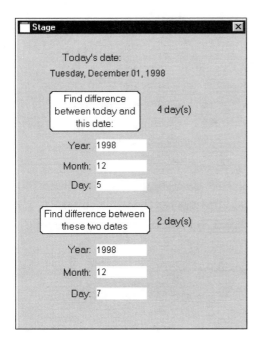

11] Stop the movie and save your work.

ON YOUR OWN

Think about how you can improve the Date Calculator program. One way would be to clear the fields when the movie starts. In the *on startMovie* handler in the movie script, you could include a command such as this:

```
member ("Result1").text = EMPTY
```

This clears any current content in the referenced field (Result1 in this example). You could also place similar commands in the two button scripts so that each button clears the Result field used by the other button. That way, only the result for the button last clicked will be displayed, and there will be less confusion for the user. A well-written program would also check the user's input and allow only numbers to be entered and would limit the number of digits for each input field.

HOW TO PREVENT YOUR MOVIE FROM RUNNING AFTER A CERTAIN DATE

You may want to place a limit on your finished program so a user cannot play it after a certain date. This may be an evaluation version of your software, for example, that you want the user to be able to use for only a certain number of days. To prevent your movie from running after a certain date, you need to compare the current date against the target date. You laid the groundwork for this action in the previous tasks.

1] Open the Cast window and select cast member 1, which contains the movie script with the *startMovie* handler. Click the Script button to open the Script editor.

You will be changing the *startMovie* handler so that it checks the current date and stops the movie if the expiration date has been reached.

2] Modify the *startMovie* handler by adding the lines shown here in bold:

```
on startMovie        --Do every time the movie starts.
  member ("Today").text = the long date
                      --Place the date in the Today text field.
                      --Check to see if this software is current.
  expirationDate = date("19981125")
                      --This is the last day the user can use the program.
  if the systemDate › expirationDate then
    halt
  end if
end
```

3] Close the Script editor and then play the movie.

The movie stops immediately, since the current date is past the expiration date. The user won't know why the movie stopped, though. You need to provide feedback to let the user know the reason the software does not run.

4] Open the Script editor again and modify the movie script as shown here in bold:

```
on startMovie        --Do every time the movie starts.
  member ("Today").text = the long date
                      --Place the date in the Today text field.
                      --Check to see if this software is current.
  expirationDate = date("19981125")
                      --This is the last day the user can use the program.
  if the systemDate › expirationDate then
    alert "The demonstration period has expired."
    halt
  end if
end
```

The *alert* command causes a dialog box to appear with the text provided in the command. When the user clicks the OK button in the dialog box, the program terminates.

5] Close the Script editor and play the movie.

The notification appears, and the movie stops.

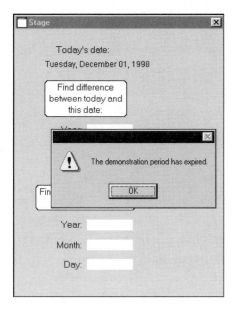

Using this simple technique, you can prevent your movie from running past a certain date. By extending this same programming technique, you could also display a message telling the user where to buy a true version of your software. You could also display a message each time the user runs your movie, such as "You are on day 20 of your 30-day evaluation period."

WHAT YOU HAVE LEARNED

In this lesson you have:

- Retrieved the current date [page 694]
- Compared dates [page 697]
- Created a date calculator [page 699]
- Made field sprites editable [page 702]
- Prevented your movie from running after a certain date [page 710]

hypertext

creating

LESSON 29

From the Internet to electronic encyclopedias to help systems, the use of hypertext is widespread. **Hypertext** is text that links particular phrases, terms, and words together with other information. By clicking a linked section of text, you can navigate to whatever information has been associated with that text via a **hyperlink** connection.

For instance, you may be able to click a topic name in an online index to immediately branch to the section that discusses that topic, without having to navigate to the section manually. Usually, the clickable term is identified in some fashion, typically

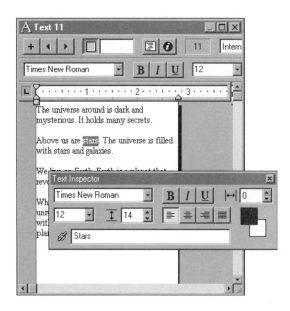

By adding hyperlinks to your movies, you can let a user click on text in one location to branch to a different location in the movie, to a different movie, or even to a location on the Internet.

by underlining, as in "Once Bill learned how to use <u>Macromedia Director</u>, he found he could create anything"; if this were hypertext, then clicking <u>Macromedia Director</u> would take you to a page with more information on Director. Hypertext links may also be identified by color or some other device. The World Wide Web provides the most extensive example of hypertext available today. Each Web page usually contains one or more hyperlinks to other Web pages.

Thanks to hypertext, you can easily explore large bodies of information, getting to just the information you need. With Director 7, you have the power to create your own hyperlinks within text that, when clicked, can execute commands, take you to other areas within your movie, or display other text. If you create a text cast member and create a Director hyperlink association for one or more of the words, you have effectively turned your text into hypertext.

In this lesson, you'll learn how to use hyperlinks to create some basic hypertext.

If you would like to view the final results of this lesson, open the Complete folder in the Lesson29 folder and play Secrets.dir.

WHAT YOU WILL LEARN

In this lesson you will:

- Set up your movie for hyperlinks
- Assign a hyperlink
- Create a handler for a hyperlink

APPROXIMATE TIME

It should take about 1 ½ hours to complete this lesson.

LESSON FILES

Media Files:
None

Starting Files:
Lesson29\Start\Start.dir

Completed Project:
Lesson29\Complete\Secrets.dir

SETTING UP YOUR MOVIE FOR HYPERLINKS

In this task, you will create a small hyperlinked document called "Secrets of the Universe." It includes a main page with this title and a short paragraph with links to pages titled "Planets," "Stars," "Galaxies," and "The Sun."

1] Choose File › Open to open Start.dir in the Start folder within Lesson29 on the CD (Windows Ctrl+O, Macintosh Command+O). Save this file as *Secrets.dir* in your Projects folder.

2] Choose Window › Cast to open the Cast window (Windows Ctrl+3, Macintosh Command+3).

The Start file already has text for the page titles, in cast members 6 through 10, and some additional text in cast members 12 through 15, but that's all.

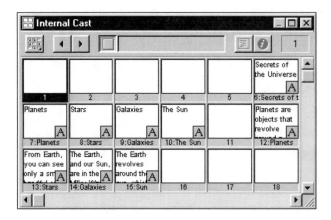

The first five cast member slots are empty. If you are working with movie scripts, as you will be in this task, it is often helpful to leave some blank slots at the beginning of the cast to hold the movie scripts. There is no real benefit to having all your cast members side by side, as is the default; in fact, it is often helpful to group similar types together and leave blank spaces in between, to make finding certain cast members easier.

3] Select cast member 6, the "Secrets of the Universe" text, and drag it to the top of stage, where it can be positioned as a title for the page.

714

4] Open the Score window. If necessary, adjust the sprite you just created in channel 1 to span frames 1 through 18.

This 18-frame duration is arbitrary; it was used because it is long enough to show the name of the cast member in the score.

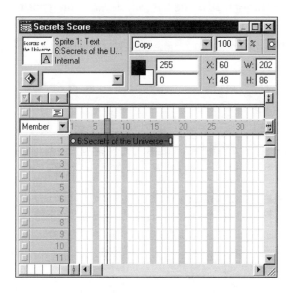

5] Select cast member 7 (Planets) in the Cast window and drag it to channel 1, frame 20, of the score. Adjust the duration of the sprite in the score to span frames 20 through 28.

715

Because the cast member was dragged into the score, the sprite is positioned in the center of the stage.

6] Select the sprite you just created and position it near the top of the stage.

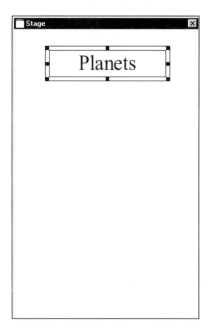

7] One by one, select cast members 8 through 10 in the Cast window and drag each to channel 1 of the score so that they span frames 30 through 38, 40 through 48, and 50 through 58, respectively. Click each sprite and make sure it is positioned so that it is visible near the top of the stage.

The actual sprite duration is arbitrary, it is long enough to show the name of the cast member and leave an empty frame between each sprite so that sprites can be easily distinguished. Because you will be using markers to identify the sprites, the actual frame locations don't matter, and because you will be looping on each marked frame, the actual sprite duration doesn't matter, either. The score should look like this:

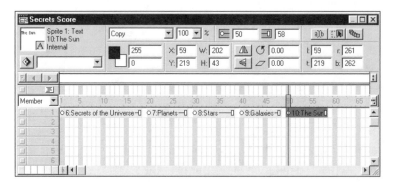

716

Next you will add markers to the frames where each sprite begins.

8] Click the marker channel for frame 1 and enter *Secrets* as the marker name.

This sets a marker for that frame. Markers allow you to refer to a frame by name rather than by frame number. This gives you more flexibility in organizing your scripts and makes the score easier to follow. You learned about markers in Lessons 5 and 18.

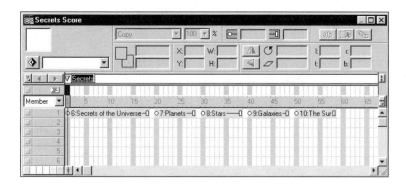

You have just placed a marker named Secrets to represent frame 1. Later you can refer to this marker by name to bring the movie back to this frame.

9] Place a marker at the beginning of each of the other sprites in the score, in frames 20, 30, 40, and 50, naming the markers *Planets*, *Stars*, *Galaxies*, and *Sun*, respectively.

Your score should now look like this:

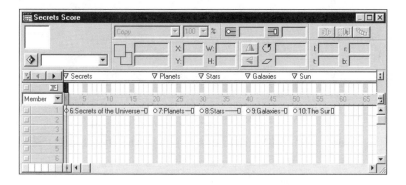

Next you need to add Lingo scripts to control looping in the movie. In previous lessons you used frame scripts, using the *go to the frame* command to loop on a particular frame. Recall from Lessons 16 and 17, however, that if a message, such as *exitFrame*, isn't handled by a sprite script, frame script, or cast script, it gets passed to the movie level. This allows you to create one movie script that handles *exitFrame* events for the whole movie.

10] In the Cast window select cast member 1 and choose Window › Script to open the Script editor (Windows Ctrl+0, Macintosh Command+0).

The Script editor opens, ready for you to edit a movie script.

11] Enter the following in the Script window:

```
on exitFrame      --Do this throughout the entire movie.
   go to the frame
end
```

By issuing an instruction in a movie script that tells Director to go to the same frame that it is just exiting, you make the movie loop on whatever frame contains the playback head.

Unless overridden by an *exitFrame* handler in a frame's behavior channel, this handler will force the playback head to stay in whatever frame it is located. You can still reposition the playback head using Lingo with a *go to frame* or *go to marker* instruction, which is how you will achieve the hypertext behavior.

12] Close the Script editor and play the movie.

The movie plays, but it doesn't leave the main "Secrets of the Universe" screen. In fact, the playback head never leaves frame 1 of the movie. Now you can start adding links to create your hypertext.

13] Save your work.

ASSIGNING A HYPERLINK

Now that the basic structure of the movie is assembled, you can add some text and create hyperlinks. Text can be edited in Director's Text window; hyperlinks are assigned by selecting text and specifying the link information using the Text Inspector. A hyperlink is not a command in itself; rather, it is a parameter that is passed to an *on hyperlinkClicked* handler that you create in your movie.

The *on hyperlinkClicked* handler can reside anywhere; it follows the usual sprite, cast, frame, movie event distribution hierarchy as discussed in Lessons 16 and 17, but usually you'll want to attach it to the text cast member's script itself, so that the handler and its instructions stay with the cast. The other likely place for this handler is in a movie script.

Since this example is small and only a few markers are shared by all the links, in this task you'll place the handler in a movie script. Here are the steps for creating a hyperlink:

• Select the text you want to define as a hyperlink.

- Choose Window > Inspector > Text to open the Text Inspector.
- In the Hyperlink box, enter any message you want to send to the *on hyperlinkClicked* handler.

Since a hyperlink that you define is passed as a parameter to a handler, it is subject to certain restrictions. It can include spaces, but not quotation marks (") directly. This means that you can pass in the name of a marker or an Internet address, but you cannot easily pass in a command with parameters. You can, however, pass in the name of a handler to invoke, and that handler can, in turn, call a more complicated command.

In this task, you'll pass in the name of the marker to which you want the playback head to go.

1] Open the Cast window and select cast member 11, which is currently empty.

2] Choose Window › Text to open the Text editor (Windows Ctrl+6, Macintosh Command+6).

You will now add text, including words that can be used as hyperlinks to the other markers.

3] In the Text editor, enter some text that uses words like *galaxies*, *planets*, *sun*, and *stars*.

For example, you might enter text like this:

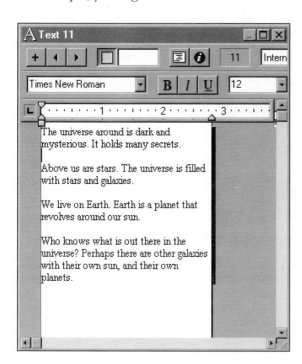

4] Choose Window > Inspectors > Text to open the Text Inspector (Windows Ctrl+T, Macintosh Command+T).

You use the Text Inspector to enter the hyperlink information.

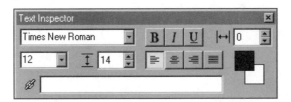

5] Double-click the word *stars* in your text to select it.

The hyperlink will be assigned to the selected region.

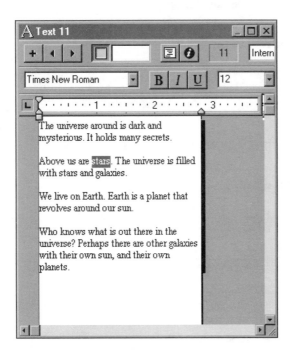

6] In the hyperlink field in the Text Inspector window, enter the name of the marker you want to transfer control to when this link is clicked; then press Enter (Windows) or Return (Macintosh). In this example, you enter the marker name *Stars*.

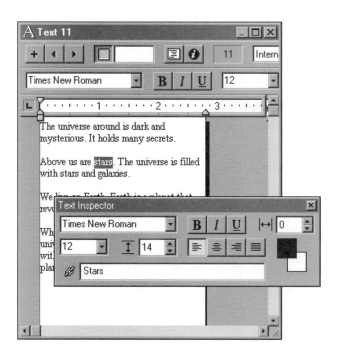

After you enter the marker name, the corresponding text is underlined in the Text editor and displayed in a different color, to identify this text as a link. By default, Director automatically adds standard hyperlink formatting to the selected text so that it initially appears with blue underlining. After the link has been used, the color of the text changes to purple. You can change or turn off this formatting in the Text Cast Member Properties dialog box.

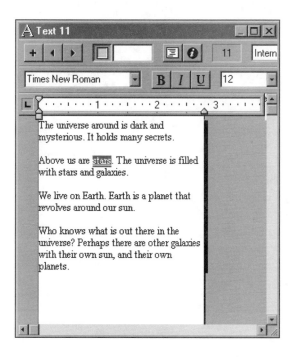

The link is now established, and clicking the linked word *stars* will generate a *hyperlinkClicked* event with *Stars* as the parameter passed to it. The *on hyperlinkClicked* handler you will write will use this parameter to transfer control to the Stars marker.

7] Repeat the hyperlinking process for other words in your text, using the marker names Planets, Stars, Galaxies, and Sun as the links you enter in the Text Inspector.
You can link whatever word or phrases seem appropriate. For instance, you can link *Earth* to the Planets marker.

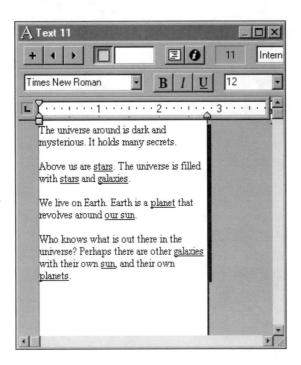

Notice that you are not restricted to linking only single words; for instance, the two words *our sun* form a single link to the Sun marker.

8] Close the Text Inspector and the Text editor.

9] Open the Score window and then open the Cast window.

10] Drag cast member 11 from the cast to channel 2, frame 1, in the score. Adjust the end point of sprite 2 so that the sprite ends at the same frame as the "Secrets of the Universe" cast member in sprite 1.

Your score should look like this:

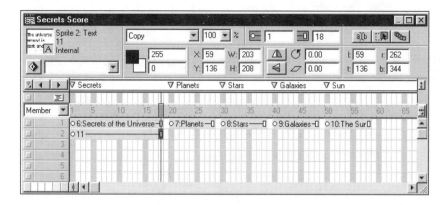

11] Select each of cast members 12 through 15 and place them in the sprite channels for the markers Planets, Stars, Galaxies, and Sun, respectively. Adjust the end points to match the sprites in channel 1.

Cast members 12 through 15 already contain hyperlinked text similar to that of cast member 11, but appropriate for their topic areas. Your score should look similar to this:

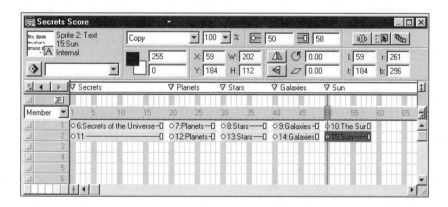

There is now hyperlinked text for each marker.

12] Play the movie. Move your cursor over some of the links and click them.

The cursor changes to a pointing hand when you are over a link, but clicking doesn't display a different frame. Although you've added the hyperlink information, you haven't yet supplied the instructions to act on it. You will do that next.

13] Stop the movie and save your work.

You are now ready to create a handler to implement the hyperlinks.

CREATING A HANDLER FOR A *HYPERLINKCLICKED* EVENT

To handle a hyperlink, you need to create an *on hyperlinkClicked* handler. This handler can reside anywhere in the movie event distribution hierarchy, or **message path**, which means that the handler can be attached to a text sprite, text cast member, the frame that contains a sprite, or a movie script. Director will try to deliver the event message to the scripts in that order, testing each for an *on hyperlinkClicked* handler.

The handler takes two parameters. One is an identifier that indicates that the parameter is a hyperlink; it does not need to be used by your handler (just accepted). The other is the actual hyperlink message that you defined in your hyperlinks. In this lesson, the messages you created were *Secrets*, *Planets*, *Stars*, *Galaxies*, and *Sun*.

The structure of the handler looks like this:

```
on hyperlinkClicked me, link      --The code goes here
end
```

The *me* parameter is the identifier; it does not need to be used within the handler but it must be in the parameter list to keep the parameters in their proper order. The *link* variable will receive the link message. For instance, it will be equal to *Stars* if a Stars hyperlink is clicked.

1] Open the Cast window and select cast member 1.

Cast member 1 contains the movie script, which you will now edit to add an *on hyperlinkClicked* handler.

2] Choose Window › Script to open the Movie Script editor.

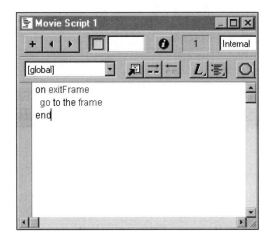

3] Click the Movie Script editor window and add the lines shown here in bold:

```
on exitFrame                --Do this throughout the entire movie.
   go to the frame
end

on hyperlinkClicked me, link   --Go to the marker specified by the link parameter.
   go to frame(link)
end
```

The instruction *go to frame(link)* tells the playback head to branch to the marker that matches the value in *link*: in other words, the same link you specified in the Text Inspector.

4] Close the Script editor.

You can now try the movie with the links enabled.

5] Play the movie and click some links.

You've created hypertext!

6] Stop the movie and save your work.

ON YOUR OWN

You can build large and elaborate documents with hypertext that your users can navigate with ease. Thanks to the hyperlink feature of Director 7, you can display hyperlinks even in scrolling text. To work on your own, try using hyperlinks to build an interactive story in which the user can decide what page to go to next (with different story results on different pages).

If you're feeling particularly ambitious and want a technical challenge, you can use the Lingo list variable type that was introduced in Lessons 24 and 25 to build a list to keep track of your last link, similar to a Back button on a browser. You will need to add each page to the list when you go to the page and to reference and remove it from the end of the list when you want to go back. In effect, you will need to build a stack of page locations, similar to a stack of plates, and then you will remove items from the top of the stack when you want to work backward.

WHAT YOU HAVE LEARNED

In this lesson you have:

• Prepared frames for a hypertext movie [page 714]

• Assigned a hyperlink [page 718]

• Created a handler for a *hyperlinkClicked* event [page 724]

director

monitoring

LESSON 30

In the Director environment, event messages are always being sent, handlers are being called, mouse clicks are being received, keys are being pressed, and frames are being displayed. Director's system of handlers and properties makes it easy for you to find just about any status information you need.

For instance, perhaps you need to know the screen coordinates of the mouse as it moves across the screen. Or perhaps you need to know what key was pressed, or the keycode. Perhaps you need to know what sprite was clicked, or whether your handler is being called as you think it should be.

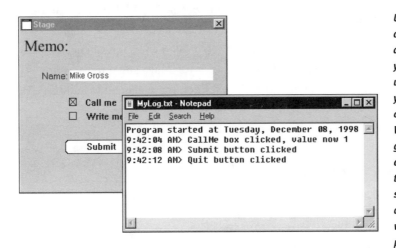

Using Lingo, you can monitor events as they occur in your movies. By using a log file, you can keep track of the events. When something goes wrong, you can use the log file to reconstruct the sequence of events and determine where the problem lies.

In this lesson, you will learn how to use some of Director's reporting features and other tools to monitor your environment. You can then use these techniques as necessary as you work on projects on your own.

If you would like to review the final result of this lesson, open the Complete folder in the Lesson30 folder and play Spy.dir.

WHAT YOU WILL LEARN

In this lesson you will:

- Monitor the mouse position
- Monitor the current sprite and frame
- Use *beep* and *alert* to monitor a movie
- Timestamp messages
- Log messages in a file

APPROXIMATE TIME

It should take about 1 hour to complete this lesson.

LESSON FILES

Media Files:

None

Starting Files:

Lesson30\Start\Start1.dir
Lesson30\Start\Start2.dir

Completed Project:

Lesson30\Complete\Spy.dir
Lesson30\Complete\Log.dir

WATCHING THE MOUSE POSITION

If you create your movies using Lingo more than the score, you will have to pay particular attention to screen coordinates (horizontal and vertical *x* and *y* positions). It is possible to position a sprite from Lingo, either by changing the coordinates of its rectangle using *sprite (x).rect* or by changing the screen location using the *loc* property, *sprite (x).loc*.

Although it is easy to visually position a sprite when working with sprites directly on the stage, in Lingo you must give actual coordinates. It helps, then, to have a way to find out what a particular coordinate is. Coordinates are also helpful for monitoring mouse-click regions (to know where the region is) and for performing calculations to ensure that a bitmap is located on the screen at a particular location relative to the mouse. For instance, the Plaid Man example in Lesson 9 used a behavior to make the man's eyes follow the mouse. Although you did not look at the behavior's script in that lesson, the script needed to determine the mouse position to do its job.

In these cases and others, you need a way to find the current mouse position. This task shows you one way to do that. In this first task, you will write Lingo code to update the contents of a field with the mouse coordinates.

1] Open the Start1.dir movie in the Lesson30 folder and save it as *Spy.dir* in your Projects folder.

This very simple movie consists of a text field for the caption in channel 1, a field in channel 2 where the mouse's coordinates will be displayed, and a script in the behavior channel to keep the movie looping.

To update the field, you need to write a script that will constantly determine the mouse's coordinates and place the results in the Coordinates field. You could do this using the *on exitFrame* handler to check the position 30 times per second, more or less, depending on the tempo setting. A better solution for real-life programming is to use an *on idle* handler. The *on idle* handler is called when Director has nothing else to do. When Director is waiting, it issues *idle* event messages. You can use these messages to take advantage of Director's quiet times by performing chores such as updating status fields without significantly affecting Director's performance.

The lower Director's frame rate, the longer Director has to wait between frames. For instance, if Director has a frame rate of 1 frame per second, it draws a frame and then waits nearly a whole second before moving on to the next frame. At 10 frames per second, the wait period is less, but still apparent, giving you plenty of time to perform other tasks.

Of course, if you do significant amounts of time-consuming work in the *on idle* handler, you can adversely affect performance, but simple tasks like checking the mouse position and updating a status field should have no noticeable effect.

2] Choose Window › Script to open a Movie Script Editor window (Windows Ctrl+0, Macintosh Command+0).

By default, this script will be cast member 4.

3] In the Script editor window, create the following handler:

```
on idle                    --Whenever the movie is not busy,
   member ("Coordinates").text = string(the mouseLoc)
                           --place the mouse coordinates in the Coordinates field.
end
```

The *the mouseLoc* property contains the current X,Y position of the mouse on the screen. This handler takes advantage of idle periods to constantly update the Coordinates field with *the mouseLoc*, thus giving you a continuous report on the location of the mouse pointer. As described in the preceding lesson, you can update the field's text with information in the string format only. The *the mouseLoc* property is normally a point (X,Y location) variable, not in string format, so it must be converted using Lingo's *string()* function. The result is not a numerical value but a text string like "point(142,218)", which can be displayed.

4] Close the Script editor and play the movie.

Move your mouse around on the screen. The Status field is continuously updated to show the current mouse location.

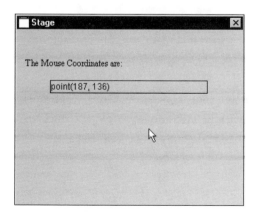

5] Save your work.

MONITORING THE CURRENT SPRITE AND FRAME

When many sprites are layered on the stage, you may sometimes need to identify which sprite is which at runtime. For instance, if a visible sprite is not receiving a click or rollover event message that you think it should be, it may be because another sprite in a higher channel is receiving the event. By applying monitoring techniques similar to those you used to determine the mouse's location, you can have Director report both the frame number and the current sprite so you can see what is happening.

1] Select cast member 4 in the Cast window and click the Script button to open the movie script in the Script editor.

2] Modify the *on idle* handler by adding the lines shown here in bold:

```
on idle                  --Whenever the movie is not busy,
   member ("Coordinates").text = string(the mouseLoc)
                         --place the mouse coordinates in the Coordinates field.
   member ("Sprite Status").text = "Current sprite:" && the rollover
                         --Place the number of the sprite the mouse is over
                         --in the Sprite Status field.
   member ("Frame Status").text = "Current frame:" && the frame
                         --Place the current frame number in the Frame Status field.
end
```

These statements will update two different status fields, Sprite Status and Field Status, with the current rollover value and the current frame number, respectively. Director always stores the number of the currently rolled-over sprite, if any, in a property called *the rollover*; Director always stores the current frame number in a property called *the frame*.

To see the results of *the rollover* and *the frame*, you need to create the fields that will display them. While you're at it, you can also create text cast members to label the fields on the stage. An easy method is to use copies of current cast members 1 and 2.

3] Select cast member 1 in the Cast window and copy it (Windows Ctrl+C, Macintosh Command+C). Paste copies in cast members 7 and 9 (Windows Ctrl+V, Macintosh Command+V). Repeat the process with cast member 2, placing copies in cast members 8 and 10.

COPY CAST MEMBER 2 TO MEMBERS 8 AND 10

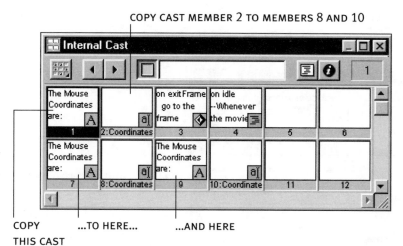

COPY
THIS CAST
MEMBER...

...TO HERE...

...AND HERE

4] Rename cast member 8 *Sprite Statue* to match the name of the field used in the Lingo you added to the *on idle* handler. Rename cast member 10 *Frame Status*.

5] Double-click cast member 7 to open the Text editor and change the text to *The Rollover Sprite is:*. Change the text of cast member 9 to *The Frame is:*.

6] Place the four new cast members on the stage so that all six sprites are visible.

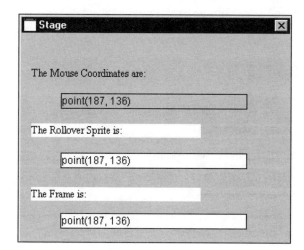

7] If necessary, adjust all of the sprites in the score so they span frames 1 through 9. Set the ink of the four new sprites to Background Transparent.

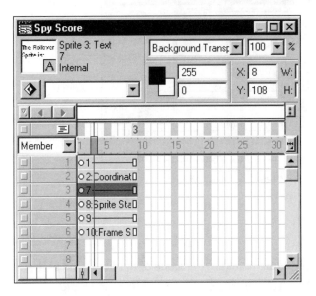

8] Play the movie. Move the mouse around so that it passes over various sprites on the stage.

As the movie runs, the Sprite Status field displays the number of the sprite the mouse is over. If the mouse is not over a sprite, the field displays 0. If you look quickly, you will see the Frame Status field begin at 1 and count up to 9. The field display remains at 9 because the movie loops on that frame.

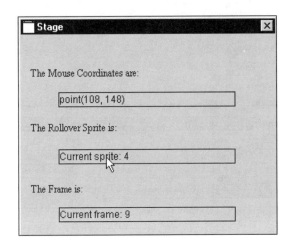

732

9] Stop playback, rewind the movie, and save your work.

Now you know some techniques for getting test information while authoring.

SENDING YOURSELF FEEDBACK

Another approach that you will find useful when authoring movies is to use the Message window to send yourself messages while your movie is running. This technique is especially handy when you want only a quick check of a particular element: for example, maybe a handler does not seem to be getting called, but since you get no obvious feedback, it is hard to tell. This task uses the *beep* command and the Message window to enable you to perform rapid testing.

1] Open Start2.dir in your Lesson30\Start folder and save the file as *Log.dir* in your Projects folder.

This movie contains an input field for a name, two check boxes, and two buttons as the interactive elements. Cast members 6 through 12 are the elements you see on the stage, and cast member 1 is a behavior script. This movie might be used to send co-workers quick memos, although this example version doesn't actually do anything. It is, however, a good template to use for generating diagnostic messages.

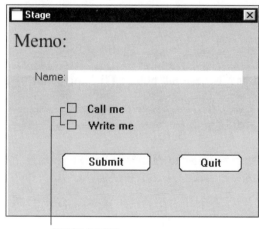

CHECK BOXES

Look at the score. The behavior script in the Behavior channel at frame 10 (cast member 1) is used to loop the movie on that frame. The choice of 10 frames is arbitrary; this duration is long enough to see the names of the cast members for the sprites. Sprites 3 and 4 (cast members 7 and 8) are check boxes created using the tool palette. By default, check boxes appear checked or unchecked as the user clicks them; you don't need to write any Lingo to implement this behavior.

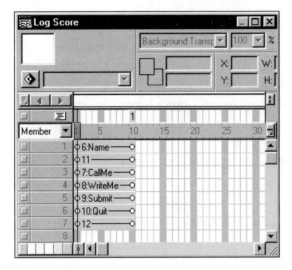

Now suppose you want to know whether one of the buttons is being clicked. Since there is no visual feedback, you can add a *beep* command to the handler for the button cast member.

2] In the Cast window, select cast member 9, the Submit button. Click the Script button to open a Script Editor window for the cast member.

By default, a *mouseUp* handler has been started for you.

3] Modify the *mouseUp* handler by adding the line shown here in bold:

```
on mouseUp
   beep          --Sound the system beep.
end
```

4] Close the Script editor; then rewind and play the movie. Click the Submit button.

The beep sounds. This device is so simple, but it can be so useful. Imagine you are looking at a *case* statement buried in a handler 100 lines long. A simple *beep* command can tell you if a particular line is being reached, and you need only a minute or two to write the code (remember to remove this script when you are done checking, though).

Sometimes, however, you may want to know more than whether a certain line is being reached. You may also want to display information about a situation. You can use the *put* command and the Message window do this just as easily.

5] Open the script for cast member 9 again and make the changes shown here in bold:

```
on mouseUp
    put "The button was clicked and this could be useful to know."
end
```

6] Close the Script editor; then rewind and play the movie. Click the Submit button.

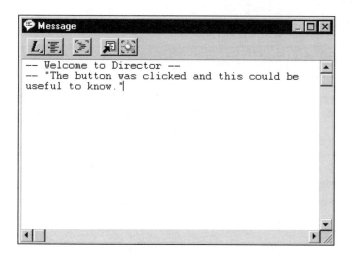

7] Stop the movie and open the Message window (Windows Ctrl+M, Macintosh Command+M).

The *put* command causes the string you provided to be displayed in the Message window. Again, it takes only a moment to create this handler, but it can quickly lead you to possible problems in your Lingo code.

USING ALERT

Sometimes you want to know about an event that happens only occasionally—maybe some portion of your code that runs only rarely. You do not want to monitor the Message window but would like to be notified when the event occurs. The *alert* command is a good choice for such situations.

1] In the Cast window, select cast member 9 again and click the Script button to open the Script Editor window.

2] Modify the *mouseUp* handler as shown here in bold:

```
on mouseUp
    alert "The button was clicked and this could be useful to know."
end
```

735

3] Close the Script editor; then rewind and play the movie. Click the Submit button.

The *alert* command causes a system beep and displays an alert box containing the specified string and an OK button. The string can be a maximum of 255 characters.

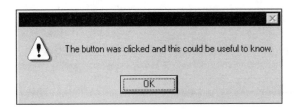

The *alert* command is also useful in your finished movie when you need to inform a user of some event, which the user then simply needs to acknowledge by clicking OK.

Once you have created a distributable movie, you may need to get feedback on what your movie was doing at a particular point, what problems it may have encountered, and what information the user may have provided to the movie. You can make sure this information is available by logging Director messages. You will see how to do this in the next task.

LOGGING MESSAGES TO A FILE

Whether your movie is a large multimedia extravaganza, a small Shockwave program, or a commercial presentation, if a user ever complains that it did not function properly, you will need a way to find out what the movie was doing and what information the user may have entered.

One approach is to create a log file where Director can store information about your movie as it runs. Since log files take up space on the user's hard drive and also cause a short delay in the movie while the information is written, you should use them judiciously. When used properly, however, a log file can be an invaluable diagnostic tool. In this task, you will learn how to create a log file.

1] In the Cast window, select cast member 7, CallMe, and click the Script button to open the Script editor.

By default, the Script editor displays an *on mouseUp* script, which is fine for this task. You will specify what diagnostic information Director should log when the CallMe box is clicked.

736

2] Modify the *mouseUp* handler as shown here in bold:

```
on mouseUp
  isClicked = member ("CallMe").hilite
                    --Save the check status of the check box in the isClicked variable.
    status = "CallMe box clicked, value now" && isClicked
                    --Create a string with the information.
    report(status)    --Call the report handler with the information.
  end
```

The *hilite* property is a property of check boxes; when the box is checked, the property is TRUE. The script assigns the *hilite* property status to the variable *isClicked* and appends it to a string that explains the event—that is, that the box was just clicked. The status string is then passed to a handler called *report()*. The *report()* handler does not exist yet; you will have to write it. The parentheses () help distinguish a handler from a variable, since parameters can be passed to a handler within the parentheses. Although the parentheses are optional, they help make your scripts more readable.

3] Select all the text in the script (Windows Ctrl+A, Macintosh Command+A) and then copy the text (Windows Ctrl+C, Macintosh Command+C). Close the Script editor.
You will now repeat steps 1 and 2 to create a cast member script for the other check box. This is a good place to use the cut-and-paste features of the editor.

4] Select cast member 8, WriteMe, in the Cast window, and click the Script button. Paste the copied text into the Script editor (Windows Ctrl+V, Macintosh Command+V). Make the changes shown here in bold:

```
on mouseUp
  isClicked = (member "WriteMe").hilite
                    --Save the check status of the check box in the isClicked variable.
    status = "WriteMe box clicked, value now" && isClicked
                    --Create a string with the information.
    report(status)    --Call the report handler with the information.
  end
```

This is essentially the same script you used for the CallMe box, modified to report the name of the WriteMe cast member.

5] Close the Script editor.
Now it is time to add scripts for the two buttons.

6] Choose cast member 9, Submit, in the Cast window and click the Script button. Modify the *mouseUp* handler as shown here in bold:

```
on mouseUp
  report("Submit button clicked")
          --Call the report handler with information about the Submit button.
end
```

You need to add only one line (plus the comment) for this script because the Submit button can only be clicked. It does not have an on or off state, so all you can report is that it was clicked.

7] Close the Script editor and repeat step 6 for cast member 10, but instead report "Quit button clicked".

```
on mouseUp
  report("Quit button clicked")
          --Call the report handler with information about the Quit button.
end
```

This adds a notice when the Quit button is clicked.

8] Close the Script editor and return to the Cast window.

Notice that each of the check box and button cast members now has a script attached.

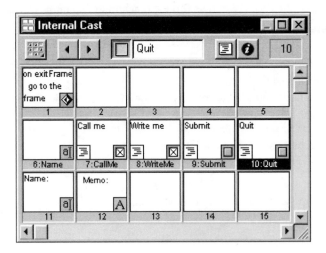

Now you will add the *report()* handler.

9] Select cast member 2 in the Cast window and choose Window › Script to open the Movie Script editor.

10] Enter the following in the Movie Script editor:

```
on report info
    alert info  --Use a dialog box to report the information.
end
```

This creates a movie-level handler called *report*.

tip *Because Lingo is not case-sensitive, the capitalization you use does not matter.*

note *Parentheses are optional when calling a handler, as in* report(), *but they are not allowed when defining the handler.*

For the moment, the *report()* handler calls an alert dialog box to display the status message passed in as the variable *info*. In this example, whenever a check box or button is clicked in the movie, an alert box will appear. The purpose of the alert here is to make sure that the report handler works as it should. In a moment you will tell Director to log the report information in a file instead of generating an alert.

You are now ready to try the movie.

11] Close the Script editor and play the movie. Click the Call me check box.
An alert appears, reporting the check box status.

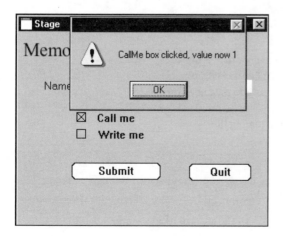

The alert reports the value as 1, or TRUE, meaning that the box is now checked.

12] Click OK to close the alert box and then click the check box again to remove the check mark.

The alert box now reports the status as 0, or FALSE, meaning that the box is not checked.

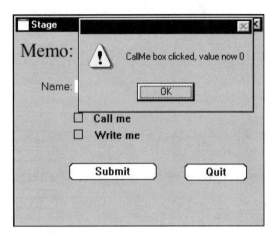

13] Experiment by clicking the other check boxes and buttons. Then stop the movie.

The reporting system seems to be working just fine. Next you'll replace the alert box with something less intrusive.

14] Open the Script editor for cast member 2 again. Change the body of the *report* handler as shown here in bold:

```
on report info
  info = the long time & "〉" && info
          --Attach time to the info being reported.
  oldInfo = getPref("MyLog")
          --Read the previous log file and store in oldInfo.
  newInfo = oldInfo & RETURN & numToChar(10) & info
          --newInfo contains old log plus info on a new line.
  setPref("myLog", newInfo)
          --Write all the information in the log file.
end
```

The first line adds the time to the *info* string and assigns it back to the *info* variable. The *time* function is similar to the *date* function you used in Lesson 28, except it reports the time rather than the date. Adding the time to the information saved adds a **timestamp**; it lets you know not only what happened but exactly when it happened as well.

The next three lines (not counting the comments) introduce a pair of functions called *getPref* and *setPref*. These functions allow you to store user preferences, or any other text information you want, in a file on the user's hard drive. You can also use these functions to log information. When you use *setPref*, it stores the string you supply in the file. When you use *getPref*, it reads the information in the file. The *setPref* function does not automatically store new information at the end of an existing file, which is what you want; to append a file, you need to first read the file (using *getPref*) into a variable, add your new information to the end of the current information, and then write the information out again.

The second line, *oldInfo = getPref("MyLog")*, retrieves the current information in the MyLog file and stores it in the *oldInfo* variable. The third line appends *RETURN & numToChar(10)*, or a line break, to the existing information and then adds the new information, storing the concatenated total in the variable *newInfo*. The line break ensures that the information is written in the file in individual lines, not in one really long line. The new, updated, information is stored in the *newInfo* variable, and the *setPref("myLog", newInfo)* command writes it back out to the file again.

One problem with the preceding scheme is that every time you play the movie, the file will grow larger as more information is added. Unless you want to keep a cumulative log, it is a good idea to reset (empty) the file every time your movie runs. This will limit the stored data to information on just the most recent use of your movie.

15] In the movie script in cast member 2, add a *startMovie* handler as shown here in bold:

```
on startMovie
  setPref("MyLog", "Program started at" && the long date)
          --Overwrite the existing file with this new information.
end

on report info
  info = the long time & "›" && info
          --Attach time to the info being reported.
  oldInfo = getPref("MyLog")
          --Read the previous log file and store in oldInfo.
  newInfo = oldInfo & RETURN & numToChar(10) & info
          --newInfo contains old log plus info on a new line.
  setPref("MyLog", newInfo)
          --Write all the information in the log file.
end
```

Now when the movie starts, the *setPref* function writes the log file without reading or saving the previous file. This overwrites the previous file, and the log file will, at that point, contain only the one line indicating that the movie was started, plus the time. If you want to add the date as well, you can easily do so.

16] Close the Script editor and play the movie. Click the various boxes and buttons.

Depending on your system, you may hear your hard drive whirring as the preferences file is updated.

17] Stop the movie. Save your work and choose File › Exit to exit Director.

The only task left is to check the preferences file to see if your entries have been stored there. The preferences files are stored with a .txt extension, so MyLog is really MyLog.txt. If the movie is running as a projector, the file is placed in the Prefs folder within the Projector folder. If you are authoring, running the movie from Director, the log file is placed in the Prefs folder within the folder from which Director is running.

18] Find the MyLog.txt file on your hard drive and open it.

You can use any text editor or word processor since the file is text only. Notepad (Windows) or SimpleText (Macintosh) will work fine.

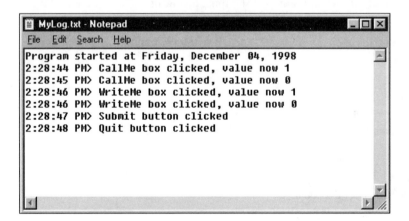

You have created an external log file to log events from your movie. Of course, logging can slow things down, and it can fill up the hard drive, so you should use it carefully. Despite these limitations, however, logging can be a valuable tool.

WHAT YOU HAVE LEARNED

In this lesson you have:

- Monitored the mouse position [page 728]

- Monitored the current sprite and frame [page 730]

- Used *beep* and *alert* to monitor a movie [page 734]

- Timestamped messages [page 740]

- Logged messages in a file [page 740]

CONCLUSION

Congratulations! You have just completed all the lessons in *Director 7 and Lingo Authorized*. In this book, you've created animations with tweening, screen transitions, film loops, color cycling, and more. You've also developed scripts and behaviors to branch to various sections of a movie, created buttons, and added sound for extra impact. You have learned numerous authoring and Shockwave tips and you've been introduced to the basics of Lingo, Director's scripting language. We hope you've enjoyed learning Director 7 and Lingo basics, and most of all, we hope the techniques in these lessons will help you in your own Director multimedia and Shockwave development.

Director offers lots of keyboard shortcuts for menu commands and common tasks. Many are already described in the lessons in this book. This appendix provides a quick reference to some of the most helpful shortcuts.

NUMERIC KEYPAD SHORTCUTS

You can use the numeric keypad to open inspector windows, play movies, and move the playback head.

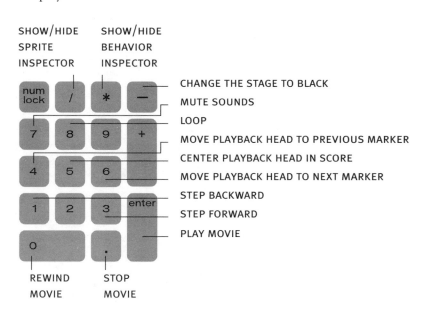

SHOW/HIDE SPRITE INSPECTOR

SHOW/HIDE BEHAVIOR INSPECTOR

CHANGE THE STAGE TO BLACK

MUTE SOUNDS

LOOP

MOVE PLAYBACK HEAD TO PREVIOUS MARKER

CENTER PLAYBACK HEAD IN SCORE

MOVE PLAYBACK HEAD TO NEXT MARKER

STEP BACKWARD

STEP FORWARD

PLAY MOVIE

REWIND MOVIE

STOP MOVIE

SHORTCUT MENUS

Right-clicking a sprite, cast member, or any window displays a shortcut menu that offers quick access to commonly used commands.

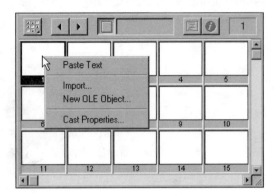

KEYBOARD SHORTCUTS

Many menu commands are also available as keyboard shortcuts. This section lists the keyboard shortcuts for commands in each menu.

FILE MENU

Command	Shortcut
New Movie	Control+N
New Cast	Control+Alt+N
Open	Control+O
Close	Control+F4
Save	Control+S
Import	Control+R
Export	Control+Shift+R
Preview in Browser	F12
Page Setup	Control+Shift+P
Print	Control+P
General Preferences	Control+U
Exit	Alt+F4

EDIT MENU

Command	Shortcut
Undo	Control+Z
Repeat	Control+Y
Cut	Control+X
Copy	Control+C
Paste	Control+V
Clear	Delete or Backspace
Duplicate	Control+D
Select All	Control+A
Find Text	Control+F
Find Handler	Control+Shift+; (semicolon)
Find Cast Member	Control+; (semicolon)
Find Selection	Control+H
Find Again	Control+Alt+F
Replace Again	Control+Alt+E
Edit Sprite Frames	Control+Alt+] (right square bracket)
Edit Entire Sprite	Control+Alt+[(left square bracket)
Exchange Cast Members	Control+E
Launch External Editor	Control+, (comma)

746

VIEW MENU

Command	Shortcut
Marker, Previous	Control+left arrow
Marker, Next	Control+right arrow
Zoom Narrower (Score Window)	Control+–(minus)
Zoom Wider (Score Window)	Control++(plus)
Zoom Out (Paint Window)	Control+–(minus)
Zoom In (Paint Window)	Control++(plus)
Grids, Show	Control+Shift+Alt+G
Grids, Snap to	Control+Alt+G
Rulers	Control+Shift+Alt+R
Sprite Overlay, Show Info	Control+Shift+Alt+O
Sprite Overlay, Show Paths	Control+Shift+Alt+H
Sprite Toolbar (Score Window)	Control+Shift+H
Paint Tools (Paint Window)	Control+Shift+H
Text Toolbar (Text & Field Windows)	Control+Shift+H
Script Toolbar (Script Window)	Control+Shift+H
Message Toolbar (Message Window)	Control+Shift+H
Keyframes	Control+Alt+Shift+K

INSERT MENU

Command	Shortcut
Keyframe	Control+Alt+K
Edit Frame	Control+] (right square bracket)
Insert Frame	Shift+Control+] (right square bracket)
Remove Frame	Control+[(left square bracket)

MODIFY MENU

Command	Shortcut
Cast Member Properties	Control+I
Cast Member Script	Control+' (apostrophe)
Sprite Properties	Control+Shift+I
Sprite Script	Control+Shift+' (apostrophe)
Sprite Tweening	Control+Shift+B
Movie Properties	Control+Shift+D
Movie Casts	Control+Shift+C
Font	Control+Shift+T
Bold Text Style	Control+Alt+B
Italic Text Style	Control+Alt+I
Underline Text Style	Control+Alt+U
Paragraph	Control+Shift+Alt+T
Join Sprites	Control+J
Split Sprite	Control+Shift+J
Extend Sprite	Control+B
Arrange, Bring to Front	Control+Shift+up arrow
Arrange, Move Forward	Control+up arrow
Arrange, Move Backward	Control+Alt+down arrow
Arrange, Send to Back	Control+Alt+Shift+ down arrow
Align	Control+K
Tweak	Control+Shift+K

CONTROL MENU

Command	Shortcut
Play	Control+Alt+P
Stop	Control+. (period)
Rewind	Control+Alt+R
Step Forward	Control+Alt+right arrow
Step Backward	Control+Alt+left arrow
Loop Playback	Control+Alt+L
Volume, Mute	Control+Alt+M
Toggle Breakpoint	F9
Watch Expression	Shift+F9
Ignore Breakpoints	Alt+F9
Step Script	F10
Step Into Script	F8
Run Script	F5
Recompile All Scripts	Shift+F8

WINDOW MENU

Command	Shortcut
Toolbar	Control+Shift+Alt+B
Tool Palette	Control+7
Inspectors, Behavior	Control+Alt+; (semicolon)
Inspectors, Sprite	Control+Alt+S
Inspectors, Text	Control+T
Stage	Control+1
Control Panel	Control+2
Markers	Control+Shift+M
Score	Control+4
Cast	Control+3
Paint	Control+5
Vector Shape	Control+Shift+V
Text	Control+6

WINDOW MENU (cont'd)

Command	Shortcut
Field	Control+8
QuickTime	Control+9
Color Palettes	Control+Alt+7
Script	Control+0 (zero)
Message	Control+M
Debugger	Control+' (single quotation mark)
Watcher	Control+Shift+' (single quotation mark)

HELP MENU

Command	Shortcut
Display Director Help	F1

DIRECTOR WINDOW SHORTCUTS

Many shortcuts are also available directly within the Stage, Score, and Cast windows. This section lists the most helpful shortcuts from these windows.

STAGE

To do this...	Do this
Select only the current frame of a sprite	Alt+click the sprite
Show/hide sprite paths	Control+Shift+Alt+H
Show/hide sprite overlays	Control+Shift+Alt+O
Change the opacity of sprite overlays	Drag the horizontal line on the right side of any overlay
Edit a sprite's cast member	Double-click the sprite
Change a sprite's ink effect	Control+click the sprite and choose from the menu
Perform real-time recording	Control+Spacebar+drag a sprite on the stage
Hide selection handles	Keypad + (plus)
Move a selected sprite by 1 pixel	Arrow keys
Move a selected sprite by 10 pixels	Shift+arrow keys

SCORE WINDOW

To do this...	Do this
Duplicate a selected sprite or keyframe	Alt+drag the selection
Select a frame within a sprite	Alt+click a frame within sprite
Turn Edit Sprite Frames on or off	Alt+double-click a frame within sprite
Select empty frames and sprite frames	Alt+drag beginning in an empty frame
Select all frames in a channel	Double-click channel number; drag to select multiple channels
Select all sprites in a channel	Click the channel number; drag to select multiple channels
Move selected sprites forward	Control+up arrow
Move selected sprites backward	Control+down arrow
Overwrite sprite frames while dragging a selection to a new location	Control+drag
Move a selected sprite by 1 pixel	Arrow keys
Move a selected sprite by 10 pixels	Shift+arrow keys
Move entire sprite (instead of keyframe)	Spacebar+drag
Extend a sprite without proportionally relocating keyframes	Control+drag the end frame
Move the playback head to the end of the movie	Tab or Control+Shift+right arrow
Move the playback head to the beginning of the movie	Shift+Tab or Control+Shift+left arrow
Go to the next marker (or jump forward 10 frames)	Control+right arrow
Go to the previous marker (or jump back 10 frames)	Control+left arrow
Edit a sprite's cast member	Double-click the sprite frame or the cast thumbnail
Open the frame settings dialog box	Double-click a frame in the tempo, palette, or transition channel

CAST WINDOW

To do this...	Do this
Edit a cast member	Double-click a paint, text, palette or script cast member or select the cast member and press Enter
Edit/create a cast member script	Control+' (apostrophe)
Display a selected cast member's properties	Control+I
Place a selected cast member in the center of the stage (using the default sprite duration; equivalent to the Place button)	Control+Shift+L
Place selected cast member in the center of the stage (with a duration of 1 frame only; equivalent to the Cast to Time command)	Control+Shift+Alt+L
Select the previous cast member	Control+left arrow
Select the next cast member	Control+right arrow
Scroll up one window	Page Up
Scroll down one window	Page Down
Scroll to show the top left of the cast window	Home
Scroll to show the last occupied cast member	End
Select a cast member by number	Type the number

macintosh shortcuts

Director offers lots of keyboard shortcuts for menu commands and common tasks. Many are already described in the lessons in this book. This appendix provides a quick reference to some of the most helpful shortcuts.

NUMERIC KEYPAD SHORTCUTS

You can use the numeric keypad to open inspector windows, play movies, and move the playback head.

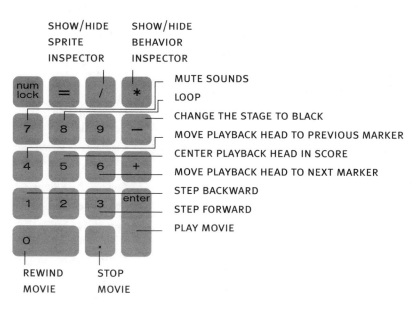

SHOW/HIDE SPRITE INSPECTOR
SHOW/HIDE BEHAVIOR INSPECTOR
MUTE SOUNDS
LOOP
CHANGE THE STAGE TO BLACK
MOVE PLAYBACK HEAD TO PREVIOUS MARKER
CENTER PLAYBACK HEAD IN SCORE
MOVE PLAYBACK HEAD TO NEXT MARKER
STEP BACKWARD
STEP FORWARD
PLAY MOVIE
REWIND MOVIE
STOP MOVIE

SHORTCUT MENUS

Control-clicking a sprite, cast member, or any window displays a shortcut menu that offers quick access to commonly used commands.

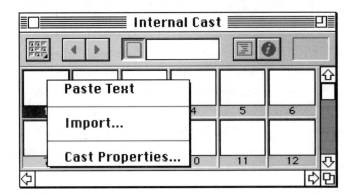

KEYBOARD SHORTCUTS

Many menu commands are also available as keyboard shortcuts. This section lists the keyboard shortcuts for commands in each menu.

FILE MENU

Command	Shortcut
New Movie	Command+N
New Cast	Command+Option+N
Open	Command+O
Close	Command+W
Save	Command+S
Import	Command+R
Export	Command+Shift+R
Page Setup	Command+Shift+P
Print	Command+P
General Preferences	Command+U
Quit	Command+Q

EDIT MENU

Command	Shortcut
Undo	Command+Z
Repeat	Command+Y
Cut	Command+X
Copy	Command+C
Paste	Command+V
Duplicate	Command+D
Select All	Command+A
Find Text	Command+F
Find Handler	Command+Shift+; (semicolon)
Find Cast Member	Command+; (semicolon)
Find Selection	Command+H
Find Again	Command+Option+F
Replace Again	Command+Option+E
Edit Sprite Frames	Command+Option+] (right square bracket)
Edit Entire Sprite	Command+Option+[(left square bracket)
Exchange Cast Members	Command+E
Launch External Editor	Command+, (comma)

752

VIEW MENU

Command	Shortcut
Marker, Previous	Command+left arrow
Marker, Next	Command+right arrow
Zoom Narrower (Score Window)	Command+–(minus)
Zoom Wider (Score Window)	Command++(plus)
Zoom Out (Paint Window)	Command+–(minus)
Zoom In (Paint Window)	Command++(plus)
Show Grid	Command+Shift+Option+G
Snap to Grid	Command+Option+G
Rulers	Command+Shift+Option+R
Sprite Overlay, Show Info	Command+Shift+Option+O
Sprite Overlay, Show Paths	Command+Shift+Option+H
Sprite Toolbar (Score Window)	Command+Shift+H
Paint Tools (Paint Window)	Command+Shift+H
Text Toolbar (Text & Field Windows)	Command+Shift+H
Script Toolbar (Script Window)	Command+Shift+H
Message Toolbar (Message Window)	Command+Shift+H
Keyframe	Command+Shift+Option+K

INSERT MENU

Command	Shortcut
Keyframe	Command+Option+K
Insert Frame	Command+] (right square bracket)
Frames	Shift+Command+] (right square bracket)
Remove Frame	Command+[(left square bracket)

MODIFY MENU

Command	Shortcut
Cast Member Properties	Command+I
Cast Member Script	Command+' (apostrophe)
Sprite Properties	Command+Shift+I

MODIFY MENU (cont'd)

Command	Shortcut
Sprite Script	Command+Shift+' (apostrophe)
Sprite Tweening	Command+Shift+B
Movie Properties	Command+Shift+D
Movie Casts	Command+Shift+C
Font	Command+Shift+T
Bold Text Style	Command+Option+B
Italic Text Style	Command+Option+I
Underline Text Style	Command+Option+U
Paragraph	Command+Shift+Option+T
Join Sprites	Command+J
Split Sprite	Command+Shift+J
Extend Sprite	Command+B
Arrange, Bring to Front	Command+Shift+up arrow
Arrange, Move Forward	Command+up arrow
Arrange, Move Backward	Command+down arrow
Arrange, Send to Back	Command+Shift+ down arrow
Align	Command+K
Tweak	Command+Shift+K

CONTROL MENU

Command	Shortcut
Play	Command+Option+P
Stop	Command+. (period)
Rewind	Command+Option+R
Step Forward	Command+Option+ right arrow
Step Backward	Command+Option+ left arrow
Loop Playback	Command+Option+L
Volume, Mute	Command+Option+M
Toggle Breakpoint	Command+Shift+Option+K
Watch Expression	Command+Shift+Option+W
Ignore Breakpoints	Command+Shift+Option+I
Step Script	Command+Shift+Option+ down arrow
Step Into Script	Command+Shift+Option+ right arrow
Run Script	Command+Shift+Option+ up arrow
Recompile All Scripts	Command+Shift+Option+C

753

WINDOW MENU

Command	Shortcut
Toolbar	Command+Shift+Option+B
Tool Palette	Command+7
Inspectors, Behavior	Command+Option+; (semicolon)
Inspectors, Sprite	Command+Option+S
Inspectors, Text	Command+T
Stage	Command+1
Control Panel	Command+2
Markers	Command+Shift+M
Score	Command+4
Cast	Command+3
Paint	Command+5

WINDOW MENU (cont'd)

Command	Shortcut
Vector Shape	Command+Shift+V
Text	Command+6
Field	Command+8
QuickTime	Command+9
Color Palettes	Command+Option+7
Script	Command+0
Message	Command+M
Debugger	Command+' (single quotation mark)
Watcher	Command+Shift+' (single quotation mark)

DIRECTOR WINDOW SHORTCUTS

Many shortcuts are also available directly within the Stage, Score, and Cast windows. This section lists the most helpful shortcuts from these windows.

STAGE

To do this...	Do this
Select only the current frame of a sprite	Option+click the sprite
Show/hide sprite paths	Command+Shift+Option+H
Show/hide sprite overlays	Command+Shift+Option+O
Change the opacity of sprite overlays	Drag the horizontal line on the right side of any overlay
Edit a sprite's cast member	Double-click the sprite
Change a sprite's ink effect	Command+click the sprite and choose from the menu
Perform real-time recording	Command+Spacebar+drag a sprite on the stage
Hide selection handles	Keypad + (plus)
Move a selected sprite by 1 pixel	Arrow keys
Move a selected sprite by 10 pixels	Shift+arrow keys

SCORE WINDOW

To do this...	Do this
Duplicate a selected sprite or keyframe	Option+drag the selection
Select a frame within a sprite	Option+click a frame within sprite
Turn Edit Sprite Frames on or off	Option+double-click a frame within sprite
Select empty frames and sprite frames	Option+drag beginning in an empty frame
Select all frames in a channel	Double-click channel number; drag to select multiple channels
Select all sprites in a channel	Click the channel number; drag to select multiple channels
Move selected sprites forward	Command+up arrow
Move selected sprites backward	Command+down arrow
Overwrite sprite frames while dragging a selection to a new location	Command+drag
Move a selected sprite by 1 pixel	Arrow keys
Move a selected sprite by 10 pixels	Shift+arrow keys
Move entire sprite (instead of keyframe)	Spacebar+drag
Extend a sprite without proportionally relocating keyframes	Command+drag the end frame
Move the playback head to the end of the movie	Tab or Command+Shift+right arrow
Move the playback head to the beginning of the movie	Shift+Tab or Command+Shift+left arrow
Go to the next marker (or jump forward 10 frames)	Command+right arrow
Go to the previous marker (or jump back 10 frames)	Command+left arrow
Edit a sprite's cast member	Double-click the sprite frame or the cast thumbnail
Open the frame settings dialog box	Double-click a frame in the tempo, palette, or transition channel

CAST WINDOW

To do this...	Do this
Edit a cast member	Double-click a paint, text, palette or script cast member or select the cast member and press Enter
Edit/create a cast member script	Command+' (apostrophe)
Display a selected cast member's properties	Command+I
Place a selected cast member in the center of the stage (using the default sprite duration; equivalent to the Place button)	Command+Shift+L
Place selected cast member in the center of the stage (with a duration of 1 frame only; equivalent to the Cast to Time command)	Command+Shift+Option+L
Select the previous cast member	Command+left arrow
Select the next cast member	Command+right arrow
Scroll up one window	Page Up
Scroll down one window	Page Down
Scroll to show the top left of the cast window	Home
Scroll to show the last occupied cast member	End
Select a cast member by number	Type the number

index

760

handlers, 116–119, 360, 376–397. *See also individual handlers*
   calling with scripts, 514–516
   combining elements into, 644–647
   creating, 389–397
   custom, 502–504
   hierarchy of, 385–388
   for *hyperlinkClicked* events, 724–725
   parameters for, 389–397
   return values and, 389–397
   stepping through in Debugger, 622–628
hardware requirements, 5
help, online, 17–18, 362
Help menu, 17–18
Hide/Show Effects Channel button, 15, 50, 75
highlights, 632–633, 649–650
hilite **property**, 737
hotspots, 217
HTML code, 344
   generating automatically, 347–348
   generating for Shockwave movies, 347–349
   hyperlinks, 712–725
   hypertext, 712–725
   viewing, 348
hyperlinkClicked **event**, 724–725
hypertext markup language. *See* HTML code

I

idle **handler**, 386
if-then-else **block**, 442
if-then **structures**
   constraining sprite movement with, 506–508
   controlling navigation with, 588–589
   replacing with *case* structures, 525–528, 549–550
Image Options dialog box, 19–20, 151–152, 246–249
images. *See also* background images; graphics
   animating, 86–89
   blending bitmaps with, 234–239
   fading out, 326–330
   setting registration points for, 94–97
Import dialog box, 78–79, 151
importfileinto **command**, 80

importing
   digital video as external cast members, 452–454
   files, 78–80
   graphics, 18–21, 78–79, 247
   media elements, 78–81, 246–249
   media for animations, 151–152
index color number, 274–275
initializing variables, 464
ink effects, 33
   applying to sprites, 229–234
   Background Transparent, 33–34, 52, 83–84, 222, 315
   Blend ink, 223, 230–233
   Copy ink, 84, 222, 240–242
   Gradient ink, 44
   Mask ink, 223, 224, 234–239
   Matte ink, 82, 84, 154, 315, 491
   Normal ink, 333
ink selector menu, 17
Insert commands. *See* commands (Director)
Interactive Library window, 193
interactivity, 7, 112–133, 180–183
Internal Cast window, 570–571
internal casts, 564, 570–561
Internet
   considerations for movies on, 341–342
   downloading Web pages and, 271
   retrieving data from, 676–679
   shocking Director movies for playback on, 344–349
   testing movies on, 667–668
   using Lingo on, 658–691
   viewing Web pages on, 349
Internet button, 577
Internet Explorer, 343, 661

J

JPEG files, 18

K

key codes
   adding for up and down arrows, 556–557
   controlling keyboard actions with, 548–549
   determining, 546
keyboard control, 544–561

Macromedia tech support number: 415-252-9080

LICENSING AGREEMENT

The information in this book is for informational use only and is subject to change without notice. Macromedia, Inc., and Macromedia Press assume no responsibility for errors or inaccuracies that may appear in this book. The software described in the book is furnished under license and may be used or copied only in accordance with terms of the license.